LAW FOR
BUSINESS STUDENTS

LAW FOR BUSINESS STUDENTS

ALIX ADAMS, STEPHANIE CAPLAN,
GRAEME LOCKWOOD

11th
edition

Pearson

Harlow, England • London • New York • Boston • San Francisco • Toronto • Sydney • Dubai • Singapore • Hong Kong
Tokyo • Seoul • Taipei • New Delhi • Cape Town • São Paulo • Mexico City • Madrid • Amsterdam • Munich • Paris • Milan

PEARSON EDUCATION LIMITED
KAO Two
KAO Park
Harlow CM17 9SR
United Kingdom
Tel: +44 (0)1279 623623
Web: www.pearson.com/uk

Previously published 2000, 2003, 2006, 2008, 2010,2012 (print); 2014, 2016, 2018 (electronic)
Eleventh edition published 2020 (print and electronic)

ISBN: 978-1-292-27224-5 (print)
        978-1-292-27222-1 (PDF)
        978-1-292-27223-8 (ePub)

British Library Cataloguing-in-Publication Data
A catalogue record for the print edition is available from the British Library

Library of Congress Cataloging-in-Publication Data
Names: Adams, Alix, author. | Caplan, Stephanie, author. | Lockwood,
    Graeme, author.
Title: Law for business students / Alix Adams, Stephanie Caplan, Graeme
    Lockwood.
Description: Eleventh edition. | Harlow, UK ; New York : Pearson Education
    Limited, 2020.
Identifiers: LCCN 2019048203 (print) | LCCN 2019048204 (ebook) | ISBN
    9781292272245 (print) | ISBN 9781292272221 (PDF) | ISBN 9781292272238
    (epub)
Subjects: LCSH: Law—England. | Commercial law—England.
Classification: LCC KD661 .A33 2020 (print) | LCC KD661 (ebook) | DDC
    346.4207—dc23
LC record available at https://lccn.loc.gov/2019048203
LC ebook record available at https://lccn.loc.gov/2019048204

10 9 8 7 6 5 4 3 2 1
24 23 22 21 20

Front cover image © d1sk / iStock / Getty Images Plus

Print edition typeset in 9.5/13 pt Avenir LT Pro by Spi Global
Printed in Slovakia by Neografia

NOTE THAT ANY PAGE CROSS REFERENCES REFER TO THE PRINT EDITION

Brief contents

Contents   ix
Publisher's acknowledgements   xviii
Preface   xxi
Table of cases   xxii
Table of statutes   xxxiv
Table of statutory instruments   xxxix
Table of European and International legislation   xli

Part 1: Introduction: getting started   1

  1   Study skills   2
  2   The nature of law   16
  3   How the law is made   26
  4   Resolving legal disputes   54

Part 2: Law of contract, agency and sale of goods   75

  5   The law of contract: Offer and acceptance   76
  6   The law of contract: Consideration, intention and privity   100
  7   The terms of the contract at common law   122
  8   Statutory terms in contracts for sale of goods and services   142
  9   Defects in the contract: Misrepresentation, mistake, duress and undue influence   172
 10   The consequences of illegality and incapacity: Illegality and incapacity   204
 11   Discharge of the contract and remedies for breach   224
 12   The law of agency   260

Part 3: The law of tort   279

 13   The tort of negligence   280
 14   Negligence and special duty situations   308
 15   Product liability   342
 16   Occupiers' liability, nuisance and vicarious liability   362

Part 4: Elements of employment law   397

17 Rights at work: The contract of employment and health and safety at work   398
18 Rights at work: Protection against discrimination in employment   422
19 Rights at work: Protection against termination of employment by wrongful and unfair dismissal including redundancy   464

Part 5: Introduction to company law   489

20 Business organisations   490
21 Forming a registered company   514
22 Running the company: Raising and maintaining capital   530
23 The management and governance of companies: Functions of directors, secretary and auditors   542
24 Company meetings, shareholder participation and minority protection   570

Part 6: General principles of intellectual property law   585

25 Statutory intellectual property protection: Copyright, designs, patents and trade marks   586
26 Common law protection of intellectual property: Passing off, malicious falsehood and breach of confidence   610

Appendix 1: Additional resources   629
Appendix 2: Worth thinking about? and Review questions – outline answers   632
Index   651

Companion Website

For student resources to complement this textbook and support your learning, please visit go.pearson.com/uk/he/resources

Lecturer Resources

For online resources tailored to support the use of this textbook in teaching, please visit go.pearson.com/uk/he/resources

ON THE WEBSITE

Contents

Publisher's acknowledgements xviii
Preface xxi
Table of cases xxii
Table of statutes xxxiv
Table of statutory instruments xxxix
Table of European and International legislation xli

Part 1: Introduction: getting started 1

1 Study skills 2
Introduction 2
Starting to study 2
Good study habits 4
Writing law assignments 5
Revision and examination technique 11
Conclusion 15

2 The nature of law 16
Introduction 16
What is law? 16
The characteristics of English law 18
Why do we need law? 19
The differences between criminal and civil law 20
Changing the law 22
Essential legal terms 22
Chapter summary 24
Review questions 1 24
Advanced questions 1 25
Further reading 25
Web activity 25

3 How the law is made 26
Introduction 26
European law 27
Parliament 32

The courts   34
The Human Rights Act 1998 (HRA 1998)   43
Chapter summary   50
Review questions 2   51
Advanced questions 2   52
Take a closer look   52
Web activity   52
Assignment 1   52

4 Resolving legal disputes   54
Introduction   54
The court system   55
Bringing a case in the civil courts   60
The Woolf reforms 1999   60
Settlement out of court   61
Payment into court and offers to settle   61
Civil litigation procedures   62
The trial of the case   64
Executing the judgment   64
Alternative dispute resolution (ADR)   66
The tribunal system   69
Chapter summary   71
Review questions 3   72
Advanced questions 3   73
Web activity   73
Assignment 2   73

Part 2: Law of contract, agency and sale of goods   75

5 The law of contract: Offer and acceptance   76
Introduction   76
The essentials of a binding contract   77
The offer   78
The acceptance   89
Chapter summary   97
Review questions 4   97
Advanced questions 4   98
Take a closer look   98
Web activity   99
Assignment 3   99

6 The law of contract: Consideration, intention and privity   100
Introduction   100
Consideration   101

Intention to create legal relations   111
Privity of contract   115
Chapter summary   118
Review questions 5   119
Advanced questions 5   120
Take a closer look   120
Web activity   120
Assignment 4   120

7 The terms of the contract at common law   122

Introduction   122
Express and implied terms   123
The relative importance of contractual terms   128
Exemption clauses: Limitation and exclusion of liability   133
Chapter summary   139
Review questions 6   139
Advanced questions 6   140
Take a closer look   140
Further reading   141
Assignment 5   141

8 Statutory terms in contracts for sale of goods and services   142

Introduction   142
Part 1: Commercial sales contracts   143
The terms implied by the Sale of Goods Act 1979   144
Other key statutes which regulate contracts involving goods   152
Part 2: Consumer sales   160
An overview of consumer sales protection before the CRA 2015   160
The Consumer Rights Act 2015   162
Chapter summary   169
Review questions 7   170
Advanced questions 7   170
Take a closer look   170
Further reading   171
Assignment 6   171

9 Defects in the contract: Misrepresentation, mistake, duress and undue influence   172

Introduction   172
Misrepresentation   173
Mistake   184
Duress and undue influence   194
Chapter summary   200

Review questions 8   201
Advanced questions 8   202
Take a closer look   202
Web activity   203
Assignment 7   203

10 The consequences of illegality and incapacity: Illegality and incapacity   204

Introduction   204
Illegality   205
Contractual incapacity   217
Chapter summary   221
Review questions 9   222
Advanced questions 9   222
Take a closer look   223
Web activity   223
Assignment 8   223

11 Discharge of the contract and remedies for breach   224

Introduction   224
Discharge of contracts   225
Remedies for breach of contract   242
Chapter summary   256
Review questions 10   257
Advanced questions 10   258
Take a closer look   258
Web activity   258
Assignment 9   259

12 The law of agency   260

Introduction   260
The creation of agency   261
The rights and duties of the agent   269
The rights and duties of the principal   272
Termination of agency   272
Some common types of specialist agents   274
Chapter summary   276
Review questions 11   277
Advanced questions 11   277
Take a closer look   277
Web activity   278
Assignment 10   278

Part 3: The law of tort   279

13 The tort of negligence   280
Introduction   280
Negligence liability   281
1 The duty of care   282
2 Breach of duty   285
3 Proving consequential loss or damage   292
Defences in tort   300
Chapter summary   304
Review questions 12   305
Advanced questions 12   305
Take a closer look   305
Web activity   306
Assignment 11   306

14 Negligence and special duty situations   308
Introduction   308
Special duty situations   309
Chapter summary   338
Review questions 13   339
Advanced questions 13   340
Take a closer look   340
Web activity   340
Assignment 12   341

15 Product liability   342
Introduction   342
Liability for defective products   343
The Consumer Protection Act 1987 (Part I)   349
Chapter summary   358
Review questions 14   359
Advanced questions 14   359
Take a closer look   360
Web activity   360
Assignment 13   360

16 Occupiers' liability, nuisance and vicarious liability   362
Introduction   362
The occupier's liability to people on the premises   363
Duties of an occupier to people outside the premises   373

Vicarious liability   386
Chapter summary   393
Review questions 15   393
Advanced questions 15   394
Take a closer look   394
Web activity   395
Assignment 14   395

Part 4: Elements of employment law   397

17 Rights at work: The contract of employment and health and safety at work   398

Introduction   398
The employment contract: a contract of service   399
The law of tort: employers' civil liability for industrial injuries   410
Criminal law regulation of safety in the workplace   416
Chapter summary   418
Review questions 16   420
Advanced questions 16   420
Take a closer look   421
Further reading   421
Web activity   421
Assignment 15   421

18 Rights at work: Protection against discrimination in employment   422

Introduction   422
The Equality Act 2010: the core provisions   423
The operation of the Equality Act 2010   426
Age   426
Disability   429
Gender re-assignment   433
Marriage and civil partnership   434
Pregnancy and maternity   435
Race   436
Religion or belief   441
Sex   445
Sexual orientation   454
Enforcing anti-discrimination legislation   457
The promotion of equality   457
The Equality and Human Rights Commission   458
Chapter summary   459
Review questions 17   460
Advanced questions 17   460

Take a closer look   461
Further reading   461
Web activity   461
Assignment 16   461

19 Rights at work: Protection against termination of employment by wrongful and unfair dismissal including redundancy   464

Introduction   464
Wrongful dismissal   465
Unfair dismissal   466
Redundancy   476
Transfer of undertakings   480
Claiming at the employment tribunal   482
Chapter summary   485
Review questions 18   486
Advanced questions 18   487
Take a closer look   487
Web activity   488
Assignment 17   488

Part 5: Introduction to company law   489

20 Business organisations   490

Introduction   490
Legal personality, incorporation and limited liability   491
The sole trader   492
The partnership   492
The registered company   497
The impact of the Human Rights Act 1998 (HRA 1998) on
business organisations   508
Conclusion   510
Chapter summary   511
Review questions 19   511
Advanced questions 19   512
Take a closer look   512
Web activity   513
Assignment 18   513

21 Forming a registered company   514

Introduction   514
Promoting the company   514
Forming the company   516
Buying a company 'off the shelf'   525
Dissolution of the company   525

Chapter summary   526
Review questions 20   527
Advanced questions 20   527
Take a closer look   528
Web activity   528
Assignment 19   528

22 Running the company: Raising and maintaining capital   530

Introduction   530
Share capital   531
Loan capital   536
Chapter summary   539
Review questions 21   540
Advanced questions 21   541
Web activity   541
Assignment 20   541

23 The management and governance of companies: Functions of directors, secretary and auditors   542

Introduction   542
The directors   543
The company secretary   558
The auditors of the company   561
Insider dealing   562
Chapter summary   565
Review questions 22   566
Advanced questions 22   567
Take a closer look   567
Web activity   568
Assignment 21   568

24 Company meetings, shareholder participation and minority protection   570

Introduction   570
General meetings   571
Protecting the rights of minority shareholders   577
Chapter summary   582
Review questions 23   583
Advanced questions 23   584
Web activity   584
Assignment 22   584

Part 6: General principles of intellectual property law   585

25 Statutory intellectual property protection: Copyright, designs, patents and trade marks   586

Introduction   586
Statutory regulation of intellectual property   587
The impact of EU law and international treaties on intellectual property rights   604
Chapter summary   606
Review questions 24   606
Advanced questions 24   608
Take a closer look   608
Web activity   608
Assignment 23   609

26 Common law protection of intellectual property: Passing off, malicious falsehood and breach of confidence   610

Introduction   610
Passing off   611
Malicious falsehood   616
Breach of confidence and protection of privacy   618
Remedies for passing off, malicious falsehood and breach of confidence   626
Chapter summary   626
Review questions 25   627
Advanced questions 25   627
Take a closer look   628
Web activity   628
Assignment 24   628

Appendix 1: Additional resources   629
Appendix 2: Worth thinking about? and Review questions – outline answers   632
Index   651

Publisher's acknowledgements

Text Credits:

28 European Union: Treaty of Nice, Article 203; **38 Incorporated Council of Law Reporting:** Royal College of Nursing v DHSS (1981, HL) Lord Diplock; **41 Court of Appeal:** Young v Bristol Aeroplane Company (1944); **45 European Convention on Human Rights:** ECtHR (Hirst v UK (No. 2) (2005)); **46 High Court of England and Wales:** DSD and NBV v Commissioner of Police for the Metropolis (2014, EWHC); **47 European Court of Human Rights:** Steel v United Kingdom 28 EHRR 603; **66 The National Archives:** Equality Act 2010 Section 144(1); **69 The National Archives:** Employment Rights Act 1996; **83 Court of Appeal:** Bigg v Boyd Gibbons (1971, CA) Russell LJ; **85 Court of Appeal:** Blackpool & Fylde Aero Club v Blackpool Council (1990, CA) Bingham LJ; **87 The National Archives:** Sale of Goods Act 1979, s 57; **87 Court of Appeal:** Dickinson v Dodds (1876, CA) James LJ; **90 Court of Appeal:** Branco v Cobarro (1947, CA); **94 The National Archives:** Electronic Commerce (EC Directive) Regulations 2002 Regulation 11; **113 Court of Appeal:** Wilson and Another v Burnett (2007, CA) Judge Nelligan; **114 European Court of Human Rights:** Steel v United Kingdom 28 EHRR 603 ; **115 Court of Appeal:** Kleinwort Benson v Malaysia Mining Corporation Bhd (1989, CA) MMC Metals Ltd; **117 Law Commission:** 1996, the Law Commission (Report No. 242); **130 Court of Appeal:** Hong Kong Fir Shipping Co. Ltd v Kawasaki Kisen Kaisha (1962, CA) Diplock LJ; **131 Court of Appeal:** Lombard North Central plc v Butterworth (1987, CA) Mustill LJ; **131 Incorporated Council of Law Reporting:** Schuler AG v Wickman Machine Tool Sales (1974, HL) Lord Reid; **133 Court of Appeal:** Edmund-Davies LJ; **144 The National Archives:** Sale of Goods Act 1979 s 2(1); **147 Court of Appeal:** Harlingdon & Leinster Enterprises v Christopher Hull Fine Arts (1990, CA); **147 The National Archives:** Section 14(2B); **152 Incorporated Council of Law Reporting:** J & H Ritchie Ltd v Lloyd Ltd (2007, HL) Lord Brown; **152 The National Archives:** The Supply of Goods and Services Act 1982 (SGSA 1982); **156 The National Archives:** Section 11 of UCTA 1977; **158–159 Court of Appeal:** Watford Electronics v Sanderson (2001, CA) Chadwick LJ; **174 Thomson Reuters Corporation:** Gordon v Selico (1986) Goulding J; **175 Incorporated Council of Law Reporting:** Edgington v Fitzmaurice (1885) Bowen LJ; **185 Incorporated Council of Law Reporting:** Bell v Lever Bros (1932, HL) Lord Atkin; **190 Court of Appeal:** Lewis v Averay (1971, CA) Lord Denning MR; **194 Privy Council of the United Kingdom:** Pao On v Lau Yiu Long (1979) Lord Scarman; **213 High Court of Justice:** Proactive Sports Management Ltd v Wayne Rooney and Others (2010); **217 The National Archives:** s 3 of the Sale of Goods Act 1979; **219**

LexisNexis: Proform Sports Management Ltd v Pro-Active Sports Management Ltd (2007); **244–245 Incorporated Council of Law Reporting:** Transfield Shipping Inc. v Mercator Shipping Inc. (2008, HL); **249 Court of Appeal:** Milner and Milner v Carnival plc t/a Cunard (2010); **251 High Court of England and Wales:** Azimut-Benetti SpA v Healey (2010) per Blair J; **263 High Court of England and Wales:** Ramsay v Love (2015) Morgan J; **266 Court of Appeal:** Quinn V CC Automotive Group (T/A CARCRAFT) (2010, CA); **274 The National Archives:** MCA, s 11; **275 The National Archives:** The Factors Act 1889, s 1; **344 House of Lords:** Donoghue v Stevenson; **282 House of Lords:** Donoghue v Stevenson Lord Atkin; **284 House of Lords:** Donoghue v Stevenson Lord Atkin; **289 Incorporated Council of Law Reporting:** Bolam v Friern Hospital Management Committee Lord Justice Denning; **290 The National Archives:** The Compensation Act 2006 Section 1; **290 Court of Appeal:** Sutton v Syston Rugby Football Club Ltd (2011) Longmore LJ; **290 Court of Appeal:** Watt v Hertfordshire County Council (1954 CA) Denning LJ; **295 House of Lords:** Lord Hoffmann; **309 Incorporated Council of Law Reporting:** Caparo v Dickman (1990, HL) Lord Oliver; **309 Incorporated Council of Law Reporting:** Sandhar v Department of Transport (2004) May LJ; **313 The National Archives:** Defective Premises Act 1972 (DPA). Section 1(1); **317 House of Lords:** Hedley Byrne v Heller (1963), the House of Lords; **323 House of Lords:** Rothwell v Chemical & Insulating Co Ltd [2008] AC 281; **329 Court of Appeal:** North Glamorgan NHS Trust v Walters (2002, CA) Ward LJ; **330 Court of Appeal:** Taylor v A. Novo UK Ltd (2013, CA) Lord Dyson, Master of the Rolls; **330 Law Commission:** 1998 a Law Commission Report (No. 249, Liability for Psychiatric Damage); **330–331 House of Lords:** Stovin v Wise (1996) Lord Goff; **332 Incorporated Council of Law Reporting:** Smith v Littlewoods Organisation (1987, HL) Lord Griffiths; **338 Cambridge University Press:** May LJ said in Merret v Bubb (2001); **344 Incorporated Council of Law Reporting:** Donoghue v Stevenson (1932, HL) Lord Atkin; **344 House of Lords:** Lord Atkin; **351 The National Archives:** Consumer Protection Act 1987 Section 2(1); **364 The National Archives:** Occupiers' Liability Act 1957; **364 The National Archives:** Occupiers' Liability Act 1957 s 1(3); **370 The National Archives:** The Occupiers Liability Act 1957, Section 2(5); **370 The National Archives:** Contract Terms Act 1977, Section 2(3); **375 Court of Appeal:** Sturges v Bridgeman (1879) Thesiger J; **383 House of Lords:** case of Rylands v Fletcher (1865) Blackburn J; **383 High Court of Justice:** RDF Media Group plc v Clements; **384 Incorporated Council of Law Reporting:** Read v Lyons (1947) Lord Porter; **402 The National Archives:** Employment Rights (Employment Particulars and Paid Annual Leave) (Amendment) Regulations 2018; **409 Incorporated Council of Law Reporting:** Malik v BCCI (1998) Lord Steyn; **409 Incorporated Council of Law Reporting:** RDF Media Group plc v Alan Clements (2007) Livesey QC; **423 The National Archives:** Equality Act 2010 Section 13; **424 The National Archives:** Equality Act 2010 Section 14; **424 The National Archives:** Equality Act 2010 Section 19; **428 The National Archives:** Equality Act 2010 Section 13(2); **429 The National Archives:** Equality Act 2010 Section 6(1); **431, 432, 440 The National Archives:** Equality Act 2010 Section 13(2); **437 The National Archives:** Equality Act 2010 Section 9(1); **441 LexisNexis:** Grainger plc and Others v Nicholson (2010) Burton J; **444**

European Union: G4S's employee code of behaviour; **454 The National Archives:** Equality Act 2010 Section 9; **455 Court of Appeal:** English v Thomas Sanderson (2008), Collins LJ; **457 The National Archives:** Equality Act 2010 Section 149; **458 The National Archives:** Equality Act 2010 Section 153; **466 The National Archives:** Employment Rights Act (ERA 1996) s 86; **469 The National Archives:** Section 98 of the ERA 1996; **480 HM Courts & Tribunals Service:** Holis Metal Industries v GMB (2007) HHJ Ansell; **497–498 The National Archives:** Companies Act 2006; **502 Incorporated Council of Law Reporting:** Williams and Another v Natural Life Health Foods Ltd and Mistlin (1998, HL) Lord Steyn; **515–516 The National Archives:** Section 51 of the CA 2006; **516 The National Archives:** Companies Act 2006 ss 9–13; **520 Court of Appeal:** Bell Houses v City Wall Properties Ltd (1966 CA); **520 The National Archives:** The Companies Act 1985, providing (s 3A); **520 The National Archives:** CA 2006 s 31(1); **524 The National Archives:** CA 2006, s (41) 2; **533 The National Archives:** The Companies Act s 610; **545 The National Archives:** Small Business, Enterprise and Employment Act (SBEEA) 2015, s 251; **550 The National Archives:** CA 2006 s 170(1); **550 The National Archives:** CA 2006 s 172(1); **551 The National Archives:** Insolvency Act 1986, Section 174(2); **573 The National Archives:** CA 2006 s 308; **573 The National Archives:** CA 2006 s 311; **578 The National Archives:** CA 2006 s 994; **579 The National Archives:** CA 2006 s 996; **587 The National Archives:** Designs and Patents Act 1988 (CDPA 1988) s 1; **592 The National Archives:** Section 213(2) of the CDPA 1988; **620 Incorporated Council of Law Reporting:** A-G v Guardian Newspapers (No. 2) (1990, HL), Lord Keith; **622 The National Archives:** House of Lords (Douglas and Another v Hello! Ltd (No. 3) (2007)) Lord Hoffmann; **622 Court of Appeal:** Law Lords in Douglas and Another v Hello! Magazine Ltd (No. 3) (2007);

Preface

We, Stephanie Caplan and Graeme Lockwood, have joined Alix Adams in writing a revised 11th edition of this textbook. The book has been updated where required and also provides restructured coverage of tort, with dedicated chapters covering negligence and special duty situations, together with product liability. Any changes were developed in response to feedback from those lecturers who used previous editions. Their responses were invaluable to the process of developing improvements to the content and presentation of the material included.

The law is covered in an accessible manner, but without over-simplification of the subject matter. The text provides coverage of the fundamental legal principles and an understanding of the practical application of the law to the business environment.

In addition, each chapter includes a new Review Questions section designed to encourage students to develop a deeper understanding of legal application.

Many thanks to all at Pearson who have helped in the preparation of this addition, we appreciate the efficiency, patience and practical assistance that has been provided.

We hope that the text will help business students (who are often required to study law covering a very diverse range of areas relating to the business environment) to understand legal concepts and principles relating to business activity and encourage them to develop their study of the law further.

Good luck with your studies, we hope you find the subject interesting and challenging and find the book retains the clarity for which Adams is renowned and which makes it such an invaluable tool across a wide spectrum of business law modules.

Stephanie Caplan and Graeme Lockwood

Table of cases

A (a child) v Ministry of Defence [2004] EWCA Civ 641, [2005] QB 183, CA, *affirming* [2003] EWHC 849 (QB) *392*

A and Others v National Blood Authority [2001] 3 All ER 289 *350, 351, 356, 360*

A v B, sub nom Garry Flitcroft v Mirror Group Newspapers Ltd [2002] 2 All ER 545 *49, 620–1, 623–4, 625, 628*

A v Ministry of Justice (2004) *392*

AB v Tameside & Glossop Health Authority (1997) 8 Med LR 91 *325*

Abouzaid v Mothercare (UK) Ltd [2000] 1 All ER (D) 2436, CA *354*

Achbita and Bougnaoui v G4S Secure Solutions and another (2017, EUECJ) *440, 443, 461*

Adams v Lindsell (1818) 1 B & Ald 681 *94, 639*

Addie (Robert) & Sons (Collieries) Ltd v Dumbreck [1929] AC 358, HL *632*

Addis v Gramophone Ltd [1909] AC 488, HL *246*

Adler v George [1964] 1 All ER 628 *37*

Aerial Advertising v Batchelors Peas [1938] 2 All ER 788 *247*

Albert v Motor Insurers Bureau [1971] 2 All ER 1345, HL *112*

Alcock v Chief Constable of South Yorkshire [1991] UKHL 5, [1992] 1 AC 310 *326–7, 332, 340, 634, 643*

Allcard v Skinner (1887) 36 Ch D 145 *200*

Alliance Bank v Broome (1864) 2 Drew& Sm 289 *103*

Allin v City & Hackney Health Authority (1996) 7 Med LR 167 *325*

Amalgamated Investment & Property Co Ltd v John Walker & Sons [1977] 1 WLR 164 *232*

Anderton v Ryan [1985] 2 All ER 355 *632*

Andreae v Selfridge [1938] Ch 11 *377*

Andrews v Singer [1934] All ER 479 *137*

Anglia TV v Reed [1971] 3 All ER 690 *245*

Anglo Overseas Transport Ltd v Titan Industrial Corporation [1959] 2 Lloyd's Rep 152 *269, 277*

Appleby v Myers (1867) LR 2 CP 651 *235, 237*

ARB v Hammersmith [2018] ECWA Civ 2803 *258*

Archer (Lady) v Williams [2003] EWHC 1670 (QB) *622–3*

Arcos v Ronaasen [1933] AC 470 *146*

Arensen v Casson Beckman Rutley & Co. [1977] AC 747 *270, 278*

Armhouse Lee Ltd v Chappell (1996) *The Times*, 7 August, CA *206*

Armstrong v Jackson [1917] 2 KB 822 *271*

Arnold v Britton & others [2015] UKSC 36 *126–7, 140*

Ashbury Railway Carriage Co. v Riche (1875) LR 7 HL 653, HL *519*

Aslam, Farrar and others v (UBER) London & others [2018] EWCA Civ 2748 *402–3*

Associated Japanese Bank (International) v Credit du Nord [1989] 1 WLR 255 *186*

Associated Newspaper Holdings v Insert Media Ltd [1991] 3 All ER 535 *612*

Associated Tyre Specialists v Waterhouse [1976] IRLR 386 *409*

Aswan Engineering Establishment Co. Ltd v Lupadine [1987] 1 All ER 135, CA *149, 171*

Ate My Heart Inc v Mind Candy Ltd [2011] EWHC 2741 (Ch) *603*

Atkin v Enfield Hospital Management Committee [1975] IRLR 217 *471*

Atlas Express v Kafco Importers & Distributors [1989] 1 All ER 641 *195*

Attorney General v Guardian Newspapers (No. 2) [1990] AC 109, HL *619, 620*

Attwood v Small (1838) 6 Cl & F 232 *179*

Atwal v Rochester [2010] EWHC 2338 (TCC) *230, 237*

Austin v Commissioner of Police of the Metropolis [2009] UKHL 5 *48*

Autoclenz v Belcher [2011] UKSC 41 *400*

Avery v Bowden (1855) 5 E & B 714 *242*

Avon Finance v Bridger [1985] 2 All ER 281, CA *196–7*

Azimut-Benetti Spa (Benetti Division) v Healey [2010] EWHC 2234 (Comm), [2011] 1 Lloyd's Rep 251 *473*

Azmi v Kirklees Metropolitan Borough Council (2007) *The Times*, 17 April, [2007] ICR 1154, EAT *442, 461*

Badger v Ministry of Defence [2006] 3 All ER 173 *303, 643*

Bairstow Eves London Central Ltd v Smith [2004] EWHC 263 (QB) *168*

Baker v National Air Traffic Services Ltd (2009) ET/2203501/2007 *427*

Balfour v Balfour [1919] 2 KB 571, CA *112*

Barber v Guardian Royal Exchange Assurance Group C-262/88 [1991] 1 QB 344, [1990] ICR 616, ECJ *413*

Barber v Somerset County Council [2004] UKHL 13, HL *413*

Barclays Bank v O'Brien [1993] 4 All ER 417, HL *198*

Barclays Bank v Various Claimants [2018] EWCA Civ 1670 *388, 644*

Barker v Corus UK Ltd; Murray v British Shipbuilders (Hydrodynamics) Ltd; Patterson v Smiths Dock Ltd [2006] 3 All ER 785, HL *294–6*

Barkway v South Wales Transport Co Ltd [1950] 1 All ER 392 *292*

Barnett v Chelsea & Kensington Hospital Management Committee [1969] 1 QB 420 *292*

Barnett v Packer [1940] 3 All ER 575 *345*

Barrett v Deere (1828) Moo & M 200, HL *264, 642*

Barrett v Enfield Borough Council [1999] 3 WLR 79 *335, 337*

Barton v Armstrong [1975] 2 All ER 465, PC *194, 641*

Batcheller v Tunbridge Wells Gas Company (1901) 84 LT 765 *383*

Batisha v Say [1977] IRRLIB 109 *446*

Baxter v Barnes [2015] EWHC 54 *153–4, 171*

Bayley v Manchester, Sheffield and Lincolnshire Railway (1873) LR 8 CP 148 *388*

Beale v Taylor [1967] 3 All ER 253, CA *146*

Beard v London Omnibus Co. [1900] 2 QB 530 *389*

Bell Houses Ltd v City Wall Properties Ltd [1966] 2 WLR 1323, CA *520*

Bell v Lever Bros 1932 AC 161 *185*

Benveniste v University of Southampton [1989] ICR 617 *452*

Berlei (UK) v Bali Brassiere Co. [1969] 2 All ER 812 *601, 607*

Bernstein v Pamson [1987] 2 All ER 220 *164*

Beswick v Beswick [1968] AC 58 *254–5*

Bettini v Gye (1875–76) LR 1 QBD 183 *129, 237*

Bickerstaff v Butcher NIIT/92/14 *430*

Bigg v Boyd Gibbons [1971] 1 WLR 913, CA *83*

Bissett v Wilkinson [1927] AC 58 *174, 641*

Blackburn and Another v Chief Constable of West Midlands Police [2008] EWCA Civ 1208 *452*

Blackpool & Fylde Aero Club v Blackpool Council [1990] 3 All ER 25, CA *85, 99*

Bloom v American Swiss Watch Co [1915] App D 100 *84*

Bogle and Others v Mcdonald's Restaurants Ltd [2002] EWHC 490 (QB) *353*

Bolam v Friern Hospital Management Committee [1957] 1 WLR 582, CA *287, 289*

Bolitho v City and Hackney Area Health Authority [1997] 4 All ER 771 *289*

Bolton v Mahadeva [1972] 2 All ER 1322 *227*

Bolton v Stone [1951] AC 850 *285*

Bowen v National Trust [2011] EWHC 1992 *366*

Boychuk v Symons Holdings [1977] IRLR 395 *471*

BP Exploration Co (Libya) Ltd v Hunt (No 2) [1983] 2 AC 352, [1982] 1 All ER 925, HL *236*

Brace v Calder [1895] 2 QB 253 *252, 642*

Bracebridge Engineering v Darby [1990] IRLR 3 *409*

Bradbury v Morgan (1862) 1 H & C 249 *85*

Branco v Cobarro [1947] 2 All ER 101, CA *90*

BRC Engineering Ltd v Schelff [1921] 2 Ch 563 *215*

Brinkibon Ltd v Stahag Stahl und Stahlwarenhandels GmbH [1983] 2 AC 34, [1982] 1 All ER 293, HL, *affirming* [1980] 2 Lloyd's Rep 556, CA *10, 93*

Bristol Conservatories Ltd v Conservatories Custom Built Ltd [1989] RPC 455 *612*

British Celanese v Hunt [1969] 1 WLR 959, CA *374*

British Home Stores v Burchell [1978] ICR 303 *471*

British Railways Board v Herrington [1972] 2 WLR 537, HL *371, 632*

Brogden v Metropolitan Railway Co. (1877) 2 App Cas 666, HL *92*

Brown v Cotterill (1934) 51 LTR 21 *344*

BTI v Sequana [2019] EWCA Civ 112 *551*

Bull and Another v Hall and Another [2013] UKSC 73 *457*

Bunker v Charles Brand [1969] 2 QB 480 *364*

Bushell v Faith [1970] 2 WLR 272, HL *557*

Butler Machine Tools v Ex-cell-o Ltd [1979] 1 All ER 965 *89*

Byrne v Van Tienhoven (1880) 5 CPD 344 *95*

C (a Debtor), Re (1994) 11 May, unreported *110*

Cambridge Water Co v Eastern Counties Leather [1994] 2 AC 264, [1994] 1 All ER 53, HL *384*

Campbell v Mirror Group Newspapers Ltd [2004] 2 All ER 995, HL *618, 621, 623–4, 628, 650*

Canadian Imperial Bank of Commerce v Beck (2010) UKEAT/0141/10/RN, [2010] All ER (D) 102 (Sep) *428*

Caparo Industries plc v Dickman [1990] 1 All ER 568, HL *283, 309, 317–19, 305, 562, 568*

Capital and Counties Bank plc v Hampshire Fire Brigade [1997] QB 1004, CA *333*

Capper Pass v Lawton [1977] IRLR 366 *449*

Car & Universal Finance Co. Ltd v Caldwell [1964] 1 All ER 290 *188*

Carlill v Carbolic Smoke Ball Co. Ltd [1893] 1 QB 256, CA *84, 99, 639*

Cartwright v Cartwright (1853) 3 De G M 982 *208*

Cavendish Square Holdings BV v Talal El Makdessi [2015] UKSC 67 *251–2*

Cehave NV v Bremer Handelsgesellschaft (The Hansa Nord) [1975] 3 All ER 739, CA *130, 133, 640*

Central London Property Trust v High Trees House [1947] KB 130 *42, 110–11*

Century Insurance v Northern Irish Road Transport Board [1949] AC 406, HL *389*

Chadwick v British Rail [1967] 1 WLR 912 *324*

Chandok & Another v Tirkey [2014] UKEAT/0190141912 *438*

Chapelton v Barry UDC [1940] 1 All ER 456, CA *135*

Chappell v Nestlé & Co. Ltd [1959] 3 WLR 701, HL *104*

Chaproniere v Mason (1905) 21 TLR 633 *148*

Chaudhry v Prabhaker [1988] 1 WLR 29, CA *262, 270, 321*

Chief Constable of Hertfordshire Police v Van Colle; Smith v Chief Constable of Sussex [2008] UKHL 50, [2008] 3 All ER 977, HL *335–6*

Chipchase v British Titan Products [1956] 1 QB 545 *415*

City Equitable & Fire Insurance Co. Ltd, Re [1925] Ch 307 *547–8, 551*

Clay v Crump [1963] 3 All ER 687 *320*

Clea Shipping Corpn v Bulk Oil International [1984] 1 All ER 129 *241*

Cleveland Petroleum v Dartstone Ltd [1969] 1 All ER 201, CA *216*

Clyde & Co v Van Winkelhof [2011] ECHC 668 (QB); [2011] All ER (D) 270 (Mar) *66*

Cohen v Roche [1927] 1 KB 169 *254*

Coleman v Attridge Law (Case C-303/06) [2008] All ER (EC) 1105, [2008] 3 CMLR 777, ECJ *431*

Collins v Associated Greyhound Race Courses Ltd [1930] 1 Ch 1 *268*

Collins v Godefroy (1831) B & Ad 950 *105*

Colour Quest Ltd v Total Downstream UK plc [2009] EWHC 540 (Comm); [2009] All ER (D) 311 (Mar), Comml Ct *384–5*

Colour Quest Ltd v Total Downstream UK plc [2009] EWHC 823 (Comm), [2009] All ER (D) 152 (Apr), Comml Ct *384–5*

Combe v Combe [1951] 2 KB 215, CA *110–11*

Commission for Racial Equality v Dutton [1989] IRLR 8, CA *437*

Community Dental Centres Ltd v Sultan-Darmon (2010) UKEAT/0532/09/da, [2010] IRLR 1024 *401*

Community Integrated Care Ltd v De Smith (2008) UKEATS/0015/08/MT, EAT *470*

Computer Associates UK Ltd v The Software Incubator Ltd [2018] EWCA Civ 518 *278*

Condor v The Barron Knights [1966] WLR 87 *229*

Confetti Records (a firm) v Warner Music UK Ltd (trading as East West Records) [2003] EWHC 1274 (Ch), [2003] All ER (d) 61 (Jun) (Ch) *92*

Cooperative Insurance Society v Argyll Stores (Holdings) Ltd [1998] AC 1, [1997] 3 All ER 297, HL *255*

Corby Group Litigation v Corby Borough Council [2009] EWHC 2109 (TCC) *382*

Corr v IBC Vehicles Ltd [2008] UKHL 13, [2008] 2 All ER 943 *297*

Cosmetic Warriors Ltd and Lush Ltd v Amazon.co.uk Ltd and Amazon EU Sarl [2014] EWHC 181 (Ch) *602*

Couturier v Hastie (1856) 5 HLC 673, HL *186*

Coventry and Others v Lawrence [2015] UKSC 50 *376*

Cox v Ministry of Justice [2014] EWCA Civ 132 *388*

Cox v Post Office (1997) (unreported) The Daily Telegraph, 5 November *430*

Craig, Re [1971] Ch 95 *197*

Cream Holdings Ltd v Davenport [2011] EWCA Civ 1287; [2011] All ER (D) 59 (Nov) *521–2*

Credit Lyonnais v Burch [1997] IRLR 167, [1997] 1 All ER 144, CA *199, 202*

Crowhurst v Amersham Burial Board (1878) 4 Ex D 5, [1874–80] All ER Rep 89, Ex D *383*

Cundy v Lindsay (1878) 3 App Cas 459, HL *188–9, 191*

Cunningham v Reading Football Club Ltd (1991) 157 LG Rev 481, [1992] PIQR P 141 *365*

Currie v Misa (1875) LR 10 Ex 153 *101, 639*

Curtis v Chemical Cleaning and Dyeing Co, Ltd [1951] 1 All ER 631, CA *136–7*

Cutter v Powell (1795) 6 Term Rep 320 *225–6, 228, 237*

D & C Builders v Rees [1965] 3 All ER 837, CA *111*

D v East Berkshire Community Health NHS Trust and Others [2005] UKHL 23; [2005] 2 All ER 443 *337*

Dalkia Utilities Services Plc v Caltech International Ltd [2006] EWHC 63 (Comm) *239*

Dalton v Burtons Gold Medal Biscuit Co. Ltd [1974] IRIR 45 *406, 645*

Dany Lions Ltd v Bristol Cars Ltd [2014] EWHC 817 (QB) *79*

Davey v Harrow Corporation [1957] 1 QB 60, CA *374*

Davis Contractors v Fareham UDC [1956] 2 All ER 145, HL *232, 258*

Davison v Kent Meters [1975] IRLR 145 *470*

De Beers Products Ltd v International General Electrics [1975] 1 WLR 972 *617*

De Francesco v Barnum (1890) 45 Ch D 430 *219*

Dennis v Ministry of Defence [2003] EWHC 793 (QB) *378, 385*

Devon Primary Care Trust v Readman [2013] EWCA Civ 1110 CA, *478*

Dickinson v Dodds (1876) 2 Ch D 463, CA *10, 87*

Dimmock v Hallett (1866) 2 Ch App 21 *176*

Director General of Fair Trading v First National Bank [2001] 1 All ER 97, HL *167, 168, 171*

Dollman v Hillman [1941] 1 All ER 355 *383*

Donoghue v Stevenson [1932] AC 562, HL *282, 306, 308, 320, 343–5, 360, 634, 642, 644*

Dooley v Cammell Laird & Co [1951] 2 Lloyd's Rep 271 *323*

Douglas and Another v Hello! Ltd [2001] 2 All ER 289, CA *612, 624, 625*

Douglas and Another v Hello! Ltd [2005] 4 All ER 128, CA *612, 625, 628*

Douglas and Another v Hello! Ltd (No. 3) [2007] 2 WLR 920, [2007] 4 All ER 545 *612–13, 638*

Doyle v Olby (Ironmongers) [1969] 2 QB 158 *180*

DSD and NBV v Commissioner of Police for the Metropolis [2014], EWHC 2493 (QB) *45–6, 52, 336*

Duffose v Melbry Events [2011] EWCA Civ 1711 *366*

Dulieu v White & Sons [1901] 2 KB 669, [1900–3] All ER Rep 353, KBD *321*

Dunlop Pneumatic Tyre Co. v New Garage & Motor Co Ltd [1915] AC 79, HL *250, 251*

Dunlop Rubber Co. Ltd v Selfridge [1915] AC 847, HL *101, 116, 639*

Dunn v Institute of Cemetery and Crematorium Management (2011) UKEAT/0531/10/DA, [2012] All ER (D) 173 (Feb), EAT *435*

Dyer v London Ambulance NHS Trust [2014] UKEAT/0500/13 *433*

Eastham v Newcastle United Football Club [1964] EC 413, [1963] 3 All ER 139, AUS HC *206, 223*

Eastwood and Another v Magnox plc; McCabe v Cornwall County Council [2004] UKHL 35; [2004] 3 All ER 991 *247*

Edgington v Fitzmaurice (1885) 29 ChD 459 *175*

Edwards v Chesterfield Royal Hospital NHS Foundation Trust [2011] UKSC 58, [2012] 2 AC 22 *247*

Electrolux v Hudson [1977] FSR 312 *597, 607*

Eley v Positive Life Assurance Co. (1876) 1 ExD 88 *521*

English v Sanderson Blinds Ltd [2008] EWCA Civ 1421 *455*

Entores Ltd v Miles Far East Corporation [1955] 2 All ER 493, CA *93, 99*

Errington v Errington & Woods [1952] 1 All ER 149, CA *88*

Erven Warnink BV v Townend & Sons (Hull) Ltd [1979] AC 731 *612*

Esso Petroleum Co Ltd v Harper's Garage (Stourport) Ltd [1968] Ac 269, [1967] 1 All ER 699, HL, varying [1966] 2 QB 514, CA, *affirming* [1965] 2 All ER 933, QBD *216*

Esso Petroleum v Mardon [1976] 2 All ER 5, CA *172, 175, 202*

Etam plc v Rowan [1996] IRLR 75, EAT *447, 646*

Europe PLC v Selskabet (Formerly Roskilde Bank) (2016) EWCA *319*

European Commission v UK (C-300/95) [1997] ECR I–2649, ECJ *350*

Evans v Triplex Safety Glass Co Ltd [1936] 1 All ER 283 *346, 643*

Evans v Xactly UKEATPA/0128/18/LA *425*

Everet v Williams (1725) cited in [1899] 1 QB 826 *205*

Eweida and Others v United Kingdom (Applications 48420/10, 59842/10, 51671/10 and 36516/10) [2013] ECHR 48420/10, [2013] All ER (D) 69 (Jan) *443–4, 461*

Eweida v British Airways [2010] EWCA Civ 80 *433*

Faccenda Chicken Ltd v Fowler [1986] 1 All ER 617, CA *212, 623*

Fairchild v Glenhaven Funeral Services [2002] 3 All ER 305, HL *294–6, 306*

Farley v Skinner (No. 2) [2001] 4 All ER 801, HL *248*

Farr v Hoveringham Gravels Ltd [1972] IRLR 104 *473, 487*

Fawcett v Smethurst (1914) 84 LJKB 473 *218*

Feldaroll Foundry Plc v Hermes Leasing London Ltd [2004] EWCA Civ 747 *161*

Felthouse v Bindley (1862) 11 CB (NS) 869 *96*

Fenty v Topshop/Topman Ltd [2015] EWCA Civ 3 *612–13, 628*

Fibrosa Spolka Akcyjna v Fairbairn Lawson Combe Barbour Ltd [1942] UKHL 4 *223, 231*

Fisher v Bell [1960] 3 WLR 919, QBD *37, 81, 639*

Fitch v Dewes [1921] 2 Ch 159, HL *211*

Flack v Baldry [1988] 1 WLR 214 *36*

Fletcher v Countrywide Estate Agents ET/3400899/2016 *468*

Flitcroft (Garry) v Mirror Group Newspapers Ltd [2002] 2 All ER 545 see A v B, sub nom Garry

Foley v Classique Coaches [1934] All ER 88, CA *80*

Ford Motor Co. Ltd and Iveco Fiat Spa's Design Application [1993] RPC 167 *594*

Forster & Sons Ltd v Suggett (1918) 35 TLR 87 *211*

Foss v Harbottle (1843) 2 Hare 461 *577, 637*

Freeman & Lockyer v Buckhurst Park Properties (Mangal) Ltd [1964] 2 QB 480 *547, 647*

Froom v Butcher [1976] QB 286, [1975] 3 All ER 520, CA *302*

Fuller v Stephanie Bowman Ltd [1977] IRLR 87 *478*

Gallie v Lee (Saunders v Anglia Building Society) [1970] 3 All ER 961, HL *193*

Gamerco SA v ICM/Fair Warning (Agency) Ltd [1995] 1 WLR 1226 *229, 235*

Games Retail Ltd v Laws [2014] UKEAT/0188/14 *471*

Gan Menachem Hendon Ltd v De Groen [2019] UKEAT 59/18 *445*

GB v Home Office [2015] QBD 31 (March) *392*

Geddling v Marsh [1920] 1 KB 668 *148*

George Mitchell Ltd v Finney Lock Seeds Ltd [1983] 2 All ER 737, HL *157*

Gibson v Manchester City Council [1979] 1 All ER 972, HL *82*

Gill v SAS Ground Services UK Ltd (2009) eat/2705021/09 *472*

Gillingham Borough Council v Medway (Chatham) Dock Co Ltd [1993] QB 343, [1992] 3 WLR 449, QBD *375*

Glasbrook Bros v Glamorgan County Council [1925] AC 270, HL *106*

Glasgow Corporation v Taylor [1922] AC 44, HL *367*

Godley v Perry [1960] 1 WLR 9 *151*

Golden Ocean Group v Salgaocar [2012] EWCA Civ 265 *78*

Goldsoll v Goldman [1915] 1 Ch 292, CA *217*

Goldsworthy v Brickell [1987] 1 All ER 853, CA *197*

Gordon v Selico [1986] 278 EG 53 *174*

Gorfin v Distressed Gentlefolks' Aid Association [1973] IRLR 290 *473, 487*

Grainger plc v Nicholson [2010] 2 All ER 253, [2010] ICR 360 *441–2*

Granada Group Ltd v Ford Motor Co Ltd [1972] FSR 103, [1973] RPC 49, Ch *614*

Grant v Australian Knitting Mills [1936] AC 85, PC *344*

Gravil v Carroll and Redruth Rugby Club [2008] EWCA (Civ) 689, [2008] IRLR 829, CA *391*

Great Northern Railway v Swaffield (1874) LR Exch 132 *267*

Great Peace Shipping v Tsavliris (International) Ltd [2002] 4 All ER 689 *185*

Greater Manchester Police Authority v Power [2010] All ER (d) 173 (Oct) *441*

Green v Cade Bros [1978] 1 Lloyd's Rep 602 *157*

Gregg v Scott [2005] UKHL 2, [2005] 4 All ER 812 *296*

GryfLowczowski v Hinchingbrooke Healthcare NHS Trust [2006] ICR 425 *232, 256*

Guinness plc v Saunders [1990] 2 AC 663 *553, 568*

Guthing v Lynn (1831) 2 B&AD 231 *79*

Hadley v Baxendale (1854) 9 Exch 341 *243, 257*

Hale v Jennings Bros [1938] 1 All ER 579, CA *383*

Halsey v Esso Petroleum [1961] 1 WLR 683 *374*

Hambrook v Stokes [1925] 1 KB 141, CA *326, 634*

Harlingdon & Leinster Enterprises Ltd v Christopher Hull Fine Art Ltd [1990] 1 All ER 737, CA *146–7*

Hartley v Ponsonby (1857) 7 EL BL 872 *106*

Hartog v Colin & Shields [1939] 3 All ER 566 *192*

Harvey v Facey [1893] AC 552 *82*

Hashman v Milton Park (Dorset) Ltd (t /a Orchard Park) (2011) ET/3105555/2009 *442*

Hatton v Sutherland [2002] 2 All ER 1 *413*

Hayes v James & Charles Dodd [1990] 2 All ER 815, CA *249*

Haynes v Harwood [1935] 1 KB 147, CA *301*

Hayward v Cammell Laird Shipbuilders [1988] 1 All ER 503, HL *450, 645*

Hedley Byrne v Heller [1963] AC 465, [1963] 2 All ER 575, HL *180, 314–17, 320–1, 340, 502, 643*

Hellard and Others v Carvalho [2013] EWHC 2876 (Ch), [2013] All ER (D) 240 *550–1*

Herman v Charlesworth [1925] 2 KB 123 *208*

Herne Bay Steam Boat Co. v Hutton [1903] 2 KB 683 *331*

Herschtal (or Herschthal) v Stewart & Ardern Ltd [1939] 4 All ER 123, KBD *344*

Heywood v Wellers [1976] QB 446 *248*

Hickman v Romney Marsh Sheep Breeders Association [1915] 1 Ch 881 *520*

Hilder v Associated Portland Cement [1961] 1 WLR 1434 *285*

Hill v Chief Constable of West Yorkshire [1988] 2 All ER 238, HL *284, 336, 642*

Hillas v Arcos (1932) 147 LT 503, HL *79*

Hirst v United Kingdom (No 2) (Application no 74025/01) (2005) 42 EHRR 849, [2005] All ER (d) 59 (Oct) *45*

Hochster v de la Tour (1853) 2 E & B 678 *238*

Hodges (Gt) & Sons v Hackbridge Residential Hotel [1939] 4 All ER 307 *269*

Hoenig v Isaacs [1952] 2 All ER 176 *227*

Hogg v Cramphorn Ltd [1967] Ch 254 *549*

Holis Metal Industries v GmB [2008] ICR 464, [2007] All ER (d) 304 (Dec), EAT *480*

Hollywood Silver Fox Farm v Emmett [1936] 2 KB 468 *377*

Holwell Securities v Hughes [1974] 1 All ER 161, CA *95*

Home Counties Dairies v Skilton [1970] 1 All ER 1227 *214, 217, 223*

Home Office v Dorset Yacht Co. Ltd [1970] AC 1004, HL *332*

Home Office v Holmes [1984] 3 All ER 549 *447, 646*

Hong Kong Fir Shipping Co. Ltd v Kawasaki Kisen Kaisha [1962] 2 WLR 474, CA *129–30, 640*

Hood v West End Motor Car Packing [1917] 2 KB 38 *176*

Hotson v East Berkshire Health Authority [1987] 2 All ER 909 *296*

Household Insurance v Grant (1879) 4 Ex D 216, CA *94*

Howard Marine & Dredging Co. Ltd v Ogden & Sons Ltd [1978] QB 574, CA *180*

Howden v Capital Copiers [1998] IRLR 586 *430*

Howmet Ltd v Economy Devices Ltd [2016] EWCA Civ 847 *345–6*

HRH Prince of Wales see Prince of Wales (HRH)

Hudson v Ridge Manufacturing Co. Ltd [1957] 2 QB 348 *411, 421*

Hufford v Samsung Electronics (UK) Ltd [2014] All ER (D) 60 *356*

Hufton v Somerset County Council [2011] EWCA Civ 789; [2011] All ER (D) 72 (Jul) *368*

Hughes v Lord Advocate [1963] AC 837, HL *297*

Humble v Hunter [1848] 12 QB 310 *259, 642*

Hunter v Canary Wharf [1997] 2 All ER 426 *380, 395*

Hurst & Others v Hone & Others [2010] EWHC 1159 (QB), [2010] All ER (D) 256 (May) *177*

Hussain and Livingstone v Lancaster City Council [1999] 2 WLR 1142, CA *380, 386*

Hutton v Warren (1836) 1 M &W 406 Exch *127*

Hyde v Wrench (1840) 3 Beav 334 *86, 639*

ICI v Shatwell [1964] AC 656, HL *302, 394*

IDC v Cooley [1972] 1 WLR 443 *549, 552, 568*

Ide v ATB Sales Ltd [2008] EWCA Civ 424 *355–6*

Immingham Storage v Clear Plc [2011] EWCA Civ 89; (2011) 135 Con LR 224 *90, 94, 99*

Ingram v Little [1960] 3 WLR 504 *189–90*

Inland Revenue Commissioners v Fry [2001] STC 1715, [2002] 06 LS Gaz R 30, Ch *92*

Insley v Accent Catering [2014] ET/3200687/2014 *472*

Interfoto Picture Library Ltd v Stiletto Productions [1988] 1 All ER 348, CA *136, 140*

Interlego AG's Trademark Application Re [1998] RPC 69, Ch *601*

Isabella Ship Owners v Shagang Shipping Co. Ltd (The Aquafaith) [2012] 2 Lloyd's Rep 61 *241*

Isle of Wight Tourist Board v Coombes [1976] IRLR 413 *409*

IWGB v Deliveroo (2017) TUR1/985 (2016) *401*

Jackson v Horizon Holidays Ltd [1975] 3 All ER 92, CA *117, 120*

James McNaughten Paper Group Ltd v Hicks Anderson & Co. [1991] 2 QB 113, CA *317–19*

Jarvis v Swans Tours [1973] 3 WLR 954, CA *247–8, 258*

JD v Mather [2012] EWHC 3063 (QB), [2012] All ER (D) 77 (Nov) *296*

Jeancharm v Barnet Football Club [2003] EWCA Civ 58, CA *250–1*

Jet2.com v Blackpool Airports [2012] EWCA Civ 417 *79*

Johnson v Unisys [2001] 2 All ER 801, HL *246*

Johnston and Others v NEI International and other Conjoined Claims [2007] UKHL 39, [2007] 4 All ER 1047, HL *322–3*

Jolley v London Borough of Sutton [2000] 1 WLR 1082, HL *298*

Jon Beauforte (London) Ltd, Re [1953] 1 All ER 660 *522*

Jones v Daniel [1894] 2 Ch 332 *89*

Jones v Lipman [1962] 1 WLR 832 *501, 512*

Jones v Tower Boot Co. Ltd [1997] IRLR 168, CA *440*

Jones v Vernons Pools [1938] 2 All ER 626 *114*

Junior Books Ltd v Veitchi Co Ltd [1983] 1 AC 520 *348, 360*

K, Re; Re M plc [2005] EWCA Civ 619, [2005] All ER (D) 23 (Mar), (2005) *The Times*, 15 March, CA *501, 512*

Kaltoft v Billund (Case C–354/13) [2014], ECJ *430*

Kaye v Robertson [1991] FSR 62 *610*

Kearley v Thompson (1890) 24 QBD 742 *209*

Kearney v Eric Waller [1966] 1 QB 29 *364*

Keir v Leeman (1809) 6 QB 308 *207*

Kelly and Another v GE Healthcare [2009] EWHC 181 (Pat), [2010] Bus LR D28 *597*

Kendall v Lillico [1968] 3 WLR 110, HL *135*

Kent v Griffiths and Others (No. 3) [2001] QB 36, CA *334*

Keown v Coventry Healthcare NHS Trust [2006] EWCA Civ 39, [2006] 1 WLR 953, CA *372*

Khorasandjian v Bush [1993] QB 727 *380*

Killen v Horseworld Ltd [2012] EWHC 363 (QB) *553–4*

King's Norton Metal Co. v Edridge, Merrett & Co. (1897) 14 TLR 98 *188*

Kiriri Cotton Co. Ltd v Dewani [1960] AC 192 *209*

Kleinwort Benson v Malaysia Mining Corporation Bhd [1989] 1 All ER 785, CA *115*

Knapp v The Railway Executive [1949] 2 All ER 508 *414*

Knowles v Liverpool CC [1993] 1 WLR 1428 *409*

Knowsley Metropolitan Borough Council v Willmore [2011] UKSC 10, [2011] 2 WLR 523 *296*

Kohli v Lit and Others [2009] EWHC 2893 (Ch), [2010] 1 BCLC 14 *579–80*

Kolmar Group AG v Traxpo Enterprises PVT Ltd [2010] EWHC 113 (Comm) *196*

Koufos v Czarnikow Ltd (The Heron II) [1969] 1 AC 350, HL *244, 258*

Krell v Henry [1903] 2 KB 740 *231*

Latimer v AEC [1953] AC 643 *286*

Lawrence v Lexcourt Holdings Ltd [1978] 2 All ER 810 *175*

Lawrence v Pembrokeshire County Council [2007] EWCA Civ 446, [2007] 1 WLR 2991, CA *337*

Leakey v The National Trust [1980] QB 485, CA *379*

Lee v Ashers Banking Company Ltd and Others [2018] UKSC 49 *456*

Leeman v Montague [1936] 2 All ER 1677 *377*

Leslie v Sheill [1914] 3 KB 607 *220*

L'Estrange v Graucob [1934] 2 KB 394 *136*

Levola Hengelo BV v Smilde Foods BV C-310/17 [2018] *608*

Lewis v Averay [1971] 3 WLR 603, CA *190*

Lewis v Six Counties [2005] EWCA Civ 1805; (2006) *The Times*, 20 January, CA *365*

Lisk v Shield Guardian Co. Ltd (2011) ET/3300873/11 *442*

Lister v Hesley Hall [2001] 2 All ER 769, HL *390, 395*

Litster v Thom & Sons Ltd [1975] IRLR 47 *469*

Littlewoods Organisation v Harris [1978] 1 All ER 1026, CA *215, 223*

Liverpool City Council v Irwin 1977 AC 739 *124*

Lofty v Harris T/A EAT 0177/17 *430*

Lombard North Central plc v Butterworth [1987] QB 527, CA *13, 140*

LRH Services v Trew, Brewer and O'Neill [2018] EWHC 600 (Ch) *554, 568*

Lucasfilm v Ainsworth [2011] UKSC 39; [2012] 1 AC 208 *588*

Luxmoore May v Messenger May Bakers 1 WLR 1009, CA *289*

Lyons & Co. v Gulliver [1914] 1 Ch 631 *382*

Macarthys v Smith [1981] QB 180, [1980] 3 WLR 929,[1981] 1 All ER 111, [1980] ICR 672 *450–1*

Maga v Trustees of the Birmingham Archdiocese [2010] EWCA Civ 256 *390–1*

Majrowski v Guy's and St Thomas' NHS Trust [2006] UKHL 34, [2007] 1 All ER 224, HL *391*

Malik v Bank of Credit & Commerce International [1998] AC 20, HL *246, 409*

Malone v Laskey [1907] 2 KB 141 *380*

Maloney v Lambeth Council (1966) 198 EG 895 *367*

Maloney v Torfaen CBC [2005] EWCA Civ 1762, CA *364, 371*

Managers (Holborn) Ltd v Hohne [1977] IRLR 230 *478*

Mandla v Dowell Lee [1983] IRLR 209, HL *437, 440*

Marc Rich & Co. AG v Bishop Rock Marine (The Nicholas H) [1996] AC 211; [1995] 3 All ER 307 *283*

Maritime National Fish Ltd v Ocean Trawlers Ltd [1935] AC 524 *234*

Marks & Spencer plc v One in a Million Ltd [1998] FSR 265 *616*

Martin v Parkham Foods (2006) ET/1800241/06 EAT *456, 646*

Mathieson v Noble [1972] IRLR 76 *472*

Mattocks v Mann [1993] RTR 13 *300*

Max Mosley see Mosley (Max) v News Group Newspapers Ltd [2008] EWHC 1777 (QB), (2008) *The Times* 28 July 2008 *618, 620, 650*

McArdle, Re [1951] Ch 669, CA *102, 120, 640*

McCarthy v Chief Constable of South Yorkshire (1996) (unreported) *328*

McCutcheon v David McBrayne Ltd [1964] 1 All ER 430 *135*

McGhee v National Coal Board [1973] 1 WLR 1, [1972] 3 All ER 1008 *293–4*

McKenna v British Aluminium Ltd [2002] Env LR 30 *385*

McKew v Holland & Cubitts Ltd [1969] 3 All ER 1621, HL *298*

McKinnon Industries v Walker [1951] WN 401 *378*

McLoughlin v O'Brien [1982] 2 WLR 982, HL *326, 643*

McMillan & Co. v Cooper (1923) 40 TLR 186 *587*

McRae v Commonwealth Disposals Commissions (1951) 84 CLR 377 *186*

McWilliams v Arrol [1962] 1 WLR 295 *292*

Merret v Bubb [2001] ILR 23/2/2001 *338*

Merritt v Merritt [1970] 2 All ER 760, CA *112*

Metropolitan Water Board v Dick Kerr & Co. [1918] AC 119, HL, *affirming* [1917] 2 KB 1, CA *232, 233*

Michael v Chief Constable of South Wales Police & Anor [2015] UKSC 2 *336*

Mihalis Angelos, The [1970] 3 WLR 601, CA *132, 133*

Miller v Karlinski (1945) 62 TLR 85 *207*

Milner and Milner v Carnival plc (t/a Cunard) [2010] EWCA Civ 389, [2010] 3 All ER 701, CA *243, 249, 253, 258*

Mint v Good [1950] 2 All ER 1159 *382*

Minter v Wellingborough Foundries (1981) *The Times* 202 *471*

Mohamud v WM Morrison Supermarkets [2014] EWCA Civ 116 *389–90*

Mondial Shipping and Chartering BV v Astarte Shipping Ltd [1995] CLC 1011 *93*

Monk v Harrington Ltd and Others [2008] EWHC 1879 (QB); [2009] PIQR P52 *324–5*

Moorcock, The (1889) 14 PD 64, CA *124*

Moore v C & A Modes [1981] IRLR 71 *470*

Morgan Crucible Co. plc v Hill Samuel Bank [1991] Ch 295 *319*

Morgan v Manser [1947] 2 All ER 266 *231*

Morris v Saxelby [1916] 1 AC 688, HL *212*

Morrish v Henlys (Folkestone) Ltd [1973] 2 All ER 137 *406*

Mosley (Max) v News Group Newspapers Ltd [2008] EWHC 1777 (QB), (2008) *The Times* 28 July 2008 *640, 650*

Moy v Stoop (1909) 25 TLR 262 *377*

Moyhing v Barts and London NHS Trust [2006] IRLR 860 *446, 645*

Muirhead v Industrial Tank Specialties Ltd [1986] QB 507 *347*

Murphy v Bradford Metropolitan Council (1991) *The Times* 11 February *366*

Murphy v Brentwood Council [1990] 3 WLR 414, HL *310, 312, 313*

Murray v Big Pictures UK Ltd [2008] EWCA Civ 446, [2008] 3 WLR 1360, CA *624–5*

NAD Electronics v NAD Computer Systems [1997] FSR 380, Ch *614, 628*

Nash v Inman [1908] 2 KB 1 *218*

National Telephone Co v Baker [1893] 2 Ch 186, 57 JP 373 *383*

Nettleship v Weston [1971] 3 All ER 581, CA *288*

Network Rail Infrastructure Ltd v Conarken Group Ltd; Network Rail Infrastructure Ltd v Farrell Transport Ltd [2011] EWCA Civ 644, CA, *affirming* [2010] EWHC 1852 (TCC); [2010] TCC 132, Tech & Constr Ct *306, 360*

Newcastle International Airport Ltd v Eversheds LLP [2012] EWHC 2648 (Ch), [2012] All ER (D) 20 (Oct) *265, 547*

Newman v Alarm Co. Ltd [1976] IRLR 45 *471*

Noble v David Gold & Sons (Holdings) Ltd [1980] IRLR 252 *449*

Nordenfelt v Maxim Nordenfelt Guns & Ammunition Co. Ltd [1894] AC 535 *215, 641*

North Glamorgan NHS Trust v Walters [2002] EWCA Civ 1792 *329*

North Yorkshire County Council v Ratcliffe [1995] ICR 833, HL *452*

Northumberland & Durham District Banking Co., ex parte Bigge (1858) 28 LJ Ch 50 *178*

Nottingham Patent Brick & Tile Co. Ltd v Butler (1886) 16 QBD 788 *176*

Numatic Ltd v Qualtex [2010] EWHC 1237 (Ch) 611–12, *584*

O'Brien v Associated Fire Alarms [1969] 1 All ER 93 *478*

Office of Fair Trading v Abbey National plc and Others [2009] UKSC 6, [2010] 1 AC 696 *168*

Office of Fair Trading v Ashbourne Management Services Ltd and Others [2011] EWHC 1237; [2011] CTLC 237 *162*

Office of Fair Trading v Foxtons [2009] EWCA Civ 288, [2009] 3 All ER 697 *162*

Ogwo v Taylor [1987] AC 431, HL *383, 395*

Olley v Marlborough Court Hotel [1949] 1 All ER 127, CA *134*

Omnibill (Pty) Ltd v Egpsxxx Ltd and Another [2014] EWHC 3762 (IPEC) *501–2*

O'Neill v Symm & Co. Ltd [1998] ICR 481, [1998] IRLR 232, EAT *430, 461*

Opel GmbH and Renault SA v Mitras Automotive [2008] EWHC 3205 (QB), [2008] CILL 2561 *106, 194–5*

Orchard v Lee [2009] EWCA Civ 295; (2009) *The Times,* 14 April *288*

Osman v Ferguson [1993] 4 All ER 344, CA *334–5*

Osman v UK [1999] 1 FLR 193 *284, 335, 337, 340*

Othman (abu Quatada) v United Kingdom application 8139/09 (2012) *50*

Ottoman Bank v Chakarian [1930] AC 277, PC *405*

Overseas Medical Supplies v Orient [1999] 1 All ER (Comm) 981 *159*

Overseas Tankship & Engineering (UK) v Mort Dock & Engineering Co (The Wagon Mound) (No 1) [1961] AC 388, [1961] 1 All ER 404, PC *42, 297, 229, 306, 643*

Owen v Professional Golf Association (2000) (unreported) *441*

Pagano v HGS [1976] I RLR 9 *411*

Page One Records v Britton [1968] 1 WLR 157 *255*

Page v Smith [1995] 2 All ER 736, HL *299, 321, 322, 643*

Palmer v Tees Health Authority [1999] Lloyd's Rep Med 351, CA *328–9*

Panesaar v Nestlé [1980] IRLR 64 *440*

Panorama Developments v Fidelis Furnishing Fabrics Ltd [1971] 3 WLR 440, CA *560, 568*

Pao On v Lau Yiu Long Long [1980] AC 614, [1979] 3 All ER 65, PC *194*

Paris v Stepney Council [1951] AC 367 *286*

Parker v Clark 1960 1 WLR 286, CA *112*

ParkingEye Ltd v Beavis [2015] UKSC *252*

Parkinson v College of Ambulance [1925] 2 KB 1 *208*

Parks-Cramer Co. v Thornton Ltd [1966] RPC 407, CA *596, 607*

Parsons v McLoughlin [1981] IRLR 65 *471*

Partridge v Crittenden [1968] 2 All ER 421 *81–2*

Patel v Ali [1984] Ch 283 *255*

Patel v Mirza [2014] EWCA Civ 1047, [2014] All ER (D) 279 (Jul) *209–10, 223*

Pearce v Brooks (1866) LR 1 Exch 213 *189, 206, 634*

Pennington v Surrey County Council and Surry Fire & Rescue Services [2006] EWCA Civ 1493, CA *409*

Pepper v Hart (1993, HL) *36, 39*

Pereira Fernandes (J) SA v Mehta [2006] 2 All ER 891 *93*

Perry v Harris [2008] EWCA Civ 907 *288, 290*

Perry v Sidney Phillips & Son [1982] 1 WLR 1297, CA *248*

Peters v Fleming (1840) 6 M & W 42 *218, 641*

Pharmaceutical Society (GB) v Boots Cash Chemists (Southern) Ltd [1953] 1 All ER 482, CA *81*

Phillips Electronics NV v Remington Consumer Products [1998] RPC 283 *600*

Phillips v Brooks [1919] 2 KB 243 *189–90*

Phillips v William Whitely [1938] 1 All ER 566 *288*

Phipps v Rochester Corporation [1955] 1 QB 450 *367*

Phones 4u Ltd v Phone4u.co.uk Internet Ltd [2006] EWCA Civ 244, CA *602*

Phonogram v Lane [1982] QB 939, CA *515, 528*

Photo Production Ltd v Securicor Transport Ltd [1980] 2 WLR 283, HL *138*

Pickstone v Freemans plc [1988] 2 All ER 803 *450*

Pierce v Doncaster Metropolitan Borough Council [2007] EWHC 2968 (QB), reversed in part [2008] EWCA Civ 1416, [2009] 1 FLR 1189, CA *337*

Pilkington v Wood [1953] 2 All ER 810 *253*

Pimlico Plumbers v Smith [2014] All ER (D) 88 (Dec) *401*

Pink Floyd Music v EMI Records [2010] EWCA Civ 1429, [2011] 1 WLR 770 *125*

Pinnel's case (1602) 5 Co. Rep 117 *107–8, 110, 640*

Piper v JRI (Manufacturing) Ltd [2006] EWCA Civ 1344 *355*

Planché v Colburn (1831) 8 Bing 14 *226*

PMS International Group v Magmatic [2016] UKSC 12 *593–4*

Polemis & Furness, Withy & Co. Re [1921] 3 KB 560, [1921] All ER Rep 40, CA *297*

Polkey v A.E. Dayton Services Ltd [1987] 3 All ER 974 *474*

Porcelli v Strathclyde Regional Council [1986] IRLR 134 *447*

Poussard v Spiers & Bond (1876) 1 QBD 410 *129, 238, 640*

Powell v Lee (1908) 99 LT 284 *91*

Power v Greater Manchester Police Authority see Greater Manchester Police Authority v Power

Power v Panasonic (UK) Ltd [2003] IRLR 151, [2002] All ER (D) 297 (Nov) *430*

Pride & Partners v Institute for Animal Health and Others [2009] EWHC 1617 (QB), [2009] NPC 56 *310*

Prince of Wales (HRH) v Associated Newspapers Ltd [2007] 2 All ER 139 *587, 618*

Proactive Sports Management Ltd v Wayne Rooney and Others [2010] EWHC 1807 (QB) *213*

Proform Sports Management Ltd v Pro-Active Sports Management Ltd [2007] 1 All ER 542 *219*

PSG Franchising Ltd v Lydia Darby Ltd [2012] EWHC 3707 (QB) *214*

PSJ v Newsgroup Newspapers Plc [2016] EWCA Civ 393 *619*

PSM International v Whitehouse & Willenhall Ltd [1992] FSR 489 *618–19*

Quilter v Hodson Developments Ltd [2016] EWCA Civ 1125 *181*

Quinn v CC Automotive Group (t/a Carcraft) [2010] EWCA Civ 1412; [2011] 2 All ER (Comm) 1412 *266, 272, 278*

R v Shivpuri [1986] UKHL 2 *632*

R (On the application of Begum) v Headteacher and Governors of Denbigh High School [2006] 2 All ER 487, HL *49, 52*

R (on the application of F and another) v Secretary of State for the Home Department [2010] 2 WLR 992 *47*

R (on the application of Laporte) v Chief Constable of Gloucestershire Constabulary [2007] 2 All ER 529, HL *47*

R (On the application of Moos and Another) v Commissioner of Police for the Metropolis [2011] EWHC 957 (Admin); [2011] All ER (D) 146 (Apr) *48–9*

R (on the application of Pearson) v Secretary of State for the Home Department and Martinez; Hirst v Attorney-General [2001] EWHC 239 (Admin) *45*

R (On the application of Unison) v The Lord Chancellor [2017] UKSC 51 *483*

R & B Customs Brokers Co Ltd v United Dominions Trust [1988] 1 WLR 321, CA *161*

R v Registrar of Companies, ex parte Attorney-General [1991] 2 QB 197 *517, 528*

Racing UK Ltd v Doncaster Racecourse Ltd and Doncaster Borough Council [2005] EWCA Civ 999 *264–5*

Radmacher v Granatino [2010] 3 WLR 1367, SC *208*

Raffles v Wichelhaus (1864) 2 H&C 906 *187*

Rainbow Estates Ltd v Tokenhold [1998] 3 WLR 980 *254*

Rainey v Greater Glasgow Health Board [1987] AC 224, HL *452, 461*

Ramsay v Love [2015] EWHC 65 (Ch) *263*

Ramsgate Hotel Co. v Montefiore (1866) LR 1 Exch 109 *86*

Ratcliff v Harper Adams Agricultural College [1999] 1 WLR 670 *302, 372, 395, 643*

Ratcliffe v Evans [1892] 2 QB 524 *616*

Rayfield v Hands [1958] 1 Ch 333, [1958] 2 All ER 194 *521, 528*

RDF Media Group plc v Alan Clements [2007] EWHC 2892 (QB), [2008] IRLR 207 *409, 421*

Read v Lyons & Co Ltd [1947] AC 156, [1946] 2 All ER 471 *383–4*

Ready Mixed Concrete v Ministry of Pensions and National Insurance [1968] 2 WLR 627 *387*

Real and Personal Advance v Palemphin (1893) 9 TLR 569 *263*

Reardon Smith Line v Hansen-Tangel [1976] 1 WLR 989, HL *133*

Redfearn v Serco Ltd (t/a West Yorkshire Transport Service) [2006] EWCA Civ 659, [2006] All ER (D) 366 (May), CA *438–9, 635*

Redgrave v Hurd (1881) 20 Ch D 1 *179*

Reeves v Commissioner of Police for the Metropolis [2000] 1 AC 360, [1999] 3 WLR 363, HL *299, 303*

Regazzoni v Sethia [1957] 3 All ER 286, HL *206*

Regus v Epcot Solutions Ltd [2008] EWCA Civ 361, CA *159*

Reid v PRP Architects [2006] EWCA Civ 1119, [2007] ICR 78, CA *415, 416, 421*

Reveille Independent plc v Anotech International (UK) Ltd [2016] EWCA 443 *90, 91, 93*

Rickards v Lothian [1913] AC 263, [1911–13] All ER Rep 71, PC *383–4*

Ritche v Atkinson (1808) 10 East 95 *226*

Ritchie (J & H) Ltd v Lloyd Ltd [2007] 2 All ER 353, [2007] 1 WLR 670, HL, reversing [2005] CSIH 3, IH *148, 171*

Robinson v Kilvert (1889) 41 Ch D 88, 58 LJ Ch 392, CA *378*

Rogers v Parish [1987] QB 933 *164*

Roles v Nathan [1963] 1 WLR 1117 *287, 367*

Rose & Frank Co. v J. R. Crompton & Bros [1925] AC 845, HL *114*

Routledge v Grant [1828] 4 Bing 653 *88*

Rowland v Divall [1923] 2 KB 500, CA *145*

Royal Bank of Scotland v Etridge (No. 2) [2001] 4 All ER 449, HL *199*

Royal College of Nursing v DHSS [1981] AC 800, HL *38, 39, 52*

Royscot Trust Ltd v Rogerson [1991] 2 QB 297 *180*

Ruxley Electronics & Construction Ltd v Forsyth [1995] 3 All ER 268 *245*

Ryan v Mutual Tontine Association [1893] 1 Ch 116 *254*

Rylands v Fletcher (1868) LR 3 HL 330, [1861–73] All ER Rep 1, HL *303, 383–5*

Sachs v Miklos [1948] 1 All ER 67 *267, 278*

Sagar v H. Ridehalgh & Son Ltd [1930] All ER 288, CA *404*

Salomon v Salomon & Co. Ltd [1897] AC 22, HL *500–1, 512, 648*

Sandhar v Department of Transport [2004] EWCA Civ 1440, [2005] PIQR 13 *309*

Saunders v UK (1997) 23 EHRR 313 *509*

Sayers v Harlow Urban District Council [1958] 1 WLR 623, CA *302*

Scott v London and St Katherine Docks Co [1885] 3 H&C 596 *313, 643*

Schuler AG v Wickman Machine Tool Sales [1974] AC 235, HL *131*

Sedleigh-Denfield v O'Callaghan [1940] AC 880, HL *379*

Selectmove, Re [1995] 1 WLR 474, CA *107, 110*

Selsdon v Clarkson Wright [2012] UKSC 16, [2012] 3 All ER 1301 *428–9*

Shanklin Pier Ltd v Detel Products Ltd [1954] 2 KB 854 *117*

Shepherd v Jerrom [1987] QB 301 *231*

Shergold v Fieldway Medical Centre [2006] ICR 304, EAT *487*

Shields v Coomes (Holdings) Ltd 1 All ER 456 *449*

Shogun Finance Ltd v Hudson [2002] 4 All ER 572, CA, *affirming* [2003] UKHL 62, [2004] 1 All ER 215, HL *191–2, 202*

Sienkiewicz (Administratrix of the estate of Enid Costello deceased) v Greif (UK) Ltd [2011] UKSC 10 *296*

Simpkins v Pays [1955] 3 All ER 10, CA *113–14, 120*

Smith and Grady v UK [1999] IRLR 734 *454*

Smith v Baker [1891] AC 325, HL *300*

Smith v Eric S. Bush [1989] 2 WLR 790, HL *316, 319*

Smith v Hughes (1871) LR 6 QB 597 *176*

Smith v Hughes [1960] 1 WLR 830 *37*

Smith v Land & House Property Corp (1884) 28 Ch D 7 *174, 641*

Smith v Leech Brain & Co. Ltd [1962] 2 WLR 148 *299, 643*

Smith v Littlewoods Organisation [1987] 1 All ER 710, HL *331–2, 643*

Smithton Ltd v Naggar and others [2014] EWCA Civ 939 *546*

Société des Produits Nestlé SA v Cadbury UK [2017] EWCA Civ 358 *600*

Soden v British Commonwealth Holdings plc [1997] 4 All ER 383 *521, 528*

Spartan Steel Alloys v Martin [1972] 3 WLR 502, CA *310–12*

Spearmint Rhino Ventures UK Ltd v Revenue and Customs Commissioners [2007] STC 1252 *261–2*

Spencer-Franks v Kellogg Brown & Root Ltd [2008] UKHL 46, [2008] ICR 863, HL *415–16, 421*

Spring v Guardian Assurance [1994] 3 All ER 129, HL *316*

St Albans City & District Council v International Computers Ltd [1996] 4 All ER 481, CA *158, 344*

St Helen's Smelting CO. v Tipping (1865) 11 HLC 642, HL *375*

St John of God (Care Services) Ltd v Brooks [1992] ICR 715, EAT *474, 487*

Stansbie v Troman [1948] 1 All ER 599, CA *333*

Stennet v Hancock [1939] 2 All ER 578 *282, 283, 344*

Stephens v Avery [1988] 2 All ER 477 *618*

Stevenson v McLean (1880) 5 KBD 346 *86*

Stewart v Casey (Casey's Patent), Re [1892] 1 Ch 103, CA *102*

Stilk v Myrick (1809) 2 Camp 317 *105, 107, 633*

Stocks v Wilson [1913] 2 KB 235 *220*

Stocznia Gdanska SA v Latvian Shipping Co. (No. 3) [2002] EWCA Civ 889, [2002] 2 Lloyd's Rep 436 *240*

Stone and Rolls (in liquidation) v Moore Stephens (a firm) [2009] UKHL 39, [2009] 4 All ER 431, HL *500*

Stone v Taffe [1974] 1 WLR 1575, CA *303*

Stovin v Wise [1996] 3 All ER 801 *330*

Stringfellow Restaurants Ltd v Quashie [2013] IRLR 99 *401*

Sturges v Bridgeman (1879) 11 Ch D 852 *375, 381*

Sumpter v Hedges [1898] 1 QB 673 *227*

Sussex Partnership NHS Foundation Trust v Norris (2012) UKEAT/0031/12/SM *430*

Sutton v Syston Football Club Ltd [2011] EWCA Civ 1182, [2011] All ER (D) 182 (Oct) *290, 293*

Sweet v Parsley [1969] 1 All ER 347, HL *40, 52*

Sylvester v Chapman (1935) 79 SJ 77 *301*

T v Surrey County Council [1994] 4 All ER 577 *314, 320*

Taittinger SA v Allbev Ltd [1993] FSR 641, CA *614–15*

Tarling v Wisdom Toothbrushes [1997] IDS Brief 597, September *432*

Taylor v Alidair [1978] IRLR 82 *470*

Taylor v Caldwell (1863) 3 B&S 826 *229*

Taylor v Ladbrokes Betting & Gaming Ltd UKEAT/0353/15/DA *430*

Taylor v Novo (UK) Ltd [2013] EWCA Civ 194, [2013] All ER (D) 167 (Mar) *329–30*

Taylorson v Shieldness Products Produce [1994] PIQR P329, CA *328*

Teggart v Teletech UK Ltd 2012 NIT 00704/11 *471*

Tesco Stores Ltd and Antoerh v Pollard [2006] EWCA Civ 393 *354*

Tetley v Chitty [1986] 1 All ER 663 *380*

Thomas v BNP Paribas (2016) *479*

Thomas v Eight Members Club and Killip (2007) et/2202603/2007 *427*

Thomas v Thomas [1842] 2 QB 85 *104*

Thomas Sanderson Blinds Ltd v English [2008] EWCA Civ 1421, (2009) *The Times*, 5 January, 2009 *455*

Thompson v Smiths Ship Repairers Ltd [1984] 2 WLR 522 *288*

Thorney Park Golf Ltd (t/a Laleham Golf Club) v Myers Catering Ltd [2015] EWCA Civ 1 *125*

Thornton v Shoe Lane Parking [1971] 2 WLR 585, CA *134, 138*

Tillery Valley Foods v Channel Four Television [2004] EWHC 1075 (Ch) *623*

Tomlinson v Congleton Borough Council [2003] UKHL 47, [2004] 1 AC 46, HL, reversing [2002] EWCA Civ 309, [2004] 1 AC 46, [2003] 3 All ER 1122, CA *365, 373*

Tool Metal Manufacturing Co. Ltd v Tungsten Ltd [1955] 2 All ER 657 *110*

Towers v Premier Waste Management Ltd [2011] EWCA Civ 923 [2012] IRLR 73 *552, 553*

Trac Time Control Ltd v Moss Plastic Parts Ltd and Others [2005] All ER (D) 06 (Jan) *147*

Transco plc v Stockport Corporation I [2003] UKHL 61, [2004] 2 AC 1, HL, *affirming* [2001] EWCA Civ 212, CA *384*

Transfield Shipping Inc. v Mercator Shipping Inc. [2008] UKHL 48, [2008] 4 All ER 159, HL *244–5*

Trebor Bassett Holidays and Cadbury UK Partnership v ADT Fire & Security [2012] EWCA Civ 1158; [2012] All ER (D) 153 (Aug) *154*

Tribe v Tribe [1995] EWCA Civ 20 *209*

Trustees of Portsmouth Youth Activities Committee v Poppleton [2008] EWCA Civ 646, [2009] PIQR P1, CA *369*

Tsakiroglou & Co. v Noblee Thorl GmbH [1961] 2 WLR 633, HL *232*

Tullet Prebon Group v Ghaleb El Hajjali [2008] EWHC 1924 (QB), [2008] IRLR 760 *251*

Tweddle v Atkinson (1861) 1 B & S 393, [1861–73] All ER Rep 369, Ct of QB *115, 640*

UK Atomic Energy Authority v Claydon [1974] IRLR 6 *405*

Vahey v Kenyon [2013] EWCA Civ 658, [2013] All ER (D) 152 (Jun) *177*

Valencia v Lupar 2012] EWCA Civ 396 *49*

Valilas v Janusaj [2014] EWCA Civ 436 *132, 140*

Venables v News Group Newspapers [2001] 1 All ER 908 *509*

Victoria Laundry v Newman Industries Ltd [1949] 1 All ER 997, CA *243*

Vidal-Hall v Google Inc [2015] EWCA Civ 311 *625, 628, 650*

Vitol SA v Norelf [1996] 3 All ER 193, HL *239–40*

Vivendi SA & Centenary Holdings III Ltd v Richards and Bloch [2013] EWHC 3006 *545*

W v Edgell [1990] Ch 359 *624*

Walker v Northumberland County Council [1995] 1 All ER 737 *412*

Walmesley v UDEC [1972] IRLR 80 *406*

Ward v Tesco [1976] 1 WLR 810 *291*

Warner Bros v Nelson [1936] 3 All ER 160 *256, 642*

Warner v Armfield Retail & Leisure Ltd [2014] UK EAT *230*

Warren v Henlys Garage Ltd [1948] 2 All ER 935 *389*

Watford Electronics v Sanderson [2001] EWCA Civ 317, [2001] 1 All ER (Comm) 696, [2001] BLR 143, [2002] FSR 19, (2001) 3 TCLR 14, [2001] Masons CLR 57 *158–9, 171*

Watson and Others v Croft Promo-Sport Ltd [2009] EWCA Civ 16, [2009] EG 86 *376, 377*

Watt v Hertfordshire County Council [1954] 1 WLR 835 *290*

Webb v EMO Cargo (No. 2) [1995] IRLR 645 *436*

Webster & Others v Liddington & Others [2014] EWCA Civ 560, CA *178*

Wells v Cooper [1958] 2 All ER 527, CA *288, 290*

West Bromwich Albion Football Club Ltd v El-Safty [2007] EWCA Civ 1299 *314*

Wheat v Lacon [1966] 2 WLR 581, HL *364, 645*

Wheeler v Saunders Ca [1996] Ch 19, [1995] 2 All ER 697 *375*

White & Carter (Councils) Ltd v McGregor 2 WLR 17, HL *240*

White Hudson & Co. Ltd v Asian Organisation Ltd [1964] 1 WLR 1466, PC *611*

White v Bluett (1853) 23 LJ Ex 36 *103–4*

White v Chief Constable of South Yorkshire [1999] 1 All ER 1, HL *324*

White v Jones [1995] 1 All ER 691, HL *313, 317*

White v London Transport Executive [1971] 2 QB 721 *409*

White v Mellin [1895] AC 154 *617*

Whitlow v Alkanet Construction [1987] IRLR 321 *473*

Whittington v Seal-Hayne (1900) 82 Lt 49 *183*

Wieland v Cyril Lord Carpets [1969] 3 All ER 1006 *298–9*

William Sindall plc v Cambridgeshire County Council [1993] EWCA Civ 14, [1994] 1 WLR 1016 *182–3, 202*

Williams and Another v Natural Life Health Foods Ltd and Mistlin [1998] 2 All ER 577, HL *502–3, 512*

Williams v Bayley (1866) LR 1 HL 200, HL *196, 641*

Williams v Roffey Bros [1990] 1 All ER 512, CA *106, 107, 110, 120*

Williams v Settle [1960] 1 WLR 1072 *589, 607*

Wilsher v Essex Area Health Authority [1988] 2 WLR 557, HL, reversing [1987] QB 730, [1986] 3 All ER 801, CA *288, 293–4*

Wilson and Another v Burnett [2007] EWCA Civ 1170, [2007] All ER (d) 372 (Oct), CA *113–14*

Wilson v Haden [2013] All ER (D) 145 (Mar) *287*

Wilson v Rickett Cockerell Ltd [1954] 1 QB 598 *148*

Wilts United Dairies Ltd v Thomas Robinson & Sons Ltd [1958] RPC 94 *617*

Wiluszynski v London Borough of Tower Hamlets [1988] IRLR 259, CA *406*

With v O'Flanagan [1936] Ch 575, CA *173, 641*

Withers v Perry Chain Ltd [1961] 1 WLR 1314 *286*

Wolman v Islington LBC [2006] EWCA Civ 1060, CA *38*

Wood v Scarth (1858) 1 F&F 293 *192*

Woodland v Essex County Council [2013] UKSC 66, [2013] All ER (D) 252 (Oct) *392*

Woods v Tiu Travel Plc [2017] EWCA Civ 11 *153*

X v Bedfordshire County Council [1995] 3 WLR 152, HL *337*

X v Mid Sussex Citizens Advice Bureau UKSC 59, [2013] 1 All ER 1038 *426*

Yapp (John) v Foreign & Colonial Office [2014] EWCA Civ 1512 *414*

Young v Bristol Aeroplane Company [1944] 2 All ER 293 *41*

Z and A v UK (2002) 34 EHRR 3 *337*

Table of statutes

Abortion Act 1967 s 1(1) *38*
Administration of Justice Act 1969 *60*
Arbitration Act (AA) 1996 *66*

Business Names Act 1985 s 4 *497*

Children Act 1989 *56*
Civil Aviation Act 1993 s 76 *303*
Companies Act 1985 *494, 508, 514, 523, 534, 547, 571, 583*
   s 3A *495, 511*
   s 317 *552*
   s 431 *580*
   s 432 *580*
   s 459 *577*
   s 994 *579–80, 583–4, 649*
Companies Act 1989 *498*
   s 3A *520*
   s 35 *523*
Companies Act 2006 *27, 494, 497–9, 508, 510, 514–16, 527, 530, 531–6, 540; 547–66, 570–2, 646*
   Part 18 *648*
   s 7 *516*
   s 8 *516*
   ss 9–13 *516–17*
   ss 14–16 *518*
   s 17 *518–19*
   s 19 *519*
   s 21 *522*
   s 28 *519*
   s 31(1) *520*
   s 31(2) *520*
   s 32 *519*
   s 33 *520*
   s 39 *523, 648*
   s 40 *523–4, 546–7*
   s 41(2) *524*
   s 51 *515–16*
   s 53 *517*

s 58 *518*
s 59 *518*
s 66 *517*
s 82 *517*
s 83 *518*
s 86 *516*
s 87 *516*
Pt 7 (ss 89–111) *524*
s 90 *524*
s 91 *524*
s 94 *524*
s 154 *543*
s 157 *543*
s 162 *543*
s 163 *543*
s 167(5) *557*
s 168 *556–7, 574, 648*
s 169 *531*
s 170(1) *550*
s 170(4) *550*
s 170(5) *545*
s 171–177 *550–4*
s 172 *550–1, 556, 564*
s 172(1) *550, 555, 637*
s 173 *551*
s 173(1) *551*
s 174 *551, 648*
s 174(2) *551*
s 175 *552*
s 175(1) *554*
s 175(2) *554*
s 176 *552*
s 176(1) *552*
s 176(2) *552*
s 176(3) *552*
s 176(4) *552*
s 176(5) *552*
s 177 *552*
s 177(1) *552*
s 178 *552, 648*
s 180(1) *552*
s 182 *552*

s 182(1) *552*
s 182(5) *552*
s 183 *528*
s 188 *544*
s 189 *555*
s 190 *555*
ss 197–214 *555*
s 217 *555*
s 239 *578*
s 251 *545*
s 252 *555*
s 260 *277, 584*
s 260(1) *577*
Chapter 11 (ss 260–264) *577–8, 583, 649*
s 261 *577–8*
s 262 *577–8*
s 263 *535, 577–8*
s 264 *577*
s 270 *558*
s 270(3) *498*
s 273 *559*
s 281 *574*
s 288(2) *574*
s 291 *574*
s 292 *574*
s 301 *575*
s 303 *572*
s 306 *572*
s 307 *571, 572*
s 308 *573*
s 310 *573*
s 311 *573*
s 318 *573*
s 336 *571*
s 477 *561*
s 485(2) *561*
s 487 *499*
s 487(2) *561*
s 488 *561*
s 489(2) *561*
s 490 *561*

s 499 561
s 510 574
s 515 574
s 518 572
s 542 531
s 553 533
s 561 581
s 580 519, 533
s 582 533
s 610 533
s 630 581
s 656 572
Pt 18, Ch 4 534
s 658 534
s 684 532
s 690 534, 648
s 691 534, 648
s 692 534
s 693 534
s 769 535
s 776 535
s 855 559
s 856 559
s 857 533
s 858 559
s 994 577, 578–80
s 995 580
s 996 579
s 1202 497
Companies (Audit, Investigations
    and Community Enterprise) Act
    2004
    ss 21–24 580
    s 499 561
Company Directors Disqualification
    Act 1986 (CDDA 1986) 558
Compensation Act 2006 289–90
    s 1 289–90, 368
    s 3 295–6
    s 3(5) 295
Competition Act 1998 205
Constitutional Reform Act (CRA)
    2005
    s 23 59
Consumer Arbitration Act 1988 67
Consumer Credit Act 1974 33, 78
Consumer Credit Act 2006 78
Consumer Protection Act 1987
    (CPA 1987) 20, 54, 342, 644
    Pt I 349–59
    s 1 349, 351–2
    s 2 351–2

s 2(1) 350–1
s 3 352–4
s 4 354–7, 644
s 5 356–7
Pt II 357
s 46 351
Consumer Rights Act 2015 (CRA)
    27, 128, 138–9, 143, 151, 153,
    156, 158, 162–71, 179, 317, 369
    Pt 1 163–7
    Pt 2 167–8
    Pt 3 168
    s 2 163
    s 9 163
    s 10 163
    s 11 163
    s 12 163
    s 13 163
    s 14 163
    s 15 163–4
    s 16 164
    s 17 163
    s 20 165
    s 22 164, 641
    s 23 164, 641
    s 24 164
    s 34 165
    s 35 165, 166
    s 36 163, 166
    s 37 165
    s 41 165, 166
    s 43 165
    s 44 165
    s 45 165
    s 46 165, 166
    s 49 166
    s 50 166, 173, 202
    s 51 166
    s 52 166
    s 55 166
    s 56 166
    s 57 166, 640
    s 61 167
    s 62 167
    s 64 167
    s 65 168, 640
    s 66 168
    s 67 168
    s 68 163
    s 83 275
    Sch 2 167
    Sch 3 168

Consumers, Estate Agents
    and Redress Act 2007
    274–5
Contracts (Rights of Third Parties)
    Act 1999 101, 103, 102, 117–18,
    120, 634, 640
    s 1 117
    s 2 118
    s 5 118
    s 6 118
    s 7 118
    s 7(2) 155
Copyright, Designs and Patents Act
    1988 (CDPA 1988) 649
    Pt I 607
    Pt II 588, 591, 607
    Pt III 591, 607, 649
    s 1 587
    s 2 587, 594
    s 3 587
    s 4 588
    ss 9–11 589
    ss 12–15 589
    ss 17–21 590
    ss 22–26 590
    ss 29–40 590
    s 85 589
    s 96 590
    s 107 590
    s 144 590
    ss 154–158 588
    s 163 589
    s 213(2) 592
    s 213(4) 592
    s 213(6) 592
    s 215 592
    s 216 592
    ss 217–220 592
    s 222 592
    s 226 592
    s 227 592
    s 229 592
    s 237 592
    s 238 592
    s 240 592
    s 243 592
Corporate Manslaughter and
    Corporate Homicide Act 2007
    (CMCH 2007)
    s 1 504
    s 1(2) 504
    s 2 504

Countryside and Rights of Way Act
    2000 *371*
Courts and Legal Services Act
    (CLSA) 1990 *56, 64*
Criminal Justice Act 1993 *648*
    Pt IV *562*

Damages (Asbestos-related
    Conditions) (Scotland) Act 2009
    323
Data Protection Act 2018 *22*
Defective Premises Act 1972 (DPA)
    s 1(1) *313*
Deregulation Act 2015 *485*
Disability Discrimination Act 1995
    (DDA 1995) *429, 431, 433*

Emergency Powers Act 1939 *33*
Emergency Powers Act 1984 *33*
Employer's Liability (Defective
    Equipment) Act 1969 *409*
Employment Relations Act 1999
    475, 479
    s 12 *476*
    s 14 *476*
    s 29 *485*
    Sch 5 *476*
Employment Rights Act 1996 (ERA
    1996) *27, 69, 486*
    s 1 *402, 420, 645*
    s 86 *465–6*
    s 98 *469, 479*
    s 98(4) *474*
    s 99 *475*
    s 100 *475*
    s 102 *475*
    s 103 *475*
    s 103A *475*
    s 104 *476*
    s 105 *475, 476*
    s 105A *475*
    s 108 *635*
    s 108(4) *476*
    s 113 *484*
    s 114 *484*
    s 117 *485*
    s 119 *484*
    s 120A *484*
    s 123 *484*
    s 136 *477*
    s 138(1) *478*
    s 138(2) *478*

s 139 *477*
s 209 *467*
s 227 *479*
s 230(3) *399, 401*
Enterprise and Regulatory Reform
    Act 2013 (E&RRA 2013) *409,
    425, 438, 459, 466, 482–3,
    485*
Environmental Protection Act 1990
    382
Equality Act 2010 *27, 82, 422,
    423–60, 645*
    s 1 *458*
    s 4 *423*
    s 5 *427*
    s 6(1) *429*
    s 7 *433*
    s 8 *434*
    s 9 *437, 438*
    s 9(2) *437*
    s 9(4) *437*
    s 10 *441–2*
    s 10(1) *441*
    s 11 *446, 645*
    s 12 *454*
    s 13 *423–4, 427, 431, 434, 436,
        439, 442, 446, 455*
    s 13(2) *428, 429*
    s 13(3) *431*
    s 13(5) *439*
    s 14 *424*
    s 15 *431–2*
    s 16 *434*
    s 18 *436*
    s 18(2) *436*
    s 18(5) *436*
    s 18(6) *436*
    s 19 *424, 427, 434, 436, 442,
        447–53, 455*
    s 19(1)(b) *439*
    s 19(2) *429*
    s 19(2)(d) *424, 440*
    s 19(3) *431–2*
    s 20 *432*
    s 21 *432–3*
    s 23 *424, 432*
    s 23(3) *455*
    s 24 *424*
    s 26 *425, 429, 447, 455, 460, 645*
    s 26(2) *447*
    s 27 *425, 429*
    s 40 *429, 447, 455*

s 44 *497*
s 45 *497*
s 60 *433*
s 64(2) *450*
s 65 *448–50*
s 66 *446, 448*
s 67 *448*
s 67(1) *451*
s 69 *451*
s 71 *451*
s 73 *452*
s 74 *452, 646*
s 75(1)–(6) *453*
s 77 *453*
s 77(3) *453*
s 78 *453*
s 109 *426, 440*
s 109(3) *426*
s 109(4) *455*
s 110 *426*
s 132 *453*
s 138(4) *453*
s 138(5) *453*
s 144(1) *66*
s 149 *457–8, 460*
s 149(1) *458*
s 153 *458*
s 159 *458, 460*
Sch 1 *429*
    para 9 *430*
Sch 9 *645–6*
    para 1 *425, 428, 431, 439, 447,
        645–6*
    para 1(3) *434, 435*
    para 2 *445*
    para 3 *445, 455*
Sch 19 *457*
Equal Pay Act 1970 (EPA 1970)
    448
Estate Agents Act 1979 *274*
European Communities Act 1972
    22, 520
    s 2 *28, 33*
    s 9(1) *523*

Factories Act 1802 *416*
Factories Act 1961 *414*
Factors Act 1889 s 1 *275*
Financial Services and Markets Act
    2000 *498, 533*
Firearms Act 1968 *36*
Food Safety Act 1990 *20*

Gender Recognition Act 2004 *434*
Growth and Infrastructure Act 2013
    400

Health and Safety (Offences) Act
    2008 *418*
Health and Safety at Work etc. Act
    1974 *55, 416–20, 505, 645*
    s 2 *416–17*
    s 3 *417*
    s 7 *417*
    s 21 *418*
    s 23 *418*
    s 24 *397*
    s 47 *414*
    s 47(2) *414*
Housing Act 1985 *380*
Human Rights Act 1998 (HRA) *17,
    43–51, 303, 336–7, 385–6, 454,
    459, 508–10, 611, 628, 635*
    s 2 *44, 49*
    s 3 *44–5, 49*
    s 4 *44*
    s 6 *44, 49*
    s 8 *45, 46–7, 619*

Insolvency Act 1986 *109, 506, 525*
    s 124A *580*
    s 213 *503*
    s 214 *551, 554, 648*
Intellectual Property Act 2014 *595,
    599, 605*
Interpretation Act 1978 *35*

Joint Stock Act 1844 *636*

Law of Property (Miscellaneous
    Provisions) Act 1989 *77–8*
Law Reform (Contributory
    Negligence) Act 1945 *253, 302*
Law Reform (Frustrated Contracts)
    Act 1943 *228, 256*
    s 1(2) *235–6*
    s 1(3) *236–7*
Limitation Act 1980
    s 11A *357*
Limited Liability Act 1855 *636–7*
Limited Liability Partnerships Act
    2000 *496*
Limited Partnerships Act 1907 *495*

Marine Insurance Act 1906 *176*

Marriage (Same Sex Couples) Act
    2004 *434*
Mental Capacity Act 2005 (MCA)
    s 2 *274*
    s 9 *274*
    s 11 *274*
Minimum Wage Act 1998 *407*
Minors' Contracts Act 1987 *222*
    s 1 *220*
    s 2 *220*
    s 3 *220*
Misrepresentation Act 1967
    s 2 *183*
    s 2(1) *180–4, 200, 319*
    s 2(2) *181–4, 200*
    s 2(3) *182–3*
    s 3 *179*

Occupiers' Liability Act 1957 (OLA
    1957) *35, 362–4, 368, 386,
    393–4, 635*
    s 1(3) *364*
    s 2(1) *369–70*
    s 2(2) *365, 644*
    s 2(3) *370*
    s 2(3)(a) *366, 367*
    s 2(3)(b) *367*
    s 2(4) *368*
    s 2(5) *370*
    s 2(6) *364*
Occupiers' Liability Act 1984
    (OLA1984) *362–4, 365, 368,
    370–1, 373, 386, 393–4, 644–5*
    s 1(3) *371*
    s 1(4) *372*
    s 2(9) *373*
Offices, Shops and Railway
    Premises Act 1963 *418*
Official Secrets Act 1920 *37*

Parliament Act 1911 *33*
Parliament Act 1949 *33*
Partnership Act 1890 *27, 493, 494,
    647*
Patents Act 1977 (PA 1977) *596,
    605, 607*
    s 1–4 *595*
    s 2 *595*
    s 13 *597*
    ss 14–19 *597–8*
    s 30 *598*
    s 39 *597*

s 40 *597*
s 46 *599*
s 48 *599*
s 55 *599*
s 60 *598*
ss 109–113 *599*
Patents Act 2004 (PA 2004) *595*
    s 1 *596*
    s 10 *597*
Pensions Act 1995
    ss 62–66 *451*
Pharmacy and Poisons Act 1933 *81*
Powers of Attorney Act 1971
    s 4 *274*
Proceeds of Crime Act 2002
    s 41(1) *501*
Protection from Harassment Act
    1997 *391*
Public Interest Disclosure Act 1998
    452

Race Relations Act 1976 (RRA 1976)
    436, 439
    s 1(1)(a) *438*
Registered Designs Act 1949 (RDA
    1949) *591, 593, 607, 649*
    s 1 *593*
    s 2 *594*
    s 7 *595*
    s 8 *594*
    s 10 *595*
    s 11A *595*
    s 34 *595*
    s 35 *595*
    Sch 1 *595*
Representation of the People Act
    1983 *45*
Restriction of Offensive Weapons
    Act 1959 s 1(1) *37, 81*

Sale and Supply of Goods Act 1994
    127, 144, 151, 153
Sale of Goods Act 1893 *142*
Sale of Goods Act 1979 (SGA)
    *127–8, 130, 143–52, 160, 162,
    169–70, 357*
    s 2(1) *144*
    s 3 *217, 218, 220*
    s 8 *80*
    s 12 *144, 145, 640*
    s 13 *144, 145–7, 147–50, 357*
    s 14 *149, 144, 150, 357*

s 14(2) *144, 147–9, 640*
s 14(2A) *147*
s 14(2B) *147*
s 14(2C) *148–9*
s 14(3) *144, 147, 149–51*
s 15 *144, 357, 640*
s 20 *165*
s 23 *165*
s 24 *165*
s 31 *165*
s 35 *151–2, 640*
s 35(6) *151*
s 50 *245*
s 57 *87*
Sex Discrimination Act 1975 (SDA
    1975) *433–4, 445–6, 451*
s 3 *435*
Small Business, Enterprise and
    Employment Act 2015 (SBEEA
    2015)
s 16 *518*
s 80 *536*
s 87 *544*
s 89 *545*
s 92 *559*
s 150 *485*
s 152 *407*
s 153 *408*

s 178 *453*
Sch 3 *536*
Social Action, Responsibility and
    Heroism Act 2015
s 2 *290*
s 3 *290*
Statute of Frauds 1677 *78*
Street Offences Act 1959 *37*
Supply of Goods (Implied Terms)
    Act 1973 (SGIT) *144, 169*
ss 8–11 *155*
Supply of Goods and Services Act
    1982 (SGSA) *140, 152–5, 169, 357*

Trade Descriptions Act 1968 *55*
Trade Marks Act 1938 *599*
Trade Marks Act 1994 *493,
    599–600, 605, 607, 615*
s 1 *600*
s 3 *601*
s 4 *601*
s 5 *601*
s 10 *601–2*
s 29 *603*
s 32 *601*
s 37 *601*
s 38 *601*
s 40 *601*

Trade Union and Labour Relations
    (Consolidation) Act 1992
    (TULR(C)A 1992)
s 152 *476*
s 238A *476*
Tribunals, Courts and Enforcement
    Act 2007 *69*

Unfair Contract Terms Act 1977
    (UCTA) *139, 143, 140, 155–9,
    160–2, 169, 369*
s 1(3) *155*
s 2 *155, 317, 370, 640*
s 2(1) *155*
s 2(2) *155*
s 3 *156, 159, 179, 319*
s 6 *156, 161*
s 6(4) *156*
s 7 *156, 161*
s 11 *156–7*
s 11(1) *156*
s 11(3) *156*
s 12 *161*
Sch 2 *156*

Wild Birds Act 1954 *81*

Table of statutory instruments

Civil Procedure Rules (CPR), SI 1998/3120, *60–3*

Collective Redundancies and Transfer of Undertakings (Protection of Employment) (Amendment) Regulations 2014, SI 2014/16, *480*

Commercial Agents (Council Directive) Regulations 2008, SI 2008/1277, *272*

Companies Act 2006 (Strategic Report and Directors' Report) Regulations 2013, SI 2013/1970, *556*

Companies (Single Member Private Limited Companies) Regulations 1992, SI 1992/1699, *498*

Company, Limited Liability Partnership and Business (Names and Trading Disclosures) Regulations 2015, SI 2015/17, *517*

Company, Limited Liability Partnership and Business Names (Sensitive Words and Expressions) Regulations 2014, SI 2014/3140, *517*

Consumer Contracts (Information, Cancellation and Additional Charges) Regulations 2013, SI 2013/3134, *162, 166, 641*

Consumer Protection Act 1987 (Product Liability) (Modification) Order 2000, SI 2000/2771, *352*

Consumer Protection (Amendment) Regulations 2014, SI 2014/870, *82*

Consumer Protection from Unfair Trading Regulations 2008, SI 2008/1277, *82*

Copyright and Related Rights Regulations 1996, SI 1996/2967, *591*

Copyright and Related Rights Regulations 2003, SI 2003/2498, *591*

Copyright and Rights in Database Regulations 1997, SI 1997/3032, *605*

Copyright and Rights in Performances (Quotation and Parody) Regulations 2014, SI 2014/2356, *590*

Electronic Commerce (EC Directive) Regulations 2002, SI 2002/2013, *90*
reg 11, *82*

Employment Equality (Age) Regulations 2006, SI 2006/1031, *426, 427*

Employment Equality (Religion or Belief) Regulations 2003, SI 2003/1660, *441*

Employment Equality (Repeal of Retirement Age Provisions) Regulations 2011, SI 2011/1069, *428*

Employment Equality (Sexual Orientation) Regulations 2003, SI 2003/1661, *454*

Employment Rights (Employment Particulars and Paid Annual Leave) (Amendment) Regulations 2018, SI 2018/1378, *402*

Equal Pay (Amendment) Regulations 1983, SI 1983/1794, *448*

Equality Act (Gender Pay Gap) Regulations 2017, SI 2017/172, *453*

General Data Protection Regulations 2016, SI 2016/679, *22*

Legislative Reform (Limited Partnerships) Order 2009, SI 2009/1940, *496*

Lettings Agency Work and Property Management Work (Requirement to Belong to a Scheme etc) (England) Order 2014, SI 2014/2359, *275*

Management of Health and Safety at Work Regulations 1992, SI 1992/2051, *414*

Management of Health and Safety at Work Regulations 1999, SI 1999/3242, *414, 417*

Partnership (Unrestricted Size) No. 17 Regulations 2001, SI 2001/2422, *494*
Provision and Use of Work Equipment Regulations 1998, SI 1998/2306
   reg 3(2), *415*
   reg 5(1), *415*

Registered Designs (Amendment) Rules 2001, SI 2001/3950, *593, 649*
Registered Designs (Fees) Amendment Rules 2001, SI 2001/3951, *593, 649*
Registered Designs Regulations 2001, SI 2001/3949, *593, 649*

Sale and Supply of Goods to Consumers Regulations 2002, SI 2002/3045, *160*
Sex Discrimination (Gender Reassignment) Regulations 1999, SI 1999/1102, *433–4*

Transfer of Undertakings (Protection of Employment) Regulations 1981, SI 1981/1794 (TUPE 1981), *480*
Transfer of Undertakings (Protection of Employment) Regulations 2006, SI 2006/246 (TUPE 2006), *480, 481–2, 486–7, 646*
Transfer of Undertakings (Protection of Employment) (Amendment) Regulations 2014, SI 2014/16, *481–2*

Unfair Dismissal and Statement of Reasons for Dismissal (Variation of Qualifying Period) Order 2012, SI 2012/989, *467, 485*
Unfair Dismissal (Variation of the Limit of Compensatory Award) Order 2013, SI 2013/1949, *485*
Unfair Terms in Consumer Contracts Regulations 1994, SI 1994/3159 (UTCCR), *143, 161*
Unfair Terms in Consumer Contracts Regulations 1999, SI 1999/2083 (UTCCR) *143, 161–2, 167–8*

Working Time Regulations 1998, SI 1998/1833, *405*

Zero Hours Contracts (Redress) Regulations 2015, SI 2015/2021, *408*

Table of European and International legislation

European Community legislation

Treaties

European Atomic Energy Treaty, *27*
European Coal and Steel Treaty, *27*
Patent Cooperation Treaty, *606*
Single European Act 1987, *29*
Treaty of Amsterdam 1997, *30, 31*
Treaty of Lisbon 2009, *30, 31*
    Art 50, *31*
Treaty of Nice, *28, 30*
    Art 203, *28*
Treaty of Rome 1957
    Art 119 (Now Art 141), *30, 451*
Treaty on European Union (Maastricht Treaty) 1992, *27, 29, 30*

Protocols

Madrid Protocol on International Registration of Trade Marks 1995, *606*

Directives

Directive 75/117/EC (Equal Pay Directive), *448*
Directive 77/91/EC (Acquired Rights Directive), *480*
Directive 85/374/EC (Product Liability Directive), *349*
Directive 89/92/EC (Insider Dealing Directive) *562*
Directive 89/667/EEC (First Company Law Directive), *523*
Directive 91/13/EC (Unfair Terms Directive), *161*
Directive 92/85/EC (Pregnant Workers Directive), *435*
Directive 93/104/EC (Working Time Directive), *405*
Directive 98/71/EC (Designs Directive), *593*
Directive 99/34/EC (Product Liability Directive), *352*
Directive 2000/31/EC (E-Commerce Directive), *94*
Directive 2001/29/EC (Copyright Directive), *591*
Directive 2002/73/EC (Equal Treatment Amendment Directive), *426*
Directive 2006/54/EC (Equal Treatment Directive), *435, 441, 454*
Directive 2011/83/EU (Consumer Rights Directive), *162*

Regulations

Alternative Dispute Resolution for Consumer Disputes (Amendment) Regulations 2015, *68–9*

International Conventions

Berne Convention for the Protection of Literary and Artistic Works 1886, *606*

European Convention on Human Rights and Fundamental Freedoms 1950 (ECHR), *17, 26–7, 43–4, 48, 50–1, 303, 337, 444, 611*

    Art 2, *44, 47, 335*

    Art 3, *45–6, 337*

    Art 5, *44, 46, 47, 48*

    Art 5(1), *48*

    Art 6, *44, 335, 509*

    Art 8, *44, 47, 337, 385–6, 435, 454, 509, 624*

    Art 9, *44, 49*

    Art 10, *44, 45, 47, 47, 509, 624*

    Art 11, *44, 47*

    Art 12, *435*

    Art 13, *454*

    Art 14, *435, 454*

    Protocol 1

        Art 1, *385, 508–9*

        Art 2, *44, 49*

European Patent Convention 1973, *605*

Interlaken Declaration 2011, *50*

Universal Copyright Convention, *606*

PART 1

Introduction: getting started

Study skills

Introduction

This chapter, which aims to help acquire the skills essential to the successful study of law, is divided into four sections:

1 starting to study;

2 good study habits;

3 writing law assignments;

4 revision and examination technique.

Starting to study

Get rid of misconceptions

Many students will be studying law for the first time and as one component of a course. Studying law is interesting and challenging. Contrary to common belief, the study of law is not primarily concerned with ancient, dry and precise regulations that have to be learnt by heart. The law as it is applied will have been decided in previous cases that have come to court because the law was not precise and consequently gave rise to the dispute. This text looks at how the law applies to real-life business and social situations, which will enable legal principles to be applied to legal situations. Effective communication of *understanding* of those principles is the main requirement for examination success.

While remembering all the cases by name and being able to quote extracts from statutes would improve answers, this is impressive, but not essential.

Law is relevant

Remember that the law responds and develops as required by the society within which it operates. For example, the Bribery Act 2010 was introduced to make the law more effective in tackling corruption in relation to corporate activities whether committed in the United Kingdom or abroad. The law affects people personally every day of their lives. For example, it determines eligibility for a student loan, rights to treatment under the National Health Service and entitlements and responsibilities as a consumer, business, employer or employee.

Widen horizons

Studies will be more rewarding if law is not considered as something to be thought about only when in class or reading a relevant text. The effects of many areas of the law are widely reported and discussed in the media. Such reports can help to see how the law works (or does not work), as well as being a reminder of what has been studied. Keep up to date with the news, try to look at a quality newspaper and look out for relevant TV and radio programmes. (Some suggestions for resources appear in Appendix 1.) The internet is an excellent research tool. (Try visiting the websites suggested by the web activity references at the end of Chapters 3–26.)

Make connections

The more one studies, the easier it gets. Studying law is rather like doing a large jigsaw without the help of a picture – progress is initially slow while the framework is established, but patience is rewarded. Once the picture begins to reveal itself, it can be seen more easily how the different pieces fit together and then the task gets easier and quicker.

Try not to think of each topic as a separate entity to be 'done' and neatly filed away in the memory. Exploit the links with other related topics; this aids both recollection and understanding. Exam and assignment questions may involve a legal problem, raising issues about a number of different topics; the ability to see connections is vital to an effective response. To help to do this, frequent cross-references appear in the text. Pondering on the questions in the 'Worth thinking about?' boxes in this textbook, and maybe discussing these with fellow students, will help with the process.

Read and practise, applying knowledge

Reading thoroughly and widely is essential; practising the written skills required by the examinations is also crucial.

The study of law is interesting but can be challenging for those unfamiliar with legal language and concepts. All may not be clear on first reading so be prepared to go back and re-read a section that is not understood. (The chapter summaries may help to understand the main points of each chapter.) Often it is best to try to get a general picture on the first reading of a topic, continuing to read on even if it is not fully understood.

Get all the writing practice that is possible. Self-directed study will help to develop legal writing skills and to prepare for assessments. Try the review questions and assignments in this textbook. Prepare written answers to tutorial questions and be prepared to participate when attending them. This is much more valuable (and more fun) than listening silently to other people's answers.

Good study habits

Create a structure for learning

Success in studies depends more on being well organised and developing a good knowledge of the subject.

Time management

It is important that a reasonable amount of time each week is set aside for private study, as this is a crucial supplement to the tuition received. Attending a lecture is the first step towards understanding a topic, but this initial learning must be reinforced in private study by reading and preparing for and participating in tutorials.

Students could produce a study timetable with realistic goals. Short bursts spread across the week may be more manageable than aiming to study in lengthy blocks, particularly in the early stages of the course.

Note-taking

Lecture notes are an essential lifeline. Perhaps use a loose-leaf folder and write on one side of the paper only. That enables more notes to be added later on having read the textbook.

Take some notes from personal reading, rephrasing with plenty of side headings. Note the sources of any extra notes taken, as they may need to be cited later in an assignment.

Take care to follow the correct academic referencing style. If an extract is copied, be sure to use quotation marks and indicate the source. This will ensure that an idea is not later represented as a student's own work in an assignment, which could be penalised as plagiarism (see below).

Reading

It is very important that the relevant section of the textbook is always read, preferably before the lecture, as well as any cases or other materials recommended by the tutor. Do not worry about understanding every word. Keep up with the reading relevant to the lectures, and understanding and applying the law will become much easier.

Although the chosen textbook should be read thoroughly, it is also always useful to consult others (see Appendix 1). Make good use of the index or contents section of additional textbooks to find the bits needed. Do not be afraid to skim. Use the search facility when reading PDF documents online. This can be a real help in isolating the legal areas of interest in a law report, for example.

Learning checks

It is a good idea to check that the reading has been understood. This textbook helps to check progress in four ways.

1 *Chapter summary*: the bullet points should act like 'triggers' and bring to mind more information from the chapter when reading them.

2 *Key terms*: check that the meanings of these have been understood. Try writing them down using different words.

3 *Review questions*: these provide a simple way to check that some of the important basic issues covered by the chapter have been understood.

4 *Join a study group*: getting together informally with a group of fellow students to discuss work can be both fun and helpful. Having to debate is a very good way of finding out how well or otherwise material is understood. In the event of a dispute, having to provide a reasoned answer is also an excellent academic exercise and good preparation for tutorials. The group can provide valuable mutual support near the exams too.

Writing law assignments

General advice

Before examining the specific techniques for writing law assignments it is useful to check awareness of what an assignment at degree or diploma level requires.

1 Style

Remember that this is not a personal account. Students should avoid saying 'I think' or 'I believe', no matter how passionately they feel about their argument. It is essential to use the third person instead and say something like 'it may be submitted/thought/argued that . . . '

2 Evidence

Back up arguments: indicate sources by referring to the relevant case reference, statute section, book title and page, date of newspaper article or website address. Make sure that arguments are developed rather than just giving a string of cases or other sources. Cited evidence must be clearly shown to support the argument.

Always use primary sources as far as possible. This means the first publication of the document. For instance, if a case is cited, some institutions insist that a footnote should be included, with the actual law report reference stated, not the page in the textbook where it was first found. Footnotes are a neat way to show references and they do not usually form part of the word limit. It is best to keep to a bare reference. While some texts seem to have more footnotes than content, don't be tempted into using this device as a subterfuge to exceed the word limit. It is unlikely to fool tutors. It is vitally important to ascertain the referencing style required from the individual institution to which the work is being submitted.

3 Avoid plagiarism

In simple terms, plagiarism means passing off someone else's work as your own. An obvious example is copying a chunk of text without using quotation marks, but altering some words in that text while leaving the sentence structure the same may also be plagiarism.

Plagiarism is easily avoided by clearly marking any direct quotes with inverted commas. However, work consisting of a large number of sections in quotation marks is unlikely to get a high grade as it is poor scholarship. Otherwise anything written should be in the student's own words, however difficult it is to find them. In the early stages of a new course of study it may be tempting to mirror someone else's text too closely but, with practice, confidence will grow as a better grasp of new concepts is acquired and self-expression improves.

This discussion so far relates to what might be called careless plagiarism, though even this may lead to work being downgraded. Sadly a minority of students set out to profit from intentional plagiarism. This is a form of cheating and carries heavy penalties including permanent exclusion in the most serious cases. This rarely goes unnoticed. Apart from the fact that tutors will notice blatant copying from sources they have recommended, all manner of plagiarism detection techniques are now being used which can spot much more subtle tricks, including essay writing services.

4 Submission requirements

Student handbooks will spell out the submission requirements for course work. It is crucial that these are known and understood, as failure to comply may jeopardise chances of success in a course. Each institution has its own very specific requirements. The devil is in the detail, so make sure the form and format required by the institution are known before submitting assignments. Promptness is crucial; miss the deadline and work may be rejected, or only accepted if a valid reason, with proof, for the delay is produced. Excuses are not acceptable reasons. Enough time must be given to avoid last-minute disasters such as a computer failure or transport issues. Despite living in an electronic age, in some institutions students may still be required to deliver hard copy rather than emailing submissions. A minimum font size may also be stipulated. A special cover sheet may be required. Check all the details before submission.

Writing technique for law assignments

Written assignments may take two forms:

1 *Problem or 'situation-based' assignments*: these involve a scenario to which students are expected to apply principles of law and draw reasoned conclusions.
2 *Discursive assignments*: essays and reports.

Very different types of answers are demanded by these two methods of testing knowledge and abilities. However, there is a need to examine the requirements which both types of work have in common at degree or diploma level.

Problem questions

A good answer to such a question will require the following:

- a clear explanation of the relevant points of law;
- an analysis of the given facts in the light of the relevant law;
- a reasoned conclusion or advice where appropriate.

Sometimes the facts will be deliberately vague to encourage students to indicate that a decision could go either way. It is crucial that reasons are given to support arguments that are made. It is not good enough to write at length about the general legal principles raised by the problem, and follow that with an assertion that X or Y will win. Giving clearly analysed reasons why such assertions are being made is what earns marks. Here are some tips to help.

1 *Read the problem thoroughly and think about what is involved.* This is crucial to spotting the relevant legal areas and in order to grasp the relationship of the parties and their names. Underline the 'triggers', the points of fact in the scenario which indicate the points of law to be applied. Refer to books and notes to make sure that these points of law are understood.
2 *Briefly jot down the relevant points of law that relate to the behaviour of the parties.* If the facts of the problem are complicated, representing the relationship of the parties in diagrammatic form may assist.
3 *Now write the answer in full.* It may be helpful to structure the answer using the CLEO formula (see below).

What is CLEO?

One approach to answering legal problem questions is the four-step CLEO method of legal analysis and writing:

- Claim;
- Law;
- Evaluation; and
- Outcome.

1 *Claim*

    (a) Start by identifying who is the claimant(s) and who is the defendant(s).

    (b) Identify the area of law, for example, contract – formation or tort occupiers' liability.

    (c) Identify what remedy the claimant is seeking.

2 *Law*

    (a) Presentation of the applicable law.

    (b) Identify relevant legal authority regarding each of the issues identified in the first step.

    (c) Relevant authority includes statute (Acts of Parliament) and case law – common law.

    (d) Use this section to demonstrate not only a depth and breadth of legal knowledge but also quality of legal reasoning.

3 *Evaluation*

    (a) Show how the legal rules apply to the facts of this problem.

    (b) Illustrate powers of analysis and persuasion by discussing the extent to which the facts in the particular question match up to the general legal standard identified in one's discussion of the law.

4 *Outcome*

    (a) Come to a reasoned conclusion / give advice as appropriate.

    (b) Identify the outcome of one's argument.

Why use CLEO?

Adhering to this analytical framework means the overall structure and arguments will be clear and easily understandable. Practice at doing this should make planning an answer in an examination situation very easy.

1 *Claim*: it is a good idea to have a brief opening paragraph identifying the parties (the claimant and defendant in a civil case), outlining the area of law in dispute and discussing the potential remedies that may be sought.

2 *Law*: outline the legal rules relevant to this dispute, using relevant statutes and cases to illustrate the points being made. When stating a point of law, indicate its primary source. Name relevant cases or statute sections, or otherwise indicate the knowledge that one is quoting a legal rule by saying, for example, 'in law'. There is usually no need to explain the facts of the case in any detail, though a brief reference may be useful to stress its relevance.

3 *Evaluation*: it is now important to get an overview of the problem faced by the parties and indicate how the law affects this. Go through the facts and proceed to the first 'trigger': stick to the point and mention the point of law that it raises. Do not write about the law at large. If the examiner expressly states the legal situation on a particular point, this does not need to be debated. For example, if a contract question specifically states that an offer has been made and a price stipulated, it is not necessary to discuss the existence of offer or consideration. Link each point of law to the relevant trigger and explain its implications. Facts of cases do not need to be included in any detail, though a brief mention explaining the relevance of the case or to show how this case can be distinguished from the facts of the problem may be useful. There is no need to worry about the evidence that would have to be proved in real life. For instance, if in a contract problem, postal acceptance is involved, do not worry about whether the offeree can actually prove that the letter was posted. Explain the outcome if the postal rules are applied. Then proceed to the next trigger point and repeat the process.

4 *Outcome*: conclude with a brief summary of the law or the advice where appropriate. This gives polish to the answer and should always form part of any legal problem question. Remember that there is not necessarily a right or a wrong answer. The student is being tested on their reasoning. The facts of the problem may be capable of more than one interpretation, each indicating a potentially different result.

   Check the answer carefully, rewriting and polishing if necessary. (See the discursive assignment tips below.)

This approach is demonstrated in the analysis of the following problem (Assignment 3 in Chapter 5). The italicised words are the fact 'triggers'.

CLEO in practice

Iris made an offer to sell her piano to Diana for £500 on Monday. Diana replied: 'I will buy it *if I can raise the money*'. Iris *promised that she would not sell to anyone else before Saturday*, and added that Diana could collect the piano *any time before noon on Saturday*. On Wednesday, Diana phoned and left a message with Iris's daughter, Athena, saying that *she had got the money* and *would come to collect the piano on Saturday morning*. *Athena forgot to pass on the message*. On Thursday, Iris was visited by Juno who said that she would pay £600 for the piano. *Iris accepted this offer*. Later that day Iris *posted a letter to Diana telling her that she could not have the piano*.
Mercury, the postman, delivered it to the wrong address and Diana, *who never received it*, appeared with a *hired van* to collect the piano at 10 o'clock on Saturday morning.

Advise Iris of her legal position.

1 *Claim*

- Diana is claiming breach of contract.

2 *Law*

- Unconditional acceptance is essential to contract formation *Jones* v *Daniel* (1894).
- Promises are not contractually binding without consideration *Routledge* v *Grant* (1828).
- Acceptance must be communicated.
- Revocation can take place up to the moment of acceptance *Payne* v *Cave* (1789).
- Notice of revocation is necessary to make it effective *Byrne* v *Van Tienhoven* (1880).
- Note that as the details state that an offer was made by Iris, it is not necessary to discuss whether or not an offer exists.

3 *Evaluation*

- *A*: conditional acceptance is not binding, therefore no contract formed yet (*Jones*).
- *Promise*: Iris is not bound to keep the offer open until Saturday, unless Diana pays to keep the offer open (*Routledge*).
- *She had got the money, and would come to collect the piano*: intention to accept?
- *Athena forgot to pass on the message*: has acceptance been communicated? (*Entores* v *Miles Far East Corporation*; *Brinkibon*).
- *Posted a letter . . . never received it*: revocation possible up to time of acceptance (*Payne*). Notice essential (*Dickinson* v *Dodds*). Postal revocation is not effective until received (*Byrne*).
- *Hired van*: acceptance by conduct (*Brogden* v *Metropolitan Railway*), or does she verbally accept before she is told of the revocation? If effective acceptance, a contract results. Iris is liable for breach and must compensate Diana for resulting losses.

4 *Outcome*

- Give a reasoned conclusion/advice as appropriate.

Writing discursive assignments

Students often incorrectly assume that writing essays and reports is easier than answering problems, but careful analysis is necessary to discover exactly what is being asked and how the relevant information is to be presented. A question does not require writing everything known about a topic. Drifting from the point or failing to present the required analysis will lose marks. The important points to remember are as follows:

1 *Make sure the question is understood*. Analyse it carefully. Look for the *key words*. These indicate what information is required and *how* to present the answer. 'How' words include: 'compare', 'discuss', 'distinguish between', 'critically assess', 'what

are the advantages/disadvantages of' and 'explain'. Sometimes information must be provided in the form of a memorandum or report. Head this appropriately with the relevant title and present it with side headings, using numbered points if appropriate.

2 *Carry out research.* Checking existing knowledge of the topic, additional sources should be referred to and notes made of relevant points with source references.

3 *Plan the answer in writing.* Write down the points to be made, paragraph-by-paragraph.

4 *Write the first draft.* Remember the warnings against plagiarism above and take care to use one's own words. Proofread and amend and correct, where necessary, and make sure sources are clearly referenced.

5 *Edit thoroughly.* This is best done after a break. Going back to the work will enable improvements to be made apart from doing the obvious things like a spellcheck. There may be a need to cut and paste to make work flow more logically. Now is the time to check for repetition and anything relating to terms and content or meaning of particular words. Word limits are important, and check all sources have been cited.

6 *Final checks.* Read through the work one more time and check the student hand-book to make sure the presentation requirements are fulfilled.

Revision and examination technique

Few people enjoy the examination process. However, everybody can make the process less stressful and more productive by ensuring that they both revise for and perform in the exam as effectively as possible. As with everything else in the study process, structure and good organisation are essential to ensuring that students fulfil their potential.

Revision

Effective preparation is essential to success: lack of it undermines confidence and thus doubly impairs examination performance. The following tips may be helpful.

Time planning

1 Make a realistic revision timetable

This must take into account other commitments and the student's likely concentration span. Short periods (20–45 minutes) are usually the most effective. Hours spent unremittingly at a desk are likely to produce little more than a sense of virtue and a headache.

2 Prioritise study time

Where there is a choice, study at the times of day when it is easiest to concentrate. While this may involve sacrificing personal time, it is important that this is viewed as a short-term loss and producing long-term gains. If a student has family commitments, it is useful to consider the benefits of taking time out for study at this important point in life. What is good for the student will be good for the family as well in the long term. Students in full- or part-time work are recommended to check if they are entitled to study leave, or consider using some holiday entitlement as study time.

3 Stick to a timetable

It is important to ensure that revision is done across the syllabus and to not get bogged down in the areas that a student feels least confident about. Keep to the schedule as tightly as possible, but be prepared to adapt and rationalise if necessary. Once the allotted time has been dedicated to a particular topic, do not tweak it, polish it or check whether it has been remembered. Press on to the next goal.

Revision technique

1 Thorough reading is essential

The primary aim is to consolidate existing knowledge. Ensure the basics of each topic have been grasped. These act as recall points: magnets and foundations to which more peripheral knowledge will stick. If a student has fully covered the revision, they may choose to read something new, to avoid getting stale. If a student is this well-prepared, they might consider taking some time off to give themselves space for assimilation and refreshment. It is possible to over-prepare, though this is likely to be a problem for only a minority of students. If struggling against time constraints or the intricacies of the subject matter, it may be best to stick to one clear source of information like lecture notes.

Don't be lulled into a false sense of security by an 'open book' exam. Just because students are permitted to take a specified text into the exam does not mean it can be ignored beforehand. The best students find it more of a comfort blanket than of practical use. There is no time to search for relevant bits in a book under the pressure of a time-constrained exam. Under these circumstances a book is generally only useful for checking things like a statute section number or case name. Check the regulations to ensure book marking or other identifying marks are permitted. If it is permissible, mark it appropriately, and be prepared to use it sparingly.

2 Note-taking while reading

This generally helps concentration and can provide useful reference points for last-minute revision. List the main points of each topic. Reduce cases to a couple of sentences, briefly conveying the essence of the facts and decision in one's own words. If this can be done it improves understanding of the essential points. Consequently, it will be more likely to be remembered. It is also good practice for the examination, when a student's own words are what will count.

3 Testing knowledge

When a topic has been covered, try to find/identify some relevant specimen questions. Draft answer plans, or try writing a timed answer. Use textbook quizzes. Suggested solutions may be helpful as a guide to question-answering technique but are not necessarily reliable in terms of content, so handle with care. Get someone to ask questions: while a fellow student is best, any long-suffering friend or family member will do. If there is a study group, encourage regular meetings. If there is no study group, maybe now is the time to form one. It can be very supportive and help to lend structure to work.

4 Working out the battle plan

Most people find taking exams hard. It is possible, however, to make some plans for effective use of time in the examination. The questions which have been given in tutorials may well resemble the sort of thing that will be found in the exam. Past papers if available are invaluable in terms of both form and content. Observe how questions are formulated. Decide which questions in each paper could be answered, avoiding any where there is uncertainty about what the examiner requires. Identify the advantages and disadvantages of different types of question. Remember that although it is often easier to pick up a good mark with a question that covers a number of different topics, this will require a reasonably lengthy exposition. If a question focuses on one small area, this can be useful when running short of time, as it may still be possible to convey the main points quickly. While it is too much to hope that these skills will become second nature, there is no doubt that studying the form and content of past papers, practising effective analysis routines and considering the best use of time will help to make the correct choices on the day.

5 Maintaining morale

During the exam period it is important to take good physical care of oneself: the brain will work more efficiently if a student has enough sleep, exercise, fresh air and the right sort of food.

Rewards are important: trying to do something enjoyable during breaks between study sessions is essential. Get away from the desk or computer. If possible, network with fellow students to avoid feeling isolated. Remember that feeling stressed can be beneficial: most people work better under a degree of pressure. Feeling too relaxed can inhibit effective revision. Do not be afraid to ask for help from lecturers or personal tutors, who will have had much experience of helping students prepare for exams. It may be helpful to use the college or university counselling service.

The examination

However thoroughly a student has revised, they will not reap their just rewards unless they acquit themselves well in the exam room. There are certain survival tactics that will help a student to keep calm and promote efficiency. Some are very obvious, but are worth thinking about in advance so that they do not get overlooked in the heat of the moment.

1 *Do make sure that the location of the exam is known and how to get there.*

2 *Do arrive in plenty of time with all appropriate equipment.*

3 *Do not be in too much of a hurry to start writing.* Read the exam paper thoroughly before starting. Check the instructions carefully. How many questions must be answered? Are any of them compulsory? Students may wish to mark the questions they feel most confident about answering.

4 *Do start with the question that is liked best.* But check that it really is as good as first thought; under stress it is easy to misread.

5 *Do plan answers.* It may be advisable to spend about 10 per cent of the time on planning, particularly if dealing with a complex problem. Always re-read a question and briefly list the points to be made before beginning to write the answer. Make sure that the question that the examiners asked is being answered, not the one the student wishes they had asked. Examiners constantly remark that failure to grasp the point of a question is the biggest cause of lost marks. Embrace the full scope of the question: check that all the 'triggers' have been spotted in a problem. It is better to cover every point the question raises superficially, than cover one or two points in great detail. Marks will be spread across the question, so they are thrown away by ignoring points raised by the question.

   In essay questions, make sure that the 'key words' have been correctly analysed, indicating the topics involved and the method of presentation required (see above). Do keep an eye on the time. Set a time limit for each question and stick to it. Remember that most people pick up the majority of marks in the first 50 per cent of the writing time per question. If running low on time, it is better to answer any remaining questions in note form. Remember that failing to answer the required number of questions potentially throws away a vital percentage of marks (maybe 20–25 per cent per question).

6 *Do not leave before the end of the exam.* Use any spare time to check the paper: correct clerical errors, ensure that each question is numbered properly. If a student finishes with more than a very few minutes in hand, the chances are that something is wrong, so this time should be used to try to put it right. Check what has been written and see if anything needs amending. If any questions have been left out, make an attempt at another answer: a few crucial marks may be gained that separate a pass from a failure (or a distinction from a pass). Even if it is the exam paper from hell, do not run away from it. Having completed a course (usually at considerable expense) there is nothing to lose from having a go. If a student writes nothing, nothing is what they will get.

7 *Do present work as clearly as possible.* Never copy the question from the exam paper; this only wastes valuable time. Questions can be answered in any preferred order, but do make sure that each question is numbered correctly. Present each question on a fresh page, leaving space to insert any forgotten points at the end of the exam. It is best to use dark ink. Take care with handwriting, and, if time allows, underline the cases and statutes that are quoted. This all helps to keep the examiners on side: remember that they may be marking hundreds of scripts and will be grateful for a clearly presented paper.

Conclusion

Hopefully the above study hints will be useful and will help you to get the most out of the course, with enjoyment along the way and a happy outcome.

The nature of law

Learning objectives

On completion of this chapter, students should be able to:

★ appreciate the distinguishing features of a legal rule;

★ explain the characteristics of English law;

★ state its purposes;

★ distinguish between civil and criminal law;

★ use basic legal terms confidently and with understanding.

Introduction

This chapter will help to provide an insight into the distinctive features of legal rules within the English legal system resulting from its long historical development. This can help to make sense of how the law operates today. It will also give a head start by introducing some of the essential technical terms that will be met in the study of law.

What is law?

English law may be defined as a body of rules, created by the state, binding within its jurisdiction and enforced with the authority of the state through the use of sanctions. Here is an analysis of this definition.

Rules

Rules are commands aimed at regulating behaviour. Rules tell people what they can and cannot do; sometimes they may permit behaviour subject to fulfilling a condition. For example, an extension of business premises is illegal unless planning permission is obtained; a shop may not sell alcohol without a licence.

Created by the state

Parliament is responsible for creating most of the law applicable in the UK. Such law is contained in *Acts of Parliament* or *statutes*. Until the UK leaves the EU the content of much of this law is determined by the European Union, and in this respect, Parliament does not have complete independence. After the UK leaves the EU it will be up to the government of the day to decide how much of the body of law created by the EU will be adopted by the UK and the remainder will be scrapped. Since the Human Rights Act 1998, the European Convention on Human Rights is directly enforceable in the English courts.

The jurisdiction of the state

The law of any country is binding only within its territory. The UK Parliament may introduce laws applicable to the UK as a whole, but this text is concerned with the relevant law as it applies in England and Wales.

State enforcement

A legal dispute may require formal resolution by the court or tribunal. The state or a party to the dispute may initiate the enforcement proceedings.

A sanction or penalty may be imposed in order to compensate the injured party or punish the wrongdoer.

The characteristics of English law

English law has characteristics that make it very different from the law of other countries in the European Union.

It has evolved slowly and without interruption over many centuries

The origins of the English legal system can be traced to the Norman Conquest in 1066. Although huge changes have taken place since then, development has been gradual and piecemeal. As a result, a rather untidy and conservative evolution has taken place, with historical relics rubbing shoulders with more modern developments. For example, two divisions of the High Court today still carry traces of the names of their forebears in mediaeval times: the Court of King's Bench (now the Queen's Bench Division) and the Court of Chancery (the Chancery Division).

Lack of Roman law influence

English law has been little influenced by the Roman law principles which dominate the legal systems of other European countries and which also have some influence on Scots law.

Judges have creative powers

Judges were the principal lawmakers until their powers were gradually superseded by Parliament from the eighteenth century; senior judges today still retain some limited powers to develop principles of case law. The powers of other European judges are restricted to interpretation of the legal codes created by the relevant state legislatures.

The doctrine of binding precedent

Precedent: previous judicial decision influential and possibly binding in later cases.

When deciding a case, English judges are bound to apply any relevant **precedent** (previous decision) of a senior court, unlike their European counterparts who are guided, rather than bound, by previous cases.

Adversarial nature

Adversarial procedure: trial in which the judge acts like the referee in the contest between two opposing litigants.

The procedure in the English courts is largely **adversarial**. A case in the courts is essentially a contest before an umpire (the judge) whose principal tasks are to see that the rules of evidence are obeyed and to decide who the winner is. Case names look rather like football fixture lists: *Bloggs* v *Snodgrass*. The main burden of proof is on the accuser, and the party who can produce the most convincing evidence wins the case. The judge plays very little part in drawing out that evidence; too much judicial intervention may lead to the decision being reversed on appeal. It has been said that the adversarial system is about proving facts rather than discovering truth.

Inquisitorial procedure: the judge helps to establish the evidence by actively questioning witnesses.

The function of judges on mainland Europe is an **inquisitorial** one; this gives the judge power to call witnesses and question them during the hearing of the case. English judges are currently being encouraged to take a more interventionist role as case managers, before the hearing of complex cases, but this extension of their function is still a long way from a truly inquisitorial approach.

Why do we need law?

Any society, or group within it, however small, will make rules for the purposes of organisation, to promote the safety and convenience of members and to regulate their relationships with each other. An affluent industrialised state requires a complex system of law that aims to fulfil a number of purposes. Figure 2.1 shows how the law may be classified.

A system of law may be needed for the following reasons:

1 to provide a governmental structure and legislative procedures: constitutional law;
2 to provide public services and to raise taxes to pay for them: administrative and revenue law;
3 to regulate and promote the economy: administrative, civil and criminal law are all involved;
4 to promote public order and preserve national security: criminal law;
5 to give individual members personal rights and duties in relation to others and to enable personal enforcement of these rights: the civil law. Civil law duties may arise through agreement between the parties (the law of contract), or be imposed directly (the law of tort);
6 to give legal validity to approved relationships and transactions between members of the society: this involves the law of contract, the law of property and succession, company and partnership law, and family law.

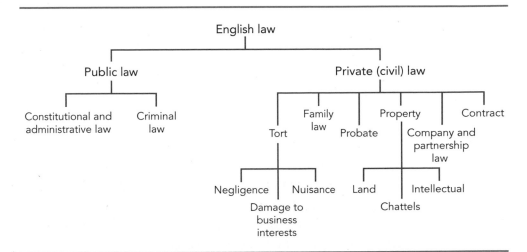

Figure 2.1 Classification of English law

The differences between criminal and civil law

It is important from the outset to understand the differences between civil and criminal law. Dual liability for a breach of both civil and criminal law may arise from the same set of facts; but since these two branches of the law have very different purposes, their procedures and penalties differ radically. The following example illustrates these crucial differences.

Real life

Alexa is treated to a hot lobster lunch at 'The Fat Cat Wine Bar Ltd' by Maria. Subsequently, both Alexa and Maria become ill with food poisoning, which they claim was caused by the dirty state of Fat Cat's kitchen.

The criminal proceedings

R[egina] v Fat Cat

Selling impure food is a criminal offence under the Food Safety Act 1990: it is in the interests of public safety to control and punish such behaviour.

In this sort of case, Fat Cat may be prosecuted in the Magistrates' Court by the local authority's trading standards department, rather than by the police. The burden of proving Fat Cat's guilt lies on the prosecutor, who has to prove *beyond all reasonable doubt* that the food poisoning was caused by the condition of the lobster.

If Fat Cat is found guilty, Fat Cat Ltd may be fined: a fine is a sum of money payable to the court; it does not go to the victims of the crime.

The civil proceedings

Maria v Fat Cat

Alexa v Fat Cat

Alexa and Maria want compensation for having been made ill. Both are self-employed and, in addition to the pain and inconvenience of their illness, they have also lost earnings while they were ill and unable to work.

Two separate claims are involved: Maria, who bought the food, will sue for breach of contract, as the lobster was clearly not of satisfactory quality; Alexa, who was harmed by the food but had no contract with Fat Cat, will sue in tort claiming negligence or breach of the Consumer Protection Act 1987.

Alexa and Maria will take action in the County Court and will have to prove that on *the balance of probabilities* Fat Cat caused their loss. This is a lower standard of proof than that required in criminal proceedings, as the court requires it to be proved only that it is more likely than not, that Fat Cat was legally responsible.

If Alexa and Maria win, damages will be payable to them by Fat Cat to compensate them for their pain and suffering and all economic loss resulting from it, including medical costs and loss of earnings. In legal terminology, this is called consequential loss. Maria will also be able to reclaim the cost of the meal.

A summary of the differences between civil and criminal law

Criminal law	Civil law
Purpose	
Regulates behaviour perceived as being anti-social and dangerous to the public.	Gives legal rights to individuals to govern their formal and informal relationships with each other.
Provides machinery by which the state may take action against offenders.	Provides the means by which they may enforce the rights arising from these relationships.
Procedure	
Generally started by the police, but some legislation is enforced by other agencies like local authorities or Revenue & Customs.	Civil proceedings are taken against the alleged wrongdoer by the party who claims that they have been wronged.
Exceptionally, a private prosecution may be brought by an individual. The victim usually plays no part in the decision to prosecute.	The case may not go to trial even if proceedings are started. Most civil law claims are settled out of court, without any threat of legal action. In many others, the proceedings are abandoned before trial.
Once started, a case will proceed to trial in the Magistrates' Court or the Crown Court.	Most civil cases are heard in the County Court and the High Court and in certain specialised tribunals.
The prosecution must prove that the accused is guilty beyond all reasonable doubt.	The claimant must prove that the defendant is liable on the balance of probability.
Penalties	
The focus is on the accused and the need to protect society against criminal conduct.	The focus is on the needs of the victim and generally requires the wrongdoer to pay damages, which are often covered by insurance.
The ultimate aim is to control the criminal, while protecting society from future anti-social conduct.	Exceptionally, the court – by injunction or other equitable remedy – may require some practical correction of the wrong. This may be used in domestic violence cases or to prevent a nuisance.
A penalty may be used to contain criminals by depriving them of their freedom, or to rehabilitate them; it may be intended to deter them or others from committing future crimes.	

Changing the law

It is important to realise that the law is subject to frequent change. Very few principles actually remain constant. These changes reflect social, political, economic and technological developments taking place within society.

Social change

Changes in moral values have influenced a number of legal developments in the last 50 years, including reform of the divorce law, decriminalisation of abortion, as well as the introduction of legislation to prevent discrimination on the grounds of sex, race, sexual orientation, disability, religion or belief, and age. Very recently, heterosexual couples have been given the right to enter into a civil partnership as a result of a Supreme Court decision in 2018.

Political change

Every parliament is sovereign and consequently after the referendum in 2016 the UK will be withdrawing from the European Union and repealing the European Communities Act 1972. The law may require radical change.

The privatisation of the water, gas and electricity utilities was achieved by repeal of previous legislation, which had introduced a policy of nationalisation.

Economic and technological change

Much of the law governing commerce and industry, including the regulation of data protection, is subject to such influence. As society and business practice develop, new challenges arise. For example, the General Data Protection Regulation (GDPR) together with the new Data Protection Act 2018 govern the way organisations deal with personal data.

In practice, these influences and political change may be interlinked: an economic or social issue is often the focus of a political policy.

Essential legal terms

This text tries to explain in lay terms some important legal terminology. However, there are a few common words and phrases explained below, which are useful shorthand. There is also a list of the key terms arising from the particular topics under examination, at the end of each chapter. It may be useful to look through these when each chapter is completed to check understanding.

The claimant and defendant

These are the parties in a civil case (*action*). The **claimant** *sues* (brings the case against) the **defendant**.

The prosecution and the defence

These are the parties to a criminal case. The '**defence**' is sometimes called the *defendant* or the **accused**. The prosecution is sometimes called the **Crown**, reflecting the fact that criminal proceedings are brought by the state in the name of the Crown. This is why criminal cases are usually reported as *R* v *(Jenkins)*.

The appellant and the respondent

These are the parties in a civil or criminal appeal hearing. The appellant is the party who is bringing the appeal against the decision of the court below, in which the respondent won his or her case.

The common law

This has two possible meanings. The relevant meaning is usually clear from the context.

Case law as opposed to statute law

When the **common law** first began to develop in the early centuries after the Norman Conquest, there was no centralised legal system and there were great variations in the law across England. Judges appointed by the Crown had the task of welding together a system of law applicable (and therefore *common*) to the country as a whole. This law gradually emerged from principles developed and applied to cases which came before the courts. Common law in this context means judge-made law.

Case law and statute law as opposed to principles of equity

The civil law sometimes allows the court to exercise discretionary powers, which are based not just on the legal rights of the parties, but on what will produce a just and moral solution. These discretionary rules are part of the **law of equity**. They protect only those parties who are *morally* as well as *legally* entitled to a remedy.

Equitable principles govern the issue of court orders like injunctions and some contractual remedies which are described later in this text. They are the foundation of the law of mortgages and trusts, since they seek to protect the vulnerable parties to the transaction from the abuse of power by lenders and trustees respectively.

The law of equity has its origins in the fourteenth century; it was initially developed by successive Lord Chancellors to put right the defects that had become apparent in

Claimant: the party who brings a civil action.

Defendant: the person against whom criminal or civil proceedings are brought.

Defence (the): the person being prosecuted in a criminal trial/ their legal representatives.

Accused (the): the person being prosecuted in a criminal trial.

The prosecution/ the Crown: the prosecutor in criminal proceedings.

Common law: various meanings determined by context: law applicable to the whole of England/ judge-made law rather than statute/ not the law of equity.

Equity (law of): complements the common law by principles based on morality as well as legal right and practical remedies granted at the discretion of the court.

the common law system. Lord Chancellors for many years were churchmen as well as lawyers, which gave this branch of the law the emphasis on moral principle that governs its operation in the civil courts today. Its principles co-exist with other principles of common law (statute and case law in this context) and may come into play at the discretion of the court where the common law principle or remedy will cause injustice.

Chapter summary

A definition of law

A body of rules imposed by the state and with authority within it and enforceable by sanctions imposed by the courts.

Characteristics of English law

Antiquity, lengthy evolution untouched by Roman law, creative power and authority of the judiciary, adversarial procedure.

Differences between criminal and civil law

Criminal law is enforced by the state and aims to protect the public from anti-social behaviour.

Civil law enables individuals to enforce rights governing their formal and informal relationships in the courts.

Review questions 1

1 What distinguishes law from other rules?

2 What are the characteristics of English law?

3 Why does a developed society need law?

4 What does the court hope to achieve when imposing a criminal sentence?

5 What does a civil litigant hope to achieve by taking a case to court?

6 What are the likely legal consequences in the following case? Sparticus, who has had too much to drink, carelessly crashes his taxi into Finch's lorry. Sparticus' passenger, Juliette, is injured and Finch's lorry is damaged. A police officer, Helen, witnesses the incident.

Answers to all review questions can be found in Appendix 2.

Advanced questions 1

(A) Define and distinguish law and morality.

(B) What are the perceived aims of the criminal and civil law?

Answers to the advanced questions can be found at **go.pearson.com/uk/he/resources.**

Further reading

Slapper G. and Kelly, D. (2016) *The English Legal System* (17th ed.). Abingdon: Routledge.

Web activity

The website of the British and Irish Legal Information Institute is: www.bailii.org

The website of the UK Ministry of Justice is: www.justice.gov.uk

How the law is made

Learning objectives

On completion of this chapter, students should be able to:

★ explain the sources of English law;

★ distinguish between the functions of the institutions of the European Union;

★ differentiate between EC regulations, directives and decisions;

★ describe the legislative process in Parliament;

★ explain the application of the doctrine of precedent in the English courts;

★ describe the differing judicial approaches to interpreting statutes;

★ appreciate the effect of the Human Rights Act 1998 on the development of English law.

Introduction

This chapter explains where law comes from and how it is made. There are currently three important sources of law:

1 European law;

2 Parliament;

3 The courts.

The European Union and the British Parliament are currently the primary sources, but the courts may have a significant law-making role, for example employment law. The courts also have a crucial role in the interpretation of legislation. The European Convention on Human Rights (which is not connected to the EU) has become increasingly influential in the development of English law since its obligations became enforceable in the domestic courts.

The rights and duties of business owners, at every point from setting up and running to selling or closing down the business, are determined by the law in various forms. For example, the Companies Act 2006 regulates setting up and closing down a corporate business; partnership formation and dissolution are governed by the Partnership Act 1890. While running the business, the owner's relationship to employees is governed by a variety of statutes including the Employment Rights Act 1996 and the Equality Act 2010, on which European law has been very influential. Buying and selling goods and services is governed by the law of contract, which combines a number of statutes including the Consumer Rights Act 2015 together with some judge-made law. Judge-made (common) law governs much of the law of tort.

European law

The law of the European Community (EC) has been a source of UK law since 1973, when the UK became a member of what was formerly called the European Economic Community (EEC). The 1992 Treaty on European Union (the Maastricht Treaty) officially changed the name to European Community to signify that the objectives of the Community are not just economic. The Maastricht Treaty also created the European Union (EU), which consists of three 'pillars'. In the middle pillar are the three existing Communities, i.e. the European Coal and Steel Community (ECSC), the European Atomic Energy Community (EURATOM) and the Economic Community. These three Communities are known collectively as the European Community. On either side of this central pillar are the Common Foreign and Security Policy (CFSP), and Police and Judicial Cooperation in Criminal Matters (PJCCM). These three pillars support the overarching constitutional order of the Union. However, Community law only governs the EC. The CFSP and the PJCCM pillars are governed by intergovernmental cooperation. This means that they are outside the jurisdiction of the Community institutions, particularly the Court of Justice. Also, none of the articles of the outside pillars are enforceable, or challengeable, in national courts. Thus, although the Union is wider than the EC, it has its roots within it. EC law is an important source of business law and its impact is noticeable in a number of topic areas in this text, such as product safety and employment law. The EEC is currently composed of 28 member states.

Under the European Communities Act 1972 (ECA 1972), s 2, EU law is part of UK law. In the event of conflict, EU law takes priority. Disputed points of EU law must be referred by the domestic courts for interpretation to the Court of Justice of the European Union (CJEU), or be decided in accordance with principles found in its existing decisions.

The principal institutions of the European Union

The Council of the European Union

Council of the European Union: consists of the government minister from each EU state whose portfolio reflects the business of the meeting (e.g. Internal Affairs).

Rather confusingly, this may also be referred to as the 'Council of the EU' or sometimes just 'the Council'. It must not be confused with the European Council, which is entirely separate. The **Council of the European Union** is the main legislative organ of the Community and within it the interests of member states find direct expression. It also has responsibility for approving the EU budget and developing foreign and community policies. It is made up of 'a representative of each Member State at ministerial level authorised to commit the government of that Member State' (Treaty of Nice, Article 203). The representatives vary according to the subject matter under discussion. For General Council meetings, a member state's representative is generally its foreign minister. The ministers of state with the relevant portfolio attend all other meetings. For example, a meeting will be made up of agriculture ministers when the common agricultural policy is under discussion. The President of the Council of Ministers chairs the meetings. The presidency rotates every six months between the heads of state or heads of government of the member states.

The European Council

European Council: an EU institution composed of the foreign ministers from each member state.

The **European Council** is composed of the heads of state or of government of the member states. It meets at least twice a year in order to discuss major Community issues in a less formal atmosphere than that which prevails at the Council of the EU. It is chaired on a six-monthly rotation by the current President of the Council of the EU, assisted by the minister of foreign affairs of each of the member states and a member of the Commission. The European Council's function is to provide the Union with the necessary impetus to define the general political guidelines for its development.

The European Commission

The Commission is composed of one nominee from each member state and is an executive and policy-making body with legislative powers. Most major decisions taken by the Council must be made on the basis of proposals from the Commission. Currently there are 28 Commissioners, but once appointed they represent Community interests rather than national interests.

The European Parliament

European Parliament: an EU institution, members of which are elected by citizens of each member state.

The **European Parliament** consists of 751 members directly elected by people with the right to vote in each member state. The number of MEPs each state is entitled to elect is determined in proportion to its population size. The UK currently returns 73 members. Parliament exercises democratic supervision over the Commission, with the appointment of the President and members of the Commission subject to its approval. The Commission is thus politically answerable to the Parliament, which can pass a 'motion of censure' calling for its resignation. Together with the Council, Parliament formulates and adopts legislation proposed by the Commission.

The European Court of Justice (ECJ)

European Court of Justice: an EU institution which hears cases from/ against member states and the EU.

The **European Court of Justice** is made up of 28 judges assisted by advocates-general. If the court so requests, the Council may, acting unanimously, increase the number of advocates-general. The judges and advocates-general are appointed by common agreement of the governments of the member states and hold office for a renewable term of six years. They are chosen from legal experts whose independence is beyond doubt and who possess the qualifications required for appointment to the highest judicial offices in their respective countries or who are of recognised competence. The judges select one of their number to be President of the court for a renewable term of three years. The President directs the work of the court and its staff and presides at hearings and deliberations of major formations of the court.

The advocates-general assist the court in its task. They deliver independent and impartial opinions in all cases in open court, where a case does not raise any new points of law, unless the court decides otherwise. Their duties should not be confused with those of a public prosecutor or similar body.

The court has two functions:

1 to interpret any point of EU law referred by the courts of member states. It is mandatory for the highest appeal court of any member state to make a referral, if the meaning of a principle of EU law is unclear;

2 to decide the outcome of cases alleging breaches of EU legal obligations, brought by EU institutions, member states or individuals.

Once the court has reached its decision, this is immediately effective. It takes precedence over any conflicting domestic legislation. Individual states have responsibility for implementing the court's decisions by changing the relevant domestic law. Reluctance to comply may result in pressure from other member states. Since the Maastricht Treaty, a penalty may be imposed on any state which does not comply with a judgment. With the passage of time it became apparent that too many demands were being placed on the court, which is why the Single European Act 1987 introduced the Court of First Instance (CFI). The CFI is made up of one judge from each member state. The judges are appointed for a renewable term of six years by common accord of the governments of the member states. There are no permanent advocates-general attached to the CFI. All cases heard at first instance by the CFI may be subject to a right of appeal to the Court of Justice on points of law only.

The sources of European law

The treaties

The most important of these are the Treaty of Rome 1957 and the Maastricht Treaty 1992, as revised by the Treaty of Lisbon 2009, which define the constitution of the EU. The Treaty of Amsterdam 1997 and the Treaty of Nice 2003 also had an important constitutional effect as well as changing and enlarging obligations of member states. Some of these obligations are directly enforceable by individual citizens, regardless of whether the relevant member state has taken legislative action to implement them. Such directly enforceable obligations include those under Article 119 (now 141) of the Treaty of Rome, which relates to the equal treatment of men and women in employment.

Regulations

Regulation:
EU legislation which is directly effective in the UK.

Regulations are intended to impose uniformity of law throughout the Community. They take effect in all member states immediately on being issued.

Directives

Directive:
EU legislation aimed at harmonising the law of member states; becomes effective once domestic law is passed to implement it.

Directives comprise the most prolific source of law in the EC. Directives apply to all member states and are intended to lead to harmonisation of law between member states, making it similar but not identical. Directives set the aims which must be achieved but leave the choice of the form and method of implementation to each member state. Thus, they have to be implemented by national parliaments. Implementation legislation may reflect the legal and social conventions of each member state.

States are required to implement directives within specified time limits, but sometimes drag their heels if a particular directive is unpopular. The Court of Justice may permit claims by individuals against an organ of a member state (though not an individual) for breaches of a directive which has not yet been implemented, provided that the wording of the directive is sufficiently clear and unconditional.

Decisions

Decision:
EU legislation binding in one state only.

A **decision** affects only particular member states, companies or individuals. It may empower the party to whom it is issued to do something, or prevent it from doing something.

The impact of EU membership on English law

The main impact so far has been felt in the areas of trade, industry, employment, the environment, provision of financial services and the promotion of equality and social justice. Membership of the EU has, therefore, had considerable influence in many areas of business law. A number of references to such developments will be found throughout this text.

As the scope of European law expands through new treaties, its impact on English law, politics and society at large increases. The Treaty of Amsterdam, which came into force on 1 May 1999, aims to place employment and citizens' rights at the heart of the Union, to remove the last remaining obstacles to freedom of movement within the Union and to strengthen security. This had a considerable impact on human rights in Britain. It required the widening of the existing principles of non-discrimination legislation in employment with regards to gender, race, ethnic origin and disability to include religious belief, age and sexual orientation. Directives on all these issues were issued to member states and implementation has taken place. (For details see Chapter 18.)

The Treaty also seeks to promote privacy of citizens' personal data. The security issues within the Treaty will have an impact on criminal law and procedure, since the Treaty requires the police and the judiciary of all member states to coordinate action on terrorism, offences against children, drug trafficking, corruption and fraud. It also requires member states to cooperate more closely in the fight against racism and discrimination in general, while promoting equality before the law and social justice.

Referendum result: UK to leave EU

To fulfil an election promise the government held a referendum in 2016 to decide whether the UK should remain in the European Union. The campaign which followed was bitter and divisive. The remain lobby was primarily concerned with the perceived economic and political consequences. It feared that leaving would spell ruination for the economy and hinder the UK's meaningful participation on the international stage. The leave lobby's concerns were primarily focused on immigration which, it claimed, would be reduced if the EU's requirement of freedom of movement were removed; it also favoured the removal of all EU control over law-making by the UK Parliament. By a very small majority (51.9 per cent against 48.1 per cent) those voting to leave were successful.

The leaving process, which is still ongoing at the time of writing, was started in March 2017 when the UK triggered Article 50 of the Lisbon Treaty to notify the European Council of its intentions. Negotiations were later tentatively initiated to determine both the terms of departure and agreement on the framework of the UK's future relationship with the EU, including trading terms, but progressed very slowly. When these terms are finally settled the Council's agreement requires a qualified majority (75 per cent of member states representing 65 per cent of the EU population) of all its members and a vote by the EU Parliament as all member states must also agree.

Until the full process is concluded the UK remains subject to all its existing EU obligations and is also entitled to all the EU's financial contributions currently contracted to it. It will not be known how far the law is likely to change until the leaving process is well advanced and relevant legislation is prepared.

Parliament

Most English law is currently made by, or with the authority of, Parliament. **Direct (parliamentary/primary) legislation** comprises Acts of Parliament, created by the passage of a Bill through certain prescribed processes in the House of Commons and the House of Lords. Indirect **(delegated) legislation** is created by a body (usually a government department or local authority) which has been given the power to legislate by Parliament under an *enabling* Act.

How an Act of Parliament is created

Most legislation is proposed by government ministers, but backbench MPs have limited opportunities to put forward **Private Members' Bills**. These usually relate to non-party-political issues. In practice, few Private Members' Bills become Acts because of the limited amount of parliamentary time available to them.

The pre-legislative stage

A Government Bill is usually preceded by the issue of a **Green Paper**, which sets out the legislative proposals for discussion. Consultation with relevant interest groups may take place. A **White Paper** is then issued, which lays down the principles on which the draft Bill is based.

Parliamentary procedure

The first stage of a Bill's journey through Parliament is *the introduction and first reading*. Most Bills are initially processed in the House of Commons and then go through the same procedures in the House of Lords. All important and controversial Bills, including all money Bills, must start off in the Commons. The first reading is a formality to announce the existence of the Bill and to set down a date for the second reading.

The *second reading* involves a full debate which starts with a speech from the minister who is proposing the Bill. This is answered by the relevant shadow minister. After contributions from any interested member, a vote is taken. Provided that a majority is in its favour, the Bill passes on to the committee stage.

At the *committee stage* a standing committee of 25–45, appointed in proportion to party representation, usually examines the Bill clause by clause. Amendments may be proposed. (Some Bills require consideration by a committee of the whole House. They do not have a report stage, but progress straight to the third reading.)

Following the committee stage the committee reports on its findings (the *report stage*), debate takes place on proposed changes, and further amendments may be proposed to the Bill.

At the *third reading* of the Bill, a short debate concentrates on the main points of the Bill. In the Commons, only superficial changes (to grammar or syntax) will be made, though greater changes may take place in the House of Lords.

The processes discussed above are repeated when the Bill reaches the House of Lords (*transfer to the other House*). Note that, under the Parliament Acts 1911 and 1949, the House of Lords cannot reject a Bill outright, although it may delay any Bill except a money Bill for up to a year: a money Bill can be delayed only for a month. The power to delay may give the Lords considerable power, as the government is likely to seek a compromise to enable it to pursue its policies.

The Bill next passes on to the *consideration stage*. Each House must consider and agree to all the amendments proposed by the other before the legislative process can proceed. This may be a lengthy process if the Bill is complex and controversial as disagreement and further amendment may occur with the Bill 'ping-ponging' between the two Houses until each has agreed to the exact wording of the disputed clauses.

Before the Bill can become an Act of Parliament and pass into law, it must receive the *Royal Assent*. By convention this is just a formality: hundreds of years have passed since the Crown took an active legislative role.

The date of implementation of the whole or any part of an Act of Parliament is usually specified in it.

Delegated legislation

This is indirect or secondary legislation made by bodies outside Parliament, through the exercise of legislative power delegated to them by Act of Parliament.

In practice, the bulk of law created every year is delegated, rather than direct. Such legislation is the means by which both central and local government agencies administer their policies. Over 2,000 such regulations are enacted annually. These may, for example, limit benefit entitlements, raise the required hygiene standards in a fast-food business, and help to keep local parks free from noise pollution.

There are four main types of delegated legislation:

1 *Orders in Council.* The Emergency Powers Acts 1939 and 1984 give law-making powers to the Privy Council in times of national emergency.

2 *Statutory instruments.* These are created by government departments to execute general principles of policy set out in the enabling Act of Parliament. The Consumer Credit Act 1974 empowers the Secretary of State to make rules to safeguard users and potential users of credit facilities. About 3,000 such instruments are created annually.

3 *Regulations to implement law from the EU.* The European Communities Act 1972, s 2, empowers ministers and government departments to implement directives and treaty provisions.

4 *Bye-laws.* These are made by local authorities and other bodies with statutory powers, like Transport for London and Network Rail, to regulate the facilities which they provide.

The use of delegated legislation is somewhat controversial as it is determined by non-elected bodies. In general, however, the practical advantages outweigh its disadvantages. The advantages of delegated legislation are:

1 *Saving of parliamentary time.* The parliamentary legislative process is slow and protracted. Parliament finds it difficult to complete its annual legislative schedule and does not have time to debate the fine details of the regulations necessary to execute government policy.

2 *Specialist knowledge.* The creation of many regulations requires specialist knowledge which the average MP may not have. They are, for example, unlikely to understand the finer points of abattoir management, or appreciate the appropriate levels of sausage in a sausage roll.

3 *Flexibility.* Such rules may be easily and quickly introduced, altered or extinguished, as and when appropriate.

4 *Legislation can take place when Parliament is not sitting.* This assists the smooth running of central and local government outside parliamentary sessions.

The disadvantages of delegated legislation are:

1 *Loss of parliamentary control.* Since details of policy administration are determined by the relevant government department, Parliament may be deprived of the opportunity to question and debate them. Scrutiny of most delegated legislation is negligible. It is laid before Parliament, but most of it is subject to a 'negative resolution' procedure. This means that it will be implemented as it stands unless an objection is sustained within the specified time limit. Exceptionally, the enabling Act may require Parliament positively to approve the regulations.

2 *Bulk and frequent change.* The huge quantity of delegated legislation produced every year makes it very difficult – even for lawyers – to keep abreast of all changes. Adapting to changes may considerably add to the burdens of running a business, despite the circulation of publicity by the regulating body. The government have nevertheless, consistently stated their commitment to reducing the amount of bureaucratic form-filling for small businesses.

The courts

Creative powers

The law made by the courts is case law, sometimes described as common law. Until the nineteenth century the courts were the primary law-makers, but were superseded by Parliament since social conditions required a different style of law-making. Case law evolves slowly and haphazardly, when relevant cases come before the courts with facts which justify further legal development. A point of case law may be very narrow in its effect since the courts can legislate only with regard to things that have already happened; they cannot legislate for what is to happen in future cases with different facts. This makes case law an inadequate form of law-making in a sophisticated industrial society, where blanket legislation is needed to regulate possible future problems.

Today the bulk of both civil and criminal law is statutory. New principles are most commonly developed in this way and much of the common law has been *codified* (converted into statutory form). The higher courts retain some limited creative powers, mainly in tort and contract law which are still not predominantly statutory. For example, the law of negligence (which is described in Chapters 13–14) has been, and mainly continues to be, developed by judges.

Interpretative powers

Since most law is now statutory, the courts are mainly concerned with the interpretation and application of points of law derived from Acts of Parliament and delegated legislation. When exercising this function, the courts must respect the sovereignty of Parliament as a superior law-making body. A judge interpreting a statute will therefore aim to give such meaning to a disputed point of legislation as to reflect what Parliament seemed to have intended.

The words used in the statute are the main focus of the interpretation exercise and limit the freedom of the court. If the statute has an apparent gap and consequently an injustice exists, the court is not necessarily free to create the law to fill that gap, unless the context gives the necessary scope. Otherwise, all that the court can do, is to recommend that Parliament amends the legislation.

Judges have a number of resources and tools, which may assist their interpretative function.

1 Intrinsic aids

These are found within the statute itself. It is common for an interpretation clause to be included which explains any special meaning to be given to words within the statute. For example, the Occupiers' Liability Act 1957 defines 'premises' as any 'fixed or moveable structure' (see Chapter 16).

2 External aids

These are materials which are not part of the statute itself. They include the following:

(a) The Interpretation Act 1978. This gives guidance on terms and phrases commonly found in legislation.

(b) Reports of the law commission or government inquiry. These may indicate why legislation is needed and thereby indicate its meaning.

(c) Parliamentary reports. Until 1993 the courts refused to admit evidence from Hansard reports of parliamentary proceedings relating to the passage of the statute. There were three main objections:

- the legislative and judicial functions of the state would be confused;
- the cut and thrust of parliamentary debate was unlikely to provide objective explanations;
- the research required to check *Hansard* would also add considerably to the cost of litigation.

Pepper v *Hart* (1993, HL)

Held (by majority): *Hansard* may be consulted by the courts if all the following circumstances exist:

- the disputed legislation is ambiguous or obscure, or the words taken at their face value produce an absurd result; and
- the *Hansard* extract consists of statements made by the relevant minister or other sponsor of the Bill; and
- the meaning of the extract is clear.

Pepper v *Hart* has been followed in a number of cases, but it is doubtful how far it is useful. The disputed section of an Act may not have been debated. Even if it was, any comments made may, in themselves, be ambiguous and confusing.

3 Judicial principles of statutory interpretation

The judiciary has developed the following practices to assist the interpretative process:

Contextual approach: vague words in a statute take their meaning from their immediate/ general context.

Ejusdem generis rule: 'of the same class'. If a class of people/things is specified by the Act any person/thing within that class comes within the Act.

(a) *The contextual approach.* Any disputed words must always be interpreted within the context of the statute as a whole (a **contextual approach**). The significance of a vague, obscure or even apparently meaningless word may become crystal clear when scrutinised in relation to the surrounding text. The ***ejusdem generis* rule** forms part of the contextual approach. General words, like 'other animals', 'other person', or 'other thing' are meaningless in themselves. Their meaning may be clarified by reference to any specific words which precede them. Thus, if the words 'other animals' were preceded by the words 'cats, dogs and guinea pigs', it would be reasonable to assume that they include any animal commonly kept as a domestic pet. Generous interpretations are sometimes made to assist the perceived purpose of the statute. Thus in *Flack* v *Baldry* (1988) an electric shock from a stun gun was held to come within the definition of 'any noxious liquid, gas or other thing' under the Firearms Act 1968.

Literal rule: the words of a statute must be taken at face value.

(b) *The literal rule.* A **literal rule** approach requires the court to take words at their face value where there is no ambiguity and the meaning is clear, even if this produces an absurd result.

Fisher v *Bell* (1960)

The defendant shopkeeper displayed a 'flick knife' (knife with a retractable blade) in his shop window and was charged with offering for sale an offensive weapon in breach of the Restriction of Offensive Weapons Act 1959, s 1(1).

Held: he was not guilty since, in contract law, a display of goods is an 'invitation to treat' and not 'an offer for sale' (see Chapter 5).

Golden rule:
rule of statutory interpretation stating that if two literal meanings exist the least ridiculous be adopted.

The application of the rule in such a case has been justified by the courts on the ground that it is for Parliament to correct any practical problems arising from the statute. Any action by the courts is an unjustifiable interference with parliamentary sovereignty.

(c) *The golden rule.* The **golden rule** developed as a means of blunting the worst excesses of the literal rule. If the statute is ambiguous, the court will apply the least ridiculous meaning in order to avoid an absurd result.

Adler v *George* (1964)

A CND demonstrator who invaded a sentry post at an army base was charged with obstructing a member of HM Forces 'in the vicinity of a prohibited place' under the Official Secrets Act 1920. It was argued that since she had actually entered the base she was on it when the obstruction took place rather than in its vicinity.

Held: to dismiss the charge on the basis of a literal interpretation would produce an absurd result; 'vicinity' must be interpreted as including the place itself, not just its environs.

Smith v *Hughes* (1960)

A prostitute who, from her window, encouraged gentlemen passing in the street to avail themselves of her services was successfully prosecuted for 'soliciting in the street'.

Held: the purpose of the legislation was to prevent annoyance to people arising from the activities of prostitutes in public places. Since the effects of the defendant's conduct were felt by people in the street, that conduct clearly fell within the purpose of the Street Offences Act 1959.

Mischief rule:
a statute must be interpreted to remedy the gap in the law which it was intended to correct.

(d) *The mischief rule.* The **mischief rule** is a sixteenth-century rule that allows the court to adopt a meaning which will enable the statute to fulfil its intended purpose. The court examines the law before the Act to discover the problem (mischief) which the statute was intended to correct; then the statute can be given the meaning which resolves the problem.

This rule largely fell into disfavour with the rise of the literal rule, which dominated judicial decision-making in the nineteenth century and for approximately the first 70 years of the twentieth century.

Wolman v *Islington LBC* (2007)

A byelaw made it an offence to park a motor cycle with wheels on any part of a pavement. When Mr Wolman parked his motor cycle on a stand hovering above the pavement it was held that the motor cycle was on the pavement. The mischief the law was trying to prevent was obstruction of the pavement.

Purposive approach:
the court interprets a statute in the way which will implement its purpose.

(e) *The purposive approach.* The **purposive approach**, which is somewhat similar to the mischief approach, but broader in its effect, has come into use since the UK's entry into the EC. The courts of other member states have traditionally used this approach, as does the European Court of Justice. It requires the court to interpret the statute by looking beyond its words to determine the general purpose behind it. To do this the court may examine relevant extrinsic documentary evidence such as government reports proposing the reform. The next case is a good example of this.

Royal College of Nursing v *DHSS* (1981, HL)

Under s 1(1) of the Abortion Act 1967 an abortion is legal only if carried out by a 'registered medical practitioner'. A change in abortion methods after the Act was passed meant that the procedure was largely carried out by nurses, subject to some supervision by a doctor. The courts had to decide whether abortions carried out by this procedure were legal under the Act.

The Court of Appeal (adopting a literal approach) held: the practice was unlawful since nurses do not have the necessary qualifications.

The House of Lords (by majority) held: a purposive approach should be used and that no illegality had occurred. Lord Diplock said: 'The approach of the Act seems to me to be clear. There are two aspects of it: the first, to broaden the grounds on which an abortion may be obtained; the second is to ensure that the abortion is carried out with proper skill and in hygienic conditions.'

(Before the Act legalised abortion in certain circumstances, many women died as a result of unregulated abortionists.)

The House of Lords' decision in *Pepper* v *Hart* (see above) may be seen as enabling and encouraging this approach. While the literal rule is still used today, a purposive approach is common where this assists a just outcome in the public interest. The court may use it to complement the literal rule: looking at the purpose of the statute will assist correct choice of meaning of an ambiguous word or phrase. It may be more radically used to correct an anomaly or fill a small gap.

Although called 'rules', it is more accurate to describe these judicial principles as 'tools' of interpretation. As *Royal College of Nursing* v *DHSS* (above) illustrates, they represent differing possible approaches to the interpretation process. They are not in any way superior or inferior to each other. Judges will choose what they view as the approach likely to produce the interpretation most beneficial to the public interest and which reflects current constitutional developments.

Real life

Hamish is enjoying the spring sunshine and bird song in his local park when Wayne and Wendy settle down on the grass nearby and entertain themselves by listening to Jazz FM on their iPhone very loudly. Hamish does not like the music and points out the park byelaws notice. This states a list of noise prohibitions, including 'singing or playing music', breach of which may be punished by a fine. Wayne, who fancies himself as a bit of an amateur lawyer, says: 'We are not playing anything mate, you'd better prosecute the radio station.'

It would no doubt be wise of Hamish to admit defeat at this point and find somewhere quieter to sit. However, he probably has the law on his side. A court considering the issue might well conclude that Wayne had breached the byelaws. 'Playing music', even literally interpreted, is capable of including music on the phone, so by using the golden rule approach an absurd result could be avoided by choosing the meaning of play as in 'a radio was playing music'. As the object of the bye-laws is to prevent noise pollution, a purposive approach would also include broadcast music.

4 Judicial presumptions

The courts will presume in the absence of clear evidence to the contrary that a statute will not:

(a) impose strict liability, i.e. where it is not necessary to prove that the accused intended to commit the offence;

(b) operate retrospectively, i.e. be said to apply to offences committed before the statute came into force;

(c) change the common law.

These presumptions may be contradicted (rebutted) only by express wording in the statute, or by clear implication to that effect.

Sweet v *Parsley* (1969, HL)

Miss Sweet let out a house which was raided by the police, who found cannabis in the possession of the tenants. Miss Sweet was charged with a statutory offence of 'being concerned in the management of premises' where the drugs were found.

Held: in the absence of a clear indication in the statute that she could be liable without reasonable knowledge of what was happening on her property, Miss Sweet was not guilty without proof of guilty knowledge. Strict liability was presumed not to have been intended.

The law of binding precedent

Persuasive decision: a non-binding but influential precedent.

Binding precedent: a judicial decision which a court must follow.

When exercising either their creative or interpretative functions, judges are bound by the law of binding precedent. This is a distinctive feature of the English legal system. In mainland European countries, judges tend to follow each other's decisions in a similar way but are not obliged to do so. Their fellow judges' decisions are all **persuasive** but they are not **binding**. Under English law, judges are not necessarily entitled to make their own decisions about the development or interpretation of the law. They may be bound by a decision reached in a previous case.

Two factors are crucial to determining whether a precedent (previous judicial decision) is binding:

1 the position in the court hierarchy of the court which decided the precedent, relative to the position of the court trying the current case. Inferior courts are bound by the decisions of superior courts (the letters SC, HL, CA and PC following the name of a case indicate that it involves an appeal in one of the higher courts);

2 whether the facts of the current case come within the scope of the principle of law in the previous decision.

The court hierarchy

1 The Supreme Court

Per incuriam: a case decision found later to have been incorrectly reached, because the court did not have the opportunity to consider potentially relevant law.

Until October 2009 this court was called the House of Lords. It is the final court of appeal in England, Wales, Scotland and Northern Ireland. Its decisions (which now include all those previously reached by the House of Lords) are binding on all courts below. Before 1966, in the interests of preserving certainty, the court followed its own decisions unless a previous decision was reached *per incuriam*. Translated literally, this means 'through lack of care' caused by a failure by counsel to draw the attention of the court to crucial statutory or case law, preventing a correct decision from being reached. Since 1966 it has indicated that it is prepared to depart from existing decisions, if this is necessary to prevent injustice or unreasonable restriction of development of the common law.

Worth thinking about?

In what circumstances do you suppose that the Supreme Court would find a previous decision unjust or restrictive?

Suggested solutions can be found in Appendix 2.

2 The Court of Appeal

(a) The Civil Division of the Court of Appeal is bound by the decisions of the Supreme Court, and its decisions bind all the civil courts below. Subject to three exceptions laid down in *Young* v *Bristol Aeroplane Company* (1944), it is supposed to follow its own previous decisions. The exceptions are:

- two of its own previous decisions are in conflict: it must then choose which to follow; the one which is not chosen ceases to be good law;
- a previous decision conflicts with a decision of the Supreme Court: the decision of the Supreme Court must be followed;
- the previous decision was reached *per incuriam*.

(b) The Criminal Division of the Court of Appeal is bound by the decisions of the Supreme Court, and its decisions bind all the criminal courts below. It may depart from its own decisions where such flexibility is in the interests of justice.

3 The Divisional Courts

These are all bound by the Supreme Court and Court of Appeal decisions. The decisions of the Divisional Courts are binding on those courts from which they hear appeals. They follow their own decisions subject to the same exceptions as the Civil Division of the Court of Appeal.

4 The High Court

Judges in the High Court are bound by the decisions of the Supreme Court and Court of Appeal, but not by the decisions of their fellow judges. High Court decisions are binding on the Crown Court, county courts and magistrates' courts.

Decisions made in the Crown Court, the county courts and magistrates' courts are not binding in other cases or in other courts. Such courts, of course, are bound by the decisions of the relevant superior courts.

The relevance of the previous decision: The scope of the *ratio decidendi*

When judges have heard cases in the High Court or any of the courts above, they may deliver lengthy judgments. These explain their reasons for deciding in favour of one party rather than the other.

Ratio decidendi: the reasons in law and fact why a judge reached a decision.

This statement of reasons, which refers both to relevant proven facts and to the applicable principles of law, is called the *ratio decidendi* (the reason for the decision). It is the *ratio decidendi* which forms the potentially binding precedent for later cases.

A later court, when hearing a case, has to decide whether the case facts are sufficiently relevant to the principle of the *ratio decidendi* of a previous case. If so, the previous decision must be applied, provided it was decided by a relevant court. If there are material differences, the latter case can be *distinguished* on its facts and the previous decision is not applicable.

Reversing and overruling decisions

An appeal court may decide to overturn a decision reached by a lower court. This may be on the ground that the case was incorrectly decided in the light of the current law. The lower court's decision is then said to be *reversed*. The victor at the previous trial is now the loser.

Reversing a decision: on appeal the party who won becomes the loser.

Overrule: the court declares an existing binding precedent to be no longer good law.

Reversing a decision does not in itself affect the validity of any precedent applied in the case. If the appeal court believes that a precedent, which bound the lower court, no longer represents the law, it may (subject to the rules explained above) **overrule** that precedent and restate the legal principle.

The importance of the law reporting system

No system of precedent can work unless there is an accurate and comprehensive collection of the key decisions of the superior courts readily accessible to all who have need of them. Authoritative reports compiled by legally qualified law reporters are produced primarily by the Council of Law Reporting. The courts may refuse to allow a non-authoritative report to be quoted in court.

Persuasive precedents

While a court may be bound to apply a precedent, other decisions called persuasive precedents are influential only. The court can choose to apply them. Persuasive precedents include:

Obiter dictum/obiter dicta: a judicial statement indicating how the judge would interpret the law in different circumstances.

1 *Obiter dicta*. In a judgment it is quite common to find statements of law relating to hypothetical facts. These are not part of the *ratio decidendi* and are called **obiter dicta** (**obiter dictum** in the singular). These indicate how the judge thinks the law should develop in the hypothetical circumstances. They are highly persuasive if they come from the Supreme Court or Court of Appeal, but a court still has a choice about applying them in a future case. Once applied, the *obiter dicta* become binding principles of law. Some important principles of law have originated from *obiter dicta*. See *Central London Property Trust* v *High Trees House* (Chapter 6).

2 The decisions of the Judicial Committee of the Privy Council. The Privy Council, which is staffed by members of the Supreme Court, hears appeals from the courts of some Commonwealth countries. As the decisions do not involve English cases

they are of persuasive influence only, despite the status of the judges. The rules relating to remoteness of damage in negligence are derived from a case called *The Wagon Mound*, an appeal from the Australian courts (see Chapter 13).

The advantages and disadvantages of the binding precedent doctrine

Conflicting opinions exist about the value of the binding precedent system. The advantages are said to be:

1 *Certainty*. The system promotes valuable certainty in the law. A party can generally be given a reasonably clear prediction of the outcome of its case.
2 *Flexibility*. The necessarily firm rules are tempered by the ability of the higher courts to overrule their own decisions. A court's ability to distinguish or reconcile decisions on their facts also promotes flexibility.
3 *Practical nature*. Principles of pure case law can be developed in response to actual problems and tailored to solve them.
4 *Speed.* The law can be developed without waiting for Parliament to legislate in a new area.

The disadvantages of the system often appear correlative to the perceived advantages:

1 *Uncertainty*. The powers of the courts to distinguish and reconcile binding precedents often lead to confusing hairline distinctions and distorted applications of case law.
2 *Rigidity*. Certainty is preserved by rigid rules which arguably inhibit development of the law.
3 *Retrieval problems.* The vast amount of case law makes it easy for relevant precedents to be overlooked during preparation for litigation, and increases the time and, therefore, the cost to the client.
4 *Haphazard development.* A change in the law depends on a case with relevant facts reaching the appropriate court. This usually means the Court of Appeal or the Supreme Court; litigants do not necessarily have the means to take their cases that far.
5 *Undemocratic.* The development of pure case law by judges (not interpreting statutes) is not appropriate since they are not democratically appointed and law-making conflicts with parliamentary sovereignty.

The Human Rights Act 1998 (HRA 1998)

This important statute, which came into force in October 2000, makes the most of the rights in the European Convention on Human Rights directly enforceable in the English courts. It has the potential directly and indirectly to be highly influential on the content and interpretation of legislation and on the way case law is developed.

The legal and political background to the Act

European Convention on Human Rights: the fundamental freedoms to be expected by the citizens of a democratic state and binding on its 47 state signatories. (*Not* EU legislation.)

The **European Convention on Human Rights** (the Convention) was drafted by the Council of Europe and came into force in 1953. It now has 47 signatories, including the UK. It requires signatory states to uphold a number of fundamental civil rights, including the rights to liberty and security (Article 5), freedom of thought, conscience and religion (Article 9), freedom of expression (Article 10), and freedom of assembly and association (Article 11). The rights to life (Article 2), a fair trial (Article 6) and privacy and family life (Article 8) are also included. There is a right to manifest one's religion under Article 9 and a right of access to religion (Protocol 1, Article 2). Until the HRA 1998, none of these was directly and specifically enforceable in the UK courts. Individuals had to take claims that the government had breached its duties under the Convention to the **European Court of Human Rights** (ECtHR) at Strasbourg, if no remedy had been found to exist in their case by the UK courts under domestic law.

European Court of Human Rights: hears cases concerning alleged breaches of the ECHR by citizens against their home state. (*Not* an EU institution.)

The Convention, even when not directly binding on the English courts, was always used as an aid to statutory interpretation and to determine the scope of the common law. Decisions of the ECtHR were used as persuasive precedents.

The Convention and the ECtHR must not be confused with the law and institutions of the EU. They are different in their origins, signatories and scope of operation. However, the European Court of Justice, based at Luxembourg, which is responsible for upholding the law of the European Union, tends to reflect the principles of the Convention in its decisions.

The operation of the HRA 1998

Section 6 of the HRA 1998 requires 'public authorities' to act compatibly with the Convention. Public authorities include central government departments and local authorities, as well as the courts, tribunals and police forces. A breach of the Convention by a **public authority** is therefore now actionable in the domestic courts.

Public authority: HRA 1998, s 6 includes the courts and any organisation or body with public functions.

The judges' functions

Interpretation of Convention rights: s 2

When the court is deciding any issue which has, 'arisen in connection with human rights' it must take into account the case law of the ECtHR.

Interpretation of legislation: s 3

The court must, 'so far as it is possible to do so', interpret legislation so that it is compatible with Convention rights. Note that the duty under s 3 is not an absolute one. To preserve parliamentary sovereignty, the Act does not permit the court to override a statute found to be incompatible with the Convention. Instead, the court has the power (s 4) to issue a declaration of incompatibility to the relevant minister, who may then at his or her discretion ask Parliament to amend the legislation. In the first year of the operation of the Act only three such declarations were issued in a total of

56 claims under the Act. For example, in *R (on the application of Pearson)* v *Secretary of State for the Home Department and Martinez; Hirst* v *Attorney-General* (2001) it was held that the Representation of the People Act 1983, which states that prisoners do not have the right to vote, was not incompatible with Article 10 of the Convention (right to freedom of expression). The Convention right is not absolute and proportionate restrictions can be imposed by the state.

Remember that the HRA does not preclude action in the ECtHR. That is still possible if all rights of action under English law have been exhausted. Hirst exercised this right and won his case in the ECtHR (*Hirst* v *UK (No. 2)* (2005)). The ECtHR held that a universal ban on prisoner voting was a breach of the Convention because it was: 'Such a general, automatic and indiscriminate restriction on a vitally important convention right.' It applied automatically to convicted prisoners in prison, 'irrespective of the length of their sentence and irrespective of the nature or gravity of their offence and their individual circumstances'. The court dismissed the UK's argument that allowing the right would 'make a mockery of the law and promote criminal behaviour' on the grounds that there was no evidence to support it and stated that UK law should be changed by August 2011. After the ECtHR decision in 2005, the UK government agreed that the law which dates from 1870 would be changed within the deadline. Consultation on this controversial issue took place, with a view to extending the right to prisoners convicted of less serious offences. Successive governments have indicated extreme reluctance about changing the current law and although a Bill was drafted in 2012 and considered by a cross-party parliamentary committee it has never been introduced for debate in Parliament. While many people in the UK are repelled by the idea of reform, if looked at in a European context, it is not such an alien notion. While a total ban is imposed in 13 countries including Belgium, in 30 others, prisoners may vote, though some restrictions are imposed in some of those states. It seems unlikely that there will be any change in the near future.

Judicial remedies: s 8

Where a breach of the Convention is proved the court has the power to grant a number of remedies, including damages and injunctions and other orders.

The methods by which the court may determine an award for damages are well illustrated by the following case.

DSD and NBV v *Commissioner of Police for the Metropolis* (2014, EWHC)

The two applicants sought damages after obtaining a declaration under the HRA against the Police Commissioner on the grounds that his force had breached the HRA and Article 3 of the Convention by subjecting them to 'inhuman and degrading treatment'.

Both women had been raped after being drugged by a serial sex offender W, and reported the crime. D was raped in 2003 and V in 2007. The police failed properly to investigate both cases. They assumed that D was lying and V's case was downgraded in priority to improve crime statistics. W was eventually arrested in 2009 after committing over 100 rapes.

Both women later brought successful civil claims against W and also received compensation from the Criminal Injuries Compensation Board.

The Court had to decide whether under the HRA s 8 and Art 5 of the ECtHR it was *'necessary'* to award damages to *'afford just satisfaction'* to the applicants.

Green J held: The fact that compensation had already been paid from other sources did not prevent a successful application. The damage caused to the parties by the police was discrete from the harm caused by the offence. Subject to proof of a link between the police failure to carry out a proper investigation of the crime and the resulting ill effects on the applicants, an award was appropriate.

When deciding the amount of damages the court had to take into account ECtHR decisions, the primary object of which was to prevent further breaches of the law, as well as domestic claims. The award must reflect the degree of culpability of the defendant as well as the degree of suffering caused to the applicants. *'The police failings were not merely operational . . . they were systemic and of a deep and abiding nature. This is an aggravating factor when it comes to damages.'* They were reflective of a culture deeply embedded in the Metropolitan Police which aggravated the seriousness of its failings.

Both women suffered acute long-term clinical depression as a result of the rape and the subsequent police actions. Fifty per cent of their subsequent suffering could be attributed to the police failings. It was also probable that V would not have been raped if the police had properly investigated D's complaint four years earlier.

Damages should be assessed as £22,000 for D and £19,000 for V.

Direct effect: under the HRA 1998 the ECHR can be enforced in cases against a public authority in an English court.

Indirect effect: the HRA 1998 makes the ECHR influential on the outcome of cases not brought under the Act as the court must act compatibly with ECHR and take account of ECtHR judgments.

The impact of the Act

The Act has both a **direct** and **indirect** effect on the way domestic law is interpreted and applied.

Direct effect

The HRA 1998 introduces an entirely new right of action for alleged breaches of Convention rights, though only against a 'public authority'. Such an action cannot be brought against a private institution or individual.

There have been some controversial cases. In *R (on the application of F and Another)* v *Secretary of State for the Home Department* (2010) the Supreme Court held that sex offenders should have a right to appeal against lifelong inclusion in the sex offenders register, because such registration was a disproportionate general requirement and each case should be considered separately. Generally and unsurprisingly, however, the direct impact of the Act on domestic law has not been a dramatic one. Apart from the innate conservatism of the English judiciary, Convention rights are very broadly worded, giving judges flexibility to find compatibility. Almost all Convention rights are not absolute, but instead are hedged around with qualifications. For example, the right to life (Article 2) may not be breached if a person dies while being lawfully arrested. The right to liberty (Article 5) may be limited in the interests of protecting the public against crime.

R (on the application of Laporte) v *Chief Constable of Gloucestershire Constabulary* (2007, HL)

Jane Laporte (and 26 other anti-war protestors) claimed that their rights to freedom of expression and freedom of assembly (ECHR, Articles 10 and 11) had been breached when the police prevented them from attending a lawful demonstration at RAF Fairford, just before the base was used to launch bombing raids on Iraq. The police stopped their coach, searched the passengers and then sealed it and escorted it back to London. The police argued that it was necessary to do so in order to prevent a breach of the peace, given the past history of some of the demonstrators and some items found on the coach (e.g. a can of spray paint). Only the three main speakers were allowed to proceed to Fairford.

Held: (unanimously): the police's entirely disproportionate conduct had breached the applicants' Convention rights. They had also been unlawfully detained. At the point that the police intervened there was no reason to view them as other than *'committed and peaceful'* demonstrators. It was irrelevant that a breach of the peace might occur sometime in the future. The HRA 1998 had created a *'constitutional shift'* and created a right to peaceful protest. The right to freedom of expression was *'an essential foundation of a democratic society'* (Lord Bingham).

The court, when determining a human rights claim, has to attempt to balance the interests of the parties to ensure neither suffers an undue limitation of their Convention rights. This is sometimes described as *'proportionality'*. For example, a claim to protect a right of privacy (Article 8) must not be decided in a way that unduly curtails freedom of expression of the other party or which will unreasonably interfere with the public's right to information (Article 10). The following case provides an example of rights to family life being compromised for public benefit.

Austin v Commissioner of Police of the Metropolis (2009, HL)

Ms Austin took part in a large May Day demonstration against global capitalism in Oxford Street in London involving about 3,000 people in 2001. The police, who had not been informed that the demonstration would take place, decided that the only workable strategy to prevent injury, damage and violence was to 'kettle' [form a cordon round] the large crowd of demonstrators near Oxford Circus and then disperse them in an orderly fashion. The dispersal took seven hours due to the behaviour of a large minority of the demonstrators who became obstructive and violent. Some prised up paving stones and hurled lumps of masonry at the police. Others obstructed arrest of violent demonstrators and refused generally to cooperate with the police.

Ms Austin claimed that by detaining her in the cordon the police had deprived her of her liberty in breach of Article 5(1) of the ECHR. Her claim was unsuccessful in the lower courts and she appealed to the House of Lords.

Held: measures by the police that impacted on an individual's liberty must be proportionate to the situation and done in good faith, in order to maintain the fundamental principle that detention must not be arbitrary. The crowd control undertaken by the police was done in the public interest with the intention of enabling orderly dispersal of the demonstrators as soon as reasonably possible. In this case the size and behaviour of the crowd had made controlled dispersal unusually difficult and slow. Consequently, the detention of the demonstrators had not amounted to a breach of the ECHR and Ms Austin's appeal must be dismissed.

The courts decide on what is a proportionate response on a case-by-case basis. The outcome is dependent on the particular facts. 'Kettling' was held to be unlawful in the next case.

R (on the application of Moos and Another) v Commissioner of Police for the Metropolis (2011, QBD)

The applicants, who were demonstrating peacefully, were forcibly contained by the police. The police believed that violent unrest would be caused by the addition of some demonstrators, just dispersed from an earlier and violent demonstration a quarter of a mile away.

Held: the police had acted unlawfully under Article 5 of the ECHR. Such containment could only be justified if a breach of the peace was about to take place, which was not the case here. Despite the sustained violence at the other earlier demonstration, no breach of the peace was actually likely to happen at the time the police contained the applicants at the second demonstration.

A school may impose proportionate rules about uniform without breaching a student's human rights.

R (on the application of Begum) v Headteacher and Governors of Denbigh High School (2006, HL)

Begum's school, while accommodating Muslim dress, only permitted girls to wear the *shalwar kameez*. Begum was happy with this initially but after two years insisted on wearing the *jilbab*. For the next two years she was excluded from the school. There were other schools nearer her home which permitted the *jilbab*. She claimed that Denbigh High School had deprived her of her right to manifest her religion (Article 9) and her right to access education (Protocol 1, Article 2) of the ECHR.

Held (by majority): her right to religious expression had not been breached. The school had acted with proportionality in devising a dress code which 'respected Muslim beliefs but did so in an inclusive, unthreatening and uncompetitive way'.

Held (unanimously): she had not been deprived of access to education. Her absence from school was due to her refusal to comply with a reasonable rule and her failure to obtain a place at a school which would have accommodated her religious beliefs.

Indirect effect

As indicated above, a court as a public authority is obligated under s 6 to act compatibly with the Convention. This, combined with its duties to take ECtHR judgments into account (s 2) and to interpret statutes compatibly (s 3), means that since 2000 Convention law has been influential on the outcome of a number of cases which were not brought under the Act. In *A* v *B sub nom Garry Flitcroft* v *Mirror Group Newspapers Ltd* (2002, CA), the court refused to grant an injunction for breach of confidence to a professional footballer to prevent publication of the story of his extramarital exploits. The court in its decision balanced the claimant's right to privacy against the rights to freedom of expression and the public interest and found that these outweighed the claimant's rights. (More detail on this and other similar cases can be found in Chapter 26.)

Looking to the future

The HRA 1998 has clearly already had a significant impact on the development of the law and a human rights culture has clearly emerged. (More examples of relevant human rights cases can be found in later chapters.)

Recently there have been some controversial decisions of both the domestic courts and the ECtHR. For example, in 2012 the ECtHR blocked the deportation of Abu Quatada, an international terrorist suspect, from the UK to Jordan, because of the substantial risk that evidence obtained by torture would be used at his trial (*Othman (Abu Quatada)* v *United Kingdom* application 8139/09 (2012)). Unsurprisingly, this gave rise to a good deal of rhetoric, both in the media and in Parliament, which suggested abandoning the Convention and repealing the HRA. It is unlikely that the UK would abandon the Convention, but it can reasonably be argued that the ECHR and its enforcement mechanisms could do with an overhaul to bring them more into line with current human rights needs. Human rights ministers from the member states of the Council of Europe issued the Interlaken Declaration in 2011, indicating commitment to reform of procedures in the ECtHR to ensure that it remained effective in the future.

In March 2012, the Commission on Human Rights set up by the Ministry of Justice in 2011 reported that seven of its nine members favoured repeal of the HRA. The Commission recommended its replacement with a Bill of Rights which would mirror the ECHR obligations and provide similar protection to the HRA, while defining some rights more clearly and redressing perceived imbalances in its application. All members agreed that the ECtHR required fundamental reform. Subsequent public consultation has taken place but no legislation has yet been tabled. The Conservative manifesto of 2015 pledged repeal of the HRA and its replacement with a Bill of Rights, but subsequent dissension in its own party ranks as well as the other parliamentary parties and pressure groups has led to withdrawal of the proposal pending further consultation. In June 2015 the government also announced that it would not seek to withdraw the UK from the ECHR. In 2017 the Prime Minister, Theresa May, affirmed that there were no plans to repeal the Human Rights Act. Changes seem unlikely in these areas in the near future.

Chapter summary

Sources of English law

EU, British Parliament and English courts.

EC institutions

The Council of the EU, the European Council, the European Commission, the European Court of Justice and the European Parliament.

European legislation

Regulations, Directives, Decisions.

British parliamentary legislation

Direct: Acts of Parliament. An Act starts life as a Bill, which must successfully pass through three readings and a committee stage in each House before receiving the Royal Assent.

Delegated: Orders in Council, statutory instruments, rules and regulations, bye-laws.

The courts

Case law: created by judges, e.g. much of contract and tort law on a case-by-case basis.

Statutory interpretation of direct and delegated legislation using literal/golden/mischief/purposive approach.

The law of precedent: judges have regard to previous decisions and must apply those which are binding.

A precedent is binding if (a) *ratio decidendi* is relevant to the current case, and (b) it comes from a higher court in the hierarchy, *or* (c) the case is being heard in the Supreme Court or Court of Appeal, which follow their own decisions.

Note: Crown/County/Magistrates' Court decisions are not binding on other courts nor on themselves.

The Human Rights Act 1998

Direct effect: ECHR rights directly enforceable by individuals against a 'public authority'.

Indirect effect: The court must act compatibly with the Convention. Therefore, its content and case law may be influential in shaping the judge's decision in any case.

Review questions 2

1 Name the three main sources of English law.

2 Define and distinguish between EU regulations and directives.

3 Name the stages through which a Bill becomes an Act of Parliament.

4 Name two kinds of delegated legislation.

5 Explain the difference between the literal rule and the mischief rule.

6 Explain how the *ejusdem generis* rule works.

Answers to all review questions can be found in Appendix 2.

Advanced questions 2

(A) Analyse the extent to which a decision of the Judicial Committee of the Privy Council might be described as an anomaly in the system of judicial precedent.

(B) To what extent can it be said to be true that judges have a role in making the law?

Answers to the advanced questions can be found at **go.pearson.com/uk/he/resources.**

Take a closer look

The following cases provide important examples of how the law in this chapter has developed. They are primary sources illustrating the law in action and give more detail about their facts, as well as helping to understand the law and to appreciate how the judges reached their decisions.

Try looking them up in the law reports or accessing them via a database, e.g. BAILII (www.bailii.org/databases.html). LexisNexis® or Westlaw® may be available in the university or college library, or extracts may be found in a case book. (See Appendix 1: Additional resources.)

DSD and NBV v Commissioner of Police for the Metropolis [2014] EWHC 2493 (QB)

R (on the application of Begum) v Denbigh High School [2006] 2 All ER 487, HL

Royal College of Nursing v DHSS [1981] AC 800, HL

Sweet v Parsley [1969] 1 All ER 347, HL

Web activity

Visit the website of Liberty and click on 'Learn more about human rights' to read about many everyday issues where human rights are relevant. There is a lot of interesting information on this site:
www.liberty-human-rights.org.uk/

Assignment 1

With reference to decided cases, discuss the impact of the Human Rights Act 1998 on the rights of claimants.

Resolving legal disputes

Learning objectives

On completion of this chapter, students should be able to:

★ identify the jurisdiction of each court;

★ appreciate the different stages of civil litigation;

★ see how the tribunal system complements and relates to the court structure;

★ be aware of the different forms of alternative dispute resolution;

★ distinguish between the different forms of arbitration.

Introduction

Legal rights are useless without an adequate means of enforcement. Similarly, legal duties need a structure within which sanctions may be imposed. This chapter explains the institutions and processes that may be relevant to the resolution of a legal dispute involving a business. It aims to give an overview of the workings of the court system and primarily focuses on how it operates in relation to the areas of law covered in this text.

While it is important to have some idea about civil procedure, remember that the great majority of civil disputes are settled without resort to the courts at all, with private agreements being reached voluntarily between the parties, sometimes with the help of arbitration or mediation. Courts and tribunals increasingly encourage such action. Inappropriate litigation is only beneficial to lawyers' bank accounts.

The court system

Hierarchy:
structure arranged so
that each component
is superior to the ones
below.

The courts described below form a **hierarchy**. This means that they are positioned in a structure in which some courts are superior to others. Through the doctrine of binding precedent (explained in Chapter 3), the decisions of the superior courts are binding on the courts below.

The courts

The Magistrates' Court

Summary offence:
a criminal offence
which can only be tried
in the Magistrates'
Court.

**Offences triable
either way/ hybrid
offences:**
a criminal offence which
may be tried either in
the Magistrates' Court
or Crown Court.

**Justices of the peace
(JPs):**
lay (not legally quali-
fied) magistrates.

District judge:
legally qualified.

Magistrates' courts are very busy courts in which over 95 per cent of all criminal offences are prosecuted. These are **summary** offences and **offences triable either way**. Summary offences are petty offences that can be tried only by the magistrates. Offences which are triable either way (sometimes called **hybrid offences**) may be tried by either the Crown Court or the Magistrates' Court, usually at the choice of the defendant; they generally involve conduct that is capable of being viewed as either serious or relatively trivial, like theft or criminal damage.

Cases are usually tried by a bench of up to three **justices of the peace (JPs)**. These act voluntarily and are not legally qualified, but they are advised on points of law by the clerk of the court, who does have a legal qualification. Exceptionally the case may be heard before a **district judge**, a lawyer with relevant court experience.

Children and young people (10–17-year-olds) are tried for the majority of criminal offences in a Youth Court which is not open to the public and where the procedures are less formal than the ordinary Magistrates' Court. A different range of sanctions apply.

The Magistrates' Court is the usual venue for trial of most environmental health and other regulatory offences under, for example, the Trade Descriptions Act 1968, and the Health and Safety at Work etc. Act 1974. Most crimes against business owners, like shoplifting and criminal damage, are usually prosecuted in the Magistrates' Court.

Bail and criminal legal aid applications are also heard by magistrates.

The sentencing powers of the magistrates' courts are restricted. They may impose imprisonment for up to six months and a fine of up to £5,000. A party tried for an offence carrying a potentially higher penalty may be sent to the Crown Court for sentencing.

With regard to civil and administrative jurisdiction, the Family Proceedings Court has wide jurisdiction over many aspects of domestic and matrimonial law and has significant powers under the Children Act 1989. The magistrates also have powers to license premises which sell alcohol or provide betting and gaming services, and also enforce payment of council tax and business rates, and charges for gas, water and electricity.

The Crown Court

There are 77 Crown Court centres, situated mainly in county and borough towns. The Crown Court is staffed principally by High Court judges, circuit judges and recorders. The seriousness of the offence determines the type of judge to officiate. A bench of justices of the peace (magistrates) may assist a judge or recorder in appeal cases.

The Crown Court has criminal jurisdiction in the following circumstances:

Indictable offence: a criminal offence which can only be tried in the Crown Court.

1 *Trial of indictable offences.* **Indictable offences** include those offences that are so serious that they must be tried in the Crown Court: for example, homicide, rape and grievous bodily harm. Hybrid offences may also be tried there. Trial is by jury if the accused pleads not guilty.

2 *Sentencing cases* committed from the Magistrates' Court.

3 *Legal aid and bail applications.*

4 *Appeals.* The defendant found guilty in the Magistrates' Court may appeal against conviction or sentence to the Crown Court. A judge (usually a recorder) sitting with a bench of justices of the peace (magistrates) hears the appeal.

The County Court

In 2010 there were 216 county courts in England and Wales, staffed by circuit judges and district judges. However, the government announced in 2015 that it planned to close 49 of these as part of a programme of financial cuts, with closures due to be completed by the end of 2017. The County Court has an extensive and purely civil jurisdiction, including contract, tort, recovery of land, trusts, mortgages and partnerships, contested wills, divorce, bankruptcy and company insolvency.

Since the Courts and Legal Services Act 1990 (CLSA 1990), almost any case which can be heard in the High Court can now be heard in the County Court provided that it falls within specified and generous financial limits. For example, cases in tort and contract may be heard if the claimant is not suing for more than £50,000. The CLSA 1990 provisions aim to free the High Court from hearing all but the most complex, costly and specialist cases.

The following cases must generally be tried in the County Court:

1 all actions worth up to £25,000; and

2 any personal injury case worth under £50,000; unless its specialist nature or complexity makes trial in the High Court appropriate.

Otherwise, provided that a case falls within the prescribed financial limits, the choice of venue is determined by:

1 the amount involved;

2 whether points of law of general public interest are involved;

3 the complexity of the case; and

4 the potential procedures and/or remedies: some are obtainable only from the High Court.

Cases starting in the High Court can be transferred to the County Court at the request of a party or at the discretion of the judge. A successful party may not get the full costs paid if the judge believes the case should have been pursued in the County Court.

The High Court

This court is staffed by High Court judges. The court's principal venue is the Royal Courts of Justice in London, but cases are also heard in provincial cities. It is divided into three divisions and is primarily concerned with the trial of civil cases outside the jurisdiction of the County Court. The three divisions of the High Court are:

1 the *Queen's Bench Division*, that is mainly concerned with the trial of cases in contract and tort. It also contains the Commercial Court, which hears cases between people in business arising out of issues like imports and exports of goods, insurance, banking and agency;

2 the *Chancery Division*, which tries cases in copyright, patents and design rights, bankruptcy and the dissolution of partnerships, sale of land, trusts, mortgages and disputed wills;

3 the *Family Division*, which deals with the most complex areas of family and matrimonial law arising, for example, from contested divorce, validity of foreign marriage and divorce, legitimacy and adoption.

Appellate functions

Separate divisional courts hear appeals from designated inferior courts. A bench of two judges is usual.

The *Divisional Court of the Queen's Bench* hears criminal appeals from the Magistrates' Court by either prosecution or defence, when the interpretation of a point of law is in dispute. (Note that this is distinct from the appellate powers of the Crown Court, which hears appeals only by the defendant, where facts as well as law may also

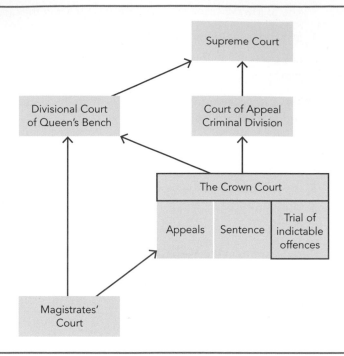

Figure 4.1 The criminal court structure

be in dispute.) It also has a supervisory jurisdiction over all inferior courts and tribunals exercised through the process of judicial review. If the Divisional Court is satisfied that a court or tribunal has exceeded its jurisdiction or has failed to conduct its proceedings impartially according to the rules of natural justice, an order may be issued overturning the outcome of those proceedings or preventing their continuance.

The *Divisional Court of the Chancery Division* hears appeals against decisions of the County Court in bankruptcy cases, and in revenue law against the decisions of the Inland Revenue Commissioners.

The *Divisional Court of the Family Division* hears appeals from the magistrates' courts in domestic and matrimonial cases.

The Court of Appeal

Lord/Lady Justice of Appeal:
Court of Appeal judge.

This is staffed by **Lord and Lady Justices of Appeal** and has two divisions. Cases are heard by a bench of three or five judges.

The Civil Division of the Court of Appeal has jurisdiction to hear appeals against decisions of the County Court and High Court. It also hears appeals from some tribunals, including the Employment Appeal Tribunal, concerning cases originally heard at employment tribunal level.

The Criminal Division of the Court of Appeal has jurisdiction to hear appeals from Crown Court trials. (Note that the Court of Appeal cannot hear an appeal from the

Crown Court where that court has itself been exercising its own appeals jurisdiction regarding cases from the Magistrates' Court. The only further avenue for such appeals is the Queen's Bench Divisional Court.)

The Supreme Court

In 2009 the Supreme Court replaced the House of Lords under the Constitutional Reform Act 2005 (CRA), s 23. The House of Lords (officially known as the Appellate Committee of the House of Lords to distinguish it from the parliamentary House of Lords) was the final court of appeal in England until then. The judges, then known as Law Lords or Lords of Appeal in Ordinary, were life peers entitled to sit and vote in the House of Lords. This was controversial, since it meant that they were involved in political decision-making.

The Supreme Court has the same jurisdiction as its predecessor and hears appeals from the Divisional Courts and the Court of Appeal, on points of law of public importance. The cases, which generally all concern statutory interpretation, are heard by a bench of three to seven judges known as **Justices of the Supreme Court**. The initial office holders are the **Law Lords or Lords of Appeal in Ordinary** (formerly judges of the House of Lords) who were holding office in 2009 when the Supreme Court started to sit. These no longer have the right to take any part in proceedings in the House of Lords. New Justices will be directly appointed to the Supreme Court by the Judicial Appointments Committee, which is responsible for judicial appointments in general.

Justices of the Supreme Court: judges in the Supreme Court.

Law Lord/ Lord of Appeal in Ordinary: judges of the House of Lords.

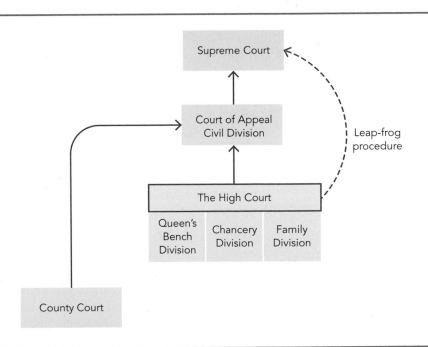

Figure 4.2 The principal civil courts and appeal routes

Leap-frog procedure: enables a case tried in the High Court to bypass the Court of Appeal and go straight to the Supreme Court for the appeal hearing.

Exceptionally, an appeal may be made directly from the High Court, bypassing the Court of Appeal (the **'leap-frog' procedure** introduced by the Administration of Justice Act 1969). This operates only where the point of law is already the subject of a Court of Appeal decision by which both it and the High Court are bound. This measure was introduced to overcome the restraints of the law of precedent, but is, in practice, very rarely used.

Bringing a case in the civil courts

The enforcement of legal rights is all too often perceived as a universal remedy, but there are many factors which can prevent a successful outcome. Many people who technically have a good claim in law may be unable to enforce it successfully for any of the following reasons:

(a) their opponents do not have the necessary funds to satisfy the claim;

(b) the law-breaker cannot be traced, e.g. an offending company may have gone into liquidation;

(c) the wronged party may not have the funds to pursue the claim. Litigation is a costly and protracted process, which may require expert assistance. Legal representatives do not simply send in a bill at the end of proceedings; regular payments are required pending the outcome of the case, and a party may run out of money even before the case comes to court. The scope of legal aid has been increasingly narrowed in recent years and entitlement means-tested and largely restricted to parties whose income does not exceed basic welfare benefit levels;

(d) the losing side may be responsible not only for their own legal costs, but also for those of their opponents. This may discourage pursuit of a case where the outcome is unpredictable.

The Woolf reforms 1999

In 1993, Lord Woolf (Master of the Rolls) headed an inquiry into the civil justice system prompted by concerns that its procedures were neither efficient nor effective. The report drew attention to a range of problems for the would-be litigant including the undue and often disproportionate cost of litigation, compounded by the unnecessary complexity of rules and procedures. It also expressed concerns that abuse by lawyers of the adversarial system could lead to litigation being controlled more by the lawyers rather than the parties or even the judge. Implementation of the report in April 1999 has resulted in radical changes to civil litigation. The new Civil Procedure

Rules (CPR) are drafted in plain English, with an emphasis on clarity and avoidance of legal jargon, to make them user-friendly for the unrepresented litigant and more accessible to all.

Note that some materials like case reports, which were published before the new rules came into effect, still use the old terminology: for example, 'plaintiff' is used instead of 'claimant'.

Settlement out of court

Litigation is time-consuming, costly and often emotionally draining for the parties. It is a step to be taken only when all alternatives have failed.

The huge majority of legal claims can be enforced without litigation, or even specialist help. Simple cases may be settled informally between the parties. A customer who is sold defective goods will usually obtain a refund from any reputable business without argument. A party who is unable to achieve a successful outcome may get a solicitor to reinforce the claim with a letter pointing out the relevant legal requirements. Sometimes the threat of litigation may produce the required result; if this fails proceedings may be started, but this does not commit either party to a court appearance. Most civil cases are settled before trial. The CPR give judges a number of powers to encourage early settlement wherever possible. For example, if a judge believes that a party has acted unreasonably in pursuing or conducting the case, penalties may be imposed as regards costs.

Payment into court and offers to settle

Payment into court: formal offer to settle made by defendant.

If proceedings have been started, the defendant may offer to make a **payment into court**. This represents the amount of compensation the defendant is prepared to pay. It is not in itself an admission of liability and the judge is not told about it prior to the conclusion of the trial. The claimant does not have to accept this offer, but may feel pressured to do so. If the case proceeds, the claimant will be liable for the defendant's costs, even if successful, if the amount of damages awarded by the court is less than the amount offered by the defendant.

Offer to settle: informal settlement out of court/ formal offer to the court by claimant.

The CPR has also introduced rights for a claimant who makes an **offer to settle** for a certain sum. If the defendant refuses the offer and the claimant then wins the case and is awarded that sum or more, the court has the discretion to increase the amount of interest payable on damages from the date of the decision by up to 10 per cent. Strategies of this kind are aimed at encouraging early settlement with a consequent saving of cost to the litigants and time for the judge.

Worth thinking about?

The great majority of potential claims are settled informally out of court. This speeds up the process, reduces stress for the litigants and saves money on legal costs. Can you see any drawbacks to the process?

Suggested solutions can be found in Appendix 2.

Civil litigation procedures

Starting a civil action

1 Letters of claim and pre-action protocols

Letter of claim:
the outline of the claim which the claimant sends to the defendant to start the civil litigation process.

Pre-action protocol:
information requirements prior to issue of a civil claim.

The CPR aims to encourage the parties to clarify the issues between them before any claim is issued. The claimant must send the defendant a **letter of claim** indicating clearly their allegations and the defendants must reply with an explanation of their conduct. **Pre-action protocols** requiring very detailed and specific information and documentation must be exchanged in certain types of cases, such as personal injury, clinical negligence, engineering and construction disputes, professional negligence, defamation, and housing disrepair.

2 Issue of claim

Issue of claim:
formal notification of the civil proceedings from the court to the defendant.

The claimant fills in the claim form with detailed particulars and submits it to the court, where it is processed and served on the defendant. This is called the **issue of claim**.

3 The defendant's response

The defendant must either admit the claim or file a detailed defence within 21 days. Failure to respond may result in the claimant obtaining immediate judgment against the defendant for any sum specified in the claim.

4 The case is allocated to the relevant track

The Woolf Report stressed that the cost of and resources for litigation should be proportionate to the complexity and size of the claim. The CPR aims to achieve this by designating a case to one of three tracks with differing procedures relative to the value and difficulty of the claim.

The small claims track

Small claims track:
civil litigation process for cases involving up to £10,000.

Since April 2013 the **small claims track** jurisdiction covers most claims for up to £10,000 or less. The limit for personal injury claims is £5,000.

All hearings, which take place in the County Court before a district judge, are informal and the normal rules of evidence do not apply. The CPR encourages an inquisitorial approach: the judge may question witnesses and limit cross-examination. The claimant may bring a friend to support him or her. A successful party may recover the costs incurred in issuing the proceedings, travel costs and a limited contribution to any expert-witness fees and loss of earnings. Legal costs are not recoverable for any money claim. This rule aims to discourage the use of lawyers but arguably loads the dice against a consumer since a business is more likely to be represented.

It does, however, provide a relatively simple procedure which can be very helpful for consumers who wish to bring a small and simple claim without the cost of paying a solicitor. Evidence suggests that it is equally useful to businesses as a means of debt enforcement against their customers.

The fast track

Fast track:
civil litigation process for cases involving £10,000–£25,000.

Cases involving claims of £10,000–£25,000 are usually dealt with in the **fast track** in the County Court. Personal injury cases are limited to those for £10,000 or less.

The judge will give directions to the parties to clarify the issues to be tried and a trial date not later than 30 weeks ahead will be announced. A party who is not ready by that point may have problems obtaining an extension; unnecessary delay may ultimately result in costs penalties.

The trial is limited to one day's duration and limits may be imposed on how long expert-witness evidence may take.

These rules aim to ensure that time (and the litigant's money) are not wasted during the preparation or conduct of relatively small and simple cases.

The multi-track

Multi-track:
civil litigation process for cases involving over £25,000.

Any case with a claim over £25,000 is allocated to the **multi-track** system in the County Court unless its complexity requires it to be tried in the High Court.

The bigger and more complex the case, the greater will be the powers of the judge to manage its progress towards trial through case management conferences involving the litigants and their legal representatives. Such case management is a strategy intended to prevent time wasting by lawyers pursuing irrelevant legal arguments and to ensure proper and full disclosure of evidence by the parties. It also enables the judge to set time limits for the achievement of any necessary processes and organise the conduct of the trial in advance.

5 The interlocutory stages

Interlocutory stage:
the period between the start of civil proceedings and the start of the trial.

The **interlocutory stages** are the periods between issue of claim and hearing, when detailed preparations for the hearing are made. In multi-track cases, there are likely to be a number of case conferences called by the judge.

At this time there may also be requests for information, disclosure, and the issue of interlocutory injunctions.

Requests for information: one party may require the other to provide further clarification of the particulars of his or her claim or defence.

Disclosure: the documentary evidence on which a party intends to rely must be made available at this stage. Third parties may also be required to give access to information.

Application to the judge may be necessary to obtain compliance.

In exceptional cases a search order may be required from the court, which permits the claimant to get entry to the defendant's premises and seize evidence. An application for such an order may be made without notice to the defendant to prevent him or her from covering their tracks.

Issue of **interlocutory injunctions**: injunctions are orders from the court which may stop the defendant from doing something or require some positive act. An injunction is an **equitable remedy**, which means that a party has no right to them. An injunction is granted at the discretion of the court. The judge must be convinced that the claimant is morally entitled to the remedy and that it will not be unjust to impose it on the defendant. A **freezing injunction** may be required at the interlocutory stage to prevent the defendant from transferring assets abroad or otherwise concealing them so as to avoid compensating the claimant.

Exceptionally, an injunction may be required as a holding measure to prevent the defendant from causing or continuing to cause serious damage to the claimant prior to the trial.

Interlocutory injunction: may be issued between starting proceedings and trial of a civil case.

Equitable remedy: discretionary judicial remedy granted only if the court believes the claimant is morally as well as legally entitled to it.

Freezing injunction: prevents the defendant gaining access to their assets pending trial.

The trial of the case

The court hears legal arguments from both parties, who will generally be represented by a barrister or a solicitor-advocate. Solicitors in general do not have the right to appear in the High Court, but under the Courts and Legal Services Act 1990 they may do so if they obtain an additional advocacy qualification by demonstrating relevant litigation experience and satisfactorily completing a training course. Witnesses may be called and questioned by both sides.

The judge who hears the case will decide which party has won and explain why that conclusion has been reached. An award of damages is the usual remedy, but, where appropriate, an injunction or any other order within the jurisdiction of the court may be issued.

Executing the judgment

A claimant who is successful at trial has won a major battle but not the war. If awarded damages, the claimant has the status of a judgment creditor, but this does not in itself compel the defendant to pay – the claimant may have to return

Distraint order: enables goods to the value of the claimant's damages to be seized to satisfy the judgment.

Charging order: made after judgment to freeze the defendant's assets until damages have been paid to the claimant.

Attachment of earnings order: court order to an employer to pay a specified sum direct from the defendant's earnings to satisfy a judgment debt.

Third party debt order: court order enabling the claimant to gain control of funds belonging to the defendant but held by a third party.

to the court to take steps to enforce the judgment. This may be done in any of the following ways:

1 A *distraint order*. A **distraint order** entitles the claimant to seize goods to the value of the debt from the defendant's premises. Bailiffs are usually employed for this purpose, at the claimant's cost.

2 A *charging order*. A **charging order** prevents the defendant from disposing of any assets, including land, trust funds, shares and debenture stock and other financial securities, pending satisfaction of the claimant's action.

3 *Attachment of earnings*. An **attachment of earnings order** requires an employer to pay a proportion of the defendant's earnings to the claimant.

4 *Third party debt order*. A **third party debt order** enables the claimant to gain control of funds belonging to the defendant but held by a third party (usually the bank).

5 *Insolvency proceedings*. If any debt (whether resulting from litigation or not) owed to the claimant is £750 or more, the claimant may institute insolvency proceedings against the debtor. This does not guarantee payment: if there are a large number of creditors the claimant will have to join the queue, and at best may recover only a proportion of the debt.

Real life

Mick was visited at home by a double glazing salesman from Transparent Deals (TD) and, persuaded by his arguments that new patio doors would reduce the house's carbon footprint, he signed a contract for £5,000 ('A bargain price, this week only, sir!'). In due course, workmen arrived and, with the help of many cups of tea and packets of biscuits provided by Mick, fitted the doors. However, the work was very poorly executed. The doors do not fit properly and there is a gap beside the frame on one side which lets warmth out and draughts in. The sliding mechanism jams, making the doors difficult to open. Mick is refusing to pay and TD is now threatening to take him to court.

There are various strategies that Mick can pursue. If TD is a member of the Direct Selling Association (DSA), it must meet certain standards of behaviour under the DSA Consumer Code, approved by the Office of Fair Trading. Mick can complain to the DSA Code Administrator. If TD is found to be in breach of the Code, the Administrator may make it refund the full cost to Mick, or replace or repair the doors without charge, or pay him compensation. The company's poor behaviour may suggest that it does not belong to the DSA. What a shame that Mick did not check that before he started. He should be advised to use the small claims track in the County Court. If TD sues Mick, he can enter a counterclaim for breach of contract as his defence, or he can immediately start proceedings himself as TD is clearly in breach of contract.

Alternative dispute resolution (ADR)

Given the cost and difficulties raised by taking a case through the courts, a cheaper, less confrontational outcome may be achieved through using an alternative method of dispute resolution. This may consist of any of the strategies set out below.

Arbitration

The parties voluntarily submit their dispute to a third party and agree to be bound by the resulting decision. Arbitration has been the most favoured method for settlement of commercial disputes for hundreds of years. Its value is recognised by the courts and it is governed by statute, which empowers arbitrators and regulates the process. More recently it has become a common method of resolving consumer disputes.

Commercial arbitration

It is common for an arbitration clause to be a term of contracts between businesses; the parties may subsequently agree to submit a dispute to arbitration. Any person acceptable to the parties may act as their arbitrator. In practice, they will tend to choose somebody with skill and experience in the relevant field. The role of arbitrator has become professionalised and the Institute of Arbitrators regulates the standards of its members.

The Arbitration Act 1996 (AA 1996) regulates to some extent the operation of arbitration procedures and the behaviour of the arbitrator. The stated purpose of the AA 1996 is to empower the parties and to increase their autonomy. It was always the case that if an arbitration agreement existed the courts would not hear the case until the arbitration procedure had taken place. Under the AA 1996, the powers of the court to intervene have been restricted further. It may determine a preliminary point of law arising in the course of proceedings. The court, on the application of a party, may revoke the arbitrator's appointment for failure to fulfil the arbitrator's duty to act with impartiality and fairness. Rights of appeal against the arbitrator's decision are limited. Appeal on a point of law underpinning the decision is possible unless the parties have previously agreed to exclude this right. It is also permitted on the grounds that the arbitrator exceeded his or her jurisdiction or committed a serious irregularity.

The Equality Act 2010 limits the ability of a party to restrict access to court action in cases concerning discrimination. Section 144(1) states:

> A term of a contract is unenforceable by a person in whose favour it would operate in so far as it purports to exclude or limit a provision of or made under this Act.

This was applied in *Clyde & Co v Van Winkelhof* (2011), where the court refused to stay W's proceedings for sexual discrimination even though her partnership contract imposed arbitration as the final means of resolving a dispute.

The advantages of the arbitration process are that it ensures privacy for the parties in dispute and it is more likely to ensure a friendly outcome between the parties than litigation. This may be valuable in a specialist business area where the choice of contracting parties is limited. The problem can usually be resolved relatively cheaply and speedily at a time and place convenient to both parties. Arbitrators' expertise in the business field enables them to understand the issues in dispute. There are possible disadvantages, though: arbitrators have fewer powers than the courts to obtain evidence from the parties and to expedite the proceedings; they may lack necessary legal knowledge, ultimately necessitating an appeal, which will increase the cost.

Commercial arbitration procedures are not necessarily appropriate unless the contracting parties are in a position of equal bargaining power. The Consumer Arbitration Act 1988 stipulates that an arbitration clause in a contract does not bind a consumer until a dispute arises, and only then if the consumer agrees in writing at that point. Consumers cannot be forced into arbitration.

Code arbitration

Some trade associations impose a code of conduct on their members and permit consumers to take disputes through an arbitration procedure run by the association. A well-known example is ABTA® (Association of British Travel Agents). Similar codes govern dry cleaning, photographic processing, car sales and a number of other trades. eBay has a dispute resolution system which appears to be very helpful.

These codes, originally developed under the auspices of the Director General of Fair Trading, are aimed at the protection of consumer buyers. A fee is payable to initiate the arbitration process, but this will be refunded if the consumer wins. The trade association appoints an appropriately experienced arbitrator registered with the Institute of Arbitrators. All communication with the arbitrator is written. If the trader is at fault, the association is responsible for enforcing any award.

A consumer can take this action only if the firm involved is actually a member of the relevant trade association. It is likely to be helpful only in relatively simple cases where the facts and evidence can readily be presented in documentary form.

Ombudsmen services

The organisations responsible for the supervision of legal, banking, insurance and financial services have each appointed officials called ombudsmen who have the power to investigate and resolve problems reported to them by dissatisfied customers.

Conciliation

A conciliator aims to assist the parties to a dispute to find a resolution. The conciliator may suggest a solution, but has no power to enforce it. Parties to a dispute which has been referred to an employment tribunal are offered the services of the Advisory,

Conciliation and Arbitration Service (ACAS). The case proceeds to the tribunal only if the conciliation process is refused or is unsuccessful.

Mediation

A mediator assists the parties to communicate with each other and find their own resolution to their dispute. Mediation is an increasingly popular means of sorting out property and custody issues when a relationship breaks down. Means-tested funding in such cases is provided by the Community Legal Service. Some health authorities use mediation to resolve complaints of clinical negligence. It increasingly plays a part in the pre-litigation process.

ADR is encouraged by the courts

In 1995, the Lord Chief Justice issued instructions that legal representatives must check that their clients are fully aware of the possible use of alternative means of resolving the dispute before proceeding to take a case to the High Court. The Woolf Report stressed the importance of encouraging parties to use ADR, and under the CPR judges have the power to require parties to attempt to resolve some or all the pre-trial issues of the case in this way before the case will be allowed to proceed. There is no requirement for mandatory mediation overall, although it is being encouraged.

In 2010 a telephone mediation service was introduced to assist parties to settle County Court fast track cases out of court and in 2012 it resolved almost all the 15,000 cases referred to it. The service now covers all fast track and multi-track cases.

New ADR initiatives to assist consumers

Alternative Dispute Resolution for Consumer Disputes (Amendment) Regulations 2015

This is an EU-led initiative which aims to give a consumer in dispute with a trader easier access to ADR through government accredited bodies. Some trading bodies do already provide such services for their members (see code arbitration above) but the Regulations require any trader, who is unable to resolve a dispute with a consumer, to provide the consumer with full written/email details of an accredited ADR provider. The trader is not compelled to engage in the process unless required to do so by membership of a trading body or by the contract with the consumer. Failure by the trader to provide the relevant information may result in court action taken by the local trading standards department, which may result in imprisonment or an unlimited fine. In October 2015 Kent County Council became the first local authority to be approved to provide ADR services by the Chartered Trading Standards Institute.

The EU's new Online Dispute Resolution Platform

This became available in February 2016 to consumers and traders in all member states to assist the settlement of cases across the EU concerning goods and services bought online. Any business which sells online must include a link to the Platform on its website. This is intended to promote trade between member states. It is to be hoped that these potentially helpful initiatives will still be available to the UK after it leaves the EU.

The tribunal system

Like the courts, the tribunal system provides a means of judicial resolution to a legal dispute and hears many more cases than are processed in the courts. It determines the rights of individuals against government departments in a wide variety of cases such as tax, immigration, social security entitlement, planning and compulsory purchase, education and aspects of mental health treatment. Employment disputes between employer and employee are also heard in this way. Tribunal judges are legally qualified and are usually assisted by a panel of two lay persons with relevant specialist knowledge.

A major reform and rationalisation took place after the Tribunals, Courts and Enforcement Act 2007, which has largely unified the system and the rules which govern it. It now operates in two generic tiers. Cases are initially heard in the First Tier in a Chamber dedicated to the relevant jurisdiction, for example Finance and Tax, Health, and Education and Social Care. Appeals are heard in the Upper Tier. Further appeal to the Court of Appeal and judicial review of decisions may be possible.

Cases involving employment law and asylum and immigration rights continue to be heard by tribunals outside the generic system because of the particular nature of their jurisdiction.

From a business perspective, the employment tribunal is the most relevant in the tribunal system. It derives its powers from a variety of statutes including the Employment Rights Act 1996.

Its jurisdiction encompasses:

(a) disputes between employers and employees concerning unfair dismissal, redundancy and discrimination at work;

(b) appeals by employers against the imposition of improvement and prohibition orders by the Health and Safety Executive.

The judge is a lawyer sitting with two other people nominated by bodies representing employers and employees respectively and hearings are open to the public. Unfair dismissal claims are generally dealt with by just one judge. Appeal on a point of law may be made to the Employment Appeal Tribunal, with further appeal to the Court of Appeal and beyond possible, including the European Court of Justice, as much of employment law is derived from the EU.

Benefits of tribunals

Tens of thousands of cases are heard by tribunals every year and the system is seen as valuable to the parties using it. The main benefits of the tribunal system as compared with the courts are perceived to be:

1 *Cheapness.* Legal representation is not essential at a tribunal and the specialist knowledge of panel members makes it unnecessary to call specialist witnesses. The parties do not generally have to travel far to the hearing.

2 *Relative informality.* Procedures are usually less formal and adversarial than those of the ordinary courts; therefore a tribunal hearing is less intimidating.

3 *Speed.* A case may take years to come to court. Cases should reach tribunals within weeks or months of proceedings being started.

4 *Flexibility.* Tribunals are not bound by their own precedents (but they are bound by relevant decisions reached by the courts).

Criticisms of tribunals

Not everyone agrees that tribunals are as effective as they should be. There are a number of criticisms that can be raised regarding the operation of the tribunal system:

1 *No access to legal aid.* There is no state-funded legal aid for most tribunal hearings, which may unfairly prejudice the chances of the claimant. At employment tribunals the employer is usually able to afford legal representation, while employees are often unrepresented unless help is provided by their trade union or other pressure group. In social security claims, applicants have to dispute their cases with a body which has considerable experience of such hearings, and do not always receive the assistance they need from panel members.

2 *Proceedings have become legalistic.* Over time some tribunal hearings have become less flexible and more formal and consequently less user-friendly to the average claimant. Employment tribunals have been particularly criticised on this ground.

3 *Urgent cases are not resolved sufficiently quickly.* Delays are common if case-loads such as immigration appeals are very heavy.

Chapter summary

The court system

The Magistrates' Court

Criminal, civil and administrative jurisdiction.

Staffed by JPs, supplemented by district judges.

Crown Court

Criminal jurisdiction only: trial (indictable offences). Sentencing/appeals from Magistrates' Court.

Staffed by High Court judges, circuit judges, recorders, JPs.

County Court

Civil jurisdiction over a wide variety of cases subject to the financial value of the claim.

Staffed by circuit and district judges.

The High Court

Three divisions (Queen's Bench, Chancery, Family) each with different jurisdiction to try civil cases outside the County Court's remit.

Divisional courts: mainly appellate jurisdiction from a variety of courts and tribunals.

Staffed by High Court judges.

The Court of Appeal

The Criminal Division: appeals from the Crown Court.

The Civil Division: appeals from the County Court, the High Court and the Employment Appeals Tribunal.

Staffed by Lord/Lady Justices of Appeal.

The Supreme Court

Appeals from the Court of Appeal and Divisional Courts.

Staffed by Judges of the Supreme Court.

Civil claims procedure

Small claims track (maximum £10,000).

Fast track (maximum £25,000).

Multi-track (above £25,000).

Most civil cases are settled before trial.

Alternative Dispute Resolution

Arbitration: the parties agree to accept the arbitrator's decision as final. Recourse to the courts is largely ruled out. This is very popular in specialised commercial cases.

Conciliation: less formal than arbitration, and access to litigation is still possible if the negotiations between the parties, and led by the conciliator, break down.

Mediation: similar to conciliation but also used as a preliminary to court action.

Tribunals

Very limited specific jurisdictions in, for example, the fields of employment, and mental health.

Less formal than the courts.

Aim to produce cheaper and speedier outcomes.

Review questions 3

1 Where will the proceedings involving the following parties take place?

   (a) Peter on a charge of causing death by dangerous driving of Doris, a pedestrian.
   (b) Sarah, who wishes to appeal against her conviction for murder.
   (c) Polly, who wishes to appeal against her conviction in the Magistrates' Court for shoplifting.
   (d) Luigi, from whom Sandrino wishes to recover a debt of £200.
   (e) Sid, who is claiming £75,000 against Eastern Railway Company for injuries caused when he fell under one of its trains.
   (f) Ranjit, who is claiming that he was unfairly dismissed by Nickleby.
   (g) Janet, regarding repossession of her house by the Wantander Building Society.

2 What are the various stages of the civil litigation process?

3 What is the purpose of a freezing injunction?

4 What is the difference between arbitration, mediation and conciliation?

5 In what ways do tribunals differ from the ordinary courts?

6 Outline the advantages and disadvantages of the tribunal system.

Answers to all review questions can be found in Appendix 2.

Advanced questions 3

(A) Evaluate the reasons why a business would choose to use alternative dispute resolution rather than court-based litigation in a commercial dispute.

(B) Analyse the grounds on which a court will order an interim injunction.

Answers to the advanced questions can be found at **go.pearson.com/uk/he/resources.**

Web activity

Visit the website of ABTA and go to 'Help and complaints' to find out about ABTA's arbitration and mediation procedures:
www.abta.com
See the Government webpages on Alternative Dispute Resolution, with links to the relevant legislation:
www.gov.uk/government/publications/resolving-consumer-disputes-alternative-dispute-resolution-and-the-court-system
www.gov.uk/government/publications/alternative-dispute-resolution-for-consumers/alternative-dispute-resolution-for-consumers

Assignment 2

How far is it true to say that most cases are best settled out of court?

PART 2

Law of contract, agency and sale of goods

The law of contract:
Offer and acceptance

Learning objectives

On completion of this chapter, students should be able to:

★ explain the essential requirements for a binding contract;

★ define offer and acceptance;

★ distinguish between an invitation to treat and an offer;

★ appreciate the importance of reasonable expectation in determining intention in offer and acceptance;

★ demonstrate how offer and acceptance may be effectively communicated.

Introduction

Simple:
a contract that does not need to be in the form of a deed to be valid.

Parol:
another name for a simple contract (see above).

A contract is a legally binding agreement between two or more parties that is enforceable by law. It often involves the sale or hire of goods, services or land. Such contracts are known as **simple** or **parol** contracts, since they are usually enforceable without having to be put into writing. People enter into many contracts on a daily basis when shopping, when getting a haircut, or taking out a mobile phone contract. Most contracts do not have any legal formalities associated with them so they are legally binding without documents, signatures or witnesses. If the goods or services provided are defective, legal rights exist arising from the contract made with the seller. To enforce those rights it is necessary to prove the existence of the contract. The receipt is evidence of this. However, if this is lost, other evidence – like a credit card receipt or proof of debit or credit card payment – will be perfectly adequate.

5

This chapter examines how such contracts are formed. They are still governed by common law principles, but statute also plays an increasingly important part. Later chapters examine areas of contract law which are additionally regulated by statute: sale of goods and services, agency, employment law, and partnerships.

The essentials of a binding contract

All contracts require the following elements:

Offer:
a full clear statement of terms on which the maker (offeror) is prepared to do business with the person(s) to whom the offer (offeree/s) is communicated.

1 an **offer**;

2 an **acceptance**;

3 **consideration** (each party will contribute something of material value to the bargain);

4 **intention to create legal relations**.

Acceptance:
unconditional assent to the terms of an offer.

Consideration:
money/goods/services/ land representing the bargain element of the contract.

Writing is not usually essential

As indicated above in the introduction, writing is not a legal requirement for the great majority of contracts, though it may well be useful proof of the contents of a complex contract. While the law does not require a building contract to be in writing, most clients would not be very happy to have settled complicated terms by word of mouth only. Many businesses use a **standard form contract** (or contract of adhesion) which stipulates terms and conditions (Ts & Cs) with no room for negotiation by the other party.

Intention to create legal relations:
the parties' intention to make their agreement legally binding.

Standard form contract:
comprised of terms imposed by a business which are not open to negotiation.

Contracts which require writing

A minority of contracts *must* be in writing in order to be valid. These include contracts to sell land under the Law of Property (Miscellaneous Provisions) Act 1989, and contracts to obtain credit which are governed by the Consumer Credit Act 1974 (as amended by the Consumer Credit Act 2006). Where such regulation applies, the written document comprises the contract. Without the contractual document the law will treat the transaction as void (i.e. of no legal effect), regardless of other available evidence.

Contracts which require written evidence

Under the Statute of Frauds 1677, contracts of guarantee – under which one party (the guarantor) agrees to guarantee the debt of another party for the benefit of a creditor – will be unenforceable without written evidence. This could be just an informal note containing the relevant information. In *Golden Ocean Group* v *Salgaocar* (2012), the Court of Appeal held that electronic signatures and an email string was capable of complying with the written evidence requirement of the Statute of Frauds 1677.

Deeds

Some transactions will be legally valid only if put in the form of a deed, such as the conveyance of land which transfers the rights of ownership to the land and is signed by the parties in front of witnesses. This is a separate transaction from the contract of sale which only requires writing for validity. Deeds are often not concerned with bargains and may be used to make a promise of a gift legally enforceable.

The offer

Offeror:
the maker of the offer.

Offeree:
the recipient of the offer.

Bilateral offer:
a contractual promise of performance of an act in return for the other party's promise of performance.

Unilateral offer:
an offer of a promise in return for the performance of an act.

This may be defined as a clear statement of the terms on which one party (the **offeror**) is prepared to make an agreement with another party (the **offeree**). An offer may be bilateral or unilateral.

Most offers are **bilateral**, i.e. such an offer consists of a promise made in return for a promise. In a sale of goods contract, for example, the offeror promises to take and pay for goods and the offeree promises to supply goods of an appropriate description and standard. A **unilateral offer** is a promise made in return for the completion of a specified act. An offer of a reward for the return of lost property falls into this category.

A legally binding offer will include:

1 clearly stated terms;

2 intention to be legally bound;

3 communication of that intention.

These must all exist for a valid offer to have been made.

Guthing v *Lynn* (1831)

The buyer of a horse promised to pay the seller an extra £5 'if the horse is lucky for me'.

Held: this expression was too vague to be enforceable. No indication was given of what this really meant. 'Lucky' could have meant anything from the horse winning the next Epsom Derby to its refraining from biting its new owner.

Clearly stated terms

A statement may be held to be too vague to comprise a valid offer.

Best endeavours' clauses

The contract may include a clause requiring a party to use their best endeavours to ensure that a contract results from its negotiations. The courts generally treat that agreement as an agreement to agree and not contractually binding because of uncertainty. In *Dany Lions Ltd* v *Bristol Cars Ltd* [2014] it was held that a best endeavours' agreement could only be binding if there were objective criteria by which the quality of the endeavours could be assessed. Dany Lions had undertaken to use his best endeavours to find a specialist classic car restorer for Bristol Cars but had not been able to do so. However, there was no way of judging his performance, such as a limit to the price that could be agreed with the restorer.

However, in contrast in *Jet2.com* v *Blackpool Airports* [2012] an airport operator was bound by its promise to use its best endeavours to promote low-cost services by a budget airline. This meant it had to allow that airline to operate outside the normal opening hours of the airport, even if that meant the airport made a loss on those services, if that was the only way to promote the business as it had promised.

Note that evidence of previous business dealings, specialist trade practice or an agreed method of independent assessment of performance might also be treated as objective evidence in cases like *Dany Lions Ltd*.

An apparently vague offer may be capable of clarification by reference to:

1 The parties' previous dealings and the nature of the relevant trade.

Hillas v *Arcos* (1932, HL)

A contract to supply wood for one year contained an option permitting the buyer to buy more wood the next year, but it did not specify the terms on which the supply would be made.

Held: this was a valid offer. Clarification of this rather vague option could readily be ascertained from the previous business dealings of the parties, as well as from custom and practice in the timber trade.

2 *Statutory implied terms.* For example, an offer to sell goods is valid even if no price is mentioned. Under the Sale of Goods Act 1979, s 8, if no price is stated, a reasonable price is payable.

3 *Arbitration clauses.* Sometimes the parties may purposely state terms vaguely and include provision for arbitration to settle disputes if and when they arise. This allows for later variations to take into account future needs, availability or price. Since the lack of clarity may be resolved, a binding offer exists.

Foley v *Classique Coaches* (1934, CA)

The arbitration clause in a long-term contract stated that F would supply petrol to the coach company 'at a price to be agreed in writing and from time to time'.

Held: the contract was binding as the arbitration clause would enable any lack of clarity about the price to be resolved when and if necessary.

Intention to be legally bound

An offer represents the parties' 'last word' prior to acceptance. A statement which does not indicate commitment to be bound by its terms (if accepted) will not be interpreted as a binding offer.

Problems arise where a party, who believes that a binding offer has been made, communicates an 'acceptance'. The party then believes that a contract exists. However, if the original statement is not a binding offer, there will as yet be no contract, since a valid contract requires both binding offer and acceptance.

There are two types of pre-contractual statement which may be confused with a legally binding offer:

Invitation to treat: encouragement to make an offer, usually by an advertisement.

(a) **invitation to treat**;

(b) negotiation.

An invitation to treat

Most advertisements for the sale of goods, land or services are not usually treated by the courts as indicating the necessary intention to form an offer. Many are just 'business puff' publicising the product or service to encourage sales by the use of catchy slogans suggesting its superiority to other similar products (e.g. 90 per cent of cats prefer Fishybits). Others may actually invite interested parties to make an offer to the advertiser, who can then legally choose whether or not to accept. Without acceptance, no contract exists; therefore, the offeror has no legal rights to the goods, etc. until acceptance is communicated.

Catalogues, share prospectuses, price lists, menus and circulars advertising so-called 'cheap offers' at local businesses are invitations to treat.

Partridge v *Crittenden* (1968)

The defendant put an advertisement in a magazine saying 'Bramble finch cocks and hens 25 shillings each'. The Wild Birds Act 1954 made it a criminal offence to offer such birds for sale and he was convicted of the offence and appealed.

Held: the defendant was found not guilty since he had not made an offer but merely encouraged others to do so. Lord Parker stated there was 'business sense' in such adverts generally being interpreted as invitations to treat.

A display of goods in a shop, with or without a price tag, is similarly merely an invitation to treat.

Fisher v *Bell* (1960)

The defendant exhibited a flick knife in his shop window and was convicted under the Restriction of Offensive Weapons Act 1959, s 1(1), for 'offering for sale' an offensive weapon.

Held: the defendant was not guilty since he had not made an offer. Goods in a shop window, even those bearing a price tag, represent an invitation to treat, not an offer. Customers make offers by saying that they are prepared to do business at the price shown. Sellers then decide if they want to accept; only if they do, will any contract result.

As new methods of marketing develop, the law needs to be interpreted to fit the new circumstances. Self-service shopping, which is the norm today, did not start to appear in the UK until the 1950s.

Pharmaceutical Society (GB) v *Boots Cash Chemists (Southern) Ltd* (1953, CA)

Boots introduced self-service including purchase of its patent medicines and was prosecuted by the Pharmaceutical Society under the Pharmacy and Poisons Act 1933 which made it illegal to sell certain drugs 'without supervision of a registered pharmacist'.

Held: no offence had been committed. The medicines on display were merely an invitation to treat. The customer made an offer when handing the goods to the checkout operator. A pharmacist was present at this point and could refuse the customer's offer if appropriate.

Electronic contracts (ecommerce) have become an important feature of marketing since the late twentieth century – Amazon sells a lot of copies of this book! So far, there is little case law. However, statutes such as the Electronic Commerce (EC Directive) Regulations 2002 have been passed to address this form of contracting.

As Lord Parker indicated (in *Partridge* v *Crittenden* above), there is considerable business sense in interpreting advertisements and display of goods as invitations to treat rather than offers. It is clearly in the public interest to ensure that some drugs are only sold under expert supervision or that a supermarket does not breach its licence by selling alcohol to the underage customer who presents it at the till. It is also convenient for a restaurant owner who is able to refuse to serve an abusive customer and a shopkeeper who doesn't have to demolish a complicated window display to retrieve an item which a customer demands. In this case it also protects the customer who otherwise might be committed to buying something which did not look so good when more closely inspected.

The Equality Act 2010 aims to prevent abuses of the right of a business to refuse a customer's offer where the business is acting in an illegally discriminatory manner. Discrimination is less favourable treatment towards certain protected groups as defined in the Equality Act 2010 (see Chapter 18). Similarly, misleading pricing notices may be a criminal offence under the Consumer Protection from Unfair Trading Regulations (as amended by Consumer Protection (Amendment) Regulations 2014).

Negotiation

Lengthy negotiations may lead up to the formation of a contract. Problems may occur where one party assumes that a statement represents the other party's offer and claims to have accepted it. The court will have to decide whether the alleged offeror had by that point indicated a sufficient intention to be bound. In a potentially complex contractual situation where protracted negotiations would normally be expected, a statement made early in the negotiations is unlikely to be held to be a valid offer.

Harvey v *Facey* (1893, JCPC)

The claimants were interested in buying an estate in Jamaica which the defendant had not advertised for sale. They sent a telegram asking the defendant to state the lowest price he would accept. When the defendant replied stating only 'Lowest price for Bumper Hall Pen £900', the claimants attempted to accept and sued for breach of contract when the defendant did not comply.

Held: no contract had been formed, since the statement of price was merely an indication of minimum price as a response to the request for information about the potential price, if the defendant ultimately decided to sell. It was at best an early step in negotiations and did not amount to a valid offer.

Gibson v *Manchester City Council* (1979, HL)

Mr Gibson requested details from the council about the proposed sale of its housing stock to existing tenants. The council replied by letter, stating that 'the council may be prepared to sell the house to you'. It included a discounted purchase price and mortgage and invited formal applications. Mr Gibson applied but after local elections the council reversed its policy and refused to sell.

Held: the council's letter was not an offer and therefore no contract had been made with Mr Gibson. His application was an offer that the council had refused. The words 'may be prepared to sell' and the request for a formal application clearly indicated that the offer was being invited from Mr Gibson.

However, it all depends on the facts; in the next case, sufficient intention was found to exist:

Bigg v *Boyd Gibbons* (1971, CA)

In the course of negotiations involving a number of letters, the claimant wrote to the defendants: 'For a quick sale I would accept £20,000.' The defendant wrote back accepting and the claimant then sent another letter in reply thanking the defendant 'for accepting my offer'.

Held: a binding offer to sell for £20,000 was made in the claimant's letter. Russell LJ said:

> I cannot escape the view having read the letters that the parties would regard themselves at the end of the correspondence . . . as having struck a bargain for the sale and purchase of this property.

The offer must be communicated to the offeree

The offeror must know of the offer to be able legally to accept. The communication of an offer may be written or spoken, but it may often be by conduct, such as taking goods to the supermarket checkout, or putting money into a vending machine. An offer is most commonly made to an individual, but a unilateral offer may be made to the world at large. In such a case, a contract will be made with all the people who can and do fulfil the terms of the offer.

Carlill v *Carbolic Smoke Ball Co. Ltd* (1893, CA)

The defendants published an advertisement, which claimed that their product would prevent influenza, and promised that they would pay £100 to any person who, having used the product correctly, still caught influenza. The advertisement also stated that £1,000 had been placed in a separate bank account to 'show their sincerity in the matter'.

Mrs Carlill bought a smoke ball from her local chemist. When she became ill with influenza despite regularly sniffing her smoke ball as instructed, she claimed £100 from the manufacturers.

Held: the advertisement was a unilateral offer by the manufacturers to the world at large. This could be accepted by any person who knew of it and who contracted influenza after using the product as directed. The £1,000 bank deposit showed intention to enter a contract and was evidence that the advertisement was not just puffing the goods.

The offeree must, therefore, know of the offer in order legally to be able to accept it. Coincidental performance of the terms of an offer, made in ignorance of its existence, does not create a binding contract.

Bloom v *American Swiss Watch Co.* (1915)

The claimant gave evidence to the authorities which led to the arrest of some jewel thieves. He then discovered that the defendant had previously advertised a reward for such information. The defendant refused payment.

Held: the defendant was not legally obliged to pay as no contract to do so existed between the parties, since the offer of the reward had not been communicated to the claimant prior to his giving the information.

Tenders

Tender:
a competitive offer (bid) to provide goods or services.

A **tender** is a competitive offer to provide goods or services. Many businesses and other organisations will advertise to invite tenders to ensure that they get the best value for money. Some publicly funded bodies may be required to do so by law. The businesses which ultimately supplied the goods and services for the Olympic and Paralympic Games in London in 2012 were all chosen as the result of tenders to the Olympic Delivery Authority.

Although the request for tenders is an invitation to treat, it may also be an offer by the advertisers to *consider* any offer submitted to them.

Blackpool & Fylde Aero Club v *Blackpool Council* (1990, CA)

The Aero Club was invited by the council to tender for a concession to provide pleasure flights for the summer tourist trade. Although the club delivered its tender before the deadline, the council, due to an oversight, failed to clear its letter box and so the tender did not reach the appropriate committee in time to be considered.

Held: the council's request for tenders implicitly contained a unilateral offer to consider any tender submitted by the deadline. The council was therefore in breach of this contract with the Aero Club which had been deprived of its chance to be the successful bidder. Bingham LJ said:

He [the tenderer] need not accept any tender . . . but whereas here the tenders are solicited from selected parties all of them known to the invitor, and where a local authority's invitation prescribes a clear, orderly and familiar procedure . . . the invitee is protected at least to this extent: If he submits a conforming tender before the deadline, he is entitled . . . as . . . of contractual right to be sure that his tender will after the deadline be considered . . . The law would I think be defective if it did not give effect to that.

The termination of offers

An offer, if not accepted, can be brought to an end in a number of different ways.

Death

If the offeree dies, the offer dies too. The death of the offeror terminates the offer if its terms require personal performance. An offer may survive if it can be performed by personal representatives.

Bradbury v *Morgan* (1862)

During his life the deceased had made a standing offer to guarantee another man's debt. The debtor failed to pay the creditor, who, not knowing of the death of the guarantor, wrote to claim his money.

Held: the guarantor's obligations could be satisfied out of his estate. At the time he accepted the offer the creditor could not reasonably have known of the offeror's death.

Rejection and counter-offer

If an offer is rejected it ceases to exist. If the offeree then changes their mind and tries to accept, they will in contractual terms be making a new offer. The same result is achieved by a **counter-offer**. This is an attempt to vary the terms of the existing offer to get more favourable terms, like a price reduction. In law a counter-offer is treated as an implied rejection.

Hyde v Wrench (1840)

The defendant offered to sell his farm for £1,000. The claimant at first said that he would pay only £950, but after a few days said he would pay the full price. He heard nothing from the defendant.

Held: there was no contract between the parties: the defendant had not accepted the offer from the claimant, who had destroyed the defendant's original offer by his counter-offer of a reduced price. The claimant's subsequent statement that he would pay the asking price could not revive the original offer. It was a new offer which the defendant never accepted.

If the offeree, while not accepting an offer, asks for further information, or clarification to see if further negotiation is possible, this is not treated as a counter-offer; it, therefore, does not destroy the offer. Therefore, in *Stevenson v McLean* (1880) an offer to sell iron at a certain price was not destroyed when the offeree enquired whether delivery and payment might be made in instalments. This was not a counter-offer of different terms, merely an enquiry as to whether the terms might be varied, which did not destroy the original offer.

Lapse of time

An offer will cease to exist if not accepted within any specified time limit. Otherwise it will lapse if not accepted within a reasonable time.

Ramsgate Hotel Co. Ltd v Montefiore (1866)

The defendant applied to buy some shares in June but heard nothing more until November when the company informed him that the shares were his.

Held: no contract had been formed since the company's unreasonable delay in notification of the allotment of the shares had made the defendant's offer lapse and the acceptance came too late. He was not obliged to take the shares.

Revocation

Offerors are entitled to change their minds and withdraw offers at any time right up to the moment of acceptance. If, at an auction sale, a bidder might place the highest bid and the auctioneer is saying 'going, going . . . ', the bidder will still have time to shout that they are withdrawing the offer, as it will not be accepted until the auction-eer's gavel hits the table (Sale of Goods Act 1979, s 57).

Notice of revocation is crucial; it is not effective unless the offeree knows of it. Personal notification is usual, but is not essential as long as the offeree knew or reasonably should have known that the offer had been withdrawn.

Dickinson v *Dodds* (1876, CA)

Dodds made an offer to sell property to Dickinson, but sold it to a third party (Allan) before Dickinson effectively responded. Berry, at Dodds' request, told Dickinson of the sale and gave him a copy of Dodds' acceptance of Allan's offer.

Held: Dickinson had adequate notice of revocation. A reasonable person would have realised that, since the property had been disposed elsewhere, the offer was no longer open. James LJ said:

It is to my mind perfectly clear that before there was any attempt at acceptance by the plaintiff, he was perfectly well aware that Dodds had changed his mind, and that he had in fact agreed to sell the property to Allan. It is impossible, therefore, to say that there was ever that existence of the same mind between the two parties which is essential in point of law to the making of an agreement.

Real life

Maria offered to sell her grand piano to her neighbour Zelda, who said she was really interested but needed to think about whether she could afford it. Later on that day, Frazer, a friend of Maria, came to visit and, hearing that the piano was for sale, said he would buy it and collect it the next day. In the morning Frazer came back with the money, a van, and a burly assistant. With Maria's help, they got the piano onto a trolley and wheeled it down to the van and loaded it up. Emmeline, Maria's next-door neighbour, who is somewhat inquisitive, asked Maria what was going on and she told her. That evening Emmeline bumped into Zelda and told her what she had heard.

As *Dickinson* v *Dodds* indicates, Maria's offer to Zelda has been revoked, since *reliable* information even from a third party, not acting on the offeror's instructions, is sufficient notice.

A *promise to keep an offer open* for a certain time or to give someone 'first refusal' will not be legally binding unless the offeree gave some payment to the offeror in return for the favour. This is called an option contract and is used in large-scale sales of property where the buyer may need time to raise the finance. Otherwise the offeror is making only a gratuitous promise: giving something for nothing. Such a promise is not a contractual one, since it lacks consideration (see Chapter 6). In the scenario above, Maria might have lost a sale to Frazer if she had waited for Zelda to make up her mind, and then she might have come back and said she was not interested after all. The offeror is therefore free to withdraw (revoke) the promise at any time before the offer is accepted. In *Routledge v Grant* (1828) the defendant offered to buy the claimant's house, promising that he would keep the offer open for six weeks. It was held that he could withdraw the promise at any time before the offer was accepted, as his promise was merely gratuitous.

Option:
a promise to allow an offeree time to consider doing business on the terms of a pre-existing offer.

If the offeree does pay for the offer to be held open, a legally binding **option** is created. This means that the offeree has a contract that allows time to choose whether or not to accept the offer. This is different from putting down a deposit on goods or land. An option agreement gives the offeree time to choose *whether* or not to buy, whereas the deposit is evidence that a contract to purchase has been made and some of the purchase price is paid in advance.

It would obviously be unjust to apply the ordinary rules of revocation to *unilateral offers*, for two reasons:

1 *Notice.* A unilateral offer is often made to the world at large. If the offeror decides to revoke such an offer, it would be impossible to notify everyone who saw it. Provided the offeror takes reasonable steps to give notice, this will be sufficient. Putting another advertisement in the same newspaper which carried the offer is treated as constructive notice and will be treated as adequate.

2 *Incomplete acceptance.* Acceptance of a unilateral offer always involves the performance of an act. If an offeree has begun but not completed the acceptance of a unilateral offer, it would be unjust to allow the offeror to revoke the offer. Therefore, revocation may not be effective if the offeree is already in the process of accepting a unilateral offer.

Errington v Errington & Woods (1952, CA)

A father bought a house and promised his son and daughter-in-law that it would become theirs if they paid all the instalments on the mortgage by which he had financed the purchase.

Held: although his unilateral offer would technically be accepted only when the last payment had been made, the father's promise was irrevocable as long as the payments were kept up. While the payments continued it would be unjust for the offer to be revoked.

The acceptance

The offeree, by acceptance, agrees to be bound by all the terms of the offer. To be legally binding, such acceptance must fulfil three rules:

1 it must be a 'mirror image' of the offer;

2 it must be unconditional;

3 it must be communicated to the offeror.

Acceptance must be a 'mirror image' of the offer

The offeree must be agreeing to all the terms of the offer and not trying to introduce new terms. In *Jones* v *Daniel* (1894) the offeree responded to an offer by submitting a draft contract which included some new terms. This response was held to be a counter-offer, not an acceptance.

Where two businesses are negotiating a contract, they may each wish to contract on their own standard terms (pre-set terms not open to negotiation). The offerors present their standard terms, but the offerees, instead of accepting on those terms, reply with their own set of standard terms. This is sometimes called 'the battle of the forms'.

Butler Machine Tools Ltd v *Ex-Cell-O Ltd* (1979, CA)

The claimants, on their standard terms, offered to sell machine tools to the defendants. These terms named a price but allowed the claimants to vary this on delivery. The defendants replied with their terms, which specified a fixed price and required the claimants to return an attached acknowledgement slip indicating that they were prepared to supply the defendants' order on these terms. The claimants did so, but when the goods were delivered, they tried to claim that the price could be increased.

Held: the claimants' offer had not been accepted by the defendants: their reply was a counter-offer accepted by the claimants when they returned the slip. The contract was on the defendants' terms and only the fixed price was payable.

Acceptance must be unconditional

Subject to contract: a provisional acceptance, prior to a contract being drawn up.

Conditional acceptance is not binding. An acceptance containing the words **'subject to contract'** is not generally a valid acceptance and use of this phrase is normal practice in sales of land. The parties will not be legally bound to each other until exchange of contracts takes place. This is meant to assist buyers by giving them time to carry out surveys and searches before deciding to commit themselves. It can also mean that the seller is free to sell to another buyer who is prepared to offer more money in the meantime. Such 'gazumping' in property contracts may cause financial loss to the first buyer, who may have spent money on legal and survey fees and is then left without means of redress against the seller, since there is as yet no binding contract with the seller. However, the intention of the parties is paramount and exceptionally the court may decide that, despite its provisional appearance, it is out-weighed by other factors and valid acceptance has taken place. In *Branco* v *Cobarro* (1947, CA) a written agreement described as 'a provisional agreement until a fully legalised contract is drawn up' was held to be a valid acceptance, since it completely reflected all the terms already agreed between the parties. In *Immingham Storage Co. Ltd* v *Clear plc* (2011) (below), the Court of Appeal again demonstrated that statements suggesting conditionality may be negatived by evidence of the parties' existing consensus on terms.

Immingham Storage Co. Ltd v *Clear plc* (2011, CA)

Between October and December 2009 the parties engaged in a succession of nego-tiations by email, letter and face-to-face concerning the availability, capacity and cost of storage facilities for a certain type of diesel fuel at Immingham's premises. Finally, in December 2009, Immingham sent an email quotation to Clear (headed 'subject to Board Approval and tank availability'). It identified Clear as buyer, the quantity of fuel to be stored and the dates during which storage was available. It stated that all other terms would be those in Immingham's general terms and conditions and that 'a formal contract will follow in due course'. Immingham's terms and conditions were attached. Clear confirmed its wish to proceed by fax. Immingham responded with an email headed 'Contract Confirmation' that started with the words 'we are delighted to accept your offer' and stated that 'a formal contract will follow in due course'. Clear later received the contract but never returned it. Clear was then unable to source the relevant fuel and Immingham claimed its charges. Clear then argued that no contract existed; the signed quote amounted only to a conditional offer because it had indicated that it was conditional on 'board approval and tank availability' and delivery of a formal contract. In addition, it claimed that Immingham's email was not a valid acceptance because it required signature of a formal contract.

Held: a contract came into existence between the parties as soon as Immingham's email validly accepted Clear's signed quotation. The signed quote was a valid offer because it included all the terms and conditions attached to it. The reference to a 'board approval' was irrelevant because these issues had already been settled. Immingham's acceptance was not invalidated by lack of a formal contract. The email as a whole evidenced full acceptance at the point it was received.

'Reasonable expectations of honest men'

Where acceptance is disputed but performance has already begun the court is increasingly inclined to apply the criterion of reasonable expectation. This means that if a reasonably honest business person would believe that a contract had been formed after examining the existing terms and the behaviour of the parties, that is conclusive evidence of a binding agreement. See below: *Reveille Independent plc* v *Anotech International (UK Ltd)* [2016] EWCA Civ 443.

Reveille Independent plc v Anotech International (UK Ltd) [2016] EWCA Civ 443

Reveille is a TV company and producer of MasterChef US; Anotech are cookware manufacturers.

Reveille disputed the existence of a contract to enable Reveille to use Anotech's cookware on MasterChef and give Anotech a limited licence to use the Master-Chef name in promoting its products.

In January 2011 the parties began negotiations and in February Reveille sent a deal memo containing some terms and stating that the deal would not be binding until executed by both parties and replaced by a formal document. At the end of February Anotech returned the deal memo, signed, but including a number of changes. Reveille started using Anotech's products on MasterChef US in accordance with the memo, although negotiations were still taking place. Negotiations eventually broke down and in July Reveille repudiated the contract. Anotech argued no contract had ever existed because of the lack of documentary evidence as indicated in the original deal memo.

The CA held (affirming the trial judge's decision): performance of the memo terms by Reveille with Anotech's knowledge clearly pointed to a contract being created by mid-March. Both parties had acted clearly and unequivocally as if already bound by the terms set out in the memo. Reveille was therefore entitled to recover monies owed by Anotech for the promotion of the cookware. The reasonable expectations criterion had clearly been fulfilled.

Acceptance must be communicated

The law relating to communication involves a number of different rules.

Communication is effective only if made by an authorised person

Powell v *Lee* (1908)

The claimant was notified that his job application had been successful by a member of an appointments board, which then later decided to give the job to someone else.

Held: the person who had informed the claimant had not been authorised to do so. Therefore acceptance had not been effectively communicated.

Methods of communication

Conduct

Brogden v *Metropolitan Railway Co.* (1877, HL)

Mr Brogden had supplied coal to the railway company for some time, when the company suggested that they should regularise their arrangements with a new contract. The draft contract was sent to Brogden who added certain terms, including the name of an arbitrator. He then marked it 'approved' and sent it back to the company. He heard no more but the company continued to order coal, which Brogden supplied on the terms of the draft agreement.

Held: Brogden's amendments to the draft contract amounted to a counter-offer which had been accepted. The company's intention to assent was in itself insufficient to be acceptance. It became sufficient only once Brogden knew of it. Here the company's conduct evidenced acceptance, either when it placed the first order, or when it accepted the first delivery.

Communication is, therefore, effective only when it reaches the offeror or the offeror's place of business. Commercial practice may enable the court to interpret conduct in relation to the making of offer and acceptance. Thus, in *Confetti Records* v *Warner Music UK* (2003) the sending of an invoice together with a music track was deemed to be an offer by Confetti to sell the material to Warner to be marketed. By producing an album containing the track Warner accepted the offer.

However, only unequivocal conduct will make the acceptance binding:

Inland Revenue Commissioners v *Fry* (2001)

Ms Fry owed the Revenue £113,000 and sent a cheque for £10,000, with an accompanying letter stating that this was the most that she could raise and that it should be regarded as full and final settlement of the debt. The Revenue cashed the cheque on receipt and the case worker to whom the letter was forwarded subsequently phoned Ms Fry to tell her that the sum could either be treated as part payment of her debt, or she could have the money back.

Held: the Revenue had not made a valid acceptance. Cashing the cheque gave rise to no more than a rebuttable presumption of acceptance and here the presumption had clearly been rebutted by the case worker's subsequent phone call. No reasonable person would believe that banking the cheque indicated intention to be bound by the terms of the offer. The Revenue's administration system would not be likely to permit a contract, under which it gave up its rights to substantial sums of money, to be concluded in this way.

Verbal communication

Acceptance is effectively communicated only when the offeror has received notice of it. In a face-to-face situation it will usually be immediately evident if any communication problems have occurred. However, if the parties cannot see each other this may be more problematic; acceptance by *telephone* is held to be effective only on being heard by the offeror. The courts have extended this principle to *telex* transmissions. In *Entores Ltd* v *Miles Far East Corp.* (1955, CA) the Court of Appeal made it clear that acceptance by telex should be treated like acceptance by telephone: instantaneous and effective on being received.

Brinkibon Ltd v *Stahag Stahl und Stahlwarenhandels GmbH* (1982, HL)

The House of Lords suggested (*obiter dicta*) that telex messages transmitted when the receiver's office was closed would be effective only once the office had reopened.

The *Brinkibon* ruling was applied in *Mondial Shipping and Chartering BV* v *Astarte Shipping Ltd* (1995) where it was held that a telex message sent just before midnight on a Friday was communicated at 9 a.m. the following Monday when the receiver's office opened for business.

Reasonable expectations of honest men: the objective standard by which the court decides whether a party's conduct evidences sufficient intention to be contractually bound.

When developing such rules the courts are guided by the '**reasonable expectations of honest men**' in the context of accepted commercial practice (See *Reveille Independent plc* v *Anotech International (UK Ltd)* [2016] EWCA Civ 443 above). In *Entores* it was stressed that if it were the fault of the offeror that the message was not received (due perhaps to lack of ink in the teleprinter), the offeror would still be bound, as the offeree would reasonably expect successful receipt. This principle, generally applied by the courts, enables objective assessment of the parties' behaviour from which it can be determined whether the intention to offer or accept is adequately demonstrated.

Electronic communications

As yet, there do not appear to be any reported cases involving communication via fax, or answerphone. Using the reasonable expectations approach, emails are likely to be treated like telex messages.

It can probably be successfully argued that messages left on *answering machines* are not communicated until, like any telephone message, the recipient actually hears them. It is, after all, immediately evident to the sender that the message is not going to be transmitted at once.

Emails have been accepted by the courts as a valid means of communication of acceptance but without any specific ruling on when communication becomes effective. In *J. Pereira Fernandes SA* v *Mehta* (2006) Judge Pelling QC in a contract of guarantee accepted without argument that email offer and acceptance is a potentially valid form of communication, but gave no indication of when communication is effective. *Immingham Storage Co. Ltd* v *Clear plc* (2011) (above) implies that receipt is required. It might be reasonable to argue that, once an email has been sent, arrival may well be instantaneous. However, delay may occur in transmission via the server, so maybe communication should be deemed to exist once the message is capable of being downloaded to the receiver's mailbox.

Internet sales were first covered by the Electronic Commerce (EC Directive) Regulations 2002 (which implemented the Electronic Commerce Directive 2000/31/EC). Regulation 11 states that electronic orders/acknowledgements of orders 'are deemed to be received when the parties to whom they are addressed are able to access them'. This suggests that when a contract is made on the internet, the website details of goods are an invitation to treat. Presumably, the customer communicates the offer by placing the order, entering name, address and payment card details and transmitting this information to the seller with a click on the relevant button. The seller will not be deemed to have accepted until it communicates acceptance by sending a message confirming that the order has been placed successfully. This will happen only after it has successfully accessed the customer's card. In some instances the website terms and conditions state that acceptance is only complete once the goods are dispatched. This is to avoid problems with pricing errors on a website.

The postal rule

Postal acceptance rule:
the default rule governing acceptance by post which is that the acceptance is binding from the moment of posting.

The **postal acceptance rule** provides an exception to the usual communication rule. In the nineteenth and early twentieth centuries the normal method of communication for parties contracting at a distance from each other was the post. In the middle of the nineteenth century the postal rules were extended to cover telegrams. The rules were clarified further by *Household Insurance* v *Grant* (1879 CA), which held that communication of acceptance by post is effective even if a letter is delayed in the post or fails to reach the offeror, as long as this is not due to some fault of the offeree's: for example, an incorrect address.

Adams v *Lindsell* (1818)

On 2 September the defendants sent a letter of an offer to sell wool to the claimant and stated any acceptance must be made by return of post. The letter was delayed because it was wrongly addressed and did not arrive until 5 September. The claimants posted their acceptance immediately and it finally arrived on 9 September. On 8 September, the defendant, believing that the claimant was not interested, sold the wool to a third party. The claimant sued for breach of contract.

Held: The claim would succeed. The claimant had complied with the terms of the offer by posting their acceptance immediately. Once a letter of acceptance is posted, a contract comes into existence immediately. The delay in communicating the letter was entirely the fault of the defendant.

Worth thinking about?

Judges always have a reason for changing the law.

Why do you think the postal acceptance rule was developed?

Suggested solutions can be found in Appendix 2.

Only postal acceptance produces an instantaneous legal effect: a postal offer or revocation is effective only on receipt.

Byrne v *Van Tienhoven* (1880)

1 October:	The defendant posted an offer from Cardiff to the claimant in New York.
8 October:	The defendant changed his mind and posted a letter of revocation.
11 October:	The defendant's offer arrived and the claimant sent a telegram of acceptance.
15 October:	The claimant affirmed his acceptance by letter.
20 October:	The letter of revocation was received by the claimant.

Held: a contract was formed on 11 October when the claimant mailed his telegram of acceptance. The revocation was not communicated to the claimant until 20 October and was, therefore, too late to be effective.

It has always been possible for an offeror to avoid the postal rules either by specifying a different means of communication, or by stating that they would not be bound until receipt of an acceptance letter. Even where an offeror specifies nothing to this effect, the courts may be prepared to imply such an intention.

Holwell Securities v *Hughes* (1974, CA)

The offeror granted an option to the offeree concerning the purchase of some land, which had to be exercised by 'notice in writing'. The claimant's letter of acceptance was posted before the deadline but failed to reach the offeror before the deadline expired, though this was not the claimant's fault.

Held: no contract resulted from the postal acceptance. The postal rule was implicitly excluded by the offeror, who, by requiring notice in writing, had indicated that for communication to be effective it must actually receive the letter of acceptance.

Today the postal rules do not play an important part in the law of contract, though they continue to feature in exam papers. Parties contracting at a distance now generally have much faster and more reliable means of communication available to them. Even where the parties choose to use the post, it is very common for offerors to state that no contract will result until they receive an acceptance.

The offeror cannot waive the communication rule

In a bilateral contract situation offerors cannot bind offerees by saying that they will assume acceptance unless the offerees tell them differently. The communication rule ensures that an offeree is not pressurised into acceptance.

Felthouse v Bindley (1862)

The claimant offered to buy a horse from his nephew, John, who was selling up all his farm stock. The claimant said that he would assume John's acceptance unless told otherwise. Intending to accept, John instructed the auctioneer to withdraw the horse from the sale, but by mistake the auctioneer sold it. The claimant sued the auctioneer in tort.

Held: the claimant's action failed because he was unable to prove that he was the horse's owner. Since John had not communicated his intention to accept to the claimant, there was no contract under which ownership of the horse could pass. The auctioneer had not disposed of the claimant's property. When the sale took place the horse still belonged to John.

In a unilateral contract, acceptance and performance constitute the same act, so no prior communication of acceptance is practicable. If a member of the public sees a notice offering a reward for the return of lost property, they will be able to accept only if they find it and actually return it, thereby performing the act for which the reward was promised. They cannot be refused it because they have not given advance notice.

The offeror may expressly require a particular method of communication

The court will usually be prepared to treat any reasonable method of communication as effective. Where no mode is specifically requested, the mode of offer and the nature of the subject matter of the contract may indicate suitable methods of response. For example, a telephone offer of perishable goods would necessitate a swift means of communicating acceptance; otherwise the offer may no longer be valid because of lapse of time.

Chapter summary

Formation of a simple contract requires the following factors to be present:

Agreement (offer and acceptance).

Bargain (consideration).

Intention to create legal relations.

Writing not essential unless required by statute.

Offer

The statement of *final* terms on which the offeror is prepared to contract which becomes effective once received by the offeree.

An offer may be bilateral (a promise in return for a promise) or **unilateral** (a promise in return for an act).

An invitation to treat or merely negotiating statement is not an offer because it invites an offer or further negotiation and does not indicate finality or intention to be bound.

An offer may be revoked up until the time of acceptance.

An offer will lapse unless accepted within a stipulated or reasonable time.

Acceptance

Acceptance is only binding in law if it is firm and completely reflects the offer terms. Any attempt to vary the terms may amount to a counter-offer.

It must be communicated. This usually requires receipt by the offeror, but a letter of acceptance is binding once posted unless the offeror specifies otherwise.

Determining the legal existence of offer and acceptance: the court interprets the behaviour of the parties objectively in accordance with 'the expectations of reasonable men'.

Review questions 4

1 Define and distinguish between an offer and an invitation to treat.

2 What is a counter-offer?

3 Explain the postal acceptance rule.

4 How may an offer be terminated?

5 Does an offer exist in the following circumstances?
   (a) Johti puts a teddy bear wearing a price ticket in her shop window.
   (b) Ying distributes flyers stating 'Cheap Offer: 10% off the cost of all our pizzas'.
   (c) Mac advertises a reward of £50 for the return of his lost bracelet.
   (d) Martha returns Mac's bracelet and then discovers that a reward was offered.
   (e) Petrov offered to sell his car to Eli for £3,000; Eli told him he would pay only £2,500.
   (f) Elizabeth offered to sell her fridge-freezer to Paul for £100. He asked her to give him three days to decide. The next day she sold the freezer to Jacob.

6 Has a valid acceptance resulted in the following situations?
   (a) Josh offers to sell potatoes to Tammy, who replies that she will take them if she can raise the money.
   (b) Eve offers to sell apples to Matthew and tells him that she will assume that he wants to buy them unless he tells her to the contrary by 10 o'clock on Saturday morning. The deadline has now passed but Matthew has not been in touch.
   (c) Lulu sent a letter to Michel offering to sell an antique clock. Michel replies accepting, but his letter is lost in the post.
   (d) Susanna offered by telephone to rewire Antony's house. He accepted, but Susanna did not hear because the line went silent.

Answers to all review questions can be found in Appendix 2.

Advanced questions 4

(A) Analyse the extent to which the postal acceptance rule has any validity in the twenty-first century.

(B) Evaluate the risks to a consumer of making a contract online as opposed to making a contract face-to-face.

Answers to the advanced questions are available at **go.pearson.com/uk/he/resources.**

Take a closer look

The following cases provide important examples of how the law in this chapter has developed. They are primary sources illustrating the law in action and give more detail about their facts, as well as helping to understand the law and to appreciate how the judges reached their decisions.

Try looking them up in the law reports or accessing them via a database, e.g. BAILII (www.bailii.org/databases.html). LexisNexis or Westlaw may be available in the university or college library, or extracts may be found in a case book. (See Appendix 1: Additional resources.)

Blackpool & Fylde Aero Club v *Blackpool Council* [1990] 3 All ER 25 CA

Carlill v *Carbolic Smoke Ball Co. Ltd* [1893] 1 QB 256 CA

Entores Ltd v *Miles Far East Corporation* [1955] 2 All ER 49 CA

Immingham Storage Co. Ltd v *Clear plc* [2011] EWCA Civ 89; 135 Con LR 224

Web activity

Read the *Carlill* v *Carbolic Smoke Ball Co. Ltd* law report on the following website, see a full colour reproduction of the famous advertisement with testimonials and find out what a smokeball actually looked like. There is also a photograph of Mrs Carlill aged 87 looking hale and hearty:

www.carbolicsmokeball.co.uk

Assignment 3

Iris made an offer to sell her piano to Diana for £500 on Monday. Diana replied: 'I will buy it if I can raise the money.' Iris promised that she would not sell to anyone else before Saturday, and added that Diana could collect the piano any time before noon on Saturday. On Wednesday, Diana phoned and left a message with Iris's daughter, Athena, saying that she had got the money and would come to collect the piano on Saturday morning. Athena forgot to pass on the message. On Thursday, Iris was visited by Juno who said that she would pay £600 for the piano. Iris accepted this offer. Later that day Iris posted a letter to Diana telling her that she could not have the piano. Mercury, the postman, delivered it to the wrong address and Diana, who never received the letter, appeared with a hired van to collect the piano at 10 o'clock on Saturday morning.

Advise Iris of her legal position. (Some hints on answering problem questions, including an analysis of the above assignment, can be found in Chapter 1.)

The law of contract:
Consideration, intention and privity

Learning objectives

On completion of this chapter, students should be able to:

★ define consideration;

★ recognise the circumstances when valid consideration exists;

★ appreciate the exceptions to the rules governing valid consideration;

★ describe the operation of the promissory estoppel doctrine;

★ appreciate the characteristics of agreements which demonstrate intention to create legal relations;

★ explain how the Contracts (Rights of Third Parties) Act 1999 has impacted on the doctrine of privity of contract.

Introduction

Mutuality:
both parties support their promises by consideration.

Consideration:
money/goods/services/ land representing the bargain element of the contract.

Bare promise:
see gratuitous promise, below.

Gratuitous promise:
a promise which is not supported by consideration.

Essentially, the law of consideration is about exchanging something of value: consideration might be the price, money, or money's worth or a service. Commercial agreements are about striking bargains, or achieving what is sometimes called '**mutuality**'. Both parties stand to gain materially from the transaction: each receives a '**consideration**'. Where one party agrees to do something for the other with nothing promised in return, that party is said to be making a '**bare**' or '**gratuitous**' promise. In effect it is a promise of a gift. A legally binding contract cannot result from such a promise, only a moral obligation. It can only be made enforceable by putting it in the form of a deed.

It is quite possible to find agreements in which the elements of offer, acceptance and consideration can be identified, but the agreement will not be binding as a contract unless that is deemed to be the parties' intention. When they entered into the

6

agreement, they may not have intended that failure to perform the agreement would make them liable to legal sanctions for breach of contract.

A contract may be made for the benefit of a third party who does not contribute consideration but the common law rule of **privity of contract** generally prevented him or her from enforcing it. This is now mitigated by the Contracts (Rights of Third Parties) Act 1999.

Privity of contract: exclusivity of contractual rights and duties to parties who contribute consideration.

Consideration

Consideration has been defined by the courts in different ways. In *Currie* v *Misa* (1875) it was held to constitute a benefit to one party or a detriment to the other. Generally, it is easy to analyse contracts on this basis. When a customer buys a laptop from a shop, the benefit they receive is the laptop, and the detriment is the money they pay the shop. The shop clearly enjoys a corresponding benefit, and suffers a corresponding detriment in taking the customer's money and parting with the laptop.

In *Dunlop* v *Selfridge* (1915, HL), the House of Lords defined consideration in terms of the price by which one party bought the other party's act or promise. This is also clearly reflected in the example of the sale of the laptop.

Executory and executed consideration

Executory consideration

Executory consideration: a contractual promise which has not yet been performed.

Executed consideration: a contractual promise which has been performed.

A binding contract may be formed by the exchange of promises to be carried out at a later date. If goods are ordered which are to be paid for on delivery, a binding contract results on the order being accepted. Failure to deliver the goods would be a breach of contract. The consideration in such a contract consists of the mutual promises and is described as '**executory**' because the promises have not yet been **executed** (performed).

Executed consideration

Sometimes no contractual obligation to pay arises unless or until another party has executed their consideration. For example, if someone advertises a reward for the safe return of a lost cat, that person is making a unilateral promise to pay money that will become binding on the performance (execution) of an act (the return of the cat). The consideration provided by the person who returns the cat is called 'executed consideration'.

The rules governing consideration

Consideration must not be past

The act claimed to represent consideration for another party's promise to pay must not precede that promise, or it will be treated as past consideration and the promise will be merely gratuitous.

Real life

> Ranjit, knowing that his elderly neighbour, Zara, is concerned about the state of her garden, offers to clear it up for her. Ranjit is busy doing this for most of the day, and Zara is so pleased with the result that she promises to pay Ranjit £15 for his trouble.
>
> If Zara fails to pay, Ranjit will not be able to sue for breach of contract as Zara's promise to pay was made after the work was completed. The work represents past consideration and, therefore, the promise to pay is merely gratuitous.

To be contractually binding, it must be shown that a promise to pay preceded the act so that the promise and act form one undivided transaction and the promise is made in return for the act as part of the 'bargain'. The principle is clearly illustrated in the following case:

Re McArdle (1951, CA)

> A house was left by Mr McArdle to his wife for life. On her death it was to be sold and the proceeds divided equally between the children of the marriage. The wife of one of the children paid for home improvements at a cost of £488. When the work had been done all the children agreed that she should recover this sum from the proceeds of the eventual sale. After Mrs McArdle died the validity of this agreement was disputed.
>
> **Held:** no valid contract existed since the home improvements were past consideration; they had been carried out before any promise to pay had been made.

There is an exception to this rule when a subsequent promise is enforceable. Valid consideration may be held to exist in the absence of an express prior promise to pay provided that:

1 the act was done in response to a specific request; and

2 the situation was one where payment would normally be expected.

Re Stewart v *Casey (Casey's Patents)* (1892, CA)

An employee contributed many hours of his own time to the development of an invention for his employers at their request. When the work was completed, the employers promised that they would pay him a share of the profits once the invention was patented.

Held: the employers were bound by the promise as the employee had done the work at their request, and the nature of their relationship implied that future payment would be made.

The subsequent explicit promise to pay in such situations is seen as an affirmation of an implied promise which accompanied the request that the work be carried out.

Consideration must move from the promisee

This rule prevents a party from enforcing a contract unless he or she has contributed consideration. However, a number of exceptions exist under common law and statute and further reform has resulted from the Contracts (Rights of Third Parties) Act 1999 (see below).

Consideration must be sufficient

Consideration must be of material value, capable of assessment in financial terms. Usually the financial nature of the consideration is obvious where goods, land or money is involved. Any legal right has a financial value. Settling a case out of court involves a contract under which one party agrees not to exercise their legal right to sue the other, provided that the other pays an agreed sum of compensation. The consideration for the promise of compensation is the promise not to sue. In *Alliance Bank* v *Broome* (1864) a bank was held to have provided consideration, for the defendant's promise to give security for a loan, by promising not to take action to recover it.

White v *Bluett* (1853)

A son whose father had cut him out of his will agreed not to bore his father by nagging him to make a new will in his favour. In return his father agreed to release him from a debt. After his father's death the executors sued the son for payment and the son claimed that the debt had been discharged by his agreement with his father.

Held: the father was not bound by his promise as the son had not provided valid consideration. He had no right to dictate how his father disposed of his property, so he had not given up anything of material value by stopping nagging his father.

Note that consideration *may be sufficient without being adequate*. Provided the alleged consideration is of financial value, it is irrelevant that it is not of equivalent value. The courts are not interested in whether the parties have made a *good* bargain, but only in whether they have made a *bargain* at all. Therefore, proof of financial value, however minute, will be enough to make consideration sufficient.

Thomas v *Thomas* (1842)

A widow was promised a house in return for ground rent and promising to keep the property in good repair.

Held: an annual rent of £1 was held to be sufficient consideration for the promise.

Advertising campaigns sometimes offer to supply goods in return for wrappers, packet tops or vouchers cut from relevant product wrapping. If a purchaser complies with what is asked, then a binding contract results and they are entitled to the tea towel, cuddly toy or other item being offered.

Chappell v *Nestlé & Co. Ltd* (1959 HL)

Nestlé ran an offer to promote a particular chocolate bar. Anybody who sent three of the relevant wrappers plus one shilling and sixpence (75 pence in today's money) was entitled to a record of a current pop hit 'Rocking Shoes'. Nestlé threw away the wrappers on receipt.

Chappell, which disputed the amount of copyright compensation, sued Nestlé and the court had to decide whether the wrappers amounted to a portion of the consideration.

Held: Nestlé would derive a clear economic benefit from any increase in sales resulting from the promotion, so it was irrelevant that the wrappers would be thrown away on arrival.

Sufficiency usually involves taking on some *new obligation* in return for the other party's promise of payment. Performing an existing legal duty does not generally amount to sufficient consideration.

Collins v *Godefroy* (1831)

The claimant was a key witness at a trial and was under a court order to attend. Failure to do so would have made him guilty of the crime of contempt of court. The defendant was a party to the proceedings; because the claimant's attendance was important to him, he promised to pay the claimant if he would attend.

Held: the defendant's promise of payment was not contractually binding. The claimant had not provided sufficient consideration merely by promising to perform his existing legal duty.

In a case like this the claimant is effectively promising the defendant that if the claimant pays him money he will not commit a criminal offence, and such agreements are treated as being *against public policy* (not in the public interest).

Similarly, where two parties have made a contract, a subsequent promise of additional payment to encourage performance is not a binding contractual promise. The promisee is already contractually bound to perform and is therefore providing no fresh consideration.

Stilk v *Myrick* (1809)

Two sailors deserted from a ship in the course of a voyage. The captain promised the remainder of the crew that he would pay a bonus to each man if they got the ship home to England from Scandinavia.

Held: this promise was not binding. Crew members were required by their contracts to cope with the normal difficulties of a voyage, which in those days included crew shortages of this kind. Therefore, there was insufficient consideration to make the captain's promise enforceable.

Economic duress: an attempt to obtain favourable contract terms by threatening financial loss to a contracting party.

The court's unwillingness to enforce promises of this kind generally results from a concern that the promisee has exerted **economic duress** – blackmailed the promisor into offering extra payment. (This topic is explained in Chapter 9.)

The court may take a more generous attitude if satisfied that the public interest is not adversely affected and that enforcing the promise would produce the fairest outcome. The court may justify such a decision in one of three ways:

1 by finding that the promisee has exceeded the scope of his or her legal duty. The excess represents the consideration; or

2 by finding that the promisee, in carrying out the legal duty, has actually conferred a new benefit on the promisor; or

3 by deciding that the act of the promisor enabled the promisee to *avoid* some material *disadvantage*.

Hartley v *Ponsonby* (1857)

The facts of this case are similar to those in *Stilk* v *Myrick*, but here the reduced number of crew and the length of the journey were so great that the crew's existing contract of employment was discharged.

Held: by getting the ship home, the crew effectively were taking on a new set of duties and thus providing sufficient consideration for the captain's promise of more pay.

Glasbrook Bros v *Glamorgan County Council* (1925, HL)

The defendant mine owners, fearing vandalism of their premises during an industrial dispute, promised that if the police authority provided a full-time guard, they would make a donation to a police charity.

Held: this promise was binding, as the police could have fulfilled their legal duty by periodic inspection of the premises: the full-time guard exceeded this and was therefore sufficient consideration.

Williams v *Roffey Bros* (1990, CA)

Roffey was a builder who had a contract to refurbish a building for a housing association. This contract contained a delay clause under which Roffey was required to pay substantial sums if the work was not finished on time. Roffey sub-contracted carpentry work to Williams, who later ran into financial difficulties and told Roffey that because of this he would be unable to continue. Roffey promised him payment of extra money to complete the contract on time. He then refused to honour this undertaking arguing that Williams was merely doing what he had originally contracted to do.

Held: Roffey's promise was binding, since by securing the completion of the contract he was obtaining a benefit, or at least avoiding a burden. He avoided having to pay the delay costs to the housing association. He had freely entered into the agreement and not been forced by economic duress.

In making this decision the Court of Appeal was breaking new ground judicially, but the ruling reflects current commercial practice. It was applied in *Opel GmbH and Renault SA* v *Mitras Automotive* (2008), where it was held that the termination agreement imposed by the defendants was supported by consideration, as it enabled the claimants to avoid breaching contracts with their clients. However, the contract was voidable for economic duress. (The full facts for this case can be found in Chapter 9.)

Note that *Stilk* v *Myrick* is not overruled by *Williams* v *Roffey Bros*. There are clear distinguishing features. It must be decided on the facts of a case which decision will apply.

Worth thinking about?

In what ways can *Williams* v *Roffey* be distinguished from *Stilk* v *Myrick*?

Suggested solutions can be found in Appendix 2.

The *Williams* v *Roffey* principle was limited and clarified by the Court of Appeal in the following case:

Re Selectmove (1995, CA)

Selectmove owed arrears of tax to the Inland Revenue which threatened to start liquidation proceedings. Selectmove negotiated with a tax inspector and stated that it would pay all future tax as and when it fell due and that it would pay off all arrears of tax at £1,000 a month. The tax inspector said that if Selectmove heard nothing more it could assume that this plan was agreeable to the Revenue. Later, the Revenue then started liquidation proceedings.

Selectmove claimed that the Revenue was bound by the tax inspector's agreement since, under the *Williams* v *Roffey* principle, it obtained a benefit or at least avoided a disbenefit. If the company went into liquidation the Revenue might not acquire full repayment of the tax arrears and would not get the benefit of future tax payments.

Held: promising to carry out an existing duty can only be binding under *Williams* v *Roffey* if the duty is to perform *an act*, not just to *pay money*. The rule in *Pinnel*'s case (below) applies to part payment of debt.

Part payment of debt is not sufficient consideration

The rule in *Pinnel*'s case (1602)

A promise by a creditor to accept less than the full sum owed on the due date, does not discharge the debtor from the legal obligation to pay the balance.

The rule in *Pinnel*'s case is illustrated by the following example:

Real life

Ranjit owes Ting £50, but he is short of money that he can pay her only £35 when the date of repayment arrives. She can still pursue him later for the £15 even if she agrees that she will take the £35 in full settlement. This looks unfair, but an analysis of Ting's promise in terms of the rules of consideration reveals the legal logic, if not the moral justice, of the outcome. Ranjit, by repaying only part of what he owes, obtains a benefit (£15) but gives nothing to Ting in return. Ting loses £15 from their agreement. Ranjit provides no consideration and so Ting's new promise is not contractually binding; it is merely a gratuitous promise.

There are some exceptions to this rule. The debt will be discharged by part payment if the creditor requests:

1 part payment at an earlier date with the creditors agreement; or
2 part payment at a different place with the creditors agreement; or
3 some goods or other material benefit to accompany the part payment with the creditors agreement; or
4 payment by a third party; or
5 composition agreements by creditors.

In these situations the debtor is providing some consideration by doing something different at the creditor's request. For example:

Real life

Ranjit did building work at Franco's delicatessen for £1,000. When payment was due Franco was unable to pay in full, so Ranjit agreed to take £900 plus £100's worth of smoked salmon for his parents' forthcoming silver wedding anniversary celebration.

Composition (with creditors): a legally binding agreement between creditors that they will each take only a proportion of what the debtor owes, in full settlement of the entire debt.

Part payment by a third party in return for a promise from the creditor not to pursue the original debtor for the balance also discharges the whole debt. An agreement (**composition**) between creditors has a similar effect. It is common business practice for the multiple creditors of a debtor to agree that they will each accept a proportionate repayment of their debts. An individual creditor cannot renege on this contract to pursue the balance of his or her debt as this would be a fraud on the other creditors.

A form of such an agreement, commonly known as an Individual Voluntary Arrangement (IVA) was introduced and is regulated by the Insolvency Act 1986. IVAs are brokered by finance businesses for a commission and allow debtors to repay a proportion of their debt to their creditors over a specified period which is usually five years. In recent years the number of people dangerously in debt has generally grown and IVAs have become very popular as an alternative to bankruptcy. (See 'In the news' below.)

In the news

IVAs: numbers continue to rise in 2018

The number of people declared insolvent hit a six-year high in the three months to June 2018 as the squeeze from high inflation, meagre wage rises and benefit cuts hit the finances of low-paid workers. Individual insolvencies totalled 28,951 in the second quarter, a jump of 4.4 per cent on the previous quarter and 27.3 per cent on the same period last year. The Insolvency Service, a government agency, said it was clear the trend had been rising steadily since 2015 to reach the highest quarterly total since the first quarter of 2012. It said the upswing was driven by a record number of people taking out individual voluntary arrangements (IVAs), where debtors agree to repay creditors some or all of what they owe.

www.theguardian.com/money/2018/jul/27/
uk-insolvencies-hit-six-year-high-as-record-number-take-out-ivas.

Between 1990 and 2003 there were under 10,000 IVAs every year. Numbers then gradually increased and since 2012 have usually been around the 50,000 mark, apart from a brief blip in 2015 when numbers dropped to 46,700 reflecting a reduction in all personal insolvencies. Numbers rose again to 52,000 by the end of 2016, comprising 55 per cent of all insolvencies.

Setting up these arrangements very quickly became an industry, with many firms charging substantial commission and some failing to advise clients appropriately, since IVAs are not suitable for everybody. The Office of Fair Trading set guidelines for advertising in 2007 and required providers to conform within four weeks. The Insolvency Service run by BEIS (Department for Business, Energy and Industrial Strategy) has issued protocols since 2008 to promote good practice in consumer IVAs. These provide a simple and straightforward framework for setting up the transaction. The current version was introduced in 2012. Advice is available from organisations like Citizens Advice. Stepchange (the debt advice charity) provides its own IVA.

Sources: www.beis.gov.uk/insolvency; www.citizensadvice.org.uk/;
www.stepchange.org/.

The cases of *Re Selectmove* (1995) (above) and *Re C (A Debtor)* (1994), indicate that the Court of Appeal is not prepared to allow the principle in *Williams* v *Roffey* to validate agreements to pay *less* than the agreed sum, rather than *more*. This would otherwise undermine the rule in *Pinnel's* case.

Promissory estoppel (*High Trees* doctrine): an equitable defence which a party may use when a contract has been gratuitously varied for their benefit and the other party seeks to enforce it in its original form.

Promissory estoppel

Promissory estoppel is an equitable defence which may be relevant in part-payment situations. Under this principle, parties who gratuitously promise that they will not enforce existing contractual rights may lose their entitlement to do so if it would be unfair to allow them to go back on their promise; they are prevented (*estopped*) from breaking the promise. This defence was developed in the following case:

Central London Property Trust v *High Trees House* (1947)

The defendants owned a block of flats on land leased to them by the claimants. By September 1939, many flats had become vacant due to outbreak of war. Consequently, the defendants were having difficulties paying their ground rent. The claimants agreed that they would accept reduced payments. The defendants continued to pay the reduced rent even when the flats refilled and the war was over.

The claimants brought a test case claiming arrears of rent for the last two quarters of 1945 (by which time the war had ended).

Held: the claimants were found to be entitled to the arrears they claimed, but it was also held (*obiter dictum*) that had they claimed for arrears prior to the end of the war this would have been refused. It would be unfair to allow them to go back on their promise on which the defendants had naturally relied. The claimants' gratuitous promise operated to suspend their rights to full payment while the extenuating circumstances in which the promise had been made continued to operate.

This *obiter dictum* (persuasive ruling) from Mr Justice Denning has been applied by the House of Lords. In *Tool Metal Manufacturing Co. Ltd* v *Tungsten Ltd* (1955) a gratuitous promise, to suspend rights to royalty payments on a patent during the war, was held to be a good defence to a subsequent claim for such payments.

However, although the doctrine of promissory estoppel has been much discussed by the Court of Appeal and the House of Lords in subsequent cases, it has been used very little and its scope is far from clear. Two elements are certain:

1 *It can operate only as a defence.* Denning LJ clarified this aspect of the doctrine in *Combe* v *Combe* (CA, 1951). Describing it as a 'shield and not a

sword', he emphasised that the doctrine 'should not be stretched too far' and the principle 'did not create new causes of action where none had existed before' and that 'the doctrine of consideration is too firmly fixed to be overthrown by a side wind.'

Therefore, if this reasoning is applied to *High Trees*, it is clear that the defendants could not have sued on the claimants' promise, but it would have been a good defence against the claimants if they had tried to enforce their original contract rights for the period in which they had been suspended.

2 *It is an equitable principle.* The court will not grant an equitable remedy unless it will produce a just result for both parties; parties seeking such a remedy must show that they have behaved morally as well as legally.

D & C Builders v Rees (1965, CA)

Mrs Rees persuaded the builders, whom she knew to be in financial difficulties, to accept payment of £300 in full settlement of a debt of almost £483, by telling them that they would otherwise get nothing.

Held: it would not be equitable to allow their promise to be used as a defence against them, given that Mrs Rees had effectively *'held the builders to ransom'* (Denning LJ) forcing them to accept the smaller sum.

Intention to create legal relations

Intention to create legal relations: the parties' intention that their agreement be binding in law, not just morally.

In determining whether the parties intend their agreement to be legally binding, the courts are guided by two presumptions concerning the parties' **intention to create legal relations**:

1 parties to a domestic or social agreement do not intend to be legally bound;

2 parties to a business agreement intend to be legally bound.

These are presumptions only and can be rebutted (disproved) by sufficient evidence to the contrary.

Domestic and social agreements

The courts believe that family members and friends do not generally intend agreements, made merely for their mutual convenience, to be legally enforceable. Property rights between family members are generally adequately covered by other areas of the law. Unless there is clear evidence of what is at heart a commercial transaction – for example, the sale of a car between family members – an intention to be contractually bound will not be presumed.

Balfour v *Balfour* (1919, CA)

Held: no intention to create legal relations existed in an agreement under which a husband working abroad promised to pay maintenance to his wife in England.

The courts take a different view if the couple does not intend to continue in the marriage. In *Merritt* v *Merritt* (1970, CA) a contractual relationship was held to arise from a post-separation maintenance agreement.

Car pool agreements may involve the necessary intention:

Albert v *Motor Insurers Bureau* (1971, HL)

Held: if lifts are provided on a regular and systematic basis under which drivers anticipate payment, an intention to create a legally binding relationship is present.

The relative financial risk to one party and the reliance by that party on the other party's promise may be relevant.

Parker v *Clark* (1960)

The Parkers (niece and nephew to the Clarks) agreed to sell their house and move in with the Clarks. The Parkers received a letter from Mr Clark confirming that, in return for moving in, sharing household expenses and taking on some household tasks, for the rest of both the Clark's lives, the house would become theirs under Mr Clark's will.

Sadly, the arrangement broke down and the Parkers, who were told to leave, sued for breach of contract.

Held: sufficient intention to be legally bound was evidenced by the clear terms of the agreement and because Mr Clark had changed his will. The Parkers had relied upon it to their considerable financial detriment having given their daughter their house sale proceeds to buy a flat.

Even a 'fun' transaction may implicitly contain a more formal intention.

Simpkins v Pays (1955, CA)

The claimant lodged in the defendant's boarding house. Every week she, the defendant and the defendant's granddaughter entered a fashion competition in a Sunday newspaper. They took it in turns to pay the entry costs and postage and agreed that any winnings should be divided equally. One week their entry, sent in the defendant's name, won £750 but she refused to pay the claimant her share. The claimant sued in breach of contract and the defendant argued that no legally binding relationship had been intended in the transaction.

Held: the claimant should succeed since the parties demonstrated sufficient intention to be legally bound. This was more than just a friendly agreement. It was a joint enterprise to which each of the parties contributed financially in the expectation of sharing prize money.

A clearly defined agreement must exist before evidence of intention to be bound can be deduced.

Wilson and Another v *Burnett* (2007, CA)

The claimants organised a girls' night out to the local bingo hall with the defendant, a workmate. The defendant won substantial prizes totalling £101,354. The claimants alleged that at the start of the evening they had all agreed to share equally any prize over £10. The defendant disputed this. At the trial Judge Nelligan said:

> I accept the defendant's evidence that there was chat or talk about sharing winnings which went no further than discussion or chat, and did not cross and cannot be inferred to have crossed that line which exists between talk and 'meaning business', or an intention to create a legal relationship, that is to share the prize money.

He therefore held that the claimants were not entitled to share the money. The claimants appealed.

Held: Judge Nelligan had been justified in coming to his decision. In agreements between friends it was presumed that there was no intention to be legally bound, though every case must be examined on its facts. Although there had been discussion about sharing winnings, there was insufficient evidence of any clear agreement sufficient to prove the existence of such intention, so the claimants lost their case.

It is easy to see clear differences between the facts in the two cases above. In *Simpkins* v *Pays* the parties had regularly entered the competition together following the same process each time and each party contributed to it and had a stake in the outcome. In *Wilson* v *Burnett* the parties were engaged in a one-off outing and the evidence of any potential agreement was conflicting.

Exam tip

If the question describes parties in a problem as friends or family members, this may be to indicate that the issue of intention to create legal relations should be mentioned in the answer.

Business agreements

In the world of business, the presumption that agreements are intended to have legal consequences means that a very clear indication of lack of intention to create legal relations is necessary to rebut the presumption that a legally binding relationship was intended.

Rose & Frank Co. v *J. R. Crompton & Bros* (1925, HL)

The claimant was a US company, selling carbon paper, and it agreed to permit the defendant, an English company in the same line of business, to market its product in the USA. The wording of the agreement stated that it was not 'a formal legal agreement and shall not be subject to legal jurisdiction in the law courts either of the United States or England, but it is only a definite expression and record of the purpose and intention of the parties concerned to which they each honourably pledge themselves'.

The defendant subsequently breached the agreement and claimed that it did not amount to a binding contract.

Held: this clause was effective to exclude intention to be legally bound as it was clear and specific.

The small print in an advertisement for a competition will usually contain similar words to those stated in the case above. In *Jones* v *Vernons Pools* (1938) it was held that no legally binding contract was created between punter and pools company: the entry coupon stated clearly that the relationship between the parties was 'binding in honour only'.

Comfort letters

In business it is not uncommon for a parent company to reassure a financial institution of the creditworthiness of a subsidiary company by issuing a 'letter of comfort'. If the subsidiary fails to repay any resulting loan, the lender may try to sue the parent company to recover the money. Despite the highly commercial context, such letters are not necessarily legally binding and the context of preceding negotiations and the wording is crucial.

Kleinwort Benson v *Malaysia Mining Corporation Bhd* (1989, CA)

A comfort letter issued by Malaysia Mining in support of its subsidiary, MMC Metals Ltd, stated that: 'It is our policy to ensure that the business [of MMC] is at all times in a position to meet its liabilities to you.'

Held: this was merely a statement of current intention and of Malaysia Mining's policy. It was not intended to have a legally binding effect and did not amount to any guarantee of the future reliability of MMC.

Privity of contract

Promisor:
a recipient of a promise.

Promisee:
a party making a promise.

Sometimes a contractual situation may arise where one party (**promisor**) agrees with another (the **promisee**) to provide a benefit for a third party. In the case of consideration (discussed earlier in this chapter), the common law rule is that parties who have not contributed consideration to a contract cannot sue on it if it is breached. This is because they are not full parties to the contract: in the rather archaic language still used by lawyers, they are not *privy to the contract*, or there is no *privity of contract* between the parties. Thus, the beneficiary cannot sue if the contract is breached.

Tweddle v *Atkinson* (1861)

William Tweddle was engaged to marry Miss Guy. The fathers of the happy couple contracted that they would each put up a sum of money when the marriage took place, but Mr Guy died before making payment.

Held: William had no right to sue Mr Guy's estate for the money since he had provided no consideration for the promise and was merely a beneficiary of the contract. As a mere beneficiary, William was not *privy to the contract*: he was not truly a party to it because he was not contributing to the consideration.

Similarly, the burdens of a contract cannot be enforced against a party to whom no consideration has been promised.

Dunlop Rubber Co. Ltd v *Selfridge* (1915, HL)

Dunlop supplied tyres at a discount (less than list price) to Dew & Co., who agreed not to resell below list price to trade buyers unless those buyers also agreed not to resell below list price. Dew supplied Selfridge, who breached the resale price agreement. Dunlop tried to take action against Selfridge.

Held: Dunlop could not sue Selfridge, as there was no privity of contract between them: Dunlop had given no consideration to Selfridge in return for the promise to stick to the resale price. (Any action could only be taken against Selfridge by Dew for breach of the contract between them.)

Exceptions to the rule of privity

To prevent injustice, a number of exceptions to the rule have been acknowledged to enable beneficiaries to enforce their rights.

1 *Agency.* Where agents make contracts on behalf of their principals with third parties, the principals may sue or be sued on those contracts as if they had made them themselves. (See Chapter 11.)

2 *Third-party insurance.* A third party may claim under an insurance policy made for their benefit, even though that party did not pay the premiums (for example: life assurance and third-party motor insurance).

3 *Assignment of contractual rights.* The benefits (but not the burdens) of a contract may be assigned to a third party, who may then sue on the contract (for example: selling debts). The original debtor may be sued by the new creditor to whom the rights to collect the debt have been assigned. The duty to perform a contract cannot be assigned.

4 *Trusts.* This is an equitable concept by which one person transfers property to a second person (the trustee), who holds it for the benefit of others (beneficiaries). The party who created the trust, which is often done by a will, lays down the rules under which it is to be administered. If these are not complied with, the beneficiaries have the right to ask the court to enforce the trust for their benefit.

5 *Collateral contracts.* The performance of one contract between A and B may indirectly bring another into being between A and C.

6 *Contracts for the benefit of a group.* Where a contract to supply a service is made in one person's name but is intended to benefit a group of people, the members of the group have no rights to sue at common law if the contract is breached; there is no privity of contract between them and the supplier of the service. The court, however, may take some of their losses into account when awarding damages to the buyer.

Shanklin Pier Ltd v Detel Products Ltd (1954)

Detel advised Shanklin Pier Ltd that their paint was suitable for maritime use and would last for at least seven years. Shanklin Pier Ltd contracted with a decorating firm to paint the pier; a term of the contract required the decorators to buy Detel's paint for the purpose. The paint began to peel off within three months.

Held: Shanklin Pier Ltd could successfully sue Detel Products on a collateral contract which was linked to the main contract between Shanklin Pier Ltd and the decorating firm. Detel had made promises about the quality of their paint and Shanklin Pier had provided consideration for this promise by requiring their decorators to use it.

Jackson v Horizon Holidays Ltd (1975, CA)

Horizon provided such a poor level of service that the Jackson family holiday was ruined.

Held: Mr Jackson, who had made the contract, was the only party who could sue but the damages he was awarded took into account the loss to the whole family resulting from Horizon's failure to deliver a holiday of the promised quality.

Statutory reform of the privity rule

In 1996, the Law Commission (Report No. 242) stated that reform was needed since the law at that time:

(a) prejudiced third parties who may have relied on contracts which they had no power to enforce;

(b) caused problems in commercial life;

(c) was out of step with other EU members and much of the common law world, including New Zealand and the USA.

As a result, reforming legislation was introduced.

Contracts (Rights of Third Parties) Act 1999

Section 1 gives a third party the right directly to enforce any contract which expressly permits this or where the contract is intended to benefit them. This gives the third party the same remedies as any other party to a breach of contract action. They must be expressly identified in the contract by name or class or description, but need not be in existence when the contract is made. Thus, a contract to provide an ongoing benefit to 'all my children' could benefit any children born after formation of the contract.

Section 2 further protects third parties by preventing cancellation or variation of the contract without their permission unless the contract *expressly* provides for this. Generally, a third party's rights cannot be withdrawn or varied without their consent if: they have communicated agreement by words or conduct to the terms, or the promisor is aware that they have relied on the terms, or the promisor should have reasonably foreseen that they would rely on the term and they have in fact done so. In exceptional circumstances (e.g. mental incapacity of the third party) the court may dispense with the right of consent.

Section 5 protects the promisor from double liability. If the promisor fails to perform the duty owed to the third party, they will not be liable to the third party for any losses that the promisee has already recovered from the promisor. This prevents the third party from recovering twice for the same losses. Third-party rights cannot be enforced in some contract situations. Section 6 specifies some exceptions: for example, a third party cannot enforce any term against an employee in an employment contract; in a contract for carriage of goods, a third party has no enforceable rights except for the protection of any exclusion or limitation clause in the contract.

Note that the 1999 Act does not abolish the privity doctrine: it just introduces a new right. Section 7 specifies that existing third-party rights and remedies remain unchanged.

Chapter summary

Consideration

The bargain element that distinguishes a contract from any other sort of agreement legally binding or otherwise.

Definition: material benefit gained/detriment arising from performance of a contract.

Price paid for the other party's promise or act. Benefit/detriment.

The rules of consideration

It must not be past: not precede the promise to pay.

It must be sufficient: represent some detriment/benefit though not necessarily an adequate price.

Generally, only a party who provides consideration may enforce the contract (see Privity, below).

Part payment of a debt does not generally discharge it (*Pinnel*'s case).

Promissory estoppel may provide a defence for a defendant sued for breach of contract, if he or she can prove that the claimant had previously gratuitously varied the contract in the defendant's favour so that it would be unjust to let them go back on their word.

Intention to create legal relations

The parties to a contract must intend it to be legally binding or it will not be enforceable in the courts. Two rebuttable presumptions operate here.

An agreement between friends or family members is presumed not to reflect that intention, while business agreements are.

Privity of contract

Generally, the doctrine of privity of contract prevents anyone except a party who contributes to the bargain from enforcing it.

The Contracts (Rights of Third Parties) Act 1999 enables a contractual beneficiary to sue for breach of a contract that was clearly made for their benefit, even though they have not provided any consideration.

Review questions 5

1 What is consideration?

2 Define and distinguish between executory and executed consideration.

3 What is past consideration?

4 What is privity of contract?

5 Are the following promises legally binding or merely gratuitous?
   (a) Rachel returned Tom's lost tortoise. Tom promised her £5.
   (b) Gurdip agreed to sell his vintage sports car to Chris for 10p.
   (c) Scarlet promised her employee, Chan, that she would give him a £10 bonus if he arrived at work on time for a week.
   (d) Hannah was owed £50 by David, but agreed to take £45 in full settlement if David made the repayment a week early.
   (e) Amira agreed that her tenant, Peter, might pay a reduced rent while he was out of work.

6 William told his tailor to make a wedding suit for William's nephew, Gareth, who chose the style and material. The cost was to be charged to William's account. When the suit was finished it did not fit Gareth, who had to hire one. Has Gareth any rights against the tailor?

Answers to all review questions can be found in Appendix 2.

Advanced questions 5

(A) Explain the doctrine of promissory estoppel and indicate the limitations of it.

(B) Analyse the legal significance of the decision in *Williams* v *Roffey Bros* (1989).

Answers to the advanced questions can be found at **go.pearson.com/uk/he/resources.**

Take a closer look

The following cases provide important examples of how the law in this chapter has developed. They are primary sources illustrating the law in action and give more detail about their facts, as well as helping to understand the law and to appreciate how the judges reached their decisions.

Try looking them up in the law reports or accessing them via a database, e.g. BAILII (www.bailii.org/databases.html). LexisNexis or Westlaw may be available in the university or college library, or extracts may be found extracts in a case book. (See Appendix 1: Additional resources.)

Jackson v *Horizon Holidays* [1975] 3 All ER 92, CA

Re McArdle [1951] Ch 669

Simpkins v *Pays* [1955] 3 All ER 10, CA

Williams v *Roffey Bros* [1990] 1 All ER 512, CA

Web activity

On the website of StepChange Debt Charity, click on 'Individual voluntary arrangement (IVA)' to find out more about how these work and their pros and cons:

www.stepchange.org/

Assignment 4

(a) Is it true to say that the doctrine of privity of contract is redundant since the Contracts (Rights of Third Parties) Act 1999?

(b) Arthur rents a house to his friend Brian for £400 a month in January. In May, hearing that Brian is in financial difficulty, Arthur offers to reduce the rent to £250 'until things pick up for you again'. In October, Cathy, Brian's wife, is left £20,000 by her uncle. In December, Arthur finds out about this windfall and asks for full rent from October onwards. Advise Arthur.

The terms of the contract at common law

Learning objectives

On completion of this chapter, students should be able to:

★ appreciate the difference between express and implied terms;

★ distinguish between conditions, warranties and innominate terms;

★ explain the purpose of exclusion clauses and the common law rules governing them;

★ be aware of the role of the EU and Parliament in the composition of the contract.

Introduction

Express term:
a contractual term included in the contract by the parties.

Implied term:
a term which was not specified by the parties to the contract, but may be implied into it by statute or common law.

Condition:
a major contractual term crucial to its existence. If this term is broken (breached), the innocent party may refuse further performance and sue for breach.

From studying Chapter 5, it can be seen that a contract is only formed when a bundle of promises (clearly defined terms) is offered by one party and accepted by the other. The size of the bundle is determined by the nature and complexity of the contract. A contract to get a haircut is obviously a much simpler transaction than one to build a housing estate. However, both will include some explicitly stated **express terms**, like the cost of the haircut or the number of houses to be built. The parties will usually also be bound by some **implied terms** that they have not expressly agreed, but which by law are included in this type of contract. So, it is assumed that the hairdresser will cut hair with reasonable competence whether they have promised this or not.

Not all contract terms are necessarily of the same importance. Some terms (**conditions**) are crucial to the contract; others (**warranties**) are less important, and therefore different legal consequences flow from breach of them. In a construction contract the number of buildings is much more important than some aspects of the

7

Warranty:
a minor contractual term, breach of which entitles the innocent party to damages.

Innominate term:
a term capable of giving rise to a variety of breaches of different degrees of seriousness so the remedy will not be determined until the actual breach occurs and the consequences are known.

Exemption clause:
a contractual term which attempts to limit or exclude a party's contract/tort liability against another.

finish to those buildings like taps or door furniture. Sometimes the importance of a term is disputed; when the court has to decide into which category such a term fits, this is called an **innominate term**.

When making a contract either as a business or as a consumer, be aware of **exemption clauses (limitation or exclusion clauses)**, which may enable the provider of goods or services to reduce or avoid liability for a breach of contract. Some of these notices are clearly displayed in a hotel or restaurant, stating that the management will not be liable for theft of customers' property. These may be effective to prevent a person making a successful claim if their property is stolen.

This chapter is concerned with the common law approach to terms, but since the nineteenth century, statute has also assumed an increasingly important role in relation to some areas of contract law, like employment and the sale and supply of goods and services. (The role of statute is considered in Chapter 8.)

Express and implied terms

The terms of a contract fall into three categories: conditions, warranties and innominate terms (explained below). These terms may be expressed or implied. Express terms are specifically communicated by the parties. Other terms may be implied by statute, custom or the courts.

The sources of implied terms

Terms implied at common law

The court may be prepared to imply a term into commonly occurring contracts, such as employment (see Chapter 17) and landlord and tenant, to protect against exploitation of the more vulnerable party.

Liverpool City Council v *Irwin* (1977, AC and HL)

The lifts, rubbish chutes and lighting in the stairs in a block of flats owned by the council were frequently vandalised with resulting inconvenience to the tenants, who withheld rent as a protest. The tenancy agreement imposed duties on tenants, including paying rent, but did not oblige the council to maintain the general facilities in the building.

Held (by the House of Lords): since proper access to the building was not possible without maintenance of these facilities, a term should be implied in any tenancy agreement requiring the landlord to take reasonable care in maintaining such facilities. However, as there was no actual breach of duty here, the tenants were not entitled to withhold payment.

Business efficacy

Business efficacy: the obvious common sense but unspoken intention of the contracting parties.

The court is not generally sympathetic to parties who claim rights under a contract that were not expressly promised to them. However, the courts have implied terms perceived as representing the will of the parties assessed objectively. A term may be implied to give '**business efficacy**' to the contract and make full sense of it. The court will do this if the contract lacks a very obvious term. For example, if the supermarket was asked to deliver 'two pints of milk', it is unlikely that there would be a need to specify that the milk must be in a container rather than left in a puddle on the doorstep.

The Moorcock (1889, CA)

The claimant hired docking space at the defendant's landing stage and suffered losses when his ship was damaged when it grounded at low tide.

Held: The claimant was entitled to assume that the state of the river-bed adjacent to the landing stage was safe for his ship and this should be implied by the contract.

This strategy prevents a party from avoiding contractual liability on a technicality and gives effect to the obvious common sense but unspoken intention of the parties.

Judges have increasingly extended this purposive approach to interpretation of ambiguous express terms.

Pink Floyd Music v *Emi Records* (2010, CA)

Held: The Court of Appeal held by majority that a term prohibiting EMI from selling 'albums', in any form other than as delivered, included sale of their contents separately as downloads or ring tones. It made 'commercial common sense' (Neuberger LJ) to enable Pink Floyd to control the integrity of their albums as delivered and how their contents were marketed in digital form.

The Court of Appeal took a similar approach more recently in *Thorney Park Golf Ltd* v *Myers Catering Ltd*, taking into account the fact that when laypersons drafted the contract ambiguity might well arise.

Thorney Park Golf Ltd v *Myers Catering Ltd* (2015, CA)

Myers Catering had a franchise to supply catering services to a golf club for a fixed term of three years, subject to termination with notice. The club was sold on to Thorney Park. The new owners terminated that agreement and the parties made a new agreement. Clause 4 stated that 'In order for this contract to be reasonable for both parties to develop and invest in a viable business development plan an initial term of three years (with the fee reviewed annually) must be agreed.' The agreement also stated that it was terminable with four months' notice.

A year later Thorney Park sought to terminate the contract. Myers claimed that this was a breach of contract given that the contract was for a fixed term and could only be terminated with four months' notice at the end of three years. Thorney Park claimed that clause this meant that it could be terminated at any time with appropriate notice.

The Court of Appeal held unanimously that Myers' interpretation was preferable. The Court must determine the parties' intention by an objective assessment of the evidence taking into account that it had been drafted by laypeople and might lack precision. The reference in clause 4 to the issue of reasonableness and time needed for investment and development was important evidence. To allow early termination would be likely to defeat that requirement. It was also striking that this reasonableness provision was expressly drafted into the agreement with Thorney when the previous one had only provided for termination by either side with notice. The parties clearly intended a change from the previous terms.

However, the Supreme Court struck a warning note in *Arnold* v *Britton & others* [2015] UKSC 36 (see below) and held that provided the wording of the contract was clear, effect should be given to it and that the courts should be wary of trying the find different meanings to help a party whose bargain later turned out to be a bad one due to future changed circumstances. In *Marks & Spencer Plc* v *BNP Parabas Securities Trust Co. (Jersey) Ltd* [2015] UKSC 72, the Supreme Court stressed that commercial practice should not be ignored unless there was clear objective evidence that this must have been the parties' intention. A term should not be implied into a commercial contract merely because the court believed that the parties would have included it if it had been suggested to them. A term should only be applied in such contracts where it would lack commercial *or* practical coherence without it.

Worth thinking about?

Can you think of any other scenario when the court might imply a term to give business sense to a contract?

Suggested solutions can be found in Appendix 2.

Business sense: A more restrictive approach

Arnold v *Britton & others* [2015] UKSC 36

Owners of 99-year leases of chalets took action against the landlord of the chalet park. Their leases issued from 1977 included a service charge starting at £90 in the first year and then rising by 10 per cent annually to cover a 'proportionate part' of the cost of providing services, taking into account inflation. This compared unfavourably with the terms of the other chalet owners with leases granted before 1977 whose service charge was increased only every three years.

The owners argued that if the disputed clause were given its face value, a lessee taking on a lease in, say, 1980 would be paying a service charge of £550,000 by 2027. It made better business sense if the term were interpreted to mean that they must pay proportionately towards service, with the initial maximum figure of £90 rising by 10 per cent every year.

The Supreme Court held: the face value of the term in the leases from 1977 onward was clear and must be enforced as it stood. The increased service charge was payable.

1 When interpreting a term in a contract the court must take the objective meaning given to it by a reasonable person with all the necessary background facts prevailing **at the time** the contract was made.

2 The court must focus on the natural meaning of the words in the context of the document as a whole, taking into account the purpose of the document and commercial common sense.

3 The approach must remain objective, as if made through the eyes of a reasonable bystander; hypothetical evidence of the parties' intention is irrelevant.

4 Commercial common sense must not undercut the natural meaning of the words. The vaguer the words, the readier the court might be to redefine them but should not look for wording problems to help change the text.

5 The fact that a transaction was imprudent or later worked out badly for a party is not necessarily a reason to say that commercial common sense required it to be altered.

The natural meaning of the disputed term was clear and must be enforced as it stood: the basic sum to cover service charges would rise yearly by 10 per cent and there was no evidence of a cap. In the 1970s inflation was running at 10 per cent so this term would have seemed a good bargain at the time and be a gamble on inflation for the future. At that time many people thought inflation would continue to rise.

Trade custom and practice

In some trades it is customary for certain practices to prevail in performance of a contract, or for risks to be allocated between the parties in a particular way.

Hutton v *Warren* (1836)

The claimant was given notice to quit his agricultural tenancy. Local custom obliged him to continue planting crops during the notice period, although he was unable to harvest them before he left.

Held: The local custom gave the tenant a reciprocal right to recoup a reasonable sum to cover the subsequent expense. This right became an implied term of the contract, so the claimant could recover his losses.

A party is generally entitled specifically to exclude the effect of any implied term unless prevented by statute from doing so. (See exclusion of liability later in this chapter.)

Statute

Parliament may provide that terms be implied in certain types of contract. For example, the Sale of Goods Act 1979 (as amended by the Sale and Supply of Goods Act 1994) is one of the most important sources of implied terms for business to business agreements. It includes special safeguards for the buyer by implying certain terms concerning the standard and quality of goods in most sale contracts. The seller may be in breach if the goods do not meet these standards, regardless of whether the seller gave any undertakings expressly to the buyer. Greater protection for consumer buyers has been a feature of recent developments in this area, which is heavily influenced by EU legislation, e.g. the Consumer Rights Act 2015. (This legislation will be examined in Chapter 8.)

The relative importance of contractual terms

The terms of a contract are not necessarily equally important. Breach of contract, therefore, gives rise to different rights according to the importance of the breached term. Generally, terms can be classified as conditions or warranties. Whether terms are to be classified as conditions or warranties is determined by the parties' apparent intentions when they made the contract. An apparently trivial matter like a sea view from the hotel bedroom may be elevated to the status of a condition of the contract if its necessity is stressed before acceptance takes place.

Conditions

Conditions are the most important terms which form the main structure of the contract. For example, when booking hotel accommodation, the dates of the stay and the type of room (single/double) are some of the most crucial requirements. If particular details are crucial to one party, this must be pointed out to the other party before the formation of the contract is completed. When booking a double room, this may result in being given single or double beds unless a preference is stipulated.

Breach of a condition gives the injured party the right to treat itself as free of any further contractual duties and to claim compensation.

Warranties

Warranties are more minor terms; they are ancillary to the contract rather than crucial to it. For example, when booking hotel accommodation, the promise of tea- and coffee-making facilities will not be vital to the performance of the contract. Their absence does not stop a guest from getting most of the enjoyment they expected from the holiday.

Breach of a warranty does not entitle the injured party to refuse to perform their side of the contract. That party is entitled only to compensation for consequential loss, i.e. loss resulting from the breach.

The next two cases illustrate the distinctions between these two types of term.

Poussard v *Spiers & Pond* (1876)

An actress was employed for a season, but was delayed by illness from taking up her role until a week after the opening night.

Held: her employers were entitled to terminate the contract: her presence on the opening night was crucial to the contract.

Bettini v *Gye* (1876)

A singer, engaged for a season, failed to turn up for the first three of the six pre-scribed rehearsal days.

Held: given the length of the contract and because no performances were missed this amounted only to a minor breach; the employer was not entitled to repudiate.

Innominate terms

Not all terms are clearly and immediately identifiable as conditions or warranties. Some, described by the courts as 'innominate', are worded broadly to cover a variety of possible consequences of the breach, some more serious than others. The court then has to decide whether a particular breach is to be treated as one of condition or warranty.

Hong Kong Fir Shipping Co. Ltd v *Kawasaki Kisen Kaisha* (1962, CA)

Charterparty:
a contract to hire a fully crewed ship.

A contract stated that a ship would be 'in every way fitted for cargo service'. This term was capable of including many types of breach, from a large hole in the hull to a malfunctioning tap in a shower room. Due to the incompetent engine room crew and a malfunctioning engine, the ship broke down and 20 weeks' use of the ship was lost from a two-year **charterparty** (hire contract). The defendants who had hired the ship abandoned the contract and the claimant owners sued them for breach.

Held: the breach of the term relating to the ship's fitness was not sufficiently seri-ous to permit the defendants to terminate the contract. The importance of the term must be judged in relation to the actual damage resulting from it. The damage caused did not strike at the root of the contract (the ship was still available for more than 18 months of the hire period), and therefore no breach equivalent to a breach of condition had occurred.

Diplock LJ stated that the judge's task in cases of this kind was 'to look at the events which had occurred as a result of the breach at the time which the charterers purported to rescind the charterparty and to decide whether the occurrence deprived the charterers of substantially the whole benefit which it was the intention of the parties as expressed in the charterparty that the charterers should obtain' (from the performance of the contract).

Hong Kong Fir was a controversial decision since it was subsequently argued that the so-called 'damage test' would promote uncertainty, since parties to a contract would not be aware of the importance of a term until it was breached.

It was applied again in:

Cehave NV v Bremer Handelsgesellschaft (The Hansa Nord) (1975, CA)

A contract stated that a cargo of citrus pellets for animal feed would be shipped 'in good condition'. On arrival some of the cargo from one hold was damaged. The buyers rejected the whole cargo, then later purchased it at a lower price and used it for its original purpose.

Held: the term was innominate and since the damage did not destroy the main purpose of the contract the buyers had no right to reject the goods.

The *Cehave* decision was clearly a just one in the circumstances since the buyers still used the cargo for its original purpose and it would have been unjust to allow them to make a profit at the other party's expense from a trivial fault.

However, the Court of Appeal indicated clearly that the damage test was a last resort where no other clear indicator existed. It set out the following criteria to interpretation of the status of an innominate term:

1 The express intention of the parties is paramount: if the contract specifies that a particular breach will entitle a party to opt out of the contract that is conclusive.

2 The use of the words 'condition' and 'warranty' to describe a term is of evidential value only – it is not conclusive in itself.

3 If a party has a statutory right to terminate the contract if a term is breached, the term is a condition (for example, Sale of Goods Act implied conditions).

4 Consistently established commercial practice will determine the status of a term.

5 Finally, if none of the above provides assistance the damage test may be used. The innocent party may repudiate their obligations only if the damage resulting from the breach is so extensive that it substantially deprives them of the benefit of the contract.

The next three cases illustrate the operation of the second criteria:

Lombard North Central PLC v Butterworth (1987, CA)

A contract for the lease of a computer stated that prompt payment of instalments was of the essence of the contract and that failure to comply would entitle the hire company to terminate the agreement. The defendant paid the third, fourth, and fifth instalments late and the sixth became six weeks overdue. At this point the claimant repudiated the agreement and sued for damages for breach of contract.

Held: late payment in such circumstances would not normally be grounds for repudiation of the contract, but here the term had been elevated to the status of a condition, because the supplier had specifically made the time factor crucial. The supplier was entitled to repudiate even if payment was minimally late.

Mustill LJ stated:

> A stipulation that time is of the essence, in relation to a particular contractual term, denotes that timely performance is a condition of the contract. The consequence is that delay in performance is treated as going to the root of the contract, without regard to the magnitude of the risk.

Schuler AG v Wickman Machine Tool Sales (1974, HL)

Wickman was given sole selling rights for Schuler's products for four-and-a-half years. A term of the contract stated that it was 'a condition of the contract' that Wickman would send its representative weekly to solicit orders from the six largest UK manufacturers.

Held (by majority): this term was not a condition in the sense that a single breach, however trivial, would entitle the innocent party to terminate the contract.

The reasonableness or otherwise of treating a term as a condition was crucial to deciding whether the parties intended breach of the term to give rise to repudiation rights.

Lord Reid said: 'We are seeking to discover intention as disclosed by the contract as a whole. Use of the word "condition" is an indication – even a strong indication – of such an intention but is by no means conclusive.'

Valilas v Janusaj (2014, CA)

A dentist rented premises and agreed with his landlord that the monthly rental would be based on his NHS earnings calculated with reference to the specified number of treatments that he was required to carry out every year. Rent was to consist of half the sum paid to the dentist monthly in advance by the NHS. The NHS contract required the dentist to make proportionate refunds if he failed to carry out the annual minimum number. The landlord agreed to repay the dentist half of any such refund.

The contract worked well initially but later the relationship soured. The dentist found that he was unable to fulfil the statutory number of treatments. He did not believe that the landlord would perform his duty to make refunds if the contract ended and so told him that in future he would pay only half the agreed rental every month, but would be entirely responsible for paying any rebate to the NHS at the end of the year. The landlord claimed that this was a breach of contract and that he was entitled to repudiate it.

The Court of Appeal held (affirming the decision of the County Court): the landlord was not entitled to repudiate the contract for this breach because timely rental payment was not stipulated in the contract and therefore time was not of the essence. The payment obligation was not a condition but merely an innominate term which only gave the right to repudiate if breach went to the root of the contract and effectively deprived the landlord of the main benefit of the contract. Although the dentist was in breach the landlord was still in effect getting the same rent; therefore the landlord had no right to repudiate.

Customary business practice (criteria 4) determined the outcome of the next case.

The Mihalis Angelos (1970, CA)

The Court of Appeal held that an 'expected readiness to load' term in a charterparty was, as a matter of commercial practice, always to be treated as having the force of a condition, provided that the party in breach had given the undertaking untruthfully, or without reasonable grounds for believing that it could be fulfilled.

Criteria 5 [the damage test] was applied in the next case and as in *Cehave* enabled the seller to avoid an unjust disadvantage.

Reardon Smith Line v *Hansen-Tangen* (1976, HL)

At the point the buyer entered a shipbuilding contract there was a boom in trade. At the point when the ship was ready for delivery, however, a recession had occurred and the vessel was now surplus to his requirements. The vessel built fulfilled all its contractual specifications except that it was built at a different shipyard from that named in the contract and he claimed he was entitled to reject it because of this breach.

Held: the breach was of an innominate term; no damage resulted so there was no right to repudiate.

The court, when applying these criteria, seeks to do justice between the parties, as well as act in the public interest. Taking these considerations into account may help to make these cases easier to grasp. Charterparty rules form part of the law which underpins an important part of the national economy. It has been formed from the custom and usage of international traders with whom good business relationships are crucial. In *Mihalis Angelos*, Edmund-Davies LJ said: 'It would be regrettable to . . . disturb an established practice.' In both the *Cehave* and *Reardon Smith* cases, the damage test was employed to prevent the buyer from unfairly avoiding contractual responsibility on a technicality and obtaining an unjust financial advantage.

Exemption clauses: Limitation and exclusion of liability

Limitation clause: a contractual term which seeks to restrict the amount of damages payable to the innocent party in the event of a civil action or to restrict the time period in which a claim can be made.

Exclusion clause: seeks to prevent any legal liability for breach of contract or negligence.

Many contracts include a term by which one party seeks to limit financial claims against it in the event of loss or damage to the other party, or to exclude itself from legal liability altogether. For example, by a **limitation clause** a holiday firm's contract may restrict customers' claims, in the event of delay, postponement and cancellation of flights to specified sums for meals and overnight accommodation. A limitation clause may specify a time limit for making claims, so a travel insurance contract may state a 30-day period after which claims for lost luggage cannot be made. When paying to use a car park, it is usual for the contract to include an **exclusion clause** stating that the proprietors have no legal liability for damage to or theft of or from customers' vehicles.

Such limitation of or exclusion from liability may be a perfectly reasonable business practice, but is subject to control, both by the courts and statute, to prevent abuse. Without such regulation a business could avoid liability for flagrant negligence, or for gross and irresponsible breach of contract.

(Please note that to make reading and writing less cumbersome a reference to 'exemption clauses' in this text covers both exclusion and limitation clauses unless there is an indication to the contrary.)

Before any exemption clause can be effective it must satisfy two criteria at common law:

1 it must be incorporated with advance notice within the contract;

2 it must be clear and unambiguous.

Incorporation

In order for any term to be incorporated in the contract (form part of it), the party to be bound by it must have reasonable notice of it. Two factors are crucial to the issue of notice:

1 timing;

2 sufficiency of notice.

Timing of notice

Notice of exclusion of liability must be given to the other party prior to that party's acceptance.

Notice may consist of a written sign of some kind displayed at the place of business, or in a contractual document. Its content should be clearly evident to customers before they commit themselves to the contract.

Here are three case examples of ineffective notice:

Olley v *Marlborough Court Hotel* (1949, CA)

A notice in Mrs Olley's bedroom stated that the hotel proprietor would not be liable for theft of guests' property. Later jewellery and furs were stolen from her room.

Held: the contract between Mrs Olley and the hotel had been concluded at the reception desk when Mrs Olley booked in, before she read the notice, which consequently did not form part of the contract. The hotel was therefore not exempt from liability for the theft.

Thornton v *Shoe Lane Parking* (1971, CA)

A notice inside a car park stated that the proprietors would not be liable for injuries to customers. This was also printed on the ticket dispensed from the automatic barrier at the car park entrance.

Held: the exemption clause did not form part of the contract: by driving alongside the machine at the car park entrance from which the ticket was dispensed, the claimant had already communicated acceptance of the defendant's offer to supply parking space.

Chapelton v *Barry UDC* (1940, CA)

The claimant, who wished to hire a deckchair at the beach, took one from a pile beside which there was a notice. This stated that payment of the specified hire charge should be made to the attendant. When he paid, the claimant was given a ticket that stated that the council would not be liable for accidents arising from use of the chairs. Later the claimant was injured when the chair collapsed because it had been negligently maintained.

Held: the ticket was not a contractual document but merely a receipt, which the claimant did not receive until after he had accepted the offer by taking the chair from the pile.

Previous business to business dealings may evidence effective notice if the court is satisfied that these have occurred regularly on the same terms, over a reasonable length of time.

Kendall v *Lillico* (1968, HL)

The parties had contracted 100 times in the previous three years on consistent terms for delivery of goods including a sales note which contained an exemption clause. The next delivery was defective, but was not accompanied by the sales note and the buyer claimed that the seller was not protected by the exemption clause.

Held: the buyer had adequate notice, since the notification had been consistently supplied throughout the long course of previous dealings.

However, such an implication is unlikely to be made in a consumer contract.

Mccutcheon v *David Mcbrayne Ltd* (1964, HL)

The claimant had shipped his car on a number of occasions on the defendant's ferry. Sometimes he had been asked to sign a risk note with a clause exempting the ferry company from liability for damage to goods. On one occasion, when a note had not been supplied, the ferry sank due to the defendant's negligence and the claimant's car was lost.

Held: the exclusion clause did not protect the defendant; the claimant had not had notice of the exemption. The previous dealings between the parties had not been sufficiently consistent, as risk notes had not been supplied regularly.

Sufficiency of notice

Generally, a clause will not be binding unless the offeror has taken reasonable steps to draw it to the customer's attention.

The more onerous the term, the greater is the degree of notice required. Exclusion clauses contained in the body of a document should be printed in clear type, which may need to be underlined or otherwise highlighted.

The next case does not involve an exemption clause, but the principle is relevant to any contractual term.

Interfoto Picture Library Ltd v *Stiletto Productions* (1988, CA)

In a contract for hire of photographic transparencies there was a clause imposing a lateness penalty of £5 per transparency per day. It was contained in the delivery note which comprised the contract.

Held: this was not binding as the supplier had not done enough to draw the attention of the hirer to this onerous clause. A special cover note was needed, or at least bold type on the delivery note.

Signature implies receipt of notice

Customers have constructive notice of the contents of any contractual document which they sign; this means that they are deemed to have notice of its contents, whether they have read it or not. There is no obligation to alert the signer to the presence of an exclusion clause.

L'estrange v *Graucob* (1934)

The claimant signed a 'sales agreement' for a cigarette vending machine without bothering to read it but was held nonetheless to be bound by an exemption clause contained in it.

It is useless for customers to claim that they misunderstood the effect of the clause, unless the seller misrepresented the effect of the clause.

Curtis v *Chemical Cleaning & Dyeing Co.* (1951, CA)

The claimant took her wedding dress to be cleaned and was asked to sign a note exempting the cleaners from liability for damage to the dress. She queried this, but signed it when told not to worry as it was there only to protect the company if beads or sequins were damaged. The dress was returned to her badly stained. She sued for breach of contract and the defendant cited the exemption clause in its defence.

Held: the defendant was liable. The exemption clause was not effective as the dry cleaner had misrepresented the scope of the clause.

An exclusion clause is not effective if it is ambiguous

Contra proferentem rule: any ambiguity of a contract term is resolved against the party who would most benefit from it.

Where its wording is unclear, the court may apply the ***contra proferentem*** **rule** to restrict the effects of an exclusion clause. The clause is construed *contra* (against) *proferentem* (the party who offered it); the meaning least favourable to the offeror is therefore adopted.

Andrews v *Singer* (1934)

A contract expressly stated that new cars would be supplied. An exemption clause stated that the supplier would not be liable for breach of any condition or warranty implied by statute. When the cars were delivered one was secondhand.

Held: the buyer could reject the secondhand car: breach of an express term of the contract had occurred. The exemption clause referred only to implied terms.

Liability for fundamental breach

Fundamental breach: so serious a breach of a condition, that it completely defeats the entire object of the contract.

Where a breach of contract is so serious that it defeats the whole purpose of the contract (**fundamental breach**), the courts may still be prepared to allow an exclusion clause to protect the party in breach. The nature of the contract and the type of breach will be evidence of what the parties are deemed to have intended. For example, in a travel contract the provider promises to take the customer to a particular destination at a particular time; such contracts usually include a clause to limit or completely exclude the liability of the provider in the event of cancellation of services in bad weather. Failure to transport the customer on time is not the fault of the provider in such circumstances, though it may defeat the customer's purposes completely. Such exclusions are likely to be treated as effective. The customer is deemed to have intended to accept the risk.

Issues of insurance are also relevant, and an exclusion clause will protect a provider where the court believes that insurance responsibilities were intended to remain with the other party.

Photo Production Ltd v *Securicor Transport Ltd* (1980, HL)

While on duty at the claimant's premises, Securicor's employee intentionally started a fire. The contract stated that there would be no liability for such damage unless Securicor was negligent; the claimant did not allege negligence. It was clearly a fundamental breach: Securicor was the cause of the destruction of the property which it had promised to keep safe. The only issue was whether the exemption clause was effective.

Held: the clause protected Securicor from liability for fundamental breach; the parties had bargained on equal terms that periodical visits should be made by a patrolman for a modest charge (26p) per visit. It was reasonable to leave the risk for fire damage with the claimant, who would be the most appropriate party to insure against such damage.

The 'Real life' example below should provide further understanding of how the common law rules apply in an everyday situation.

Real life

Gwen goes shopping by car to the Buymore-Stuff shopping centre. A notice near the entrance to the underground car park states:

Parking: £2.70 per hour. Please pay at machines inside car park and display ticket on your vehicle windscreen. Buymore-Stuff will not be liable for death or injury to any person using these premises, nor for any damage to any vehicle or other property however caused.

After displaying her ticket, she shuts the car door with a loud bang, which triggers a fall of masonry from the badly maintained roof above. This damages the car and a piece of masonry crushes her foot.

If the notice is clearly displayed so that people can see it before they are committed to entering the car park, the exclusion clause forms part of Gwen's contract with Buymore. (See *Thornton* v *Shoe Lane Parking*, above.) However, Buymore may not be relieved of liability. If the roof fall is caused by Buymore's negligence in failing adequately to maintain its premises, then, applying the *contra proferentem* rule, a court would be likely to hold that since the wording of the clause does not precisely specify exclusion from negligence liability, this is not covered. So Gwen should get compensation for harm to herself and the car.

The outcome would be the same if Gwen brought her claim under the Consumer Rights Act 2015. (See Chapter 8.)

To be effective any exclusion clause must also comply with the Unfair Contract Terms Act 1977 or the Consumer Rights Act 2015 (both of which are fully covered in Chapter 8). This means that a party may be able to defeat an exclusion clause using both common law and statutory provisions. In this case there can be no exclusion of liability for death or personal injury caused by negligence.

Chapter summary

A contract is composed of promises called 'terms'. These may be express or implied.

Classification of contract terms

Conditions.

Warranties.

Innominate terms.

Exemption clauses

Use is controlled by the common law and statute.

Common law controls of exemption clauses

Incorporation of the terms requires timely and sufficient notice unless a party signs the contract.

The *contra proferentem* rule protects a vulnerable party from being disadvantaged by ambiguous language.

Review questions 6

1 Distinguish between conditions and warranties.

2 What is an innominate term?

3 How do the courts determine the status of an innominate term?

4 What is the difference between a limitation clause and an exclusion clause?

5 Are exclusion clauses incorporated in a contract when notified in the following ways:

(a) in a notice on the counter of a shop?

(b) in a signed document?

(c) in a hotel bedroom?

(d) in a receipt?

6 What is the *contra proferentem* rule?

Answers to all review questions can be found in Appendix 2.

Advanced questions 6

(A) To what extent can it be said that the concept of the innominate term causes uncertainty for business?

(B) Consider the relevance of the traditional business efficacy and reasonable bystander test in the twenty-first century.

Answers to the advanced questions can be found at **go.pearson.com/uk/he/resources.**

Take a closer look

The following cases provide important examples of how the law in this chapter has developed. They are primary sources illustrating the law in action and give more detail about their facts, as well as helping to understand the law and to appreciate how the judges reached their decisions.

Try looking them up in the law reports or accessing them via a database, e.g. Bailii (www.bailii.org/databases.html). LexisNexis or Westlaw may be available in the university or college library, or extracts may be found in a case book. (See Appendix 1: Additional resources.)

Interfoto Picture Library Ltd v *Stiletto Productions* [1988] 1 All ER 348, CA

Lombard North Central plc v *Butterworth* [1987] QB 527, CA

Valilas v *Janusaj* [2014] EWCA Civ 436

Arnold v *Britton & others* [2015] UKSC 36

Further reading

McCaughran J. (2011) Implied Terms: The journey of the man on the Clapham Omnibus. *Cambridge law Journal*. 70(3), pp. 607–622.

Assignment 5

Widgets plc entered into a three-year contract with Crankit plc under which Crankit agreed to service Widgets' production line machinery. Widgets signed a document headed 'Service Agreement' consisting of 150 terms, including the following:

10. It shall be a condition of the contract that Crankit will attend in response to any call-out request by Widgets within 24 hours.

36. Crankit will not be responsible to Widgets for any defect in quality of any spare parts supplied by Crankit when servicing customers' machinery.

142. Crankit reserves the right to terminate the contract immediately if Widget delays in paying or fails to pay the agreed monthly retainer fee or any part thereof on the agreed date.

Advise the parties how these terms will affect the outcome of a claim in the following circumstances:

(a) When carrying out the first annual service, Crankit fits a new fuel pump. This malfunctions 48 hours later, causing an explosion which completely destroys the factory.

(b) Twenty months into the contract, Crankit is called upon by Widgets, which reports that a major mechanical failure has brought its production line to a halt. Crankit replies that due to a lack of staff, it will be unable to attend for three days. Next day, Widgets tells Crankit that it is opting out of the contract as immediate servicing is obtainable from Best and Sons Ltd.

(c) Twelve months into the contract, Widgets changes its banking arrangements and due to a mistake in the transfer arrangements the new bank only pays Crankit half its monthly retainer on the next due date. Crankit immediately cancels the contract.

Statutory terms in contracts for sale of goods and services

Learning objectives

On completion of this chapter, students should be able to:

★ distinguish between different types of sales contracts and the legislation governing them;

★ appreciate the difference between a business and a consumer buyer;

★ understand how the provisions of the SGA 1979 and related statutes protect the trade buyer;

★ get an overview of consumer buyer protection before 2015;

★ explain the rights of the consumer in contracts regulated by the CRA 2015.

Introduction

How many contracts to buy goods have been made in the last week? Huge numbers of contracts involve such sales; they are essential to healthy national and international trade.

This chapter is concerned with elements of the role of statutory legislation in the regulation of contracts for the sale of goods and related business transactions. The first Sale of Goods Act in 1893 was primarily concerned with the needs of commercial buyers and sellers; the *caveat emptor* principle (buyer beware) was highly influential, so the parties were treated very much on equal bargaining terms and free to negotiate. In the latter half of the twentieth century Parliament acknowledged that many buyers did not enjoy unlimited freedom to bargain. With the end of post-war austerity there was a much greater range of goods available in the domestic and leisure markets and the consumer (customer buying for personal use) was particularly vulnerable to exploitation especially with regard to quality and safety issues.

As a result the Sale of Goods Act 1979 (SGA 1979) (later amended by the Sale and Supply of Goods Act 1994) ensured that certain terms must be implied in sales contracts to extend protection for buyers. It also enhanced the buyer's rights to reject defective goods.

The Unfair Contract Terms Act 1977 (UCTA 1977) introduced the first statutory regulation of exclusion clauses for all buyers. Greater protection followed for consumers in the Unfair Terms in Consumer Contract Regulations 1999 (UTCCR 1999). By 2013 consumer contracts were regulated by a rather confusing web of different statutes and various sets of regulations reflecting EU impact.

In consequence The Consumer Rights Act 2015 (CRA 2015) was passed. It aims to simplify and enhance legal protection for consumers by consolidation and enhancement of the existing legislation.

Part 1 of this chapter is concerned with sales contracts between businesses. It will examine statutorily implied terms and the buyer's right to reject under the SGA 1979 (as amended) and related legislation. The statutory regulation of exclusion clauses in UCTA 1977 contracts between businesses involving goods concludes this section of the chapter.

Part 2 focuses on similar issues in sales contracts between a consumer buyer and a business seller which are governed by the CRA 2015.

Part 1: Commercial sales contracts

Commercial sales refer to those contracts made between parties who run businesses as opposed to those made by a business seller with someone buying for their own domestic use. Businesses enjoy less protection and choices if the contract runs into difficulties since the law perceives them as trading with each other on more equal terms than in consumer contracts.

Sales of goods between a non-business seller (a private seller) and a consumer buyer remain regulated by the SGA 1979 and are not within the scope of the CRA 2015.

A number of different types of selling are potentially involved in commercial sales contracts and are governed by different statutes. For example a clothing manufacturer will make contracts with other businesses to buy materials and sell on the finished stock (SGA 1979). It will need to make a contract for goods and services if it is buying new machinery from a company which is also installing it on site (Supply of Goods & Services Act 1982 [SGSA 1982]). This Act will also apply in the case of a construction company needing to hire heavy plant like cranes. Businesses sometimes buy goods on hire purchase, in which case the Supply of Goods Implied Terms Act 1973 (SGIT 1973) will apply to the goods aspect of the contract. In these statutes certain terms are implied in the relevant contracts which give a good degree of protection to the buyer. They also govern the right of the buyer to repudiate the contract. The SGA 1979 is the key statute with related legislation largely mirroring its terms concerning buyer rights. The key elements of this legislation are explored below.

The terms implied by the Sale of Goods Act 1979

A sale of goods contract is defined as 'a contract by which the seller transfers or agrees to transfer the property in goods to the buyer for a money consideration called the price' (s 2(1)).

Under ss 12–15 of the SGA 1979, a seller automatically assumes certain obligations to the buyer as a result of what are stated to be 'conditions' which are automatically implied in every such contract. The buyer may therefore assume that:

1 the seller has lawful authority to transfer ownership of the goods (s 12);

2 the goods will match their description (s 13);

3 the goods will be of satisfactory quality (s 14(2));

4 the goods will be suitable for any purpose specified by the buyer (s 14(3));

5 the goods will match any sample shown to the buyer prior to the contract being made (s 15).

These terms apply to all sales of new or secondhand goods, apart from terms 3 and 4 which apply only to sellers who are acting in the course of a business.

Breach by the seller of any of these terms puts the buyer in a strong position because:

1 *These terms all impose strict liability on the seller.* The seller is liable for breach of contract without the buyer having to prove that the seller is at fault. Indeed, it is irrelevant for the seller to prove that it is blameless and that it was not aware of the alleged defect in the goods. The seller will still be liable.

2 *All of these terms are defined by the Act as being conditions of the contract.* Breach of a condition enables victims to refuse further performance of their contractual obligations and enables them to recover any money or other property which they have tendered. (See Chapter 7.)

These implied terms are now examined in more detail.

Title: s 12

In a contract of sale, the seller implicitly promises that he or she has the right to sell the goods (to transfer **title** in them to the buyer) or, in an agreement to sell, the seller implicitly promises that he or she will have such a right at the time when the property is to pass. The seller can fulfil this promise only if he or she has ownership (title) himself or herself, or is acting with the real owner's permission, at the time of transfer.

Rowland v *Divall* (1923, CA)

The defendant had bought in good faith a car which had in fact been stolen. The thief could not pass good title, and neither could the defendant when he sold the car on to the claimant. After the claimant had used it for four months, the real owner turned up and took the car back.

Held: the claimant was entitled to recover the full purchase price from the defendant. No discount was allowed against his four months' use, as he had never received what he had contracted to buy – full ownership of the car.

Description: s 13

Almost all goods are sold by description, and the seller is in breach of contract if this is inaccurate.

The form of the description

The description may be given by word of mouth ('these boots are waterproof'), or by a written notice put in place by the seller ('silk shirts'). The seller is also responsible for any descriptions which the seller personally did not attach to the goods but which came from a manufacturer or other source: for example, labels attached to the goods or wording on the packaging ('produce of Spain', 'machine washable').

In a self-service situation, where the goods are picked out by the customers, the customers rely on the label on the tin to tell them whether they are buying baked beans or sweet corn. Some selling situations (like catalogue or mail order sales) are entirely reliant on descriptions of goods which the buyer will not see before making the contract.

Sales by sample and description

Where the sale is by sample as well as by description, the seller will be in breach of s 13 even though the goods match the sample, if they do not match the description. Many selling situations involve sample and description. For example it is possible to examine a carpet sample, but gain knowledge of its composition only from an accompanying notice. If this information is incorrect, a breach of contract exists even though in all other respects the carpet meets the statutory requirements.

The relationship of description to quality

The seller's obligations concerning quality and description may overlap. Stating the age of a car can be said to involve a description and also a reference to its quality; the two factors are inextricably interlinked. This may be advantageous to the buyer, as s 13 obliges all sellers to be accurate in their descriptions, whether or not they are selling by way of business.

Description may be a completely separate issue from quality. Goods can be rejected on the ground of incorrect description even though they are not defective in any other way.

Arcos v *Ronaasen* (1933)

An order was placed to buy wooden staves, described by the seller as 'half an inch thick'. When delivered, the width of the staves varied from between half an inch to nine-sixteenths of an inch.

Held: the goods could be rejected as they did not match their description.

Liability depends upon reliance

If the buyer did not know of the description or did not rely upon it (having checked it with a third party), the sale is not by description. Examination of the goods does not automatically preclude reliance by the customer. The average customer does not have sufficient knowledge to spot that the description is inaccurate. In *Beale* v *Taylor* the fact that the buyer had examined the car prior to purchase did not prevent his being held to have relied on the seller's description of it. However, if a buyer with expert knowledge buys from a non-expert seller, that buyer is not likely to be held to have relied on the seller's description. The customs of the trade may be relevant here. Note the comment of Nourse LJ in *Harlingdon & Leinster Enterprises* below.

Harlingdon & Leinster Enterprises v *Christopher Hull Fine Arts* (1990, CA)

An art dealer who, to the buyer's knowledge, was not an expert on German impressionist painting, offered to sell two paintings which he claimed were by a famous German impressionist. After inspecting the pictures, the seller bought them. The description later turned out to be incorrect.

Held: the buyer had relied on his own skill and judgement when deciding to buy, so sale was not by description.

Nourse LJ commented:

> Many dealers [in the art market] habitually deal with each other on the principle *caveat emptor*. For my part, being confident that that principle would receive general acceptance amongst dealers, I would say that the astuteness of lawyers ought to be directed towards facilitating, rather than impeding, the efficient working of the market. The court ought to be exceedingly wary in giving a seller's attribution any contractual effect.

The goods must be of satisfactory quality: s 14(2)

Satisfactory quality: meets the reasonable expectation of a person buying the particular goods.

Where goods are sold in the course of business, there is an implied condition that the goods are of **satisfactory quality**.

The meaning of 'satisfactory quality'

The goods must meet the standard which a reasonable person would regard as satisfactory, taking into account all 'relevant circumstances', including price and any description attached to the goods (s 14(2A)). The court objectively assesses the quality of the goods with reference to the expectations of the average buyer. Section 14(2B) gives examples of some factors which might be 'relevant circumstances':

- whether the goods are fit for the purposes for which such goods are normally used;
- appearance and finish;
- freedom from defects;
- safety and durability.

Trac Time Control Ltd v Moss Plastic Parts Ltd and Others (2005)

The defendant supplied what he described as high-quality polycarbonate mouldings to the claimant light manufacturer. Floodlights with housings made using the materials were returned to the claimant by dissatisfied customers who claimed that the housings had broken because they were brittle. The claimant sued the defendant for breach of contract.

Held: the defendant was liable as the goods did not match their description under SGA 1979, s 13 and neither were they of satisfactory quality under s 14(2) nor fit for their purpose under s 14(3).

How liability arises under s 14(2)

Goods which are physically dangerous, or which do not work at all, are clearly not of satisfactory quality, whether they are expensive or cheap, reduced in a sale, new or secondhand. A buyer of secondhand goods may, however, be expected to put up with some defects in finish or performance. Even with new goods, the buyer is entitled only to get what they pay for. The finish and durability of a cheap item will not be the same as that to be expected at the luxury end of the market.

The buyer merely has to prove that the defect exists, not how it happened nor that the seller was in any way at fault. Section 14(2) protects the buyer against inherent defects of quality; therefore no proof of reliance on the seller's judgement is required. If the seller is found liable, he or she can recover his or her losses from the party who supplied the goods.

Liability may arise from goods that are of satisfactory quality in themselves but are contaminated by foreign bodies, since these impurities prevent normal use. In *Chaproniere* v *Mason* (1905), a bun made of otherwise normal ingredients contained a stone and was held not to be of appropriate quality.

Wilson v Rickett Cockerell Ltd (1954)

A delivery of coal included fragments of detonators left from the mining process. This resulted in an explosion when the coal was burnt, which caused serious structural damage to the buyer's premises.

Held: the coal was not of satisfactory quality, being inseparably contaminated with the explosives.

The goods include their *packaging* and *instructions*. Defects in these may render the goods defective or dangerous. Liability may arise even if the packaging remains the property of the seller. Therefore, in *Geddling* v *Marsh* (1920), the seller of carbonated mineral water was liable for failing to supply goods of satisfactory quality when the returnable bottle, in which the water was supplied, exploded and injured the buyer.

The limits to liability under s 14(2)

Section 14 applies only where the sale arises *in the course of business*, not where sale is by a private seller.

The seller is not liable if *the buyer knows about the defects* (s 14(2C)). Such pre-sale notice may be acquired in two ways:

1 *Notice of the defects may be given by the seller*. Such notice must explicitly describe the defects. For example, a notice might be displayed on a washing machine saying 'instruction manual missing' or 'dents in casing at rear'. The notice

only covers those defects. If the motor turned out to be faulty, the seller would be liable for breach of s 14 even if the fault were traced to the accident that caused the dents.

2 *Inspection by the buyer.* Buyers are not generally under any obligation to inspect the goods, but if they do, they cannot claim that the seller is liable for any defects that should have been reasonably evident, given the level of inspection to which they subjected the goods. Thus, a superficial inspection can reveal only superficial defects, but latent defects will not generally be revealed even by thorough inspection. The buyer's level of skill and expertise is relevant: a lay car buyer looking at a car engine would not be expected to spot the clues that would alert a professional dealer.

If the buyer *fails to follow the instructions supplied* with the goods, the seller is not liable for any resulting damage. The seller will also not be liable for damage caused by the buyer's *mistreatment* of the goods.

Aswan Engineering Establishment Co. Ltd v *Lupdine Ltd* (1987, CA)

The sellers supplied waterproofing material in plastic pails. These collapsed spilling their contents, having been stacked by the buyer in piles six pails high in bright sunshine and temperatures up to 150° F for several days.

Held: the sellers were not in breach of their duty. The packaging was appropriate for normal storage practices.

The buyer is expected to take any precautions that would normally be employed when using the relevant type of goods. Therefore damage arising from failing to follow good industrial practice or even plain common sense is unlikely to give rise to seller liability.

The goods must be suitable for their purpose: s 14(3)

Where goods are sold in the course of business, they must be reasonably suitable for any purpose for which such goods are normally sold. They must also fulfil any special purpose that the seller claims for them, provided that the buyer reasonably placed reliance on the seller's skill.

The buyer will only succeed with a claim if it can be shown that the buyer placed reliance on the seller. Such reliance may be implicit or explicit.

Implicit reliance

Such reliance occurs where the buyer neither knowledgeably inspects the goods to check their suitability, nor asks any questions about them. The condition will be breached if the goods turn out to be unsuitable for the usual purposes of such goods, or for any particular uses specified by the buyer. A supermarket buying food designed for humans can assume that it is suitable for human consumption. Similarly a shampoo, labelled 'suitable for use on small children', should be safe for them. If the buyer does not specify particular needs, the seller is not liable if the particular needs of the buyer exceed what is normally required.

Explicit reliance

The buyer may question the seller about what the goods may be used for, or ask the seller to recommend the goods which will best suit the buyer's purposes. If a customer visits a sports shop and asks to buy a watch suitable for use when diving, what is sold should not leak or respond unfavourably to changes in water pressure.

Real life

Hamish runs a shop called Happy Camper Supplies. He recently bought some stock from a wholesaler including anoraks all labelled 'waterproof'. He also bought some tents which the wholesaler describes as 'simple to erect' and 'ideal for the first time camper'. Hamish decides to use one as part of his own sales display but after half an hour of bitter struggle eventually gives up the attempt. He then discovers that a crucial piece of information is missing from the instruction leaflet.

Two days later a customer brings back one of the anoraks complaining that after one outing a seam has split letting in water and demanding her money back.

The wholesaler is in breach of the SGA 1979, s 13 as clearly neither the anorak nor the tent live up to their description. They also do not fulfil s 14 since the anorak ripped after minimal use, indicating that it is clearly neither of satisfactory quality nor fit for its purpose and the misleading instructions for the tent mean that it does not meet the reasonable expectations of the novice camper.

The goods must correspond with their sample: s 15

Many types of goods are sold by sample, including carpets, wallpaper, perfume and some types of make-up and toiletries. It is an implied condition in a contract for sale by sample that:

1 *The bulk will correspond with the sample in quality.* The buyer will have to show that any defect complained of in the bulk of the goods was not present in the sample.

2 *The goods will be free from any defect rendering them unsatisfactory which would not be apparent on reasonable examination of the sample.* Therefore, buyers cannot reject the goods for defects that they should have spotted in the sample, but can reject if other defects are present.

Godley v *Perry* (1960)

A shopkeeper was able to show that he had tested a sample catapult for strength by pulling back the elastic.

Held: this was sufficient to check that the sample was not defective.

Generally, a sale by sample will also be a sale by description, so these requirements need to be studied in conjunction with those concerning s 13 (above).

The right to reject the goods: s 35

Breach of any of the above terms is a breach of condition, which means that buyers are entitled to reject the goods wholly or partially and recover the price from the seller, unless the defect is a trivial one. Buyers have a limited time to exercise this right. If they delay too long, they will be deemed to have accepted the goods regardless of defects. In that situation they will be entitled to be compensated for the defects, but cannot reject the goods. Once acceptance has taken place, the breach becomes one of warranty rather than of condition.

The courts have often held that acceptance has resulted from the buyer using the goods for anything more than a very short time and/or retaining and continuing to use the goods after having complained about them, or agreeing to them being repaired.

The issue of repair is often contentious. It may cause inconvenience to the buyer, who is temporarily deprived of the use of the goods: sometimes a whole saga of delay and incompetence starts to unfold. At this point the buyer may find out that he or she need not have agreed to the repair in the first place and seeks to reject the goods. To safeguard the buyer in such situations a 1994 amendment to the SGA 1979 states that a buyer is not to be assumed to have accepted the goods merely by agreeing to their being repaired (s 35(6)). This may increase the opportunities for a buyer to reject the goods.

The House of Lords held in *J & H Ritchie Ltd* v *Lloyd Ltd* (2007) (below) that when goods are returned to a buyer for inspection with a view to repair, this constitutes a separate agreement from the contract of sale itself. It puts the seller under an implied duty to inform the buyer of the nature of the defect so that the seller can then decide whether or not to repudiate the sale of goods contract. Special rights to request a repair in consumer sales are found in the Consumer Rights Act 2015.

J & H Ritchie Ltd v *Lloyd Ltd* (2007, HL)

The claimant farming contractor bought a seed drill and harrow from the defendant. As soon as it was used, the claimant noticed that it vibrated very loudly, and he operated it only for a short time before reporting the matter to the defendant. The defendant agreed to remove the equipment for inspection, with a view to possibly repairing it. In due course, it was returned, having been repaired to what the defendant described as 'factory gate specification' but without any explanation about what had caused the defect. When pressed, the defendant refused to explain what the problem had been, but the claimant found out informally, from a mechanic, that bearings had been missing. The claimant then rejected the goods because of concerns that this fault might have caused damage to other parts of the equipment and compromised the manufacturer's guarantee.

Held: the claimant was entitled to reject the goods. It was implied in the agreement to repair that the defendant would inform the claimant about the cause of the problem and that the claimant would retain his right to reject until he had the necessary information to make a '*properly informed choice*' (Lord Hope) as to whether he wanted to keep the goods or not.

Lord Brown commented:

> Even though the harrow after repair was . . . in as good as new condition, the seller's failure to follow the procedure implicitly agreed justified the buyer in refusing to accept the goods sold. The buyer was still prepared to accept the goods, if the seller at its expense obtained a clean engineer's report, but the seller refused to do this either. The buyer was in this situation justified on 26 May 1999 in rejecting the goods.

Other key statutes which regulate contracts involving goods

Not all contracts involving goods come within the SGA 1979. The following types of contract all involve goods but are regulated by other statutes giving similar protection to buyers.

The Supply of Goods and Services Act 1982 (SGSA 1982)

This relates to the following transactions:

(a) goods and services contracts;

(b) services contracts;

(c) hire contracts;

(d) barter contracts.

Goods and services contract: the sale of the goods is incidental but necessary to the performance of a service.

Goods and services contracts

In a **goods and services contract** the sale of goods is incidental to the provision of a service, for example having double-glazing installed, or getting new brake pads fitted to a car. Such contracts are regulated by the Supply of Goods and Services Act 1982. Contracts to hire goods also come within this statute.

This is clearly illustrated by *Wood* v *Tui Travel Plc* (below).

In the news

Wood v *Tui Travel Plc* [2017] EWCA Civ 11

Mr and Mrs Wood booked an all-inclusive holiday to the Dominican Republic with Tui Travel Plc. During their stay the hotel served them contaminated food which made them very ill, al-though the hotel was not actually at fault. The Woods claimed that Tui Travel had failed to supply goods of satisfactory quality.

Tui Travel argued that its contract was to supply services such as hotel accommodation, and did not involve any actual sale of goods and therefore did not include any term relating to the quality of food supplied by the hotel. The Woods did not buy the food, their contract merely gave them a licence to help themselves to food from the hotel buffet.

The Court of Appeal held: Tui Travel was liable as the contract involved supply of goods, ownership of those goods passing to the Woods whenever they acquired food and drink from the hotel.

Note that these days the Woods could claim under the CRA 2015 which was not in force when their claim was first initiated. The result would be the same.

The following terms, which are designated as *conditions* under SGSA, are implied in any contract of goods and services:

- title;
- description;
- satisfactory quality and suitability for purpose;
- sample.

The buyer has the same rights to reject the goods where a breach of the above terms occurs as a buyer in a sale of goods contract.

Baxter v *Barnes* (2015)

The claimant was a tree surgeon who hired a mobile elevated platform for use while pruning a tree from the defendant. As the ground was soft the defendant supplied plastic bearing plates for the platform to prevent them sinking into the uneven sloping ground where the claimant was working. The claimant was seriously injured when he fell from the platform which toppled sideways when one of its feet slipped off the plate.

> **Held:** the claimant's injuries were a result of the goods not being of satisfactory quality in breach of the Supply of Goods and Services Act 1982. There was nothing wrong with the platform as such but the bearing plates were unsuitable for their purpose.

The following terms are also implied in all contracts involving a supply of services, whether or not goods are involved:

- the work will be performed with all reasonable care and skill;
- the work will be carried out within a reasonable time;
- the price charged will be reasonable.

Under SGSA 1982 these are *terms* only: they are not designated as conditions or warranties. Their status depends on what, if anything, was agreed in the contract. Sometimes the amount of damage caused by the breach will be used as evidence of their importance. They are a good example of *innominate terms*. (See Chapter 7.)

Supply of services

The seller's obligations are limited to the implied terms concerning service which also apply to contracts for supply of goods and services outlined above.

In *Trebor Bassett Holidays and Cadbury UK Partnership* v *ADT Fire & Security* (2012) the Court of Appeal held that a contract for *design and supply of a fire suppressant system* was not a contract for sale of goods and services but merely one for the supply of services and so did not contain an implied term regarding satisfactory quality.

Hire contracts

Hire contract: entitles the hirer to possession of the goods for the hire period but not title.

In a **hire contract**, the hirer is entitled to the same rights concerning description, sample quality and suitability for purpose as a buyer and possession, but not title to the goods, for the hire period.

Contracts to barter

Bartering: exchanging goods or services for other goods and services.

In a **bartering** situation the parties exchange goods or services; even if goods are involved, it is not a sale of goods contract as no money changes hands. A part-exchange contract is generally treated as a sale of goods contract under which the buyer is given the option to tender goods in part satisfaction of the contract price.

A 'free' gift linked to a sale contract

Such transactions are probably regulated by the Supply of Goods and Services Act 1982 since this covers contracts not regulated elsewhere under which title to goods will pass.

Worth thinking about?

It is a common sales tactic to offer the customer something 'free' as in 'buy one get one free' promotions. What is the contractual position if the shop tries to charge you for both?

Suggested solutions can be found in Appendix 2.

The Supply of Goods (Implied Terms) Act 1973

Hire-purchase contracts

The goods aspect of such contracts is regulated by ss 8–11 which state the same implied terms concerning title, description, quality and fitness for purpose and sample as in a sale of goods contract. Under a **hire-purchase contract**, the person supplied with the goods is, in the eyes of the law, the hirer not the buyer. The contract initially gives the hirer possession of the goods only. The hirer may choose to buy the goods when all the instalments have been paid. If they do so they then become the owner.

Hire-purchase contract: the hirer gains immediate possession of goods with the option to take ownership when all price instalments are paid.

Unfair Contract Terms Act 1977

The scope of the Act

The Unfair Contract Terms Act 1977 (UCTA 1977) applies almost exclusively to contracts giving rise to *business liability* (s 1(3)). Thus, it is primarily concerned with sellers or suppliers who seek to limit or exclude liability incurred in the course of business. Private sellers or suppliers are generally not restricted in the use of exclusion clauses (see s 6, below).

Certain types of contract are *expressly excluded*: for example, contracts of insurance and contracts for the sale or lease of land.

Although the title of the Act refers to 'contract terms', the Act also regulates non-contractual notices which attempt to restrict liability for negligence. For example, a notice, outside premises, stating that people enter at their own risk may be ineffective because of UCTA 1977.

The substance of the Act

Negligence liability (s 2)

Under s 2(1), liability cannot be excluded if death or personal injury is caused by negligence. Damage to property through negligence is addressed by s 2(2). Under that provision, negligence liability may be excluded if this is *reasonable* in the circumstances. Note that under s 7(2) of the Contracts (Rights of Third Parties) Act 1999 (see Chapter 6) the reasonableness defence is not effective against a claim by a third party beneficiary.

Breach of contract (s 3)

Liability for breach of contract may not be excluded where a party enters into a contract made on the other party's **standard terms** (when no negotiation will have been possible), or where the party deals as a consumer, unless the exclusion is *reasonable*. UCTA 1977 gives guidance on how the term 'reasonable' is to be interpreted and this is explained later in the chapter.

Breach of implied terms in contracts for sale/hire purchase/supply/hire of goods (ss 6–7)

A commercial seller is restricted in imposing exclusion of the conditions relating to title, description, suitability and sample implied under the Sale of Goods Act 1979 and related legislation. **Consumers** enjoyed special protection in a contract with a business seller and none of these conditions could be effectively excluded against them. The rights of a consumer are now governed by the Consumer Rights Act 2015.

A commercial buyer has never enjoyed such comprehensive protection. The condition regarding title (under ss 6–7) can never be excluded; the others may be excluded if the clause is 'reasonable' in any contract with a non-consumer buyer.

Note that a *private seller* is free to exclude liability for breach of any of the relevant terms above in a sale of goods or hire-purchase contract (s 6(4)). This only covers the terms regarding title, description and sample, since the term regarding satisfactory quality is implied only in contracts where the seller/supplier is a business.

What is 'reasonable' for the purposes of UCTA 1977?

Section 11 of UCTA 1977 provides guidance as to what is 'reasonable' for the purposes of the Act:

1 a contract term will satisfy the requirement of reasonableness if it is fair and reasonable with regard to all the circumstances which should have been considered by the parties when they entered the contract (s 11(1));

2 if the claim relates to a non-contractual notice, reasonableness is judged with reference to all the circumstances prevailing when the damage was caused (s 11(3)).

Schedule 2 to the Act offers further guidelines:

1 *Imbalance of bargaining power.* The parties to a contract may not enjoy equal bargaining power. In a standard terms contract, one party is presented with a set of terms and given no opportunity to negotiate existing terms or add others. The buyer of goods or services may be heavily reliant on the technical knowledge and expertise of the seller, and that ignorance produces power imbalance.

2 *Inducements and choices.* If a customer is given an unfair inducement to accept the exclusion clause, this may make it unreasonable. If that party could have made a similar contract with another party without being subject to such a term, this

may make the exemption reasonable. Similarly if a customer is offered, for example, a price reduction in order to accept the exclusion clause, the clause may be reasonable.

3 *Prior knowledge.* If the customer should reasonably have been aware of the existence and extent of the term, taking into account previous dealings between the parties and trade custom, it may be reasonable to impose the exclusion.

4 *Special requirements.* If the goods were made or adapted to meet the customer's special requirements, an exemption may be binding.

The courts have also taken other factors into account, including the issue of insurance and whether the customer should have taken independent advice.

The following cases illustrate the approach of the courts to the interpretation of reasonableness.

Green v *Cade Bros* (1978)

A standard form contract, which complied with the requirements of the National Association of Seed Potato Merchants, restricted the right of rejection of seed potatoes to three days from delivery; any compensation was limited to the return of the contract price. The stock supplied to the buyer was infected by a virus which was not detectable until the growing process had started.

Held: the three-day time limit was not reasonable given the type of damage suffered. The limit on compensation was reasonable: it was usual in the trade, the parties enjoyed equal bargaining power, and the buyer had received no inducement to accept the limitation. The buyer could have bought guaranteed seed potatoes for a higher price.

George Mitchell v *Finney Lock Seeds Ltd* (1983, HL)

The claimant ordered cabbage seed from the defendant which did not match its description. It was also inferior in quality. The claimant lost his entire crop, sustaining a £61,000 loss. The contract limited liability for breach to replacement of the goods or a refund of the price.

Held: this was not reasonable because:

1 the breach arose from the seller's negligence;
2 the seller could have insured against crop failure at a modest cost;
3 in the past the seller had settled claims in excess of the limitation sum – this indicated that the seller did not always consider the clause fair and reasonable.

St Albans City & District Council v International Computers Ltd (1996, CA)

Computer software, supplied and installed by the defendant company to provide a database facility for the local authority, was defective. It caused errors in the estimation of the number of eligible poll-tax payers, and as a result the local authority lost substantial funds. A limitation clause in the contract restricted the defendant's liability to £100,000.

Held: the limitation clause was unreasonable because:

1 the defendant was a multinational company with substantial resources;

2 the defendant carried product liability insurance of £50 million and the limitation of liability was too small relative to the possible risk and the loss actually suffered;

3 the claimant's specialist needs greatly limited its choice of providers;

4 it was fairer to put the risk on the defendant who stood to make a profit on the contract. If the risk lay with the local authority, its taxpayers would be unjustly burdened by the loss.

As should be evident from the above examples, the facts of each case are crucial to its outcome. The issues of the knowledge and resources of both parties are crucial to determining bargaining power. Issues of policy may also play a part. For example, compare the *St Albans* case, where, in effect, losses would have fallen on council taxpayers, with the *Watford Electronics* case (below), where the claimant was a private company and bespoke software was involved.

Watford Electronics v Sanderson (2001, CA)

A specially designed computer software package was provided by the defendant under a contract that excluded liability for indirect and consequential losses and limited any general liability to the value of the contract price (£104,600). Due to defects in the software the claimant suffered £4.5 million losses from lost profits, replacement of the system and increased working costs.

Held: each clause was reasonable, as the clauses were negotiated between parties of appropriate experience representing equally substantial companies. There was equal bargaining power between the parties.

Chadwick LJ commented:

Where experienced businessmen representing substantial companies negotiate an agreement, they may be taken to have had regard to matters known to them.

They should be taken to be the best judge of whether the terms of the agreement are reasonable. The court should not assume that either is likely to commit his company to an agreement which he thinks is unfair or which he thinks included unreasonable terms. Unless satisfied that one party has in effect taken unfair advantage of the other or that a term is so unreasonable that it cannot properly have been understood or considered the court should not interfere.

The issue of one party seeking to use a clause to take unfair advantage is illustrated by *Overseas Medical Supplies* v *Orient* (1999) where an exclusion clause stating that the defendant would not be liable for loss of goods in transit was held to be unreasonable given that another term in the contract required the defendant to insure the goods, which had not been done. The existence of an alternative remedy may make what would appear to be an unreasonable term acceptable.

Regus v *Epcot Solutions* (2008, CA)

Regus (R) were IT trainers who rented accommodation for their courses from Epcot (E). The air conditioning system broke down, making work conditions on the premises very difficult for R's employees and customers. E failed to rectify the situation after a number of requests by R who then refused to pay the rent. E sued R for breach of contract and R counterclaimed for their losses. E claimed that it was protected by a clause 23(3) which stated that it would not be liable 'in any circumstances' for any loss of business or profits, third-party claims and any consequential loss. Clause 23(4) stated that in any event R's losses would be limited to 125 per cent of the fees or £50,000 whichever was higher.

R successfully claimed in breach of contract in the High Court which held that clause 23 was unreasonable under UCTA, s 3 because it deprived R of any remedy at all and covered intentional acts because it was to operate 'in any circumstances'.

E appealed.

Held (dismissing the appeal): clause 23 was not unreasonable because it did not leave R without a remedy as it was still entitled to claim for diminution in value of the services provided. 'In any circumstances' could not be construed as excluding liability for fraud/wilful/reckless/malicious damage. However, this argument was irrelevant since E had not refused to repair the air conditioning from a wish to harm R's customers but from a desire to save money.

It was not unreasonable for E to restrict liability for breach of contract. There was no inequality of bargaining power between the parties and E had made it clear that customers should make their own insurance arrangements to protect themselves against business losses.

Part 2: Consumer sales

The word 'consumer' in this context refers to somebody purchasing goods intended primarily for their own personal as opposed to business use. Such buyers have been afforded increasing special legal protection since the 1970s. This area of the law has grown haphazardly and piecemeal in a complex web of statutory amendment and sets of regulations which have often been prompted by EC legislation. Simplification and some enhancement of rights to take into account modern marketing methods were necessary and this led to the enactment of the Consumer Rights Act 2015.

An overview of consumer sales protection before the CRA 2015

The Sale of Goods Act 1979 and related legislation

The implied terms

Consumers enjoyed the protection of all the implied terms explained above but with certain enhancements.

Satisfactory quality

After amendment in 2003 to reflect the Sale and Supply of Goods to Consumers Regulations 2002, 'satisfactory quality' was extended to covers 'public statements' by the manufacturer relating to 'specific characteristics of the goods' like advertising, labelling and any other sales information accompanying the goods. The seller could only avoid liability for a misleading statement if he could prove that he did not know or was not reasonably aware of the statement, or, before the relevant contract was made, the seller had publicly corrected or withdrawn the statement.

The right to reject goods

The consumer was entitled to reject goods with trivial defects while the commercial buyer could not and the courts were sometimes prepared to be more flexible concerning time limits in a consumer sale.

Repair and replacement

The consumer buyer had the right to demand repair or replacement of goods that did not conform to the contract at the time of delivery.

Exclusion of liability and the Unfair Contract Terms Act 1977

UCTA 1977 gave the same protection against exclusion for liability for negligence to all parties but some additional protection to consumers concerning the implied terms in contracts involving sale and supply of goods.

Sections 6–7 prevented exclusion of liability for breach of any of the implied terms in in the SGA 1979 and related legislation in any contract for sale of goods and hire made by a business with a consumer. A consumer was defined as someone not contracting in the course of a business (UCTA 1977, s 12) and this was interpreted generously.

Thus, in *R & B Customs Brokers Co. Ltd* v *United Dominions Trust* (1988, CA) 'consumer' was held to include anyone obtaining goods for use in their business, as long as these they were not integral to the course of the business, or regularly bought for incidental purposes. A contract to buy a car for private and business use made by a company owned by a husband and wife was therefore deemed to be made by a consumer. This reasoning was affirmed by the Court of Appeal in *Feldaroll Foundry plc* v *Hermes Leasing (London) Ltd* (2004) on the grounds that it furthered the intention of UCTA, which was to safeguard a buyer's protection under the terms implied under relevant sale and supply legislation.

The Unfair Terms in Consumer Contracts Regulations 1999 (UTCCR 1999)

These regulations implemented EC Directive 91/13/EC and replaced the 1994 regulations of the same name. They only protected *consumers* who entered a contract deemed to be unfair according to criteria laid down in the regulations. Such a term was voidable by consumers, i.e. they were not bound by it unless they chose to comply, but the rest of the contract remained binding.

The substance of the regulations

Consumers were defined as human beings (as opposed to a company) making contracts for non-business purposes (with a seller or supplier) in the course of its business. If the contract was written the seller or supplier had to use clear, intelligible language. Any ambiguity is resolved in favour of the consumer.

Unfairness of a term

A term was unfair if it failed to fulfil the requirements of good faith and this caused a significant imbalance in the parties' contractual relationship, prejudicial to the consumer's interests. In assessing whether the seller or supplier acted in good faith, the court had to have regard to all the circumstances relevant to formation of the contract.

The effect of an unfair term

The consumer was not bound by an unfair term and the rest of the contract remained effective if it was still effective without the problem term.

The regulations contained an illustrative but not comprehensive list of potentially unfair terms.

It was up to the consumer to prove that the term was unfair, taking into account the nature of the subject matter of the contract, the legal and commercial context in which the contract was made and the reasonable expectations of both parties; all the circumstances surrounding the contract are relevant to determining any imbalance.

Enforcement of the regulations

The regulations could be used by consumers directly to enforce their contractual rights. The Office of Fair Trading (OFT) also had a crucial investigatory role (performed since 2014 by the Competition and Markets Authority (CMA)) requiring it to investigate complaints from consumers and trading standards departments about allegedly unfair terms. If the complaint was upheld the CMA could take legal action to require the offending business to change or withdraw the term. Successful interventions include *Office of Fair Trading* v *Foxtons* (2009) where the Court of Appeal held that an injunction should be granted to prevent the enforcement of unfair terms in an estate agent's contract and also *Office of Fair Trading* v *Ashbourne Management Services Ltd and Others* (2011) which concerned gym contracts.

The Consumer Rights Act 2015 repealed these regulations entirely and largely replicates their substance.

The Consumer Contracts (Information, Cancellation and Additional Charges) Regulations 2013

These regulations which came into operation in 2014 largely implemented the Consumer Rights Directive (2011/83/EU) and increased the duties of the seller in consumer sales.

Greater provision of accurate pre-contract information about the goods and the contract terms to the buyer was required in all contracts.

Stricter controls were introduced in distance contracts (those not made by a consumer actually on the seller's premises) to ensure transparency of pricing and to prevent imposition of hidden extra charges. For example, the seller in an online contract is prohibited from using ticked boxes in an order form to make customers buy additional items like cancellation insurance.

Cancellation rights in all distance contracts were extended to 14 days.

Other measures covered by the regulations introduced new rights concerning the purchase of digital content in either tangible form such as DVDs and CDs, or in downloadable form such as ring tones, games, music and video. In all such contracts the seller must give specific information about how the materials function: for example the scope of their regional operation and compatibility with certain other devices must be clearly stated. The buyer loses their right to a 14-day cancellation period once they have downloaded the goods.

These regulations run in tandem with the CRA 2015 which does not amend or repeal them but includes some of the same rights and implements some other aspects of the directive.

The Consumer Rights Act 2015

This legislation radically alters the consumer rights landscape. As explained above, it consolidates all the special protection for consumers in the Sale of Goods Act 1979, UCTA 1977, UTCCR 1999 and some other related statutes and regulations involving provision of goods and services. It also introduces some new rights.

CRA Part 1: Consumer contracts for goods, services and digital content

This part of the Act applies to all contracts between a trader and a consumer which involve supply of goods, services and digital content. Therefore it affords protection to the consumer in contracts for the sale of goods, goods and services, hire and hire purchase and any other contract involving the transfer of goods. Such contracts may be written or oral.

Section 2 definitions of certain key terms

Trader: a person who is 'acting for purposes relating to that person's trade, business, craft or profession'.

Consumer: 'an individual acting for purposes that are wholly or mainly outside that individual's trade, business, craft or profession'. In the event of dispute it is up to the trader to prove that the buyer is not a consumer. A person buying second-hand goods at *an auction sale which they had the option to attend* is not a consumer for the purposes of the Act. It is important to note that unlike the preceding legislation, a consumer under the CRA 2015 cannot be a company (s 36).

Goods: covers not only all tangible moveable items but also gas, electricity and water.

Digital content: any data in digital form.

The consumer's rights in all contracts for supply of goods

Pre-contractual information about the goods and the content of the contract is to be treated as part of the terms of the contract. This includes details about the seller as well as information about the goods, price and delivery (s 12).

Every contract involving supply of goods is to be treated as containing the following terms:

- s 9 – goods will be of satisfactory quality;
- s 10 – goods will be suitable for their particular purpose;
- s 11 – goods will match their description;
- s 13 – goods must correspond to sample;
- s 17 – the trader has the legal right to transfer the contract goods which means that the trader must have the right to transfer possession of goods in a hire contract and the right to transfer ownership (title) in a sales contract.

These all carry the same meanings as those used in the interpretation of terms in consumer contracts under the SGA and related statutes.

New rights are also introduced:

- Section 14 – goods must match any model previously shown to the consumer or examined by them.
- Section 15 – where the contract requires the trader to install the goods they will not conform to the contract if they are installed incorrectly by the trader or their

agent. Therefore if a consumer has asked for installation of their new washing machine and it fails to work because of defective fitting they are entitled to reject it even though the machine itself is without fault.

- Section 16 – any goods which include any digital material will not conform to the contract if the digital content does not conform. If a computer is bought with programs installed on it which do not work, the consumer may have rights to reject the computer. This section does not apply to contracts purely for the sale of digital content which are covered by a discrete part of the Act (see below).

Rights to reject the goods

Where the goods fail to 'conform to contract' by breaching the requirements of the implied terms or containing incorrect or misleading pre-contract information the consumer has three choices:

1 a 'short term' right to reject the goods within 30 days of delivery (s 22);

2 a timely and effective repair or replacement of the goods (s 23);

3 a 'final right' to reject the goods after one attempt to repair them which fails or which is not carried out within a reasonable time (s 24).

This should help to clarify the position of the consumer where goods turn out to be defective. The 30-day limit seems reasonably generous and gives a welcome certainty previously lacking, as illustrated by the plight of the unfortunate claimant in the *Bernstein* case:

Bernstein v *Pamson* (1987)

After 21 days and with only 140 miles on the clock, the engine of the claimant's brand-new Nissan seized up on the motorway, due to sealant coagulating in the cooling system.

Held: the engine was clearly not of appropriate quality and the claimant was entitled to damages. However, he had lost his right to reject the car since a reasonable time had elapsed since taking delivery. The judge held that a reasonable time meant long enough to give the car a reasonable road test, not necessarily long enough to discover latent defects.

Before the Act, agreeing to a repair would sometimes trigger a saga of unsuccessful attempts to correct the defect before the trader would, if the customer was lucky, agree to their rejection of the goods. In *Rogers* v *Parish* (1987) it was held that a top of the market Range Rover could be rejected after seven months, with a 5,000 mileage, since it had been beset by endless mechanical problems from the moment of delivery, and had spent much of its life in the garage while many unsuccessful repairs were attempted.

The consumer's exercise of either right to reject brings the contract to an end (s 20). All moneys or any other property that was tendered to the trader must be returned within 14 days from the trader's acceptance of the consumer's choice. No refund fees can be claimed nor deductions made by the trader.

Section 23 requires that any repair or replacement must be completed within a reasonable time and without significant inconvenience to the consumer. The trader must bear the cost unless this is impossible or disproportionate in which case the consumer can exercise their rejection rights or seek a price reduction.

No liability exclusions

The trader cannot exclude, limit or undermine its liability for any of the above terms in contracts involving sale of goods (s 31).

Contracts to supply digital content

This covers data in any digital form so includes everything from CDs and DVDs to downloads of music, apps and ring tones. It covers any digital content supplied free with other goods or with other digital content for which a price was paid.

Terms as to pre-contractual information, quality (s 34), purpose (s 35), description (s 36), pre-contract information (s 37) and the trader's right to supply (s 41) automatically form part of the contract and the goods will not conform to the contract if they are breached. In addition, s 46 states that if the goods cause damage to a device belonging to the consumer and this would not have occurred if the trader had acted with reasonable care and skill, this is a breach of contract. If, for example, a consumer bought a computer program and due to some fault by the trader it was contaminated by a virus, they would have a remedy as a result of this provision.

Rights of the consumer if the digital content does not conform to the contract

Free replacement or repair

As with any other defective goods under the Act this must be done within a reasonable time and the seller may refuse if the cost is disproportionate or it is impossible to repair or replace the item (s 43).

In that situation the consumer may ask for a partial reduction or refund (ss 44–45) which is payable within 14 days of the trader agreeing that the consumer is entitled. A refund may only be a partial price reduction if only part of the digital content supplied is defective. However, apart from that the seller must not make deductions or impose extra costs.

Repeat performance

The consumer may ask for repeat download if performance was defective. The trader must carry this out within a reasonable time and without causing undue inconvenience unless it is impossible (s 45).

Compensation

If the goods cause damage to a device or other digital content belonging to the consumer the trader may be required to repair the other goods or pay compensation for the damage (s 46).

Note that the Act does not give a consumer in such contracts any rights to reject the goods. Limited and sufficient rights are given by the Consumer Contracts (Information, Cancellation and Additional Charges) Regulations 2013 (see above).

Exclusion of liability in digital content contracts

The trader is not permitted to exclude liability for defective goods in respect of satisfactory quality (s 35), description (s 36), right to supply (s 41) or damage to the consumer's device or other digital property if the contract involves digital content (s 46).

Contracts to supply services

This part of the CRA applies to any contract under which a service is to be performed whether or not goods are also supplied as part of it. It is largely a consolidation of the previous legislation, but, as with all consumer contracts regulated by the Act, includes the additional requirement that pre-contractual information becomes a term of the contract (s 50). Other sections stipulate:

- the service must be carried out with all reasonable care and skill (s 49);
- a reasonable price is payable (s 51);
- performance must take place within a reasonable time (s 52).

Remedies for defective performance

A repeat performance may be requested if the initial performance is defective (s 55), which must be carried out within a reasonable time and avoid inconvenience to the customer as far as practicable.

A reduction or refund (s 56) may be payable to the consumer where repeat performance is not appropriate because it is impossible, or (s 55) the trader has failed in its obligation to carry out the repeat performance requested.

'Reasonable' as in other contracts regulated by the Act means that the service and price meet the expectations of the average consumer taking into account all the particular circumstances pertinent to the contract.

Exclusion of liability (s 57)

The seller is not permitted to exclude liability for:

- the duty to use reasonable care and skill (s 49); or
- pre-contractual information (s 50); or
- reasonable price (s 51); or
- carrying out the service within a reasonable time (s 52).

General contractual remedies

The CRA makes clear that, in addition to the remedies which it prescribes, a party is still free to pursue an action for damages or seek a decree of specific performance or injunction for breach of any contract covered by the Act.

CRA Part 2: Unfair terms

This part of the Act is relevant to all terms of all contracts between a trader and consumer. It repeals and largely replicates the UTCCR 1999 and those parts of UCTA 1977 which provided consumer protection and which are repealed by the Act. It allows the consumer to avoid the effect of such terms if they are found to be unfair as defined by the Act (s 61). It also covers any notice given or displayed by the trader which relates to rights and obligations owed to the consumer by the trader, or by which the trader tries to exclude or limit liability to any consumer.

Meaning of unfair

Good faith:
general honest dealing. Under the CRA 2015 a term's failure to evidence this makes that term voidable.

Significant imbalance:
a lack of equal bargaining power, which may evidence unfairness.

No unfair term or notice is binding on a consumer.

Section 62 defines unfair as being 'contrary to the requirement of **good faith**' and causing 'a **significant imbalance** in the parties' rights and obligations . . . to the detriment of the consumer'. The nature of the contract, its subject matter and all the surrounding circumstances must be taken into account in determining whether this has occurred.

This is the same rather vague definition used in the UTCCR 1999. The courts have given some help with interpretation of this which is still relevant. For example, in *Director General of Fair Trading* v *First National Bank* 2001 Lord Bingham said that good faith was reflected by 'good standards of morality and commercial practice' and would be evidenced by 'fair and open dealing'. Just because a term is not beneficial to the consumer and may come, as their Lordships commented, as 'a nasty surprise' does not necessarily indicate unfairness or breach of good faith.

Written terms must be expressed in plain and intelligible language (s 68). The concept of good faith requires fair dealing and equality between the parties. Transparency of the terms of the contract is therefore crucial. If the meaning is unclear the court will choose the interpretation most favourable to the consumer.

Examples of unfair terms

There is a long list of examples of terms that may be judged unfair in Schedule 2 of the Act. For example, a term which permits a trader to hold on to a deposit if the trader withdraws from the contract before performance, or one which imposes a penalty sum on a consumer who withdraws.

Core terms:
relate to subject matter or price and are not subject to a fairness test under the CRA 2015.

Core terms of the contract cannot generally be assessed for fairness. These include the main subject matter and the price as long as they are legible, transparent and sufficiently prominently presented in any documentation (s 64). However, if they appear in the list of potentially unfair examples in Schedule 2 then they do come within this section's scope.

The courts have tended to give a restrictive interpretation to what comes within the scope of 'price or remuneration' to prevent consumer protection from being undermined. This was stressed by the House of Lords in *Director General of Fair Trading* v *First National Bank*, which held that the disputed term relating to payment of interest was not excluded from the court's jurisdiction.

This approach was followed in *Bairstow Eves London Central Ltd* v *Smith* (2004) where an escalating commission rate charged by an estate agent was deemed not to come within the core terms exclusion.

However, the Supreme Court took a tougher line with regard to overdraft charges in *Office of Fair Trading* v *Abbey National plc and Others* (2009, SC). After lengthy litigation the Supreme Court decided that charges imposed on customers going overdrawn without an arranged overdraft came within the core terms of the contract, provided that this was clearly and intelligibly notified to the customer prior to acceptance.

Negligence liability for personal injury cannot be excluded (s 65)

This applies to notices like 'Persons entering these premises do so at their own risk' or any contractual term directly or indirectly attempting to avoid liability in any degree for death or other personal injury. Therefore liability for harm negligently caused by the trader not just to the buyer but to any visitor to the premises cannot be excluded.

This does not apply to insurance contracts or to situations where the trader is not issuing the notice as part of their trade or profession (s 66). This covers situations where, for example, a farmer allows a village fete to take place in their field.

The consequences of an unfair term (s 67)

Any term or notice which is deemed to be unfair is not binding on a consumer who therefore may avoid the effect of that term but the rest of the contract continues to be effective.

CRA Part 3: Enforcement

The consumer is entitled to take action personally if rights are breached, but as under UTCCR 1999 some public authorities and industry watchdogs are designated in the CRA Schedule 3 as **regulators**. These include the Competition and Markets Authority (CMA) the Financial Conduct Authority (FCA), the Gas and Electricity Markets Authority (GEMA), the Office for Rail Regulation (ORR) and the Consumers Association (CA).

Regulator:
a body authorised by the CRA to investigate complaints about breaches of the Act and to seek remedies.

Schedule 3 gives regulators powers to investigate and resolve complaints within their jurisdiction. This includes the power to seek an injunction if necessary to prevent continued use by any trader of any term or notice attempting to restrict liability for breach of any contract regulated by the Act or any term or notice seeking to exclude liability for death or personal injury or any other term judged to be unfair.

Chapter summary

Contracts concerning goods made between businesses and those between a business and a consumer are governed by different statutes and regulations which give extra protection to the consumer buyer.

Regulation of inter-business contracts

The Sale of Goods Act 1979.

The Sale of Goods and Services Act 1982 (includes hire contracts).

The Supply of Goods (Implied terms) Act 1973 (includes goods supplied under hire-purchase).

Implied conditions of contracts regulated by these statutes

Title will validly pass.

Goods match description.

Goods of satisfactory quality.

Goods suitable for purpose.

These statutes also give rights to rejection, replacement or repair of goods supplied in breach of these terms and all other common law remedies such as damages.

Exclusion clauses

Inter-business contracts are governed by UCTA 1977 which limits the extent to which liability can be excluded in contract and tort.

Consumer buyers' rights (primarily protected by the Consumer Rights Act 2015)

Pre-contractual statements become terms of the contract.

Protection is introduced for contracts for sale of digital content.

All the implied terms above are automatically included in a contract concerning goods between a consumer buyer and business seller but with enhancements to ensure added protection.

Rights to reject are also enhanced to permit rejection of goods generally within 30 days of acceptance, but longer where the buyer requests a repair which is not successful.

Negligence liability causing death or physical injury cannot be excluded.

Any other exclusion clauses or terms found to be unfair terms because they breach good faith are voidable by the consumer.

The CMA and certain other bodies have powers to enforce the Act.

Review questions 7

1 What terms are implied in a B2B (Business to Business) contract under the Sale of Goods Act 1979?

2 When does a business buyer have the right to reject goods bought under a contract with another business seller?

3 In what circumstances may a business seller exclude liability for negligence?

4 What legislation currently protects consumer rights in contracts concerning computer games?

5 Rosanna had a new washing machine installed in her home 14 days ago but today it ceased to work. Explain her rights.

6 Ali entered a two-year phone contract with Concoms plc. From the outset signal levels have been very limited: he has been with no or very little connectivity for days at a time. After three months of fruitless complaints he wants to terminate the contract. Concoms say he is liable to a contractual penalty of one year's full rental. What can he do?

Answers to all review questions can be found in Appendix 2.

Advanced questions 7

(A) Evaluate the extent to which exemption clauses are regulated by statute.

(B) How far does the law's involvement in consumer contracts contradict the principle of freedom of contract?

Answers to the advanced questions can be found at **go.pearson.com/uk/he/resources.**

Take a closer look

The following cases provide important examples of how the law in this chapter has developed. They are primary sources illustrating the law in action and give more detail about their facts, as well as helping to understand the law and to appreciate how the judges reached their decisions.

Try looking them up in the law reports or accessing them via a database, e.g. Bailii (www.bailii.org/databases.html). LexisNexis or Westlaw may be available in the university or college library, or extracts may be found in a case book.
(See Appendix 1: Additional resources.)

Aswan Engineering Establishment Co. Ltd v *Lupdine Ltd* [1987] 1 All ER 135, CA

Baxter v *Barnes* [2015] EWHC 54 (QB)

Watford Electronics v *Sanderson* [2001] 1 All ER (Comm) 696, CA

J & H Ritchie Ltd v *Lloyd Ltd* [2007] UKHL 9

Director General of Fair Trading v *First National Bank* (2001) 1 All ER 97, HL

Further reading

Davies, P.S. (2016) The Control of Exclusion Clauses and Unfair Terms, in: *JC Smith's The Law of Contract*. Oxford: Oxford University Press, Chapter 15, p. 201.

Assignment 6

In practice the Consumer Rights Act 2015 is unlikely to confer many benefits on a consumer buyer that they could not access under previous legislation. Discuss.

Defects in the contract:
Misrepresentation, mistake, duress and undue influence

Learning objectives

On completion of this chapter, students should be able to:

★ explain the difference between the legal consequences for parties to a void and a voidable contract;

★ identify the different forms of misrepresentation and the remedies applicable to each;

★ understand the concept of operative mistake;

★ recognise the circumstances where operative mistake occurs;

★ be aware of the forms which duress may take;

★ appreciate how duress differs from undue influence.

Introduction

Although on the face of things a contract has been formed, it may contain elements that make it defective. These may be caused by a number of factors varying from deliberate dishonesty or negligence, through to an honest mistake. They have differing legal consequences; some, while upsetting to a party, will not affect the validity of the contract at all. Others may render a contract voidable or exceptionally, void. It is important to grasp the difference between these concepts.

1 *A voidable contract:* here the parties have successfully made a contract but it contains a defect (often, though not always, caused by one of the parties) that enables the innocent party to withdraw from or avoid the contract. Usually the court will order the return of any property that was transferred. This chapter examines misrepresentation, duress and undue influence, all of which may make a contract voidable.

9

2 *A void contract:* although the parties believe they made a contract, the defect is so serious that in the eyes of the law no contract ever came into existence. Even if both parties wish to enforce the contract, this is not possible. If property has changed hands, ownership is not usually transferred and the property may be recovered. In this chapter the law of mistake provides an example of how a void contract may arise. As can be seen, in practice it is very rare for the court to decide that a contract is void. In law, as in life, people often have to live with their mistakes.

Misrepresentation

During pre-contractual negotiations, statements (representations) may be made which induce a party to enter the contract. Such statements may, for example, be made by sales staff by word of mouth, or be included in catalogues or brochures. If untrue, they are called misrepresentations. A remedy in **misrepresentation** is available to the innocent party whether or not the statement was incorporated as a term of the contract. If it is a term, an action for breach of contract provides alternative remedies. Section 50 of the Consumer Rights Act 2015 (CRA 2015) makes such statements in contracts for the supply of services in consumer contracts, a term of the contract and not just a mere representation, which if untrue may be a misrepresentation.

Misrepresentation: an untrue statement and a material inducement to a party to enter a contract.

Misrepresentation makes the contract **voidable**. The **misrepresentee** (the party to whom the statement was made) is entitled to avoid the contract or to continue with it.

Voidable contract: a contract exists but the innocent party may refuse to perform it.

An actionable misrepresentation is:

Misrepresentee: person to whom a misrepresentation is made.

1 An untrue statement of fact, which

2 is a material inducement to enter the contract.

These principles have legal implications which it is important to grasp.

Statement of fact

This can be written, spoken or pictorial, and may also arise from other conduct. Here are a few brief examples.

Gordon v Selico (1986)

Held: the seller of premises, who deliberately concealed dry rot by painting over it, was guilty of misrepresentation to the buyer. In effect he was saying that the premises were of an appropriate standard.

Goulding J said:

> I believe it to be the law that conduct alone can constitute a fraudulent misrepresentation . . . The concealment of dry rot . . . was a knowingly false representation by Mr Azzam that Flat C did not suffer from dry rot, which was intended to deceive purchasers and did deceive the plaintiffs to their detriment.

A statement of fact does not include *statements of genuinely held opinion*.

Bisset v Wilkinson (1927)

The vendor sold land to the buyer, having told the buyer that, if properly worked, he estimated the land would carry 2,000 sheep. In fact, it was capable of supporting many fewer.

Held: the vendor had not made a misrepresentation. Since he had never used his land for sheep farming, he was not making a statement of fact merely stating an honest opinion when he told the buyer how many sheep he believed the land would support.

However, statements of opinion may be treated as statements of fact if the maker, with knowledge of the underlying circumstances, could not reasonably have held the opinion.

Smith v Land & House Property Corp. (1884)

A vendor of a house described its tenant, Frederick Fleek, as a 'most desirable tenant', knowing that Fleek was in arrears with rental payments.

Held: the vendor was liable for fraudulent misrepresentation, as he was clearly lying. It was obvious to the vendor that Fleek was far from desirable as a tenant.

Statements of intention may be treated as statements of fact if at the time of making the statement the maker had no such intention.

Edgington v *Fitzmaurice* (1885)

A company prospectus said that the proceeds from the sale of debentures were to be used to improve buildings and extend the business; in fact the directors intended to use the money to pay off pressing company debts.

Held: a misrepresentation had been made. Bowen LJ said: 'The state of a man's mind is just as much a fact as the state of his digestion . . . A misrepresentation as to the state of his mind is therefore a statement of fact.'

More recent cases indicate a willingness by the courts to treat an estimation of future performance as a statement of fact, where it was reasonable for the other party to rely on it.

Esso Petroleum v *Mardon* (1976, CA)

A sales forecast for a filling station, given by Esso's experienced manager to a prospective tenant of the garage, turned out to be radically incorrect.

Held: Esso was liable for misrepresentation as a person as skilled as the manager should be able to be relied upon to give a reasonably accurate forecast.

Statements of law are not usually regarded as statements of fact. Everybody is supposed to know the law and therefore to be aware when it is incorrectly stated. However, a statement relating to existing civil law rights of the **misrepresentor** concerning the subject matter of the contract is likely to be treated as a statement of fact.

Misrepresentor: person who makes a misrepresentation.

Lawrence v *Lexcourt Holdings Ltd* (1978)

The vendor's statement that 'existing planning permission covers use of this building as an office' was held to be a statement of fact.

Although there is a duty to answer questions truthfully, *failure to volunteer information* is generally not misrepresentation, even if the representee is clearly under a misapprehension.

Smith v Hughes (1871)

A race horse trainer assumed that he was buying old oats, when actually they were new, but he did not ask the seller their age.

Held: no misrepresentation had occurred. The seller had said nothing about the age of the oats and it was irrelevant that he was aware of the importance of this to the buyer.

Liability for failure to disclose information may arise, however, in any of the following circumstances:

1 *Half-truths.* A statement may be true as it stands, but still mislead because it is incomplete.

Nottingham Patent Brick & Tile Co. Ltd v Butler (1886)

A solicitor who, without checking, told the buyer of some land that he 'did not know' of any restrictive covenants affecting it, was liable for misrepresentation.

Similarly, misrepresentation was held to have occurred in *Dimmock* v *Hallett* (1866), where the seller described the land as occupied by certain named tenants, but did not also tell the buyer that they had given notice.

2 Circumstances change between making the statement and acceptance.

With v O'Flanagan (1936, CA)

A doctor, who was selling his practice, gave the buyer correct information about its value. However, before the buyer notified acceptance the value had considerably diminished, as many patients went elsewhere when the doctor became ill.

Held: his failure to notify the buyer of the drop in value amounted to a misrepresentation as his original statement was no longer true and the buyer should have been notified of this.

Fiduciary relationship: a legal relationship with a very high degree of trust by one party in another's expertise, knowledge etc., giving that other party the capacity to influence their decisions.

3 A *fiduciary relationship exists between the parties.* A **fiduciary relationship**, involving a high degree of trust between the parties, exists, for example, between partners, and between solicitor and client. It is also relevant to insurance contracts, which are voidable unless full disclosure is made of all material facts, meaning those 'which would influence the judgment of a prudent insurer' (Marine Insurance Act 1906). For example, in a contract for carriage of goods by sea, the fact that goods are to be transported on deck, not in the hold, would be material *(Hood* v *West End Motor Car Packing* (1917)).

It is irrelevant that the failure to disclose was not careless or intended to deceive. Some people have found that they were deprived of insurance cover because they quite innocently failed to reveal that their cars had modified features (e.g. alloy wheels and sun roof) that were not standard on a particular model.

The statement acted as a material inducement

The misrepresentation must be a sufficiently important influence on the misrepresentee. It must be enough to incline a reasonable person to enter the contract, but it need not be the only reason for them doing so.

Vahey v Kenyon (2013, CA)

Mr Vahey was negotiating buying land from Mr Kenyon and asked him about its flooding history, because it was near a flood plain. Mr Kenyon said that, despite local flooding 30 years previously, his land had not been affected. Later, when the house was found to be damp, Mr Kenyon admitted, after further questioning, that the stream which flowed through the grounds occasionally burst its banks but had never flooded the house. The sale went ahead subject to a £10,000 discount. Soon after completion the property was flooded and Mr Vahey discovered that the garage and house had been flooded some years before, during Mr Kenyon's occupancy.

Held: the contract was voidable for fraudulent misrepresentation. It was clear from his enquiries that the issue of flooding concerned Mr Vahey and that the reassurances from Mr Kenyon had been material in getting him to enter the contract otherwise he would have sought to negotiate a higher discount.

Evidence that a misrepresentee was prepared to take unreasonable risks in pursuit of large profits may incline the court to discount the weight of the misrepresentor's statement. In *Hurst & Others v Hone & Others* (2010) a well-known former footballer was persuaded by the defendants' fraudulent statements suggesting huge financial gain in return for a substantial loan to further a building project in Spain. He lost all his money but it was held that the misrepresentations had not materially induced him. The prospect of quick and substantial profits had encouraged him to participate in the deal and he had been prepared to ignore third party advice about the risks.

Where the misrepresentor has technical knowledge the court is inclined in favour of a consumer who trusts in that, especially where third party advice is unlikely to be sought, as in the following case.

Webster & Others v *Liddington & Others* [2014] EWCA

The claimants were all women who had been treated with a skin-rejuvenating product by the defendants who were clinics using a particular manufactured product.

Prior to buying the treatment, the claimants had all been given information brochures by the clinic they were contracting with. Some brochures had been produced by the manufacturer, others composed by the clinic based on the manufacturer's information. These all stressed the efficacy of the product due to its natural purity and claimed that, unlike Botox and similar treatments, it did not contain non-natural substances and that it contained only the patient's skin. The product was an injectate based on a small sample of the patients' skin which was sent by the clinic to the manufacturer. Bovine products were used in the process of creating the injectate; traces of these products sometimes remained, which in 3–10 per cent of cases could cause an allergic reaction. None of this information appeared in the brochures.

The claimants sued the clinics for misrepresentation. None had suffered ill effects but all wanted damages for having been sold an adulterated product of a different quality from what they had been led to believe.

Held: the defendants were liable for misrepresentation since they were liable for the contents of all the brochures which they had distributed and thereby implied were an accurate, safe, reliable information source for patients. The patients were consumers who trusted in the superior specialist knowledge of the clinicians. The defendants had not issued any disclaimer for inaccuracies in the brochures. The misrepresentation about the content of the injectate was material. Had the patients known about the bovine product content and the medical risk they might well have decided against buying the treatment.

The misrepresentee must both *know* of the statement and *rely* on it.

Re Northumberland & Durham District Banking Co., ex parte Bigge (1858)

A contract with a shareholder was not voidable: he was unable to prove that when he bought the shares he had already seen reports which had been issued about the company which later proved to be false.

Attwood v *Small* (1838)

The seller of a mine misrepresented its capacity. However, the contract was not voidable because the buyer had not relied on the seller's statement, but had commissioned his own survey which also turned out to be inaccurate.

The misrepresentee is entitled to take the statement at face value and has no obligation to check the truth of the statement, even if the misrepresentor offers the opportunity to do so.

Redgrave v *Hurd* (1881)

A solicitor who was selling his practice gave information about its income and told the buyer that he could check the figures against relevant documentary evidence. The buyer did not choose to do so, and it was held that this did not prevent the contract from being voidable.

Exclusion of liability for misrepresentation

The Misrepresentation Act 1967, s 3, as amended by the Unfair Contract Terms Act 1977, permits exclusion or limitation of liability for misrepresentation so far as is reasonable in a contract between business parties. Reasonableness must be proved by the party who seeks to enforce the exemption. The Consumer Rights Act 2015 has further amended s 3 so that it does not apply to a term in any consumer contract covered by the CRA 2015, so misrepresentation cannot be excluded in a consumer contract governed by the CRA 2015.

The remedies for misrepresentation

Fraudulent misrepresentation: an untrue statement made intending to deceive or recklessly not caring whether it is true or false.

Rescission: an equitable remedy requiring a party to a voidable contract to give back money/property to the other party who has avoided the contract.

The remedies available to the misrepresentee depend on the perceived state of mind of the misrepresentor at the point at which the statement was made. A misrepresentation may be made fraudulently, carelessly or wholly innocently.

Fraudulent misrepresentation

Misrepresentation is **fraudulent** if the misrepresentor knows that the statement is untrue, or makes the statement recklessly, not caring whether it is true or false. The misrepresentee may sue in the tort of deceit and obtain damages and/or **rescission** of the contract. Rescission is an equitable remedy issued at the discretion of the court; it seeks to return the parties to their pre-contractual position. This enables the misrepresentee to recover any money paid to the fraudulent party.

In practice, successful deceit actions are quite rare, though fraudulent misrepresentation is common. It happens, for example, every time somebody obtains goods with a stolen credit card, thus fraudulently representing themselves as the card holder. In situations like these, the misrepresentors quickly disappear and action against them is not possible. If action is taken, the burden of proof of intention is a very heavy one for the claimant to discharge.

Negligent misrepresentation

Under s 2(1) of the Misrepresentation Act 1967, a representor who induces the claimant to enter into a contract, by a statement which the representor did not reasonably believe, may be liable in damages. Rescission may also be granted. It is up to the representor to prove reasonable belief in the statement.

Howard Marine & Dredging Co. Ltd v *Ogden & Sons Ltd* (1978, CA)

> The defendant was informed that barges chartered from the claimant had a certain capacity. The claimant's manager made this statement on the basis of insurance documentation. In fact, this was incorrect, as reference to the ship's papers would have shown. (Ship's papers are the equivalent of a birth certificate issued with a new vessel at sale and held by the current owner.)
>
> **Held:** the claimant was liable under s 2(1). The claimant had not discharged its burden of proof that it had reasonable belief: in such an important matter reference to a primary source of information was necessary.

Negligent misrepresentation: an untrue statement made without reasonable belief in its truth.

Section 2(1) thus provides a remedy for **negligent misrepresentation**. Also, since a potentially fraudulent misrepresentor cannot be said to have had a reasonable belief in the truth of the statement, the victim may claim under s 2(1) instead of pursuing an action in deceit. This relieves the claimant of the burden of proof but gives access to an identical remedy. In *Doyle* v *Olby* (*Ironmongers*) (1969, CA) it was held that, since deceit is an intentional tort, the defendant was liable for all the direct consequences of its behaviour. In *Royscot Trust Ltd* v *Rogerson* (1991) the Court of Appeal decided that damages under s 2(1) should be calculated in the same way as damages for fraud. This sometimes means that a party may recover a more generous measure of damages than if calculated according to contract principles that attempt to put the claimant in the position he or she would have enjoyed if the contract had been properly performed.

The victim of negligent misrepresentation may also have a remedy in negligence under the rule in *Hedley Byrne* v *Heller* (which is explained in Chapter 14). This is helpful where parties have been misled and suffer loss, but then find out that the statement is incorrect before they enter the contract. It may also be used by someone who was misled by a third party. Such parties are not assisted by s 2(1) which relates *only* to misrepresentors who have actually succeeded in making the misrepresentee contract with them.

Quilter v Hodson Developments [2016] EWCA Civ

Ms Quilter bought a flat from a developer in a complex of buildings, served by a common heating system, for £240,000. Her pre-purchase questionnaire asked whether there were any past or ongoing disputes concerning the building or its use and the reply from the developer was there were none. However, when she moved in, Ms Quilter discovered that the central heating system was defective due to the boiler not working properly and that this issue had arisen before she bought the flat and was known to the developer, since other tenants had already complained and the problem had not been addressed. Two years later she sold the property for £275,000. The boiler was still causing problems but she was able to reassure her buyer that the problem was now being dealt with through the National House Building Council guarantee scheme.

Ms Quilter then claimed damages in misrepresentation from the developer and the court awarded her £15,000 to represent the difference in value of the property at the point she bought it and the sum which she paid. The builder appealed and argued that as she sold the property for a sum that made good her previous loss these damages were not legitimate.

The Court of Appeal held: the trial judge's decision was correct: the flat was £15,000 less valuable than the purchase price at the point of Ms Quilter's purchase. It was irrelevant that due to a rise in property prices she was getting back more than she had paid originally. She was entitled to take full advantage of this and had no duty to account for it to the developer. The misrepresentation had induced her to buy something which was not in the condition it claimed that it was and therefore not worth the price.

Wholly innocent misrepresentation

Innocent misrepresentation: an untrue statement not made fraudulently. May be made carelessly or with reasonable belief.

Even if a misrepresentation is made in good faith, with no intention to deceive and without carelessness (**innocent misrepresentation**), the contract is rendered voidable. Rescission is the usual remedy.

Damages may be an alternative remedy under s 2(2) of the Misrepresentation Act 1967, which states that it is applicable to any misrepresentation which is *not made fraudulently*, so it can apply to careless misrepresentations as well as wholly innocent ones. It gives the court the discretion to award damages instead of rescission. This discretion is likely to be used if the misrepresentation did not have a major impact on the contract and would, if it were a contract term, be classified as a warranty rather than a condition. This section therefore may apply to a careless misrepresentation.

The Act gives no specific guidance on quantum though s 2(3) implies that it is different from s 2(1). It seems fair to assume that the level of damages should be lower.

Some judicial guidance about how this section operates emerged in *William Sindall plc* v *Cambridgeshire County Council* (below), though as no liability was held to exist it is an *obiter dictum* (for guidance only).

William Sindall plc v *Cambridgeshire County Council* (1993, CA)

Sindall, in March 1989, contracted to buy land for development from the council for £5 million. A term of the contract stated that the land was sold subject to any existing liabilities over it, but the vendor had a duty to disclose any they knew of. The council, after carrying out checks, stated that, as far as they knew, there were none. Eighteen months later, market values had radically dropped and Sindall had discovered a sewer that necessitated a six-foot wide maintenance strip being left uncovered; Sindall tried to avoid the contract on the grounds of misrepresentation but was unsuccessful.

Held: no misrepresentation had occurred since the council had made reasonable investigations before making their statement so rescission would not be granted.

Obiter dictum: if liability had existed, the following factors would have been considered by the court when deciding to exercise its discretion of awarding damages in lieu of rescission under s 2(2):

(i)   *The nature of the misrepresentation.* The importance of the misrepresentation relative to the contract as a whole must be examined. Here the diminution in value of the land to Sindall of £18,000 was very small relative to the purchase price of £5 million.

(ii)   The potential loss to the misrepresentee of upholding the contract. The cost to Sindall was £18,000 to divert the sewer, plus the loss of one plot and delay and interest charges of £2,000 a day until diversion was complete.

(iii) The potential loss to the misrepresentor of rescinding the contract. If rescission took place, Cambridgeshire CC would lose a bargain at top of the market price. They would have to repay £8 million and would receive in return land which due to market fluctuations was now only worth £2 million.

Taking all this into account, damages would be a more just award than rescission.

Quantum of damages. *Obiter dictum* it was held:

(i)   Section 2(2) is concerned only with the damage resulting from the property not being what it was represented to be while s 2(1) relates to damage directly resulting from having entered into the contract. Here Sindall would not have been entitled to claim damages for the drop in value of the land as this was not a result of the misrepresentation but due to market fluctuations.

(ii) The measure of damages must be different from that under s 2(1) because s 2(3) contemplates that damages under s 2(2) will be less than damages under s 2(1). Section 2(2) is aimed at redressing the lot of the non-fraudulent misrepresentor against 'the harsh consequences of rescission for a wholly innocent misrepresentation' (Evans LJ).

(iii) The relevant Law Commission report indicated that the Act was intended to correct the anomaly of a minor defect making a contract voidable for misrepresentation where breach of contract would not produce the same result.

(iv) Damages should not generally exceed those recoverable for a breach of warranty. The possibility of compensation for loss of market value could not be ruled out in all cases as the court must be free to determine what was equitable in the circumstances of each case.

Damages for non-fraudulent misrepresentation

Before the Misrepresentation Act 1967 there was no remedy other than rescission for a victim of non-fraudulent misrepresentation. Any such misrepresentation merited only, at best, an order for rescission which, even if available, might still not be an adequate remedy. Rescission is an equitable remedy, available only at the discretion of the court, unlike damages which are available as long as it can be proved that the relevant misrepresentation has occurred. There are many circumstances when it may be refused which are described at the end of this chapter. Even if rescission is applicable, its purpose is only to put the parties in their pre-contractual position, not to compensate them for any actual damage. The only money that can be recovered is that which was paid to enable performance of the contract. In practice a party may suffer other incidental losses that are not covered.

In the next case the claimant could now claim damages to make good his losses under s 2.

Whittington v *Seal-Hayne* (1900)

The claimant rented a poultry farm on the strength of a non-fraudulent misrepresentation by the defendant owner that the premises were in a sanitary condition. In fact the water supply was contaminated. As a result, the farm manager employed by the claimant became ill and the prize-winning poultry either died or became valueless. To add insult to injury, the local council condemned the premises as being unfit for habitation and ordered the claimant to carry out repairs. Under the terms of the lease the claimant was responsible for repairs.

Held: he was entitled to rescind the contract and could recover the rent he had paid and the costs of repair. However, the costs of lost stock and medical expenses were not recoverable as they were incidental to performance of the contract, which did not require him to stock the farm or appoint a manager.

Parity with remedies for breach

Before the 1967 Act, the victim of a misrepresentation was always able to avoid the contract regardless of the seriousness of the effect on it of the misrepresentation. This produced the anomalous result that the victim of a misrepresentation might be in a better position than a victim of a breach, who could only treat the contract as voidable if a condition was breached rather than a minor term. Section 2(2) enables the court to withhold rescission for non-fraudulent misrepresentation and award damages instead, thus solving this problem.

Mistake

Although it is common for a party to make a contract under a misapprehension, it is unusual for the resulting contract to be void. Such a contract may be voidable for misrepresentation; remedies for breach of contract may also be available.

Real life

Harvey was buying a new house and after a lengthy search thought that at last he had found the ideal home, a pretty Victorian terraced house in a quiet street, with roses growing round the front door. Ivana, the vendor was delighted to accept Harvey's offer, as she had had a long difficult relationship with her next door neighbours, Sid and Harry, who were often very noisy in the evenings; they started actively to harass Ivana after she had reported them to the local Council. A sale of land contract requires the vendor to complete a Sellers' Property Information Form. Ivana, desperate to escape, answered 'no' to the question about whether she had had any disputes with, or had made any complaints to/about her neighbours, or had sent any letters that might affect the property. The sale was duly completed but Harvey is now enduring substantial noise nuisance from his neighbours who threatened him when he politely requested them to keep the noise down.

Harvey can rescind this contract for fraudulent misrepresentation and claim damages. Though it may be possible to have some sympathy for Ivana, at the same time she clearly was lying. In less clear-cut circumstances Harvey would be better off suing under the Misrepresentation Act 1967, s 2(1) which requires the misrepresentor to prove reasonable belief in their statement.

Void contract: no contract exists in the eyes of the law.

Operative mistake: one which makes a contract void because it prevents true agreement between the parties.

An operative mistake makes the contract void

Exceptionally, a mistake will be so fundamental that the contract will be rendered **void**. Such a mistake is said in law to be **operative** because it strikes at the root of the contract, effectively preventing any true agreement. In practice this is very rare.

Mistakes as to *quality* do not make the contract void. A mistake as to the *attributes* of the subject matter of the contract or of a party to it is never an operative mistake, even if the other party induces the mistake (misrepresentation), or fails to correct the mistaken party's false impression. If a customer buys a food processor from a shop, under the mistaken belief that it has a juice-making facility, this mistake does not make the contract void. If the shop assistant said that a juice maker was included, the contract is voidable for misrepresentation. If the customer is not actively misled, the contract is binding. The shop may be prepared to let them exchange the goods, or even give a refund, but there is no legal obligation on it to do so.

Here are some cases of mistakes as to quality that have come before the courts.

Bell v *Lever Bros* (1932, HL)

Bell and Snelling, directors of a subsidiary company of Lever Bros, without its knowledge, fraudulently used their position to speculate to make secret profits. Later, when leaving the company they negotiated a generous severance package. Lever Bros sought to recover this when it discovered the fraud, arguing that this contract was void because of a common mistake as to entitlement to the money. It did not know at the time of payment that they had committed fraud and the evidence was that Bell and Snelling had forgotten about it.

Held: the contract was valid as the mistake was merely as to the quality of the employment contract which could have been terminated summarily on grounds of fraud, with no compensation payable.

Lord Atkin said that a mistake as to quality by both parties will never make a contract void unless it 'is to the existence of some quality which makes the thing without the quality essentially different from the thing it was believed to be'.

It is quite hard to imagine circumstances which would satisfy the Atkin criteria. The courts have stuck firmly to his line ever since.

In contracts for the sale of land, the courts were sometimes prepared to treat a contract as voidable under equitable principles. Rescission was sometimes granted if both parties made the same mistake. This was possible only if it produced the most just result. Similarly, the court would not allow a party to obtain a decree of specific performance, if this would permit a party to exploit a mistake unfairly. This equitable doctrine was abolished by the Court of Appeal in *Great Peace Shipping* v *Tsavliris* (*International*) *Ltd* (2002). (Full information about equitable remedies can be found at the end of Chapter 11.)

Operative mistake may occur in the following circumstances.

Common mistake concerning the existence of the subject matter

Common mistake: both parties make the same mistake.

In **common mistake** both parties reasonably but wrongly believe that the subject matter exists at the time they make the contract.

Couturier v *Hastie* (1856, HL)

The parties made a contract for the sale of a cargo of corn which was being conveyed on named ship from a foreign port. Unknown to either party, the corn had already been disposed of by the carrier because it had started to ferment and become a risk to the safety of the ship.

Held: there was no possibility of a contract coming into being if the specific goods did not exist at the point when the parties reached agreement. It was impossible to buy that cargo any longer.

The contract may be void even if the subject matter never existed as long as it was reasonable for the parties to believe that it did.

Associated Japanese Bank (International) v *Credit du Nord* (1989)

The claimant bank contracted to buy £1 million-worth of computers from a rogue (Bennet) and lease them back to him, with a guarantee from the defendant bank to cover his repayment. The computers were the security for the guarantee but never actually existed. Bennet went bankrupt and the claimant tried to enforce the guarantee.

Held: the contract was void for common mistake from the outset, since the computers did not exist and never had existed, although this was unknown to the parties to the case. Existence of the security for the loan had been crucial to the contract. Without that promise the defendant would never have agreed to the guarantee.

Leaseback contracts of this kind are a very common commercial transaction, with goods passing unseen to the lessee (the party who bought them and is now renting them back from the other party). Provided there is nothing to alert the lessor (the buyer of the goods to be leased) to the integrity of the other party, they are not expected to check that the relevant goods exist.

However, the contract will not be void if one party has responsibility to check that the subject matter exists.

McRae v *Commonwealth Disposals* (1951)

The parties entered a contract under which the defendant gave the claimant rights to salvage a wrecked ship and its cargo of oil, which the defendant said would be found on a reef at a given map reference. After much costly searching by the claimant, the wreck could not be found at that site.

Held: the defendant was liable for breach of contract since it had been careless in promising the existence of the wreck.

Worth thinking about?

What is the legal situation if the parties make a contract about property, which is currently in existence but ceases to be before the contract is performed?

Suggested solutions can be found in Appendix 2.

Mutual mistake concerning the identity of the subject matter

Mutual mistake: both parties each make a different mistake.

In **mutual mistake** both parties operate under different misapprehensions and are at cross-purposes. This objectively assessed is seen as preventing any real consensus and is not due to the fault of either party. Essentially there is no meeting of minds, essential for the formation of a valid contract.

Raffles v *Wichelhaus* (1864)

Two ships called *Peerless* were both carrying cotton from Bombay. The parties contracted for the sale of such a cargo. The buyer believed that he was buying one consignment while the seller was disposing of the other.

Held: this mistake prevented any agreement coming into being and therefore the contract was void. No true agreement existed between them since they were entirely at cross purposes about what was being bought and sold.

Unilateral mistake

Unilateral mistake: one contracting party is mistaken.

In **unilateral mistake** only one party makes a mistake. Such mistakes are very common, but usually they only make a contract at best voidable or even leave it unaffected.

A unilateral mistake can only make the contract void if:

1 One party enters a contract crucially mistaken and would not have made the contract if they had known the truth.

2 The other party should reasonably have known of the mistake.

3 The mistaken party is not at fault.

There are two types of such mistakes: identity of a party or of a term of the contract.

Unilateral mistake by one party regarding the identity of the other

Although mistaken identity is very common, it is very unlikely to make a contract void, particularly if the parties have contracted face to face.

Mistaken identity usually arises from a fraudulent misrepresentation, which enables a fraudster (commonly called 'a rogue' in law books) to take possession of the victim's property. The resulting contract, between claimant and rogue, is voidable for misrepresentation. Ownership of the goods passes to the rogue, under what is called a **voidable title**. Unless the claimant takes steps to avoid the contract made with the rogue *before* the goods are sold on, the party who buys the goods from the rogue becomes the legal owner. Since the victim of the fraud cannot usually contact the rogue directly, giving information about the fraudulent activity to the police has been held to be sufficient to avoid the contract (*Car & Universal Finance v Caldwell* (1964)).

In practice, the victim is usually unable to avoid the contract with the rogue before the goods are sold on, so an innocent third party becomes owner of the goods. The only hope for the victim is to persuade the court that the contract is void for mistake, since this would mean that the goods have not become the property of the party who bought from the rogue and could be recovered. The problem for the court is how best to do justice between two innocent parties – the rogue's victim (the claimant) and the person who bought the goods from the rogue in good faith (the defendant). Generally, the courts are more likely to sympathise with the defendant, unless the claimant is able to prove that it was entirely reasonable for the claimant to be duped by a virtually foolproof deception by the rogue. The rationale for this approach is that it is fair that the original seller carries the risk of the buyer not being creditworthy, by letting the buyer remove the goods.

A contract will not be void for mistaken identity unless the claimant can prove the following:

The claimant intended to deal with some person other than the contracting party. The claimant must be mistaken not merely as to the attributes (quality) of the other party, but also as to that party's actual identity. Therefore, the claimant's case will collapse unless he or she can prove that there are two persons – one with whom he or she contracted and one with whom he or she intended to contract.

Voidable title: provisional ownership of goods lost by the misrepresentor if the misrepresentee avoids the contract before a bona fide third party buys them.

King's Norton Metal Co. v Edridge, Merrett & Co. (1897)

A rogue represented himself to the claimant company as the agent of a successful business enterprise which did not actually exist. The claimant entered into a postal contract which was held not to be void since the claimant clearly intended to make a contract with somebody and the only entity with whom this was possible was the rogue.

Compare:

Cundy v Lindsay (1878, HL)

A rogue, Blenkarn, represented himself as Blenkiron & Co., a reputable company already known to the claimant and trading from an address in the street where the rogue had set up his premises. He ordered, by post, linen handkerchiefs from the claimants, never paid for them and sold them on to a third party whom the claimants sued.

Held: the contract between the claimant and Blenkarn was void, as the claimants reasonably believed that they were dealing with another party than the rogue. This meant that the claimant could recover the goods which had been sold on to the defendant.

1 *The other party was aware of the claimant's mistake.* This is not generally a problem, since usually the other party is bent upon deception.
2 *The issue of identity must have been crucial when the contract was made.* The claimant will have to satisfy the court that at the point the contract was made he or she intended to contract only with the person whom the rogue claimed to be. In *Cundy v Lindsay*, which was a postal contract, the court was prepared to accept this. In later cases, the courts have adopted a different approach where the contract is made face to face and have placed a heavy burden of proof on the claimant, who must show that it was reasonable to place reliance on the rogue's representations. Otherwise, it is presumed that the claimant intended to contract with the person before them and the contract will not be deemed void for mistake, but will merely be voidable for misrepresentation.

The conduct of the parties is judged objectively to determine whether the claimant has acted reasonably.

Phillips v *Brooks* (1919)

The claimant jeweller contracted to sell a ring to a rogue who claimed to be Sir George Bullough. He then pawned the ring with the defendant and the claimant sued to recover it.

Held: the claimant could not recover the jewellery since the contract he had made with the rogue was not void. The issue of identity was clearly not crucial to the claimant who had merely checked the name and address in a street directory and was satisfied by such flimsy evidence which did not demonstrate any real link between the rogue and the person he claimed to be. It proved nothing more than that a Sir George Bullough did live at a particular address.

The Court of Appeal reached an apparently conflicting decision in:

Ingram v *Little* (1960, CA)

A rogue offered to buy a car from three elderly sisters. They initially refused to take a cheque so the rogue claimed to be P.G.M. Hutchinson and said he was a successful businessman. He also supplied an address. While two of the sisters kept the rogue talking, the third went to the post office and checked the particulars in the telephone directory and found that the name and address given by the rogue were correct. This, of course, proved nothing except that the rogue knew

Hutchinson's name and address, but the sisters agreed to sell. The cheque was not honoured and the rogue sold the car to the defendant, a car dealer.

Held (by majority): the contract was void and therefore the car was recoverable from the defendant. The test was whether the rogue should reasonably have believed at the time of entering the contract that the offer from the seller was to the person they represented themselves as being. The sisters had intended to deal only with Hutchinson, as was evidenced by their initial refusal to accept the cheque until they had checked the phone book. Every case in these circumstances must be determined on its facts and *Phillips* v *Brooks* could be distinguished as the jeweller had agreed to sell before he checked the street directory.

While it is difficult to see any material difference between the facts of the two cases above, the decision in *Ingram* v *Little* may be justified as reflecting the customary approach of protecting the more vulnerable party at the expense of the business party. Remember it was a dealer who bought the car from the rogue.

Lewis v *Averay* (1971, CA)

The claimant (Mr Lewis) sold his car to a rogue, who had claimed to be Richard Green, a film actor well known for portraying Robin Hood in a popular TV series. Before the sale was agreed, the rogue showed the claimant a chequebook in the name of R.A. Green, and a pass to Pinewood Studios. The pass bore an official stamp, the name Richard Green and the rogue's photograph. The rogue then sold the car to the defendant (Mr Averay) and the claimant sought to get it back.

Held: his claim must fail. The contract with the rogue was not void and therefore the defendant purchaser of the car had acquired ownership. The claimant had not proved that it was crucial to him to contract with the rogue as he accepted less than convincing evidence of the rogue's identity. All it showed was that the rogue's name was probably Richard Green and that he worked at Pinewood. 'Green' is a common name and there are many jobs at film studios which do not involve leading acting roles.

Lord Denning MR said:

Mr Lewis made a contract with the very man, the rogue, who came to the flat. We say he 'made a contract' because . . . we do not look into his intentions or into his mind to know what he was thinking, or into the mind of the rogue. We look to the outward appearances. It was still a contract though voidable for fraud . . . under which this property passed to the rogue and in due course to Mr Averay before the contract was avoided. Though I very much regret that either of these two good and reliable men should suffer, in my judgement it is Mr Lewis who should do so.

The court (by majority) refused to apply *Ingram* v *Little* and instead applied the *Phillips* v *Brooks* decision. *Ingram* v *Little* was perceived as anomalous as the facts of all three cases were indistinguishable.

In the next case the Court of Appeal refused to follow this decision, distinguishing it on its facts.

Shogun Finance Ltd v *Hudson* (2002, CA)

A rogue, who represented himself as Mr Patel, using a driving licence stolen from Mr Patel as evidence, obtained a car on hire purchase from the claimant finance company, which had made very limited identity checks on the electoral regis-ter and county court judgment records. He later sold it to Hudson. The finance company succeeded in its claim to recover the car from Hudson as the contract between it and the rogue was deemed void.

Held (by majority):

1 Identity was a crucial issue for the finance company. In these circumstances the rogue would reasonably believe that the offer was being made not to him personally but to Mr Patel.

2 This was not a face-to-face contract as the car dealer was not acting as agent of the finance company when dealing with the rogue. Therefore, the presumption that the claimant intended to deal with the person before him did not apply.

All the judges hearing this case commented on the confusing state of the law in this area and the need for statutory reform to enable a clear and fair system of loss distribution in such cases. Hudson appealed to the House of Lords.

Shogun Finance Ltd v *Hudson* (2004, HL)

The House of Lords (by majority) affirmed the Court of Appeal's decision.

Held: no hire-purchase contract had been created between the finance company and the rogue, but a contract had been concluded with Mr Patel, who was clearly identified in the agreement in accordance with the way prescribed by the finance company. Mr Patel was the only person the company had been willing to do business with. The delivery of the car to the rogue by the dealer did not create any contract with the rogue.

It was not appropriate to depart from the House of Lords' previous decision in *Cundy* v *Lindsay*, since it made good sense to maintain the presumption, in face-to-face contracts only, that the seller intended to contract with the person before them.

The determination of the courts to protect Shogun Finance in this case may seem surprising. This sort of fraud is widespread and it could be argued that hire-purchase companies should be encouraged to take greater precautions to prevent it regard-less of how the contract is made. The evidence it relied upon, in reality, only told the company that Mr Patel had a current driving licence, was on the electoral register and had no unsatisfied court judgments against him. None of it proved that the rogue was Mr Patel.

Unilateral mistake regarding the terms of the contract

Parties will not usually be able to treat a contract as void by claiming that they were mistaken about the terms on which the contract was based. Exceptionally, the contract will be treated as void if the error would have been clearly evident to the other party, who will not be allowed to rely on it.

Hartog v *Colin & Shields* (1939)

A written contract to sell hare skins stated that the price would be calculated by the pound. It should have stated that the goods would be sold by the piece. This had been agreed orally between the parties and reflected the customs of the trade.

Held: the buyer was not entitled to take unfair advantage of what he must have realised, with his experience of the trade, was a clerical error in the written contract which must be treated as void.

Only a very obvious mistake will invalidate the contract.

Wood v *Scarth* (1858)

The defendant's written offer to let premises did not include a premium, and the claimant was not informed of such a requirement when he concluded the contract with the defendant's agent.

Held: the contract was not invalidated by this mistake, since the claimant could not reasonably have been expected to have anticipated that a premium would be payable.

The equitable remedy of rectification

Rectification: an equitable remedy to amend a document to reflect the parties' true intention.

If a contract is found to be void for operative mistake the court will require any money or property which has changed hands to be returned: as no contract exists in law, title does not pass.

However, the court may be prepared to order a decree of **rectification** to amend a written contract which contains a unilateral mistake relating to its terms. It will only be granted if there is clear evidence that, as it stands, it does not represent the intention of the parties and that injustice would result from enforcement of the written document in its existing form.

Documents signed by mistake

Non est factum:
'This is not my deed.' May be pleaded by a party who has mistakenly signed a contract for a radically different purpose than he or she was led to believe.

The courts are generally very unsympathetic to people who try to avoid the effect of a mistakenly signed document. It is usually binding, unless misrepresentation or undue influence makes it voidable. Exceptionally, a plea of **non est factum** (this is not my deed) may be applicable.

The House of Lords has specified certain proof points for this plea, which if satisfied will result in the mistakenly signed document being void. Signers must prove that:

1 the document signed is radically different in its effect from what they believed they were signing;

2 the signers were not careless. The standard of care exercised by a signer is judged subjectively, taking into account age and physical and mental capabilities.

Gallie v *Lee (Saunders* v *Anglia Building Society)* (1970, HL)

Mrs Gallie, who was 78, had poor sight and had mislaid her spectacles, signed a document without reading it. She assumed it to be a deed of gift assigning her house to her nephew, Wally. She had previously agreed to give him the house so that he could raise money on it for a business venture, provided that she would be able to continue living there. In fact, the document presented to her for signature by Lee, Wally's friend and business colleague, actually assigned the house to Lee for £3,000. He never paid Mrs Gallie the money, but mortgaged the house to the building society. He then failed to make any repayments and so the building society attempted to repossess the house. By the time the case reached the House of Lords, Mrs Gallie was dead and the parties to the case were her executor and the building society.

Held: the plea of *non est factum* failed.

1 The document was not sufficiently different in purpose from what Mrs Gallie believed she was signing: it transferred the ownership of the house, which was what she intended. It was irrelevant that it transferred the house to a different person, by sale not gift.

2 Mrs Gallie had not taken sufficient care before signing. She should at least have checked the contents of the document by asking someone to summarise it for her if she was not able to read it for herself.

The courts have shown great reluctance to allow a plea of *non est factum* to succeed in most of the cases where it has been raised. The fact that Mrs Gallie was clearly vulnerable to the wiles of her nephew and his mate seems to have cut no ice with the court. Initially the contract would have been voidable for misrepresentation or undue influence (see below) but by the time the building society foreclosed it was too late.

Duress and undue influence

The essence of a contract is that it is a voluntary agreement. Evidence that a party entered a contract under compulsion may make it voidable.

Duress

Duress:
physical threat to
force a party to enter a
contract.

Duress is a common law doctrine, under which threats or use of violence to force a party to make a contract may make it voidable. In practice, physical duress is very rare, though exceptions do exist. In *Barton v Armstrong* (1975, PC) the claimant, who had been subjected to a campaign of physical threats to persuade him to part with a valuable shareholding, was able to avoid the resulting contract.

Traditionally, the doctrine of duress encompassed only threats and violence against the person, but the courts, in the latter half of the twentieth century, extended the doctrine to cover economic duress. Such duress usually consists of threats by one party not to perform the contract with the other party unless the terms of the contract are varied in favour of the coercive party. In the past, the courts have tended to treat such variations as void in law because of an absence of consideration, but increasingly they are tending to hold them voidable because of economic duress. In *Opel GmbH and Renault SA v Mitras Automotive* (2008) (facts below) the judge (Donaldson QC) described it as '*a more refined control mechanism*'.

In *Pao On v Lau Yiu Long* (1979) Lord Scarman held that the following criteria are relevant to deciding whether the contract is voidable:

1 The extent of the pressure employed. This must exceed the acceptable levels of pressure normally to be expected in commercial dealings.

2 The level of protest evidenced by the aggrieved party.

3 Whether the aggrieved party had any real choice about complying with the other party's threats.

4 Whether independent advice was available to the aggrieved party.

The cases below illustrate how much must be at stake for a claim of economic duress to succeed.

Atlas Express Ltd v *Kafco Importers & Distributors* (1989)

The claimant had contracted to transport goods for the defendant at a certain price calculated (by the claimant) on the basis of an estimated size of load. The first load was actually much smaller than was economic. The claimant then said that they would not make any further trips unless the price was renegotiated with a raised minimum cost per load. The defendants felt obliged to accept this as there was not time to find another carrier; they were also heavily dependent on a current order to Woolworths, where the next delivery was to be made.

Held: where a party is forced to renegotiate terms to its disadvantage and is left without bargaining power with no alternative but to accept the new terms offered, economic duress has occurred. Kafco's business would have been in danger of collapse if it was unable to supply its main customer.

A greatly disproportionate rise in cost may be convincing evidence of duress.

Opel GmbH and Renault SA v *Mitras Automotive* (2008)

The claimants, Opel and Renault, had contracted for some time with the defendant Mitras (M) for the supply of bumper mountings for vans. Eventually, they repudiated the contract with six months' notice because of changes in design to their vans. M responded with a 'termination agreement' demanding several hundreds of thousand pounds 'in recompense' for losing the contract and increased costs of production. The claimants were placed in a very difficult position as they only had supplies sufficient for 24 hours of production, and M was refusing further delivery. They reluctantly agreed to M's terms and paid but subsequently claimed that this leaving agreement was not binding as it was made under economic duress.

Held: economic duress invalidated the agreement, making it voidable. The defendants had applied illegitimate pressure to the claimants by threatening to breach the supply contract, as the claimants would have suffered huge losses if production had ceased; consequently they were placed in a no-choice position. No alternative supplier was immediately available. The agreement was voidable and the claimants could recover the money they had paid.

Serious loss of business reputation is also influential.

Kolmar Group AG v Traxpo Enterprises PVT Ltd (2010)

The claimant, Kolmar, agreed to buy a specified amount of ethanol at a specified price from the defendant, Traxpo. Time of delivery was crucial, as Kolmar intended to sell the ethanol to a very important client in urgent need. Later, Traxpo told Kolmar that it could only deliver a smaller amount than specified and at a higher price. Kolmar went ahead with the purchase, as he felt he had no choice, but later sued for the difference in price.

Held (Clarke J): Traxpo had placed Kolmar under economic duress by subjecting him to illegitimate pressure and placing him in a take it or leave it position which it had no alternative but to accept in order to supply its client: 'and, if it failed to do so, would not merely suffer a severe loss of reputation with a client of great potential importance but would in all probability be exposed to very large claims.'

Kolmar was entitled to damages to cover the increased price.

Undue influence

Undue influence:
inequitable influence
making a contract
voidable.

Undue influence is an equitable doctrine, applicable where one party abuses his or her personal influence or authority over another to make that other party enter a transaction. If the influence is effective, the transaction is voidable.

Williams v Bayley (1866, HL)

A father was told by his bank that his son would be prosecuted, unless he (the father) paid back money that the son had fraudulently obtained from the bank by forging his father's signature.

Held: the resulting contract was voidable against the bank by the father because he had not entered into it freely.

Avon Finance v Bridger (1985, CA)

An elderly couple were buying a retirement home; their son was making the financial arrangements and was providing part of the money. To do this, he obtained a loan from the claimant, but did not tell his parents, who signed a legal charge as security, that it related to their home. The son then failed to keep up the repayments and the claimant took action to possess the house.

> **Held:** the security agreement was voidable for undue influence by the son, which was attributable to the claimant. The son was in effect acting as the claimant's agent. The claimant should have been aware that the son would exercise influence over his parents, who had not received independent advice.

Where there is *no fiduciary relationship* between the parties the burden of proof of undue influence is on the complainant. He or she will have to satisfy the court that, but for the influence to which he or she had been subjected, he or she would not have entered the transaction. Proof that the complainant had no independent advice before entering the transaction may be evidence that he or she did not act with free will.

Where a *fiduciary relationship* exists between the parties, undue influence is presumed, provided that the complainant can prove that the resulting transaction was disadvantageous to him or her. The transaction will be voidable unless the other party can prove that the complainant was not prevented from exercising freedom of will. Evidence that the complainant had access to independent advice will be proof of this.

A fiduciary relationship is deemed in law to exist automatically in some situations. These include:

1 doctor and patient;
2 solicitor and client;
3 principal and agent.

However, the court may be prepared to acknowledge that particular circumstances give rise to a fiduciary relationship in the case before it. In *Re Craig* (1971) a secretary companion, who persuaded her frail and elderly employer to make gifts to her from the bulk of his savings, was held to be in a fiduciary relationship to him. He was both physically and emotionally dependent on her. She had to repay the money to his estate. In the next case the amount of control taken by the defendant over an elderly man's business affairs was sufficient to create a fiduciary relationship.

Goldsworthy v *Brickell* (1987, CA)

> The claimant, who was elderly, owned a large and valuable farm which had become very run down. He came to rely heavily on the defendant (his neighbour) for advice. Within a few months the defendant was effectively managing the farm. The claimant then gave the defendant a tenancy of the farm on terms very favourable to the defendant, but took no independent advice.
>
> **Held:** the tenancy was voidable because undue influence was presumed. A fiduciary relationship was held to exist because of the very close working relationship of the parties in which the defendant clearly dominated the claimant.

In general, the courts have not often been persuaded to find a fiduciary relationship to exist between husband and wife or same sex couples, even if the relevant transaction was to benefit only one of the parties.

Barclays Bank v O'Brien (1993, HL)

Surety:
a person who provides security to a creditor for a loan.

The facts of this case are set out below. The House of Lords indicated that a more generous approach may be appropriate where a wife stands **surety** for a husband's debts:

1 The informal nature of business dealings between spouses raises a substantial risk that the husband might fail accurately to inform his wife of the extent of the liability she is undertaking.

2 Many wives place trust and confidence in their husband's judgement in financial matters.

3 Similar principles would apply to transactions between cohabitees where there is an emotional bond, whether heterosexual, lesbian, gay, or transgender.

Occasional exceptions are made but no fiduciary relationship is usually acknowledged to exist between a bank and its customers. The bank does not even have a duty to ensure that a customer takes independent advice prior to entering into a transaction with it. However, failure to do so may prevent the bank from enforcing a contract in its favour, if it is perceived as having constructive notice of undue influence or misrepresentation which led the customer into the transaction. Such notice may be given by the nature and substance of the agreement and the relationship between the customer and any other party involved in or benefiting from the transaction.

Barclays Bank v O'Brien (1993, HL)

Mr O'Brien persuaded his wife to sign a mortgage on the jointly owned matrimonial home, as security for the overdraft for her husband's company in which she had no interest. He told her that the overdraft was limited to £60,000 for a period of three weeks. In fact, it was unlimited in both respects. When it rose to £154,000, the bank sought to enforce the mortgage. The branch where Mrs O'Brien had entered the transaction had failed to carry out instructions from head office to make sure that both parties were fully aware of the nature of the transaction and to recommend independent advice.

Held: if the circumstances surrounding the transaction should have put the bank on notice that a wife had been subject to undue influence or misrepresentation, she could avoid the transaction, unless the bank had warned her in confidence of the need to take independent advice. Mrs O'Brien was entitled to avoid the transaction as the bank had been put on notice of her husband's likely misbehaviour and had not taken adequate steps to safeguard her.

Later cases indicate that it is hard to persuade the court that the bank did have constructive knowledge unless the circumstances are exceptional.

Credit Lyonnais v *Burch* (1997)

The defendant was a junior employee in a small company and a family friend of the owner, who was also her boss. She was persuaded by him to take out a second mortgage on her flat and to give the bank an unlimited guarantee of the company's debts, to enable the company to increase its overdraft from £25,000 to £270,000. Neither he nor the bank ever revealed to her the heavy state of indebtedness of the company. The bank urged her to take legal advice before signing the relevant documents but when she refused, in a letter clearly written in consultation with her employer, it allowed her to enter what it knew to be a precarious contract.

Held: that the bank had constructive notice of the influence her employer was capable of exercising over her and of the lack of legal advice and, therefore, could not enforce the mortgage and guarantee against her.

In the majority of cases the court has held that the bank does not have constructive notice once the vulnerable party has been advised to take independent advice. The courts have usually interpreted the concept of independent and adequate advice in favour of the bank. However, in the *Etridge* case the House of Lords has restated and clarified some of the issues and has revived a little of the spirit of the *O'Brien* decision. Nevertheless, there are still concerns about whether the surety is sufficiently protected with regard to the issue of independent legal advice. As the law now stands, the surety's only remedy in most cases may be an action in negligence against the solicitor, rather than being able to avoid the transaction with the bank.

Royal Bank of Scotland v *Etridge* (No. 2) (2001, HL)

Held:

(a) The bank is automatically put on notice when the surety is not acting in the course of business.

(b) The bank must reasonably ensure that the surety has understood the consequences of what he or she is signing, has been warned of the risks in non-technical language and has freely chosen to sign. However, the bank need not personally meet with the surety. Confirmation from the solicitor advising the surety will normally be sufficient.

(c) Independent advice may be supplied to the surety by the borrower's solicitor. That solicitor must determine whether there is any conflict of interest which indicates that the surety should be separately advised.

Once the bank was informed that the surety had been advised, the bank could assume that the advice had been delivered competently.

The limits of rescission

The only remedy for undue influence is *rescission*. This is an equitable remedy and, therefore, available only at the discretion of the judge. The right to avoid the transaction may be lost in the following circumstances:

1 *Affirmation.* The complainant performs the contract with no complaint once freed from the other party's domination.

2 *Delay.* In *Allcard* v *Skinner* (1887) the claimant joined a religious order and made large gifts to it. She stayed in the order for eight years and then left. Six years later she tried unsuccessfully to recover the money despite evidence of undue influence.

3 *A third party has acquired bona fide rights over the contract property.* If property was transferred under a contract voidable for undue influence and sold on before the complainant had time to avoid the contract, the right to rescind is lost.

Chapter summary

Misrepresentation

An untrue statement of fact, made by the misrepresentor, which induces the misrepresentee to enter the contract and makes the contract voidable. A misrepresentation may be fraudulent or innocent.

Fraudulent misrepresentation: made intentionally/recklessly.

Innocent misrepresentation: misrepresentation made carelessly without reasonable belief or wholly innocently with reasonable belief.

Remedies for misrepresentation

Fraudulent: action in deceit, rescission and damages.

Careless: action under Misrepresentation Act 1967, s 2(1). Burden of proof of reasonable belief is on defendant. Rescission and damages.

Wholly innocent: action under Misrepresentation Act 1967, s 2(2). Rescission is the usual remedy but damages may be substituted if rescission is not justified by the nature of the misrepresentation.

Mistake

An operative mistake makes a contract void.

Mistake may be operative in the following circumstances:

Common mistake about the existence of the subject matter.

Mutual mistake about the existence of the subject matter.

Unilateral mistake about the identity of a contracting party.

Unilateral mistake about a term of the contract.

Remedies

The court requires any property or money which has changed hands between the parties to be returned. Rectification may keep a contract alive if there is unilateral mistake regarding its terms.

Duress

Forcing a party to enter a contract by physical threats to their person or by threatening their business interests may make the contract voidable.

Undue influence

A contract resulting from more subtle forms of illicit persuasion than duress may be voidable.

Presumed undue influence: exists if the parties are in a fiduciary relationship and the resulting contract is disadvantageous to the less powerful party.

Actual undue influence: exists if the parties are not in a fiduciary relationship but one party can prove unfair exercise of power by the other party to get them to enter into a contract.

Remedy

Rescission.

Review questions 8

1 What effect does a successful claim of (a) misrepresentation, (b) mistake, and (c) *non est factum*, have on a contract?

2 On what grounds may the following contracts arguably be defective?
   (a) Crockford sold his house to Wisden, having placed a large and heavy bookcase to conceal subsidence cracks in the wall.
   (b) Kelly contracted to sell Bradshaw 1 tonne of jelly babies, which both parties believed to be in a warehouse in Scunthorpe. Earlier the same day, a massive fire had destroyed the contents of the warehouse.

(c) Chambers wrongfully told Webster that he was Pears, the famous flute player. As a result, Webster agreed to sell him his antique flute.

(d) Whittaker, who is frail, elderly and heavily dependent on his son, Moore, sold Moore valuable shares for a fraction of their market price, because Moore threatened that otherwise he would go and live abroad.

3 Explain how a misrepresentation can be distinguished from a statement of opinion.

4 In what circumstances might silence constitute misrepresentation?

5 Define and distinguish between duress and undue influence.

6 Explain the remedy of rectification.

Answers to all review questions can be found in Appendix 2.

Advanced questions 8

(A) Evaluate the effect of s 50 of the Consumer Rights Act 2015 in contracts for services.

(B) A claim for breach of contract is to be preferred to an action for misrepresentation. Analyse this statement.

Answers to the advanced questions can be found at **go.pearson.com/uk/he/resources.**

Take a closer look

The following cases provide important examples of how the law in this chapter has developed. They are primary sources illustrating the law in action and give more detail about their facts, as well as helping to understand the law and to appreciate how the judges reached their decisions.

Try looking them up in the law reports or accessing them via a database, e.g. Bailii (www.bailii.org/databases.html). LexisNexis or Westlaw may be available in the university or college library, or extracts may be found in a case book. (See Appendix 1: Additional resources.)

Esso Petroleum v *Mardon* [1976] 2 All ER 5, CA

William Sindall plc v *Cambridgeshire County Council* [1994] 1 WLR 1016, CA

Shogun Finance Ltd v *Hudson* [2004] 1 All ER 215, HL

Credit Lyonnais v *Burch* [1997] 1 All ER 144, CA

Web activity

Click on 'News' and explore the Action Fraud archives. Have a look at some of the scams on offer and see if any involve misrepresentation or undue influence like those in this chapter. It also includes useful information about how to protect yourself against fraud:

www.actionfraud.police.uk/

See 'What's Wrong with the Consumer Rights Act 2015?' on the blog of law lecturer David Gibbs:

http://gibbslawandlife.blogspot.com/2016/04/whats-wrong-with-consumer-rights-act.html

Assignment 7

(a) Explain the remedies for misrepresentation.
(b) James sold his car privately by cheque to a rogue who represented himself as Robert Gould, whose chequebook and banker's card the rogue had recently stolen. For additional proof of identity the rogue showed James a travel pass in Robert's name on to which the rogue had put his own photograph. The rogue then sold the car on to a secondhand car dealer called Harry. The cheque was not paid when James presented it to the bank and he has traced the car to Harry's showroom.

Advise James.
Would it make any difference to your answer if James had become suspicious shortly after selling the car and had notified the police?

The consequences of illegality and incapacity:
Illegality and incapacity

Learning objectives

On completion of this chapter, students should be able to:

★ appreciate the scope of the concept of illegality of contracts;

★ recognise the circumstances in which making a contract is illegal;

★ identify the difference between contracts which are illegal and those which are merely void;

★ understand when a contract in restraint of trade is enforceable;

★ explain what kinds of contracts are enforceable against minors and mentally impaired people.

Introduction

This chapter examines some more contractual defects: illegality and incapacity.

In the law of contract, the word 'illegal' has a wider meaning than that understood by lay people. It includes not only contracts which are actually *prohibited* by law, but also contracts to achieve a *purpose which is against the law*, as well as contracts seen to be against the public interest but which do not actually break the law. A contract found to be illegal is void.

In general, any person is legally *capable* of making a contract and, therefore, may sue or be sued on any contract to which he or she is a party. However, some types of person have *limited contractual capacity* and will not necessarily be bound by all the contracts that they make. This chapter examines the rules concerning two categories of people whose capacity is limited to protect them against exploitation – minors and mentally impaired persons.

Illegality

Illegal contract: includes contracts which are not prohibited by law but which are against the public interest.

The rules governing **illegal contracts** are found in statute and common law.

Contracts illegal by statute

These are numerous and include the Competition Act 1998, which prohibits a variety of contracts which restrict, distort or prevent competition such as price-fixing agreements.

Contracts illegal at common law

The court determines the existence and extent of the illegality by reference to public interest considerations, sometimes described as 'the public policy'. Contracts invalidated for public policy reasons fall into two categories: illegal and merely void. An illegal contract is one where the parties agree to do something which is directly or indirectly against the law. One which is merely void is one with a purpose perceived as undesirable and therefore against the public interest.

The following types of contract are illegal.

A contract to commit a crime, a tort or a fraud

Everet v Williams (1725)

Two highwaymen agreed to rob a stagecoach and share the proceeds. One held up the coach at gunpoint while the other collected all the valuables from the unhappy passengers. They were successful in carrying out their plan, but the one who had grabbed the valuables refused to part with any of them so the other one sued him in contract.

Held: since the contract was to commit a crime, it was illegal and void.

A contract which is damaging to the country's foreign relations

Regazzoni v *Sethia* (1957, HL)

India's export regulations prohibited exports from India to South Africa. To avoid the prohibition, the claimant and defendant agreed to export the goods initially to Italy. From there they would be sent on to South Africa. The buyer sued for breach of contract when the seller failed to deliver.

Held: the buyer's claim must fail because the contract was illegal. Its performance would breach the law of India and was likely to endanger its friendly relationship with Great Britain.

A contract for a sexually immoral purpose

Pearce v *Brooks* (1866)

The claimant coach builders supplied a carriage to the defendant, knowing that she would use it to ply her trade as a prostitute.

Held: the contract was illegal. The coach builders could neither recover payment from the defendant nor repossess the carriage. They had effectively aided and abetted soliciting.

These days such a contract might not be treated so severely. The court operates according to current moral standards and tries to avoid unjust enrichment.

Armhouse Lee Ltd v *Chappell* (1996)

The defendant refused to pay the claimant for advertising the defendant's sex chat phone lines.

Held: the contract was legally binding. It was not a criminal or civil offence to place such adverts. There was no evidence that 'any generally accepted moral code condemned these sex lines'.

A contract which prejudices the administration of justice

Keir v *Leeman* (1809)

After a riot, criminal proceedings instigated by the claimant against the defendant were compromised when the defendant promised £50 to the claimant in return.

Held: this contract was illegal and void because it undermined the administration of justice and the claimant was not entitled to the money.

However, please note that civil cases may be legally compromised through an out of court settlement and arbitration agreements are actively encouraged by the law (see Chapter 4).

A contract to defraud the Revenue

Miller v *Karlinski* (1945)

The defendant employer agreed to pay a salary of £10 to the claimant and told him that he could claim expenses in which he could include the amount he should have paid in tax on the salary. The employer then failed to pay and the defendant sued for breach of contract. He claimed 10 weeks' salary and just over £21 expenses.

Held: the contract was void for illegality: it was clearly intended to evade paying tax. Over three-quarters of the expenses claimed represented what the claimant should have paid in income tax.

A contract endangering public safety

Contracts most often invalidated for this reason have been those made in wartime with an enemy alien. It is important to distinguish contracts made during wartime from those made before a war broke out. In the latter case the contract though valid when made will be discharged once the war starts (see Chapter 11).

Contracts promoting corruption in public life

Sale of honours or public office are good examples.

Parkinson v *College of Ambulance* (1925)

The defendant charity persuaded the claimant to make it a donation of £3,000 on the understanding that the charity would ensure that he got a knighthood, but then failed to deliver on its promise. The claimant sued for breach of contract.

Held: this was an illegal contract because it tended to promote corruption and the claimant could not recover the money.

Contracts prejudicial to marriage

A contract to restrict marriage such as one requiring a person not to marry at all or to marry a particular person or a member of a group is void, but other contracts which used to be deemed illegal may now be regarded differently.

A marriage brokerage contract (where a fee is paid to the person who arranged the marriage) was held to be void in *Herman* v *Charlesworth* (1925). A contract made prior to marriage which stated financial arrangements in the event of separation was also held to be illegal in *Cartwright* v *Cartwright* (1853).

However, attitudes have changed and subject to certain conditions both types of arrangement may now have some legal effect. Contracts with dating agencies are now enforceable. The growth of pre-nuptial agreements has led the courts to give them considerable influence in deciding how matrimonial property should be distributed, although they have stopped short of declaring them enforceable contracts.

Radmacher v *Granatino* (2010, SC)

The Supreme Court held that pre-nuptial agreements should be given full evidential weight by the court when determining the parties' financial post-divorce arrangements, provided there is no evidence of misrepresentation or undue influence.

The consequences of an illegal contract

The general principle is that illegality taints the whole contract, rendering it void. A party may find him or herself indirectly penalised for having made the contract. For example, if a party was aware of the illegal purpose before entering the contract, he or she was not generally able to recover any property which has changed hands. This was seen as a deterrent to discourage parties from making such contracts and often resulted in the instigator of the illegality profiting from it. From the mid-twentieth century onwards the courts have increasingly looked for ways to enforce contracts of this kind; a point has now been reached where it may appear that illegal intent will almost always be overlooked in the interests of preventing unjust enrichment.

The court may also be more lenient in what it perceives as less serious involvement by one party. For example, a party who withdraws from the contract before it is carried out may recover (*Kearley* v *Thompson* (1890)). Sometimes the court will waive the illegality to protect the more vulnerable party against exploitation.

Kiriri Cotton Co. Ltd v *Dewani* (1960, CA)

A tenant was allowed to recover the cost of an illegal premium a landlord had demanded before granting a tenancy because the statute which banned the premium was intended to protect the tenant against just such exploitation.

If a party withdraws from the contract before performance they may be treated more leniently by the courts. Historically this only covered cases where a party pulled out because they thought better of their dishonest behaviour, but proof of such regret is no longer necessary (*Tribe* v *Tribe* (1996)). In *Patel* v *Mirza* (2014), this was extended by the Court of Appeal to a situation where the contract had become frustrated (impossible to perform due to circumstances outside the parties' control). The Supreme Court recently broadened the principles determining the recovery of property by a party to an illegal contract when *Patel* v *Mirza* came before it (see below).

In the news

Patel v *Mirza* (2016, SCUK)

Mirza (M) was involved in the foreign exchange business and told Patel (P) and their mutual friend G that they could use his spread-betting account to bet on changes in price of RBS shares. P paid him £620,000 to place bets because M told him that he had contacts in the bank able to give him information about an expected rise in share values. The contract was illegal because it involved insider dealing which amounts to conspiracy to commit a criminal offence.

Ultimately the plan fell through as the expected raised share value did not occur. M then mistakenly repaid P's money to G instead of P and P claimed it back from M.

The Supreme Court by majority held: that P could recover his money from M. The defence of illegality exists for public policy (public interest) reasons. It prevents a wrongdoer from profiting from their bad behaviour and stops the law from being self-defeating by permitting unlawful behaviour. To decide whether the illegality defence should defeat a claim it was necessary to decide the following:

(a) is the public interest prejudiced by allowing the defence?

(b) does withholding the defence conflict with some other principle of public policy?

(c) is denying the defence an appropriate response to the illegality?

> Many factors would need consideration such as the seriousness of the illegal conduct of the parties, its centrality to the contract, whether it was intentional and how far the parties were equally to blame. It was the function of the criminal law to impose punishment while the civil law was concerned with determining the private rights and duties of the parties.

This judgment seems at first sight so broad as to encourage rather than discourage illegal behaviour. However, each case is decided on its facts in the light of these criteria. Remember, the illegal contract was not performed. As in so many cases of this type, unjust enrichment is the key. Allowing Mr Mirza to hide behind the defence of illegality instead of taking responsibility for his negligence would result in unjust enrichment of his friend, or even himself. All three parties can be regarded as being equally culpable, but it was Mr Mirza's carelessness which caused the loss to Mr Patel so that on balance he is the guiltier party. The Supreme Court also emphasised the difference in function and focus between the civil law and the criminal law.

Contracts which are merely void

Such contracts do not involve law breaking but are perceived to be against the public interest since they are perceived as encouraging undesirable activities. The parties will not be penalised by the courts for making them. The contract will be enforceable as far as it is not void. Property which has changed hands is always recoverable. The most important type of contract in this category is one said to be in restraint of trade.

Contracts in restraint of trade

Restraint of trade:
restriction on freedom to work for/do business where/with whom one chooses.

Restraint of trade is commonly a feature of the following agreements:

1 *Contracts of employment.* Employees may be required to give undertakings not to reveal trade secrets or to compete with their employers on leaving their service.

2 *Contracts for the sale of a business.* Where a business is sold as a going concern, the seller may undertake not to set up in competition with the buyer.

Solus agreement:
contract under which one party agrees to deal with only one supplier, etc.

3 *Solus agreements.* A seller of a particular product may agree to deal with only one supplier in return for a discount or some other financial benefit (a **solus agreement**). This is very common in contracts for the supply of petrol. The owner of a filling station obtains a discount price, or financial assistance from the supplier to develop a site, in return for a promise to sell only that supplier's brand.

The use of such restraints is generally regarded as not being in the public interest, because they tend to hamper competition and freedom of movement of labour. All such restraints are said to be *prima facie* void – i.e. they will initially be treated as against the public interest – but will be enforced if proved reasonable. This means that the court will not give a remedy (like an injunction) to help a party enforce the restraint, unless there is evidence that in the particular circumstances the restraint is reasonable.

Three questions are relevant to determining reasonableness:

1 Is the business interest one which can legally be protected? Such interests are limited to trade secrets and influential relationships in employment contracts. If the contract concerns the sale of a business, the goodwill may be protected.
2 How long is the restraint intended to last?
3 How wide a geographical area is covered by the restraint?

Provided that a legally recognised business interest is found to exist, the issues of time and geographical area are determined in the light of the particular facts of the case. The courts have exceptionally upheld lifelong or worldwide restraints. In practice, however, most restraints operate only within a very limited time and area.

Restraints in employment contracts

An employer may in a contract of employment seek to impose restrictions on employees who have moved to a new employer.

With regard to *trade secrets*, an employer may restrain employees with access to unique information concerning the manufacturing process or composition of goods from revealing this information to others or using it for their own purposes.

Forster & Sons Ltd v *Suggett* (1918)

The employee had access to secret bottle-glass manufacturing processes invented by his employer.

Held: it was reasonable to restrict the employee from being involved in such a trade for five years after he stopped working for the employer, anywhere in the UK.

Business connections created by an employee through close relationships forged with customers during the relevant employment may also be protected. This is to prevent an ex-employee from poaching customers.

Fitch v *Dewes* (1921, HL)

Held: a solicitor's managing clerk could reasonably be restrained from working as a solicitor for the rest of his life, within a seven-mile radius of Tamworth town hall, as he had dealt confidentially with many clients within his employer's practice. They might follow him if he were allowed to practise locally.

Employees who have learnt skills and obtained business knowledge from their employment cannot be legally prevented from using these skills elsewhere, unless trade secrets were imparted or close relationships with customers resulted.

Morris v *Saxelby* (1916, HL)

Held: a draughtsman and engineer could not be restrained from working in the crane components manufacturing business. Knowledge about the way in which his ex-employers organised a similar business was not an interest which could be protected.

Eastham v *Newcastle United Football Club* (1963)

Football Association rules stated that players who left a club at the end of a contract could be placed on a retainer list. This prevented them from seeking employment with any other club in the UK or abroad, for as long as their ex-club paid them 'a reasonable wage'.

Held: this rule was not binding since no legitimate trade interest was protected by it.

Faccenda Chicken Ltd v *Fowler* (1986, CA)

The claimants sold frozen chickens door to door. Mr Fowler was their sales manager but had no direct contact with customers. He left Faccenda's employment and set up a similar business in the area, using his ex-employers' customer lists. Eight of the claimants' other employees left to work for him.

Held: Fowler could not be restrained from this activity: the information he had used was not a trade secret and he was not breaching his ex-employers' confidence by using it. He was at liberty to offer jobs to any person that he thought suitable.

The issue of reasonableness must be determined in the way most likely to produce a fair outcome for both parties. In each of the three cases above, the employer was merely trying to prevent legitimate competition by an ex-employee. This would have unduly restricted the employee selling his labour, or setting up in business elsewhere.

Real life

Chang trained as a graphic designer, but left the industry and for the past five years has worked as a personal trainer at the FitQuick Gym in Oldcastle. His friend Kofi owns a company running a chain of fitness clubs with branches in nearby towns and has just opened a new one in Oldcastle. He offers Chang a job as promoter and publicity manager.

Chang's contract of employment with FitQuick states that he cannot work as a personal trainer or in any related job connected with the fitness industry in Oldcastle, or within 30 miles of it for one year after leaving FitQuick's employment.

As Chang will have built up a personal relationship with clients at FitQuick, it is reasonable for it to protect this business interest, and seeking to prevent him from working as a personal trainer for one year within Oldcastle itself is not an excessive time or too wide a locality. However, trying to prevent Chang from working as a personal trainer outside the town, or taking a job in the fitness business not involving a close personal relationship with clients, may well be deemed unreasonable. It rather depends on how far away the nearest gym in Kofi's chain is located and whether his new job would permit him to exploit his relationship with his old clients.

The courts recognise that employees do not usually share equal bargaining power with their employers. The wording of a contract is therefore strictly interpreted to prevent unreasonable restraints upon employees, particularly if their youth and inexperience make them prey to exploitation.

Proactive Sports Management Ltd v *Wayne Rooney and Others* (2010)

Proactive claimed that Rooney was in breach of a contract which entitled it to 20 per cent of all profits from the exploitation of R's image for eight years. Rooney had entered the contract with Proactive at the age of 17 and neither he nor his parents appeared to have been legally advised during the process.

Held (Judge Hegarty QC):

> The contract between Proactive and Rooney was in restraint of trade and unenforceable because it was unreasonable in its duration, area and scope.

As it stood, the restraint would last about half of his footballing career, as he would be 25 when the contract term finally expired. It gave worldwide exclusive control to Proactive, and imposed significant restrictions on Rooney's freedom to exploit his talents in any way he chose. He had agreed 'not, without Proactive's prior consent, to negotiate or enter into contracts with any other firms or agents or representatives or persons or any other businesses which might reasonably be regarded as competitors of Proactive or might wish to exploit his intellectual property rights.'

The court, however, must balance the parties' interests and do not allow one party to twist the meaning of the restriction to construct an unreasonable meaning.

PSG Franchising Ltd v Lydia Darby (2012)

The claimant sought an injunction against the defendants, claiming that they were in breach of a restraint clause in a franchise agreement concerning the provision of property search services.

The restriction, lasting one year from termination of their franchise, prevented them from selling such services or being interested in any company providing similar services 'within the territory' which covered Milton Keynes and its adjacent postcodes. The defendants argued that this was unreasonable in scope as it would prevent them from providing any such services *anywhere* to those that PSG supplied within the Milton Keynes district.

Held: an injunction would be granted to the claimants as the restriction was reasonable: it only restricted the defendants from doing similar business within the Milton Keynes area.

Where ambiguity arose from contract wording, the court must adopt the meaning that any reasonable person, knowing the background to the transaction, would take from the words in question. Its aim should be to interpret the words to limit the restriction to protect legitimate business interests.

The court may not always take the literal meaning of the words if this would allow an employee to abuse the employer's legitimate interests. Instead, a purposive approach may be adopted. The contract is interpreted in the way which prevents the employee from avoiding a reasonable degree of restraint.

Home Counties Dairies v Skilton (1970)

Skilton's employment contract required him not to sell milk or dairy products to any person whom he had served during his time with the dairy, for one year after leaving the dairy's employment.

Held: the object of the clause was to prevent the dairy's loss of customers from Skilton's old milk round, not to prevent him from taking up work, for example, in a grocery shop selling butter and cheese. It was therefore valid in so far as it prevented him from poaching his ex-employer's customers when working as a milkman.

Littlewoods Organisation v *Harris* (1978, CA)

The claimant, who had planned the contents of Littlewoods' mail order catalogue for the next year, left to work for Littlewoods' main competitor, Universal Stores. His contract with Littlewoods stated that he must not work for Universal Stores for one year after leaving Littlewoods.

Held: this very generally drafted restraint, if interpreted literally, would prevent Harris working in any capacity for Universal Stores. It must be interpreted with implied reference to Harris's very high degree of access to crucial trading information in the mail order market sector. Once this was taken into account, the clause became reasonable as it protected Littlewoods' secret information.

Restraint on the seller of a business

Buyers of the goodwill of a business may protect themselves against loss of customers by restraining the sellers from setting up in a similar business too close and too soon. The only business interest that can be protected here is the existing custom enjoyed by sellers: they can be restrained only from running a business of *exactly the same kind* as they are selling.

BRC Engineering v *Schelff* (1921)

Schelff sold his business, which was concerned with the sale of loop concrete road reinforcements. The contract of sale contained a clause that attempted to restrain him from being involved in the sale or manufacture of *any type* of concrete reinforcement.

Held: the only business interest that could validly be protected here concerned the sale of loop reinforcements. Any wider restraint was unreasonable as it related to business interests that were not being sold.

Nordenfelt v *Maxim Nordenfelt Guns & Ammunition Co. Ltd* (1894)

Nordenfelt sold his arms manufacturing business to the Maxim Nordenfelt Co. The contract restrained him from being involved, for 25 years, in any way with the armaments trade. No geographical limit was mentioned.

Held: given the wide scope of the business (a large variety of armaments were manufactured by Nordenfelt) and the very small number of customers involved (state governments), this was held to be a reasonable restraint.

Solus agreements

These most commonly arise in contracts between petroleum companies and retail petrol outlets.

Esso Petroleum v Harper's Garage (Stourport) Ltd (1968, HL)

Two solus agreements were made between Harper's and Esso: agreement 1, which was to last four-and-a-half years, was made in return for a price discount on the petrol; agreement 2, which was to last 21 years, was made in return for a mortgage loan of £7,000 from Esso secured on the filling station and which was repayable over that period.

Held: agreement 1 was binding as it was entirely reasonable. Agreement 2 was held to be unreasonable in relation to its time span. It was longer than necessary to allow Esso to protect their business interest in maintaining stable levels of distribution. It was irrelevant that it had been agreed in relation to a mortgage.

It should be noted that in the above case Harper's already occupied the land at the point that they took the mortgage. They were giving up their freedom to trade from there with whomever they chose. The restraint rules do not apply where a party agrees to a restraint *as a condition* of being given possession of land.

Cleveland Petroleum v Dartstone Ltd (1969, CA)

The defendants took a lease of a garage from Cleveland. The lease stated that they could sell only Cleveland's petrol for the duration of the lease.

Held: it was not an unreasonable restraint of trade, since the defendants had not previously been in occupation of the land and had taken on the tenancy with full knowledge of the restriction.

The same principle applies to tied pubs.

The consequences of a void restraint

The fact that a restraint is void does not prevent the rest of the contract from being valid. A party can sue successfully for breach of a contract of employment or sale of a business, as long as the alleged breach does not relate to the void restraint.

The court may be able to sever (cut out) the unreasonable part of a restraint. The remainder of the restraint can then be enforced.

Goldsoll v *Goldman* (1915, CA)

The defendant sold an imitation jewellery business situated in London. Much of the business was conducted through mail order in the UK. In the contract of sale he undertook that he would not for two years be involved in the sale of real or imitation jewellery in any part of the UK, France, the USA, Russia, or within 25 miles of Berlin or Vienna.

Held: this was clearly too wide to be reasonable as regards:

1 *business interest*: the claimant was buying an imitation jewellery business only, and could restrict the defendant's trading only in that respect;

2 *the geographical area covered by the restraint*: this was wider than reasonably necessary to protect a business interest where sales had previously been limited to the UK.

The reference to real jewellery must be severed, as must the geographical references, apart from the UK.

Severance means what it says – cutting out; the court does not take it upon itself to rewrite a restraint to make it reasonable.

Even if severance is not applicable, the purposive approach adopted by the courts in cases like *Home Counties Dairies* v *Skilton* (described above) may enable a widely drafted restraint to be interpreted reasonably.

Contractual incapacity

Minors

Minor:
person under the age of 18.

Minors (people under the age of 18) are legally capable of making most kinds of contracts and may take steps to enforce them against the other party. The law protects minors by restricting the extent to which their contracts may be enforced against them. Some – like a contract to lend money to a minor – are never enforceable by the creditor; others are binding only to a limited extent.

Contracts capable of binding a minor

Necessaries:
goods/services proved to be appropriate to the minor's needs.

Contracts to purchase **necessaries** are capable of binding a minor. 'Necessaries' are defined by s 3 of the Sale of Goods Act 1979, as 'goods suitable to the condition in life of the minor . . . and to his actual requirements at the time of sale and delivery'.

There are two issues here:

1 Are the goods capable of being necessaries? The lifestyle and social standing of the minor may be relevant.

Peters v *Fleming* (1840)

Held: a watch chain was capable of being a necessary to the defendant undergraduate and his social standing made it reasonable for it to be a gold one.

2 Were the goods necessary to the minor's requirements at the time of sale and delivery?

Nash v *Inman* (1908)

The claimant supplied clothing to the defendant minor, a Cambridge undergraduate. The clothing included 11 fancy waistcoats.

Held: as the defendant was already amply supplied with clothing appropriate to his station in life the clothing purchased could not amount to necessaries and the action must fail.

The concept of necessaries also, by analogy, covers services. All of the following are capable of being necessaries: food, clothing, lodgings, transport to work, legal advice, education.

A minor's liability in a contract for necessaries is limited to payment of a *reasonable* price. The minor is not necessarily bound by the price specified in the contract. The Sale of Goods Act 1979 s 3 states that a 'reasonable price' is payable for goods 'sold and delivered'. The court may require the minor to pay less than the price agreed with the seller. The words 'sold and delivered' suggest that the minor has a duty to pay only when delivery of the goods has been made.

A *harsh or onerous contract* will not be enforced at all.

Fawcett v *Smethurst* (1914)

A contract for hire of a car made the minor liable for any damage sustained to it whether caused by the minor or not.

Held: although this contract was for necessaries, it was void as it put an unreasonably heavy burden on the minor.

Beneficial contracts of employment are also capable of binding a minor. These include training and apprenticeship contracts, but not trading contracts. The contract is binding on the minor if overall it is for the minor's benefit, but not if it is unduly burdensome.

De Francesco v Barnum (1890)

Under a dancing-apprenticeship contract, a girl of 14 promised that she would not marry during the apprenticeship, or accept any engagements, without her master's permission. He was under no obligation to find her engagements, or to pay her if she was unemployed. When employed her pay was very poor (9d per night) even by then existing standards. She refused to go on working under these conditions and he sued her for breach of contract.

Held: the contract was void; it was onerous and unfair to the minor who was at the total disposal of the claimant.

Voidable contracts include a number of different types of contracts that create continuing obligations. Tenancy agreements, partnership agreements and contracts for the purchase of shares are examples. A minor can opt out of such a contract at any time before majority, or within a reasonable time after, but is liable for any obligations (rent, calls on shares) which accrued before then.

Proform Sports Management Ltd v Pro-Active Sports Management Ltd (2007)

Wayne Rooney, who was under contract to Everton, entered into a 'representation agreement' with the claimants giving them the right, for a certain period of time, to represent him in any transfer negotiations into which he might enter. During the agreement's currency, Rooney was approached by the defendant company which persuaded him to enter an exclusive transfer agreement. The claimant sued the defendant arguing that the defendant had induced Rooney to break his contract with the claimant.

Held: no breach of contract had occurred. The representation agreement amounted to a voidable contract only. It was insufficiently analogous to a contract for necessary services, apprenticeship or education to be binding on a minor and Rooney was entitled to avoid it at any time.

Judge Hodge said: 'Players' representatives do not undertake matters that are essential to the player's training or his livelihood. They do not enable the minor to earn a living or to advance his skills as a professional footballer.'

Unenforceable contract: contract to loan money/supply non-necessary goods to a minor cannot be enforced *against them*. The minor has the right to sue.

Contracts which are not enforceable against a minor

All contracts which do not fit into the categories discussed above are not binding on minors. The commonest **unenforceable contracts** are for loans of money or the sale of non-necessary goods and services.

Historically, parties who did business with minors did so at their peril, and often found themselves out of pocket. Today they may be able to obtain payment or recover goods under the Minors' Contracts Act 1987, which aims to redress the sometimes excessive immunity enjoyed by minors:

1 *Guarantee of minors' debts.* Under s 2 of the Act, contracts by a third party to guarantee payments by minors under contracts not enforceable against them are binding on the third party.

Restitution:
an equitable remedy requiring a party to hand back specific property to another party.

2 *Restitution orders against minors.* This is an equitable remedy available at the court's discretion whereby a minor may be required to return to the other party any property acquired under the contract (Minors' Contracts Act 1987, s 3). This remedy was available prior to 1987 and was sometimes granted in cases of fraud, where minors obtained property under a contract by lying about their age. The court may also order minors to hand over the proceeds of sale of any goods supplied to them (*Stocks* v *Wilson* (1913)). It does not generally enable a creditor to recover a money loan, since the actual coins or notes supplied are no longer recoverable from the minor, having been spent (*Leslie* v *Sheill* (1914)).

Ratification of debt:
the binding acknowledgement on reaching majority, of the obligation to pay a debt contracted while a minor.

3 *Ratification of debts* contracted during minority. Section 1 of the 1987 Act provides that if, on attaining majority, persons ratify debts transacted in their minority, this ratification (confirmation) is binding on them.

Worth thinking about?

How does the law treat contracts supplying mobile phone services to minors?

Suggested solutions can be found in Appendix 2.

Mentally impaired persons

The contractual capacity of a person who is mentally impaired is limited in two situations:

1 *Where the other party knew of the impairment.* If the other party to the contract knew or reasonably should have known of a party's mental impairment, the contract is voidable by the impaired party, i.e. the impaired party can choose to opt out of it. If the other party was not aware of the impairment, the contract is valid and enforceable.

2 *Contracts for necessaries.* Under s 3 of the Sale of Goods Act 1979, a mentally impaired person is obliged to pay a reasonable price for necessaries when they are supplied by a seller who is aware of that person's mental state. The court will not interfere with the price if the seller was not aware of the buyer's mental state.

Chapter summary

Illegality of contracts

A contract may be void for illegality because:

- It is prohibited by statute.
- It is against public policy because its purpose is to break the law.

Consequences: such contracts are absolutely void – property may not be recoverable.

Other contracts are merely void because they do not involve law-breaking but are against the public interest.

For example: contracts in restraint of trade because they potentially inhibit competition.

Consequences: valid if it can be shown that the restraint is reasonably necessary:

(a) to protect a business interest;

(b) and does not cover too wide a geographical locality;

(c) and does not last too long.

A *purposive approach* is used to interpret the words of the restraint.

Severance of unreasonable aspects of the contract is also possible.

Capacity to contract

The law protects some vulnerable classes of person by limiting the types of contracts which fully bind them.

Minors

Binding on a minor

Contracts for necessary goods/services.

Beneficial contracts of employment.

Voidable by a minor

Contracts creating some continuing interest or obligation are voidable at the minor's option.

Unenforceable against a minor

All other contracts (including contracts to loan money) are unenforceable against the minor.

Mentally impaired persons

Bound to pay a reasonable price for necessaries even if the seller is aware of the incapacity.

All other contracts are voidable by them if the other party should have been aware of the incapacity.

Review questions 9

1 How does illegality affect the validity of a contract?

2 Why may the following contracts be illegal?

   (a) a contract to rob a bank;

   (b) a contract to make a pornographic film;

   (c) a contract by an English firm to supply arms to terrorists in the US.

3 Are the following contracts enforceable against Alfie who is 17?

   (a) to buy a suit to wear at job interviews;

   (b) to buy 50 Christmas cakes which he intends to distribute to local old people's homes;

   (c) to work for Busby Ltd as a packer in their dispatch department;

   (d) to borrow £50 from Jemima.

4 In what circumstances will a contractual term restricting an employee's future employment be binding?

5 What contracts are capable of binding a minor?

6 Explain when the contractual capacity of a person who is mentally impaired is limited.

Answers to all review questions can be found in Appendix 2

Advanced questions 9

(A) Analyse the circumstances in which a contract may be deemed void, voidable or illegal using examples from decided cases.

(B) Evaluate the Minors' Contracts Act 1987.

Answers to the advanced questions can be found at **go.pearson.com/uk/he/resources.**

Take a closer look

The following cases provide important examples of how the law in this chapter has developed. They are primary sources illustrating the law in action and give more detail about their facts, as well as helping to understand the law and to appreciate how the judges reached their decisions.

Try looking them up in the law reports or accessing them via a database, e.g. Bailii (www.bailii.org/databases.html). LexisNexis or Westlaw may be available in the university or college library, or extracts may be found in a case book. (See Appendix 1: Additional resources.)

Eastham v Newcastle United Football Club [1963] 3 All ER 139

Home Counties Dairies v Skilton [1970] 1 All ER 1227

Littlewoods Organisation Ltd v Harris [1978] 1 All ER 1026, CA

Patel v Mirza [2016] SCUK 42

Web activity

This article provides a good example of an enforceable contract tainted by illegality: www.inhouselawyer.co.uk/legal-briefing/illegality-in-contracts/

Assignment 8

Barry is employed by Sweeties Ltd and has learnt secret toffee-making processes exclusively used by Sweeties in the UK. His contract states that if he leaves Sweeties he must not be involved in the manufacture of toffee or any other confectionery in the UK or the US for one year.

1 Is this restraint lawful?
2 If unlawful, is it capable of being made lawful?

Discharge of the contract and remedies for breach

Learning objectives

On completion of this chapter, students should be able to:

★ understand the ways in which a contract may be discharged;

★ appreciate the concept of complete performance and the exceptions to it;

★ describe how a contract may be discharged by agreement;

★ give examples of when a contract may be frustrated;

★ explain the rights of the parties to a frustrated contract;

★ grasp when a breach is capable of discharging the contract;

★ apply the remoteness of damage rules;

★ distinguish between the different types of damages available for breach of contract;

★ be aware of when the court may impose an equitable remedy for breach of contract.

Introduction

This chapter examines how contractual obligations come to an end. When a contract is made, normally the obligation would end with full performance: one party pays the contract price and the other party provides the goods or service requested. However, life is not always quite so simple; sometimes performance is interrupted in some way or only partial performance takes place.

One party may change their mind and agree not to perform the contract or want to vary it in some way; how does the law ensure this agreement is binding?

Sometimes things go wrong. What is the legal position if a photographer is booked to take pictures at a wedding and on the day he is too ill to attend, or alternatively, in excellent health, does attend with results that are a testimony only to his incompetence instead of being a wonderful record of the special day?

This chapter examines how the law resolves issues like these.

Discharge of contracts

Discharge by performance

The general rule: a contract is discharged only by complete performance; all the obligations in the contract must have been carried out. A party's failure to perform may make him or her vulnerable to an action for breach of contract by the other party, who may also be entitled to withhold payment. Although it may generally be fair to hold someone to the letter of a bargain, this rule is capable of producing some unjust results.

Cutter v Powell (1795)

The defendant, Captain Powell, engaged Lieutenant Cutter as part of his crew for a voyage from Jamaica to Liverpool. The contract stated that payment was due only on completion of the voyage, but the Lieutenant died 19 days before the ship reached Liverpool.

Held: his widow, who sued on behalf of his estate, could not claim any part of his salary since payment of it was not due until the voyage had been completed when the entire obligation would have been discharged.

Exceptions have been developed to prevent injustice.

1 Divisible contracts

Entire contract: contract consists of one obligation only and no payment is due unless/until that obligation is fully performed.

Divisible contract: the contract consists of a number of distinct obligations and payment must be made for as many as are properly performed.

The contract made by Lieutenant Cutter was an **entire contract**; he was obliged to perform one whole obligation in order to be able to claim payment – complete the voyage from Jamaica to Liverpool. The outcome for Mrs Cutter would have been happier if this obligation had been **divisible** – broken down into smaller units (for example, weeks), on completion of each of which payment of a proportion of his wages would have been due. She would then have been able to claim for three weeks' wages.

Ritchie v Atkinson (1808)

A contract stated that goods would be shipped at a cost of £5 per tonne. When only part of the agreed cargo was transported, the owners claimed that they were not bound to pay.

Held: since the obligation was divisible, payment was owed for each tonne of the cargo which had been carried.

Contracts of employment are divisible, with payment due on a weekly or monthly basis. Building contracts are another example: specified sums become payable on completion of performance of specified portions of the work.

2 One party prevents the other from completing performance

Significant opportunities for fraud would occur if a party to a contract could claim that they were not bound to pay when they themselves had prevented the other party from completing the necessary work. To prevent such injustice, the party who prevents performance is deemed to be in breach, which releases the other party from the obligation to tender complete performance.

Planché v Colburn (1831)

The claimant entered into a contract to write a book for the defendant publisher and was to be paid £100 when the book was completed. He had researched and written part of the book when the defendant told him that it would not be required.

Held: he was entitled to a sum to represent the value of the work he had done towards completion of the contract.

3 Acceptance of part performance

Part performance:
incomplete performance which may discharge the contract if accepted.

Where the contract is entire, part performance does not discharge a party's obligation. However, **part performance**, if voluntarily accepted by the party to whom it is offered, does release the other party from the remainder of the obligation. The accepting party must then pay an appropriate price. The accepting party must have a genuine choice to accept or reject the part performance. A buyer can refuse to take delivery of a consignment of goods, but may have no real choice in a contract to supply goods and services if materials have become part of their own property.

Sumpter v *Hedges* (1898)

The claimant contracted to build a barn for the defendant, but then abandoned the project when it was only half completed.

Held: no payment was due since the defendant, who had completed the barn himself, had no choice but to accept part performance and make the building safe by finishing the work. The defendant did have to pay for materials which the claimant had left behind and which the defendant had chosen to use to complete the building.

4 Substantial performance

Substantial performance:
Almost complete performance which must be accepted.

Provided a party has received **substantial performance** (the bulk of what was agreed) payment is due, even if final performance deviates marginally from the letter of the contract. The payer is then entitled to a discount to cover the minor failure to perform. The court has to decide whether the performance is sufficiently substantial to discharge the obligations. Compare the following two decisions.

Bolton v *Mahadeva* (1972)

Held: a contract to install a central heating system was not substantially completed: fumes escaped into the house, which was also substantially less warm than was promised as a condition of the contract.

Hoenig v *Isaacs* (1952)

Held: a contract to decorate and furnish a flat had been substantially performed since the defects (repairs to a bookcase and replacement of a wardrobe door) were superficial and easily remedied. The total cost of the contract was £750 and the cost of the defects £55.

Note that none of these exceptions would have helped in the *Cutter* v *Powell* case:

- Lieutenant Cutter's contract was an *entire* obligation; payment was made on the basis of completion of the whole voyage, not on a weekly or daily basis;
- the captain did not *prevent completion* of the contract: fate intervened;
- the captain had no choice but to accept part performance;
- performance was not *substantial*; Cutter had not performed more than about two-thirds of what was required of him.

Today a remedy would be provided under the Law Reform (Frustrated Contracts) Act 1943 (see below).

Discharge by agreement

Having formed a contract, the parties to it may agree not to go through with it. This agreement (which is in effect a secondary contract) will be binding as long as the necessary requirements of a valid contract are satisfied. The issue most likely to be problematic is consideration.

Bilateral discharge

Where the first contract is still wholly or partially executory (neither party has performed all his or her obligations), consideration will consist of each party's promise not to insist on the other party's performance of those obligations. Each party is giving up legal rights under the first contract.

Unilateral discharge: accord and satisfaction

Accord and satisfaction:
a legally binding agreement to discharge an existing contract.

Where one party has completely performed his or her obligations under the original contract and the other party wants to be released from their obligations, a promise by the first party to allow this is binding only if the other party promises some material benefit (consideration) in return. Such a transaction is described as **accord and satisfaction**. A promise, to pay a sum of money, or to provide some other consideration in return for the other party giving up his or her rights, will immediately discharge the contract.

Discharge by frustration

Frustration:
impossibility of contract performance occurs subsequent to formation but before performance.

If, between formation and performance of the contract, events outside the parties' control render further performance impossible or futile, the contract may be discharged by **frustration**. The party claiming that the contract has been frustrated must satisfy the court that the supervening events have radically changed the nature of the contractual obligation. This doctrine was developed in the nineteenth century to prevent injustice where a party is prevented from carrying out a contract through no fault of his or her own.

Frustration may discharge the contract in the following situations:

1 destruction or unavailability of the subject matter;

2 the death or illness of one of the parties;

3 supervening illegality;

4 government intervention;

5 the event on which the contract is based fails to occur;

6 delay in performance.

1 Destruction or unavailability of the subject matter

Taylor v Caldwell (1863)

Held: a contract to let a music hall was found to be frustrated when the hall was destroyed by an arsonist.

Gamerco SA v ICM/Fair Warning (Agency) Ltd (1995)

Held: a contract under which the Guns N' Roses band was going to perform was frustrated when the stadium where the concert was supposed to take place became unsafe and it was impossible to find another suitable venue in time.

2 Death or illness of one of the contracting parties

This affects contracts involving a service which can be performed only by the relevant party. Illness does not necessarily frustrate the contract. The average employment contract is not frustrated by an employee having a week off with influenza. Relevant factors to consider include the length of the illness relative to the length of the contract and whether the essential nature of the contract is threatened by the loss of performance. A seven-year contract with an actor in *The Mousetrap* will not be frustrated by one night's laryngitis, but this would prove fatal to a contract for a one-night performance by a famous soprano at the Royal Opera House.

Condor v The Barron Knights (1966)

Condor, drummer with the Barron Knights pop group, became ill with nervous strain. His doctor said that he should perform no more than four nights a week.

Held: the contract was frustrated, since such limited performance was incompatible with the nature of the work. In the music business, performance dates might not arise at regular intervals. It might involve performance seven nights a week at busy periods.

The law relating to disability discrimination now prevents an employer from sheltering behind the doctrine of frustration to avoid observing the rights of an employee who acquires a disability (see case below).

Warner v Armfield Retail & Leisure EAT (2014)

Mr Warner had worked for some years as a carpenter for Armfield. He then suffered a minor stroke which made him unable to use his left hand or pick up heavy objects. He received discretionary sick pay from Armfield for several months, until his entitlement ran out. Armfield then sent him his P45 and dismissed him, arguing that the contract was frustrated because he could no longer perform his job. Mr Warner argued that Armfield had discriminated against him by failing to perform its duty to investigate whether reasonable adjustments could be made to enable him to return to work. The employment tribunal agreed with the employer that the contract was frustrated because there were no reasonable adjustments that could have been made in the circumstances and dismissed the case. The EAT affirmed the employment tribunal's decision. The contract was frustrated by the claimant's disability: there was nothing the employer could reasonably have done to get Mr Warner back to work even if it had carried out an investigation into possible adjustments. The doctrine of frustration could never discharge the contract where disability discrimination was relevant unless reasonable adjustment was not practicable.

A contract with a sole trader may be frustrated through their illness if their input is sufficiently crucial.

Atwal v Rochester (2010)

Mr Rochester, a sole trader, became very ill with heart disease while carrying out a building contract for Mr and Mrs Atwal. After bypass surgery he was advised by his doctor to give up work. The Atwals had to get their work completed by another builder at a greatly increased price which they tried to recover by claiming that Mr Rochester had wrongfully repudiated the contract.

Held: the contract was frustrated not breached. It was in effect a personal service contract. He had no members of staff who could carry out the work on his behalf. He did much of the work personally, assisted by casual labourers and subcontracted out the specialist work.

3 Supervening illegality

A contract which is completely legal when formed may become illegal by a change in the law occurring before performance. A contract with a foreign national will be made illegal if Britain subsequently declares war against that person's country, since performance would in effect have involved trading with the enemy. Therefore, in *Fibrosa Spolka Akcyjna* v *Fairbairn Lawson Combe Barbour Ltd* (1943, HL) a contract by a British firm to sell machinery to a Polish firm was frustrated when Germany, with whom Britain was at war, annexed Poland in 1939.

4 Government intervention

This has often arisen in wartime due to the internment or conscription of personnel and requisitioning of property. In *Morgan* v *Manser* (1947) the conscription in wartime of a comedian frustrated his contract. At the point when he received his call-up papers there was no indication of how long hostilities would last.

Other exercise of power by government agencies may have the same effect. In *Shepherd* v *Jerrom* (1987) the imposition of a prison sentence was held to frustrate a contract of apprenticeship. Compulsory purchase of land may invalidate a contract of sale.

5 The event on which the contract is based fails to occur

Here the letter of the contract can usually still be performed, but performance has become futile and in no way reflects the object which the parties intended to achieve.

Krell v *Henry* (1903)

Held: a contract for the one-day hire of a room for the purpose of viewing Edward VII's coronation procession was frustrated when the coronation was postponed due to the King's illness. While it would have been possible for the hirer and his party to have sat and watched the traffic on the booked date, this clearly was not what the parties had intended.

If part of the purpose of the contract can still be achieved, however, the contract will not be frustrated.

Herne Bay Steam Boat Co. v *Hutton* (1903)

Hutton hired a boat to take a party of guests to view the fleet and watch the naval review on Edward VII's coronation day but due to the postponement of the coronation the review was also cancelled.

Held: the contract was not frustrated since it was for two purposes only one of which had failed to happen. The fleet could still be toured.

6 Delayed performance

Delay, caused by some supervening event which suspends or unreasonably delays performance of a contract, may lead to frustration of the contract, if it makes the outcome radically different from what the parties originally planned. See *Davis Contractors* v *Fareham District Council* (1956, HL), *Metropolitan Water Board* v *Dick Kerr & Co.* (1918) and *GryfLowczowski* v *Hinchingbrooke Healthcare NHS Trust* (2006) below.

The limitations of the frustration rule

The courts do not willingly free parties from their contractual obligations. An event which should have been foreseeable when the contract was made will not frustrate the contract unless its occurrence was outside the parties' control. Even then the court may still take the view that this eventuality (e.g. bad weather) should have been covered by the contract. It is also irrelevant that subsequent events have caused mere inconvenience or delay, or made the performance of the contract more expensive, or less profitable, than was planned. In *Tsakiroglou & Co.* v *Noblee Thorl GmbH* (1961, HL) it was held that closure of the Suez Canal did not frustrate a shipping contract although it added to the length, and therefore to the cost, of the journey.

Davis Contractors v *Fareham District Council* (1956, HL)

Davis had contracted to build houses for the council and had specified a fixed price. Due to bad weather, lack of materials and reduced manpower because of postwar shortages, the contract took much longer to complete than the builders had expected and was much more costly.

Held: frustration had not occurred. Inconvenience and expense were not sufficient: frustration occurs only where the end result of the contract is radically different from what the parties intended. If the contract had been frustrated, the council would have had to pay a price truly in line with the cost to the builder. (Remedies for frustration are explained later in the chapter.)

Amalgamated Investment & Property Co. Ltd v *John Walker & Sons* (1977)

Held: applying *Davis* (above), a contract to buy a property with a view to development was not frustrated by the building later being listed by the local authority, which in effect prevented any real development taking place. The listing did not prevent the contract being carried out. Listing was an inherent risk that would certainly drastically reduce the price but there was no express or implied term in the contract that the property would continue to be capable of development. The listing therefore did not make the contract radically different.

The above case illustrates particularly well how the court is unsympathetic to the plight of an experienced business, which in effect gambles and loses on a risky contractual deal. The nature of the premises meant that listing was a considerable probability, and the buyer had asked the vendor whether it knew of any plan by the local authority to do so. The buyer still chose to go ahead, clearly aware that it was a risky enterprise. It was fair to treat the buyer as having accepted the inherent risk.

Force majeure clauses

Force majeure clause: a contract term which states the rights of the parties in the event of specified problems.

An effective ***force majeure* clause** may prevent a contract being frustrated. It determines the rights of the parties in the event of specified circumstances outside their control. A *force majeure* clause can be useful in two ways:

1 To exempt a party from, or limit its liability for, breach of contract to cover situations where failure to perform arises from circumstances which are unlikely to be treated as frustrating the contract. Hazards which commonly prevent performance are deemed by the courts to be foreseeable and therefore incapable of frustrating the contract. For example, bad weather is a common cause of delay in the performance of transport, travel and construction contracts. They may also be interrupted by trade union action, or through outbreak of civil or national hostilities. (Remember that exemption and limitation provisions are subject to the controls outlined in Chapters 7 and 8.)

2 To avoid the contract being discharged by events which would otherwise frustrate it. This will be effective only if the court is satisfied that the parties really intended to keep the contract alive in the circumstances which are now threatening its existence.

Metropolitan Water Board v *Dick Kerr & Co. Ltd* (1918)

A contract made in July 1914 for the construction of a reservoir within six years contained a provision that the time limit could be extended in the event of delay arising from difficulties, delays or impediments, however caused. On the outbreak of war the following September, the work was halted by government order.

Held: the clause did not prevent the contract being frustrated, since the delay occasioned by interruption of the work appeared likely to be much more lengthy than the parties could have contemplated when they made the contract.

Self-induced frustration

The courts are not sympathetic to a party who causes the allegedly frustrating event.

Maritime National Fish Ltd v *Ocean Trawlers Ltd* (1935)

The defendants hired a trawler equipped with a type of net which required a licence. The defendants applied for five licences, to cover their own ships and the hired ship, but only four were granted. The defendants, therefore, used these to license their own ships. They claimed that the lack of a licence for the claimant's ship frustrated the contract of hire by making its performance illegal.

Held: the contract was not frustrated as the defendants had chosen which ships to license and could have licensed the hired ship instead of one of their own.

The difference between frustration and mistake

It is important to note the difference between a contract which is void for mistake and one which is frustrated due to destruction of the subject matter. The distinguishing feature is one of time (as can be seen in the 'Real life' example outlined below).

(For operative mistake, see Chapter 9.)

The consequences of the contract being frustrated

When a contract is discharged by frustration, it ceases to exist from that moment on. Rights that have already arisen with regard to a party remain that party's property, but the party loses any rights which are due to arise later. This means that a party who has received property is entitled to retain it; a party with no entitlement to claim payment before the contract was frustrated loses its right to do so under the contract. Prior to 1943 such loss was said to 'lie where it fell' at the time when the contract was frustrated. There was no means by which a party could recover prepaid money, or payment for services rendered in preparation for performance of the contract.

Real life

Manesh works as a sales representative for Stephen's Toys Ltd. He contracts to sell a consignment of teddy bears to Zoe. He believes that they are safely stored in a warehouse at Stephen's factory but unknown to both parties the warehouse has just caught fire after being struck by lightning and the goods ceased to exist before Manesh made his offer. Here no contract ever came into existence. It was void from the outset for operative mistake, as it was based on non-existent subject matter. It was impossible for a contract to result.

If destruction of the teddies had occurred after Zoe had accepted Manesh's offer, the contract would be frustrated, since it was formed with reference to goods which existed at the time the contract was made, but destroyed before it was performed.

Appleby v Myers (1867)

The claimants contracted to install machinery on the defendant's premises. Payment was to be made on completion of the work. The defendant's premises were destroyed by fire prior to completion. It was held that the claimants were unable to recover any of the cost of their labour and materials.

The injustice of this principle was reduced by the decision in *Fibrosa*:

Fibrosa Spolka Akcyjna v Fairbairn Lawson Combe Barbour Ltd (1943, HL)

(The facts in this case are set out above.)

Held: since consideration had completely failed and the Polish firm should recover the £1,000 which it had already advanced and was not liable for the remaining £600 advance payment since it had received no benefit whatever from the contract.

While the common law still determines the situations where frustration may occur, the rights of the parties to a frustrated contract are now regulated by statute.

The Law Reform (Frustrated Contracts) Act 1943

Payer's right to recover prepaid sums (s 1(2))

Any money paid in advance is recoverable subject to s 1(2). Any sum due to be paid is no longer payable.

Payee's right to recover expenses (s 1(2))

A proviso protects the payee. If the payee has incurred expenses in performance of the contract before the frustrating event they may, at the discretion of the court, retain or claim up to the maximum of any prepaid or prepayable sum to cover those expenses, if with regard to all the circumstances it is fair and just to do so.

Gamerco SA v ICM/Fair Warning (Agency) Ltd (1995)

(The facts in this case are set out above.)

The defendant had been paid $412,000 in advance while the claimant promoters had incurred approximately $450,000 expenses. The defendant's expenses were assumed to be about $50,000.

Held (by Garland J, somewhat controversially): given the extent of the claimant's expenses and the absence of any real evidence of those of the defendant, the defendant must repay the whole $412,000.

Note the limits to the protection of this proviso in s 1(2): if the work done by the payee exceeds the prepaid/pre-payable sum the difference cannot be claimed. However, its effect may be to make the payer part with money without seeing any benefit.

Payee's right to cost of a valuable benefit (s 1(3))

A party who, prior to the frustrating event, has conferred a valuable benefit on the other (apart from the payment of money) may claim its value, if it is just to do so. This right exists as an alternative to, or in addition to, the rights conferred under s 1(2). Unfortunately, the 1943 Act does not define what is meant by a 'valuable benefit'. Some guidance was given in the next case, which also illustrates how a just sum should be calculated.

BP Exploration Co. v Hunt (1982, HL)

Hunt owned an oil concession in Libya. His contract was with BP, under which it was to explore the concession to see if it was commercially viable and, if so, to develop it. This would be done at BP's risk and cost. If oil were found in commercial quantities, BP would be repaid out of Hunt's share. A substantial oil field was developed and went into production, but the contract was frustrated when the Libyan government withdrew the concession. BP claimed that the oil Hunt had received was a valuable benefit.

Held: the Act must be interpreted purposively to prevent either party obtaining an unfair financial advantage.

The valuable benefit was the end product of the service as opposed to the service itself. Hunt had been given his share of the oil and, therefore, received a valuable benefit from BP's performance of contractual services.

The value of the benefit must be determined at the moment the contract was frustrated. This represented the upper limit of any award. The value of Hunt's share of the oil so far was $85 million, but this must be reduced to take into account gains made by BP so far and the terms of the contract.

The just sum to be awarded to BP was $35 million, since it had already recovered $62 million of its $85 million development costs but had also paid Hunt $10 million. The fact that BP bore the main risks attached to the contract was also relevant to determining this sum.

The next case clearly illustrates the operation of s 1(3) and the nature of a valuable benefit.

Atwal v Rochester (2010)

(The facts in this case are set out above.)

The total cost of building work prior to frustration of the contract by his illness was £89,450, some of which had been paid. The part-completed building work was clearly of financial value representing a 'valuable benefit' under s 1(3) and the builder was entitled to £13,550 for it.

The Act, therefore, always protects a payee who has asked for some prepayment. The payee will be covered, whether or not he or she has actually provided any valuable benefit. However, if the payee has (perhaps unwisely) not stipulated any advance payment, the Act will assist only if the payer has received a valuable benefit. Therefore, if *Appleby* v *Myers* (1867) (see above) was being decided today, the outcome would be the same unless the builder had obtained some payment up front.

It is instructive to see how the doctrine of frustration would affect the outcome of *Cutter* v *Powell*, which was explained at the beginning of this chapter. Today, Lieutenant Cutter's contract would be frustrated by his death. By serving on the ship, he would have provided a valuable benefit to his employer prior to his death; so now a proportion of his wages would be recoverable by his widow.

Discharge by breach

Not every breach of contract is capable of resulting in its discharge. The distinction between conditions and warranties (which were described in Chapter 7) is important here:

1 *Breach of warranty.* The innocent party has the right to claim damages if he or she has suffered any actionable damage or loss. The breach is not capable of bringing the contract to an end.

Bettini v Gye (1876)

Bettini had a three-month contract to perform as an opera singer. Bettini was ill for six days of the rehearsal period and his employer terminated his contract and replaced him with another performer.

Held: Bettini was in breach of a warranty and consequently the employer was not entitled to terminate the contract. Failure to attend some rehearsals did not go to the root of the contract.

Repudiate:
refuse to recognise or
perform an obligation.

2 *Breach of condition.* Where a term has the status of a condition and, therefore, is crucial to the contract, the innocent party is entitled to **repudiate** (refuse further performance of his or her obligations); he or she may recover any property transferred under the contract and obtain damages. Notice that the innocent party, in theory at least, has a choice. An innocent party can free himself or herself from his or her obligations if he or she wishes, or may attempt to hold the other party to the bargain. In many cases no real choice exists, as the breach will be so ruinous to the contract that the injured party will be only too glad to be able to avoid his or her obligations. A breach of condition may consist of a refusal to perform, or arise from performance which is so inadequate that the innocent party is effectively deprived of the bargain. It may occur before or at the date of performance.

Poussard v *Spiers & Pond* (1876)

Madame Poussard had a contract to perform as an opera singer for three months. During that time she was ill, five days before the opening night and was unable to sing for the first four nights of the opera. Spiers replaced her with another opera singer.

Held: Madame Poussard was in breach of a condition of her contract. Failure to attend on the opening night went to the root of the contract, as the critics were there and reviews were written on that basis. Spiers was entitled to repudiate/terminate the contract.

Anticipatory breach

Anticipatory breach:
notice that a contract
will not be performed
once performance
is due.

So-called **anticipatory breach** of a contract occurs where one party indicates, before the time for performance is due, that he or she repudiates the contract. This may consist of either a total refusal to perform or a statement that performance will be different from that set out in the contract. Once this occurs the innocent party may repudiate his or her side of the contract and sue for damages.

Hochster v *De La Tour* (1853)

The parties made a contract in April, under which the defendant agreed that the claimant should act as his courier on a foreign tour, due to begin on 1 June. On 11 May, the defendant informed the claimant that his services would not be required.

Held: the claimant could sue for damages immediately: he did not have to wait for the performance date.

Refusal of performance must be clear and unambiguous to amount to repudiatory breach.

Dalkia Utilities Services plc v *Caltech International Ltd* (2006)

In 1995 Dalkia entered a contract to provide energy services for 15 years, payable by monthly instalments. The contract gave Dalkia the right to terminate the contract and claim a termination fee if Caltech committed a material breach.

Caltech was late paying some instalments between 2000 and 2003, and in June 2003 Caltech warned Dalkia that Caltech was experiencing financial difficulties and was considering sale of the business or putting it into administration. By 1 August, three months' instalments were owing and Caltech told Dalkia that it did not have the means to pay and was facing insolvency. It asked for a moratorium and suggested a scheme for repayment. Within days Dalkia served a demand for the arrears and issued a termination notice as prescribed by the contract. Caltech then paid the arrears.

Held: the contract was not discharged. Caltech's statement on 1 August was not sufficient to amount to refusal of further performance. While clearly Caltech had breached the contract it had not repudiated it. Caltech had not refused payment permanently nor shown any intention to deprive Dalkia of the substantial benefit of the contract. Caltech had 'sailed close to the wind' in its reference to insolvency but regarded this 'no doubt as lever in the negotiations'. It had given 'a mixed message' lacking 'the necessary clarity to constitute repudiation'.

Obiter dictum: even if Caltech had committed a repudiatory breach, Dalkia had not evidenced acceptance of it but arguably had chosen to affirm the contract by using the termination clause instead of pursuing the normal remedies for breach.

Victims of an anticipatory breach therefore are entitled to repudiate their contractual obligations only if the other party has already indicated his or her own repudiation. The innocent party must then give notice of intention to repudiate. This may be implied from the conduct of the parties and/or commercial practice.

Vitol Sa v *Norelf* (1996, HL)

The buyer of a cargo wrongly repudiated the contract because of unfounded fears about delay in loading and notified the seller, by telex, of what he was doing. The seller took no further action to perform the contract and, therefore, did not send the buyer the bill of lading which would, in this sort of contract, normally be sent once the cargo was loaded.

> **Held:** the absence of the bill of lading should have made the buyer aware of the seller's intentions. The seller's behaviour in the context of trade practice 'clearly and unequivocally' evidenced intention to treat the contractual obligations as discharged by the buyer's breach.
>
> Formal communication of notice is not necessary and may be effective even if it comes from an unauthorised third party. The issue is whether a reasonable person would have believed that the innocent party was opting out of further performance.

Note that the Court of Appeal in *Stocznia Gdanska SA* v *Latvian Shipping Co. (No. 3)* (2002) has stated that affirmation is not irrevocable.

When the nature of breach is such that performance may still be possible, a party, who affirms but later gets tired of waiting, may then repudiate.

If the innocent party chooses to wait for the performance date in the hope that the other party will, after all, perform, three consequences may follow:

Mitigate:
reduce the loss arising from a breach of contract.

1 The innocent party may have no duty to **mitigate** any loss before the date when the other party's obligations become due. The innocent party's duty to take reasonable steps to avoid adding to the loss arising from the breach may not arise until he or she acknowledges the breach or until the date of performance, whichever comes first. The innocent party may continue with his or her performance, where this can be done without the cooperation of the other party, and claim his or her full costs.

White & Carter (Councils) Ltd v McGregor (1962, HL)

> Mr McGregor, who owned a garage, was persuaded to advertise it through White's advertising plates, which the company contracted to display on council litter bins for three years. McGregor's obligation to pay arose only once the plates were installed. He attempted to cancel the contract the same day that he had made it, but the company refused to accept his repudiation.
>
> **Held:** the company, having performed its obligations, was able to claim the full sum. As the company had not chosen to repudiate the contract, no duty to mitigate arose, i.e. the company was under no obligation to look for another advertiser so as to avoid losing money.

The facts of the above case were exceptional since performance was completely within White & Carter's control and the product was only of any use to McGregor. The House of Lords (*obiter dictum*) stated that such a claim should not be successful unless the innocent party had a legitimate interest in keeping the contract alive.

Clea Shipping Corpn v Bulk Oil International (1984)

Twelve months into a 24-month charter the ship went out of commission after a breakdown and the charterers immediately repudiated the contract. Nonetheless, the owners carried out extensive repairs and kept the ship manned and ready for the remainder of the charter period and took no steps to find another hirer.

Held: the owners should have mitigated their loss by seeking another charterer. They had no legitimate interest in behaving as they had rather than just claiming damages for the wrongful repudiation.

However, the facts of the case determine whether a legitimate interest should be acknowledged. (See *Isabella Shipowner v Shagang Shipping Co. Ltd* (2012), below, where the High Court came to the contrary decision in what superficially seems to be a very similar case.)

Isabella Shipowner v Shagang Shipping Co. Ltd (2012)

Shagang terminated a 61-month charter 94 days before the finish date and argued that the owners should have mitigated their loss instead of refusing to accept repudiation.

Held: the owners had a legitimate interest in keeping the contract alive, as there was nothing perverse or unreasonable about their decision in the circumstances. Market conditions and the short time left in the charter period made it very unlikely that another hirer could be found.

The differences are clear: in *Clea Shipping* the ship breakdown, which was the owner's risk in this sort of charter, was the initial cause of all the problems and prompted the repudiation. In *Isabella Shipowner* the repudiation was spontaneous, instigated by the hirers, and there was only three months of a much longer charter left to run and real problems in finding new charterers.

2 The contract remains alive for the benefit of both parties. The innocent party is not discharged from his or her duties under the contract until he or she repudiates the contract. If he or she does not repudiate, but fails to perform obligations as they fall due, the innocent party could be liable for breach.

3 If the contract is frustrated before the performance date, the innocent party loses any rights to sue for breach.

Avery v *Bowden* (1855)

The claimant hired a ship to the defendant at a port in Russia. Before the hire date the defendant told the claimant that he would not be able to fulfil the contract, but the claimant chose to wait to see if he would change his mind. The Crimean War then broke out.

Held: the outbreak of war frustrated the contract and the claimant no longer had any right to sue. The contract from which his rights had been derived had ceased to exist.

Actual breach

Actual breach: failure to perform at all or properly once performance is due.

Actual breach occurs when performance is due, or in the course of performance. It takes one of two forms: a failure to tender any form of performance, or performance which is so inadequate that it largely destroys the purpose of the contract. An example of the latter occurred in December 1994, when passengers on the QE2 were transported to New York while the ship was still in the process of refitting; the ship resembled a construction site rather than a luxury liner. Although the passengers were delivered to their destination on the correct date, the conditions under which they had travelled were so appalling that their contractual expectations were largely defeated. There is little doubt that a court would treat such poor performance as amounting to a breach of condition. A very high standard of comfort, with access to the facilities to be expected on such a trip, is central to such a contract. Cunard immediately offered all the passengers a full refund of their fares.

Remedies for breach of contract

The most common remedy for breach is damages, but an equitable remedy is sometimes appropriate.

Damages

The purpose of damages is to compensate the injured party for loss or damage arising from the breach. The court awards a sum that is aimed at putting the injured party in the financial position that he or she would have enjoyed if the contract had been performed. The court must assess the damage alleged to result from the breach and decide whether any of it is too remote. It may not be justifiable to blame defendants for all the results of their actions, which may be knock-on effects of the breach. Having decided how much of the damage is attributable to the defendant, the court must decide on the quantum of damage, i.e. determine how much money the damage is worth. *Milner and Milner* v *Carnival* (2010) (see later in this chapter) provides a good example of how this is done.

Remoteness of damage

Hadley v *Baxendale* (1854)

The defendant contracted to carry the claimant's mill shaft from Gloucester to London, where it was to be used as a pattern to construct a new one. Due to the fault of the defendant, there was a considerable delay in the return of the shaft. The claimant claimed damages for his lost profits due to the mill being out of action.

Held: the defendant was not liable for this loss because it was too remote. There was nothing to alert him to the problem, since the claimant had not indicated that failure to return the shaft within the promised time limit would produce this result.

In *Hadley* v *Baxendale*, the court distinguished between the two types of damage that might follow a breach: usual and non-usual (special) damage.

Usual damage:
(Hadley v *Baxendale)*
damage normally expected to arise from a breach.

Special damage:
(Hadley v *Baxendale)*
damage which is too remote unless the defendant should have known of special circumstances which made it likely.

1 *Usual damage.* **Usual damage** is the damage that anybody might reasonably anticipate would arise from a contract of the relevant kind. For example, breakage is an obvious hazard in a contract to transport china.

2 *Special damage.* **Special damage** arises because of particular circumstances which will not necessarily be known to the other party, unless these are drawn explicitly or impliedly to that party's attention before the contract is made. For example, in a contract to transport china, failure to disclose that the delivery time is crucial to a highly profitable re-sale would prevent a claim for more than normal profits in the event of a late delivery.

The following cases illustrate how these principles may be applied.

Victoria Laundry v *Newman Industries Ltd* (1949, CA)

Victoria Laundry, wishing to extend its business, asked the defendant to deliver a boiler by a stated date in June. Delivery did not take place until November, due to damage caused by the defendant. Due to this delay, the claimant was unable to take on some particularly lucrative dyeing contracts. The defendant knew that expansion of the business would be delayed if the boiler was not promptly delivered.

Held: the defendant was liable for the profits that would have resulted from the use of the boiler between June and November. However, the defendant knew nothing about the dyeing contracts, so it was not liable for those losses.

Koufos v Czarnikow Ltd (The Heron II) (1969, HL)

The defendants contracted to carry a cargo of sugar for the claimants. They knew that the claimants were sugar merchants and that there was a sugar market at the destination port. Due to delay caused by the defendants, the sugar was sold at a loss.

Held: the claimants were entitled to recover their lost profits because of the defendants' knowledge of the nature and purpose of the contract. This should have alerted them to the consequences of delay.

The remoteness rule in contract is more stringent than the reasonable foreseeability test in tort, because of the parties' relationship to each other. (See *Transfield Shipping* v *Mercator Shipping* below.) When negotiating a contract, the parties have the opportunity to discuss risk allocation and may refuse to do business if this cannot be resolved satisfactorily.

Transfield Shipping Inc. v Mercator Shipping Inc. (2008, HL)

Transfield (T) chartered a ship from Mercator (M). It was agreed that it would be returned by 4 May 2004. M entered into another charter with a third party running from 8 May 2004. However, due to delays on the voyage T did not return the ship until 11 May 2004. The new charterers agreed to take the ship, but at the new market price which was lower than when they had initially entered the contract.

M claimed damages of the difference in market price for the whole of the new charter period, while T maintained that it should only be liable pro rata for the number of days delay before it had returned the ship. The issue was initially determined by arbitrators who supported M's claim on the grounds that the loss should have been reasonably foreseeable to T. T appealed.

Held: T was only liable for the three days' loss. The remaining loss was too remote.

Reasonable foreseeability alone was too crude a test to apply to remoteness of damage in contract. Under the rule in *Hadley* v *Baxendale* as affirmed by the House of Lords in the *Heron II*, the issue must be determined not by probability but also by what the contracting parties presumably had in mind with regard to the nature and object of their transaction when they entered into it.

Lord Hope said:

In this case it was within the parties' contemplation that an injury which would arise generally from late delivery would be loss of use at the market rate, as compared with the charter rate . . . This is something that everybody who deals in the market knows about and can be expected to take into account. But the charterers could not be expected to know how, if there was a subsequent fixture, the owners would deal with any new charterers. This was something over which they had no control and, at the time of entering into the contract, was completely unpredictable.

Quantum of damages

Quantum of damages: the amount of money necessary to compensate for the damage caused.

When establishing the **quantum of damages** (the financial value of the claimant's loss) the court is governed by a number of criteria:

1. the loss must be financially quantifiable;
2. agreed damages will not be altered, but penalty sums will not be enforced;
3. the injured party has a duty to mitigate any loss;
4. contributory negligence may reduce the amount of damages.

1 Quantifiable loss

Quantifiable damage: loss or harm capable in law of being compensated by money.

It must be possible to assess the loss to the injured party in financial terms (**quantifiable damage**). This is easy where goods are damaged, since the costs of repair or replacement are easily verified. The measure of damages for breach of a building contract is normally the cost of reinstatement (correcting the defect) rather than the diminution in value of the end product, but this is subject to exceptions in the interest of producing a just result.

Ruxley Electronics & Construction Ltd v *Forsyth* (1995)

A contract to build a garden swimming pool specified that it would be 7 foot 6 inches at its deepest part, but on completion it was found to be 9 inches shallower there and 18 inches shallower at the point where diving would take place.

Held: reinstatement damages were unreasonable here as they would be 'out of all proportion to the benefit to be obtained'. Ruxley was entitled to £2,500 for loss of amenity.

Claims for loss of profit are common in contract. Under s 50 of the Sale of Goods Act 1979, a buyer who refuses to take delivery of goods may be liable to the seller for any loss on the resale of the goods due to fluctuation of the market price.

Reliance loss: the amount lost by the claimant preparing to perform their side of the contract prior to the defendant's breach.

A party may also recover **reliance losses**: expenses incurred while preparing to perform a contract which never takes place due to the breach of the other party. So in *Anglia TV* v *Reed* (1971) Robert Reed, who unlawfully repudiated a contract to appear in a film, was held liable for the costs Anglia TV had incurred in preparing for the production.

Other damages are less easily quantifiable. Where a party suffers personal injuries, his or her resulting financial losses may also often be calculated with reasonable accuracy. There are, though, some rather arbitrary rules that exist to enable the court to compensate for non-financial losses like pain and suffering.

Until recently, the courts were reluctant to award damages for mental distress, hurt feelings and disappointment. In *Addis* v *Gramophone* (1909, HL) it was held that damages were not available to compensate for the claimant's hurt feelings and distress at being wrongfully dismissed, nor for the fact that the mode of his dismissal made it difficult for him to obtain future employment.

This principle was for many years deemed to apply to all contracts but a number of distinctions and exceptions have gradually developed.

Damages may be awarded for loss of reputation. The House of Lords recently developed the concept of **stigma damages**.

Stigma damages: Damages for the claimant's loss of reputation caused by the defendant's misconduct.

Malik v *Bank of Credit & Commerce International* (1998, HL)

The defendant bank went into liquidation after its dishonesty and corrupt dealings emerged. The claimant, an ex-employee, was awarded damages for the losses he incurred, caused by a continuing difficulty in securing employment, because of the misdeeds of his previous employer.

Held: *Addis* did not apply here. This was not a distress claim. Malik's claim could succeed on the grounds that the bank was in breach of the employment contract. Employer and employee have a mutual duty of trust and confidence. Failing to conduct business honestly was a breach of this. (See Chapter 19.)

The basic principle of *Addis* continues to be upheld by the court and damages for distress arising from the *manner* of dismissal are not recoverable.

Johnson v *Unisys* (2001, HL)

The claimant suffered a nervous breakdown after being summarily dismissed by the defendant and he was unable to get a new job. He was awarded the statutory maximum (just under £12,000 the limit at that time) under the statutory scheme for unfair dismissal at the employment tribunal.

He argued that he also had a claim for breach of contract at common law and claimed £400,000 in lost earnings on the grounds that the manner of his dismissal was a breach of the employer's duty of trust and confidence.

Held (by majority): the duty of trust and confidence did not relate to the termination of the contract. The needs of the claimant concerning dismissal were already covered by the statutory scheme and the claimant could not avoid the statutory limit to compensation by bringing a common law action.

In *Edwards* v *Chesterfield Royal Hospital NHS Foundation Trust* (2011) the Supreme Court affirmed this principle. However, if the breach of duty arises *while the contract is still running*, a right of action at common law may exist. See the linked decision of two similar cases, *Eastwood* v *Magnox* and *McCabe* v *Cornwall County Council* (2004, HL) below.

Eastwood and Another v Magnox Plc (2004, HL) and McCabe v Cornwall County Council (2004, HL)

In *Eastwood* two employees claimed that before they were unfairly dismissed, their employer had conducted a campaign to demoralise and undermine them, which caused them psychiatric illness. The employee in *McCabe* claimed that he had suffered psychiatric illness because his employer failed to carry out a proper investigation into the allegations against him and had not conducted the disciplinary proceedings appropriately.

Held: the employees had a right to sue for the breach of contract caused by the behaviour of the employers and which had preceded the unfair dismissal.

The claimants in the above cases had two causes of action: one for breach of contract at common law in the court and a statutory one for unfair dismissal in the employment tribunal. The House of Lords pointed out that, if they brought both types of action, any overlapping heads of damage could not be recovered twice. (For more information about statutory unfair dismissal rights, see Chapters 19.)

Breach of an advertising contract may result in an award of damages for lost reputation, since the contract is intended to enhance reputation not to detract from it. In *Aerial Advertising Co.* v *Batchelors Peas* (1938) the defendant had contracted to advertise the claimant's product by flying an aircraft with a suitably worded banner over a number of locations. In breach of the contract, the defendant flew the aircraft over Salford during the two-minute silence on Remembrance Day. People were so scandalised by this disrespectful behaviour that Batchelors suffered a boycott of their product and damages were awarded for the damage to their reputation.

On the same principle, distress losses are recoverable in contracts with consumers, provided that the purpose of the contract is to provide pleasure or peace of mind or freedom from distress, but where the breach has in fact caused any of these to be lost.

Jarvis v Swans Tours (1973, CA)

When he bought a skiing holiday package, Mr Jarvis was promised a house party atmosphere with full bar facilities, a welcome party, afternoon tea and cakes, and a yodeller evening. There were only 13 guests in the first week. During the second week Mr Jarvis was the only guest. The yodeller turned up in working clothes rather than national dress, and sang only a few songs. The afternoon tea consisted of crisps and dry nut cakes. The bar was open on one evening only and the skiing facilities were very poor.

Held: Mr Jarvis was held to be entitled to damages both for his disappointment at the absence of all the promised facilities which were central to the contract's performance, and the full cost of his holiday, a total of £125.

Heywood v *Wellers* (1976)

The claimant contracted with the defendant solicitor to obtain an injunction to prevent her ex-boyfriend from harassing her. Due to the solicitor's negligence the procedure failed and she continued to be molested. Damages were awarded for her distress since the entire purpose of the contract was to prevent this occurring.

Even where the court is not prepared to categorise a contract as one for peace of mind, it may award damages for distress directly resulting from physical inconvenience caused by the breach. In *Perry* v *Sidney Phillips* (1982, CA) the defendant, who was under contract to the Perrys to survey premises they wished to buy, overlooked roofing faults and a defective septic tank. Once they moved in the need for repairs became evident, especially as the smell from the septic tank was causing nuisance to the neighbours. The court refused to categorise an ordinary surveyor's contract as one for peace of mind and freedom from distress. However, damages were awarded for the distress arising from the physical inconvenience of the execution of the repairs.

Cases since the late 1990s generally indicate greater readiness by the courts to recognise peace of mind obligations in contracts. In *Farley* v *Skinner (No. 2)* (2001), below, the House of Lords held that the particular circumstances of the contract should determine whether it placed such obligations on the surveyor.

Farley v *Skinner (No. 2)* (2001, HL)

The claimant specifically requested the defendant surveyor to advise whether the property he was interested in buying was badly affected by aircraft noise from Gatwick airport.

Held: the claimant was entitled to £10,000 since the surveyor's favourable report proved grossly inaccurate. It was sufficient that a major or important part of the contract was to give peace of mind, pleasure or relaxation, for recovery of such damages to be permissible.

The Court of Appeal (*Milner & Milner v Carnival, t/a Cunard* (2010)) has clearly indicated the limitations on such damages in consumer contracts.

Milner and Milner v Carnival plc t/a Cunard (2010)

Mr and Mrs Milner, the claimants, booked what was described by Cunard as a glamorous world maiden-cruise and a 'legendary experience exceeding expectations'. Sadly, due to structural problems with the ship, their cabin was very noisy and uncomfortable and they abandoned the cruise at Hawaii.

At appeal the amount of damages for distress and inconvenience was reduced by more than half to approximately £4,000 each.

Held (Ward LJ):

Physical inconvenience and discomfort is necessarily ephemeral. Disappointment, distress, annoyance and frustration are likewise the feelings one experiences at the time and which last painfully for some time thereafter. But one is not disabled, the psyche is not injured and one gets on with life.

The courts have resisted attempts to extend peace of mind damages into contracts between two businesses.

Hayes v James & Charles Dodd (1990, CA)

The defendant solicitors failed to warn a commercial client of acute access problems to land that the client was buying.

Held: damages were not payable for the mental distress caused.

2 Agreed damages: Liquidated damages and penalties

Liquidated damages: pre-estimated damages for breach agreed when the contract is made.

It is quite common for a contract to specify that, in the event of a breach, a sum of agreed or **liquidated damages** will be payable. If the court is satisfied that this sum represents a genuine attempt by the parties to determine a reasonable pre-estimate of the loss likely to result from such a breach, that sum will be awarded whether or not it represents an appropriate level of compensation. If the sum is not adequate, the injured party cannot claim more, since it contractually agreed to accept it. If it is more than necessary, the injured party does not have to return the difference. However, the court is not prepared to enforce a sum that is held to represent a **penalty**, i.e. a punishment to be suffered by the guilty party if it fails to perform its obligations, rather than an appropriate level of compensation. This sum is put into the contract *in terrorem* – to frighten a party with the consequences of not performing the contract. The object of awarding damages in contract is to compensate an injured party, not intimidate the other party into performance. If the court decides that the

Penalty: a contractual sanction intended to enforce performance.

sum represents a penalty, this will be disregarded; instead a sum will be awarded which is representative of the injured party's actual loss. In *Dunlop Pneumatic Tyre Co. Ltd* v *New Garage & Motor Co. Ltd* (1915) below, Lord Dunedin proposed the following tests to distinguish between liquidated damages and penalties:

1 the words used to describe the sum are evidence of what the parties intended but are not conclusive;

2 the sum should be treated as a penalty, if grossly disproportionate to the greatest damage likely to result from the breach;

3 where the breach consists of a failure to pay money, the prescribed sum is a penalty if it exceeds the sum payable;

4 where one sum is payable in the event of the commission of any of a number of different breaches, some of which are trifling and some of which are more serious, it is probably a penalty;

5 even if accurate pre-estimation is almost impossible, this does not prevent a sum from being treated as liquidated damages, as long as it represents a genuine attempt to make a reasonably accurate assessment.

Dunlop Pneumatic Tyre Co. Ltd v *New Garage & Motor Co. Ltd* (1915, HL)

Dunlop had a clause in its contract of sale which attempted to impose a minimum price restraint on resale of its tyres by New Garage. It stated that breach of this term would make New Garage liable to pay '£5 by way of liquidated damages for every tyre, cover or tube'.

Held: this sum was liquidated damages. It was impossible to forecast precisely the damage resulting from each sale in breach of the agreement and there was no reason to suspect that this was not a genuine bargain to assess damages. (Application of criterion 5 above.)

Since £5 was quite a substantial sum in 1915, this seems a rather surprising decision. Perhaps the House of Lords felt such a restraint was appropriate to the development of a completely new area of the market, the future of which was unpredictable at the point when the contract was formed.

The following cases illustrate how the courts apply the criteria in the *Dunlop* case.

Jeancharm v *Barnet Football Club* (2003, CA)

Jeancharm contracted to supply football kit to the club. A term in the contract stated that in the event of late payment the club should pay interest at 5 per cent per week (equivalent to 260 per cent per year). In the event of late delivery, Jeancharm promised to pay 20p per garment per day.

Held: the 260 per cent interest was an unrealistic sum to pay for Jeancharm's administrative costs, and the term must be treated as a penalty clause which was therefore unenforceable. It was totally disproportionate in comparison to the greatest loss that Jeancharm was likely to suffer.

Tullet Prebon Group v *Ghaleb El Hajjali* (2008)

El Hajjali (E), the defendant, was a specialist broker who, after taking legal advice, entered an employment contract with Tullet Prebon Group (T). This stated that if he failed to take up the job he would be liable for liquidated damages equal to at least 50 per cent of his net annual salary. His solicitor drew this clause specifically to his attention prior to signing. E having accepted, later told T, the claimant, that he wasn't interested in the job after all. T attempted unsuccessfully to find a replacement and claimed liquidated damages for breach of contract from E who refused to pay the money arguing that it was a penalty sum.

Held: E was crucial to the performance of a particular function or project. By failing to take up the job he made T suffer loss. T had made all reasonable efforts to mitigate its loss. The liquidated damages clause was not a penalty clause since it was not a disproportionate sum in the circumstances. E had entered the contract after legal advice and with full notice of the term so the parties enjoyed equal bargaining power.

Azimut-Benetti SpA v *Healey* (2010) makes it clear that in a commercial contract where the parties are on equal terms the relevant payment should be treated as liquidated damages: 'The evidence clearly shows that the purpose of the clause was not a deterrent, and that it was commercially justifiable as providing a balance between the parties upon unlawful termination by the builder' (per Blair J).

Cavendish Square Holdings BV v *Talal El Makdessi* and *ParkingEye Ltd* v *Beavis* [2015] UKSC

These two conjoined cases concerned penalty clauses. This is the first time that the Supreme Court has reviewed this area of the law since *Dunlop Pneumatic Tyre Co. Ltd* v *New Garage & Motor Co. Ltd* (1915, HL).

Held: the *Dunlop* test was adequate as guidance in the general run of damages cases, but a more flexible approach was needed in more complex cases where a true pre-estimate of loss was unpredictable and the concept of deterrence unhelpful.

The Court stressed that a penalty clause could only be imposed on a 'secondary obligation'. If the contract is aimed at enforcing performance this is a primary obligation only and the sum is not payable. A secondary obligation arises where the contract requires payment of a specified sum of money or transfer of particular assets if a contractual duty is not performed, where breach is likely to be damaging to the more long-term legitimate interests of the party who seeks to enforce it. Such a penalty sum could then be justifiable provided it was 'not totally disproportionate to any legitimate interest of the innocent party in the enforcement of the primary obligation'.

In the case of *Cavendish Square*, imposing a penalty for breach of a restrictive covenant protected the legitimate interest of the claimant to cover any potential losses flowing from a breach such as loss of profits. The penalty which was determined by a price formula for the shares retained by the claimant after the breach was a flexible method to ascertain the sum necessary to protect this legitimate interest proportionately.

In *Parking Eye* (Lord Toulson dissenting), an overstay penalty of £85 (reduced by 50 per cent for prompt payment) was not disproportionate to protect the provider firm's legitimate interest to increase its profits by mitigating the cost of maintaining the car park and optimising turnover of car park space. Car owners had clear advance notice of the term which pointed to evidence of reasonableness and they could be taken to have accepted the risk of the penalty sum in return for the convenience of parking within the shopping centre.

It remains to be seen how far this decision will assist the courts in future.

3 The duty to mitigate

The injured party cannot claim the cost of damage which it could reasonably have avoided. It is up to the party in breach to prove that the damage was avoidable.

Brace v *Calder* (1895)

A clerk with a fixed contract of employment with the defendant's partnership lost his job when the partnership was dissolved when one of the partners left. The partnership was immediately reformed by the remaining partners who had offered the clerk a job on his old contractual terms. He refused and sued to claim the wages which would have been payable had his contract run for its remaining two years.

Held: the clerk was not entitled to damages since he had been given a perfect opportunity to mitigate his loss completely and had failed in his duty to do so.

However, only reasonable steps need be taken to fulfil the mitigation duty. In *Pilkington* v *Wood* (1953) it was held that it was unreasonable to expect the claimant to take legal action against the seller of land to correct a defect in title, which the defendant solicitor had negligently failed to notice when acting for the claimant during the purchase of the land. In *Milner and Milner* v *Carnival, t/a Cunard* (2010) (see the facts above) the Court of Appeal held that the claimants acted unreasonably in refusing the defendant's offer of alternative accommodation on the ship, abandoning their cruise and incurring the unnecessary expense of the flight home.

4 Contributory negligence

It is possible that this may reduce the amount of damages awarded by the court. The Law Reform (Contributory Negligence) Act 1945, which regulates this defence in the law of tort, does not refer to contract liability. It is arguable whether in its current form it can legitimately be extended to cover contractual situations. The courts have been prepared to reduce damages where claimants' own lack of care has aggravated their loss. This appears to have been restricted to cases where a defendant is in breach of an obligation to act with reasonable care and skill which would entitle the claimant to sue in tort or contract. In 1993, the Law Commission recommended a new statute explicitly extending the defence to claims arising from any breach of a contractual duty to act with reasonable care and skill. So far Parliament has not implemented this recommendation.

Equitable remedies

A dominant characteristic of such remedies is that they are discretionary. The court has a choice whether or not to award them, unlike damages, which must be awarded if a party proves its case. A party may be refused access to an equitable remedy unless the court believes that it is just to both parties. The party claiming the remedy must show that:

1 damages would not be an adequate remedy;
2 he or she acted completely honestly: dishonest, though legal, behaviour will defeat a claim.

For example, the seller of a house has no legal duty to declare its defects unless asked. If, however, a seller knowingly failed to disclose such defects, a decree of specific performance would not be awarded against a buyer who discovered the defects later and refused to perform his or her contractual obligations.

Imposition of the equitable remedy must not be unnecessarily oppressive to the other party.

The victim of a breach of contract may exceptionally be awarded one of the following remedies.

1 Rescission

The court sets the contract aside and restores the parties to their pre-contractual positions. Note that the courts are more generous to a breach victim than to a party who claims rescission on other grounds, like misrepresentation. Rescission may be granted in a breach action even though the party at fault cannot be restored to his or her pre-contractual position: for example, where the victim of the breach has consumed the goods.

2 Specific performance

Specific performance:
an equitable remedy which orders a party in breach to perform their contractual obligation.

The court orders a party to perform his or her contractual obligations. **Specific performance** is rarely granted except in relation to contracts for the sale of land. It will never be granted to enforce a contract of employment since it would be an unreasonable restriction of personal liberty to enforce performance of such a contract. It is also unlikely that the outcome of such enforced performance would be satisfactory. A sale of goods contract concerning a unique item, like a rare antique or a work of art, might attract the remedy. Generally, damages are regarded as adequate, as the buyer can obtain similar goods elsewhere. In *Cohen* v *Roche* (1927) a contract to sell a set of Hepplewhite chairs was held not to be specifically enforceable since the chairs were regarded as 'ordinary articles of commerce'.

Specific performance is unlikely to be granted to enforce a continuing obligation which requires continuing supervision. So in *Ryan* v *Mutual Tontine Association* (1893) specific performance was held not to be appropriate to enforce a requirement in a lease relating to the provision of a janitor in fulltime attendance at a block of flats.

However, the need for limited supervision will not deter the court from issuing the order to carry out work. In *Rainbow Estates Ltd* v *Tokenhold* (1998) specific performance was granted to a landlord to make a tenant carry out repairs as required by the lease. It was held that the schedule of work was sufficiently clear and specific to make it readily capable of enforcement. Once complete, no further supervision would be required.

Specific performance has been used to enforce a debt owed by a third party to the estate of a deceased person.

Beswick v *Beswick* (1968)

Peter and John Beswick made a contract, under which John promised Peter that he would pay an annuity to Peter's wife after Peter's death. John failed to perform this obligation and Peter's widow sued him for breach of contract.

Held: as she was not privy to the contract between Peter and John, she had no rights to claim on her own behalf. However, she could succeed in her claim as the administratrix of her husband's estate which entitled her to pursue the action on behalf of her husband's estate. As the estate itself had suffered no loss through the breach, any damages would be nominal, so in the interests of justice, specific performance of the contract should be ordered to prevent John from getting away with the breach.

Worth thinking about?

Beswick v *Beswick* is a good example of the court using an equitable remedy to avoid the unjust result which would arise from strict application of the law. What statute could Mrs Beswick use to enforce payment if she was bringing this case today?

Suggested solutions can be found in Appendix 2.

As indicated above, an equitable remedy will not be granted unless it will do justice to both parties in all the circumstances of the case. Therefore the court may, in its discretion, refuse to enforce a contract where this would cause unreasonable hardship to the party who is refusing to perform. Thus, in *Patel* v *Ali* (1984) Mrs Ali contracted to sell her house, but almost immediately she suffered considerable domestic trauma including the death of one of her children. She no longer wanted to move, as she spoke little English and had friends and neighbours nearby whom she relied upon for help. Specific performance was refused.

Hardship can also be relevant to commercial contracts.

Cooperative Insurance Society v *Argyll Stores (Holdings) Ltd* (1997, HL)

The defendant opened a supermarket in a shopping centre owned by the claimant. The 35-year lease contained a covenant by the defendants that during the currency of the lease the store would be kept open for trade during normal retail hours. Six years into the lease the defendant closed the store and the claimant requested specific performance. Damages were not an adequate remedy as it was virtually impossible to quantify them accurately for the remaining 29 years of the lease.

Held: the contract would not be enforced. It would be unjust to force someone to run an unprofitable business, and supervision of performance was impracticable in the circumstances.

3 Injunction

Injunction:
an equitable remedy which orders a person to do or refrain from doing something.

An **injunction** is a commonly requested remedy for breach of restraint of trade contracts (see Chapters 10). It will not generally be granted to force one party to employ or work for another, as this would amount to enforcing a contract of employment indirectly. In *Page One Records* v *Britton* (1968) it was held that an injunction would not be granted to restrain The Troggs (a pop group) from employing a new manager, since this would force them to go on employing the claimant. But compare *Page One Records* v *Britton* with the following case.

Warner Bros v *Nelson* (1936)

The film star, Bette Davis (Nelson), breached her contract, under which she had agreed not to act on stage or screen for anybody except Warner Bros for one year, by agreeing to make a film with a UK company.

Held: an injunction would be granted to restrain Bette Davis from making films for the rival company. The contract restrained her from acting for anyone other than Warner, but did not prevent her from earning her living in other ways. The injunction did not force her to perform the contract if she was prepared to earn her living in a less profitable way.

Very exceptionally, a court may use an injunction actually to compel performance of a contract where this is in the interests of justice. In *GryfLowczowski* v *Hinchingbrooke Healthcare* (2006) Mr Justice Grey clearly felt that an injunction was necessary to assist the claimant to obtain a fair outcome in a situation where his employers had treated him very inappropriately.

Chapter summary

Discharge of contracts

Performance: must generally be complete.

Exceptions: contract divisible, acceptance of part performance, prevention of performance, substantial performance.

Agreement: mutuality essential.

Frustration: performance becomes impossible or futile due to circumstances beyond the control of either of the parties and not due to their fault.

The Law Reform (Frustrated Contracts) Act 1943 determines how far the parties may recover any resulting financial losses.

Breach of a condition gives the innocent party the option of avoiding the contract and suing immediately or awaiting performance date.

Remedies

Damages: the innocent party may claim damages for any quantifiable loss or harm resulting but not too remote from a breach of condition or warranty.

Remoteness of damage: *Hadley* v *Baxendale* (1854) states that damage may be too remote if it is 'non-usual' ('special'), i.e. not a normally anticipated consequence of breach in the particular contract situation.

Quantum of damages: the amount necessary to put the claimant in his or her pre-contractual position. Covers lost profits, reliance losses, tangible damage to person/property and exceptionally intangible damage such as loss of reputation, or pleasure or peace of mind.

Equitable remedies

Awarded in exceptional cases at the court's discretion:

- rescission;
- injunction;
- specific performance.

Review questions 10

1 Is Frankie discharged from his contractual obligations in the following circumstances?

    (a) He delivers 50 kilos of turnips to Elvis who had ordered 70 kilos, and:

        (i) the turnips were sold at 50 pence per kilo, or

        (ii) the turnips were sold at £250 for 70 kilos, but Elvis agrees to take the smaller order.

    (b) He contracts to decorate Georgie's house. When the work is half complete, Georgie refuses to let him in.

2 On 1 May, Barry contracted to hire his vintage Rolls-Royce to Laura on 30 May. On 15 May, Barry tells Laura that he is not prepared to supply the car on the due date. Laura says she will wait and see if Barry will change his mind. On 29 May, Barry's chauffeur writes off the car. What is the legal position? What difference would it make to your answer if the accident had already happened at the point Barry and Laura had made the contract?

3 Distinguish between the concepts of remoteness and quantum of damage.

4 When may the court refuse to award a decree of specific performance?

5 When will the courts order an injunction as a remedy for breach of contract?

6 What is the duty to mitigate loss and on whom does it fall?

Answers to all review questions can be found in Appendix 2

Advanced questions 10

(A) Critically evaluate the rules for determining the amount of damages to be awarded for a successful claim for breach of contract.

(B) Analyse the distinction between reliance loss damages and expectation loss damages.

Answers to the advanced questions can be found at **go.pearson.com/uk/he/resources.**

Take a closer look

The following cases provide important examples of how the law in this chapter has developed. They are primary sources illustrating the law in action and give more detail about their facts, as well as helping to understand the law and to appreciate how the judges reached their decisions.

Try looking them up in the law reports or accessing them via a database, e.g. Bailii (www.bailii.org/databases.html). LexisNexis or Westlaw may be available in the university or college library, or extracts may be found in a case book. (See Appendix 1: Additional resources.)

ARB v Hammersmith [2018] ECWA Civ 2803

Davis Contractors Ltd v Fareham UDC [1956] 2 All ER 145, HL

Jarvis v Swan Tours [1973] 3 WLR 954, CA

Koufos v Czarnikow Ltd (The Heron II) [1969] 1 AC 350, HL

Milner and Milner v Carnival plc, t/a Cunard [2010] EWCA Civ 389; [2010] 3 All ER 701

Web activity

You may have noticed that a number of cases in this chapter concern builders. Search for 'builders' on the Citizens Advice website to find out practical steps that can be taken in the event of problems arising from contracts of this kind:

http://www.adviceguide.org.uk/

Assignment 9

Janet and Arthur engaged Cuthbert to carry out extensive repairs to the electrics in their house. Cuthbert promised that the work would be finished in four weeks. To avoid the disruption, Janet and Arthur and their son George (aged nine months) moved to a hotel. A month later, the work was still not complete, but they could no longer afford to stay in the hotel and had to return home. The work was not finished for another two weeks. They had to buy a camping stove, lamps and bottled gas and pay for a laundry service. Janet became ill with stress and they were left £600 out of pocket.

Advise Cuthbert.

Would it make any difference to your advice if new safety regulations were implemented after the contract was made, which required Cuthbert to install additional failsafe devices, and it was this extra work that made the contract run past the deadline?

The law of agency

Learning objectives

On completion of this chapter, students should be able to:

★ describe how an agency relationship may be created;

★ explain the rights and duties of the agent and the principal;

★ distinguish between the ways by which the agency relationship may be terminated;

★ appreciate the nature of some particular types of agency relationships.

Introduction

There are a number of situations where an agent may be employed – when buying a house an estate agent may be employed; perhaps insurance is obtained through an insurance broker; or shares bought through a stockbroker. An employer may choose to obtain staff through an employment agency. In many sales of goods situations, agents may be employed by sellers or buyers to obtain customers or to arrange transport for international trading deals. In all these situations an agent is employed because of their expertise in the relevant business area.

However, an agent is not necessarily a professional, engaged for commercial purposes. An agency relationship may arise, for example, where a person agrees to handle the affairs of a friend who is currently unable to act personally, because of being abroad or in ill health.

An agency relationship may therefore arise in any situation where one party (the principal) authorises another person (the agent) to act on his or her behalf. Any contract made by the agent on the principal's behalf is binding by or against the third party with whom the agent negotiated. The agent may also be liable to the principal if the agent acted negligently or in breach of any contract of agency.

The creation of agency

Agent:
a person with the authority to carry out business on behalf of another person.

Principal:
person for whom an agent acts. May be disclosed or undisclosed.

The authority of the **agent** is the keystone of the agency relationship. Provided an agent has legal authority to do business on the principal's behalf, any resulting contract is binding by and against the **principal**.

The agent must make the principal a party to a contract it makes with a third party or no agency relationship exists. Even if one party exercises some control over another and receives a benefit from the contracts which the other party makes, this may not be sufficient evidence of authority to give rise to an agency relationship.

Spearmint Rhino Ventures UK Ltd v *Revenue and Customs Commissioners* (2007)

Lap dancers worked on a self-employed basis in Spearmint Rhino Clubs to dance and provide entertainment for customers. They had to do a minimum number of shifts per week and were paid a fee per shift plus a fee for every 'sit down' (a period of 'dancing and companionship' in a private room). In return, Spearmint provided the necessary facilities, security, advertising and administration.

The Revenue claimed that lap dancers were Spearmint's agents and, therefore, it should pay VAT on the services they provided to customers.

Held: VAT was not payable as no agency relationship existed between the club and the dancers. Their agreement with Spearmint was a licence, from which Spearmint derived some benefits, to allow the dancers to ply their trade on club premises. In no way did it give a dancer any authority to act on Spearmint's behalf. She decided which and how many customers she would entertain individually and kept the resulting fees and gratuities. The fact that a fee was payable to Spearmint per 'sit down' did not mean that the 'sit down' was organised on behalf of Spearmint. A dancer worked only on her own behalf.

Worth thinking about?

Spearmint Rhino Clubs pay lap dancers to work in their clubs. If they failed to pay, could the lap dancers sue in breach of contract for their earnings?

Suggested solutions can be found in Appendix 2.

Legal authority to do business on the principal's behalf normally arises from agreement between the parties, but exceptions exist in the interests of commercial efficiency. The relationship may be deemed to exist to avoid injustice to a third party or the agent. Sometimes a principal can create authority retrospectively to allow the principal to take advantage of an unauthorised transaction.

Agency by agreement between the parties

An agency relationship is most commonly created by an agreement between the parties under which the agent is given *actual authority* by the principal. The agency agreement may be made in the following ways:

Power of attorney: authority created by deed enabling agent to manage affairs for a principal who is currently incapable of doing so, because of ill health, for example.

1 *Formally by deed.* This gives a **power of attorney** to the agent. This is essential where an agent is appointed to act on behalf of a person who has become incapable of managing his or her own affairs. More detail on this topic appears at the end of the chapter.

2 *Informally by written or spoken agreement.* No particular written formalities are generally required: it is possible to appoint an agent by word of mouth. The parties may choose to evidence the agreement in writing, but this does not necessarily include all the terms binding the parties. In *Chaudhry v Prabhakar* (1988, CA) an agreement between friends, under which one who claimed knowledge of cars agreed to find a suitable secondhand model for the other, was held to have created an agency relationship.

3 *By implication.* The relationship of the parties may give rise to an implied agency agreement. This commonly arises from the employer and employee relationship.

The agency agreement may exist without any contractual relationship between principal and agent. An agency may be purely gratuitous, with the agent receiving no payment for his or her services. For example, if colleague X asks colleague Y to buy a lunchtime sandwich for her, in law she is appointing Y as her agent, but neither of them will anticipate that payment will be made for performance of the service. However, when a homeowner tries to sell a house through an estate agent, a contract exists between both parties. Under its terms, the agent is entitled to payment of commission from the homeowner if a sale takes place with a buyer introduced by the agent.

Where the agency is created by agreement the agent has actual authority. Actual authority is divided into two kinds: express and implied.

1 *Express.* The power is derived from the principal's explicit directions.

2 *Implied.* The principal is unlikely to spell out every detail of what is required. The principal is, however, deemed to have impliedly given the agent authority to accomplish anything necessarily incidental to the performance of the principal's directions.

The extent of implied authority is indicated by all the circumstances in which the agency arose, such as the relationship between the parties, the usual authority of the agent in the relevant area of business and the nature of the principal's orders. For example, if a homeowner asks an estate agent to find them a buyer, they give the agent actual authority to do so. They also impliedly authorise the agent to photograph their house and use this for advertisement purposes. In *Real and Personal Advance* v *Palemphin* (1893), the matron of a hospital was held to have implied authority to contract in her employer's name to buy essential supplies for the hospital.

Ramsay v Love (2015)

Gordon Ramsay the celebrity chef claimed that he was not bound by a personal guarantee because it had been given by Mr Hutcheson, the chief executive of his company and his father-in-law, without authority.

Gary Love, a property developer bought some premises to convert into a small hotel and restaurant. Hutcheson entered into a contract on behalf of Ramsay's company to buy these premises provided that the finished work met his approval. The defendant asked for a personal guarantee from Ramsay which Mr Hutcheson provided using an electronic writing machine to reproduce Gordon Ramsay's signature. Later Hutcheson repudiated the contract as he found the work unsatisfactory. The developer claimed on the guarantee. Ramsay sought a declaration from the court that he had not given authority for the guarantee.

Held: the evidence showed that Hutcheson had a wide remit to enter into a variety of commercial contracts on Ramsay's behalf. Ramsay's own testimony showed that he had complete trust in Hutcheson and openly admitted that he relied upon him because of his own lack of business acumen. In the past, Hutcheson had signed many legal documents with the electronic machine with Ramsay's knowledge. Personal guarantees were common practice in deals of this kind. Ramsay had given a number in the past sometimes when not even expressly asked.

Morgan J said:

> I find that when Mr Hutcheson committed Mr Ramsay to the guarantee in the lease of the premises, Mr Hutcheson was acting within the wide general authority conferred on him by Mr Ramsay at all times . . . I also find, in particular, that in Mr Ramsay's own words . . . that authority extended to Mr Hutcheson offering, on behalf of Mr Ramsay, Mr Ramsay's guarantee in relation to a lease when the business required it.

Agency by estoppel

In certain circumstances a third party may presume that a person has the authority of an agent even if this is not so. If the principal's behaviour reasonably appears to give this impression, the third party may enforce a resulting contract against the principal. Provided there was nothing to alert the third party to the true facts, the principal is **estopped** (prevented) from denying that the relationship exists. The agent in such circumstances has **apparent** or **ostensible authority**.

Apparent authority may exist in the following situations:

1 An agency relationship has ceased to exist but the principal has failed to give notice of this to third parties.

2 No agency relationship has ever existed, but the 'principal' allows a third party to believe the 'agent' was acting on the principal's behalf.

3 An agency relationship exists and the principal allows a third party to believe that the agent's authority is greater than it is. As long as the agent's behaviour seems to comply with relevant business practice, apparent authority generally exists unless the principal does something to rebut this presumption.

Estopped: prevented in law from denying the existence of a right of another person.

Apparent authority: the agent has no real authority but it appears that they do, because the principal has given the impression that authority exists or has failed to give notice that the authority no longer exists.

Ostensible authority: see apparent authority.

Barrett v Deere (1828, HL)

The defendant went to the claimant's counting house to pay a debt and handed his payment over to a rogue, who was in the claimant creditor's counting house and appeared to be responsible for transacting business there.

Held: this was sufficient to discharge the debt. It was reasonable for the debtor to believe that the rogue was the creditor's agent and had the creditor's authority, since the creditor had the right to control all transactions taking place on the premises.

Common knowledge in the business world may be sufficient to provide reasonable belief.

Racing UK Ltd v Doncaster Racecourse Ltd and Doncaster Borough Council (2005, CA)

The Chief Executive (CE) of Doncaster Racecourse Ltd signed, 'as duly authorised representative', an agreement granting TV rights to Racing UK Ltd. It was claimed by Racing UK and the racecourse that this contract bound the council. The council, which owned the race course, claimed that it was not bound as the CE did not have any authority to act as its agent.

Held: (by the Court of Appeal): since it was common knowledge in the racing world that the council owned the racecourse and in the business world that the owner of a course held the television rights, the CE had ostensible authority to enter the contract on behalf of the council. Therefore, the contract was binding on the council.

A company's lawyers may be justified in believing that an executive director has authority to instruct them.

Newcastle International Airport Ltd v Eversheds LLP (2012)

The Airport (N) claimed that Eversheds (E) had been negligent in accepting instructions from D, an executive director on N's remuneration committee, which awarded payment of very significantly increased bonuses to executive directors as part of a new refinancing agreement. In fact, committee members had only agreed in principle to a bonus distinct from the refinancing agreement.
E argued that it had not been negligent as D had apparent authority to give these instructions.

N argued that E knew that the remuneration committee's function was to obtain the best possible terms for the airport and that D had a conflict of interest. Therefore, E should have checked with the chair of the committee before going ahead.

Held: E had not been negligent. D had apparent authority because:

1 The chair had apparently deliberately chosen to leave communication to D and the other executive directors had not questioned the proposals. It was common practice for remuneration committees to instruct solicitors through their executive directors. E had advised D on what the effects of the drafted changes meant believing that, he would pass this on to the committee. R had signed off the draft agreement when E sent it to her. There was nothing more that E could have done to fulfil its duty of care to N.

2 It was very important for solicitors to be able to place reliance on the apparent authority of a company's agent unless it was unreasonable or irrational not to do so. No evidence that D was acting without authority was in any way apparent here.

Sometimes the agent's behaviour should put the third party on notice that no authority exists.

Quinn v CC Automotive Group (t/a Carcraft) (2010, CA)

On 5 July 2005 Mr Quinn consulted Mr Khan, who was employed by the defendant, Carcraft, in Leeds, about the sale of his silver Jaguar in part exchange for a new red one to drive to his daughter's wedding on 22 July 2005. As no red Jaguar was available, he agreed to buy a blue one, with finance arranged through Carcraft, who agreed to pay off the money still owed on the silver car. Shortly afterwards, Mr Khan phoned him and said that he had located a red Jaguar in Bury and showed Mr Quinn the car via the internet. He agreed to buy it. Shortly afterwards, Mr Khan told Mr Quinn that the finance company required an additional £700. When Mr Quinn said he could only afford £400, Mr Khan agreed to accept it, with the balance to be paid subsequently. Two days before the wedding, they met at a service station between Bury and Leeds and exchanged cars. Mr Quinn paid £400 in cash and signed documents to cancel the old contract and agree to the purchase the new one.

Mr Khan sold the silver Jaguar to a *bona fide* purchaser in a private deal and pocketed the money. Mr Quinn cancelled the finance agreement on his silver Jaguar and the finance company sued him for the outstanding payment of £15,000. The red Jaguar had never been part of Carcraft's stock and its provenance was uncertain.

Mr Quinn sued Carcraft, arguing that it was vicariously liable for Mr Khan, who had acted as its agent with apparent authority to make the deal.

Held: Carcraft was vicariously liable for Mr Quinn's loss. Mr Quinn honestly trusted in Mr Khan's authority, thinking he was being particularly helpful in getting the car in time for the wedding.

Gross LJ stated:

> the . . . factors relied upon by the defendant as putting Mr Quinn on inquiry, are to be considered in context and without the benefit of hindsight . . . The transaction was within the class of acts – and squarely so – that a car salesman . . . is usually authorised to do.

Agency arising from necessity

An agency relationship may arise in an emergency situation, where one party spontaneously takes steps to preserve somebody else's property interests. This enables that party to avoid liability for the reasonable costs of the intervention on the owner's behalf. This can only occur where it is impossible to get in contact with owner of goods in an emergency situation, so is rarely relevant today.

Agency of necessity may arise if *all* the following conditions are satisfied:

Agency of necessity: agency created by an emergency requiring the agent to take reasonable steps to preserve the principal's property.

1 while one party has possession of another party's goods an emergency occurs; and

2 this forces that party to take action regarding the goods *for the benefit of their owner*; and

3 it is impossible to communicate with the owner first.

Such an agent has authority to take such reasonable and prudent steps as are necessary in the best interests of the owner of the property.

Sachs v *Miklos* (1948)

The defendant gratuitously stored the claimant's furniture. During the war he wanted the space it was occupying, but was unable to contact the claimant. He sold the goods.

Held: no agency of necessity arose here because there was *no emergency* justifying the sale and the claimant was acting for *his own benefit*. Therefore, the defendant was liable to the claimant in the tort of conversion (unlawful disposal of the claimant's goods).

In the past, such agency often arose in situations where carriers were forced to make decisions to pay for the food and accommodation for livestock (*Great Northern Railway* v *Swaffield* (1874)) or to dispose of perishable goods. Such circumstances are unlikely to occur today, given that generally it is possible for a carrier to communicate directly with the owner and obtain emergency instructions.

If agency of necessity exists:

1 the agent may claim expenses;

2 the agent has a defence if sued for trespass for disposing of the goods;

3 a third party who has acquired goods from such an agent gets good title to the goods.

Agency by ratification

Ratification:
acknowledgement that a prior obligation is binding.

Even if a party had no authority or exceeded the given authority to act for another when making the contract, authority can be given subsequently if the other party wants to adopt the transaction. This **ratification** creates antecedent authority for the agent: the law treats the agent as having had authority from the outset.

For ratification to be valid the following requirements must be fulfilled:

1 the agent must expressly or impliedly indicate that it is acting as someone's agent, so the principal must be disclosed;

2 the principal must both exist and have the capacity to make the contract when it was made (promoters of a company making pre-incorporation contracts are not acting as company agents as the company as yet has no legal existence (see Chapter 20);

3 ratification must be within a reasonable time;

4 ratification must be complete: the principal must agree to all, not part, of the contract with full knowledge of what is involved;

5 notice of ratification must be communicated: this may be done by conduct, such as retaining goods which have been delivered.

The consequences of ratification are as follows:

1 the agent is freed from any liability for acting without authority;

2 the agent is entitled to remuneration from the principal where appropriate;

3 a third party obtains title to any property which has been transferred under the contract;

4 a contract made by the agent on the principal's behalf is retrospectively binding on the principal.

The disclosed and undisclosed principal

Disclosed principal

When agents enter into contracts on behalf of principals, they usually name the principals or at least indicate that they are acting as agents. Here the principal is said to be disclosed even if not actually named.

In general, the disclosed principal is liable on any resulting contract and the agent is not. Exceptions may arise where words, conduct or surrounding circumstances indicate that the agent and principal are jointly liable, or that the agent is to remain solely liable. Thus, if an agent signs a deed without indicating that he or she is signing as an agent, he or she will be personally liable.

Undisclosed principal

Sometimes the agent behaves as if no principal is involved, although in fact one is; here the principal is undisclosed. The contract will be binding by and against the principal if:

1 the agent was acting under the principal's actual authority at the time the contract was made;

2 the terms of the contract do not preclude the existence of the principal.

In *Humble* v *Hunter* (1848) an agent signed a charterparty so that he appeared to be sole owner of the ship involved. It was held that the principal could not enforce the contract. However, if the third party can show that it intended to do business only with the agent personally, the principal cannot enforce the contract against the third party. In *Collins* v *Associated Greyhound Race Courses Ltd* (1930) a contract to underwrite a share issue involved exclusive reliance on the agent's business reputation and integrity. The principal was held to be excluded.

The rights and duties of the agent

Rights

Payment

The agent does not have an automatic legal right to payment. Such a right exists only where the agency agreement indicates such an intention. If the agency is gratuitous, no payment is intended. Even if the agency is contractual, payment is due only if the terms of the contract governing payment are fulfilled. Payment may be conditional on a particular result being achieved.

G.T. Hodges & Sons v *Hackbridge Residential Hotel* (1939)

The owner of a hotel asked an estate agent to find a buyer. A representative from the War Office was introduced by the agent and began negotiations which then lapsed. Some months later the War Office announced that it would compulsorily purchase the hotel.

Held: this compulsory sale did not entitle the agent to their commission, as this was not the sort of sale contemplated by the parties when the owner put his property in the agent's hands.

Where the agency is contractual, the agent may sue for breach if the principal fails to make appropriate payment. The agent may also be entitled to exercise a lien (legal right to retain) over any property still in his or her possession that was purchased for the principal and for which the agent has not yet been paid.

Indemnity

Indemnity:
payment to make good expenses/losses incurred by one party while acting for the benefit of another.

Whether the agency is gratuitous or contractual, an agent is entitled to **indemnity** and therefore may recover any expenses incurred or losses suffered, if these are sufficiently incidental to the agent's authorised conduct.

Anglo Overseas Transport Ltd v *Titan Industrial Corpn* (1959)

An agent was engaged to make arrangements for shipping of the principal's goods. The principal was late in delivering the goods to the port which, by the customs of the trade, made the agent liable for losses incurred by the ship owner.

Held: the principal must indemnify the agent for its loss.

A gratuitous agent may request the court to order the principal to pay restitution.

Duties

The agent is in a fiduciary relationship with the principal: he or she enjoys the trust and confidence of the principal, and consequently has a number of legal duties which must be performed whether the agency is contractual or gratuitous.

Performance

An agent must carry out the principal's orders within the limits of the agent's authority. Generally, the agent is required to perform the duties personally and without delegation because of the agent's confidential relationship with the principal. Delegation may be permissible, however, if the principal consents, or if delegation is in keeping with trade practice. For example, if a case is being handled by country solicitors but it is to be heard in London, it is normal for some tasks to be delegated to a London firm. It may also be allowed if the delegated tasks require no exercise of special skill or discretion by the agent. Thus, solicitors may delegate claim-form-serving duties to their clerks.

Reasonable skill

Agents must perform their duties with reasonable care and skill and may be liable in breach of contract, or negligence, if they fail to do so.

An agent with trade or professional skills is expected to act with the level of skill reasonably to be expected of a person from such a trade or profession.

Where a contract of agency exists, failure to perform duties appropriately will be a breach of contract.

Chaudhry v Prabhakar (1988, CA)

The defendant was a friend of the claimant and claimed to be knowledgeable about cars. He was asked by the claimant to find a car for her that had not been involved in an accident. He found what he claimed was a suitable vehicle, although he noticed that the bonnet had probably been replaced and that it came from a garage which did crash repairs. Within a few months it turned out to be unroadworthy because of previous crash damage.

Held: the defendant was liable to the claimant in negligence as he had not exercised the level of care and skill to be expected from somebody with the level of expertise he had claimed to possess and on which the claimant had reasonably relied.

Arensen v Casson Beckman Rutley & Co. Ltd (1977)

A professional share valuer placed too low a valuation on his principal's shares.

Held: he was liable for breach of his duty to act with the degree of skill to be expected from a person with his level of professional experience.

Accountability

The agent must account for any profits resulting from the exercise of authority and transfer to the principal any monies or financial benefits derived from performance of the agent's duties. This duty is closely related to the agent's duty to avoid conflict of interest.

Real life

Max's great uncle William wants to sell his antique pocket watch and asks Max to find a suitable buyer. He tells Max that he wants at least £1,000 for it. Max takes the watch to an antique market where Cathy, a stall holder, offers him £1,200 pounds. Eddie, another stall holder, interrupts at this point and says he will pay £1,400 and give Max a bonus of £50 for taking his offer. Max sells to Eddie, but he should tell his uncle about the £50 when he hands over the proceeds of the sale. The £50 is an advantage which he obtained while acting as his uncle's agent and he must account for all profits. Maybe his uncle will let him keep the extra £50 but in law it is the uncle's property as it is treated as a secret profit in law if it is not disclosed.

Avoidance of conflict of interest

The agent must ensure that the principal's interests take priority over the agent's and must not exploit the relationship for the agent's own profit.

An agent who takes a bribe is in flagrant breach of the duty to avoid a conflict of interest. If an agent accepts payment from a third party in return for making a contract with that party in the principal's name, the contract is voidable for fraud. The principal is entitled to dismiss the agent without payment and recover the amount of the bribe. The principal may also repudiate the contract with the third party and claim damages for any loss which has resulted from the contract being made.

Armstrong v *Jackson* (1917)

A principal instructed his agent to buy shares in a particular company. Unknown to the principal, the agent owned some shares in the company and sold these to the principal instead of obtaining them elsewhere.

Held: the agent had failed to avoid a conflict of interest and must pay the principal the profit obtained on the sale.

The rights and duties of the principal

In relation to the agent

The principal's rights and duties largely mirror the duties and rights of the agent. Therefore, the principal is entitled to the benefits to be derived from the agent's performance of his or her fiduciary duties. In return the principal must make any necessary payment to the agent.

In relation to third parties

Contractual duties

Any contract made by the agent with a third party is binding on the principal provided that it was made within the limits of the agent's apparent authority. The principal is therefore liable for any misrepresentation or breach of contract, even though this was caused by the agent.

Tort liability

A principal may be vicariously liable for any torts committed by the agent closely connected with the exercise of the agent's apparent authority.

   Quinn v CC Automotive Group (t/a Carcraft) (2010) provides a good example of vicarious liability.

The Commercial Agents (Council Directive) Regulations 1993 (as amended)

The common law rights and duties between agent and principal have been put on a statutory footing, but only in commercial agencies for the sale of goods. The regulations amended by the Commercial Agents (Council Directive) (Amendment) Regulations 1998 gave the parties additional protection, including a right to a written contract and to a minimum period of notice if the agency contract is to be terminated. The agent has rights to commission. This must be paid within specified time limits. The agent is entitled to check the principal's books to ensure that he or she has been paid at the correct rate.

Termination of agency

The agency relationship may come to an end either:

1 by operation of law; or

2 by the acts of the parties.

By operation of law

Death

Since the relationship of principal and agent is a confidential one, the death of either party brings the agency to an end.

Mental incapacity

If a person's mental condition precludes him or her from having a reasonable level of understanding, he or she will be treated as no longer having the ability to be a party to a contract. If either party to an agency agreement becomes mentally incapable, this usually terminates the relationship. However, where the agent has been granted an irrevocable or lasting power of attorney, a principal's mental incapacity does not discharge the agency. (See below.)

Bankruptcy

The bankruptcy of either party terminates the agency, since the bankrupt's property passes into the control of the trustee in bankruptcy to enable payment of creditors.

Frustration of the agency agreement

Any event rendering further performance of an agency contract illegal, impossible or futile will terminate the agency. (See Chapter 11).

By the acts of the parties

Performance

Once the object of any short-term agency has been achieved, the agency ends.

Agreement or revocation

Both parties may agree to terminate the relationship. One party may revoke the agreement regardless of the other party's wish to continue. If the agency is contractual, this revocation may be a breach of contract entitling the other party to claim damages. No notice period is required, except where principal and agent are also in an employer–employee relationship.

Exceptionally, an agency cannot be revoked. An irrevocable agency exists in the following circumstances:

1 *The agent's authority is linked to the agent's own interest.* The purpose of this agency is to provide security for some pre-existing interest which the agent has with the principal. The agency cannot be revoked until the interest (usually the principal's debt with the agent) is discharged. For example, a debtor who currently is unable to repay a creditor may authorise the creditor to liquidate some of the debtor's assets

in order to raise the funds to repay the debt. Such an agency will be terminated by operation of law, however, if the principal subsequently becomes bankrupt or insane, unless the agent has obtained an irrevocable power of attorney.

2 *The agent has been granted an irrevocable power of attorney.* Under the Powers of Attorney Act 1971, s 4, an **irrevocable power of attorney** may be granted by the principal (donor of the power) to the agent (donee), which prevents an agency relationship from being terminated by the death, incapacity or bankruptcy of the principal. Similarly, if the principal is a corporate body the agency will survive its dissolution or winding up. An irrevocable power of attorney will be granted only to a donee who can prove that it is necessary to assist the donee to preserve a pre-existing interest in the principal's property. An irrevocable power of attorney exists for the benefit of the agent and must be distinguished from a lasting power of attorney.

3 *The agent has been granted a lasting power of attorney.* The Mental Capacity Act 2005 (MCA 2005), s 9 allows a donor to grant a **lasting power of attorney** (LPA). Since 2007, this replaces the previous system of enduring power of attorney. LPAs provide greater protection for the donor. For example, an LPA is only effective if registered with the Office of the Public Guardian and must contain the name of a person to be notified and asked for their permission before the power is invoked.

An LPA has a broader scope than an enduring power of attorney since it enables the donee to make decisions, not only about managing the donor's property, but also regarding his or her personal welfare: for example, deciding whether/what medical treatment is to be undertaken. Under the MCA 2005, s 11 the donee has no authority to act unless the donor is deemed to lack the capacity to make the relevant decision as defined by s 2. This states: 'a person lacks capacity in relation to a matter if at the material time he is unable to make a decision for himself in relation to the matter because of an impairment of, or a disturbance in the functioning of the mind or brain.' This may be a permanent or temporary state of affairs.

Irrevocable power of attorney:
to protect the agent's interest in the principal's property; it cannot be revoked by the principal/ their incapacity/ death/ bankruptcy.

Lasting power of attorney:
enables the agent to make decisions about an incapacitated principal's welfare as well as managing their property.

Some common types of specialist agents

Estate agents

Estate agents act for the seller of a property; their function is to find a buyer. They are regulated by the Estate Agents Act 1979, which requires estate agents to be insured against the loss of any deposits which they may be required to handle. They must also inform the seller of their commission charges before agreeing to act for them. Commission is payable only if a sale takes place to a purchaser whom they have introduced. Further controls were introduced under the Consumers, Estate Agents and Redress Act 2007, which required estate agents to register with an Estate

Agents Redress Scheme. This enables complaints against them to be investigated by the Property Ombudsman. Registration imposes a range of duties on estate agents including transparency of terms and conditions of business including payment of fees in addition to the other legal duties of agents as described in this chapter. Since 2014 lettings agents have also been required by law to sign up to a government recognised redress scheme (the Redress Schemes for Lettings Agency Work and Property Management Work (Requirement to Belong to a Scheme etc.) (England) Order 2014). This handles complaints by both tenants and landlords about lettings and management agents. The Consumer Rights Act 2015, s 83 requires letting agents to display fees clearly to their clients.

Auctioneers

The auctioneer initially acts as the agent of the seller, with the authority to sell to the highest bidder unless any reserve price is not reached. Once a sale has taken place the auctioneer becomes the agent of the buyer too.

An auctioneer is not authorised to transact a sale by credit. The buyer must pay immediately after the sale has taken place, although a cheque is acceptable instead of cash.

Brokers

Broker:
an intermediary who introduces parties to enable them to do business.

There are a number of different types of **broker**, all of whom act primarily as intermediaries between two parties, one of whom has something to sell – like stocks and shares, insurance or commodities – which the other party is interested in buying. The broker effects the introduction and may assist in the formation of the contract in return for a commission. Unlike factors (below), brokers do not generally have physical possession of the property which is being sold. Brokers' authority may be defined by customs relating to their particular trade.

Factors

Factor:
a 'mercantile agent' who sells goods on behalf of a customer and also lends money on the security of goods pledged with him or her.

The Factors Act 1889, s 1, defines a **factor** as 'a mercantile agent having in the customary course of his business as such agent authority either to sell goods or to consign goods for the purpose of sale or to buy goods or to raise money on the security of goods'. A factor, therefore, not only has apparent authority to sell goods – which any agent may have apparent authority to do – but he or she also has apparent authority to pledge goods or the documents of title to goods. Such pledges are very commonly used to raise money on imports of commodities like cocoa or wheat.

A factor is given physical control of the goods. The sale or other disposition of the goods within the factor's apparent authority to a purchaser acting in good faith is binding on the owner, even if the factor has disregarded orders and exceeded their actual authority.

Chapter summary

Creation of agency agreement:

By deed (power of attorney); or

in writing; or

by word of mouth.

The authority of the agent is usually:

Actual: express/implied and derived from the agreement.

Exceptionally agency arises without actual authority:

By estoppel: if the principal allows a person to behave like their agent that person has apparent/ostensible authority.

From necessity: where one party in control of another's property has to take steps to protect it in an emergency.

By ratification: a party subsequently ratifies a contract made by another for their benefit.

Duties of the agent

The agency relationship is fiduciary: the agent must account for any profits arising from his or her work for the principal and avoid any conflict of interest.

He or she must carry out their work with reasonable care and skill.

Duties of the principal

To the agent: perform reciprocal fiduciary duty.

Pay agreed remuneration.

Indemnify expenses.

Principal's liability to third parties:

Liable to perform authorised contracts.

Vicariously liable for the agent's torts.

Termination of the agency relationship

Operation of law: incapacity/death, bankruptcy, or frustration of the agency agreement.
Act of the parties: performance, agreement or revocation.
Enduring/irrevocable/lasting power of attorney may prevent termination.

Review questions 11

1 Under what types of authority do the following agents act?

   (a) Norbert, who was asked by Sharon to take Sharon's DVD player to be repaired.

   (b) Eric, who was asked to drive William's car to the airport to collect William's business client and had to buy petrol as the tank was almost empty.

2 Patricia, while in Sanjay's employment in a jewellery shop, always collected necklaces from the wholesalers Sparkles, once a week. She is dismissed by Sanjay but the following week collects the necklaces from Sparkles as normal. Sparkles have not been told that Patricia is no longer working for Sanjay. Patricia disappears with the necklaces. Advise Sanjay of his rights to refuse to pay for the necklaces.

3 When is a third party not bound by a contract with an undisclosed principal?

4 When is an agent entitled to delegate performance duties?

5 When will mental incapacity not bring the agency relationship to an end?

6 Explain when an agency of necessity may arise.

Answers to all review questions can be found in Appendix 2.

Advanced questions 11

(A) Analyse the various ways in which a principal agent relationship can arise.

(B) Critically evaluate the rights and duties of an agent.

Answers to the advanced questions can be found at **go.pearson.com/uk/he/resources.**

Take a closer look

The following cases provide important examples of how the law in this chapter has developed. They are primary sources illustrating the law in action and give more detail about their facts, as well as helping to understand the law and to appreciate how the judges reached their decisions.

Try looking them up in the law reports or accessing them via a database, e.g. Bailii (www.bailii.org/databases.html). LexisNexis or Westlaw may be available in the university or college library, or extracts may be found in a case book. (See Appendix 1: Additional resources.)

Anglo Overseas Transport Ltd v *Titan Industrial Corpn* [1959] 2 Lloyd's Rep 152

Arensen v *Casson Beckman Rutley & Co.* [1977] AC 747

Computer Associates UK Ltd v *The Software Incubator Ltd* [2018] EWCA Civ 518

Quinn v *CC Automotive Group (t/a Carcraft)* [2010] EWCA Civ 1412

Sachs v *Miklos* [1948] 1 All ER 67

Web activity

Visit GOV.UK to see examples of lasting powers of attorney:
www.gov.uk/government/publications/lasting-power-of-attorney-valid-examples
Read 'The Commercial Agents Regulations: a step behind the times?' by Alex Williamson:
www.tltsolicitors.com/insights-and-events/insight/the-commercial-agents-regulations-a-
step-behind-the-times/

Assignment 10

(a) 'If an agent is clothed with ostensible authority, no private instructions prevent his acts within the scope of that authority from binding his principal.' Discuss and illustrate this proposition.

(b) Patricia was part of a group that went on a two-year trip to search for lost tribes in the Amazon jungle. She left her cat, Tabitha, with her friend Brian and asked him to take good care of her and not to let her out in case she got lost. Six months after Patricia left, Tabitha managed to escape from Brian's house and was run over by a car and badly injured. Brian immediately took her to the vet, who said that it would cost £4,000 to treat her. If treated, she stood a very good chance of full recovery, but the only other option was to put her to sleep.

Advise Brian on his legal responsibilities as Patricia's agent.

PART 3

The law of tort

The tort of negligence

Learning objectives

On completion of this chapter, students should be able to:

★ understand duty of care in negligence, and the criteria of reasonable foresee-ability and proximity;

★ explain the circumstances when a breach of duty may occur, including the burden of proof and *res ipsa loquitur*;

★ distinguish between causation in fact and causation in law;

★ apply the rules of remoteness of damage, including the 'eggshell skull' principle;

★ describe the circumstances where defences to liability may exist, i.e. contribu-tory negligence and statutory authority;

★ explain voluntary assumption of risk (*volenti non fit injuria*).

Introduction

This chapter examines the law of tort, which is concerned with breaches of civil law that cause personal injuries, damage and interference to property and other sorts of personal loss. This, like the law of contract, is a crucial area of law for individuals and organisations that may be liable, not only to customers in a contractual rela-tionship with them, but also to a wide variety of other people who suffer legally recognised loss or damage much more indirectly by their activities and business

13

practices where relevant, as well as products, the state of premises and the conduct and safety of staff.

In any society of people living together, numerous conflicts of interest will arise, and the actions of one person may cause or threaten damage to others. This damage may take many forms: for example, injury to the person, damage to physical property, financial loss, injury to reputation. The law of tort aims to provide redress, i.e. it is concerned with the allocation or the prevention of losses. Negligence has developed as a specific tort tending to overshadow all other torts.

Negligence liability

The tort of negligence gives rights to persons who have suffered damage to themselves or to their property, against a party who has failed to take reasonable care for those persons' safety. (In very limited circumstances, pure financial loss is also recoverable in negligence, see Chapter 14.) Negligence is the commonest tort claim and is relevant to the whole *range* of accidental injury situations: for example, road accidents, illness and injuries caused by workplace conditions and harm arising through medical treatment. It also plays an important part in product liability: a person who suffers damage because of defects in a product, caused by the carelessness of the manufacturer or other party responsible for the state of the goods, may have a right to sue in negligence. (See Chapter 15.)

To be successful in a claim of negligence, the claimant must prove that:

Duty of care:
a person undertaking an activity or course of behaviour owes a duty not to harm any person reasonably expected to be caused loss/damage as a result.

1 the defendant owed the claimant a **duty of care**; and

2 the defendant failed to perform that duty; and

3 as a result, the claimant suffered damage.

1 The duty of care

The claimant must be able to show that he or she is someone who, in the circumstances, the defendant should have had in mind when embarking on the course of conduct which led to the alleged damage. This concept was established by the House of Lords in the landmark case of *Donoghue* v *Stevenson* (1932, HL). (See Chapter 15.).

Neighbour principle: formulated in *Donoghue* v *Stevenson* by Lord Atkin, indicated that the defendant only owes a duty of care to persons with sufficient proximity to him or her.

Donoghue v *Stevenson* established a general principle of establishing whether one person owed another a duty of care which forms the basis of the modern law of negligence today, this is sometimes known as the '**neighbour principle**'. This is because Lord Atkin said that a duty was owed only to one's neighbour, which in law means: 'persons who are so closely and directly affected by my act that I ought reasonably to have them in my mind as being so affected when I am directing my mind to the acts or omissions called into question.'

Lord Atkin's judgment has had a huge impact on the civil law. The 'neighbour principle' has enabled successive judges to use it as a springboard for the development of negligence in *all* its forms.

Stennett v *Hancock* (1939)

The claimant, a pedestrian, suffered a leg injury when he was hit by part of a wheel which came off a passing lorry.

Held: the garage which had recently negligently fitted the wheel owed a duty to the claimant, since it was reasonably foreseeable that any road user in the vicinity of the lorry could be harmed if a wheel became detached.

Worth thinking about?

Why is *Donoghue* v *Stevenson* regarded as such an important decision in English law?

Suggested solutions can be found in Appendix 2.

Development of the duty of care

In modern times the neighbour principle still forms part of the current test for establishing the existence of the duty of care in a new duty situation, as developed in the following case.

Caparo v *Dickman* [1990] 1 ALL ER

(See also Chapter 14).

Shareholders in a company purchased further shares and then launched a successful takeover bid for the company having examined the audited accounts prepared by the defendants. Subsequently they sued the auditors on the basis they had relied on the accounts which had shown a significant surplus rather than the loss which was actually the fact.

The House of Lords held: that the auditors did not owe a duty of care since company accounts are not prepared for the use of potential investors and cannot be relied upon for such a purpose.

The House of Lords also determined that when deciding whether a duty of care exists in any negligence action, the court must take into account whether the following criteria are satisfied:

1 reasonable foreseeability;

2 proximity;

3 public interest taking into account fairness, justice and reasonableness.

The decision in *Caparo* has since been followed in:

Marc Rich & Co. AG v *Bishop Rock Marine* (1995, HL)

A shipping vessel was negligently classed as seaworthy, and then sank. The classification society did not owe a duty of care to the owners of a cargo that sank with the ship. This was economic loss. The House of Lords applied the three-part test from *Caparo* v *Dickman* and determined that it was not just and reasonable in the circumstances of the case to impose a duty.

These factors are interlinked and interdependent.

Reasonable foreseeability

Reasonable foreseeability: limits the scope of duty of care as this is owed only when it is reasonable to anticipate damage to the claimant.

No duty of care will exist unless it is **reasonably foreseeable** that the particular claimant was vulnerable to the risk created by the defendant. For example, in *Stennett* v *Hancock* (above) it was reasonably foreseeable that, if the lorry wheel was not securely fitted, an accident endangering any pedestrian in the vicinity might result.

Proximity

Proximity:
a sufficiently close relationship must exist between claimant and defendant at the time the dangerous behaviour occurred for a duty of care to exist.

There must be a close enough relationship of **proximity** between the defendant's acts and the claimant at the time of the wrong complained of. Lord Atkin (*Donoghue v Stevenson*) stated that proximity was not restricted to 'mere physical proximity, but [should] be used . . . to extend to such close and direct relations that the act complained of directly affects a person whom the person bound to take care would know would be directly affected by his careless act'. The claimant in *Stennett* v *Hancock* (above) provides a good example of such proximity. While the claimant lacked close physical proximity to the defendant they nonetheless stood to suffer from its negligence.

Public interest/policy

Public interest/policy:
For the benefit of people in general. Influential on the court's decision to permit/refute a duty of care.

This criterion covers a wide range of circumstances involving what may be described as policy or **public interest** issues and is relevant whenever *a new duty situation* is to be decided by the court. A duty of care will not be acknowledged unless it is fair, just and reasonable to the parties but also not damaging to the interests of the public at large, however beneficial it might be to the individual claimant.

The court may refuse to develop the scope of negligence to provide a right of action already covered by an existing area of the law, or to develop the law so as to discourage people from taking reasonable precautions, such as insurance, to protect their own interests.

A duty may be developed because it will actively promote the *public interest*.

Hill v *Chief Constable of West Yorkshire* (1988)

Jacqueline Hill was the last victim of Peter Sutcliffe – the Yorkshire Ripper. Her mother argued that Jaqueline would still have been alive had the police investigation been carried out competently.

The House of Lords held: police do not generally owe a duty of care to the general public in relation to the manner in which they undertake investigations. (See also *Osman* v *UK* (1999).)

Robinson v *Chief Constable of West Yorkshire* (2018 SC)

The Supreme Court decided that in determining the existence of a duty of care, the law should be developed incrementally and by analogy with previous cases. The Caparo test should only be applied in novel situations, that is in circumstances where the court is being requested to make a decision where there is no previous case law to follow.

2 Breach of duty

Reasonable man: the standard by which reasonable care is judged. This is said to reflect the behaviour of the average person in the given circumstances.

It is up to the claimant to prove that the defendant failed to take reasonable care in performing the duty of care. What is reasonable is measured objectively against the standards of the so-called '**reasonable man**' in the circumstances of the particular case. Certain criteria exist to guide the court.

The likelihood of an accident happening

The greater the likelihood of an accident, the more care the defendant may need to take. The court will need to be satisfied that the chance of risk was reasonably reduced. The risk of damage need not be completely removed for the standard to be met.

Bolton v *Stone* (1951)

The claimant was injured by a cricket ball hit from the cricket club grounds controlled by the defendant. The boundary fence was 17 feet high and the ball had travelled over 80 yards from the wicket. There was evidence to show that such a hit was a very rare occurrence.

Held: the defendant was not liable as reasonable care had been taken to reduce the chances of such an occurrence, given the height of the fence and the distance from the wicket and the previous history of balls rarely escaping from the ground.

However, a similar accident occurring in different circumstances gave rise to liability for the defendant since the chances of an accident were very likely.

Hilder v *Associated Portland Cement* (1961)

Children frequently played football on land belonging to the defendant company which was close to a road and bordered by a wall less than three feet high. A motorcyclist was killed when a ball was kicked into the road.

Held: the defendant was liable since it had not taken reasonable care to reduce the chances of a very likely accident despite being aware of the risk. It had neither prevented the children from playing on its land nor provided a boundary fence sufficient to prevent footballs escaping into the highway.

The extent of the potential harm

The greater the extent of the likely damage the more the defendant is expected to do to reduce its risk.

Paris v *Stepney Council* (1951)

The claimant was employed in a manual job by the defendant company. He had only one eye and was then blinded in his good eye in an accident at work.

Held: the defendant had failed to act with reasonable care by failing to supply safety glasses to the claimant. It was irrelevant that the work he was doing would not necessitate use of these glasses by a normally sighted person. The consequence of injury to his eyes was much more serious than to other employees.

The practicability of taking precautions: risk–benefit analysis

The court when determining reasonable care seeks to impose a standard of care that gives reasonable protection to the claimant while not unduly burdening the defendant. This may be described as a **risk–benefit analysis**. A risk-free environment can never be fully guaranteed.

Risk-benefit analysis: a balancing exercise to determine the required level of care relating to an activity to determine what precautions are necessary, without unreasonably inhibiting its beneficial effects.

Withers v *Perry Chain Ltd* (1961)

The claimant, who was employed in a factory where contact with grease was involved at every stage of the production process, became allergic to grease and developed a skin condition. Her employer moved her to the most grease-free job that fitted her capabilities but the allergy persisted.

Held: the defendant company had done everything that it could reasonably be expected to do to prevent harm to the claimant and was therefore not in breach of its duty and Ms Withers' claim must accordingly fail.

Latimer v *AEC* (1953)

A factory floor was slippery after a flood. The defendant spread sawdust over most of the walkways in the factory and issued warnings to employees. The claimant, who was injured when he slipped in an area which had not been made safe because it was less often used, argued that the building should have been closed until it had dried out.

Held: the extent of the risk and likely injury did not justify this extreme response. The precautions taken were all that was practicable in the circumstances.

The defendant's resources and the nature and size of business may be relevant factors for the court to take into account. However, the greater the risk and extent of damage the less relevant the cost factor to the defendant. This is an area of the common law where standards have been influenced by statutory developments in health and safety regulation (see Chapter 17). This commonly requires prior risk assessment for certain activities. Evidence that this process was sufficiently comprehensive and resulted in relevant precautions is often sufficient to discharge the duty of care. Risk assessment is accepted practice even where it is not statutorily required.

Wilson v *Haden* (2013)

The defendant ran an adventure centre. The claimant scoutmaster was injured by falling from a slippery fireman's pole on an obstacle course in wet weather.

Held: the defendant was negligent. Failure by staff to take proper account of the centre's risk assessment process and to give proper instructions to visitors was a breach of duty.

Skilful claimants

If a claimant has a skill which should make him or her aware of an inherent danger, the defendant will not be expected to take steps to protect him or her from it.

Roles v *Nathan* (1963)

Two sweeps died when they were overcome by fumes while attempting to seal a hole in a flue while the boiler on the defendant's premises was still alight.

Held: the defendant was not negligent. The sweeps were experienced tradesmen and knew that the boiler should have been extinguished before work was started. It was not up to the defendant to put it out or issue warnings.

The qualifications claimed by the defendant

Defendants will be held liable if they fail to act with the reasonable degree of care and skill to be expected from a person with the qualifications which the defendants claim to have – *Bolam* v *Friern Hospital Management Committee* (1957) (see below).

Phillips v *William Whitely* (1938)

The defendant jeweller who pierced the claimant's ears was not liable for the abscess which resulted.

Held: the defendant was not negligent. He had acted in accordance with the level of care and skill to be expected from a person with his training. The standards of a surgeon could not be expected of him.

Only the level of qualification is relevant. Lack of experience is not taken into consideration: the same standards are expected of a newly qualified professional or craftsperson as of one with considerable experience. In *Wilsher* v *Essex Area Health Authority* (1986) the Court of Appeal held that it was irrelevant that the doctor who treated the claimant was newly qualified and had been working excessively long hours when she treated the claimant (for facts see below).

This extends to learner drivers, who are required to demonstrate the same standard of care as those who have passed a driving test (see *Nettleship* v *Weston* (1971, CA)). This is to prevent insurance companies avoiding liability to third parties.

A defendant claiming no special training or skill is expected to take such care as can reasonably be expected in the circumstances. In *Perry* v *Harris* (2008) the Court of Appeal held that the defendant was not liable for the injuries sustained by a child hurt when using a bouncy castle at a children's birthday party. She had acted as a responsible adult in her supervision of the children at the time and constant supervision was not required as serious injury was not reasonably foreseeable. Similarly, the standard required of an amateur carpenter's repairs is not as high as that required of a professional tradesperson (*Wells* v *Cooper* (1958, CA)).

Children are expected to exercise a level of skill commensurate with their age. In *Orchard* v *Lee* (2009), the Court of Appeal decided that a 13-year-old boy, who seriously injured a dinner lady on colliding with her in the playground when he was playing, had not breached his duty of care. A reasonable 13-year-old would not have reasonably foreseen that such harm would be likely to result from his conduct.

Good practice

Conformity with accepted and current good practice may be indicative of reasonable care. Thus, in *Thompson* v *Smiths Ship Repairers Ltd* (1984) the defendant employer's failure to provide ear protectors was held not to amount to a failure to take reasonable care until they had been alerted to the necessity by government circular.

There may be more than one type of good practice: both claimant and defendant may produce expert witnesses with conflicting views. The judge does not have the relevant professional skill to decide whose procedure was correct. The claimant must prove that on the balance of probability the defendant was in breach. If there is proof that what the defendant did would also have been done by another similar professional in compliance with good practice then the claimant fails.

Bolam v Friern Hospital Management Committee (1957, CA)

> The claimant, who suffered a fractured pelvis when undergoing electro-convulsive therapy, brought expert evidence that his limbs should have been restrained during treatment.
>
> **Held:** on the balance of probability there was no proof of a failure to take reasonable care. The hospital was able to prove that its practice of cushioning limbs was equally well accepted in respected medical circles.

The House of Lords approved the *Bolam* principle in *Bolitho v City and Hackney Area Health Authority* (1997), but stressed that it is not enough to show that other professionals subscribe to the practice: an expert witness must be able to justify its use in the circumstances of the particular case, having weighed up its risks and benefits.

Unhappy outcomes

In *Bolam v Friern Hospital Management Committee* Lord Justice Denning neatly summarised the nature of reasonable care when he said 'the doctor does not promise to cure the patient nor the lawyer to win the case'. All reasonable care may be taken but the claimant may still suffer damage. Proof of damage to the claimant or even proof of a mistake by the defendant does not necessarily prove that the defendant has failed to take reasonable care.

Luxmoore May v Messenger May Bakers (1990, CA)

> The defendant auctioneers claimed to be expert picture valuers. They failed to judge correctly the potential of two paintings owned by the claimant, who consequently obtained only a tiny fraction of their true value when they were sold.
>
> **Held:** the claimants had failed to prove that the defendants acted without reasonable care. Evidence from the defendant indicated that a competent valuer could have made the same mistake.

Legislation relating to the standard of care

The Compensation Act 2006

Section 1 states that when a court is deciding whether a defendant has taken reasonable care it may:

have regard to whether a requirement to take those steps might –

(a) prevent a desirable activity from being undertaken at all, to a particular extent or in a particular way, or

(b) discourage persons from undertaking functions in connection with a desirable activity.

This statute merely reflects current judicial practice, so may appear to be an unnecessary piece of legislation. Parliament's intention was presumably to improve awareness of this aspect of the law and to attempt to ensure that normal activities are not inhibited by fear of litigation and excessively risk-averse behaviour. There does appear to be an increase in such restrictions of late usually as a result of defensive behaviour by public authorities and businesses rather than by the courts. These encourage the popular belief that life should be risk free, and that, since any and every accident is preventable, somebody must be legally liable.

Reflecting this legislation, the Health and Safety Executive published (August 2006) proposals for a code of principles for risk management which states that, while the safety of workers and members of the public should be properly protected, sensible risk management is not about 'creating a totally risk free society' or 'stopping important recreational and learning activities' or 'scaring people by exaggerating or publicising trivial risks'.

This view has been reinforced by the courts on a number of occasions. In *Sutton* v *Syston Rugby Football Club Ltd* (2011) (see below) Longmore LJ said:

> It is important that neither the game's professional organisation nor the law should lay down standards that are too difficult for ordinary coaches and match organisers to meet. Games of rugby are, after all, no more than games and, as such are obviously desirable activities within the meaning of s 1 of the Compensation Act 2006.

The Social Action, Responsibility and Heroism Act 2015 is another statute many lawyers think that we could manage without. It was prompted in part by a report on volunteering (*Helping Out: A national survey of volunteering and charitable giving*, September 2007) which found that the perception of the danger of personal liability and risk discouraged some people from participating. It requires the court in a case of negligence or breach of statutory duty to have regard to whether the defendant was engaged in activity beneficial to the public (s 2) or was attempting to protect 'the safety or interests of others' (s 3) when deciding whether reasonable care was taken. As stated earlier in this chapter, existing case law shows that the courts do not expect the same standard of care from a lay person as from a professional (*Perry* v *Harris* (2008), *Wells* v *Cooper* (1958)). Where acts of heroism are concerned, any person who intervenes in a manner reasonably commensurate with the urgency of the situation and to their own abilities is unlikely to find themselves liable for any injury they cause. In *Watt* v *Hertfordshire County Council* (1954, CA) Denning LJ said:

> It is well settled that in measuring due care one must balance the risk against the measures necessary to eliminate the risk . . . One must balance the risk against the end to be achieved. The saving of life or limb justifies taking considerable risk.

It should also be noted that the common law protects volunteers if they are injured as a result of their philanthropic behaviour through the negligence of others. They are entitled to the same safety precautions as anyone else involved in the organisation relative to their needs and experience. Anyone who goes to the rescue of another person in a dangerous situation in a reasonable manner will, if harmed, have a remedy against any person who caused the original accident negligently. (See Chapter 14).

The burden of proof in negligence and *res ipsa loquitur*

The burden of proof in negligence actions normally falls on the claimant. However, the burden of proof can be shifted by the doctrine of '*res ipsa loquitur*' (the thing speaks for itself). In such circumstances an inference of negligence can be drawn from the facts and the burden of proof transfers from the claimant to the defendant to explain how the accident could have happened without negligence on the defendant's part.

The following conditions must be satisfied for the rule to apply.

(a) Defendant must have exclusive control over the thing that caused the damage.

(b) The cause of the accident must be such as would not normally happen without negligence.

(c) The cause of the accident must be unknown.

Scott v London and St Katherine Docks Co [1885] 3 H & C

The claimant was a dockworker who was injured when large heavy bags of sugar fell from the open door of the defendant's warehouse.

Held: the court applied the doctrine of *res ipsa loquitur*, the facts speak for themselves, i.e. bags of sugar could not have fallen from the door of the warehouse without fault on the part of the defendant. The defendant was liable for the claimant's injuries.

Ward v Tesco [1976] 1 WLR 810

A customer slipped on yoghurt that had been spilt onto the supermarket's floor. Tesco claimed they had a procedure in place whereby the floors were cleaned regularly throughout the day and staff were instructed to stay with such spillages when they were found until they were cleared. Nevertheless, the customer was also able to provide evidence of other spillages that had not immediately been cleaned up.

The court accepted that such incidents could only result from negligence.

Barkway v *South Wales Transport Co Ltd* [1950] 1 ALL ER 392

Without apparent reason a bus mounted a pavement and this resulted in injury to the claimant. Following examination of the tyre it was revealed that it had burst due to a defect in the wall of the tyre that could not have been discovered.

Since the exact cause of the accident was known (a burst tyre), *res ipsa loquitur* could not apply. However, there was evidence that the bus company should have instructed drivers to report significant impacts suffered by tyres that might weaken them. Failure to do so meant the defendants were liable.

3 Proving consequential loss or damage

The claimant must prove the link between the defendant's failure to take reasonable care and the damage which the claimant has suffered. Two elements are involved: the claimant must first prove that but for the defendant's behaviour, the damage would not have occurred (*causation in fact*) and secondly that the damage is a reasonably foreseeable result (*causation in law/ remoteness*).

1 Causation in fact: the 'but for' rule

The defendant's failure to take care must be the material cause of the damage. A claimant must show that he or she would not have been injured **but for** the defendant's act or failure to act.

'But for' principle: damage to the claimant must be a result of the defendant's breach.

Barnett v *Chelsea & Kensington Hospital Management Committee* (1969)

A man died from arsenic poisoning which the hospital negligently failed to detect.

Held: the hospital was not liable. According to expert evidence he would still have died even if the hospital had diagnosed the problem and treated him appropriately.

McWilliams v *Arrol* (1962)

The claimant's husband fell from a roof that he was repairing; he had not been wearing a safety belt. There was evidence that, although belts were normally available, on the day of the accident, the shed where they were stored was locked. The claimant argued that if the belts had been available her husband would not have fallen.

Held: her claim failed since the defendant employer was able to prove that her husband did not usually bother to wear a belt.

Sutton v Syston Rugby Football Club Ltd (2011, CA)

Mr Sutton was injured during rugby training when he fell on a broken cricket marker near the pitch boundary while attempting to score. He claimed that club's negligence in failing to carry out a proper pitch inspection had caused the accident.

Held: failure to inspect was a breach of duty, but the Club was not liable because there was no causative link between the failure to inspect and Mr Sutton's injuries. The evidence indicated that, even if a reasonably careful inspection had been carried out, it would probably not have revealed the stump of broken marker, which was largely concealed by the grass.

Multiple causes

The 'but for' principle works well as long as there is only one likely cause of the damage. Where there are multiple causes, the claimant may be unable to prove on the balance of probability that it was the defendant's behaviour which was a material cause of the accident.

Wilsher v Essex Area Health Authority (1988, HL)

Failure by the hospital to give the claimant, a premature baby, the correct oxygen mixture was alleged to be the cause of his becoming visually impaired.

Held: the claimant could not succeed since the 'but for' test had not been satisfied, as he was suffering from a number of other conditions, any of which could have caused the same damage. It had not been proved on the balance of probability that the oxygen mixture was a material cause.

In a previous case the House of Lords had adopted a different approach.

McGhee v National Coal Board (1972, HL)

The claimant worked in very hot and dirty conditions in a brick kiln. No showers were provided and he could not get clean until he had cycled home from work. He contracted dermatitis. He could not prove on the balance of probability that showering before leaving work would have prevented the dermatitis.

Held: the NCB was liable as the medical evidence indicated that lack of showers greatly increased his chances of developing the condition.

In *Wilsher* v *Essex Area Health Authority* the House of Lords described the *McGhee* approach as 'robust and pragmatic': correct on its facts but not a principle of law.

This cast doubt on the standing of *McGhee*, and produced a puzzling distinction for many students.

However, in 2002 the House of Lords clarified the law. Its decision and the cases and legislation which followed it had a big impact both on relevant businesses and their insurers.

Fairchild v *Glenhaven Funeral Services* (2002, HL)

The claimants in this case all contracted mesothelioma (a form of invariably fatal cancer) after being exposed to asbestos fibres at work. There was clear evidence of flagrant breach of safety standards by all the employers. Causation was problematic, however, as all the claimants had been employed by more than one employer. Each employee could only have contracted the disease during one period of employment, and it was impossible for them to prove which one was the source of the disease.

Held (unanimously): given the impossibility of proof, the claimants should succeed. It was fair and just to use the less stringent *McGhee* rule here, as by breaching safety standards all the employers had materially increased the claimants' chances of contracting the condition. The facts could clearly be distinguished from those in *Wilsher* where a number of possible causes, apart from the oxygen, could have led to the claimant's disability. In *Fairchild*, asbestos was the only possible cause. The House of Lords in *Wilsher* was incorrect in failing to acknowledge *McGhee* as establishing a new principle of law.

The defendants were jointly and severally liable. Therefore, the claimants were entitled to full compensation from the employer who was being sued, since that employer could seek contribution from any other employer who had exposed the claimant to the risk.

The *Fairchild* decision is important as it firmly establishes the *McGhee* approach as a principle of law. It is also a good example of a public interest or 'policy' decision. Had the employers escaped liability, others might be encouraged to ignore safety standards in similar situations, secure in the knowledge that the causative link could not be established. Insurers, too, would have unjustly profited.

Four years later in *Barker* v *Corus UK Ltd*, *Murray* v *British Shipbuilders Ltd*, *Patterson* v *Smiths Docks Ltd* (2006, HL) a differently constituted House of Lords decided three cases in which the facts were subtly different from *Fairchild*. This resulted in the principle in *Fairchild* being both expanded in one respect and restricted controversially in another.

The expansion

Mr Barker had been exposed to the risk of mesothelioma not only by his employers but also during a period of self-employment, but this was held to be irrelevant to his employers' liability. It was held that, provided there was evidence of negligence by the defendant which materially increased the risk of contracting mesothelioma, it was irrelevant that the claimant had also been exposed to the risk from another source. It was irrelevant that that other exposure might have been caused by tortious or non-tortious behaviour or some natural cause.

The restriction

In *Barker*, etc. the House of Lords by majority held that joint and several liability could only be imposed if the defendants had actually *caused the claimants to contract* the disease. It also held that only a minority of the House of Lords in *Fairchild* had actually decided that the defendants had done so. The majority (three out of five) had merely held that the defendant had exposed the claimants to the *risk of contracting* the disease. Therefore, their Lordships restated the decision in *Fairchild*, holding that each defendant could only be held liable severally (only for the damage it had personally caused) and so would pay compensation proportionately to the period of time the claimant had been employed by them. This impacted unfavourably on the current claimants as all previous employers bar the current defendants were insolvent and, as mentioned above, Mr Barker had been self-employed for a time.

This was a very controversial decision as regards the several liability issues. Lord Hoffmann said that it would 'smooth the roughness of the justice which a rule of joint and several liability creates'. It certainly pleased the defendant insurers. However, it may be argued that it roughened the justice for the claimants and their dependants, as Lord Rodger clearly indicated in his dissenting judgment where he called upon Parliament to come to their assistance. Richard Leyton (president of the Association of Personal Injury Lawyers) declared that it was 'an insult to the victims' families' and Parliament was quick to intervene to remove the *Barker* restriction.

The Compensation Act 2006, s 3

Section 3 in effect imposes joint and several liability for negligence and breach of statutory duty arising from the circumstances of exposure covered by the *Fairchild* and *Barker* decisions but s 3(5) expands this to cover liability for failure to protect from exposure.

The Act received Royal Assent in July 2006 and s 3 has retrospective effect, which means that all future cases must be decided in accordance with it, even if the damage occurred before the section came into force. It also means that the outcomes of some past claims may need to be varied.

This was a very welcome parliamentary intervention for those of us who agree with the House of Lords in *Fairchild*, that perfect justice cannot be obtained in this problematic causation situation and that any injustice should be borne by a party who is culpably in breach of their duty of care, rather than their innocent victims.

The *Fairchild* and *Barker* cases must not be disregarded in future. Section 3 clearly reflects them pretty precisely as regards exposure issues and the causation principle. Parliament has in effect made that part of those decisions statutory, so they will still be as relevant in future cases to courts interpreting and applying s 3. In *Sienkiewicz v Greif (UK) Ltd* and *Knowsley Metropolitan Borough Council v Willmore* (2011) the Supreme Court directly applied its previous decision. It held that both single or multiple defendants were liable if the claimant proved under the *Fairchild* causation rule that the defendant's breach of duty had been a material cause of the claimant's illness. Section 3's reference to 'material' was intended to rule out insignificant risks but not to require proof that the defendant had doubled the risk of exposure to the claimant.

Lost chances

The more liberal approach to causation in *Fairchild* has not been extended to claims for a lost chance. Although damages may be award for such losses the claimant must as usual in civil cases, establish that the defendant was on the balance of probabilities the material cause of the loss.

In *Hotson v East Berkshire Health Authority* (1987) the claimant fractured his hip and the hospital negligently failed to spot that he had associated nerve damage which resulted in long-term damage to his hip joint, severely reducing his mobility. He claimed that he had been deprived of his mobility by the hospital's failure to treat the condition. He lost his claim because he was unable to prove that but for the defendant's negligence he would have been cured, since expert evidence showed that treatment was only successful in 25 per cent of cases. Therefore, he could not prove that on the balance of probability he would have regained full mobility, because he was unable to prove that treatment was successful in at least 51 per cent of cases. This principle was affirmed by the House of Lords in 2005 in *Gregg v Scott*. Due to the defendant's negligence, Mr Gregg's cancer was diagnosed late, reducing his chance of a cure to 25 per cent. Prompt diagnosis would have increased this chance to 46 per cent. His claim failed since even swift intervention would not on the balance of probability have resulted in his cure.

This principle was applied in a similar case more recently:

JD v Mather (2012)

Due to the defendant doctor's failure to diagnose the claimant's cancer, there was a seven-month delay before a different doctor correctly identified it. By then it had spread and by the time the case reached trial the claimant was not expected to live much longer.

Held: the defendant was liable for reducing the claimant's life expectation.

Expert predictive evidence indicated that, on the balance of probability, prompt diagnosis would not have enabled a cure but would probably have slowed down the progress of the disease and increased life expectation by three years.

2 Causation in law (remoteness of damage)

The damage must not be too remote. The defendant is not held legally responsible for all the results of the breach.

The law treats intentional and unintentional torts differently as regards determining remoteness. We are presumed to intend all the direct consequences of our intentional acts, so in a tort like trespass the defendant will be liable for all the direct consequences regardless of whether they could reasonably have been foreseen (*Re Polemis* (1921, CA)). However, it was decided in *The Wagon Mound* (1961) (below) that damage caused to the claimant by a non-intentional tort like negligence or nuisance must be of a reasonably foreseeable type.

Overseas Tankships & Engineering v *Morts Dock & Engineering Ltd (The Wagon Mound (No. 1))* (1961, PC)

Fire damage was caused to the claimant's dock when a spark from a welding torch being used on the claimant's dock ignited oil which the defendants had negligently discharged into the harbour.

Held: the chance of fire breaking out in such circumstances was not reasonably foreseeable by the defendants who were therefore not liable.

In *Corr* v *IBC Vehicles Ltd* (2008) the House of Lords held Mr Corr's employer (IBC) liable for his death. The acute clinical depression arising from the disfigurement and post-traumatic stress resulting from the negligence of his employers made it reasonably foreseeable that he would commit suicide.

Provided that the *type of damage* is reasonably foreseeable, the defendant will be liable. It is irrelevant that the defendant might not have been able to foresee its cause or its severity.

Hughes v *Lord Advocate* (1963, HL)

The defendant telephone engineers left an inspection hole for the night, covered only by a tent and surrounded by lighted paraffin lamps. The child claimant was severely burned when he fell down the hole carrying a lamp which exploded as it hit the ground, producing a fireball.

Held: the defendants were held liable as it was reasonably foreseeable that a child would be attracted by the lamps and might be burned when playing with them. It was irrelevant that the explosion and the severity of the burn damage were not reasonably foreseeable.

Their Lordships reaffirmed this principle in the following case:

Jolley v *London Borough of Sutton* (2000, HL)

The defendant council failed to remove an abandoned boat from its land. The claimant (aged 14) was seriously injured when it fell on him after he had jacked it up to try to repair it.

Held: the council was liable, as the precise circumstances causing the accident did not have to be foreseeable. The boat was a safety hazard and likely to attract children.

Intervening acts

Intervening act: event aggravating the claimant's damage which occur between the defendant's act and resulting damage.

Sometimes subsequent behaviour of the claimant or a third party may lead to an aggravation of the damage set in train by the defendant. The question for the court to decide is whether that **intervening act** breaks the chain of causation and thus prevents the defendant from being liable for the resulting damage. However, if the act is reasonably foreseeable and/or the defendant has a duty to prevent it then liability remains with the defendant, as the damage is not too remote.

McKew v *Holland & Cubitts Ltd* (1969, HL)

The defendant negligently injured the claimant's leg. As a consequence, it would quite often give way. In full knowledge of this, the claimant attempted to descend a steep stairway without using the hand rail. His leg gave way and he fell down the stairs, sustaining further injuries.

Held: the defendant was not liable for the injuries sustained in the fall; the claimant's descent of the stairs was an intervening act which was not reasonably foreseeable to the defendant. It was unreasonable of the claimant to behave as he had.

A different result was reached in *Wieland* (below) due to the claimant being unaware of the full effects of her previous accident.

Wieland v *Cyril Lord Carpets* (1969)

Due to negligence of the defendant, the claimant suffered injuries. She was sent to hospital and was fitted with a surgical collar. This impeded her head movement and, consequently, use of her bifocal spectacles. The next day when she was returning home from a check-up at the hospital, she felt so unwell that she called in at the defendant's showrooms, where her nephew worked, to get him to take her home. Unable to see properly, she fell down some steps and hurt herself.

Held: the defendant was liable for all the claimant's injuries, since its negligence had left her unable to cope with the normal necessities of life. Descending the stairs was not unreasonable and did not break the chain of causation. She had not had time to adjust to the effects of her treatment and was still suffering from some residual shock at the time of the second accident.

When a third party is involved, the issue of whether the defendant had a duty to control them or to prevent such acts is relevant to determining liability.

Reeves v *Commissioner of Police for the Metropolis* (1999, HL)

Reeves committed suicide while in police custody. He was known at the time to be in a mentally unstable condition.

Held: the police were liable for his death. It was their negligence, in failing to supervise him appropriately, which enabled him to end his life. His intervening act was both reasonably foreseeable and the very thing that they were meant to prevent.

The 'eggshell skull' rule

'Eggshell skull' rule: exception to remoteness rule, which makes the defendant liable for unforeseeable damage to a claimant arising from a pre-existing medical condition or weakness.

The **'eggshell skull' rule** is an exception to the *Wagon Mound* principle. If the claimant has some particular weakness that makes him or her susceptible to a type of harm which is not reasonably foreseeable, the defendant will nevertheless be liable.

Smith v *Leech Brain & Co. Ltd* (1962)

Due to the defendants' negligence, an employee suffered a minor burn to his lip which would normally have caused only superficial damage. However, pre-cancerous cells in his lip which might otherwise have remained dormant were activated and he died. It was held that the defendants were liable for their employee's death although such serious damage was not foreseeable.

In *Page* v *Smith* (1995) the House of Lords held that the 'eggshell skull' principle applied to both mental and physical conditions. The principle has also been held to apply to a claimant whose financial situation makes him or her more vulnerable to the damage caused by the defendant.

Mattocks v *Mann* (1993)

The claimant's car was damaged by the negligence of the defendant. When it had been repaired, there was a delay before she could recover it, as the garage refused to part with it until the insurance company came up with the money. The claimant did not have the funds to pay the bill herself.

Held: the defendant (in reality, his insurers) was liable for the cost of the claimant hiring a car until she could recover her own.

Defences in tort

Even if a claimant can satisfy the court that the defendant's conduct does amount to a tort, the defendant may be able to prove that there are mitigating circumstances which remove, or at least reduce, liability. The following defences may be relevant to any of the torts covered in this text.

1 Voluntary assumption of risk/consent – *volenti non fit injuria*

If the claimant expressly or impliedly consented to the defendant's behaviour, the defendant is not liable. The claimant must make the decision with full knowledge of the likely outcome and be free to make a choice.

Smith v *Baker* (1891, HL)

The claimant quarryman was injured by rocks falling from overhead machinery. He had protested about the danger, but continued to work after being ordered to do so and being told that he could leave if he was unhappy with his working conditions.

Held: the claimant had not consented to the risk of injury as, although he knew of the danger, he had never freely consented to the risk. He had no real choice in the matter.

Rescue cases

If the claimant is injured rescuing somebody from a hazard created by the negligence of the defendant, the claimant only consents to the risk, if:

1 *They had no legal or moral duty to intervene.* The nature of the claimant's job may impose a legal duty to assist in an emergency: fire-fighters and the police are obvious examples; a schoolteacher supervising children on an outing would also

qualify as they have a legal duty to act as a responsible parent to their pupils. Most people seeing a third party in danger could be said to be under a moral duty to take *some* action.

2 *Their method of intervention was unreasonable in the circumstances.* The greater the danger and the more able the rescuer, the more reasonable it will be to take risks. Nobody expects a non-swimmer to plunge into deep water to rescue someone in distress, as one potential drowning may turn into two certain ones. However, a non-swimmer may have a moral duty at least to throw a lifebelt and summon assistance.

Compare the next two cases to see the difference between reasonable and unreasonable risk.

Haynes v *Harwood* (1935, CA)

A policeman was injured when attempting to stop bolting horses which were pulling a van in a busy street.

Held: the defendant was liable for the policeman's injuries; the policeman had not consented to the risk as he had a legal duty to prevent danger to the public and his intervention was a natural and foreseeable result of the defendant's negligence in failing to secure the horses.

Would-be heroics must be justified in the circumstances or will be treated as reckless.

Sylvester v *Chapman* (1935)

The claimant, while visiting a zoo, attempted to extinguish a cigarette end that he noticed was smouldering near straw bales beside a leopard's cage. To do so he climbed a safety barrier. The leopard, displeased by the disturbance, reached out between the bars of the cage and clawed him.

Held: the claimant had consented to the risk. While he had a moral duty to alert the staff to the fire risk, by putting himself unnecessarily in danger he had acted unreasonably.

Consent to negligence

It is not generally in the public interest to allow defendants to avoid liability for their careless behaviour. Where claimants have clearly acted recklessly, though, without regard for their own safety, or have willingly participated in the defendant's careless behaviour, the defendant may be provided with a defence.

ICI v Shatwell (1964, HL)

The claimant shot firer was injured when helping to carry out a controlled explosion. The claimant was experienced in the work and had encouraged the team leader to use inappropriate equipment.

Held: the claimant had consented to the risk of injury by acting recklessly in regard to his own safety.

Ratcliff v Harper Adams College (1999, CA)

A student, who was paralysed after breaking his neck when trespassing in his college swimming pool outside opening hours, was deemed to have consented to the risk of diving into shallow water.

2 Contributory negligence

Under the Law Reform (Contributory Negligence) Act 1945, the court may reduce the damages payable by the defendant if the claimant has failed to take reasonable care for *their own safety* thus aggravating the damage suffered. In cases where failure to wear a seat belt has aggravated injuries to a claimant it is usual to reduce damages by 25 per cent (*Froom* v *Butcher* (1975, CA)). The defence may succeed where their argument of consent fails and is applicable to any tort not based on intentional behaviour, e.g. deceit.

Here are two illustrative cases.

Sayers v Harlow Urban District Council (1958, CA)

The claimant visited the defendant's public lavatory and was trapped when the lock jammed. After trying to attract attention for 15 minutes, she attempted to climb out over the partition. Unfortunately, she fell when the toilet roll, which she was using as a foothold, rotated and threw her to the floor.

Held: the claimant's escape attempt was reasonable; she had not consented to the risk of injury. Her choice of foothold, however, involved an unreasonable risk, so the damages payable by the defendant would be reduced by one-quarter.

Stone v *Taffe* (1974, CA)

The claimant's husband was killed when, after a party hosted by the Royal and Antediluvian Order of Buffaloes, he catapulted himself down the unlit staircase in the defendant's pub. The claimant's wife and a friend who had preceded him had completed the descent safely.

Held: damages should be reduced by 50 per cent to take account of the lack of care taken by the deceased for his own safety.

The defence applies to cases of industrial disease if the claimant's own behaviour has made him or her more open to the risk.

Badger v *Ministry of Defence* (2006)

Mr Badger (B) died from cancer mainly caused by the negligence of the defendant in exposing him to asbestos, but B also was a long-term smoker which was a contributory factor.

Held: his damages must be reduced by 25 per cent to reflect his contributory negligence for his death since, by the 1970s (when health warnings already appeared on cigarette packets), he was medically advised to give up smoking and received further warnings from doctors in 1991, 1992 and 1995, but still did not comply.

It may also apply where the claimant harms themselves intentionally. In *Reeves* v *Metropolitan Police Commissioner* (2000), the police were liable for negligently allowing a suicide to occur but damages claimed by the deceased's next of kin were reduced by 50 per cent.

3 Statutory authority

Public authorities are empowered by statute to carry out specific duties and powers and while this is no defence to negligence or breach of statutory duty, the statute may provide a defence to nuisance or *Rylands* v *Fletcher* liability, e.g. the Civil Aviation Act 1993, s 76 states no action may be brought in nuisance in relation to low flying aircraft, as long as this is reasonable in relation to weather conditions and all the other circumstances of the flight.

A defence of statutory authority may be challenged under the Human Rights Act 1998 on the grounds that the provision is incompatible with the ECHR with a further claim to the European Court of Human Rights if the action fails in the domestic courts.

Chapter summary

Negligence

Duty of care: A 'three part' test for establishing a duty is now used – is there proximity, is the damage foreseeable, is it just and reasonable to impose a duty?

Breach of duty: A breach of duty occurs when the defendant falls below the standard of care appropriate to the duty owed.

Doctrine of res ipsa loquitur and burden of proof: 'the thing speaks for itself'.

Damage: The claimant must prove that it was the defendant's breach of duty which actually caused the damage suffered.

Breach of duty of care

The claimant must prove that the defendant failed to take reasonable care taking into account:

(a) seriousness of the risk arising from the defendant's conduct;

(b) the extent of the reasonably foreseeable damage to the claimant;

(c) any relevant skill of the claimant; and

(d) the skill/qualifications of the defendant.

Causation: the link between the breach and the damage to the claimant must exist:

(a) **in fact:** the damage must be the result of the breach ('but for' test);

(b) **in law:** the damage must not be too remote from the breach of duty.

Test for remoteness: damage must be of a reasonably foreseeable kind in unintentional torts like negligence and nuisance.

Intervening acts: make damage too remote unless they were reasonably foreseeable to the defendant.

Defences

Voluntary assumption of risk/consent – volenti non fit injuria: express/implied consent by the claimant to the defendant's behaviour may be an effective defence.

Contributory negligence: damages may be reduced proportionately in relation to the claimant's failure to take care for their own safety.

Review questions 12

1 What must a claimant in an action for negligence prove?

2 In an action for negligence, what factors are important to establish a duty of care?

3 Explain the 'eggshell skull' rule.

4 What is the difference between the defence of consent and contributory negligence?

5 What defence may be open to Cherry, whose car collided with Wilma who was riding her motorbike and not wearing a crash helmet?

6 Explain the purpose and effect of the doctrine of *res ipsa loquitur*.

Answers to all review questions can be found in Appendix 2.

Advanced questions 12

(A) Discuss how the courts determine whether there was a breach of the duty of care.

(B) Critically evaluate the rule relating to police immunity from being sued in negligence and the justification for this.

Answers to the advanced questions can be found at **go.pearson.com/uk/he/resources.**

Take a closer look

The following cases provide important examples of how the law in this chapter has developed. They are primary sources illustrating the law in action and give more detail about their facts, as well as helping to understand the law and to appreciate how the judges reached their decisions.

Try looking them up in the law reports or accessing them via a database, e.g. BAILII (www.bailii.org/databases.html). LexisNexis or Westlaw may be available in the university or college library, or extracts may be found in a case book. (See Appendix 1: Additional resources.)

Donoghue v *Stevenson* [1932] AC 562 HL

Fairchild v *Glenhaven Funeral Services* [2002] 3 All ER 305, HL

Network Rail Infrastructure Ltd v *Conarken Group Ltd and Another* [2010] EWHC 1852; [2010] TCC 132

Overseas Tankships & Engineering v *Morts Dock & Engineering Ltd (The Wagon Mound) (No. 1)* [1961] 1 All ER 404

Web activity

Read 'Suing the Police for negligence: The legal line that still can not be crossed . . . ' by David Corrigan:
www.farleys.com/suing-police-negligence-legal-line-still-can-not-crossed/

Assignment 11

Max is driving his girlfriend Kate to the railway station on a misty rainy day.

They were held up in traffic and Kate is convinced that she will be late for her train. After they have waited at a red light for some time, Kate shouts: 'Get on with it. Go through the red light. The lights are obviously not working. There's no traffic around. Get a move on!' Max cannot see any traffic approaching and drives across the junction. He strikes a bicycle ridden at speed by Edward, who is wearing dark clothing, no helmet and has no lights on his bicycle. Kate, who was not wearing a seat belt, is injured and Edward who has a heart condition, suffers a heart attack and dies of his injuries.

Advise Max of his potential liability in negligence.

Negligence and special duty situations

Learning objectives

On completion of this chapter, students should be able to:

★ recognise the relationship from which a duty of care for pure economic loss may arise;

★ decide when a duty of care arises for negligent statements;

★ appreciate the scope of nervous shock liability;

★ describe when a duty exists for omissions and third-party acts;

★ understand when a public authority may be liable in negligence when exercising statutory discretion.

Introduction

As indicated in the previous chapter, under *Donoghue* v *Stevenson* principles, a third party reasonably likely to suffer loss or injury may be owed a duty of care in negligence if he or she directly suffers personal injury or damage to property.

Sometimes there may be a large pool of potential claimants. The garage which services X's car owes a duty of care to carry out the work safely not only to X, but also to X's passengers as well as other road users and pedestrians in the vicinity of X's vehicle when it is in use. However, the law is unwilling to make defendants vulnerable to every possible claim of damage resulting from their negligent behaviour. Liability in negligence is greatly restricted by the courts in some situations. The problem of recovering pure economic loss is addressed in this chapter. There are also a number

14

of other special duty situations relevant relating to negligent statements, shock-induced injuries, liability for damage caused by third parties and the exercise of statutory discretion by public authorities such as local councils and the police.

Proof of duty alone does not guarantee a successful claim. If a claimant brings a negligence action, they must also prove that the defendant breached the duty by failing to take reasonable care and that the claimant suffered damage as a result, which is not too remote.

Special duty situations

As will be seen in this chapter, the tort of negligence has traditionally covered claims for death, personal injury and damage to property. In claims of this sort the existence of duty of care is not in doubt. In *Caparo* v *Dickman* (1990, HL) Lord Oliver said: 'the existence of a nexus of duty between the careless defendant and the injured plaintiff can rarely give rise to any difficulty', and in *Sandhar* v *Department of Transport* (2004) May LJ affirmed this: 'Personal or physical injury directly inflicted is the first building block of negligence . . . it will almost always be a component of breach of duty of care owed by the person inflicting the injury to the person or owner of the material object injured.'

However, although the law of negligence today embraces liability for less traditionally recognised types of damage and their cause, the courts are wary of imposing liability in these less traditional areas. The criteria relevant to existence of new duty situations (reasonable foreseeability, proximity, justice and reason) may be stringently applied. In order to limit the scope of duty to make it just and reasonable, the court may take a very restricted view of what is reasonably foreseeable and require proof of a very close relationship of proximity. These criteria often underpin such judgments even if not expressly mentioned by the judge.

Pure economic loss

Negligence liability does not usually arise from the poor *quality* of a service, but from the *physical damage* to people and property caused by it. Any purely financial loss arising from defective performance is not generally recoverable, as indicated by the decisions in *Spartan Steel Alloys* v *Martin* (1972 CA) and *Murphy* v *Brentwood Council* (1990, HL) (below).

Distinguishing between consequential and pure economic loss

Students initially studying this area often find it difficult to tell consequential from pure economic loss. Judges usually just talk about 'economic loss' without clearly indicating what sort they mean and leave others to work it out from the context. It may help to think about this in terms of the cost of the damage to the claimant and their goods caused by the defendant's product or service (consequential economic loss) as opposed to a loss of money alone, which is often related to future and possibly notional income (pure economic loss).

Pure economic loss caused by negligent acts

The next case clearly evidences the courts' reluctance to allow negligence claims for pure economic losses.

Pride & Partners v *Institute for Animal Health* (2009)

Held: the defendants were liable for the consequential financial losses to farmers whose stock were culled as a result of a foot and mouth disease outbreak, which was caused by the virus escaping from the Institute. However, claims by other farmers who suffered purely financial losses due to the movement restriction orders, such as reduced milk production and extra feeding costs, did not succeed. Tugendhat J acknowledged that claims for lost market value, caused by stock losing condition (exceeding optimal market weight) due to delayed sales, were potentially consequential losses, but would still not succeed because they were only an indirect consequence of the defendants' negligence.

The next case provides a helpful example of how to distinguish between the two different types of economic loss and illustrates some of the many ways used by judges to avoid liability in this area.

Spartan Steel Alloys v *Martin Ltd* (1972, CA)

Early one morning the negligent operation of a power shovel outside the claimant's steelworks resulted in a power cut which put its furnace out of action for the rest of that day. The metal, which had been in the furnace when the power was cut off, was spoilt and no further consignments could be processed that day.

Held: the claimant was entitled to damages for the cost of the spoilt metal and for the profit which would normally have been made on its sale in good condition as this was a directly consequential loss. However, the claim for the lost profits on the melts which could not be processed that day must fail, as it was purely economic loss and did not result from any damage to the claimant's property.

Lord Denning said: 'at bottom I think the question of recovering economic loss is one of policy. Whenever the courts draw a line to mark out the bounds of duty, they do it as a matter of policy so as to limit the liability of the defendant.'

Lord Denning held that no duty of care existed concerning the unprocessed melts because:

1 It would be unfair to impose a duty on the defendants since statutory providers of electricity and other utilities enjoy exemption from liability for pure economic loss arising from interruption of supply.

2 Such interruption is well known and commonplace. Most people temporarily deprived of electricity supply 'do not go running round to their solicitor'. They may insure against possible losses or install a back-up generator as a precaution 'or make up the economic loss by doing more work the next day. This is a healthy attitude which the law should encourage'.

3 A huge number of claims would arise if a duty existed in this situation 'some might be genuine, but many might be inflated or even false . . . it would be well-nigh impossible to check the claims'.

4 It would place an unreasonable burden on the contractor. 'The risk of economic loss should be suffered by the community who suffer the losses, usually many but comparatively small losses rather than . . . on the contractor on whom the total of them . . . might be very heavy.'

5 'The law provides for deserving cases', i.e. those where physical damage results to the claimant or material property.

Should the claimant have been insured?

While there may be some sympathy for the claimant in *Spartan Steel*, it is important to understand that in many cases of pure economic loss insurance plays a part, as Lord Denning indicates. Business interruption insurance is readily available to the likes of Spartan Steel. No doubt Martin carried insurance too, but the court tends to take the view that the claimant should carry the risk in situations where it expects them to be insured, to prevent too great a burden being placed on the defendant. Something else to bear in mind is that prior to litigation the claimant will often have made a successful claim on their own insurance and then their insurers take the case in the insured's name to recover what was paid out. The court is unlikely to feel that it is fair to allow the insurers to recoup a loss that may well have been more than covered by insurance premiums.

Murphy v *Brentwood Council* (1990, HL)

The claimant's newly built house subsided when the foundations turned out to be defective. As a result, he had to sell the house for £35,000 less than its proper market value. He claimed that the local authority building inspection department had been negligent in its checks on the foundations.

Held: the house was defective, but no personal injuries had been caused to Mr Murphy and none of his property had been damaged. Therefore, the local authority did not owe a duty of care to the claimant, since his only loss was purely economic: only the diminution on the value of the house was affected.

There was insufficient proximity between the parties, since it was not reasonably foreseeable to the council that Mr Murphy would place reliance on its checks which were carried out in order to comply with the building regulations to safeguard public health rather than protect the financial position of future home owners. No liability in tort would rest on a builder for damage to someone like Mr Murphy who had no contractual relationship or other sufficiently proximate relationship and it would be unfair to impose liability on the council which was less directly involved. It also was not just and reasonable to burden local taxpayers with homeowners' financial losses in such circumstances. Lord Oliver said: 'I am not sure that I see why the burden should fall on the community at large rather than be covered by private insurance.'

Again, in *Murphy* the issue of policy is extremely influential and the issue of personal insurance is relevant to determining what is fair, just and reasonable. Many taxpayers would rather see their council tax being used on public services rather than assisting individual home owners. However, as consumer groups afterwards pointed out, normal buildings insurance does not cover structural problems which arise from defective materials or workmanship, but only those caused by natural phenomena like drought or geological features.

Is there an alternative remedy?

The court may be unwilling to expand the boundaries of negligence liability if the claimant could have pursued compensation by another established route.

Home owners may be able to sue under the Defective Premises Act 1972 (DPA 1972). Section 1(1) imposes a duty on 'any person taking on work in connection with the provision of a dwelling . . . to see that the work is done in a workmanlike . . . or professional manner . . . so that the dwelling will be fit for human habitation when completed'. This covers pure economic loss but was no help to Mr Murphy as his claim arose after the six-year limitation period had elapsed.

Property bought subject to a transferable guarantee from the builder who constructed or substantially renovated it is also protected. Such compensation schemes provide more generous terms than the DPA 1972. Claims can be made by the buyer and subsequent purchasers for the lifetime of the guarantee, so no contractual relationship with the builder is required.

A high degree of proximity between the parties is crucial in pre-economic loss claims

In *White* v *Jones* (1995, HL) (below) the claimants were successful in their pursuit of a lost inheritance as the House of Lords acknowledged that there was a very close relationship between them and the defendant.

White v *Jones* (1995, HL)

An elderly man, after a quarrel with his two daughters, left them no money in his will. Three months later he forgave them and informed his solicitor that he wished to make a new will under which the daughters were each to be given a legacy of £9,000. Two months after giving his instructions he died, before the solicitor completed the necessary work. Due to this negligent delay, the daughters did not receive their inheritance. They successfully sued the solicitor.

Held: the solicitor was brought into a special relationship of close proximity with the sisters. By agreeing to draft the will, he was deemed voluntarily to have accepted the responsibility for ensuring the creation of a valid will. It was reasonably foreseeable that any potential beneficiary would suffer pure economic loss if the will was invalid.

Note the different but equally valid criteria applied by the House of Lords for determining proximity in these cases:

- *Murphy* v *Brentwood Council*: reasonable reliance by the claimant;
- *White* v *Jones*: voluntary assumption of responsibility by the *defendant*.

The *White* v *Jones* approach is more realistic, where the defendant is asked by a third party to do something which affects the well-being of a claimant, who is unaware of the request and so cannot realistically be said to be placing reliance on the defendant.

In some cases both factors may be present (see, for example, *Hedley Byrne* v *Heller*, below).

West Bromwich Albion FC v *El-Safty* (below) indicates that a special relationship requires clear evidence that the defendant actually assumed responsibility for very specific consequences to make it reasonably foreseeable that the claimant is likely to rely upon it.

West Bromwich Albion Football Club Ltd v *El-Safty* (2007)

Michael Appleton damaged his knee during a training session with the claimant club. His contract required him to be treated by one of the medical advisers employed by the club's insurance scheme. The defendant was a service provider to the insurers and his fees in respect of the treatment were settled by that company. The defendant negligently recommended reconstructive surgery and as a result Appleton became unable to play professional football. Had the appropriate conservative treatment been carried out, he would have been match fit within four months.

As a result, the club claimed that they had lost millions for the loss of Appleton's services, including the expense of finding a replacement and covering the costs of his lost salary.

Held: the defendant did not owe a duty of care to the claimant for these losses. He was paid under the insurance scheme to treat WBA's players, not to advise it about its players' treatment or its financial affairs. No special relationship existed between the claimant and defendant as the defendant had not assumed responsibility to the claimant for this type of loss. Also it was not fair, just and equitable to impose a duty in these circumstances.

Negligent statements

In principle, there is no difference between liability arising from negligent statements and from negligent acts. A party may suffer physical damage by reliance on incorrect advice just as he or she may be injured by other negligent conduct.

T v *Surrey County Council* (1994)

T was injured by the actions of a child-minder whom the defendant council had negligently recommended to his mother.

Held: the council owed a duty of care to T. By advising his mother, the council had been brought into close relationship to T, and it was reasonably foreseeable that he would be affected by the quality of the advice acted upon by his mother.

In practice, the duty is generally limited because a negligent statement has the potential to have more far-reaching effects than a negligent act. One snail-infested bottle of ginger beer will poison only one or two people, but a negligent statement may affect thousands and its effects may be long-lasting. The courts are not willing to make the defendant liable to potential claims from a large and unidentifiable class of persons, for an indefinable period of time.

Duty of care for negligent statement covers both pure and consequential economic loss

The duty arises from the claimant's close relationship to or reliance on the defendant. In *Hedley Byrne* (below) the relationship was described variously as a '**special relationship**', or '**quasi-fiduciary**' in character and 'akin to contract'.

Special relationship: essential to liability for pure economic loss claims in negligence. The claimant reasonably places a high degree of reliance on the defendant's knowledge or expertise.

Quasi-fiduciary: describes a relationship involving a high degree of trust, though not a fiduciary relationship as such.

Hedley Byrne v *Heller* (1963, HL)

A firm called Easipower entered into a contract with the claimant, an advertising agency, to book advertising on TV and the national newspapers on terms which made the claimant personally liable for the cost if their client defaulted. Satisfied by an initial reference from Easipowers's bank the claimant went ahead. Three months later it sought further reassurance asking whether Easipower could be relied on 'to the extent of £100,000 per annum'. The bank replied repeating its initial statement that it believed Easipower 'to be respectably constituted and good for its normal business engagements', but adding 'your figures are larger than we would normally expect to see'. The reference was headed 'Confidential. For your private use and without responsibility on the part of this bank or its officials.' Reliant on this, the claimant continued to work for Easipower, but lost over £17,000 when it went into liquidation. The claimant sued the defendant bank for giving negligent advice.

Held: the defendant did not owe a duty of care to the claimant because of the disclaimer. However, in the absence of an effective disclaimer, a duty not to make a careless statement which causes pure economic loss might exist, provided that a special relationship of close proximity 'akin to contract' existed between the parties.

The criteria determining existence of a 'special relationship'

This relationship which is essential to success in *all* pure economic loss claims in negligence must satisfy certain criteria.

Proximity

The parties must have been brought sufficiently into a close relationship of proximity with each other. A high degree of trust will be involved. This relationship may arise in a number of ways:

1 *The statement may be made directly to the claimant by the defendant.*

This is illustrated by the facts of *Hedley Byrne* v *Heller*.

2 *The statement may be made to a third party who passes it on to the claimant.*

Smith v *Eric S. Bush* (1989, HL)

The defendant surveyors' valuation report prepared for a building society was shown with his knowledge to the claimant buyer. In reliance on this she bought the property. The surveyor had overlooked major weakness in the support of the chimneys, one of which fell causing much damage to the interior of the house.

Held: the defendant owed a duty of care to the claimant since she could reasonably be expected to rely on the advice. She was a consumer first-time buyer with no knowledge or experience of the construction business. Most people in her position relied on the lender's valuation report and could not be expected to commission an independent survey.

3 *The statement may be made to a third party who relies upon it thus causing consequent loss to the claimant.*

Spring v *Guardian Assurance* (1994, HL)

The claimant had worked for the defendant insurance company but was made redundant. He applied for a job with Scottish Amicable. LAUTRO (the regulatory organisation for insurance companies) requires a reference from a previous employer for applicants to such jobs. The reference was described by the trial judge as 'so strikingly bad as to amount to . . . the kiss of death to his career in insurance. Scottish Amicable wanted no truck with the man it described'. This slur on his character was completely unwarranted so the claimant sued the defendant in negligence in preparation of the reference.

Held (by majority): the defendant owed a duty of care to the claimant under the *Hedley Byrne* principle. It had special knowledge of the claimant's character, skill and diligence evidenced by the way he had worked while employed by it. The defendant had assumed responsibility to the claimant by giving the reference to Scottish Amicable and the claimant had relied upon it to compose the reference with reasonable care and skill.

Reasonable reliance and assumption of responsibility

It must have been reasonable for the claimant to rely on the statement and thus reasonably foreseeable to the defendant that reliance would be placed. The defendant will then be taken to have responsibility.

These factors usually form two sides of the same coin, but note *White* v *Jones* (above), which indicates that the circumstances may be such that the defendant will be assumed to have taken responsibility even though the claimant may not at that time have placed reliance upon it.

In *Hedley Byrne* v *Heller* (1963), the House of Lords indicated criteria helpful to establishing when reliance can reasonably be placed.

1 *The defendant's ability to give reliable advice.* Specialist knowledge, professional qualifications or other expertise are all relevant.

2 *The circumstances in which the advice was given.* Specialist advice cannot reasonably be relied on when given off the cuff, or on a purely social occasion. Even if given in a business context, it may not be reasonable to rely on it if it is given without proper checks on relevant data.

3 *Disclaimer or condition.* If the defendant indicates expressly or impliedly that the advice should not be relied upon, this may make the claimant's reliance unreasonable and, therefore, not reasonably foreseeable. In *Hedley Byrne* v *Heller* a **disclaimer** by the bank was a factor preventing imposition of a duty of care.

Disclaimer:
a statement by which a party seeks to avoid liability for the consequences of negligent advice or behaviour.

A disclaimer is not automatically effective. The Consumer Rights Act 2015 makes it impossible to exclude liability for negligence for death or personal injury and only covers property damage if this is proved to be reasonable. In a claim between businesses, liability for death and personal injury cannot be excluded but for other damage or loss may be excluded if reasonable (Unfair Contracts Act 1977 UCTA, s 2) (see Chapter 8).

Even if no disclaimer is given, any doubt raised by the way the advice is worded – for example, statements like 'as far as I know', or 'if performance reflects last year', or 'without checking my figures', or 'you might want a second opinion' – may make it unreasonable for the claimant to rely upon the defendant.

Restriction of the *Hedley Byrne* principle

In *Hedley Byrne* and the other cases so far examined, the only person likely to be harmed was the claimant him or herself. In *Caparo* v *Dickman* (1990) (facts below) the court was confronted for the first time by a statement issued to the public. This necessitated restriction of the *Hedley Byrne* principle to prevent a defendant from being potentially liable to a large and unascertainable group of people. The House of Lords held that no duty of care arises unless the following conditions are satisfied:

1 when the advice was given the defendant must reasonably have anticipated what it would be used for (e.g. *Caparo Industries plc* v *Dickman* (1990, HL);

2 the defendant must reasonably have known the recipient of that advice – a specific (not necessarily named) individual, or a member of a clearly ascertainable group (e.g. *Caparo Industries plc* v *Dickman* (1990, HL));

3 the defendant must reasonably have anticipated that the advice would be acted upon without the claimant seeking further clarification or independent advice (e.g. *James McNaughten Paper Group Ltd* v *Hicks Anderson & Co.* (1991, CA).

It must be just and reasonable to impose a duty

Some apparently conflicting case decisions may be found in this area. This is because the courts may interpret the concepts of proximity and foreseeability more strictly in some cases than others in order to prevent the duty of care from developing in ways that are perceived not to be in the public interest. While glad to assist a vulnerable consumer like Ms Smith (see above) without many financial resources, the courts do not wish to encourage a lack of responsibility in economically powerful parties with access to independent advice, particularly those pursuing a speculative deal with high stakes, as in *Caparo* v *Dickman* (1990) (see below).

Similarly, remember that if alternative legal remedies are available, a right of action in negligence may be perceived to be redundant, even though the other remedies may not be applicable to the particular claimant due to the particular circumstances of the case.

Caparo Industries plc v *Dickman* (1990, HL)

The claimant company owned shares in Fidelity plc. The defendants were the accountancy firm which had audited the annual accounts. These negligently stated that Fidelity had profits of £1.3 million; it had actually made a loss of over £465,000. The claimant increased its shareholding and later made a successful takeover bid. It then discovered that its acquisition was much less valuable than it had been led to believe by the accounts.

Held: no duty of care was owed to the claimant. The purpose for which the information was given was crucial here. The accounts were to enable shareholders to decide how to vote at the annual general meeting, not to give them personal investment advice.

If a duty was imposed, it would protect not only the shareholders but also the potential buyers on the open market, thus creating potential liability to a diffuse group of people which would not be appropriate.

The following cases illustrate the operation of some of the *Caparo* criteria.

James McNaughten Paper Group Ltd v *Hicks Anderson & Co.* (1991, CA)

No duty was owed by accountants to a company director for whom they prepared draft accounts for consideration prior to a takeover bid.

Held: the defendant was not liable because it was not reasonably foreseeable that the claimant would rely on the draft accounts, particularly as he had access to expert advice to evaluate them. The defendant was also aware that the accounts had been swiftly compiled in draft form, providing a guide to the company's financial health rather than a definitive statement.

Compare the two decisions above with the following:

Morgan Crucible Co. plc v Hill Samuel Bank (1991, CA)

The claimants' takeover bid was made in reliance on a profit forecast issued to them by the defendant company. The defendant accountants and bank stated that this had been made in accordance with the company's accounting procedures, after full and careful enquiry.

Held: the defendants were liable. They had intended the claimants to rely on the information when making the bid, which they had done. The claimants' reliance was reasonable since, although they had independent advice, much of the information was available only to the defendants and could not be independently verified.

See also *Smith v Eric S. Bush* (1989) (above) and *Europe plc v Selskabet (Formerly Roskilde Bank)* (2016, CA) (below).

Europe plc v Selskabet (Formerly Roskilde Bank) (2016) EWCA

A bank advertised the sale of some loan notes to encourage investors in a video presentation shown first at a road show and later reproduced on the bank's website. The video included a disclaimer. A third party bought some of the notes and then sold them on to the claimant investment company which had previously seen the original material on the bank's website. The information turned out to be inaccurate and this caused loss to the claimant which sued the bank for damages under the Misrepresentation Act s 2(1), claiming that it had been induced to buy the shares by false information.

Held:

1 The claimant had no contractual relationship to the bank. Therefore it was necessary to decide if there was sufficient proximity between the claimant and the bank to create the necessary duty of care (*Caparo v Dickman* (1990)). Merely placing information on a website does not create proximity to readers. The advertiser must have intended the reader to respond in a particular way. Here the bank put out the information to attract potential investors both at the road show and among those who saw the website and the claimant was a member of that class. Therefore potential liability did exist.

2 However, the defendant bank was not liable since it was covered by the disclaimer accompanying the advertisement. UCTA 1977, s 3 covered contractual terms and non-contractual notices and therefore could apply in a misrepresentation claim by a third party not in a contractual relationship with the bank. A disclaimer was legitimate if reasonable; in a commercial contract the parties were entitled to make their own bargains provided the terms were sufficiently clear.

Most of the reported cases on negligent statement concern pure economic loss; the next one concerns a personal injuries claim.

T v *Surrey County Council* (1994)

T was a small baby. His mother consulted the council to check on the suitability of a registered child-minder. The council failed to tell T's mother that previously a young baby had been brain-damaged while in the minder's care and, although there was no conclusive evidence against her, it had been suggested that she should in future only look after children over two years old. T subsequently suffered severe brain damage when shaken violently by the child-minder.

Held: the council owed a duty of care to T since it had given advice directly relevant to his safety and thus created a relationship of sufficient proximity. The council should reasonably have foreseen that the advice, which came from one of their professional officers with special knowledge, would be relied upon. If incorrect, it would clearly jeopardise T's safety.

Although the judge in the above case said that a *Hedley Byrne* relationship existed in this case, where physical rather than pure economic loss has occurred it is sufficient that a straightforward analysis of *Donoghue* v *Stevenson* principles is applied. In *Clay* v *Crump* (1963) the defendant architect was held liable to workers on a demolition site injured after a wall, which he had negligently stated was stable, collapsed on to them. It was held that it was reasonably foreseeable to the defendant that the workmen would be endangered if his advice was incorrect.

Interesting and as yet unsolved questions of liability are raised by specialist information on financial and legal issues broadcast to the public on radio and TV programmes and published in some periodicals. There are also books which claim to help members of the public do their own conveyancing, or to make a will. Here the large class of potential claimants which exists might make the courts unwilling to entertain claims. On the other hand, such publications often encourage reliance on the given information by offering help and suggesting that this will be provided by experts. The more focused such information is (e.g. one-to-one on a radio phone-in), the greater the likelihood of a duty arising unless an appropriate and effective disclaimer is given.

Real life

Hardeep is an enthusiastic computer user and reads a lot of computer magazines. When he meets Stella at a party she is impressed by his apparent knowledge, and asks him if he will help her buy a computer for her new design business. Hardeep tells her that he knows where to find her a bargain and the following week takes her to the premises of Mouse Technology, where on his advice she buys a model which he assures her will do everything she needs. However, within a couple of weeks' use it becomes evident that it is entirely unsuitable for the sort of programs that she needs to use and she has to buy a different machine which puts her £1,500 out of pocket.

Hardeep may unwittingly have made himself liable to Stella by helping her in her computer quest. Although he is not an expert in the relevant technology, he has held himself out as having that knowledge and a *Hedley Byrne* relationship has been held to exist in non-business relationships. In *Chaudhry* v *Prabhakar* (1988) amateur advice on buying a second-hand car gave rise to liability. (See Chapter 12.) However, unlike Ms Chaudhry, Stella was present when the computer was purchased and could have checked the advice with a shop assistant, so her reliance on Hardeep might well not be regarded as reasonable.

Nervous shock (psychiatric harm)

A duty of care readily exists where the claimant has suffered physical injury from the defendant's careless behaviour. It may be harder to establish a duty of care when the claimant suffers illness induced by acute shock or distress caused by the defendant. Damages are *not* recoverable for the *actual shock or distress*, but liability may arise from the *medically recognisable* illness or condition triggered by it. Such illness could be physical, like a heart attack, but most recent claims concern psychiatric conditions like post-traumatic stress syndrome.

In *Page* v *Smith* (see below) the House of Lords held that the rules determining duty of care for **nervous shock** are different according to whether the claimant is categorised as a **primary** or a **secondary victim** of the accident caused by the defendant. Primary victims were defined as those directly involved in the accident, who, as a result, have been physically hurt or reasonably put in fear for their own safety.

Nervous shock: psychiatric or physical harm caused by the shock of being involved in or witnessing an accident caused by the defendant's negligence.

Primary victim: nervous shock victim directly endangered by the defendant's negligence.

Secondary victim: a claimant in a nervous shock claim who sustains damage as a result of directly witnessing the accident caused by the defendant's negligence.

Dulieu v *White* (1901)

The defendant negligently failed to control his horse and cart, which demolished the wall of the pub where the claimant was working as a barmaid. She managed to shelter from the shower of masonry and was not directly hurt. Later, however, she suffered a miscarriage from the shock.

Held: the defendant was liable because it was reasonably foreseeable that the claimant would suffer shock from fear for her own physical safety in the dangerous situation created by the defendant's negligence.

Secondary victims are not so closely involved since they merely witness the accident or are involved in the aftermath but not endangered by it. Stricter rules are therefore necessary to limit the duty to them, as large numbers might claim and it would not be fair, just and reasonable to make the defendant responsible for them all.

Primary victims

Since the defendant has caused a dangerous situation to arise, the duty is largely based on basic negligence principles. A duty of care arises because there is reasonable foreseeability of some physical or psychiatric injury to the claimant.

Page v *Smith* (1995, HL)

The defendant's negligent driving caused his car to collide with that of the claimant. Minor damage resulted to the vehicles but the claimant appeared unhurt. Shortly afterwards, however, he suffered a recurrence of ME (myalgic encephalomyelitis, then perceived as a psychiatric condition) from which he had enjoyed a lengthy remission.

Held: the defendant owed the same duty of care to the claimant as he would to any other fellow road user, since it was reasonably foreseeable that he might suffer personal injuries if the defendant drove negligently. It was not necessary for the claimant to prove that psychiatric damage might result. The distinction between physical and psychiatric injury was irrelevant in these circumstances.

The House of Lords indicated the limits of *Page* v *Smith* in *Johnston* v *NEI International* (2007, HL) which comprised four claims by various employees who had developed pleural plaques as a result of exposure to asbestos by their employers. Prior to this decision, claims for pleural plaques were potentially successful.

Johnston and Others v *NEI International* (2007, HL)

The claimants were all diagnosed with pleural plaques (hardening of lung tissue), which while harmless in themselves indicate exposure to asbestos. Diagnosis occurred years after the employer's negligent behaviour. Fear that they might develop asbestosis resulted in Mr Johnston and two others suffering anxiety and distress and one (Mr Grieves) developing clinical depression and irritable bowel syndrome.

Held: all the claims failed.

1 Mr Johnston and the two other claimants, who argued that the defendants were liable for the pleural plaques and their consequent anxiety and distress, failed because legal liability requires some actual injury recognised by law.

> The plaques were just a simple physical change, not the cause of illness. They were harmless in themselves and neither they nor the fear of future illness amounted to actionable damage. Even when combined, they did not amount to actionable harm.
>
> 2 Mr Grieves' claim failed because it was not reasonably foreseeable that a person of reasonable fortitude would develop a medically recognised disease as a result of the fear of future illness.
>
> His other argument that he was a primary victim and therefore owed a duty because physical harm, i.e. asbestosis, was a reasonably foreseeable result of asbestos exposure, also failed because the principle in *Page* v *Smith* was limited to injury resulting directly and immediately from the negligence of the defendant where the claimant's injury was 'an immediate response to a sudden and alarming incident of which the plaintiff had no opportunity to prepare himself' (Lord Hope). Twenty years had passed between exposure to the asbestos and the diagnosis of pleural plaques and, therefore, there was no causative link between them.

The *Johnston* decision was controversial. The insurers who had previously had to pay out for these claims were delighted but potential future claimants and their supporters loudly protested. The Scottish government promptly legislated and passed the Damages (Asbestos-Related Conditions) (Scotland) Act 2009 which in effect reversed the *Johnston* decision in Scotland from the date of the judgment. The Northern Irish Assembly passed a similar Bill in 2011.

In 2010 the government announced that pleural plaques would not give rise to legal liability in England and Wales because the plaques did not in themselves cause illness.

Involuntary participants

Involuntary participants: a primary nervous shock victim, who, though blameless, feels implicated in an accident caused by the defendant's negligence.

The claimant, an **involuntary participant**, who is made to feel responsible for the accident although it is the defendant's conduct which is the real cause, may also be treated as a primary victim.

Dooley v *Cammell Laird* (1951)

> The claimant was operating a crane which had been negligently maintained by his employer. The crane cable snapped and he saw the heavy crate attached to it hurtle into the hold. His shock at the anticipated fate of his workmates (who miraculously escaped injury) induced an acute nervous breakdown.
>
> **Held:** the employer was liable since the claimant's response was prompted by his feelings that he had helped to cause the accident, and fear for his colleagues was reasonably foreseeable.

It is not easy to persuade the court that sufficient foreseeability exists in this area. In *Monk v Harrington Ltd and Others* (2008) (see below), Mr Monk's genuine belief that he was responsible for the accident, which had aggravated his trauma, was not justified in the circumstances and he lost his claim because it was held that it was not reasonably foreseeable that anyone in his situation would suffer psychiatric injury.

Rescuers

Until the House of Lords' decision in *White v Chief Constable of South Yorkshire* (below) rescuers were automatically deemed to be primary victims, provided they had a sufficient degree of involvement in the accident. The rationale of this principle was that it was in the public interest to encourage people to act humanely in an emergency.

Chadwick v British Rail (1967)

The claimant became acutely clinically depressed after spending a gruelling night giving first aid and comfort to severely injured and dying victims within the compacted wreckage of a horrific train crash.

Held: it was reasonably foreseeable that volunteers would render assistance and might suffer psychiatric injury as a result and, therefore, a duty of care was owed to the claimant.

The duty of care to rescuers was restricted by the House of Lords in *White v Chief Constable of South Yorkshire*, which held that a duty of care to rescuers exists only if the rescuer was actually in danger or reasonably believed that they were.

White v Chief Constable of South Yorkshire (1999, HL)

At Hillsborough football stadium 96 people were killed and hundreds injured in the crush resulting from the failure of senior police officers adequately to control admission to the stadium. The claimants, who were junior police officers, claimed for post-traumatic stress syndrome resulting from the harrowing scenes in which they had been heavily involved for many hours as rescuers.

Held: these claims must fail, since the claimants had not been exposed to or put in fear of danger and therefore no duty of care was owed to the claimants by their employers.

This decision can be justified on policy (public interest) grounds. The House of Lords was concerned to limit the increasing number of claims for compensation from members of the emergency services whose employment as a matter of course involves potential exposure to harrowing, though not necessarily dangerous, situations. The cost of settling such claims could, if not checked, undermine the provision of the services themselves and put an unreasonable burden on the taxpayer. However, someone like Mr Chadwick might not win his case today unless the court was prepared to acknowledge sufficient danger or reasonable fear. This point is well illustrated by the next case.

Monk v Harrington Ltd and Others (2008)

During the building of Wembley stadium an accident was caused by the negligence of the defendant construction firm. Two of Mr Monk's workmates fell 60 feet when a platform collapsed. One died shortly afterwards and the other broke a leg. M tried to help both men. Subsequently, as a result of what he had seen, he began to suffer from post-traumatic stress disorder and depression.

Held: when M rendered assistance, it was unlikely that he believed himself to be in danger and there were no reasonable grounds for his subsequent belief that he had caused the accident. Therefore, he was not a primary victim and no duty of care was owed to him.

This case illustrates the problems caused by the limitation of the rescuer category. By so doing, their Lordships have effectively barred the courts from assisting all litigants in areas where policy might well suggest that liability should be imposed. The construction industry, although better regulated than it used to be, is still well known for a poor accident record. While it is questionable that imposing liability necessarily drives up safety standards, at least deserving claimants like Mr Monk would be entitled to compensation for the loss of their livelihood as a result of their acting humanely.

Negligent statements and nervous shock

Liability may arise from statements as well as acts. There is a duty of care to deliver bad news with sufficient sensitivity to prevent reasonably foreseeable psychiatric damage (*AB* v *Tameside & Glossop Health Authority* (1997)). Similarly, there is a duty to deliver news accurately. In *Allin* v *City & Hackney Health Authority* (1996), it was held that the defendant was liable for nervous shock suffered by the claimant when she received the sensitively delivered but *inaccurate* news that her baby was dead. Where negligent statements are involved duty may be based more on a *Hedley Byrne* relationship than the normal rules relating to nervous shock.

Liability to primary victims may be costly for service providers. This is evidenced by the Kings Cross fire, where London Transport was liable for multiple successful claims, including fire-fighters. A mass claim was brought by traumatised victims and relatives of the 193 people who drowned when the *Herald of Free Enterprise* ferry to Zeebrugge capsized in 1987. The sinking of *The Marchioness* pleasure boat on the Thames in 1989, with 51 dead, is another case in point.

Secondary victims

These merely witness the accident or, if involved, are not in danger or reasonable fear of it. The next case was the first secondary victim claim and laid down most of the basic principles governing such claims today.

Hambrook v *Stokes* (1925, CA)

A mother saw the defendant's driverless lorry careering down the hill in the direction of her two daughters who had just disappeared round the corner of the road. Although she did not see the accident, she heard the impact when the vehicle crashed through a wall after mounting the pavement close to her daughters. Miraculously, the girls were unhurt, but their mother suffered a fatal heart attack due to the shock resulting from fear for her children's safety.

Held: the defendant was liable. A duty of care was owed to a person who suffered nervous shock from directly witnessing an accident caused by the defendant's negligence, where such trauma was *reasonably foreseeable in a person of reasonable fortitude. The shock might result from the claimant witnessing the build-up to the accident and/or the immediate aftermath, but without seeing the accident itself.* The shock must be a product of what the claimant actually witnessed *with their own senses*, not what was reported to them by a third party.

In a later case, the House of Lords further developed the law, stressing the need for proximity of the claimant both in place and time to the accident and imposed limits on the concept of immediate aftermath.

McLoughlin v *O'Brian* (1982, HL)

The claimant suffered acute depression and personality change resulting from the shock of witnessing serious injuries caused to her husband and children by the defendant's negligent driving.

Held: her claim was successful. Although she was not present when the accident occurred, the harrowing scenes she witnessed at the casualty department an hour afterwards were horrific enough to make her sufficiently proximate, and her response reasonably foreseeable.

In *Alcock* v *Chief Constable of South Yorkshire* (1992) the House of Lords rationalised the criteria determining duty of care to secondary victims.

Alcock v *Chief Constable of South Yorkshire* (1992 , HL)

The 16 claimants had loved ones who had perished in the horrific occurrences at the Hillsborough stadium (see Web activity below). None was successful because they did not fulfil the necessary criteria laid down by the House of Lords, which restrict the concepts of reasonable foreseeability and proximity applicable in such circumstances.

Held: claimants must be able to prove the following:

Sudden and immediate attack: the nature of the trauma which may give rise to nervous shock liability.

(a) They have suffered some medically recognised illness or condition as a result of a **'sudden and immediate attack'** upon their senses. This excludes claimants who do not suffer a quick and sudden trauma, but whose illness is caused by a build-up of stress and fear.

Close bond of love and affection: the required relationship between claimant and accident victim in nervous shock claims.

(b) It was reasonably foreseeable that they would react in this way: there must be a **'close bond of love and affection'** between them and the accident victim. This is presumed only between spouses and parents and children; all other claimants must prove that the bond exists in the relevant circumstances. (Not all the *Alcock* claimants could satisfy this test.)

(c) Their reaction was that of a reasonably brave person given the level of trauma that they witnessed.

Sufficiently proximate: closeness of the claimant to the accident in terms of both time and space.

(d) *They were* **sufficiently proximate** *to the accident.* Proximity is measured both in terms of time and space. The claimant must usually be present at the scene when the accident occurs, although seeing the build-up to it and/or the immediate aftermath may be sufficient. The claimant must have witnessed the accident directly with his or her own senses and not have had the scene interpreted for him or her by a third party. (This ruled out some of the *Alcock* claimants, who had seen events unfold through a simultaneous TV broadcast, or who had identified a body at the mortuary eight hours after the accident.)

Worth thinking about?

Why do you think the House of Lords in Alcock (above) insisted that secondary victims must witness the accident directly and ruled that TV transmitted pictures did not count?

Suggested solutions can be found in Appendix 2.

The *Alcock* criteria make a very useful checklist for students to refer to, particularly when answering problem questions on this topic. Their application is usefully illustrated by the next two cases.

Taylorson v Shieldness Products (1994, CA)

The claimants were the parents of a 14-year-old boy who died three days after being crushed by a lorry driven by the defendant's negligent employee. The parents, who did not witness the accident, only briefly glimpsed their son after initial treatment when he was transferred to a second hospital. They were not present while he was being treated. The father visited on the night of the accident but the mother did not see him until the next day. They both remained with him for the next two days while he was on a life support system. They claimed that they suffered clinical depression as a result of the experience.

Held: no duty of care existed, as there was insufficient proximity of the parents in time and space to the accident. It was also probable that the damage to the claimants was more the result of grief than shock.

The only successful reported claim from a Hillsborough victim was that of John McCarthy (*McCarthy* v *Chief Constable of South Yorkshire* (1996)), who received over £200,000 damages for his ongoing post-traumatic stress. His half-brother, Ian, died from asphyxiation in one of the grandstands. John satisfied the *Alcock* criteria as he was at the ground though in a different stand with a view of the events as they unfolded. He was therefore deemed to be sufficiently proximate, and the close nature of his relationship to Ian evidenced a close bond of affection.

In practice, very few claims by secondary victims have succeeded.

Palmer v Tees Health Authority (1999, CA)

The claimant's daughter was abducted and murdered by a psychiatric patient. The claimant suffered acute post-traumatic stress disorder and alleged that the defendant authority were negligent in failing to diagnose that the patient was a risk to children. She claimed that within 15 minutes of discovering that her daughter had disappeared she was told that she had been abducted and this produced an immediate shock to her nervous system. When the child's body was discovered three days later, the claimant was within the vicinity of the patient's house but was not allowed to see her daughter's body at that point. She claimed that the psychiatric illness was caused by her presence at the scene and the immediate aftermath of the abduction and the search for and discovery of the body, which she later identified.

Held: her claim must fail on two counts:

(a) she had not witnessed the abduction, nor the murder, nor the discovery of the body, nor was she involved in the immediate aftermath, so she was not sufficiently proximate;

(b) what she had witnessed and experienced did not amount to a sudden and shocking event within the scope of *Alcock*.

Her situation was similar to that of unsuccessful Hillsborough claimants who went through a period of acute anxiety before their worst fears were realised. Her imagination of what had happened was not the same as 'the sudden appreciation by sight or sound of the horrifying event'.

However, the Court of Appeal has been prepared to interpret the *Alcock* principles more generously to deal with extreme circumstances.

North Glamorgan NHS Trust v *Walters* (2002, CA)

Due to the negligence of the Health Trust, the claimant's son died of liver failure. During the 36 hours leading up to his death, the claimant witnessed a number of traumatic events after the child had been admitted to the hospital, starting with her waking to find her son having a violent epileptic fit and vomiting blood all over his cot and ending when he died in her arms when life support was eventually terminated. She was given conflicting information about the likely outcome for her son. In effect, she was on an emotional roller coaster throughout: *'her hopes were lifted and then dashed and finally destroyed'* (Ward LJ). As a result, she suffered a pathological grief reaction.

Held: these circumstances must be treated as one entire 'horrifying' event and, therefore, the *Alcock* criteria were satisfied and a duty of care was owed to her.

A close link between the alleged traumatic event and the original accident is crucial to establish liability where a succession of events has led to the trauma. The *Walters* case was later distinguished on its facts in *Taylor* v *Novo UK* (2013).

Taylor v *A. Novo UK Ltd* (2013, CA)

The claimant's daughter suffered severe injuries when, due to her employer's negligence, a stack of shelving fell on her. Initially she was making a good recovery, but three weeks later she died as a result of thrombosis and an embolism caused by a blood clot. The claimant was present at the death and suffered severe traumatic stress.

Held: the defendant was not liable because the claimant could not prove sufficient proximity. Witnessing the death was the immediate trigger for the claimant's trauma rather than the previous accident. In the interests of policy the accident and the death could not be treated as one event. Otherwise a claim might be successfully brought if death occurred years after the accident, while a claim by someone coming upon an accident scene shortly after the accident could not recover. The idea that Ms Taylor could recover in the first situation but not in the others would strike the ordinary reasonable person as unreasonable and indeed incomprehensible. In this area of the law, the perception of the ordinary reasonable person matters' (Lord Dyson, Master of the Rolls).

This is a complex and controversial area of the law of negligence. The rules often seem arbitrary and may sometimes produce apparently unjust results. In 1998 a Law Commission Report (No. 249, *Liability for Psychiatric Damage*) was published which proposed statutory reform of the duty of care regarding secondary victims to replace the *Alcock* rule. The Report included the following recommendations:

(a) *The class of persons presumed to have a close bond of love and affection should be extended* to include siblings and cohabitees of at least two years' standing (including same-sex partners).
(b) *The claimant's illness need not be caused by a sudden shock* but might arise from a build-up of anxiety and stress over a period of time.
(c) *The claimant's proximity to the accident or its aftermath should be irrelevant.*
(d) *If physical injury were reasonably foreseeable, there would be liability* even if only psychiatric injury resulted.

So far, none of these proposals has been implemented by Parliament.

Omissions to act and liability for damage caused by third parties

Omissions

The law of tort is concerned with compensating acts by a defendant that have actively damaged the claimant (*misfeasance*), rather than with the defendant's failure to act for the claimant's benefit (*nonfeasance*). Consequently, it is rare for a duty of care to result from an omission to act. In *Stovin* v *Wise* (1996) Lord Goff said:

> There are sound reasons why omissions require different treatment from positive conduct. It is one thing for the law to say that a person who undertakes some activity shall take reasonable care not to cause damage to others. It is another thing for the law to require that a person who is doing nothing in particular shall take steps to prevent another from suffering harm.

He went on to say that there are political, moral and economic reasons for this approach. Imposing liability would unduly restrict personal freedom. There is no moral justification in making one person bear the economic burden of compensating a claimant when he or she may be one of a number who might morally be expected to intervene.

> Liability to pay compensation for loss caused by negligent conduct acts as a deterrent . . . But there is no similar justification to require a person who is not doing anything [wrong] to spend money on behalf of someone else.

As Lord Goff indicates, it is important to distinguish between moral and legal duties as the two do not necessarily overlap. For example, a passer-by would not be liable in negligence or any other tort if they failed to stop a blind person from walking into a road in front of an oncoming bus, if they had no pre-existing legal responsibility for their safety.

'False omissions' may give rise to a duty of care

There are situations where a failure to act does give rise to a duty, though if we examine them closely, we see that the omission was not an isolated failure to act but was part of a chain of events already giving rise to liability or that the claimant was in a dependent relationship with the defendant. In both these situations a duty of care already exists between the parties. For example, a driver will be liable for harm to any pedestrian they knock down with their car, if the accident happened because they omitted to use their brakes, or to keep a proper lookout. Similarly, a school teacher may be liable for failing to stop a pupil from climbing into the bear pit on a visit to the zoo, as might a doctor who harms patients by failing to warn them that the drug prescribed cannot be safely combined with certain foods.

Acts of third parties

There is a presumption in law that we are all responsible for our own behaviour, therefore, it is rare to find cases where one party is liable for the tort of a third party (apart from circumstances giving rise to vicarious liability (see Chapter 16).

This is an area of liability which may impact on a business where the claimant is adversely affected by third party activity on premises controlled by the defendant.

Smith v Littlewoods Organisation (1987, HL)

Littlewoods bought a disused cinema with a view to opening one of its stores on the land. While the cinema was being demolished, at a time while no contractor or Littlewoods employees were present, vandals entered the premises and started a fire. This spread to Smith's adjoining premises. Smith alleged that Littlewoods were in breach of a duty to prevent this damage, by making the premises secure against trespassers. Both parties agreed that only a twenty-four-hour guard could have prevented entry by trespassers.

Held: although occupiers of premises have a duty to take reasonable care that their premises are not a source of danger to neighbouring landowners, Little-woods did not owe a duty of care as there were no special circumstances indicating that such vandalism was reasonably foreseeable.

Lord Griffiths stated:

> I do not say that there will never be circumstances in which the law will require an occupier to take special precautions against such a contingency, but they would have to be extreme indeed . . . there was nothing inherently danger-ous . . . stored on the premises, nor can I regard a cinema stripped of its equipment as likely to be any more alluring to vandals than any other recently vacated building in the centre of a town. No message was received . . . from the local police, fire brigade or any neighbour that vandals were creating a danger on any premises.

To require a 24-hour guard would be 'an intolerable burden' in the circumstances.

The *Littlewoods* case is a good example of the court taking a restricted view of what is reasonably foreseeable. Vandalism is a well-known problem in urban areas. However, in cases involving property damage the court expects a claimant to be insured, so it is usually unsympathetic to claims for negligent omissions and third party damage.

The aim of this policy is to encourage property owners to be prudent and to prevent insurance companies from fronting a successful action to recover their losses.

Occupiers do not generally have a duty to secure their premises in order to safeguard neighbouring premises unless alerted by evidence that they represent a risk. If the defendant's premises have previously been subject to trespass and vandalism, this would be more likely to make the court take the view that the damage to the claimant was reasonably foreseeable.

A *duty* may arise in the following circumstances:

1 The defendant had a responsibility to control the third party's behaviour because of a pre-existing relationship with the party. Businesses will be keen to avoid liability in cases such as:

Home Office v *Dorset Yacht Co. Ltd* (1970, HL)

The Home Office was held liable when the claimant's yacht was damaged by improperly supervised Borstal trainees who had escaped from a nearby work camp.

2 The defendant's pre-existing relationship to the claimant makes the defendant responsible for preventing the damage.

Stansbie v *Troman* (1948, CA)

Stansbie was a decorator who was left in sole charge of Mrs Troman's house. He left it unlocked when going out to buy wallpaper and was held liable for the loss arising from the burglary which took place in his absence.

Public authorities and statutory discretion

Public service providers, such as the fire brigade, the police and local authorities, operate in the context of statutory duties and powers. Such duties are mandatory but often widely drafted, leaving a large element of discretion to the authority about how it is implemented. For example, a local authority must provide full-time education for children in its catchment area, but how it does so is left largely to its discretion. The authority decides, for example, whether single-sex education shall be an option and determines the selection methods, if any, for transfer to secondary schools. Some local authorities provide special schools for pupils with some acute physical disabilities and learning difficulties, while others choose to place such students in mainstream schools. Such choices are made with regard to the perceived needs of the particular community and may be limited by budgetary concerns.

Statutory discretion: flexibility in implementation of a statutory duty derived from the wording of the relevant Act of Parliament.

The statutory duty exists to benefit the public at large through the provision of services relevant to local needs. The courts have traditionally been unwilling to permit a duty of care in negligence to be owed by a public authority to individual members of the public who claim to be harmed by the way the authority has used its **statutory discretion** in performing its public duties. Usually, such claims arise where an omission to exercise the power is allegedly the cause of the damage or where a third party is actually responsible for the harm. These factors combined with the desire of the courts not to fetter discretion derived from Parliament makes them particularly reluctant to impose a duty of care. Policy plays a very important role in such circumstances.

The fire brigade and ambulance services owe a limited duty

Capital and Counties Bank plc v *Hampshire Fire Brigade* (1997, CA)

Here the brigade fought a fire on the claimant's premises but left having turned off sprinklers in the roof area, which was still smouldering. Later it reignited and the building was destroyed.

Held: the defendant fire brigade was liable, as its intervention had increased the damage to the claimant. A fire brigade has no civil duty to attend a fire. Duty of care is limited to situations where acts of the fire brigade directly worsened the claimant's problems.

Remember that the court's decision in cases like this will be influenced by the expectation that the claimant will have insurance against fire damage. Maybe if a case concerning death or physical injury occurs we may see a different approach.

Ambulance services owe a duty to provide a timely service once a caller has been told that an ambulance will be dispatched, because their remit involves giving assistance to people requiring medical care.

Kent v Griffiths and Others (No. 3) (2001, CA)

The claimant had an acute asthma attack and suffered severe brain damage when delay caused by negligence by the ambulance service prevented her from receiving timely treatment.

Held: provided an ambulance was available and a caller was told that it would be sent, it should attend within a reasonable time. The ambulance service is part of the health service. It was therefore appropriate to regard it as providing services of the same kind as those provided by hospital services rather than being equivalent to those of the fire brigade and police.

The police

While the police authority will be liable in the same way as any other employer for negligent driving by its officers or failure to protect a person in custody from coming to harm, the court has refused to hear cases where the police were apparently negligent in preventing crimes from occurring. It was perceived that this would unduly restrict discretion in an area where much flexibility was needed and could lead to defensive behaviour by the police that would be prejudicial to the public.

Robinson v Chief Constable of West Yorkshire (2018)

The recent Supreme Court decision in this case held that the police owe a duty of care to a third party injured during the execution of an arrest as the police officers were aware of the claimant's presence but failed to take that into account which resulted in her being injured in the ensuing scuffle.

Osman v Ferguson (1993, CA)

A schoolmaster became obsessed with a pupil, harassed him and his family, carried out acts of vandalism against their property and tried to ram their car while it was being driven. The police were informed and interviewed the man but did not take steps to arrest him. He continued his campaign of harassment which culminated in his shooting both father and son, killing the former and injuring the latter. An action in negligence was taken against the police.

Held: the action must be struck out. Arguably, there was sufficient proximity between the police and the victims of the shooting to give rise to a special relationship. However, it was not fair, just and reasonable to impose a duty of care by the police to the victims of crime. It would not improve standards and could dangerously divert police resources from the general investigation and suppression of crime necessary to protect the public.

This case seemed to indicate that the police enjoyed complete immunity from litigation concerning policing discretion.

The courts have been compelled to take a less prescriptive approach since *Osman v UK* (1999), where the European Court of Human Rights held that giving the police immunity was in effect a breach of Article 6 of the ECHR (right to a fair trial). The House of Lords (*Barrett v Enfield Borough Council* (1999)) subsequently held that any claim where immunity of any public authority is in question must be tried to determine whether a duty of care exists. This, of course, does not mean that a duty will necessarily be held to exist, but it gives the claimant the opportunity to have his or her own case considered, thus enabling his or her right to a fair trial.

Given the House of Lords' decision (below), it seems almost impossible to persuade the court that a duty of care in negligence or liability by the police for breach of Article 2 of the ECHR exists.

Chief Constable Hertfordshire v Van Colle and Smith v Chief Constable of Sussex (2008, HL)

These two cases involved claims against the police for failing to intervene to protect a party in danger of alleged violent attack. The first case concerned X, a witness who was murdered days before he was due to give evidence at a trial for theft by a party later convicted for his murder. In evidence, it was alleged that X had been subjected to a number of threats and intimidation by Y which the police had known about.

Smith repeatedly told the police that A (his former partner) had threatened to kill him and provided sufficient evidence to justify his arrest. For example, he had received over 130 text messages from A. Some contained very explicit threats such as: 'U are dead'; 'Look out for yourself psycho is coming'; 'I am looking to kill you and no compromises'; 'I was in the Bulldog last night with a carving knife. It's a shame I missed you.' However, the police chose to ignore Mr Smith's complaints. Eventually, A attacked him with a claw hammer causing serious injury. X's representative claimed breach of the ECHR, Article 2 (right to life) and Mr Smith claimed in negligence.

Held: both appeals must be dismissed.

X's claim: under *Osman* v *UK* the test of liability stipulated that the court should not acknowledge a breach unless 'at the time' the police should have known of a 'real and immediate risk to life of an identified individual from criminal acts of a third party'.

Y was a seriously 'disturbed and unpredictable individual'. Therefore, it could not be said that the police by involving X as a witness and making him a member of a special class separate from the public at large, should have anticipated that Y was a sufficient risk to X's safety. The *Osman* test did not impose an invariable standard and the particular facts were relevant to determining whether or not it was satisfied.

Mr Smith's claim (Lord Bingham dissenting): under the rule in *Hill* v *Chief Constable West Yorkshire* (1989, HL) the police owed no common law duty of care to protect individuals from attacks by criminals, unless there were very special circumstances justifying departure from the principle which protected the public interest. A specific and evident threat would have to exist for the police to owe a duty. It had not existed here.

The Supreme Court affirmed this principle in *Michael* v *Chief Constable of South Wales* (2015).

Michael v *Chief Constable of South Wales* (2015)

The police received a call for help from Ms Michael after she had been attacked by her ex-partner. He had briefly left the premises threatening to return at once to kill her. Fifteen minutes later she called again and was heard screaming. Eight minutes later the police arrived to find her dead. Police records showed a history of violent attacks on her by her partner. A claim in negligence was made against the police on behalf of her estate.

Held (by a majority of five to two): no duty of care was owed by the police to an individual member of the public even where that individual had given credible evidence of imminent physical danger. No special exception should be created to cover crimes of violence. There was insufficient proximity between police and victim to permit a duty unless the police gave a very specific representation to them that they would assist. The call handler saying that the information would be sent to the police was insufficient to amount to this.

Apart from the potential restriction on police discretion the cost of imposing liability on the police was not justifiable.

While this can look unjust, bear in mind that the victims of such crimes as these do have alternative means of dispute resolution, such as the Criminal Injuries Compensation Board, formal complaint systems or under the Human Rights Act. See *DSD and NBV* v *Commissioner of Police for the Metropolis* (2014, EWHC) where the court awarded a considerable sum of damages against the defendant police force for failing to prevent the claimants being attacked by a serial rapist (see Chapter 3 for a detailed account).

Education and social services

The courts in the past generally refused to allow claims to proceed in negligence against a local authority's education and social services departments, on the ground that this would fetter executive discretion in the use of resources, and interfere with social policy. In *X* v *Bedfordshire County Council* (1995) the House of Lords struck out two claims concerning allegedly negligent decisions by local authorities in failing to take children into care. It was held that no duty of care existed in such cases or social services departments would be unduly constrained. They might be inclined to act defensively and unnecessarily take children into care.

As indicated above, this attitude has had to change since the ECtHR decision in *Osman*. This was evidenced by the House of Lords decision in (*Barrett* v *Enfield Borough Council* (1999) (above)).

A case of failing to take a child into care may now succeed (*Pierce* v *Doncaster Metropolitan Borough Council* (2008, CA)). However, a claim by a parent that their child was wrongly taken into care is still unlikely to be successful. In *Lawrence* v *Pembrokeshire County Council* (2007, CA) the claimant's children were mistakenly put on the at-risk register when Ms Lawrence was wrongfully suspected of abusing them. Her action was struck out since no duty of care was deemed to exist. The claimant appealed, arguing that application of Article 8 (right to family life) of the ECHR in domestic law since implementation of the HRA 1998, should result in an incremental change in the law of negligence. The Court of Appeal held that the House of Lords (*D* v *East Berkshire Community Health NHS Trust and Others* (2005)) had already decided (albeit prior to implementation of the HRA) that no duty of care in negligence was owed to parents wrongly suspected of abuse provided the local authority had acted in good faith. An extension in the scope of duty of care would be a step too far. There was a lack of proximity between Ms Lawrence and the council. It would also militate against the public interest, which required that a child protection authority should be able to exercise its discretion freely during the investigation and prevention of abusive behaviour, without being inhibited by threat of potential litigation.

In such cases, alternative remedies are often available. Ms Lawrence had already received compensation after an ombudsman investigation and an action under the HRA was also possible.

The impact of the Human Rights Act 1998

Since 2000, an action under the Human Rights Act 1998 for breach of the Convention is now possible in cases against a public authority. This may well be more appropriate than an action in negligence and more likely to be successful, where the claim involves omission to act, failure to prevent damage by a third party or negligent exercise of a statutory discretion. In *Z and A* v *UK* (2002) the claimants (two of the child claimants involved in *X* v *Bedfordshire County Council* (1995)) successfully claimed that the council had breached its duty under Article 3 (the right not to be subjected to inhuman or degrading treatment) by failing to protect them from prolonged and serious ill-treatment and abuse. Article 8 (right to respect for family life) was breached in respect of another child who was wrongly taken into care. Her mother also succeeded with an Article 8 claim. Such claims can now be brought in the English courts, which must have regard to decisions of the European Court of Human Rights (see Chapter 3).

In conclusion: duty criteria are guidance only

As shown in the various special duty situations examined in this chapter, judges determining the existence of duty of care often refer to such criteria as reasonable foreseeability, proximity and justice and reason (policy). Students often ask their lecturers to tell them what exactly these words mean in the hope that this will provide a magic key to unlock a secret door to understanding. Be warned that this is a fruitless quest. Such words cannot be defined as legal terms and in themselves, do not provide certain answers to the question of whether a duty of care exists in a particular case. The context in which they are applied, i.e. the circumstances of the particular case, heavily influences their definition and limits, so that apparently conflicting decisions are made. As May LJ said in *Merret* v *Bubb* (2001): it would be 'reaching for the moon . . . to expect to accommodate every circumstance which may arise within a single short abstract formulation.'

It may help to keep in mind that the courts take an *incremental* approach to the development of duty of care, particularly in the controversial areas of duty examined above. Therefore, any change is likely to be a small step at a time rather than a leap into the dark.

A duty is unlikely to be acknowledged for any case which:

- is *not* concerned with *physical damage directly caused* to the claimant or their property;
- involves loss insurable by the claimant;
- could be remedied by a claim in a different area of the law;
- opens up claims to an indefinable class;
- is perceived as being against the public interest in any other respect.

Chapter summary

Special duties of care

The requirements for proof of duty of care in these special areas are rigorous and based on a high degree of foreseeability and proximity and public interest.

Pure economic loss

A special relationship of close proximity between the parties is essential, involving reliance by the claimant on the defendant's expertise and/or assumption of responsibility by the defendant. A disclaimer or conditional undertaking by the defendant prevents creation of the relationship.

Liability may result from negligent advice as well as other negligent behaviour.

Nervous shock

Shock causing physical/psychiatric injury which must be medically recognised.

Primary victims: if duty for physical harm exists it includes nervous shock.

Secondary victims: for a duty to exist the claimant must satisfy the *Alcock* criteria:

(a) sudden shock causing medically recognised condition;

(b) reasonable foreseeability of this reaction;

(c) claimant's reaction that of a reasonably brave person;

(d) claimant close to the accident in time and space.

Omissions/third-party acts

The defendant must generally owe a duty of care to the claimant/ have a duty to control the third party.

Public authority exercise of statutory discretion

Duty of care is rarely upheld.

Limited duty: fire and ambulance services.

Human rights action may be more viable.

Review questions 13

1 May a duty of care exist in the following circumstances?

(a) To Ruby, who was wrongly advised by Samie on the value of her antique clock?

(b) To Evie, who witnesses a horrific accident caused by Dai in which Evie's daughter Crystal was killed?

(c) To Ali, who suffered theft from his premises when thieves gained access to his premises through a hole in the next-door fence which belongs to Guy?

2 What is the relevant standard of care against which a defendant who is a professional adviser will be judged in a negligence action?

3 Explain what is meant by psychiatric harm.

4 Who in law is a primary victim?

5 Who in law is a secondary victim?

6 Explain the circumstances in which an omission to act will give rise to negligence liability.

Answers to all review questions can be found in Appendix 2.

Advanced questions 13

(A) Critically evaluate the extent to which the concept of the duty of care in negligence has developed so that both claimant and defendant are treated fairly in special duty situations.

(B) Critically evaluate the decision in *Alcock* v *Chief Constable of South Yorkshire* (1992).

Answers to the advanced questions can be found at **go.pearson.com/uk/he/resources.**

Take a closer look

The following cases provide important examples of how the law in this chapter has developed. They are primary sources illustrating the law in action and give more detail about their facts, as well as helping to understand the law and to appreciate how the judges reached their decisions.

Try looking up the law report or accessing it via a database, e.g. BAILII (www.bailii. org/databases.html). LexisNexis or Westlaw may be available in the university or college library, or extracts may be found in a case book. (See Appendix 1: Additional resources.)

Alcock v *Chief Constable of South Yorkshire* [1992] 1 AC 310, HL

Hedley Byrne v *Heller* [1963] 2 All ER 575, HL

Osman v *UK* (2000) 29 EHRR (ECtHR)

Robinson v *Chief Constable of West Yorkshire* (2018) UKSC4
https://www.supremecourt.uk/cases/docs/uksc-2016-0082-press-summary.pdf

Web activity

Type 'Hillsborough Disaster' into the BBC's search facility. You will find some interesting materials on the background to the case and subsequent official inquiries:
www.bbc.co.uk
www.supremecourt.uk/watch UK SC

Assignment 12

Anil was considering using an inheritance to buy a business, CDE Ltd, which specialised in converting the garages of residential properties into additional living space. However he needed additional finance to complete the purchase and wanted to make sure he was investing wisely. He therefore commissioned Bobby, a self-employed business consultant, to prepare a report advising on the prospects of the business and whether CDE Ltd was a suitable investment. Anil told Bobby the report would be shown to potential investors, including Clive. Bobby's report was highly favourable and concluded the business was presently sound and had good prospects for the future.

Unfortunately when Bobby prepared the report on CDE, he did not inspect the company accounts so he did not see that the business was not in a very good financial position in that people were concerned about losing storage space available in a garage and were instead opting to extend their properties. Also he had not read a recent article in the Business Consultants Gazette talking about forthcoming legislation preventing the conversion of garages as a way of protecting the environment, and stating that businesses offering garage conversions were no longer considered a sound investment. In fact, Bobby, who was rather new to the profession, was unaware of the Business Consultants Gazette although it was widely read in the profession.

Within three months, business declined and CDE went into liquidation. Anil and Clive lose their investment. Anil and Clive blame Bobby's report for their losses and would like to claim compensation from Bobby.

Advise Bobby.

Product liability

Learning objectives

On completion of this chapter, students should be able to:

★ appreciate the relationship of the law of contract to tort liability for defective products;

★ understand the scope of duty of care in negligence relating to defective products;

★ recognise the difference between consequential and pure economic loss;

★ know and be able to apply the main principles of the CPA 1987;

★ distinguish between the circumstances where liability in negligence and/or the CPA 1987 may arise.

Introduction

This chapter looks at liability in tort for defective products. To take a very simple example: an office worker buys sausage rolls from a nearby bakery to share at lunchtime. Unfortunately the food is contaminated with salmonella. As a result of eating this, the worker and their colleagues become very ill for three weeks, are unable to work and lose the commission they would normally make. Do they as the consumers of the *contaminated food*, have a claim in law? There is no claim in contract since that area of law protects only the buyer of the defective goods. Other people harmed by the goods cannot generally sue in contract because of the lack of privity (a contractual relationship) between themselves and the seller. However, they may sue in tort, since they are protected by the law of negligence, and selling contaminated food seems to indicate failure to observe hygienic processes in the bakery. They may also have a claim under the Consumer Protection Act 1987 (CPA 1987), as the food is clearly defective. Which is the most effective claim?

Liability for defective products

Product liability in negligence relies on proving the same essential elements as for claims in negligence (see Chapter 13). This means that to be successful in a product liability claim in negligence, the claimant must prove that:

1 the manufacturer owed the claimant ('ultimate consumer') a duty of care; and

2 the manufacturer was in breach of that duty; and

3 as a result, the claimant ('ultimate consumer') suffered damage which is not too remote.

1 The duty of care

The claimant must be able to show that he or she is someone who, in the circumstances, the defendant should have had in mind when embarking on the course of conduct which led to the alleged damage. This concept was established by the House of Lords in the following key case.

Donoghue v *Stevenson* (1932, HL)

Mrs Donoghue and a friend stopped for refreshment at a café one hot afternoon. The friend purchased from the proprietor some ginger beer manufactured by the defendant. This was supplied in stone bottles which were opened at the table. Having happily consumed a glassful, Mrs Donoghue tipped the bottle to make sure nothing was left; to her horror what appeared to be the decomposing remains of a snail slithered into her glass. She consequently became ill with gastro-enteritis and sued Stevenson (the manufacturer) in negligence.

Held: (by a majority): the manufacturer did owe Mrs Donoghue a duty of care. As she was the user of its product, she was somebody who reasonably foreseeably would be affected by the way the manufacturer processed its product.

> Lord Atkin stated:
>
> A manufacturer of products, which he sells in such a form as to show that he intends them to reach the ultimate consumer in the form in which they left him, with no reasonable possibility of intermediate examination and with the knowledge that the absence of reasonable care in the preparation or putting up of the products will result in an injury to the consumer's life or property, owes a duty of care to the consumer to take reasonable care.

In these consumer-conscious days it comes as a surprise that prior to the decision in *Donoghue* v *Stevenson* a person in Mrs Donoghue's position had no rights in tort. Defective goods only gave rise to contract liability. Mrs Donoghue's friend could have sued but only to recover the cost of the drink, apart from that she had suffered no damage or loss and she could not claim reparation on behalf of Mrs Donoghue. Before 1932, liability in negligence for defective goods was restricted to harm caused by those products which were dangerous in themselves, such as guns or explosives.

The scope and influence of Lord Atkin's judgment

To understand the influence of Lord Atkin's judgment, it is necessary to analyse some of the terms used by Lord Atkin and see how they have been interpreted in later case law.

Manufacturer

The duty was soon extended from the maker of goods to those delivering services such as fitting and installing or repairing goods (see *Stennet* v *Hancock* (1939) in Chapter 13), and defendants with responsibility to check the goods prior to sale. Today it covers the whole range of products and service industries.

Product

Case law illustrates that liability in negligence covers a huge variety of products in normal daily use for example, cars (*Herschtal* v *Stewart & Ardern Ltd* (1940)), computer software (*St Albans City Council* v *International Computers* (1996)), and includes some less likely items such as tombstones (*Brown* v *Cotterill* (1934)), and itchy underpants (*Grant* v *Australian Knitting Mills* (1936)).

Lord Atkin referred to the '*preparation or putting up of the products*' so the duty of care extends to the packaging and any instructions accompanying the product. The goods may be perfectly safe in themselves but become dangerous because inappropriately packaged, or because they do not carry correct instructions or a warning (e.g. medicines, weed-killer).

The ultimate consumer

Ultimate consumer: any person directly or indirectly harmed by a defective product or service.

Mrs Donoghue is the perfect example of an **ultimate consumer** – the actual user of the defective goods who is harmed by the defects, but who is not necessarily the buyer.

'Consumer' in this context has a very wide meaning, which extends beyond mere users of the goods or service. A consumer may be defined as someone reasonably likely to be affected by the goods in question. Consumers will be owed a duty, since the supplier should have taken their needs into account.

Barnett v Packer (1940)

A shop assistant laying out chocolates for display was injured by a wire protruding from one of them.

Held: the manufacturer owed a duty of care to the shop assistant, as well as to people who ate the goods. Anybody handling the chocolates could have suffered injury from *the presence of this object*.

Limitations to liability for defective products

1 *The goods are no longer under the defendant's control.* The defendant ceases to have control if, prior to use, the goods have been tampered with or examined by a third party or claimant, in such a way as would probably cause or reveal a defect. Remember that in *Donoghue* v *Stevenson* the ginger beer was supplied to Mrs Donoghue in an opaque bottle which was opened in Mrs Donoghue's presence. There was no possibility that its unwanted inhabitant could have got there through the intervention of a third party. The bottle arrived at the table in the same state as when it left the manufacturer. The stone bottle prevented the hazard from being evident until its contents were removed.

Howmet Ltd v Economy Devices Ltd [2016] EWCA Civ

The defendant manufactured products used in aerospace engineering and supplied a device to the claimant factory to prevent fire risk from overheated molten metal. It was intended to detect and give warning when the liquid level fell below a certain point. The claimant factory purchased and installed the device, but six weeks later it malfunctioned and a fire occurred which was extinguished without any resulting damage. Employees ordered a new part without informing the senior management and meanwhile instituted a back-up system to check on liquid levels in the tank during working hours and to drain the tank and turn off the heater at weekends. A new part later arrived, but before it was installed a fire broke out in the tank and destroyed the whole factory.

The Court of Appeal held: the manufacturer was not liable as once a product had left its factory it had no control over how it would be used. An end-user who persists in using a defective product when aware of its defect can no longer claim that the manufacturer is responsible. The employees' knowledge of the defect was attributable to the owner of the factory. Even if a duty of care had existed the claim would still have failed on the issue of causation. The second fire did not result from the defective device but from a failure in the system introduced by the employees after the first fire.

2 *Too much time has elapsed since the product left the defendant.* Whether the goods have been used or not, it would be unfair to place the manufacturer under a duty for an indefinite time.

Evans v Triplex Safety Glass (1936)

Mr Evans bought a new Vauxhall car fitted by the manufacturer with a windscreen made of toughened safety glass manufactured by Triplex. One year later, he and his family were injured during a car journey when the windscreen shattered.

Held: Triplex did not owe Evans a duty of care because:

- any weakness in the glass might have been caused by Vauxhall when fitting the windscreen;
- a defect might have been detectable on inspection by Vauxhall prior to fitting;
- too much time had elapsed between the product leaving their control and the accident – the glass could have been weakened in use.

3 *The claimant has failed to take reasonable precautions prior to or when using the product.* A claimant must be able to show that the product has been used appropriately, in accordance with instructions. This may constitute contributory negligence (see Chapter 13).

Pure economic loss rarely gives rise to a duty of care

Pure economic loss: loss of money alone, not arising from personal injury to the claimant or damage to other property.

The courts have not usually regarded it as just and reasonable to impose a duty of care where the defect results in **pure economic loss**. Such loss, which is derived from the goods being defective rather than dangerous, merely causes the claimant to be out of pocket. The courts treat such losses as contractual only as they relate to the *quality* of the goods rather than any actively dangerous fault, which causes damage. However, this limitation is not helpful to a party who did not buy the goods from the defendant in the first place.

Real life

Max was given a tablet device for his birthday by his friend Sebastian, who bought it from Flash Electricals plc. The tablet was manufactured by Quality Ltd. Due to a production defect, it set fire to Max's bedroom with resulting damage to carpets and furniture. Max was made ill due to smoke inhalation. He is entitled to claim damages from Quality Ltd which made the tablet, for:

1   the pain and suffering caused by the smoke inhalation;
2   loss of earnings while he recuperated and the cost of replacing furnishings and decorating his bedroom.

These are the resultant costs from the damage caused by the defendant's negligence and are described as *consequential economic loss.*

Max would not be entitled to recover the cost of replacing the defective tablet, which is categorised as *pure* economic loss; *the defect* does not of itself give rise to liability of the manufacturer in negligence. It is *the physical damage to a person or other property* which imposes the duty. The lack of *quality* in the goods does not in itself give rise to negligence liability.

Consequential economic loss: financial loss resulting from injury to the claimant and/or damage to some property other than the defective product.

This difference between pure and **consequential economic loss** is also illustrated by the following case.

Muirhead v *Industrial Tank Specialities Ltd* (1986)

The claimant, who ran a lobster farm, was supplied with oxygen pumps manufactured by the defendant through a contract with a third party. The pumps proved to be incompatible with the English electricity system and kept cutting out. The claimant's lobsters died and he was unable to restock for a substantial period of time while he attempted to work out what was wrong.

Held: the claimant was entitled to recover the consequential cost of restocking the lobsters and for the loss of profits on those that died. He was not entitled to recover for profits lost during the time that lobster production was suspended, or the cost of replacing the pumps, since these were pure economic losses only.

Exceptionally, the claimant may be able to claim for pure economic loss if it can be shown that the claimant obtained the goods after having personally and directly consulted the manufacturers and placed reliance on their expertise. This creates a high degree of proximity between the parties, which is deemed to make it fair, just and reasonable to impose the duty.

Junior Books v *Veitchi* (1982, HL)

Junior Books made a contract for the construction of a warehouse. They told the building contractor that they wanted flooring to be supplied by the defendant, who was consequently a nominated sub-contractor. The flooring was so defective that the warehouse was unusable until the floor was replaced causing considerable expense.

Junior Books had no claim in contract as, by nominating Veitchi, Junior Books had relieved the building contractor of responsibility for the appointment, and no contract had been formed between Junior Books and Veitchi. Consequently, Junior Books claimed in negligence.

Held: the claimant's reliance on the defendant's expertise was sufficient to bring the parties into close proximity, and so a duty of care existed for the pure economic loss.

Veitchi was not applicable in the *Muirhead* case as Muirhead had not nominated the manufacturer to his supplier. The court usually takes the view that a contract between the claimant and supplier provides the appropriate route to compensation. The supplier should have been able to negotiate terms to give himself or herself adequate protection, or, if this is not workable, to insure against possible pure economic losses, such as business interruption.

2 The claimant must prove breach of duty

It is not enough for the claimant to prove that the defendant owed them a duty of care. The claimant must prove that by objective standards the defendant failed to take reasonable care, i.e. did not provide a reasonable level of protection against reasonably foreseeable accidents. This includes taking into account the particular needs of a target group and giving adequate warning or instructions about the use of the product. For example, a soft-toy manufacturer must consider that baby and toddler users of its teddy bears may literally try to consume them. Thus, it must ensure that non-toxic materials are used and that the bears' eyes and noses are very firmly attached. (See Chapter 13 which examines breach of duty in more detail, and Chapter 14 with regard to negligent service delivery.)

3 The claimant must prove consequential damage

The claimant must also prove that it was the defendant's breach of duty which actually caused the damage suffered. In the scenario of Max and the tablet outlined earlier, Max would not be successful, despite proof of a defect in the tablet making it a fire risk, if there was evidence that the fire was actually caused by defective wiring in Max's house.

Defendants are not necessarily liable for all the consequences of their behaviour: some may be deemed *too remote* from their original act. In negligence a defendant is generally liable for all reasonably foreseeable damage, but not for highly improbable or fluke results.

(The issues of breach and consequential damage are explored in greater depth in Chapter 13.)

The Consumer Protection Act 1987 (Part I)

Strict liability:
exceptionally (as in claims under the CPA 1987) the claimant can succeed merely on proof that the tortious behaviour occurred and that damage resulted.

Fault liability:
most tort actions require the claimant to prove that the defendant was at fault, i.e. acted intentionally, carelessly or without reasonable foresight.

The Consumer Protection Act 1987 Part 1 (CPA 1987), which was enacted to implement the EC Product Liability Directive (85/374/EC), has introduced a measure of **strict liability** for defective products into English law.

The difference between fault and strict liability

Most torts, including negligence, are based on **fault liability**. The claimant has to prove not only that the defendant's behaviour broke the law and caused damage, but also that the defendant either intended to cause harm to the claimant, or was blameworthy in overlooking the risk to the claimant.

Strict liability is exceptional in tort. Where it exists the claimant is relieved of the need to prove any intent or carelessness on the part of the defendant; the claimant merely has to prove the causal link between the defendant's tortious behaviour and the damage suffered. This may increase the claimant's chances of a successful claim, as proof of failure to take care is often problematic.

Cases involving injuries caused by the side-effects of drugs like Thalidomide, which caused serious injuries to many unborn foetuses during the 1960s, raised public perception of the problems caused by fault liability and encouraged recommendations for reform from the Pearson Commission of 1978, as well as from judges and pressure groups. Successive governments ignored these recommendations, and change came only after intervention by the EC prompted the enactment of the CPA 1987.

As cases emerged some commentators perceived that the way in which the law was being interpreted seemed to provide no more protection for claimants than an action in negligence. This was a concern since the Product Liability Directive had indicated that its purpose was to enable claimants to avoid the need to prove fault by the defendant, thus overcoming one of the main obstacles to a successful claim. The Act (s 1) stated that it was intended to comply with the directive. The lack of successful claims prompted intervention from the EU.

European Commission v *UK* (1997, ECJ)

The Commission claimed that the UK was failing in its obligations to implement the purpose of the directive with respect to the concept of a defective product and the scope of the state of the art defence. This controversially protects a manufacturer who proves that current technical knowledge did not indicate any fault in the product.

Held: it was essential that the Act be construed in accordance with the purpose of the directive and that the directive must prevail in the event of conflict.

In the next case the judge constantly referred to the directive for assistance when interpreting the meaning of 'defective' and the scope of the state of the art defence.

A and Others v *National Blood Authority* (2001)

The claimants contracted Hepatitis C after being given transfusions of contaminated blood products supplied by the defendant.

Held: the product was defective under the Act. The claimants did not have to prove fault or negligence, merely that the product did not meet the reasonable expectations of the public to be safe for any foreseeable use. A reasonable person would expect that blood used for transfusion would not be infected.

Both the Act and the directive required the court to take into account 'all the circumstances attendant upon the reasonable person's expectations of safety'. These did not include the questions of whether the defendant could have avoided the danger, nor whether this would have been impracticable, costly or difficult.

The state of the art defence should be narrowly interpreted in order to avoid defeating the purpose of the directive. It only protects the defendant against unknown risks in the context of the most advanced available knowledge which should have been accessible to them when marketing the product.

The main provisions of Part I of the Consumer Protection Act 1987

Who may sue? s 2(1)

Any person suffering damage giving rise to liability under the Act to their person or property and resulting from defective goods has a right to claim.

Methods of supply: s 46

The goods may have been supplied by way of sale, barter, hire, prize or gift provided that the supplier was acting in the course of business.

Potential defendants: s 2

Section 2(1) provides that 'where any damage is caused wholly or partly by a defect in a product', the following persons shall be liable:

Producer:
manufacturer/
processor.

1 *The* **producer**. This includes the manufacturer and persons responsible for winning or abstracting a product, for example, mineral water or electricity.

2 *The self-branding supplier or marker* 'who, by putting his name on the product or using a trade mark or other distinguishing mark in relation to the product has held himself out as the producer of the product'.

Therefore where goods are marketed under an 'own brand' label (like many supermarket goods), the business whose name appears on the label is likely to be treated as the producer. If the label indicates that the goods were manufactured by another producer ('produced for Sainsbury's by X plc'), it may be arguable that the supplier is not the producer as they are not 'holding themselves out as the producer'.

Importer:
first party to import
the product into an EU
country from a non-EU
country.

3 *The* **importer**. The party who initially imported the product into the EU may be liable. (This is not necessarily the party responsible for the goods entering the UK.)

4 *The supplier*. Suppliers are liable only if they fail, on request from the injured party, to identify the manufacturer, producer or importer.

The meaning of 'product': s 1

Product:
covers a wide variety
of goods, including
agricultural produce,
utilities like water and
gas, and even blood.

'**Product**' includes packaging and instructions and potentially covers a huge variety of manufactured and other goods and utilities.

1 *Manufactured products*. This includes components of another product. Although buildings are not goods, building components which become fixtures to the land like window frames or girders are 'products' under the Act.

2 '*Substances won or abstracted*'. This includes things like electricity and water.

3 Things which owe their 'essential characteristics' to an 'industrial or other process'. In *A and Others* v *National Blood Authority* (2001) blood and blood products supplied by the defendant were 'products' within the meaning of s 1 because they had been subject to an industrial process. Anti-coagulants are mixed with blood on collection and it may be subject to other processes before storage.

4 Agricultural products like growing crops and game, which were not originally included, have been covered since 2000 when the Act was amended by the Consumer Protection Act 1987 (Product Liability) (Modification) Order 2000 to implement Directive 99/34/EC.

It is unclear how far goods conveying information such as books and computer programs are covered by the Act. It is possible for information transmitted in this form to cause harm through its defects. A book on fungi might incorrectly describe a species as edible, with disastrous consequences. There is medical evidence which suggests that some computer games may trigger fits and migraine. Unless and until such matters are conclusively determined by the courts, this will remain an uncertain area.

Causation and liability: s 2

The claimant must prove that the defect was the cause of the damage claimed. Since liability is strict the claimant does not have to prove that the defendant was careless, merely that the product comes within the statutory meaning of defective.

Defective means dangerous: s 3

Defective:
goods dangerous
physically to person/
property.

The CPA is not concerned with the *quality* of the product but with its *safety*. Therefore, a product is not **defective** under the Act unless it is unsafe: there is no liability unless it actually causes damage to the consumer or the consumer's other property. The Act specifies the following factors to be relevant to determining safety:

1 *The packaging and any warnings or instructions.* A medicine may be perfectly safe in and of itself, but rendered dangerous because it lacks clear instructions or a warning that it is unsuitable for people with certain medical conditions.

2 *The normal uses of the product.* The needs of the relevant class of consumer must be taken into account in deciding whether the manufacturer has rendered the product safe. Toys marketed for use by small children require different safety standards, in relation to things like sharp edges, non-toxic materials and the size of removable parts, to goods for the entertainment of adults. If the consumer is harmed by use of the product for purposes which are not normal, liability does not arise. By indicating the purpose of a product and the age group for which it is intended, the manufacturer may limit the 'normal use' of the product.

3 *The time when the product was issued.* This is relevant to issues like shelf life, or situations where the product met appropriate standards of safety when issued but current research now indicates that those standards were not high enough.

The standard of safety under the Act is that which people 'generally are entitled to expect' which is actually set by the court rather than necessarily reflecting public expectation, which may be regarded as unreasonably high. The next two cases aptly illustrate this point.

Bogle and Others v McDonald's Restaurants Ltd (2002)

This case concerned a number of child litigants who had sustained scalding injuries after tea and coffee purchased from McDonald's had been spilt on them. Many of the injuries were serious involving severe pain and the need for skin grafts. However, in no case was the spillage directly caused by McDonald's staff but resulted from other restaurant users, or the claimant dropping or knocking over the drink.

The claimants argued that the hot drinks, a product of McDonald's, were defective because of the temperature at which they had been served and the mode of delivery, including the nature of the cups, lack of appropriate staff training and failure to give warning of the likelihood of scalding.

Held: (Field J): McDonald's had not supplied a defective product under the CPA because:

1 Staff obtained very thorough training, with supervision in their first six months of training and regular assessment after that. This training included ensuring that tops were firmly attached to cups before handing them over to customers and giving a tactful warning about the danger of spillage where appropriate. The drinks were served at a temperature which customers would expect. Buyers of tea and coffee were usually people old enough to appreciate such risks and take precautions against them.

2 The cup design did not encourage spillage. A standard cup would only tip over at an angle of 20 degrees and a large one at 18 degrees. With the lid on, the contents would not spill if knocked over or dropped. Even if the lid was removed (to add sugar, for example), it was still effective when replaced.

3 'Persons generally expect tea or coffee purchased to be consumed on the premises to be hot. Many prefer to consume a hot drink from an unlidded cup rather than through a spout in the lid. Persons generally know that if a hot drink is spilt onto someone, a serious scalding injury can result. They accordingly know that care must be taken to avoid such spills, especially if they are with young children. Given that the staff were trained to cap the drinks securely and given the capabilities of the cups and lids used, I am satisfied that the safety of the hot drinks served by McDonald's was such as persons generally are entitled to expect.'

Tesco Stores Ltd and Another v Pollard (2006, CA)

The claimant, aged 13 months, was injured by consuming some dishwasher powder after he had managed to remove the 'child-proof' cap from the container, which did not meet the relevant British standard.

Held: Tesco was not in breach of the CPA, since the reasonable expectation test was satisfied since the bottle was harder to open than one with an ordinary screw top. It could reasonably be expected to defeat the attentions of so young a child who was unlikely to be unsupervised for long enough to get it open.

Some products do have inherent risks attached to their use which cannot be entirely prevented, like power tools. Other products would require disproportionate expenditure to eliminate or reduce risk which would make them over expensive. Risk/benefit analysis is necessary in such cases to determine a reasonable standard.

Abouzaid v Mothercare (UK) Ltd (2000, CA)

The claimant, who was 12 years old, was blinded in one eye while attempting to attach the defendant's product (a Cosytoes sleeping bag) to his little brother's push chair. An elastic fastening strap sprang from his hand and the attached buckle struck his eye.

Held: the product was defective under s 3, since the reasonable expectations of the public that the product was safe to use were not satisfied, given the vulnerability of the eye and potential seriousness of such injuries. There was a risk attached to use of the product but no warning was given to the user to enable them to avoid the risk.

Defences

Under s 4 of the Act, the defendant will have a defence if able to show the following:

1 The goods comply with EC or UK safety standards and the defect is attributable to compliance with those standards.

2 The goods became defective after they were supplied. The defendant is liable only if the defect is present when the goods are put in circulation. If it arises later due to use or abuse by the consumer or a third party, the defendant is not liable because they did not cause the defect.

This may be a problematic area of proof for the claimant.

Piper v JRI (Manufacturing) Ltd (2006)

Mr Piper had a total hip replacement using a prosthesis made by JRI. Not long after it had been implanted it sheared in two and had to be removed and replaced, causing him increased loss of mobility, as well as the additional pain and suffering of undergoing more surgery.

He claimed that the prosthesis was defective under the CPA 1987. JRI argued that they were protected by s 4 as Mr Piper could not prove that a defect was present at the point the goods were released from the factory. They argued that the defect was more likely to have been caused when the prosthesis was implanted.

Held: Mr Piper's claim must fail as he was not able to prove that the defect arose from the production process. Defects arising during manufacture which might have weakened the prosthesis would most probably have been picked up by the scanning process used by the defendant to check the goods.

This may place a very heavy burden of proof on the claimant and endangers the principle of strict liability. It comes very close to requiring proof of negligence.

Worth thinking about?

Who else might Mr Piper consider claiming from?

Which tort would his claim be based on?

What problems might he have in proving the case?

Suggested solutions can be found in Appendix 2.

The Court of Appeal gave some assistance to claimants in *Ide v ATB Sales* (2008) (below) by stressing that as the claim was made under the CPA there was no need to prove the nature of the defect, only that a defect was present and that the damage arose from that, and not some other competing cause. It was up to the judge to analyse the evidence and determine which, on the balance of probability, was the more likely cause.

Ide v ATB Sales (2008, EWCA)

The claimant was injured when the handles of his mountain bike snapped as he was riding over the South Downs. He claimed that this was due to a manufacturing defect and the defendant's expert witness argued that the snapping happened after he fell and was caused by the bike hitting either the ground or his body. The claimant was an experienced rider, the bike had been properly maintained and metallurgy tests indicated how the snapping could have arisen. The judge assessed the evidence and held that the more probable cause was an inherent defect.

The Court of Appeal affirmed the judge's decision saying that his reasoning regarding assessment of the evidence was entirely appropriate.

This was applied in *Hufford* v *Samsung Electronics (UK) Ltd* (2014) where the court held that the evidence that a fire arose from a defect in a freezer was a more probable cause than that claimed by the defendant, that it was caused by an improperly extinguished cigarette. The claimant was a smoker but always did so outside the house because of his parents' objections.

3 The 'state of the art/developments risk' defence. This is a special defence under the Act which potentially undermines the strict liability element. The defendant will not be liable if it can be shown that when the product was released the defendant had done all that was required to fulfil safety standards in accordance with current research and technological expertise, and in consequence the defect was not discoverable.

This defence is meant to be a safeguard for manufacturers of new products. It is argued that without it manufacturers fearful of litigation might restrict important new product development of great potential benefit to the public. However, this remains a controversial subject. The directive does not prohibit such defences and the approach of other EU countries varies. Prior to the Act, both the Law Commission (Law Com. 82) and the Pearson Commission rejected exemption from liability on the grounds of development risk. It is highly arguable that a drug like Thalidomide could slip through the liability net through the use of this defence. No such defence is available under the law of contract and it can be argued that with appropriate insurance a manufacturer can protect itself against liability. The need to interpret the defence in accordance with a purposeful application of the directive was stressed in *A* v *National Blood Authority* (2001) (above).

4 The defendant did not at any time supply the product to another in the course of business.

Contributory negligence and consent are also relevant. (These are examined in Chapter 13.)

Actionable damage: s 5

This covers death, personal injuries and damage to property (including land) which the claimant is *not* using for business purposes. A claim for property damage must be for at least £275; there is no upper limit.

Since pure economic loss is not recoverable, the cost of replacing or repairing the defective item cannot be claimed. The same principles apply here as in negligence.

Time limits

Under the Limitation Act 1980, s 11A, claimants must take action within three years of the date when they first became aware of the damage, the defect, and the identity of the defendant. There is a final cut-off date of 10 years from the date on which the product was supplied to the claimant and no action can be started after that time.

Liability for defective products is summarised in Figure 15.1.

Area of law	Contract	Tort	Tort
	Sale of Goods Act 1979 (SGA 1979) Supply of Goods and Services Act 1982 (SGA 1982)	Negligence	Consumer Protection Act 1987
Who can sue?	Buyer only	Injured party (ultimate consumer)	Injured party
Who can be sued?	Seller	Manufacturer of goods Servicer of goods Supplier – if duty to inspect	Producer of product Manufacturer Own-brand labeller Importer Supplier
What must be proved?	Goods – breach of SGA 1979, ss 13, 14, 15 Goods and services – breach of CPA 1987, ss 4, 5 Goods – like SGA 1979 SGSA 1982 Services – lack of reasonable care and skill, reasonable timeliness, reasonable charging	(i) Duty of care (ii) Breach of duty (iii) Consequent damage	(i) Product defective and unsafe (ii) Damage suffered as a result
Damage compensated	Any loss or damage to buyer as long as not too remote, including purchase price	Any loss or damage to injured party as long as not too remote; excluding purchase price and other pure economic loss	Death/personal injury Damage to land, goods (over £275)
Liability	Goods – strict Services – fault Civil only	Fault Civil only	Strict Criminal liability also possible under CPA 1987, Part II

Figure 15.1 Liability for defective products

The impact of the Consumer Protection Act 1987

After a disappointing start, judicial interpretation in the light of the original directive has provided a more level playing field for the consumer who is the party which the directive was aiming to assist. It can also be seen as a sensible loss distribution system since the losses of the claimant are made the responsibility of the manufacturer that sought to make a profit from its product. The manufacturer is not unreasonably burdened as the losses are insurable and that cost is passed on to the consumers.

Real life

Max was injured and suffered damage to his property when a tablet device, manufactured by Quality Ltd and which was a present from his friend Sebastian, caught fire on its first use. As well as a claim in negligence, Max also has a claim under the CPA 1987, as his losses certainly exceed the £275 minimum.

Quality, the manufacturer, is liable as producer under the CPA 1987 if the tablet is proved to be defective. Even if Quality is not clearly identifiable as producer of the tablet, it may still be best to claim under the CPA, as this may give Max more flexibility in his choice of defendant.

Flash Electricals, from which Sebastian bought the tablet, would be the 'marker', if the tablet was marketed as Flash's own brand. If there is no label saying who the producer is, Flash may still be personally liable as 'supplier' unless it identifies the producer. Even if Flash merely imported the tablet, it could still be sued as 'importer' if it obtained the goods directly from any country outside the EU.

As long as he can prove that the tablet was defective and actually caused the fire, he will be successful and will not have to prove failure to take reasonable care as the CPA 1987 imposes strict liability.

Chapter summary

A person harmed by a defective product may claim in:

(a) **breach of contract** against the seller (provided claimant purchased the goods); or

(b) **tort** (negligence/CPA 1987, Part 1).

Negligence

Defendant: the manufacturer.

Claimant must prove: duty (owed by manufacturer to ultimate consumer of the goods), breach (failure to take reasonable care), resulting damage.

Liability: based on fault: proof of failure to take reasonable care.

Compensation: covers personal injury and all consequential economic loss. Generally, pure economic loss cannot be recovered.

The CPA

Claimant: any person harmed by the product.

Defendant: producer/ 'own brand' provider/supplier/importer.

Liability: strict. Claimant must prove that the product is dangerous (does not conform to reasonable public expectation of safety) and caused the relevant damage.

Claims are limited: to those over £275. Pure economic loss is never recoverable.

Review questions 14

1 What circumstances may bring a duty of care for defective goods to an end?

2 Basil buys a chicken pie from Tarragon Stores. The pie was manufactured by Marjoram Foods. Basil shares the pie with Rosemary and they both become ill. What are the civil law rights of Basil and Rosemary?

3 How is liability for a defective product proved in negligence?

4 How is liability for a defective product established under the Consumer Protection Act 1987?

5 What defences are available under the Consumer Protection Act 1987?

6 What remedies are available for a defective product?

Answers to all review questions can be found in Appendix 2.

Advanced questions 14

(A) Critically evaluate the distinctions between a claim for a defective product in negligence and a claim under the Consumer Protection Act 1987.

(B) Analyse the state of the art/ development risk defence under the Consumer Protection Act 1987.

Answers to the advanced questions can be found at **go.pearson.com/uk/he/resources.**

Take a closer look

The following cases provide important examples of how the law in this chapter has developed. They are primary sources illustrating the law in action and give more detail about their facts, as well as helping to understand the law and to appreciate how the judges reached their decisions.

Try looking them up in the law reports or accessing them via a database, e.g. BAILII (www.bailii.org/databases.html). LexisNexis or Westlaw may be available in the university or college library, or extracts may be found in a case book. (See Appendix 1: Additional resources.)

A v National Blood Authority [2001] 3 All ER 289

Donoghue v *Stevenson* [1932] AC 562 HL

Junior Books v *Veitchi* [1983] 2 All ER 301 HL

Network Rail Infrastructure Ltd v *Conarken Group Ltd and Another* [2010] EWHC 1852; [2010] TCC 132

Web activity

Read 'Product liability claims: a global product and a world of legal jurisdictions' by
    Amy Haughton:
www.thompsons-scotland.co.uk/blog/25-compensation-claims/2922-product-liability
    -claims-a-global-product-and-a-world-of-legal-jurisdictions
https://iclg.com/practice-areas/product-liability-laws-and-regulations/england-
    and-wales

Assignment 13

Florence visits a supermarket with her daughter Daisy, aged eight. A promotion for Funny Mug face paints is taking place and children are being offered a free make-over. Florence lets Daisy take part. Florence buys some frozen puff pastry and a bag of mixed salad leaves that bears a notice saying 'Wash thoroughly before consumption'. Then she visits the deli counter to buy some ham for Edwina, her elderly next-door neighbour. When she gets home an hour later she immediately delivers the ham to Edwina and puts the puff pastry in her freezer in accordance with the instructions on the packet. She uses the leaves to make a salad for supper for herself and her husband, Gordon.

That evening, Florence and her husband, Gordon, become ill from bacteria in the salad.

Next day, Daisy develops an allergic rash, which her doctor says is caused by the face paints.

Later in the week, Edwina contracts salmonella poisoning which is traced to the ham.

A month later, Florence retrieves the puff pastry from the freezer and defrosts it. When she rolls it out, she discovers that it smells strongly of petrol and is therefore unusable.

Discuss the remedies available to Daisy, Edwina, Florence and Gordon.

Occupiers' liability, nuisance and vicarious liability

Learning objectives

On completion of this chapter, students should be able to:

★ appreciate the different ways in which an occupier may be liable for damage caused by the state of his or her premises or activities taking place there;

★ distinguish between the effect of the Occupiers' Liability Act 1957 and the Occupiers' Liability Act 1984;

★ recognise the situations where liability for public and private nuisance will arise;

★ describe the circumstances where the defences to liability may exist;

★ apply the doctrine of vicarious liability to hypothetical situations.

Introduction

This chapter explains three areas where a legal duty is owed in tort. Firstly, the duties imposed by the law of tort on occupiers in relation to the maintenance and use of their premises are owed under the law relating to *occupiers' liability*. An occupier has a duty to maintain the premises safely for the benefit of third parties on or outside the premises. The occupier must also ensure that the use of premises does not cause unreasonable inconvenience to other people. For the operator of a business this is particularly important, as the premises are likely to be visited more often than residential premises and may actually be open for public access.

Secondly, not only must a business take account of the safety of staff, customers and other business visitors. It must also consider the neighbours and the wider public and take reasonable steps to prevent any business activity from causing harm, disruption or unreasonable disturbance to them which may be actionable in the tort of *nuisance*.

Thirdly, if a legal action is brought against a business, it will not be found liable if it can show a good defence. However, it is no defence to argue that an employee committed the tort, as the business is generally *vicariously liable*. An overview of the doctrine of vicarious liability concludes the tort section of this text.

The occupier's liability to people on the premises

Negligent activities

Occupiers who undertake *activities* on their land without taking reasonable care may be liable to a third party under the general principles of negligence (which were examined in Chapter 13). If the harm is caused by the structural condition of the premises then liability may exist under the Occupiers' Liability Acts of 1957 and 1984. If caused by some activity on the premises the more appropriate claim is negligence.

Ogwo v *Taylor* (1987, HL)

The defendant negligently set the roof space on fire while using a blowtorch to burn off paint from weatherboarding on his house. The claimant, a fire-fighter, was injured in the ensuing extensive fire.

Held: negligence was a more appropriate cause of action than the Occupiers' Liability Act 1957, given that the fire was triggered by the defendant's negligent use of the blowtorch, rather than the condition of the premises. The defendant was liable as the claimant's injuries were a reasonably foreseeable consequence of the defendant's negligent behaviour.

Dangerous premises

Occupiers have a legal duty to maintain the structure of their premises in a reasonably safe condition. For example, a hotel owner must take care to avoid harm to the guests from over-polished floors, low beams or slippery tiles. This part of the law is covered by statute.

The Occupiers' Liability Act 1957

Occupier (OLA 1957/1984): the person who is in control of the premises at the relevant time.

Visitor: a person entering premises with the permission of the occupier under the OLA 1957.

The 1957 Act (OLA 1957) covers the liability of an **occupier** to whom the Act calls '**visitors**', i.e. those people who are on the premises with the occupier's consent – family members, employees, customers, the window cleaner and the meter reader are obvious examples. However, under s 2(6) any person exercising a right conferred by law is also covered. This includes the police and fire fighters and anybody entering premises that are open to the public.

Maloney v *Torfaen CBC* (2005, CA)

M, who was drunk, was returning home in the dark. When taking a short cut from the road to his house he fell down a steep grassy slope onto the concrete floor of a subway, sustaining injuries.

Held: the defendant was not in breach of the OLA 1957, since M was not a visitor; the grassy slope was intended purely to be landscaping, not access, and so there was no implied permission to be on it.

Who is the occupier?

In *Wheat* v *Lacon* (1966) the occupier was defined as the person *in control of the premises* at the time of the accident. If premises are left empty during refurbishment, the builder, shop fitter or plumber who causes a hazard will be liable to an injured person rather than the occupier. There may be more than one occupier at a time. In *Wheat* v *Lacon* the licensee and brewery owner of a pub were both held to be the occupiers of a pub since, under the lease, the brewery was responsible for repairs and thus controlled the state of the premises, while the licensee should have alerted the landlord to what was required.

What are premises?

Premises: under the OLA 1957 any fixed or moveable structure, widely construed by the courts.

Premises are widely defined by the Act and cover not only buildings and open spaces but also 'any fixed or moveable structure', and include 'any vessel, vehicle or aircraft' (s 1(3)). This has been held to include a wide variety of things, including scaffolding (*Kearney* v *Eric Waller* (1966)) and a large excavating machine (*Bunker* v *Charles Brand* (1969)).

The extent of the occupier's duty

The occupier must take reasonable care to ensure that the visitor is reasonably safe for the purposes for which the visitor is on the land (s 2(2)). There is no duty to eliminate all the risks attached to the visit. The occupier can reasonably assume that the average able-bodied adult will be aware of hazards which are normally found on the relevant premises and will take care to avoid them. So, a hotel owner who fails to ensure that an upstairs window has restricted opening has not breached his duty to an adult who leans out so far that he falls from it (*Lewis* v *Six Counties* (2005, CA)).

Notice that the occupier's duty is limited to taking reasonable care to ensure reasonable safety and only for the purposes of that visit. The occupier's consent to a visitor's presence is limited by the purpose of the visit. If a visitor strays into a part of the premises where he or she is not reasonably expected and suffers injury, the occupier is unlikely to be liable under the 1957 Act as the visitor has exceeded the scope of his or her permission to be on the premises. There may be liability instead under the Occupiers' Liability Act 1984, which covers duty of care to entrants to premises, without the occupier's permission (see *Tomlinson* v *Congleton Borough Council* (2003), below).

The standard of care

As in negligence, there exists a duty to take *reasonable* care. The occupier is not liable just because the accident happens; the injured visitor will have to prove that the occupier failed to take reasonably adequate precautions to prevent it. What is reasonable is determined with reference to all the circumstances.

Cunningham v *Reading Football Club* (1991)

Due to the club's failure to maintain its terraces, loose lumps of masonry were used as missiles for the use of football hooligans. As a result the claimant, a policeman on duty at the ground, was injured and sued the club.

Held: the club was in breach of its duty. It was reasonably foreseeable that troublesome elements in the crowd which were known to cause problems at matches, would use the masonry for dangerous purposes.

The type of hazard, the nature of the premises and the needs of the visitor are all relevant. Each case has to be decided on its own facts.

Murphy v *Bradford Metropolitan Council* (1991)

A school caretaker had twice cleared snow from a notoriously slippery path before 8.30 a.m. on the morning when the claimant was injured by a fall.

Held: reasonable care had not been taken: the nature of the path, the numbers of people using it and the severity of the weather demanded the use of grit, not just regular clearance.

An occupier whose premises are open to the public must take account of the needs of a wide cross-section of people, including children, the elderly and those with disabilities, since it is reasonably foreseeable that such people may form part of the clientele and a greater duty of care is owed to them (s 2(3)(a)).

Dufosse v *Melbry Events* (2011, CA)

Ms Dufosse, an elderly lady, visited Santa's grotto in a department store with her family and was injured when she slipped on a fallen icicle decoration. The grotto was staffed by Santa, assisted by an Elf, whose job included checking the grotto for tripping hazards in the 90 seconds between customer visits. Santa was also responsible for checking the area immediately around his throne.

Held: the defendant was in breach of the OLA. Since Ms Dufosse had stepped on the icicle, on the balance of probability it was visible during the Elf's inspection and therefore should have been removed prior to Ms Dufosse's arrival. The lighting in the grotto was quite dim, its dimensions such that with a family party of six plus Santa and Elf it was overcrowded, probably making the icicle less visible to visitors.

Risk assessment and compliance

Bowen v *National Trust* (2011)

A tree branch fell down entirely without warning on a group of school children camping on National Trust property. The branch seriously injured three children and killed the claimant.

Held: the National Trust were not liable. Tree inspectors took reasonable care when assessing safety in the park, and the injury was not reasonably foreseeable.

Children and visitors with special skills

The Act gives particular guidance on the extent of duty owed to these two categories.

1 *Children.* An occupier must expect children to be less careful of their own safety than adults; consequently a higher standard of care may be needed (s 2(3)(a)). Things which present no hazard to an adult may be a dangerous allurement to a child.

Glasgow Corporation v *Taylor* (1922, HL)

The corporation was held liable for the poisoning of the child claimant by attractive berries on a tree in a public park.

An occupier is not liable for all accidents to children: the standard of care required of an occupier is no greater than that of a reasonably careful parent. It may be reasonable for the occupier to assume that very small children will be appropriately supervised by an accompanying adult.

Phipps v *Rochester Corporation* (1955)

An occupier was held not to be liable to a five-year-old child who fell into a trench on a building site on the corporation's land.

Held: 'responsibility for the safety of little children must rest primarily upon the parents' (Devlin J).

However, it all depends on the nature of the premises. A building site is not meant to be safe for unsupervised children, as it would be unusual to find them there, but stairways in public housing should be child friendly. Therefore, in *Maloney* v *Lambeth Council* (1966), the local authority (as occupier of a block of flats) was liable when a four-year-old child fell through a gap in banister railings that posed no danger to an adult.

2 *Visitors with special skills.* An occupier is not liable to contractors carrying out a service on the premises for accidents arising from job-related hazards, since the contractors should be aware of these given their trade skills and experience (s 2(3)(b)).

Roles v *Nathan* (1963, CA)

The claimants were overcome by fumes and died when they carried out flue repairs in a boiler room while the boiler was alight.

Held: the occupier was not liable for their deaths: their knowledge and experience of this kind of work should have made them extinguish the boiler before starting work.

Liability for contractors

Under s 2(4) of the 1957 Act, the occupier is not generally liable if a visitor suffers damage arising from construction, repair or maintenance work carried out by an outside firm, provided that the occupier took reasonable precautions to select a competent firm and checked the completed work.

Section 1 of the Compensation Act 2006 applies not only to common law negligence but also to breach of statutory duty. It is therefore relevant when determining standard of care in cases brought under the Occupiers' Liability Acts of 1957 and 1984.

Discharging the duty

The duty of care may be discharged in a variety of ways. Ideally, the hazard should be removed – a shop entrance should be carpeted if the floor may get slippery on a wet day. However, removal of the hazard may not always be practicable, either immediately or in the long term – for example, if the occupier removed the low beam in an old building, the roof may fall in, presenting much greater risks to visitors than the occasional bruised head. It may be possible to protect visitors adequately by the erection of suitable barriers, or even warning notices.

Under s 2(4) of the 1957 Act, occupiers may be found to have taken reasonable care of their visitors by giving *adequate warning* of the hazard. To be adequate the warning must be sufficient to allow the visitor to be reasonably safe. Such notice must be given in sufficient time and with sufficient clarity to enable the visitor reasonably to avoid the hazard. It should indicate the nature of the hazard ('take care: wet floor') and give an indication, where appropriate, of how it should be safely avoided ('please use other exit').

Hufton v *Somerset County Council* (2011, CA)

The claimant student was seriously injured after slipping on a small patch of rain at an entrance to the school assembly hall. It was the practice on rainy days for signs to be displayed at the entrance to the Council's school buildings, requiring pupils to take a detour and not enter the school assembly hall directly from the playground. There was absorbent rubber matting at the entrance to the hall.

Held: the defendant was not liable. The school's risk assessment of this issue was appropriate and had been properly implemented. If rain started during a break there would reasonably be a short delay before the detour notices were displayed and during this time some students might already have entered the hall with wet feet.

Written warnings are not effective for those who cannot reasonably be expected to read or understand them: for example, children or the visually impaired.

A warning is not required where the hazard should have been obvious to the user.

Trustees of Portsmouth Youth Activities Committee v *Poppleton* (2008, CA)

P (an adult) was injured while using a climbing wall at the appellant's indoor premises. The floor was covered with thick matting. Rules forbidding jumping were displayed outside the climbing room. P attempted to jump off the climbing wall to a support on the opposite wall, but fell and became paralysed from the neck down as a result. He argued that he believed that the matting would protect him if he fell and that he should personally have been told of the danger.

Held: no breach of duty had occurred. The risk of falling was entirely evident. No reasonable person could imagine that matting, even in large quantities, could protect against injury from an awkward fall.

Actionable damage

Damage to the person or to goods may give rise to liability under the 1957 Act.

Excluding liability

Business liability for breach of the Occupiers Liability Act 1957 cannot be excluded if the visitor dies or suffers personal injuries from the occupier's failure to take reasonable care.

It is possible to exclude liability for breach of the duty causing damage to property imposed by the 1957 Act (s 2(1)), subject to the Unfair Contract Terms Act 1977 and the Consumer Rights Act 2015.

Liability for damage to property may be excluded if this is judged to be reasonable in the circumstances: for example, if the damage is caused by a third party who is not subject to the occupier's control.

Real life

Boris recently moved house. The path leading to the front door is slippery in wet weather. The other day after a heavy shower, Jacob, who was delivering advertising flyers for the local pizza parlour, slipped and fell, straining his back. He has not been able to work since. As an occupier, Boris has a duty under the OLA 1957 for Jacob's reasonable safety, unless he has a notice on his gate saying 'No Junk Mail'. An occupier impliedly consents to people entering the premises to deliver items unless notice to the contrary is clearly given. He may be in breach of his duty if he should have taken precautions to reduce or remove the risk.

He might genuinely not know that it exists if it is only apparent in wet weather and maybe it had not rained since he moved in. If he should have known, a suitably clear notice ('Take care slippery path!') would probably be sufficient at least as an interim measure.

However, if Boris displayed a notice saying 'No Junk Mail' on the front gate, Jacob becomes a trespasser by entering.

Under the OLA 1984, Jacob has no claim unless he can prove that Boris owes him a duty. If there has previously been sufficient rain to alert Boris to the problem, he may owe a duty as the problem with the path is one which could quite easily be rectified. Boris might argue that the notice refusing junk mail means that he need not anticipate people delivering it, but this will not be any use if he knows that the notice has already been ignored by other people. If a duty does exist, it could be discharged by displaying a suitable warning notice.

Defences under the 1957 Act

The following defences may be available to an occupier:

(i) *Volenti non fit injuria (the visitor willingly accepts the risk).* The Occupiers Liability Act 1957, s 2(5), provides that: 'The common duty of care does not impose on an occupier any obligation to a visitor in respect of risks willingly accepted as his by the visitor.'

(ii) *Contributory negligence.* This may be raised to apportion damage between the parties. Section 2(3) of the Act provides that in determining whether an occupier has breached the common duty of care, the courts may take into account the degree of care a reasonable visitor can be expected to show for their own safety.

(iii) *Exemption of liability.* An occupier may exclude or restrict his liability to visitors to his premises if he gives proper notice of the danger, e.g. 'wet paint'. A warning is not to be treated as absolving the occupier unless in all the circumstances it was enough to enable the visitor to be reasonably safe.

The Occupiers Liability Act 1957, s 2(1), allows the occupier to exempt his or her liability under the Act in so far as they are allowed to do so. Note that exemption of liability *on business premises* is restricted by the Unfair Contract Terms Act 1977, s 2 (exemption of liability for negligence), and s 2(3): 'Where a contract notice or term purports to exclude or restrict liability for negligence a person's agreement to or awareness of it is not of itself to be taken as indicating his voluntary acceptance of any risk.'

The Occupiers' Liability Act 1984

This Act regulates the duty of an occupier of premises to people who do not have permission from the occupier to be on the premises. The Act embraces not only trespassers but also other entrants such as visitors to national parks or people exercising a 'right to roam' under the Countryside and Rights of Way Act 2000. Not surprisingly, the occupier owes only a very limited duty of care. It would not be in the public interest to encourage a burglar to claim damages after falling down the stairs of the house which he was burgling. However, more innocent parties, straying onto premises containing dangerous tools and/or equipment, clearly deserve some protection. This is illustrated by the following case, which preceded the 1984 Act but was based on similar principles.

British Railways Board v Herrington (1972, HL)

The claimant, a child of six, was injured when he strayed onto the railway from a public park through broken fencing belonging to the railway. Drivers previously had reported trespassers on the line.

Held: the Board was liable for the child trespasser's injuries since it knew of the possibility of trespassers and could have avoided the risk at 'small trouble and expense' (i.e. by mending the fence).

When is the duty owed?

Under s 1(3) of the 1984 Act, the following criteria must all be satisfied for the duty to be activated:

1 the occupier must have reasonable knowledge of the danger;
2 the occupier must know or reasonably suspect that potential entrants, etc. are in the vicinity of the premises or are reasonably likely to come into the vicinity;
3 the risk is one against which, in all the circumstances, it is reasonable for the occupier to offer some protection.

The courts will take account of the resources of the occupier, relative to the likelihood of entrants and the extent of the danger. A lake in a remote hill area presents much less of a danger than an electrified railway running through a heavily populated locality. The following two cases will indicate possible approaches to determining whether the criteria in s 1(3) have been satisfied.

Maloney v Torfaen CBC (2005, CA)

(For facts see above.)

Held: the defendant did not owe a duty under the OLA 1984 as the danger, which was heightened by the claimant being drunk and the accompanying darkness, was not so obvious that the defendant should reasonably have known of it. Further, the presence of the claimant on the slope could not reasonably be anticipated. A safe path nearby led directly to the claimant's premises.

Keown v Coventry Healthcare NHS Trust (2006, CA)

K, aged 13, fell when climbing the underside of a fire escape on premises owned by the hospital and used by the public as a cut through.

Held: the defendant was not liable. No duty of care was owed to K, as the danger did not arise out of the state of the premises. K was injured as a result of what K chose to do on the premises rather than the condition of the premises.

Premises not dangerous to an adult might present a hazard to a child and it was a matter of fact or degree whether or not they did. It was not necessarily appropriate, however, to ignore a child's choice to indulge in dangerous behaviour, just because he was a child.

In *Keown* the court may have been influenced by the fact that the claimant had strayed from a public access area onto the fire escape. Making the latter inaccessible to trespassers might have created a worse risk to people in the building in the event of fire.

The extent of the duty

The occupier's duty under the 1984 Act is limited to taking such care as is reasonable to see that the entrant *does not suffer injury* from the relevant danger (s 1(4)). It is interesting to compare this with the *positive* duty owed to the lawful entrant under the 1957 Act whereby the occupier must ensure that visitors are *reasonably safe*. The occupier's responsibility to the entrant is a *negative* one: to take reasonable steps to prevent harm.

Performing the duty

Such a duty under the 1984 Act can be performed by taking reasonable steps to keep people out. A sufficiently explicit warning clearly displayed will generally be deemed enough for adults, while properly maintained boundary fencing should be a sufficient deterrent to children.

The following case illustrates how these principles are applied.

Ratcliff v McConnell and Harper Adams Agricultural College (1999, CA)

The claimant was a student at the college. One night he entered the grounds of the college pool by climbing over a seven-foot wall. He was paralysed when he broke his neck after diving into the pool where the water was too shallow.

Held: the college was not liable. Even if it should have been aware that students trespassed in this manner, it was not in breach of its duty. Their duty did not extend to warning adult trespassers against evident risks, or to lighting the premises at night to make them safe for trespassers.

The House of Lords took a similarly robust approach in the following case.

Tomlinson v *Congleton Borough Council* (2003, HL)

Mr Tomlinson dived into shallow water in a lake in a public park. He was paralysed when he struck his head on a rocky outcrop. The lake was a flooded quarry and signs beside it clearly prohibited swimming and warned that it was dangerous.

Held: no duty was owed. Since the claimant must have known of the risk of striking his head on the lake bottom before he dived, there was no duty to warn of risks that were obvious and against which the defendant could not reasonably be expected to offer some protection.

It would be unreasonable to impose a duty on public authorities to protect people from self-inflicted injuries that resulted from taking risks voluntarily in the face of obvious dangers.

Actionable damage

Liability under the 1984 Act is restricted to death and personal injuries only (s 2(9)).

Defences under the 1984 Act

The general defences in tort – voluntary assumption of risk and contributory negligence – are also available under the 1984 Act. Under the 1984 Act, the occupier might discharge his or her duty by displaying signs, warning of the dangers on the premises.

Duties of an occupier to people outside the premises

An occupier owes a variety of duties in tort to people who are not actually on the premises. Where physical damage to people or their property occurs which is caused by an adjoining occupier's failure to take reasonable care, action may be taken in negligence.

A heavier burden of liability, based purely on the reasonable foreseeability of damage, is imposed through the law of nuisance. This imposes liability not only for tangible harm, but also for unreasonable levels of inconvenience arising from the occupier's use of premises. The law of nuisance is composed of two separate torts (private and public nuisance) which have some characteristics in common.

Private nuisance

This protects an **occupier** of land against unreasonable interference with the use or enjoyment of his or her premises, caused by the state of a nearby occupier's land or activities taking place on it. A nuisance is usually caused unintentionally, indirectly and as a by-product of an on-going state of affairs on the defendant's land.

Proof of liability

The claimant must prove, first, that the defendant has caused *damage*. This includes:

1 *Damage to the structure of the claimant's premises.*

2 *Damage to goods on the claimant's land.* In British *Celanese* v *Hunt* (1969, CA) metal foil stored on the defendant's premises blew onto power cables causing a cut in the electricity supply to the claimant's factories. The defendant was liable for damage to machinery and components.

   Liability for personal injury may also arise, though this is only actionable if the injury was caused by the defendant's negligent or intentional conduct. Private nuisance protects interests in land, rather than personal injuries.

3 *Amenity damage.* Liability may arise for **amenity damage** where the defendant's behaviour has unreasonably reduced the comfort and convenience of use of the claimant's premises. This may accompany, or exist independently of, property damage and can cover a wide range of annoying activities, commonly including noise, smells, smoke and vibrations. In *Halsey* v *Esso Petroleum* (1961) Esso were held liable for a variety of nuisances emanating from their processing plant. Pungent and nauseating smells invaded the claimant's premises and at night noise from the boilers made the claimant's doors and windows vibrate, preventing sleep. All day the passage of heavy lorries caused a high level of noise.

Davey v *Harrow Corporation* (1957, CA)

Mr Davey sued Harrow Corporation for subsidence damage caused to his house by trees growing on the corporation's land.

Held: the council was liable as it had unreasonably interfered with the claimant's land by allowing the encroachment of the tree roots onto the claimant's land.

In a private nuisance claim, the claimant must show that the defendant's activities caused *an unreasonable level of interference.* It is usually sufficient to prove some tangible damage.

St Helen's Smelting Co. v *Tipping* (1865, HL)

Fumes from the defendant's chemical works damaged the claimant's trees.

Held: this damage indicated an unreasonable interference with the claimant's enjoyment of his land. It was irrelevant that the defendant's activities were not out of keeping with the locality.

However, where amenity damage only is claimed, it is harder to prove unreasonable interference. Some people would claim to suffer disturbance from their neighbours' activities; few of them, however, would be able to persuade the court that the level of interference was unreasonable. The law aims to maintain a fair balance of interest between parties and requires a certain amount of give and take. While a shop is being refitted, the next-door neighbour may be somewhat inconvenienced by noise or dust, but, provided the builders are doing what they reasonably can to keep it under control, the shop owner is within his legal rights. In six months' time, when the neighbour is having major work done, the shop owner will be expected to show a similar understanding.

Each case is decided on its own facts, but any of the following criteria may be relevant:

1 *Locality.* In *Sturges* v *Bridgeman* (1879) Thesiger J declared: '*What would be a nuisance in Belgrave Square would not necessarily be so in Bermondsey.*' If one lives in an industrial and commercial area with a high density of population, the level of peace and quiet is bound to be reduced. Similarly, agricultural activity is to be expected in a rural area and some level of related smell or noise must be endured. Note, however, that locality is relevant only in a claim restricted to amenity damage. It is not appropriate where some tangible loss has been caused to the claimant (see *St Helen's Smelting Co.* v *Tipping*).

Planning permission is no defence to nuisance. In *Wheeler* v *Saunders* (1996) the defendant had been granted planning permission to expand his pig farm. This resulted in a pervasive unpleasant and intense smell in the neighbourhood. The Court of Appeal held that the planning permission only allowed the building and operation of the farm, not the creation of the nuisance. If one can persuade the court that the planning permission was so radical that, in effect, it authorised a change in the nature of the locality, this may be a justification for resulting disruption. In *Gillingham Borough Council* v *Medway Chatham Dock Ltd* (1993) the Dock Company was granted planning permission to operate around the clock. What had been a largely quiet and residential area became busy, noisy and dirty due to the constant passage of heavy lorries to and from the dock, but the claimants lost their case because it was held that the planning permission had changed the character of the area and the issue of reasonableness must be judged by reference to this new character. However, this will only apply in exceptional cases because the court is generally unwilling to acknowledge a character change.

Watson and Others v *Croft Promo-Sport Ltd* (2009, CA)

The defendants were granted planning permission to run motorcycle racing on a former airfield, in an essentially rural location. The claimants, whose houses were 300 metres from the race track, complained of the noise.

Held: the grant of planning permission does not automatically affect third-party rights to quiet enjoyment of land. Here it had in no way changed the nature of the locality and the level of the defendant's activity was unreasonable. Therefore an injunction would be issued limiting use to 40 days per year.

The Supreme Court produced a useful checklist of factors for the court to take into account concerning the relevance of planning permission to the creation of nuisance in *Coventry and Others* v *Laurence* (2014). It indicates something of a shift in judicial approach by indicating that while planning permission may be highly relevant it is only one piece of the evidence under consideration and is not conclusive in and of itself.

Coventry and others v *Lawrence* [2014] SC

For over 13 years the defendants had operated motor racing activities on their premises in rural Suffolk with planning permission which limited time and frequency of use. These restrictions were observed by the defendants. Subsequently the claimants moved into a house about half a kilometre from the stadium and claimed that they had been unaware of the activities taking place there before moving in. They sued the defendants for noise nuisance and were successful in the High Court which granted damages with the option of applying for an injunction. On appeal this judgment was overturned. The claimants then appealed to the Supreme Court which re-instated the High Court decision and held the defendants liable.

Held: the planning permission only justified the defendants' activity in so far as it did not amount to a nuisance. Planning permission does not automatically permit creation of nuisance.

A planning authority should not be able to deprive an occupier of their rights to object to what would otherwise amount to a nuisance without providing compensation, when nothing in the relevant legislation suggested this possibility.

A planning decision in and of itself did not determine the civil law rights of the occupier.

The evidence before the planning authority did not dictate the outcome to the court but was merely for the court's consideration. Each case, regardless of the size of the development or a change in the nature of the locality, turns on its facts and is open to the judge's discretion.

2   *The timing, level, duration and frequency of the nuisance.* Night-time noise is more likely to be actionable than noise during the day. See, for example, *Leeman v Montague* (1936) on the nocturnal crowing of cockerels. The more substantial the inconvenience to the claimant the less important is lengthy duration or frequency. The court may be prepared to allow the activity to continue subject to reduction of such factors to a reasonable level (see *Watson and Others v Croft Promo-Sport Ltd* (2009, CA) (above)).

3   *The practicability of preventing the nuisance.* In *Andreae v Selfridge* (1938) the defendant was held liable in nuisance through failure to prove that it had taken reasonable steps to reduce the noise and dust arising from building operations. The law acknowledges that some annoyance to the claimant may be an inevitable consequence of the defendant's activity. A defendant who can prove that they have taken all reasonable precautions to avoid causing annoyance is rarely liable for intangible, as opposed to tangible, damage.

Moy v Stoop (1909)

The claimant complained about the noise of children crying in the defendant's day nursery next door.

Held: the noise was an unavoidable consequence of the defendant's activity. It was not caused by neglect by the defendant of the children's welfare, and therefore the defendant was not liable.

4   *The defendant's motive.* Most nuisance is caused by unthinking behaviour, but occasionally the defendant may actually be trying to cause distress to the claimant. If the claimant can prove such motivation, this may cast new light on the defendant's behaviour, rendering potentially reasonable behaviour unreasonable.

Hollywood Silver Fox Farm v Emmett (1936)

Believing that the presence of the claimant's farm was inhibiting the sale of building plots on his own land, the defendant carried out intensive shooting operations on his land throughout the silver fox breeding season. He knew that this would disturb the animals and discourage successful breeding and thus cause damage to the claimant's business.

Held: the defendant was liable since his malicious intentions made his behaviour unreasonable.

5   *The claimant's sensitivity.* The claimant will have to prove that the level of nuisance is higher than that which the average person could reasonably be expected to endure. A sensitive claimant cannot impose a heavier duty on the defendant to accommodate his unusual need. However, if the level of interference would be unreasonable to the average claimant, the defendant will be liable to one who is sensitive, provided the damage is reasonably foreseeable.

Robinson v *Kilvert* (1889)

The defendant installed a boiler in his basement. This caused a rise in temperature and a drop in humidity in the claimant's adjoining basement. Most people would have been pleased, but the claimant complained because the previous conditions were essential for the storage of paper which became damaged by the warmer and drier air.

Held: the defendant's behaviour was not a nuisance as warming the premises did not amount to unreasonable behaviour. The claimant's damage arose from the peculiar sensitivity of his goods.

But compare this superficially similar case which produced a contrary result.

McKinnon Industries Ltd v *Walker* (1951)

The escape of noxious fumes from the defendant's premises caused damage to the claimant's orchids.

Held: the defendant was liable as any plants would have suffered similarly, not just exotic blooms.

6 *Public benefit.* This will be taken into account to some extent in assessing competing interests and reasonableness. The fact that planning permission exists for the particular land use may be relevant here. However, if the defendant's behaviour is found to be unreasonable, the fact that it is of public benefit does not prevent liability, though it may affect the nature of the remedy.

Dennis v *Ministry of Defence* (2003)

RAF low-flying training activity caused noise of great severity and frequency over the claimant's estate.

Held: the disturbance amounted to unreasonable interference. However, it was in the public interest that such training flights should continue, so damages must suffice in lieu of an injunction.

Reasonable foreseeability

The burden of proof is easier for the claimant to discharge in nuisance than in negligence, since in nuisance the claimant does not need to prove that the defendant failed to take reasonable care. The claimant needs show only that the type of damage caused was a *reasonably foreseeable consequence to a person in the defendant's position*. The state of the defendant's knowledge is crucial.

Defendants will naturally be expected to anticipate the consequences of their own actions. Where the nuisance arises from a state of affairs created by a third party like a previous occupant or a trespasser, a defendant will not be liable unless they should reasonably have known about this and of the risk to the claimant.

Sedleigh-Denfield v O'Callaghan (1940, HL)

A ditch ran across the boundary of the defendant's property. The local authority installed a culvert (drainage pipe) in the ditch near the point where the ditch left the defendant's land. The end of the pipe extended into the defendant's property and a grid should have been placed at the other end of the pipe. The workman, however, left it on top of the pipe where it was completely useless. The defendant had not given permission to the local authority which was therefore trespassing when it entered his land. The defendant was aware that there was a danger of flooding if debris blocked the pipe. Usually, the defendant kept the pipe clear, but once this job was overlooked, rubbish built up and caused a flood on the claimant's property during heavy rain.

Held: the defendant was liable in private nuisance as it had failed to take reasonably practicable steps to remove a known hazard from the land. It would have been very easy to put the grid into place and the flood would not have occurred.

The courts have extended this principle to cover entirely naturally occurring events.

Leakey v The National Trust (1980, CA)

The claimant owned a house at the foot of a steep hill in the care of the National Trust. The claimant alerted the Trust to evidence of minor landslips which had occurred due to drought. A major slippage then occurred and large quantities of debris landed in the claimant's garden.

Held: as the Trust knew of the risk of such damage, it would be liable as it had failed to take reasonable steps to prevent landslips.

Who may sue in private nuisance?

Private nuisance protects the right to peaceable enjoyment of land and has traditionally been seen in law as the exclusive right of the owner-occupier, or tenant, since it pertains to the capital or amenity value of the land. Other residents do not have the right to sue in private nuisance.

Malone v *Laskey* (1907)

The claimant and her husband lived in premises owned by the defendant, her husband's employer, but without a tenancy. The claimant was hit on the head by a lavatory cistern which became detached from its fixings due to the vibration of machinery on adjoining premises, and she claimed against the defendant in private nuisance.

Held: her claim could not succeed, because she was 'a mere licensee' and had no proprietary rights over the premises.

The principle was upheld by the House of Lords in *Hunter* v *Canary Wharf* (1997), which disapproved the Court of Appeal's decision in *Khorasandjian* v *Bush* (1993) to extend the right to sue to members of the occupier's family.

Who may be sued?

The current occupier is the most usual defendant, but the party who caused the nuisance (for example, a previous occupant) may be sued. A landlord who lets premises knowing that their use will create a nuisance is also liable. Thus, in *Tetley* v *Chitty* (1986) a landlord, who had let some premises for development as a go-karting track, was liable for the resulting noise nuisance.

However, to be actionable the nuisance must be an inevitable result of the letting and must relate to the land use by the tenant.

Hussain and Livingstone v *Lancaster City Council* (1999, CA)

The claimants were victims of a sustained campaign of racial harassment by a number of people including the defendant's tenants. The council had statutory powers under the Housing Act 1985 to evict tenants and other occupants causing nuisance or annoyance to neighbours.

Held: the defendant was not liable in nuisance. This was restricted to the use of land by the defendant which interfered with the claimants' land. The harassment complained of fell outside the tort of nuisance; the campaign was not the result of the letting.

The defence of prescription

Prescription: the right to continue to commit a nuisance which has already persisted for 20 years.

Defendants will not be liable if they can prove that they have been causing the nuisance for *20 years* without anybody taking action against them. It is not enough to show that an activity has been carried on for that length of time; the court will have to be satisfied that it caused a nuisance to the claimant or his predecessors for the whole of that time for **prescription** to be a defence.

Sturges v *Bridgeman* (1879)

A confectioner had a workshop in premises adjacent to the claimant dentist. Noisy equipment in the workshop had been in use for over 20 years, but caused no problems until the dentist built a new consulting room in his garden, near the boundary wall where the noise was highly audible. He sued the confectioner.

Held: the defendant was liable in private nuisance since the noise level was unreasonable. Prescription was not an appropriate defence as it was the activity rather than the nuisance which had continued for 20 years. It was irrelevant that the claimant had moved into the noisier environment.

Public nuisance

The scope of liability

The tort of public nuisance resembles private nuisance as it may arise from similar situations, including the escape of noise, smells, dust and vibration. However, the scope of public nuisance is wider, covering any activity that unreasonably interferes with the comfort and convenience of the public. This includes the obstruction of highways or waterways. Behaviour giving rise to a public nuisance always involves criminal behaviour. Today there are a large number of statutory criminal offences to protect public health, covering pollution of all kinds and regulating businesses involved in the preparation and marketing of food. Until the twentieth century, these activities were prosecuted under the umbrella of public nuisance. Civil action may also be taken.

Potential defendants

Action may be taken against the person who created the nuisance, or the current occupier of land from which a nuisance emanates.

Potential claimants

Tort action may be taken to protect the public at large and an injunction may be sought, by the Attorney-General or by a local authority. Individuals are entitled to take action only where they have suffered special damage greater than that suffered by the public at large.

Notice that, unlike private nuisance, claimants are not required to have any occupational rights to the land where they suffer damage, to entitle them to sue. Sufficient geographical proximity to the nuisance is all that is required.

Mint v Good (1950, CA)

A garden wall belonging to the defendant collapsed onto the pavement and injured the claimant.

Held: the claimant should succeed in his claim. Blockage of the pavement was a public nuisance: any members of the public passing by would be inconvenienced. The claimant who was injured clearly physically suffered special harm.

Proof of liability

To establish public nuisance, the following points must be satisfied:

1 *The nuisance must be capable of affecting 'the public'.* The nuisance must potentially affect too many people to make it reasonable to expect any one person to take action to stop it.

Corby Group Litigation v Corby District Council (2009)

The 18 young claimants in this case were all born with limb deformities between 1986 and 1999 to mothers who lived in, or regularly visited, Corby while pregnant. They claimed that the council was liable for the birth defects that they had suffered resulting from their mothers' ingestion or inhalation of toxic substances released by the council's reclamation of land, which had previously been occupied by a vast steelworks.

Held: subject to proof of causation by each individual claimant, the council was liable in public nuisance, negligence and breach of the Environmental Protection Act 1990 from 1985–1997. It had not taken reasonable care to prevent reasonably foreseeable airborne exposure of the claimants' mothers to a variety of dangerous toxins, including cadmium, chromium and dioxins. These had been present in the dust and mud disturbed at the sites that were being reclaimed and were spread by wind across the locality or along local roads when materials were being moved by lorry. The statistically significant size of the cluster of birth defects, in children born between 1989 and 1998 in the defendant locality, supported this conclusion.

2 *The level of inconvenience must be unreasonable.* Similar criteria are relevant here as apply to private nuisance.
3 *Damage must result.* This includes physical damage to the person, land or goods, as well as amenity damage. Pure economic loss may also be actionable. Thus, in *Lyons & Co.* v *Gulliver* (1914) the defendants were held liable for causing loss of custom to the claimant's tea shop, access to which was blocked by long queues outside the defendants' theatre.

4 *The damage must be reasonably foreseeable to the defendant.* As in private nuisance, the claimant is not required to prove any failure to take reasonable care. Defendants may avoid liability by showing that they took all reasonably practicable precautions to prevent reasonably foreseeable damage. A very high standard is required where the nuisance occurs on the highway.

Dollman v Hillman (1941)

The claimant was awarded damages for injuries caused by slipping on a piece of fat, which had been dropped on the pavement outside the defendant's butcher's shop.

The rule in *Rylands* v *Fletcher*

This principle is derived from the case of *Rylands* v *Fletcher* (1865) concerning a mill owner who employed contractors to construct a reservoir on his land. In the course of the construction disused mine shafts were uncovered and negligently sealed. When the reservoir was filled, water leaked through the shafts and flooded an adjoining mine owned by the claimant, causing considerable loss and business interruption. It was held that the defendant was *strictly liable* for this damage, because 'a person who for his own purposes, brings onto his land and collects or keeps there anything likely to do mischief if it escapes, must keep it in at his peril and if he does not do so is prima facie liable for all the damage which is the natural consequence of its escape' (Blackburn J). This was affirmed on appeal by the House of Lords, with qualification that the defendant's use of land must be 'non-natural'.

The proof points of the rule

1 *'Things' within the rule.* Potentially this covers anything likely to do harm on escape. Something perfectly safe if contained can do much damage if it escapes. There are innumerable examples, e.g. gas (*Batcheller* v *Tunbridge Wells Gas Company* (1901)), electricity (*National Telephone Co.* v *Baker* (1893)), as well as some rather bizarre cases such as *Hale* v *Jennings* (1938): escaping chair-o-plane demolishing an adjacent shooting gallery at a fair, and *Crowhurst* v *Amersham Burial Board* (1878): yew branches falling from the defendant's graveyard and poisoning the claimant's cattle in the field next door.

2 *Accumulation.* The defendant must have brought the thing onto the land; it must not have got there in the course of nature.

3 *Non-natural use of land.* This has gradually been defined more and more strictly by the courts. As early as 1913 it was held that it must be more than unusual: 'it must be some special use bringing with it increased danger to others and must not be the ordinary use of land or such a use as is proper for the general benefit of the community' (Lord Moulton in *Rickards* v *Lothian* (1913)). In *Read* v *Lyons* (1947)

which concerned storage of explosives at a munitions factory in wartime, Lord Porter held that 'all the circumstances of time and place and the practices of mankind must be taken into consideration, so that what might be regarded as dangerous and non-natural may vary according to the circumstances'. Unsurprisingly, *Rylands* v *Fletcher* liability was not held to exist. In *Transco plc* v *Stockport Corporation* (2003) Lord Nicholls held the defendant's use of land must be '*extraordinary and exceptional*' to give rise to liability, and Lord Hoffmann suggested that only those risks against which it would be unreasonable to expect the claimant to be insured against should be covered.

4 *Escape*. The thing must escape from a place occupied by the defendant to a place outside their occupation and control. The defendant need have no proprietary interest over land from which escape takes place; it is their *control* of the thing which is crucial. Escape may be onto the highway, so the claimant also need not have a proprietary interest in land.

At first, *Rylands* v *Fletcher* was treated by the courts as a new legal principle governing a vaguely defined category of what at the time were regarded as exceptional and dangerous activities. Large numbers of cases concerned escapes from industrial installations. In the nineteenth and early twentieth centuries these were more prevalent and successful litigation commonplace, so initially there were many successful claims. Today, we would regard such use of land as commonplace and such activities as generally safe.

The strict liability principle has been judicially undermined and liability today is based on reasonable foreseeability as it is in nuisance (*Cambridge Water Co.* v *Eastern Counties Leather* (1994)). A whole range of defences has also developed, such as statutory authority which gives protection to some public bodies from liability, provided no negligence is involved. Claimants who succeed do so because they can prove nuisance or negligence and today *Rylands* v *Fletcher* is generally regarded merely as '*a sub-species of nuisance*' (Lord Bingham in *Transco plc* v *Stockport Metropolitan Council* (2003)). Some judges have suggested that it should be abolished altogether, but the House of Lords in the *Cambridge Water* and *Transco* cases did not approve of such a move. It was acknowledged as a viable cause of action in *Colour Quest and Others* v *Total Downstream UK plc and Others* (2009), though as negligence liability existed, strict liability was not in issue.

Colour Quest Ltd v *Total Downstream UK plc and Others* (2009)

In December 2005 a huge explosion and resulting fire occurred at an oil storage facility in Hertfordshire controlled by Total UK. Staff at the facility failed to notice that a gauge had stuck, causing a tank to overfill. The back-up switch also failed and the facility was flooded with oil. The vapour ignited and there was a massive explosion (2.4 on the Richter scale and audible across the English Channel). Forty people were injured and the blast destroyed oil storage facilities belonging to other parties on the site, as well as considerably damaging businesses and property within a radius of seven miles.

Held: Total UK was liable in negligence to Colour Quest for its failure to employ appropriate procedures to prevent tank overflow, despite the fact that this was a recurring problem. It was liable in *Rylands* v *Fletcher* to persons who had suffered damage outside the site and in nuisance to those on and outside the site. Total had to pay several hundred million in damages to the other oil companies on the site and hundreds of local businesses and householders.

Remedies

In claims in public and private nuisance and *Rylands* v *Fletcher*, the remedies are damages and/or an injunction.

The impact of the Human Rights Act 1998

The courts have acknowledged the relevance of the Human Rights Act 1998 in some nuisance cases.

McKenna v *British Aluminium Ltd* (2002)

The claimants were all children from over 30 families who claimed nuisance by British Aluminium in permitting a factory to emit fumes and noise which had caused them mental distress and physical harm. They argued that this breached their rights under Article 8 (right to respect for privacy and family life) and under Protocol 1, Article 1 (right to peaceful enjoyment of possessions) of the ECHR.

British Aluminium argued that the claims should be struck out as none of the children had the necessary proprietary interest in the land to enable them to sue in nuisance.

Held: the action should not be struck out since there were strong arguments supporting the claim. Potentially the law of nuisance was in conflict with the Convention rights and arguably needed to be developed compatibly. Otherwise, a person living in his home where enjoyment of property was interfered with would be unable to protect his Convention rights unless he also had proprietary rights. The matter could only be decided at trial.

Note that the *McKenna* case does not in itself change the law of nuisance. That could only happen after a full trial decision, which might well result in appeal to the House of Lords. No such proceedings have taken place. However, this case does indicate the potential for development in the light of the Human Rights Act 1998.

In *Dennis* v *Ministry of Defence* (2003) (see above) the judge held that a declaration that the Ministry of Defence had breached Article 8 and Protocol 1 would have been in order, had the nuisance action not provided an appropriate remedy.

Legal area	1957 Act	1984 Act	Public nuisance	Private nuisance
Potential defendant	Person(s) in control of premises	Person(s) in control of premises	Owner/tenant/creator of nuisance	Owner/tenant/creator of nuisance
Potential claimant	Lawful entrants	Trespassers	Any member of public suffering special damage	Occupiers of adjacent premises
Where damage occurred	On defendant's premises	On defendant's premises	Anywhere inside or outside defendant's premises	On premises occupied by claimant
Type of damage	Personal injuries, damage to goods	Personal injuries only	Personal injuries, damage to property, interference with enjoyment of premises	Damage to property, interference with enjoyment of premises, possibly personal injuries
Cause of damage	State of premises	State of premises	State of premises and activities taking place there or obstructing highway	State of premises and activities taking place there
Nature of liability	Failure to take reasonable care of visitor's safety	Failure to take reasonable care to avoid causing injury to trespassers	Failure reasonably to foresee damage to claimant	Failure reasonably to foresee damage to claimant

Figure 16.1 The occupier's civil legal liability for premises

An action under the Human Rights Act 1998, therefore, may provide an alternative where a public authority is the defendant. Had the Hussains (*Hussain and Livingstone* v *Lancaster City Council* (1999 CA) (see above) been able to sue the Council for breach of Article 8, they might well have been successful, but sadly their claim arose before the Act was implemented.

Vicarious liability

Usually people are liable only for their own torts, but in certain situations they may be sued for the torts of others for whom they are said to be *vicariously* liable. **Vicarious liability** most commonly arises in relation to employers, with regard to the wrongful behaviour of their employees, but it also extends to the agency relationship.

Vicarious liability: liability for the tort of another person.

The difference between employees and independent contractors

Employee:
Part-/full-time waged/salaried worker whose job description is defined by a contract of service.

An employer may be liable for the torts of its own **employees** but not usually for those of independent contractors. It is therefore important to be able to distinguish the two.

A person running a business will employ their own staff but may also need to bring in others to carry out some essential services. For example, a shop owner may employ sales assistants, while window cleaning is done by an outside firm. The shop owner may be vicariously liable for any torts committed by the shop assistants because of the employer–employee relationship arising from the **contract of service**. Such a relationship does not exist between the shop owner and the window cleaner, who is an **independent contractor** and works under a **contract for services**. The window cleaner is an accessory to the business rather than integrated within it.

Contract of service:
a contract between employer and employee.

Independent contractor:
self-employed person providing services to a business/individual.

Contract for services:
a contract between a party and an independent contractor.

This distinction may be difficult to see in large organisations, where services, like catering and cleaning may be contracted out to other firms. The distinction between the staff of the contractor and the 'real employees' is not immediately apparent; so determining those employees for whose actions the owner of the workplace is vicariously liable may be problematic. The terms of the contract may provide crucial evidence of the intention of the parties. Where work is contracted out, the contractor generally remains the employer of the relevant employee. A party who provides plant, tools and materials and undertakes financial risks in carrying out a job may be deemed to be an independent contractor, even though the employer may exercise considerable control over the contractor's business enterprise.

Ready Mixed Concrete v *Ministry of Pensions and National Insurance* (1968)

Drivers employed by Ready Mixed Concrete had to buy their own vehicles from a supplier nominated by Ready Mixed and paint them in Ready Mixed's colours. They could not use the vehicles for their own purposes, and had to make them available whenever required by Ready Mixed, with a substitute driver if necessary.

Held: the drivers were independent contractors. Despite the high degree of control by Ready Mixed, the financial stake that they acquired by the purchase of their own vehicles and the fact that they could get a substitute driver to perform their contractual duties indicated that the parties intended the contract to be for services.

The Court may be prepared to impose vicarious liability on the grounds that a relationship analogous to employment exists between an employer and a party acting under their directions.

Cox v Ministry of Justice (2014, EWCA)

The claimant C was on the catering staff of a prison assisted by prisoners who were paid nominally for their work. A prisoner injured C by accidentally dropping a loaded sack onto her back when she was kneeling down to clean up a spillage.

C's original claim that the defendant was vicariously liable failed because the prisoner was not employed by the defendant. C appealed.

The Court of Appeal held: the defendant was vicariously liable because the relationship between the prisoner and the Ministry of Justice was akin to the employment relationship. The law relating to vicarious liability had developed incrementally and there were sufficiently similar circumstances in those decisions to justify a finding of liability in this case. It was fair, just and reasonable to impose liability. The prisoner was carrying out work for the benefit of the defendant saving it the expense of paying the full market rate. There was no reason why the defendant should not carry the financial burden resulting from this as well as the benefits.

In the recent case of *Barclays Bank* v *Various Claimants* (2018, CA) the bank was held vicariously liable for assaults on 153 patients sent to a self-employed doctor for medical assessments by the bank.

The extent of the vicarious liability

The traditional *test* for determining the course of employment is the Salmond test, which states that a tort will be committed in the course of employment if it is either:

(a) a wrongful act authorised by the 'master' (employer); or

(b) a wrongful and unauthorised mode of doing some act authorised by the master.

This has been developed by the courts and the 'close connection test' is now used where the activity consists of intentional wrongdoing.

As long as the activity which gave rise to the tort was sufficiently closely connected with carrying out designated contractual duties, the employer is liable, even if the employee was negligent or disobeying orders concerning the execution of those duties. This may seem harsh on the employer, but the law takes the view that employers are obliged to supervise their workforce properly.

Bayley v Manchester, Sheffield and Lincolnshire Railway (1873)

Mistakenly believing that Mr Bayley had boarded the wrong train, the defendant's porter hauled him from it when it had begun to move away, causing him injuries.

Held: the porter had been carrying out his duties, although in a careless and incompetent manner, and the railway company was vicariously liable.

Century Insurance v *Northern Irish Road Transport Board* (1949, HL)

While discharging petrol from a tanker the defendant's employee was smoking. This was forbidden under work rules. An explosion causing serious damage resulted.

Held: the defendant employer was vicariously liable. The employee was carrying out his duties in an unauthorised way.

If, however, the employee's behaviour is not sufficiently coincidental to his job, the employer is not vicariously liable. In *Beard* v *London Omnibus Co.* (1900) the company was not liable for injuries caused to Mr Beard when a bus conductor tried his hand at reversing the bus at the terminus, since he was not employed to drive the bus.

Warren v *Henlys Garage Ltd* (1948)

A pump attendant challenged Mr Warren, believing that he intended to drive off without paying for his petrol. Mr Warren then said he would report him to the manager for insolence; the attendant, in response, hit him on the chin.

Held: the employer was not vicariously liable; the attendant had not been acting to protect his employer's interest when he hit Mr Warren, but to avenge himself and therefore was acting outside the scope of his employment.

Similarly in *Mohamud* v *Morrison Supermarkets plc* (2015) the Supreme Court reversed the decision of the Court of Appeal deciding that a close connection between a supermarket assistant's duties and an unprovoked verbally and physically abusive attack on a customer resulted in the supermarket being vicariously liable to the customer.

Mohamud v *Morrison Supermarkets plc* [2016] UKSC

Mr Mohamud was a customer at the defendant's supermarket petrol station. He approached the defendant's employee who was responsible for serving customers and ensuring the smooth running of the petrol pumps. The employee responded to Mr Mohamud's request for information by verbally racially abusing him and telling him to leave. He then followed him across the forecourt and violently physically attacked him.

Held: there was sufficient close connection between the employee's behaviour and the tasks which he was employed to do to make the defendant vicariously liable. Interacting with customers to provide information and assistance was within the scope of the employee's job description, though the accompanying abuse was an inexcusable way of carrying out his duties. The violence which followed on the forecourt was all part of a continuous sequence of behaviour. It was a gross abuse of his orders but he was purporting to carry out his job when he pursued the claimant and told him to leave the premises and not come back. It was irrelevant that he appeared to be motivated by racism rather than a desire to assist the employer's business.

The application of the doctrine of vicarious liability is increasingly dictated by policy and this is well illustrated by the Supreme Court's decision in the case above. Where the court believes that the employer should be publicly accountable it will be generous when interpreting the issue of close connection, even where on the face of things the employee has acted only to further his own interests.

Lister v *Hesley Hall* (2001, HL)

A warden of a care home sexually abused boys for whom he was responsible.

Held: the employer was vicariously liable because there was a very close connection between the acts of abuse by the warden and the work he was employed to do. By abusing the boys he was failing in the very obligation he had contracted to fulfil which was ensuring the care and safety of the children.

Sufficiently close connection in such cases may occur outside residential care.

Maga v *Trustees of the Birmingham Archdiocese* (2010, CA)

The claimant appealed against a High Court decision that the defendant Archdiocese was not vicariously liable for sexual abuse of the claimant by one of its priests.

The claimant was befriended and groomed by the defendant's priest when he was about 12 years old. Initially, the priest got into conversation with the claimant in the street when he was admiring the priest's car. The priest gradually befriended him, encouraging the boy to do odd jobs for him and to come to parish youth discos. The relationship became abusive when he took him back to the presbytery after the boy had stayed behind to help clear up after a disco.

Held: the defendant was vicariously liable since the abusive acts were within the course of the priest's employment, being closely linked to his official responsibilities.

The defendant's priest had been given special responsibility for youth work and was performing this duty when he befriended M. It enabled him to develop a relationship with the boy by encouraging him onto church premises to take part in organised church functions and had the opportunity to escalate the relationship to an abusive one.

A contract may specifically forbid certain wilful behaviour and indicate that the employer is vicariously liable for such occurrences even though there may be an element of personal revenge. In *Gravil* v *Carroll and Redruth Rugby Club* (2008, CA), G claimed damages against the rugby club in trespass to the person after he sustained a broken cheekbone from a punch by C as a scrum broke up when the whistle had blown for close of play. The Court of Appeal held that the rugby club was liable for C's behaviour: it was sufficiently closely connected to his employment since incidents of this kind were commonplace in such circumstances and the terms of his contract made it clear that such behaviour was not authorised.

The House of Lords has affirmed that an employer may be liable for an employee's breach of statutory duty as well as common law torts. In *Majrowski* v *Guy's & St Thomas' NHS Trust* (2006, HL), the trust was vicariously liable for the employee's breach of the Protection from Harassment Act 1997.

Worth thinking about?

How does the doctrine of vicarious liability benefit the claimant?

Suggested solutions can be found in Appendix 2.

Liability for independent contractors: non-delegable duties

Although a person who employs an independent contractor is never *vicariously* liable for the contractor's torts, there are circumstances where the employer may be held *personally* liable for damage resulting from the contractor's work. Such liability arises where a non-delegable legal duty is imposed on the employer because they have particular responsibility, which cannot be transferred to anybody else. In practice the courts are very reluctant to acknowledge such a duty. It was traditionally limited to the following circumstances:

1 *Public nuisance affecting the highway.* For example if scaffolding used by building contractors working on your premises causes an obstruction, you will be personally liable.

2 *Injury to a servant.* Employers have a non-delegable duty to provide a safe working environment for their servants (employees, etc.) and will be personally liable for injuries caused by contractors' work. (This is covered in more detail in Chapter 17.)

3 *Hospitals have a non-delegable duty to ensure that proper care is taken of patients* (A v *Ministry of Defence* (2004)) and so will be personally liable for the torts caused by medical staff of all kinds even if no contract of service exists to give rise to vicarious liability.

However in *Woodland* v *Essex County Council* (2013) the Supreme Court introduced a new category covering situations where a vulnerable claimant, in the custody of the defendant, is adversely injured by the negligence of a third party over whom the claimant has no control, who was performing a task ordered by the defendant, in circumstances where the defendant is deemed to have assumed responsibility for that vulnerable person. The Supreme Court gave examples of persons likely to be regarded as vulnerable including: patients, children, care home residents and prisoners.

Woodland v *Essex County Council* (2013)

Annie Woodland, aged 10, a pupil in a school controlled by Essex County Council, suffered serious brain damage as a result of nearly drowning during a swimming lesson at Basildon pool supervised by a swimming teacher and lifeguards who were independent contractors. She included Essex County Council in her claim for negligence because she argued that the school had a non-delegable duty making it responsible for the damage caused by the negligent behaviour of the swimming teacher and lifeguards working at Basildon Council's pool under the management of Harlow Council. Essex argued that a school did not owe a non-delegable duty to its pupils and claimed that this part of the claim should be struck out before the case was heard.

The Court of Appeal held that a non-delegable duty did not exist in this case and the claimant appealed to the Supreme Court which overturned the Court of Appeal decision.

Held: the Council did owe a delegated duty of care to the claimant. It had a duty to ensure that swimming lessons, which were part of the school curriculum, were carried out with all reasonable skill. It had delegated responsibility for the supervision and teaching of those lessons to Harlow Council and the swimming teacher. The alleged negligence occurred during the performance of the actual function for which the school had assumed responsibility and which it had delegated. Therefore if there was negligence in performance the school and vicariously Essex Council remained liable for it.

The *Woodland* principle was applied in the case of *GB* v *Home Office* (2015) where the High Court held that the claimant, a detainee in an immigration removal centre, was a vulnerable person in Home Office custody. The Home Office owed her a non-delegable duty for any negligence in her compulsory medical care provided by a local medical practice authorised by the Home Office.

Chapter summary

Tort liability and premises

Negligence: damage to a person or their property caused by some activity taking place on the defendant's premises.

Occupiers' Liability Acts of 1957 and 1984: defective structure or condition of the defendant's premises, which adversely affects 'visitors' (OLA 1957) and trespassers (OLA 1984).

Public and private nuisance: covers interference emanating from the defendant's premises and interfering unreasonably with the right of peaceful enjoyment of occupiers of nearby premises/highway.

Please see Figure 16.1 (above) for a detailed summary of the scope of the OLA 1957 and 1984 and public and private nuisance.

Defences

Consent: express/implied consent by the claimant to the defendant's behaviour may be an effective defence.

Contributory negligence: damages may be reduced proportionately in relation to the claimant's failure to take care for their own safety.

Vicarious liability

An employer is liable for the torts of those working for him or her under a contract of service, provided that the tortious behaviour of the employee is sufficiently closely connected to the employee's work.

Personal liability for independent contractors

Exists if the employer owes a non-delegable duty to the claimant.

Review questions 15

1 What is the likely tort liability of Reed in the following circumstances?

   (a) Marie is hit by a can of paint dropped from the top of a ladder into the street by Cherry, who was up the ladder painting Reed's shop front.

   (b) Seema slipped on a spillage while climbing the stairs in the shop. A notice at the bottom of the stairs said 'Take care: wet floor, please use other stairs'.

(c) Lennie, aged seven, went through a door in the shop marked 'Private' and cut himself on some broken glass in a storeroom.

(d) Mario, Reed's next-door neighbour, has discovered wet rot in his premises caused by condensation from an unlined boiler flue on Reed's premises.

2 Wilma was a passenger in Chester's car, which was being driven carefully when it skidded on oil on the road and Wilma was thrown forward as the seatbelt malfunctioned. Chester was aware that the seatbelt was not working properly and failed to remedy this. Advise Wilma.

3 What is the difference between an employer's liability for the torts of employees and for those of independent contractors?

4 How does the doctrine of vicarious liability benefit the claimant?

5 When is the duty owed to trespassers activated under the OLA 1984?

6 Explain the term 'occupier'.

Answers to all review questions can be found in Appendix 2.

Advanced questions 15

(A) 'The Occupiers' Liability Act 1957 modifies the common law to the extent that the safety of lawful visitors is ensured.'

Discuss how the law on occupiers' liability has developed in light of the above statement.

(B) The doctrine of vicarious liability 'has not grown from any very clear, logical or legal principle, but from social convenience and rough justice' (Lord Pearce, *ICI* v *Shatwell* (1965) AC 656 at 685).

Critically evaluate this statement.

Answers to the advanced questions can be found at **go.pearson.com/uk/he/resources.**

Take a closer look

The following cases provide important examples of how the law in this chapter has developed. They are primary sources illustrating the law in action and give more detail about their facts, as well as helping to understand the law and to appreciate how the judges reached their decisions.

Try looking them up in the law reports or accessing them via a database, e.g. BAILII (www.bailii.org/databases.html). LexisNexis or Westlaw may be available in the university or college library, or extracts may be found in a case book. (See Appendix 1: Additional resources.)

Hunter v *Canary Wharf* [1997] 2 All ER 426

Lister v *Hesley Hall Ltd* [2001] 2 All ER 769

Ogwo v *Taylor* [1987] AC 431

Ratcliff v *Harper Adams Agricultural College* [1999] 1 WLR 670

Web activity

Read 'Protection from Harassment Act – Sainsbury's not liable for employee stabbing' on the employment law blog of Fieldfisher:

https://employmentlawblog.fieldfisher.com/2013/protection-from-harassment-act-sainsburys-not-liable-for-employee-stabbing

See the House of Lords judgment in *Tomlinson* v *Congleton Borough Council* (2003, HL) at:

https://publications.parliament.uk/pa/ld200203/ldjudgmt/jd030731/tomlin-2.htm

Read 'Judges, child trespassers and occupiers' liability in the built environment' by Luke Bennett (2010), available at:

http://shura.shu.ac.uk/2862/1/Bennett_-_Judges_%26_Child_Trespassers_-_COBRA_2010_paper.pdf

Assignment 14

Healing plc recently opened an anti-stress clinic on the edge of the village of Raunchy. Farmer Oswald's farm is immediately adjacent to the clinic's premises, which includes a swimming pool. For three weeks during the summer, Grinders Farming Contractors Ltd are employed by Oswald to bring in the harvest. The work involves daily use of huge machines. The noise of the machinery upsets the clinic's patients, many of whom cancel expensive courses of treatment. The dust and dirt from the harvesting process forms a thick film on the swimming pool making it unusable, and clogs the filter causing it to break down and require expensive repairs. Ned, one of Grinders' employees, drops a cigarette end which starts a fire in the field. It spreads into the clinic's grounds and destroys a summer-house.

Advise Healing plc about its possible rights in tort.

PART 4

Elements of employment law

Rights at work:
The contract of employment and health and safety at work

Learning objectives

On completion of this chapter, students should be able to:

★ distinguish between an employee and an independent contractor;

★ be aware of the main terms in an employment contract;

★ understand the common law contractual duties of employer/employee;

★ examine the extent of the employer's civil liability for industrial illness and injury;

★ appreciate the role of the Health and Safety at Work etc. Act in promoting the welfare of employees.

Introduction

The operation of employment law is very important, whether from the perspective of a business owner or employee, as it provides the basic structure of the employer and employee relationship from the time an employee is interviewed for a job until the time they leave. Although the common law of contract is still highly relevant to employment law, statutory regulation since the 1970s attempted to promote a more equal balance of power between employer and employee. Employers lost their traditional freedom to select, recruit and dismiss staff at will and to contract purely on their own terms. Employees were given a greater range of remedies. The current government sees a need to push the pendulum in the opposite direction as part of its 'red tape challenge'. This is aimed at reducing regulation on employers which it perceives as restricting business development, growth and productivity. Legislation implementing some of these proposals will be covered later in this section of the text. At the time of writing (May 2019) it is as yet uncertain how Brexit will impact upon the landscape of employment law. However, much European regulation has been incorporated into the law of England and Wales and is unlikely to change immediately on the UK exiting the European Union.

The employer and employee relationship is based on the **contract of employment**. In this chapter the focus is on how this contract of employment is formed and the terms which the law requires it to contain to protect both parties.

Many accidents occur in workplaces, so what happens if a worker suffers injury or become ill due to workplace conditions? This chapter also examines employers' liability in tort and criminal law for the health and safety of their employees.

Contract of employment: a contract of service or apprenticeship, whether express or implied, and (if it is express) whether oral or in writing.

The employment contract: a contract of service

Workers, employees and independent contractors

Worker: works under a contract of service but with fewer rights than an employee.

Employee: an individual who has entered into or works under a contract of employment.

Independent contractor: business/individual providing services under contract to another business/individual.

Contract for services: contract between an independent contractor and another party.

A business may employ **workers** and **employees** under a **contract of service**, and **independent contractors** under a **contract for services**.

The employer is responsible for paying National Insurance contributions and sick pay (to employees only) and for deduction of income tax.

Workers

Workers may generally be employed on a part-time/casual and agency basis. Their contract of service does not entitle them to sick pay and certain other benefits, and they may not claim unfair dismissal. They may however claim holiday pay and be entitled to other benefits, including the National Minimum Wage. The definition of a worker can be found in s 230(3) of the Employment Rights Act 1996 (ERA 1996):

an individual who has entered into or works under (or, where the employment has ceased) –

(a) a contract of employment, or

(b) any other contract, whether express or implied and (if it is express) whether oral or in writing.

Employees

An employee's contract of service entitles them to the full range of existing employment rights including sick and holiday pay and the right to claim for unfair dismissal and redundancy.

Employee shareholders

The Growth and Infrastructure Act 2013 introduced this new category of employees. This intervention is intended to give small, rapidly growing companies more flexibility, by enabling them to dismiss staff more readily. Such employees choose to forgo their rights to claim unfair dismissal (except when related to discrimination) in return for an allotment of shares, but otherwise generally enjoy many of the same rights as other employees including holiday and sick pay.

In October 2014 the Department for Business, Innovation and Skills (BIS, now BEIS) announced a wide-ranging review aimed at clarifying and enhancing rights for workers. It said that there appeared to be widespread confusion among both workers and employers about the extent of workers' as opposed to employees' rights.

Independent contractors

An independent contractor may be a company or partnership with its own staff or a single self-employed person providing services to an employer on or off site. An employer is generally not vicariously liable for unlawful behaviour by an independent contractor (see Chapter 16) and the contractor does not enjoy the same legal rights as an employee.

Modern workplace practice has made the distinctions between employee, worker and contractor less evident. Increasingly, large firms have taken to contracting out a variety of services like catering. The contractor's staff may work on site for similar hours to other staff and may even be required to wear a uniform in the business livery. Litigation to determine the status of the parties and their resulting rights and liabilities is common.

Factors which may help the court to determine status

1 *The contract*: the court uses a purposive approach to ascertain the intention of the parties. Calling a party 'self-employed' does not always make them an independent contractor in law. The label given to the person working is not conclusive and may be considered to be a sham (*Autoclenz* v *Belcher* (2011)).

2 *Financial risk and capital outlay*: Who pays? Does the employer provide all the necessary equipment? An employee is generally entitled to payment and to have equipment provided by the employer.

3 *Delegation or personal performance?* A contractor is often free to delegate while an employee must perform in person. Thus in *Community Dental Services* v *Sultan Darmon* (2010) the claimant was held to be an independent contractor because his contract with Community Dental Services allowed him to appoint a locum to do his work if necessary. Under s 230(3), a contract under which an employee or worker is employed will always require personal performance of all contractual duties. This has been particularly problematic in the gig economy cases, where in *Pimlico Plumbers* v *Smith* (2014, EAT) Smith was held to be a worker for Pimlico, rather than an independent contractor, because of the lack of specific substitution rights, despite otherwise having a high degree of autonomy. This was upheld by the Court of Appeal in *Pimlico Plumbers* v *Smith* (2017) and subsequently by the Supreme Court in 2018. However, in *IWGB* v *Deliveroo* (2017) the right of the Deliveroo drivers to substitute another driver resulted in them being designated as self-employed.

4 *Control:* the extent to which the employer controls working hours and directs a party in the manner of discharge of their duties may help to indicate status.

The next case unsurprisingly attracted a lot of coverage in the popular press. It is also a good illustration of how the court approaches cases of this kind.

Stringfellow Restaurants Ltd v *Quashie* (2012, CA)

Ms Quashie worked as a lap-dancer in one of the defendant's clubs. She claimed unfair dismissal when the defendant dismissed her services after suspicion was raised that she was involved with drugs on the premises.

Held: Ms Quashie was not entitled to claim. She did not have a contract of employment with the defendant because:

1 The club did not pay her. She negotiated her own fees for private dances with customers and these were remitted to her by the club minus agreed deductions. She was required to provide her own dance outfits as deemed suitable by the employer.

2 Her contract, which stated that she was self-employed, did not entitle her to sick or holiday pay and she paid her own tax.

3 The control element was insufficient to make her an employee. Although she was required to work one shift at weekends she could otherwise choose when and how many hours a week she would work. She could take such leave as she wished by prior written notice.

Where the employment status is uncertain, particularly in the age of the gig economy, concerns have been raised both in government and the courts. If status is not disputed, this provides a potential means for the employer of avoiding paying National Insurance contributions and tax deductions, saving administration and other financial costs to the business. Those employed may also avoid declaring earnings to HMRC. However, the courts have also seen an increase in those claiming to be deprived of their statutory employment rights.

The form of the contract of service

The validity of a contract is not dependent on its form. It can arise quite informally by word of mouth; writing is not essential to the existence of the contract. However, s 1 of the ERA 1996 obliges an employer to provide an employee with a *written statement* of the key terms of the employee's contract within two months of starting work. From 6 April 2020, these particulars must be provided on the first day of employment (Employment Rights (Employment Particulars and Paid Annual Leave) (Amendment) Regulations 2018).

This statement must include:

1 the parties' names and addresses;

2 the date when the employee started the job;

3 the date on which the employee's continuous employment began. This may not be the same as 2 above if, for example, the employee was already employed by the same employer but in a different post. The length of continuous employment is crucial to rights relating to unfair dismissal and redundancy, which are discussed below but which are not relevant to workers and various other terms;

Aslam, Farrar and others v (UBER) London & others (2016)

UBER is a company operating a taxi hire company via a phone app. The claimants were drivers for UBER and claimed that they were workers but were being treated by UBER as if they were independent contractors. UBER argued that they were independent contractors and that it merely acted as the drivers' agent and found them work.

The Employment Tribunal held: the terms under which the drivers worked clearly indicated that they were workers and therefore entitled to the minimum wage and the other workers' rights. The primary reason for the decision was the element of control exercised over them. For example, there was a clear contradiction between UBER's claim that it was the drivers' agent and the condition in their contracts giving UBER 'sole and absolute discretion' over the acceptance of bookings. The drivers were interviewed prior to being taken on. Very strict limitation was placed on what vehicles could be used. Drivers had no choice about whether to accept a ride and were given no information about the passenger except a first name and address. Failure to comply was punished by being logged off the system. Drivers had to follow the prescribed route for a price set by UBER. The passenger paid UBER and not the driver. Any complaints were dealt with by UBER and all risk was carried by UBER. In a contract for services risk always falls upon the independent contractor.

This decision was subsequently upheld by the Employment Appeal Tribunal in 2017 and the Court of Appeal in 2018. The Court of Appeal has granted UBER permission to further appeal. It is anticipated that the Supreme Court will hear the further appeal in late 2019.

4 a note of any disciplinary and grievance procedures;

5 full particulars of:

(a) pay entitlement;

(b) hours of work;

(c) any holiday entitlement and pay;

(d) any sick leave and pay entitlement;

(e) any pension rights (unless these are controlled by a statute which itself ensures notification);

(f) length of notice required to be given to and by the employee;

(g) the title of the employee's job and a brief description of what it involves;

(h) if the job is not intended to continue indefinitely, the period for which it is expected to last, or the date it is intended to end if it is for a fixed term;

(i) the place(s) where the employee will be required to work (employees required to work outside the UK for more than one month must be told how long this will be for, what currency they will be paid in, any entitlement to additional benefits and any terms relating to their return to the UK);

(j) any collective agreement directly affecting the job.

Failure to provide this statement does not invalidate the contract. It is merely intended to provide employees with sufficient written evidence of some of the conditions under which they are employed to enable them to enforce their statutory rights. The statement does not represent all the terms of the contract, which are described below. Failure to provide these particulars entitles the employee to 2–4 weeks' pay in the Employment Tribunal.

Sources of the terms of the employment contract

The terms of the contract will not generally be found in one written document since they may be both express and implied and may be traced to a number of sources.

Express terms are stated in any written contract of employment, but are also to be found in the written statutory information described above. They may also consist of promises made by word of mouth prior to acceptance.

The court may imply a term from any of the following sources:

Custom and practice: business behaviour accepted locally/ nationally/in the particular industry.

Collective agreement: made with an employer, by a trade union on behalf of its members.

- **custom and practice**;
- works and staff rules;
- **collective agreements**;
- statute;
- common law rights and duties of employers and employees;
- business efficacy (see Chapter 7).

Custom and practice

Relevant business practices acceptable nationally, locally or in the particular trade or workplace may be implied as terms of the contract. To be enforceable they must be reasonable, certain and not contrary to law. For example, in Lancashire, weaving factories employers customarily made deductions from pay for poor work. This was held to be a term of the contract (*Sagar v H. Ridehalgh & Son Ltd* (1930, CA)).

This source of terms has diminished in importance with the increased formalisation of the employment contract. In the event of conflict with the written contractual terms, the written terms prevail.

Works and staff rules

While not necessarily terms of the contract, failure to obey works and staff rules is likely to be treated as evidence of failure to obey reasonable orders. If the rule does not have the status of a contractual term this is advantageous to the employer, since a rule may be introduced and varied at will without the consent which would be required from the employee to make a contractual term or variation binding. Policy considerations may influence judicial decisions on such issues.

Collective agreements

The terms of a collective agreement between union and employer may expressly or impliedly form part of a contract of employment. With the decrease of union recognition in recent years, only a small minority of workers' contracts is likely to be influenced by such agreements.

Statute

Legislation increasingly restricts the freedom of employers to impose the terms of their choice on employees. For example, the Working Time Regulations 1998 (implementing the Working Time Directive) impose limits on the hours which an employee can be asked to work and include requirements for minimum rest breaks and annual paid holidays.

Terms implied at common law

The common law implies certain terms into contracts of employment which impose duties on both employer and employee. For example, the common law requires employees:

1 to do their job with reasonable care and skill;

2 to obey all reasonable orders;

3 to act in good faith towards the employer.

Each of these duties is implied in the contract. They are discussed in detail below.

The common law duties of the employee

The duty to work with reasonable care and skill

Essentially this means that an employee must not be negligent. What is a reasonable standard depends on the status of the employee within the organisation and the level of qualification, skill and experience held by the employee. Grossly negligent performance may entitle an employer summarily to dismiss the employee.

The duty to obey reasonable orders

An order is usually treated as reasonable as long as it does not require the employee to do something outside their job description, since under the terms of the contract the employee has expressly or impliedly agreed to do anything necessarily incidental to performing the job. In *UK Atomic Energy Authority* v *Claydon* (1974) the employment contract stated that Claydon could be asked to work in any base in the UK. It was held that by refusing a transfer he had failed to obey a reasonable order.

An order is not reasonable if its performance is likely to endanger the personal safety or liberty of the employee. The employee must be able to show that *imminent* danger will result from carrying out the order. Compare the following two cases.

Ottoman Bank v *Chakarian* (1930)

The defendant was an Armenian refugee who had escaped from Turkey where he was under sentence of death.

Held: in the circumstances it was not reasonable to expect him to accept a posting in Turkey.

Walmesley v *UDEC* (1972)

Walmesley was ordered to accept a transfer to Ireland, which he refused because he was frightened of being harmed by the IRA.

Held: he was acting in breach of his contract since he was unable to prove any imminent and specific threat of harm.

An employee cannot be ordered to break the law.

Morrish v *Henlys (Folkestone) Ltd* (1973)

An employee who had refused to falsify the company's accounts was held not to be acting in breach of contract.

In determining what is reasonable, current standards of good industrial relations practice are taken into account.

An employee cannot choose how far to perform an employer's reasonable orders. Some forms of industrial action, short of going on strike, may entitle the employer to dock pay for part performance. The employees must receive prior notification of the employer's refusal to accept part performance. In *Wiluszynski* v *London Borough of Tower Hamlets* (1988, CA) it was held that council employees who refused to answer councillors' enquiries could legally be deprived of all their earnings for the five weeks that this action continued, even though they were carrying out all other aspects of their work. The employees had received specific and prior notice of the consequences of their action.

The duty to act in good faith

Employees must act with complete honesty towards their employers when carrying out their contractual duties. The motivation of employees is irrelevant to their liability.

Dalton v *Burtons Gold Medal Biscuit Co. Ltd* (1974)

Dalton falsified a clocking-in card to benefit another employee.

Held: he had breached his duty of good faith by cheating his employer. It was irrelevant that he obtained no personal benefit from the dishonest action.

The duty to act in good faith may be divided into three separate obligations:

1 *Not to act in conflict with the employer's interests.* Employees must not compete with the employer's business, even if they do so in their spare time. If the contract requires the employee to work for the employer exclusively, doing any paid work for another person is a breach of duty.

2 *Not to reveal confidential information.* The employee must not reveal confidential information about the employer's profits, customers, work systems, products or services. This duty remains enforceable, though to a more limited extent, even after an employee has left the employer's service. (There is detailed information about breach of confidence by employees in Chapter 26.)

3 *To account for all profits.* Taking bribes is obviously a gross breach of duty, but this duty may be breached by an employee who makes any unauthorised profit from the job. Employees, therefore, are not entitled to any secret commission. Tips may be retained in jobs where these are seen as part of payment, as in the restaurant trade.

The common law duties of the employer

It is implied in the contract of employment that the employer will:

1 pay the employee as agreed by the contract;

2 not undermine the trust and confidence of the employee;

3 provide the employee with safe working conditions.

The duty to pay the employee

Minimum wage/ living wage: statutory entitlement under the Minimum Wage Act 1999. Subject to updating by the BEIS.

Most employees (not just those with a contract of service) are entitled to a **minimum wage/living wage**, under the Minimum Wage Act 1998. Some people are not entitled under the Act, for example the self-employed, volunteers, students doing work as part of an undergraduate or post-graduate course and workers on certain government training schemes.

The hourly rates in 2019 were: £8.21 for workers aged 25 and over. This is a new banding introduced in 2016 and labelled the 'Living Wage' by the government. Workers aged 21–24 are paid £7.70; 18–20-year-olds are entitled to £6.15; under 18s get £4.35 and apprentices of any age get £3.90. Since October 2009 it has been illegal for an employer to use tips paid through payroll to make up the minimum wage.

A name and shame system was introduced in 2011 to deter employers from flouting their legal responsibilities on fair pay. Lists are published by the Department for Business, Energy and Industrial Strategy (BEIS) throughout the year. As well as being named, an employer may also be fined. Originally this was limited to a one-off fine of up to £20,000 but the Small Business, Enterprise and Employment Act (SBEEA) 2015, s 152 amends the Minimum Wage Act 1998 to make the fine payable per employee, so the bigger the employer the greater the penalty for flouting the law.

The employer has no right to make pay deductions unless, like income tax or National Insurance contributions, these are authorised by statute or agreed in writing with the employee. In practice, the contract of employment often provides for employer's deductions, and the employee thus waives the protection of the common law in this respect.

The obligation to pay the employee exists *whether or not the employer has provided work*. In general, there is no duty to provide work but, if the nature of the work means that the employee is likely to obtain a benefit other than payment from doing the work, the employer may be under a duty to provide work. For example, actors and other performers require the publicity that performance brings. Similarly, apprentices are entitled to the opportunity to practise the skills they have contracted to learn.

Zero hours contracts may enable an employer to avoid their obligation to pay for hours where no work was provided. It all depends on how the contract is structured; they vary greatly in their terms but do not create mutuality of obligation as they may require an employee to work on demand within the terms of the contract while not requiring an employer to pay if no work is provided. This is clearly contentious as at worst it fails to provide the employee with any financial security. Some employees find them a convenient means of fitting part-time working round caring or study commitments. Employers like them because of the flexibility it gives them to draw on a pool of labour according to need. Originally the use of such contracts was largely restricted to businesses with fluctuating seasonal demand, but they are now much more widespread. A number of high-profile businesses now use them, including Cineworld, Sports Direct, the Tate Gallery and Buckingham Palace. They have been taken up by the NHS and a number of local authorities.

The Office for National Statistics reported in 2018 that there were approximately 901,000 people on such contracts during the period September–December 2018. In 2016 there were 1.7 million people on such contracts and in 2014 approximately 670,000 on such contracts. The controversy surrounding the use of such contracts led BIS (now BEIS) to hold an enquiry; reform was recommended to redress the imbalance of power. The SBEEA 2015, s 153 bans exclusivity clauses in zero hours contracts. This means that an employer cannot tie an employee into a contract which prevents that employee from concurrently entering a contract with another employer. Further protection was provided by the government in 2015.

The exclusivity terms in Zero Hour Contracts (Redress) Regulations 2015

These regulations give protection to a worker (it is not limited to employees) on zero-hour contracts against unfair dismissal from day one of their employment. The service qualification required for a claim for unfair dismissal claims does not exist in these circumstances.

Dismissal is automatically unlawful if it is for breach of (unlawful) prohibition in their contract against working for a third party. Imposing any detriment on the employee for breaching such a prohibition is also unlawful.

Not to undermine the trust and confidence of the employee

In *Malik* v *BCCI* (1998) Lord Steyn held that the employer shall not, 'without reasonable and proper cause, conduct itself in a manner calculated or likely to destroy or seriously damage the relationship of confidence and trust between employer and employee'.

This is aimed at preventing the employer from indulging in unreasonable and abusive conduct towards the employee; and is reciprocal to the employee's duty to act in good faith. A wide variety of behaviour can give rise to a breach of this duty: for example, failing to provide extra support to staff at busy times (*White* v *London Transport Executive* (1982)), criticising a supervisor in front of employees who worked under him (*Associated Tyre Specialists* v *Waterhouse* (1976)), failure to protect an employee against harassment (*Bracebridge Engineering Ltd* v *Darby* (1990)).

Isle of Wight Tourist Board v *Coombes* (1976)

A manager, within earshot of the claimant who was his personal secretary, said to another employee: 'She is always an intolerable bitch on Monday mornings.' He did not attempt to apologise.

Held: his behaviour shattered a close and confidential working relationship thus undermining the employee's trust and confidence.

In *RDF Media Group plc* v *Alan Clements* (2007) Livesey QC held that while a press article vilifying the claimant (even if truthful) did amount to a breach of his employer's duty, deliberations by the board of directors discussing his character in very negative terms did not, because: 'the Board of Directors is the controlling mind of the Company and representations between individuals on the Board are merely equivalent to the Company thinking aloud to itself. It is not yet the law that an employer is prohibited from thinking even negative and unworthy thoughts about an employee on his payroll.'

Breach of this duty may be grounds for a claim that the employee has been *constructively* dismissed. If the employer's conduct is sufficiently serious, the employee is entitled to leave without giving notice and treat this as a dismissal for the purposes of bringing an unfair dismissal claim. (See Chapter 18.) However, the duty is a mutual one, so if the employee himself acted in breach of this duty prior to the alleged breach by the employer, he will not succeed in his claim. In *RDF Media Group plc* Clements lost his case for constructive dismissal since by taking a job with a competitor in breach of his contract with RDF he had already breached his own duty of loyalty and fidelity to RDF. His own breach had prompted the behaviour he complained of.

To provide safe working conditions

Employers must take all reasonable care to provide safe working conditions for their employees. Liability for breach of this duty is also imposed through the law of tort, both at common law and statute. In practice, actions for personal injury to employees are brought by an action in tort rather than for breach of contract. In the following section this is explained in that context.

The law of tort: employers' civil liability for industrial injuries

Two possible rights of action in tort may be open to an employee injured at work:

1 an action for breach of the employer's common law duty of care;
2 an action for breach of statutory duty.

Employers' common law liability

Non-delegable duty: a personal duty, liability for breach cannot be passed by requiring a third party to carry it out.

This is a **non-delegable duty**. This means that an employer cannot avoid liability merely by showing that a hazard has been created by a third party. The responsibility to maintain safety remains with the employer. Therefore, if independent contractors cause a spillage on which a member of the employer's staff slips and breaks a leg, the employer may be liable. The employee will have to prove that in the given circumstances, in a properly managed workplace, the employer would have ensured that the spillage was cleared up. Liability, therefore, is not strict, but requires an employer to take reasonable care to avoid reasonably foreseeable harm, as in a negligence action.

The common law duty comprises three interlinked obligations:

1 to provide competent staff;
2 to provide safe premises, plant and equipment;
3 to provide a safe system of work.

Competent staff

The employer must take reasonable care to ensure that its staff is competent to do their work so that they are not a danger to their fellow employees. Reasonable care must be taken in the selection, training, supervision and discipline of the workforce. The duty includes preventing hazards arising from activities that are not necessarily closely connected to the job in hand.

Hudson v Ridge Manufacturing Co. Ltd (1957)

An employee, who had previously been reprimanded more than once for such behaviour, injured a fellow employee when playing a practical joke.

Held: the employer was liable since it had been alerted to the fact that the employee was a potential danger by his previous mischievous behaviour and should have taken adequate steps to control him.

Safe premises, plant and equipment

This includes providing appropriate tools, machinery and materials maintained to an adequate standard. The premises must also be reasonably safe. In *Pagano* v *HGS* (1976) an employer which failed to maintain its vehicles in a safe condition, despite having been alerted to the problem by complaints from its workforce, was held liable for breach of duty.

Under the Employers' Liability (Defective Equipment) Act 1969, if equipment is defective due to the fault of a third party such as a manufacturer or repairer, the employer may be held liable even though it is not personally to blame and could not have known of the defect. The courts interpret 'equipment' purposively so any item or materials that employees are required to handle while carrying out their duties is usually covered. In *Knowles* v *Liverpool CC* (1993) a paving stone which shattered during installation was deemed to be work equipment.

A safe system of work

This encompasses a huge variety of activities. It includes providing protective clothing with instructions about its use, setting up safe working procedures and appropriate training, ensuring sufficient washing and first aid facilities, and appropriate use of warning signs.

Pennington v Surrey County Council and Surrey Fire & Rescue Services (2006, CA)

The claimant fire-fighter was injured when his finger got caught in the moving part of a power ram which he was using to assist in a motor accident rescue operation. He had not been trained to use such a heavy ram although he was used to operating a lighter model.

Held: the employer was in breach of his duty to the claimant by allowing him to use equipment that he had not been trained to use, in a stressful situation. This was not a safe system of work.

An employer's liability may arise from a mixture of breaches of these three interdependent duties. For example, a computer operator claiming repetitive strain injury might be able to prove (i) lack of proper equipment (the seating and desk not being at an appropriate height), and (ii) failure to maintain a safe system of work (if employees are required to use keyboards for lengthy periods without a proper break).

Real life

Sukhi works as an administrative officer for Smallville Borough Council. Recently she had a bad day at the office. On her way to a meeting with her boss, she tripped over some large packages left in a dark corner of a corridor by Jester, a new employee. Her hand was badly sprained and it was four weeks before she could use it fully.

The council appears potentially to be in breach of all three aspects of its duty as employer.

First, Jester does not appear to have been trained to an appropriate level of competence. If the corridor is so dark that obstructions are not readily spotted this amounts to failure to provide safe plant or equipment. Finally, leaving obstructions in a passage way may be evidence of failure to impose a safe system of work. Similarly, if the passage was dark because the lighting had not been appropriately checked for faults, this would also point to lack of a safe system of work.

Stress-related illness

Historically, claims against employers have been for physical injuries, but recently cases have come before the courts in which employers have been found liable for stress-related illness.

Walker v *Northumberland County Council* (1995)

The employers, who knew that Mr Walker had already suffered psychiatric illness due to stress at work, increased his workload. This caused the illness to recur so badly that he had to take early retirement. The judge, who awarded substantial damages, said that there was no difference in principle between mental and physical injury in the context of the employer's duty to provide reasonably safe working conditions.

Increasing numbers of similar claims have come before the courts since the decision in *Walker*.

In *Hatton* v *Sutherland* (2002) the Court of Appeal laid down guidelines which stressed the need to avoid imposing too great a burden on employers:

- No occupation should be regarded as intrinsically dangerous to mental health.
- The employer should be alerted to the risk to an employee when a reasonable employer would foresee that risk.
- Injury to health (not just emotional stress) must be reasonably foreseeable.
- It is reasonable for the employer to assume that the employee could cope with the level of stress normally associated with the job. Often it will be up to the employee to bring the issue to the employer's attention rather than suffering in silence.
- A breach of duty must be judged by the normal criteria: the magnitude of the risk, the gravity of harm and the practicability of taking precautions.
- If the only way to resolve the risk is to dismiss the employee, the employer will not be in breach if the employee is allowed to continue working.
- The duty can often be performed by the offer of counselling or other treatment.
- The issue of causation is often problematic for employees given that stress-related illness can come from a number of sources, not just the working environment.

Application of these principles by the House of Lords is illustrated by the following case:

Barber v *Somerset County Council* (2004, HL)

In 1995, restructuring took place at the school where Mr Barber worked and he was obliged to take on extra duties to enable him to continue at his current salary. In May 1996 he took three weeks' certificated sick leave due to anxiety and depression. When he returned to work, he met with the school's senior management team, which was unsupportive and did nothing to help him. Over the next three months, Mr Barber visited his GP on a number of occasions with stress-related issues and eventually left the school in November 1996 after losing control and shaking a pupil.

Held: the employer had a duty to take some action to assist the claimant, from the time it was put on notice of his condition. This occurred when he had met with senior staff. The employer had breached its duty by failing to make enquiries into his condition to discover what could be done to support him. It was irrelevant that all the staff were stressed and overworked because of the severe problems currently facing the school.

The employer had breached its duty by falling below the standard to be expected of a reasonable and prudent employer, and had not taken positive precautions to safeguard the safety of its employees, in the light of what it knew or ought reasonably to have known.

In *Yapp* v *Foreign & Colonial Office* (2015, CA) the Court of Appeal held that stress-related illness would generally be regarded as too remote a category of damage unless the claimant had evidenced signs of it previously to their claim or where the conduct of the employer was so extreme as to be likely to have such an effect on a person of reasonable robustness.

Civil liability for breach of statutory duty

Any criminal or administrative legislation, which does not expressly give rights to take action in tort for damages, may be treated by the courts as capable of doing so. This means that an employee who is the victim of an industrial accident or illness may be able to sue the employer for breach of a duty imposed on the employer by legislation designed primarily to impose public rather than civil law duties on an employer. The claimant will have to prove the following:

1 *The legislation gives the right to sue for damages.* The legislation may make this explicit one way or the other. Section 47 of the Health and Safety at Work, etc. Act 1974 clearly rules out an action for damages for breach of the employer's *general duty*; no action is possible here. However, s 47(2) states that action is possible for breach of any regulations made under the authority of the Act unless expressly excluded. Many successful actions imposing strict liability resulted from breaches of duties imposed by the Factories Act 1961 and subsequent related legislation. Breach and subsequent damage required proof, but not any fault by the employer. In recent years many of these duties have been replaced by regulations governing most aspects of workplace safety and derived from implementation of a whole raft of EC directives, for example the Management of Health and Safety at Work Regulations 1999. These have often proved a fertile ground for claims by injured employees and were resented by employers.

   The Enterprise and Regulatory Reform Act 2013 (E&RRA) amended s 47(2) to prevent liability unless the employee can prove that the employer was negligent, unless the relevant legislation specifies otherwise. The government claimed that this removed an unjust burden from employers. Parties representing employees argue that this will lower health and safety standards and prevent just claims. It is likely that this will in practice only affect claims against private sector employees; EU directives concerning health and safety legislation incorporated into English law still have a direct effect on the state and thus its public authorities. Therefore public service employees may be able to sue their employer for strict liability in circumstances where those in the private sector cannot.

2 *The employee is part of the class of persons protected by the legislation.* Sometimes legislation is very limited in its application. For example, breach of a regulation to protect a machine operator might not protect a different type of employee. In *Knapp* v *The Railway Executive* (1949) a train driver injured in an accident caused by failure to close level-crossing gates, was held not to be protected by legislation intended to protect members of the public.

3 *The defendant is in breach of the duty.* The extent of the duty is specified by the statute. It may be advantageous to sue under statute if the burden of proof is placed on the employer to show that he or she discharged the duty. The employee must prove fault by the employer unless the statute specifies otherwise.

Chipchase v *British Titan Products* (1956)

Building safety regulations required the provision of platforms of at least 34 inches wide when work was being conducted six-and-a-half feet above ground level. The claimant, who was working at a height of six feet, was injured when he fell from a platform which was only nine inches wide.

Held: he had no right to claim for breach of the regulations since he had been working six inches below the regulated height when the accident happened.

Provided the conditions above are fulfilled, the court is often prepared to interpret unspecific statutory terms purposively as a matter of policy and justice. In the next case it seems common sense that an employer should be responsible for its employee's safety while she was taking an appropriate route out of the building in which she worked and over which her employer had at least some control of health and safety.

Reid v *PRP Architects* (2007, CA)

Precious Reid was injured at the end of the working day, due to poor maintenance of a lift which she was using to vacate the multi-occupancy office building where her employer, PRP, was based, and which was in the common part of the building.

She argued that PRP was in breach of the Provision and Use of Work Equipment Regulations 1998, reg 5(1), which requires an employer to ensure work equipment is efficiently maintained and in good repair. Work equipment is defined (reg 3(2)) as 'any machinery, appliance, apparatus, tool or installation for work (whether exclusively or not)'.

Held: PRP was liable because a lift was capable of coming within the meaning of an 'installation' which was being used for work under the regulations. On the facts of this case, it was not appropriate to draw a line on the employer's liability at the point an employee left its offices to take the lift. It provided the main route out of the building.

Similarly, in *Spencer-Franks* v *Kellogg Brown & Root Ltd* (2008, HL) the claimant was injured when repairing a door closer in an oilrig control room. The House of

Lords held that if an item was used at work it was work equipment and everyone using the control room door used it for the purpose of their work. The regulations (and the directive on which they were based) in no way suggested that repairing should be interpreted narrowly or deprived of its ordinary meaning. Here, the ordinary meaning was that the door closer was work equipment. The employer's argument that the door closer was part of the premises, was not workable. The fact that Mr Spencer had been repairing the door at the time of his accident meant that he still was using the necessary component in order to do his job.

Worth thinking about?

What other civil action was open to Precious Reid? (See *Reid* v *PRP Architects* (2006).)

Suggested solutions can be found in Appendix 2.

Criminal law regulation of safety in the workplace

Since the Factories Act 1802, the welfare of employees has increasingly been regulated by statute as well as by the common law. In recent years the UK's membership of the EC has led to an increase in development of the law in this area.

The Health and Safety at Work, etc. Act 1974 was intended to implement a general policy of integrated statutory control of health and safety in the workplace. Powers are delegated under the Act to enable the Department of Employment (now the Department for Work and Pensions (DWP)) to make regulations covering specific areas of workplace safety. The Act was an important development in three respects:

1 it imposed general duties on both employers and employees to maintain health and safety;

2 it created the Health and Safety Executive, with powers to enforce the legislation;

3 it gave wide powers to the Department of Employment to make detailed legally binding regulations to cover particular hazards.

The employer's and employee's statutory duties

The employer's general duty to employees: s 2

Employers have a duty 'to ensure as far as is reasonably practicable the health, safety and welfare of all their employees'. (This means only those under a contract of service to an employer.) Employers are not made strictly liable by the 1974 Act. They are responsible only if they have failed to take *reasonably practicable* precautions. This has been criticised for its vagueness. It is very similar to the common law duty of reasonable care, but the reference to practicability indicates that the resources of employers may be relevant in judging how much can be expected of them.

The scope of the duty is spelt out in s 2 and encompasses particular areas of employer responsibility that closely mirror the employer's common law duty in tort.

The employee's duty: s 7

Employees are also placed under a two-part duty:

1 to take reasonable care for their own health and safety and for that of others likely to be affected by their acts and omissions at work;

2 to cooperate with the employer as far as is necessary to enable it to carry out its legal responsibilities.

The employer's duty to persons other than employees: s 3

Section 3 places the employer under a duty to conduct its business as far as practicable in a way that does not endanger persons other than employees who might be affected by it. This includes independent contractors, as well as visitors to the premises. Section 3 imposes a similar duty on self-employed persons. The s 3 duty is a negative requirement not to expose them to risks, compared with the positive duty in s 2 'to ensure as far as practicable'.

Health and safety policies: s 2

The 1974 Act seeks to ensure that employees are involved in and kept informed about health and safety provision in their workplace. An employer with a workforce of five or more must have a written health and safety policy and ensure that this is kept up to date and brought to the attention of the employees. A workplace safety committee must assist in the process. The employer must consult health and safety representatives from trade unions if required by BEIS regulations.

The powers of the Health and Safety Executive (HSE)

HSE inspectors are given wide powers to enter and investigate workplaces and to enforce sanctions under the 1974 Act; and this has been widened by other subsequent legislation, for example, the Management of Health and Safety at Work Regulations 1999.

The HSE has the following powers:

Prosecution of any offence specified in the Act

Offences may arise not only from breach of duty, but also from obstruction of the inspectors.

The Health and Safety (Offences) Act 2008, which came into force in January 2009, empowered the Magistrates' Court to impose a fine of up to £20,000 and a prison sentence of up to 12 months. The cap on fines was removed in 2015. The Crown Court already had the power to impose an unlimited fine, but since January 2009 it may impose a prison sentence of up to two years. Certain offences which previously could only be tried in the Magistrates' Court are now triable in either the Crown Court or Magistrates' Court, which increases the possibility of a heavier penalty for more offences.

Improvement notices: s 21

If in an inspector's view the statute is being breached and this state of affairs is likely to continue, the inspector may issue a notice requiring the contravention to be corrected within specified time limits. Compliance may be enforced by prosecution if necessary.

Prohibition notices: s 23

If the inspector believes that the way the business is being conducted is likely to result in serious personal injury, a prohibition notice may be issued. This prohibits continuance of the relevant activity until the situation is resolved. These notices have to set out clearly the nature of the problem and may include advice about how it can be remedied. Section 24 gives rights to appeal against an order to an employment tribunal.

Ministerial regulations

The 1974 Act empowers the Department of Employment (now BEIS) to make specific regulations to ensure performance of duties under the Act. Progress was initially slow in this area, but the need to comply with EC directives issued between 1989 and 1991 forced the Department to issue the Management of Health and Safety at Work Regulations 1992. These came into force progressively between 1993 and 1997 and replace most of the provisions of statutes like the Factories Acts and the Offices, Shops and Railway Premises Act 1963. These regulations expand the scope of obligations imposed on employers by the Health and Safety at Work etc., Act 1974, since they incorporate aspects of EC law not envisaged by the 1974 Act.

Chapter summary

A business is served both by employees and independent contractors and has different contractual relationships with each.

The *contract of service* governs the relationship of employer and employee. It is valid without writing but ERA 1996 requires an employer to provide each employee with a written statement of the key terms.

It contains express and implied terms which may be derived from:

(a) custom and practice;

(b) works/staff rules;

(c) collective agreements;

(d) statute and common law.

Common law duties of employee:

(a) reasonable care and skill to fulfil all reasonable orders;

(b) good faith (confidentiality, account for profits, no conflict of interest).

Common law duties of employer:

(a) payment;

(b) trust and confidence;

(c) safe working conditions.

Employer's liability for injuries at work

Civil liability: common law duty.
The employer has a non-delegable duty to take reasonable care to provide reasonably safe working conditions including:

(a) competent staff;

(b) safe plant and equipment;

(c) safe systems of work.

Breach of statutory duty

An employee may also sue an employer for failing to perform a statutory duty provided:

(a) Parliament intended a civil remedy to be possible (can the statute be interpreted like this?);

(b) the employee is a member of the class protected by the statute;

(c) the employer has breached the statute;

(d) damage has resulted from the breach.

Criminal liability

May arise under a variety of regulations and the HSWA 1974.
The HSE is empowered to enter premises, issue improvement orders and prosecute employers.

Review questions 16

1 What are the main differences in the legal obligations of an employer to an employee and to an independent contractor?

2 What must the s 1 written statement of the Employment Rights Act 1996 (ERA 1996) include?

3 Identify the main sources of contractual terms.

4 Angelica is employed by Juniper plc as personal assistant to the managing director. What contractual duties may Angelica have breached in the following circumstances?

   (a) She takes an evening job with Coltsfoot Ltd.
   (b) When serving refreshments at a meeting at Juniper plc, she drops a full coffee pot into the lap of Lupin, the chairman of the board.
   (c) After the meeting, Hawksbeard, a visiting consultant, who had enjoyed Lupin's discomfiture, gives Angelica a £10 tip.

5 Heather, who is employed by Rush, was run over on work premises by a forklift truck driven by Bogbean. Her injuries were aggravated by difficulties in locating the first aid kit. What are Rush's liabilities?

6 What powers are available to HSE inspectors who discover that a health and safety offence has been committed?

Answers to all review questions can be found in Appendix 2.

Advanced questions 16

(A) Examine what distinguishes employees from other types of workers. Why is that distinction important?

(B) Critically assess the importance of implied contractual terms in employment law.

Answers to the advanced questions can be found at **go.pearson.com/uk/he/resources.**

Take a closer look

The following cases provide important examples of how the law in this chapter has developed. They are primary sources illustrating the law in action and give more detail about their facts, as well as helping to understand the law and to appreciate how the judges reached their decisions.

Try looking them up in the law reports or accessing them via a database, e.g. BAILII (www.bailii.org/databases.html). LexisNexis or Westlaw may be available in the university or college library, or extracts may be found in a case book. (See Appendix 1: Additional resources.)

Hudson v *Ridge Manufacturing Co. Ltd* [1957] 2 QB 348

RDF Media Group plc v *Alan Clements* [2007] EWHC 2892 (QB); [2008] IRLR 207

Reid v *PRP Architects* [2006] EWCA Civ 1119; [2007] ICR 78

Spencer-Franks v *Kellogg Brown & Root Ltd* [2008] UKHL 46; [2008] ICR 86

Further reading

Lockwood, G., Henderson, C., and Thornicroft, G. (2017) An Assessment of Employer Liability for Workplace Stress. *International Journal of Law and Management.* **59**(2), pp.1–15.

Web activity

Click on 'News' on the HSE website and check out 'health and safety myths' to see some of the dafter ideas falsely attributed to health and safety requirements: www.hse.gov.uk

Assignment 15

Employment protection legislation is largely confined to those working in a traditional employment relationship. This is an inadequate basis for those working in atypical employment.

Analyse this statement with particular reference to recent parliamentary reports and those working in the gig economy.

Rights at work:
Protection against discrimination in employment

Learning objectives

On completion of this chapter, students should be able to:

★ appreciate the scope of legal protection under the EA 2010 in relation to employment;

★ understand what is encompassed by the 'protected characteristics';

★ define the nature of behaviour prohibited under the Act;

★ grasp the difference between direct and indirect discrimination;

★ understand the notion of 'occupational qualifications';

★ describe the functions of the Commission for Equality and Human Rights.

Introduction

The Equality Act (EA 2010) has brought the law relating to unlawful discrimination within the compass of one statute, and aims to create a harmonised body of law from the patchwork of previous legislation, which developed in a piecemeal fashion from the middle of the twentieth century. It covers all aspects of discrimination law, including education and services, but this chapter focuses solely on discrimination in the workplace.

The Act repeals, re-states and to some extent simplifies the provisions of the previous legislation in this area and creates some new obligations for employers. The law generally remains the same in substance, so existing case law must therefore be regarded as valid unless the Act or subsequent litigation indicates to the contrary. Any statutory references in this chapter are to the EA 2010 unless stated otherwise.

The Equality Act 2010: the core provisions

This part of the chapter will examine the operation of the central provisions of the EA 2010, which state who is covered by the provisions and the nature of conduct made illegal by EA 2010 and relevant claims available.

The protected characteristics: s 4

Protected characteristic: designation of a person or group protected against less favourable treatment under the EA 2010.

This section lists the areas of discrimination protection covered by the Act which are described as '**protected characteristics**'. They are: age, disability, gender re-assignment, marriage and civil partnership, pregnancy and maternity, race, religion and belief, sex and sexual orientation.

Prohibited conduct

This is behaviour which is unlawful under the Act: direct and indirect discrimination, harassment and victimisation.

Direct discrimination: s 13

Section 13 states that 'a person (A) discriminates against another (B) if, because of a protected characteristic, A treats B less favourably than A treats or would treat others'.

It occurs where A treats B less favourably because of B's protected characteristic than he would treat others without that characteristic. The definition includes *discrimination by association* (treating one person unfavourably because of their association with another person who does have a protected characteristic) or *perception* (treating someone unfavourably because of an incorrect and maybe stereotypical belief about their attributes, abilities, beliefs, etc. relating to a protected characteristic).

This largely mirrors previous equality legislation, although before the Act, associative discrimination could not be claimed in cases involving age, disability, gender re-assignment or sexual discrimination. Perceptive discrimination did not apply to disability, gender re-assignment and sexual discrimination claims.

There is no defence to **direct discrimination** except on the grounds of occupational requirement.

Direct discrimination: openly treating an employee less favourably than others because of a protected characteristic.

Combined discrimination: s 14

This is mentioned in the Act but not yet law. This occurs 'if, because of a combination of two relevant protected characteristics, A treats B less favourably than A treats or would treat a person who does not share either of those characteristics'. For example, a person might allege that they were discriminated against simultaneously because of their race and disability. However, in March 2011, the government announced that this section would not be implemented on the grounds of cost to, and over-regulation of, employers. This means that a person who is claiming for sex and race discrimination will have to bring two separate claims. This is a serious weakness in the law, which denies a person protection from an important form of discrimination.

Indirect discrimination: s 19

This arises 'if A applies to B a provision, criterion or practice (PCP) which is discriminatory in relation to a relevant protected characteristic of B'.

In other words, this would put B at a disadvantage compared with others who do not share the protected characteristic. For example, a minimum height restriction as a criterion for a job may be judged as indirectly discriminatory on the grounds of sex, as men are on average taller than women and so would put a large number of women at a disadvantage. Unlike direct discrimination, an employer who indirectly discriminates might raise a defence. The defence of justification applies when the employer can show that the practice is a *proportional* response to a *legitimate aim* in the particular circumstances (s 19(2)(d)).

While this section clearly reflects the previous legislation, it extends protection to disabled and transgender people.

Comparators: s 23

Liability in all cases of direct or indirect discrimination is determined by comparing the defendant's treatment of the claimant with that of an actual or hypothetical person who does not share their protected characteristics. So an employer will, for instance, be liable if they treat a person with a disability in a way that puts them at a disadvantage compared with an able-bodied person doing similar work.

Irrelevance of alleged discriminator's characteristics: s 24

The fact that A, who has allegedly discriminated against B, has the same protected characteristic as B is irrelevant to determining liability. So, for example, a woman may be liable for acting in a discriminatory way to another woman.

Occupational requirement: Schedule 9, s 1

Discrimination may be legal if the defendant can show that the nature of the job makes it essential to restrict employment to people of a certain characteristic. For example, it would be reasonable on the grounds of authenticity to advertise jobs as a waiter in a Chinese restaurant to people of Chinese ethnicity. This is the only justification available to a claim of direct discrimination.

Other prohibited conduct

All the following behaviour was unlawful under the previous legislation but is newly defined in the Act.

Harassment: s 26

There are three types:

Harassment:
verbal/non-verbal behaviour which creates an intimidating/ hostile/degrading/ offensive environment and is intended/has the effect of violating a person's dignity.

1 unwanted conduct related to the claimant's gender which has the intention or effect of violating their dignity or 'creating an intimidating, hostile, degrading, humiliating or offensive environment';

2 unwanted conduct of a sexual nature that has the same intention or effect as in 1 above;

3 less favourable treatment or **harassment** on the grounds of sexual or gender reassignment. A contentious provision imposing liability on the employer for harassment by a third party (anyone other than an employee – such as a customer or a supplier) was later repealed by the Employment and Regulatory Reform Act 2013.

Evans v Xactly (2018)

Mr Evans, a salesman, was subject to a variety of derogatory remarks from co-workers, including being referred to as 'fat ginger pikey'. However, it was held that this comment did not qualify as harassment in accordance with s 26 of the Equality Act. While the tribunal accepted that at face value the comment is a potentially discriminatory and harassing remark the context of the workplace needed to be considered. The comment was not unwanted because Mr Evans participated in and was comfortable with the workplace culture and banter.

Evans v *Xactly* might be considered a surprising decision, and employers should remain vigilant about workplace banter and take action against inappropriate remarks or conduct.

Victimisation: s 27

This protects anyone who has asserted their rights under the EA or someone supporting them from subsequent unfavourable treatment by their employer. There is no need to find a comparator to determine liability but the victim must have suffered some detriment.

Vicarious liability: s 109

An employer may be vicariously liable for the torts of their employees working under a contract of service or an agent with the authority of the principal (see Chapter 17). This common law principle was replicated in the previous equality legislation and repeated in the EA and extended to cover any breach of the Act.

It is no defence that the employer or principal did not know about the discriminatory behaviour (s 109(3)), although the employer will not be liable if they took 'all reasonable steps' to prevent it. In such circumstances a claimant may sue the offending claimant directly (s 110).

Potential claimants and defendants

The employment provisions of the Act generally cover anybody in or seeking work, not necessarily under a contract of service. It therefore not only covers employees in the strict sense but also job applicants, the self-employed with a contract for services, workers, and also for example agents, agency workers, apprentices, partners or prospective partners, barristers' pupils, people in work experience placements and police personnel. Members of the armed forces are included but enjoy only limited protection. It does not cover volunteers (*X* v *Mid Sussex Citizens Advice Bureau* (2013, SC)).

In this chapter, for ease of expression, all potential claimants will generally be referred to as 'employees'. Similarly, those for whom they are working will be referred to as 'employers'. An employee who commits a breach of duty under the Act is personally liable and therefore may also be a defendant (s 110).

The operation of the Equality Act 2010

This part of the chapter explains the protected characteristics in more detail and illustrates the way the Equality Act is likely to operate in practice with reference to case law and examples. Revisiting the definitions of prohibited behaviour and other concepts explained above may prove useful, since, to avoid repetition, these are not spelt out in relation to each protected characteristic. It may be assumed that they apply unless the contrary is stated.

Age

Until the Employment Equality (Age) Regulations 2006 (implementing the Equal Treatment Amendment Directive (2002/73/EC)) came into force on 1 October 2006, age discrimination was legal under English law. In its core principles explained above, the EA 2010 largely replicates the protection given by the Regulations but protects people of any age, while the regulations only gave protection to people up to 65 years old.

The definition of the protected characteristic of age: s 5

Where the Act refers to the protected characteristic of age, it means a person in a particular age group. Such a group includes people of the same age and people of a particular range of ages. When people fall in the same age group they share the protected characteristic of age. For example, 18-year-olds or 50-year-olds are two different age groups but an over-60s age group includes anybody of 60 upwards.

The comparator (s 23) in age discrimination cases would be someone from a different age group from the claimant who is treated more favourably for that reason.

Prohibited behaviour

Direct discrimination and indirect discrimination: ss 13 and 19

The next case is a good example of indirect discrimination.

Baker v National Air Services Ltd (2009)

The defendant employer refused to allow Mr Baker, aged 50, to train as an air traffic controller. It claimed that the age limit of 35 was a legitimate and proportionate aim, because of safety concerns and the need for applicants to be in the job sufficiently long to justify the cost of training.

Held: the defendant had committed indirect discrimination: the defendant's aim was legitimate but not proportionate. It reflected 'the received wisdom that air traffic controllers must start young and older individuals will not be suitable'. The existing safety precautions were sufficient in themselves, as they ensured scrutiny of all employees' health at all times and further restriction was superfluous. Such an arbitrary universal age ban was unreasonable: it would unnecessarily prejudice older applicants.

The introduction of the Employment Equality (Age) Regulations 2006 was largely prompted by concerns about discrimination against older people. However, one of the first cases brought under the regulations concerned a young woman.

Thomas v Eight Members Club and Killip (2007)

Megan Thomas, aged 19, was sacked from her job as membership secretary of an exclusive City club after four months. The managers told her that she was too young to deal appropriately with the club's clientele. The tribunal held that she was the victim of direct discrimination and awarded her a compensation for hurt feelings, which was all that was required, as she had mitigated her loss by immediately obtaining better paid employment with a City firm.

Canadian Imperial Bank of Commerce v Beck (2010)

Achim Beck was 42 when his employers claimed that they were making him redundant from his job as marketing director and then replaced him with someone of 38.

The Employment Appeal Tribunal affirmed that Mr Beck had been dismissed on account of his age because of proof of instructions from the employer to an employment agency stating that it wanted to head-hunt 'a younger entrepreneurial profile'. This raised sufficient evidence of age discrimination to shift the burden of proof to the bank, which had not proved that the question of age was sufficiently significant. Indeed, the bank's evidence did not appear genuine, but more a rationalisation after the event. Mr Beck had suffered both direct and indirect discrimination.

Occupational qualification: Schedule 9(1)

It may be a good defence to an employer if they can prove that it is appropriate to appoint someone in a particular age group. For example in a dramatic production, because it is essential to the integrity of the production, casting an older actor to play King Lear.

Retirement age

The Employment Equality Age Regulations prevented compulsory retirement at 65 (men) or 60 (women), stating that this was the default retirement age (DRA). People wishing to continue working after that could *request* their employer for an extension.

A government review concluded in 2010 that the DRA should be abolished for both men and women. This coincided with government plans to raise the age of entitlement to the state retirement pension. The Employment Equality (Repeal of Retirement Age Provisions) Regulations 2011 were subsequently passed, which abolished the DRA from April 2011, and EA 2010 was amended to mirror this change.

Although there is no longer a default retirement age, an employer may be entitled to impose retirement, as long as this requirement is a 'proportionate means of achieving a legitimate aim' under the EA, s 13(2). Some guidance in determining this provision in such cases was provided by the Supreme Court in 2012.

Selsdon v Clarkson Wright (2012, SC)

The Supreme Court held that the following criteria must be taken into account:

1 *Social policy.* It may be reasonable for an employer to impose a retirement age in the interest of 'intergenerational fairness'. This means ensuring a wide age range of employees with equal opportunity of promotion and

advancement within the business. It also enables the employer to retain able, younger staff members who otherwise might be tempted to seek better opportunities elsewhere. Only broad social policy considerations are relevant to deciding whether direct discrimination on the basis of age is justified under s 13(2). Particular concerns of the employer such as saving money or upping competition are not relevant (although they may be in cases of indirect discrimination under s 19(2)).

2 *Dignity of the employee.* Imposition of a retirement age may enable an employer to ease out older workers who have become incompetent or who are under-achieving. This is preferable to a formal dismissal which might result in litigation.

It can be seen that the Supreme Court's criteria are by their nature rather wide and ambiguous. The particular facts of each individual case will be crucial.

Harassment and victimisation: ss 26, 27 and 40

Employees with the protected characteristic of age now enjoy full protection against harassment and victimisation.

Disability

Disability:
physical/mental impairment having substantial long-term adverse effect on a person's ability to do his or her job.

The **Disability** Discrimination Act 1995 (DDA), with amendments, governed the rights to equal treatment of people with disabilities prior to 2010. Protection has been clarified and increased by the EA 2010.

The protected characteristic of disability

This is defined by s 6(1) of EA 2010, which states:

1 A person (P) has a disability if:
   (a) P has a physical or mental impairment, and
   (b) the impairment has a substantial and long-term adverse effect on P's ability to carry out normal day-to-day activities.

This rather superficial definition is clarified by Schedule 1 to the EA 2010 and largely replicates the DDA definition. However, the EA does not require proof that the impairment affects a specific capacity, such as hearing, mobility or eyesight, which should make it easier for claimants to prove that their disability is covered by the Act.

What is 'impairment'?

Guidance issued by the Department for Work and Pensions (DWP) indicates that the words 'physical or mental impairment' should be given their usual meaning. Previous litigation is also relevant to deciding this. Therefore, to give rise to liability, the impairment must be medically recognised and relate, for example, to mobility, manual dexterity, eyesight, hearing, memory, concentration or comprehension. Progressive conditions are also included (e.g., multiple sclerosis, HIV/AIDS). Severe disfigurement such as birthmarks, scars, skin diseases may be a disability. Some previous case examples include asthma (*Cox* v *Post Office* (1997)); soft tissue injuries (*O'Neill* v *Symm & Co. Ltd* (1998)); acute abdominal pain (*Howden* v *Capital Copiers* (1998)); recurrent infections (*Sussex Partnership NHS Foundation Trust* v *Norris* (2012)); type 2 diabetes (*Taylor* v *Ladbrokes Betting & Gaming Ltd* (2016)) and pre-cancerous lesions (*Lofy* v *Harris T/A (2018)*). Mental impairment includes clinical depression, bi-polar disease and learning difficulties.

In 2014 the ECJ held that discrimination on the grounds of obesity is not necessarily unlawful (*Kaltoft* v *Billund* (2014, ECJ)). However, it could be unlawful if the obesity gives rise to long-lasting physical or psychological impairment which hinders 'the full and effective participation of the person concerned in professional life on an equal basis with other workers'. This ruling was applied in *Bickerstaff* v *Butcher NIIT* (2015) where it was held that the claimant had suffered harassment arising from his morbidly obese condition.

Certain conditions, such as addiction to alcohol, nicotine and other similar substances are not covered, although it is possible to claim if such a condition triggers a statutory impairment. In *Power* v *Panasonic* (2002), the Employment Appeals Tribunal (EAT) held that because the claimant had clinical depression, it was irrelevant whether she was depressed because she was an alcoholic or had become an alcoholic because she was depressed.

The effect of the impairment must be 'substantial', which means that a person's ability to carry out ordinary daily tasks must be considerably inhibited compared with people without the impairment. So, for example, the DWP guidance suggests that the length of time taken to complete the task, the means necessary to achieve it and its cumulative effect on the claimant are relevant. For example, someone with asthma could successfully claim that its effect was substantial if it took them much longer to climb a flight of stairs than an able-bodied colleague who did not have to pause to catch their breath every few steps and use their inhaler to recover from severe breathlessness once they had got to the top. Recurrence is also a relevant issue.

How long is 'long term'?

Schedule 1, para 9 says that the disability should have lasted, or be expected to last, for at least 12 months.

Prohibited conduct

Direct discrimination

The EA 2010 core provisions concerning direct discrimination (s 13), which includes discrimination by perception and by association, are basically similar in scope to those in the DDA and give rise to liability if their effect is to treat a disabled person less favourably than someone who is able-bodied.

In this context, discrimination by perception relates to general incorrect assumptions about the nature of the relevant disability. It would include, for example, refusing to shortlist a severely visually impaired person for a job involving computers, in the belief that this disability would automatically render the applicant incapable of using the computer.

A new development under the EA 2010 is the inclusion of discrimination by association. This occurs where an able-bodied person claims that they have suffered discrimination because of their connection to someone with a disability. This corrects the problem that arose in *Coleman* v *Attridge Law* (2008), where Ms Coleman claimed that she had been discriminated against on the grounds of her son's disability, because her employers refused her the flexible working hours that she needed in order to cope both with her job and her responsibilities as his carer. She won her case only when, in compliance with the judgment of the ECJ, the EAT found in her favour by interpreting the DDA in accordance with the relevant EC directive.

Under s 13(3) it is not unlawful to treat a disabled person *more* favourably than able-bodied colleagues.

The occupational requirement exception: Schedule 9(1)

This may be exceptions where direct discrimination is not unlawful. For example, a flawless complexion may reasonably be required to advertise facial cosmetics, so a person with a severe facial disfigurement might reasonably be rejected for that job.

Consequential unfavourable treatment: s 15

This is a new provision, relevant only to people with a disability. It makes it illegal knowingly to treat a person unfavourably because of anything arising *as a consequence of that person's disability*, provided this is not a *proportionate means of achieving a legitimate aim*. A person is treated unfavourably if put at a disadvantage. For example, a person being treated for cancer might need to take more sick leave than other, fitter colleagues. It would be discriminatory to dismiss her for that reason because it is a result of her disability.

Indirect discrimination

The EA 2010 (s 19(3)) extends this to cover people with disabilities.

It occurs if an unjustifiable 'provision, criterion or practice' (PCP), applied to everyone, particularly disadvantages people who share the disabled person's disability compared to others who do not. Proving that the discriminatory behaviour is a proportionate means of achieving a legitimate aim is a good defence. Thus, prescribing rigorous physical fitness criteria for fire-fighters may be justifiable.

Comparators: s 23

To determine whether a claimant has been unfairly treated, a comparison exercise must be carried out to decide whether another person without the claimant's impairment but with the same abilities or skills would have been treated in the same way.

Note that no **comparator** is needed when determining consequential discrimination (s 15).

Comparator: an actual or hypothetical person with whom the claimant is compared who does not share their protected characteristic.

The duty to make reasonable adjustments: s 20

This requires the employer to ensure that a person with a disability is not put at a 'substantial disadvantage' compared with able-bodied employees. The duty can be divided into three areas:

(a) *Adjustments to working arrangements.* For example, allowing an employee caring for a person with a disability to work flexible hours.

(b) *Making physical alterations to the premises.* It might be appropriate to install a ramp for a wheelchair user.

(c) *Provision of aids to facilitate carrying out employment duties.*

Tarling v Wisdom Toothbrushes (1997)

Ms Tarling had a club foot, which made it difficult for her to stand for long periods. This impaired her work performance, which led to her dismissal.

Held: her dismissal was discriminatory and due to the failure of the employer to make reasonable adjustments. Her employer knew that a special chair was available, on four weeks' free trial at a subsidised cost which reduced the price to £200, but took no steps to obtain one.

Failure to make reasonable adjustments amounts to discrimination: s 21

What is reasonable is dependent on the circumstances and any changes must be proportional not only to the needs of the employee but also to the employer. The size and nature of the business and its premises must be taken into account and expense is a factor to be considered, though not necessarily decisive. The Code of Practice issued by the Department of Work and Pensions (DWP) suggests that the cost of appointing and training a new employee may be an appropriate indication of the cost of the adjustment. Issues of health and safety are also relevant.

Occasionally there may be nothing an employer can reasonably do to enable an employee to work. In *Dyer* v *London Ambulance NHS Trust* (2014, EAT) the claimant, who worked in a large control room with numerous staff, often visited by members of the public, became acutely allergic to aerosol sprays and perfume. The employer notified staff repeatedly about the need to avoid use of these but the order did not have the necessary effect and the claimant suffered five attacks of anaphylactic shock, requiring hospitalisation. The fifth attack was almost fatal. At this point the employer dismissed the claimant on the grounds of incapability. She claimed discrimination. The EAT held that no discrimination had occurred as there was nothing more her employers could reasonably do to accommodate her disability.

Enquiries about disability and health: s 60

This is a new provision. Previously, an employer was able, legally, to ask such questions prior to, or at, a job interview, but not to discriminate against an applicant in response to their answer. This new provision is intended to add transparency to the recruitment process and prevent information about health and ability from acting as a disincentive to the employer at this stage. Under s 60, an employer generally must *not* ask a job applicant about their health or disability prior to offering them a job.

Such questions can only be asked:

(a) to find out whether the applicant would be able to participate in an assessment to test their suitability for the job;

(b) to make reasonable adjustments to enable the disabled person to take part in the recruitment process;

(c) to find out whether a job applicant would be able to cope with functions intrinsic to the job, with any reasonable adjustments;

(d) to monitor diversity in the appointments process;

(e) to support positive action in employment for disabled people; and

(f) to assist an employer where there is a genuine occupational requirement for the person to be disabled.

While on the face of it this appears to be an improvement on the DDA provisions, it is questionable whether the information given under the exception rule may not sometimes lead to a biased response.

Gender re-assignment

The protected characteristic of gender re-assignment (s 7) includes both male to female and female to male transsexuals and is continuous from the time they decide that they wish to change gender and live as a member of the opposite sex, whether or not they are undergoing or have undergone medical treatment. This increases the previous rights under the Sex Discrimination Act 1975 (as amended by the Sex

Discrimination (Gender Re-assignment) Regulations 2007), which only protected a transsexual person who was undergoing or had previously undergone relevant medical treatment. Now the process of moving from one gender to another is perceived as personal rather than medical. There is no obligation to tell an employer of the status but it may be appropriate to ensure that arrangements are made to avoid unfavourable treatment.

Prohibited behaviour

In addition to the usual protection against direct discrimination under s 13, protection against indirect discrimination (s 19) has been extended to transgender people.

They are also protected by s 16, which states that it is discrimination to treat someone absent from work due to gender assignment treatment less favourably than anyone else taking sick leave.

Transsexuals also now enjoy full protection against harassment and victimisation.

Occupational requirement defence

Under Schedule 9, para 1(3), if an employer can show that *not* being a transsexual is an occupational qualification for a job, less favourable treatment may be justified as long as the employer proves that this is a proportionate and justifiable means of pursuing a legitimate aim. For example, a pre-operative male to female transsexual man could legitimately be refused employment as a female model for nude life-drawing classes.

The Gender Recognition Act 2004

This enables transsexuals to apply at least two years after transition for a gender recognition certificate that gives them full legal recognition of their change of gender. They may also obtain a new birth certificate reflecting the change. Generally a birth certificate is sufficient for most employment purposes. An employer should not legitimately need to require sight of a gender recognition certificate more than once. Additional requests may amount to harassment.

Marriage and civil partnership

The protected characteristic

Any person who is currently married or is currently in a civil partnership has this protected characteristic (s 8) and is entitled not to be treated unfavourably because of it.

The Marriage (Same Sex Couples) Act 2014 extended rights to civil marriage to LGBT couples.

Dunn v Institute of Cemetery and Crematorium Management (2011, EAT)

Ms D claimed marital discrimination in breach of the Sex Discrimination Act 1975, s 3 (now EA, s 8) on the grounds that she had been treated unfavourably by the defendant employer because she was married to Mr Dunn, who was also in dispute with the defendant, before her own difficulties at work had begun.

Held: she had the right to claim. Correct interpretation of the law (in accordance with the ECHR Articles 8, 12, and 14) covered situations where discrimination had arisen, not just because the claimant was married, but because of whom she was married to.

Marriage includes any form of marriage regarded as legal under UK law.

Prohibited behaviour

Indirect discrimination is prohibited, but people with this protected characteristic only have a claim for basic direct discrimination, not for discrimination by perception and association. They are protected against victimisation but not harassment. However, members of a civil partnership or same-sex marriage could claim harassment on the grounds of their protected characteristic of sexual orientation.

Occupational qualification: essential personal requirement for a job which may permit employer to discriminate against those employees who lack it.

Occupational qualification defence

Under Schedule 9, para 1(3), if an employer can show that *not* being married or not being in a civil partnership is an **occupational qualification** for a job, less favourable treatment may be justified as long as the employer proves that this is a proportionate and justifiable means of pursuing a legitimate aim.

Pregnancy and maternity

Pregnancy and maternity is listed in s 4 with the other protected characteristics.

Anti-discrimination rights in this area remain virtually the same as they were before the Act, under the Sex Discrimination Act 1975 and related legislation. These rights are derived from EU law, which includes the Pregnant Workers Directive (92/85/EEC) and the amended Equal Treatment Directive (2006/54/EC).

A woman enjoys a protected status in relation to unfavourable treatment at work during pregnancy and for a limited time afterwards. This gives her special protection while pregnant or on maternity leave, in addition to that covered by other relevant aspects of the protected characteristics.

Prohibited behaviour

The 'protected period'

Unfavourable treatment of a woman because of her pregnancy, or because of illness resulting from or relating to her being on maternity leave is illegal if it takes place during '**the protected period**' (s 18(2)). Such treatment includes dismissal (*Webb* v *EMO Cargo (No. 2)* (1995)), demotion and refusal of training opportunities.

Protected period: period of protection for a woman while pregnant or on maternity leave.

The protected period starts when a woman becomes pregnant and continues until the end of her maternity leave, or when she returns to work if that happens sooner (s 18(6)). During this time liability is strict, the employer's motivation or intention is irrelevant and a comparator is not necessary to determine liability.

Once the protected period is over any further claim of unfavourable treatment is treated as one of gender discrimination, unless it arises from a decision made during the protected period (s 18(5)).

Direct and indirect discrimination: ss 13 and 19

A woman with this protected characteristic may claim direct or indirect discrimination under s 18, but not discrimination by perception or association.

Note, however, that any employee who is treated less favourably through associating with a pregnant woman, or a woman who has recently given birth, may claim for sex discrimination. This would protect, for example, a member of the woman's family who provides care to the woman after the birth.

Victimisation

Section 18(4) covers victimisation during the protected period arising from unfavourable treatment caused by her exercising her rights to maternity leave.

Harassment

There is no specific protection against harassment for women with this protected characteristic but the sex discrimination provisions of the Act (see above) are relevant.

Race

The EA 2010 largely replicates the Race Relations Act (as amended) in prohibiting discrimination on the grounds of race.

The protected characteristic: s 9

Race includes (s 9(1)):

- colour;
- nationality;
- ethnic or national origins.

A person with this protected characteristic will be a member of a racial group (s 9(2)). A racial group may consist of two or more distinct racial groups (s 9(4)).

The interpretation of these terms

Nationality

Nationality indicates a person's legal relationship to the state in which they were born or of which they became a citizen through naturalisation. It determines their voting rights and rights to access state-provided services. It is also relevant to determining duty to perform military service.

Ethnic or national origins

Ethnicity is interpreted more widely than race.

Mandla v *Dowell Lee* (1983, HL)

Held: an ethnic group existed if it was regarded by its members and by outsiders as a clearly distinguishable community with its own cultural traditions and a long-shared history. Other relevant factors were said to include a common geographical origin, or language, religion, or literature.

Therefore, Sikhs constituted a distinct ethnic group. School rules forbidding Sikh boys from wearing turbans and requiring their hair to be cut to a specified length indirectly discriminated against them.

In *Commission for Racial Equality* v *Dutton* (1989, CA) the Court of Appeal applied the *Mandla* decision and held that 'gypsies' (we would call them 'Roma' today) constituted an ethnic group that had not merged wholly with the general population, although it was no longer derived from a common racial stock.

Other legally recognised ethnic groups include Jews, and Scottish and Irish Travellers.

National origin must be distinguished from nationality. An individual cannot change their national origin but they might take on a new nationality. For example, a person born in Turkey is of Turkish national origin, but might immigrate to the UK, become naturalised and thus acquire British nationality.

National origins have both historical and geographical identifiable elements, which indicate that a nation currently exists or previously existed. For example, the English and the Scots have separate national origins because Scotland was originally a separate nation.

Racial group

All racial groups are protected against unfavourable treatment under the Act.

A racial group is made up of people who have colour or nationality, or their ethnic or national origins in common. A person may be a member of more than one racial group, for example black, with British nationality, of Indian national origin and a Jew.

Caste discrimination is not specifically prohibited by the EA 2010 but it is possible to interpret s 9 to include caste in some circumstances. In *Chandok & another v Tirkey* (2014, EAT) the claimant, a nanny, sued her employers claiming they had mistreated her because of her caste. The EAT held that while caste is not currently a protected characteristic in its own right, discrimination is illegal where caste is determined through birth or where it involves an identifiable ethnic identity.

Shortly before the case, s 9 was amended by the Enterprise and Regulatory Reform Act 2013. This states that the government 'must by order amend Section 9 [of the Act] so as to provide for caste to be an aspect of race'. In 2017 the government carried out a public consultation that was published on 28 March 2017 and ran until 18 September 2017. The government published its response on 23 July 2018, concluding against further legislation, preferring to rely on developments in case law. The government has therefore committed to repealing the duty, under the amended s 9 of the Equality Act, to legislate to prohibit caste discrimination.

As the intention of the Act is primarily intended to protect racial minorities, the courts may need to interpret it purposively.

Redfearn v Serco Ltd (2006, CA)

R was dismissed by the defendant bus company when it discovered that he was a member of the British Nationalist Party and a local councillor. The defendant argued that he was a risk to health and safety, as it was feared that Asians, who made up the majority of the customers and staff, might react violently to him. He had not worked for the defendant long enough to enable him to bring a case of unfair dismissal so he attempted to claim discrimination on 'racial grounds' under s 1(1)(a) of the RRA 1976.

Held: R had not been discriminated against on racial grounds (because he was white) but because of his particular views, which were shared by a tiny proportion of the white population.

However, Mr Redfearn later made a successful claim to the European Court of Human Rights (*Redfearn* v *Serco* Ltd (2012)), which held that his rights to freedom of assembly and association had been violated and that a legal system that allowed dismissal merely because of political belief was defective. A change in the law was necessary to enable implementation of this decision. As a result, the government amended ERA 1996, s 108 to provide that an employer may be liable for unfair dismissal of an employee, regardless of the length of time they have been employed, if the principal reason for the dismissal was political belief. The employer will be liable unless it proves that its procedures and reasons for the dismissal were fair. This does not make dismissal for political belief automatically unfair, nor does it mean that dismissal on these grounds is categorised as discrimination.

Worth thinking about?

A claim under the Race Relations Act was always going to be a long shot for Mr Redfearn. It was many years before his claim in the European Court of Human Rights was resolved. What other legal claims, not available in 2006, might Mr Redfearn pursue today? What are his chances of success?

Suggested solutions can be found in Appendix 2.

Prohibited conduct

This means treating a person less favourably because of their colour, nationality, ethnic or national origins than others without the protected characteristic of race.

Direct discrimination: s 13

This includes discrimination by association and perception. Special protection includes prohibition of deliberate segregation (s 13(5)) of either an individual or racial group. This is automatically unlawful and no comparator is required.

Occupational qualification is a defence: Schedule 9, para 1

An employer has the right to make a specific racial characteristic a requirement of employment provided it fulfils a legitimate aim and is a proportional requirement of the job. It may be relevant to jobs involving the provision of welfare services to a specific racial group, where applicants may be required to be members of that group themselves.

Indirect discrimination: s 19(1)(b)

This occurs when a 'provision, criteria or practice' (PCP) is imposed which discriminates against people with the protected characteristic of race because they cannot comply with it, to their personal detriment. This is clearly illustrated by the next case.

Mandla v *Dowell Lee* (1983, HL)

Held: school rules forbidding Sikh boys from wearing turbans and requiring their hair to be cut to a specified length indirectly discriminated against them on the grounds of their ethnic origins.

The 'proportionate means' defence

If the condition can be shown to be a 'proportionate means of achieving a legitimate aim', indirect discrimination may be justifiable (s 19(2)(d)). In *Panesaar* v *Nestlé* (1980) a rule forbidding long beards and hair in the defendant's factory, while indirectly discriminating against Sikhs, was nonetheless justifiable on hygiene grounds. This decision would be differently decided today on the grounds that while the aim (preserving high standards of hygiene) is legitimate, the means to achieve it is disproportionate. Suitable head and face covering (a beard guard) would readily solve the problem and are commonplace in the food industry.

The European Court of Justice recently heard a case concerning dress codes in the context of religious discrimination (see *Achbita and Bougnaoui* v *G4S Secure Solutions and another* (2017, EUECJ), below).

Vicarious liability: s 109

In *Jones* v *Tower Boot Co. Ltd* (1997 CA) the claimant was subjected to verbal and physical racial abuse in his workplace from other employees. His employer was vicariously liable. However, an employer may be vicariously liable for torts caused by employees even if not personally at fault.

Real life

Nick has just been made chief executive at Smallville Borough Council, which is Harriet's employer. Nick, who is keen to impress, has made a variety of organisational changes, including a new dress code. This bans women from wearing trousers to work. Harriet, as union representative for her department, has been approached by two female employees adversely affected by this rule. Ravinder, a Sikh, who works as a telephonist complains that her line manager won't let her wear the *shalwar kameez* because it includes trousers. Her religion requires her to cover her legs and the *shalwar kameez* is required dress in her community. Alice works in the stores department and has always worn smart trousers to work. She finds this convenient given the nature of her job, which involves actively handling stores and transporting them round the building. Since she has complied with the code, her colleague Kevin has made a number of comments about her legs, and the other day was peering up her skirt while she was up a step ladder.

Harriet takes up both these issues with the human resources department. She argues that the dress code indirectly discriminates against Ravinder on both racial and religious grounds in breach of ACAS guidelines. That seems a sound claim. Imposing a rule of this kind is justifiable only if it is a proportionate response by an employer, whereas this seems to be a rigid rule imposed for no good reason except uniformity.

Harriet claims on behalf of Alice that the dress code directly discriminates against women and treats her less favourably than male colleagues. Current case law suggests that this would be successful. In *Owen* v *Professional Golf Association* (2000) the employment tribunal held that instructing a female employee to return home and change from a smart trouser suit into a skirt was sex discrimination.

Kevin's behaviour is sexual harassment and Smallville will be liable if steps are not taken to resolve the situation.

Religion or belief

Protection against discrimination in this area has existed since 2003, when Employment Equality (Religion or Belief) Regulations 2003 were introduced to implement the Equal Treatment Directive of 2000. The EA largely replicates the regulations.

The protected characteristic of religion or belief: s 10

The definition reflects Article 9 of the ECHR (freedom of thought, conscience and religion).

Religion

This is defined in the Act as including lack of religion (s 10(1)). It includes all religions, and any religious or philosophical belief, including atheism and agnosticism. Denominations or sects of religions like Baptists or Sephardic Jews are also protected. While it includes religions that are not mainstream, a religion must have a clearly defined belief system and structure. The EAT (*Greater Manchester Police Authority* v *Power* (2010)) recognised that spiritualism was a religious belief, pointing out that the Spiritualist Church was the eighth largest worshipping group in Great Britain.

Belief

Both religious and non-religious belief comes within this definition. A belief does not have to involve faith or worship but must fulfil certain broad criteria. In *Grainger plc and Others* v *Nicholson* (2010) Burton J helpfully described belief:

> It must be a belief as to a weighty and substantial aspect of human life and behaviour. It must attain a certain level of cogency, seriousness, cohesion and importance. It must be worthy of respect in a democratic society, be not incompatible with human dignity and not conflict with the fundamental rights of others.

He refused to strike out Mr Grainger's claim that he had suffered discrimination at work because of his belief in climate change. Belief in the sanctity of life and that fox-hunting should consequently be banned was held to be a protected belief in *Hashman v Milton Park (Dorset) Ltd* (2011); however, the belief that a poppy should be worn as a mark of respect for military war dead was not (*Lisk v Shield Guardian Co. Ltd* (2011)).

Prohibited behaviour

When the protected characteristic is religion or belief, it is illegal for one person to treat a person with this characteristic less favourably than they would, or do, treat others without that protected characteristic.

Direct and indirect discrimination: ss 13 and 19

Unfavourable treatment arising from direct or indirect discrimination including discrimination by perception or association is actionable. Indirect discrimination may be justifiable if the employer can show that it is proportionate and necessary to fulfil a legitimate aim. Cases have often arisen on grounds of rules regarding uniform or dress requirements, which may amount to unfavourable treatment by preventing a person from manifesting their religion. The next case is a good example of how such cases are determined and how discrimination can be justified.

Azmi v Kirklees Metropolitan Borough Council (2007, EAT)

Ms Azmi was suspended from her job as a teaching assistant when she persisted in wearing a full veil, despite instructions not to do so.

She claimed that the council had directly and indirectly discriminated against her, as her religion required her to wear a veil while the class teacher, who was male, was in the room.

The council denied the claim arguing (from observing her at work) that the veil which covered her face and mouth interfered with her ability to communicate properly with the children and interfered with their learning to read.

Held: no direct discrimination had occurred. She had not been treated any differently, on the grounds of her religious belief, than any woman employee, Muslim or otherwise, who covered her face for non-religious reasons. They would have been subject to the same rule. No indirect discrimination had occurred. While the council's dress policy contained a provision which some Muslim women might not be able to fulfil, it did not target the veil but acknowledged that the policy had an impact in that area and that every case would be dealt with on its merits. The policy was neutral or at least applicable to non-Muslims. The council had acted with proportionality in order to achieve a legitimate end (the children's learning).

In *Eweida* v *British Airways* (2010) the Court of Appeal held that Ms Eweida, a devout Christian who usually wore a crucifix, had not suffered indirect discrimination due to BA's uniform rules, which forbid wearing any jewellery round the neck. The intention of the provision against indirect discrimination was to offer protection to a group of people rather than one person alone. There was no evidence that other Christians were adversely affected by the policy. However, the court stated that, had indirect discrimination been determined, BA could not have justified it as a proportionate restriction. Subsequently, BA revised its uniform policy to accommodate wearing religious symbols. Ms Eweida appealed successfully to the European Court of Human Rights.

Eweida and others v UK (2013, ECtHR)

Held: freedom of religion is a crucial right in any democratic society, but in determining whether the right has been infringed restrictions may be justified where its exercise unduly impinges on the rights of other people. An appropriate balance must be established between the extent of duty of the employer to protect the rights of others and the rights of the applicant to practise their religion.

BA had breached Ms Eweida's rights to freedom of religion under Article 9. A fair balance had not been struck between BA's legitimate aim to project a corporate image by its uniforms and Ms Eweida's right to manifest her belief. Other employees were allowed to wear religious specific clothing such as hijabs and turbans with no deleterious effect on the company image. Clearly the restriction on Christian symbols had not been sufficiently important to BA, particularly given that the dress code had later been amended to permit them.

Ms Chaplin, another party in the above case, lost her claim. She was a nurse and health and safety concerns had motivated her employers' ban on jewellery of any kind for employees performing clinical duties. The European Court of Human Rights court held that asking her to remove her cross was a proportionate response by her managers, who were in a better position to make safety judgements and therefore her case must fail.

These cases illustrate that while the right to hold to a religion or belief is in itself absolute, the right to manifest that belief is a qualified one. The issue was later revisited in the European Court of Justice (see *Achbita and Bougnaoui* v *G4S Secure Solutions*, below).

Sometimes a conflict may arise between the needs of people with different protected characteristics. In *Eweida and Others* v *UK* (2013) (above), two of the unsuccessful parties, Ms Ladele and Mr Macfarlane, had lost their jobs because they believed that their Christian beliefs did not allow them to condone homosexuality. Ms Ladele, an employee of Islington Council, had refused to perform civil partnerships and Mr Macfarlane, employed by Relate, had refused to counsel lesbian and gay couples. It was held that their Convention rights had not been breached because their employers' equal opportunity policies were designed to protect the rights of both employees and their clientele, including same-sex couples whose rights were also protected by the Convention. Previous decisions of the ECHR indicated that adverse treatment on the grounds of sexual orientation could only be permissible when serious justification could be proved. Same-sex couples should be treated equally with mixed-sex couples regarding the protection and legal recognition of their relationship.

The issue of religious discrimination was more recently the subject of a European Court of Justice case.

Achbita and Bougnaoui v *G4S Secure Solutions and another* (2017, EUECJ)

The claimants worked for G4S in Belgium and France respectively. Ms Achbita worked as a receptionist for G4S and Ms Bougnaoui as a consultant design engineer for a firm called Micropole.

G4S's employee code of behaviour stated: 'employees are prohibited, in the workplace, from wearing any visible signs of their political, philosophical or religious beliefs and/or from giving expression to any ritual arising from them.' Ms Achbita was dismissed for insisting on wearing the Muslim hijab (headscarf).

Ms Bouganoui claimed that she had been asked not to wear her scarf because many of the company's customers did not like dealing with someone dressed that way and it also embarrassed her workmates.

The ECJ held: A dress code which applied potentially to all employees in the same way was not directly discriminatory but could be indirectly so if it affected an individual or group more adversely than the others, unless the employer was able to prove that it was a reasonable and proportionate response to ensure religious and political neutrality in the workplace. Ms Achbita had not suffered discrimination because the policy was 'genuinely pursued in a consistent and systematic manner' for all employees. The case of Ms Bougnaoui was remitted to the French court to determine whether she had refused to obey work policy and if this policy was justifiable.

Note that this ruling does not give *carte blanche* to employers to ban the hijab from the workplace. If it amounts to indirect discrimination employers will only succeed if justification is evident.

Occupational requirement

Special dispensation is granted by the Act in relation to organised religions and certain institutions with a religious ethos.

Organised religions

Schedule 9, para 2 enables an employer which is an organised religion to require its ministers and holders of key posts to be of a specified gender and sexual orientation. Transgender people and lesbian, gays and bisexuals may be legally excluded. Marital status may also be specified to exclude people who are divorcees, if their spouse is still alive.

For example, the Church of England can legally refuse to employ a priest who is lesbian or gay. The Roman Catholic Church can require its priests to be unmarried and not divorced.

Such a requirement can only be imposed by a recognised religion to comply with religious doctrine and to avoid conflict with the majority of the religion's followers.

It is construed narrowly and only applies to posts which involve direct ministry carrying out religious services and related pastoral care.

Employers with a religious ethos

Under Schedule 9, para 3, an employer with an ethos based on a recognised religion or belief is also entitled to protect its key posts with the occupational requirement. Ethos may be defined as the reflection of the religion or belief evidenced by the culture and philosophy of the relevant institution as derived from its constitution and functions.

This, for example, covers church schools, higher-educational institutions training people for the priesthood and other organisations reflecting a particular religion or belief in the nature of their work, like the Humanist Society.

Gan Menachem Hendon Ltd v De Groen (2019, EAT)

A teacher at a religious Jewish nursery school was dismissed after disclosing to parents that she lived with her boyfriend, which was contrary to orthodox religious Jewish beliefs. She subsequently refused the school's request to lie in a letter to be sent to parents, saying this was not the case.

Held: her claim for religious discrimination failed because she had not been dismissed because of her lack of belief but because of the nursery's own religious belief forbidding cohabitation of non-married couples.

Sex

Before the EA 2010, the Sex Discrimination Act 1975 (as amended) was the relevant legislation in this area. Its coverage included marriage, pregnancy and maternity and transgender discrimination. Under the EA, sex discrimination becomes discrete.

Although the SDA was enacted primarily to combat sexual discrimination against women, men are given equal rights under its terms. In some years, men brought more successful cases than women. The EA closely mirrors the SDA regarding sexual discrimination with a few enhancements.

The protected characteristic of sex: s 11

This includes male and female persons of any age. In relation to a group of people it refers to men/boys or women/girls.

The EA 2010 makes it illegal to discriminate directly or indirectly against persons on the grounds of their sex. Treating men and women differently does not amount to unlawful discrimination unless it results in members of one sex being treated less favourably than the other.

The sex equality clause: s 66

This is intended to ensure that the terms in an employment contract are not more or less favourable to an employee on the grounds of their gender. All contracts with employees must include such a clause or such a term will automatically be implied. It requires that a term in the employment contract which is less favourable than that of a comparator of the opposite sex doing the same or similar work must be altered to reflect the term in the comparator's contract. Similarly, if the comparator's contract includes a favourable term which is not in the employee's contract, such a term must be implied in the employee's contract of employment. Proof of a material difference may be a justification.

Prohibited behaviour

Direct discrimination: s 13

Direct (overt) discrimination occurs if a person is treated on the grounds of their sex less favourably than a person of the opposite sex. Reserving a job for male candidates only is an obvious example. In *Batisha* v *Say* (1977), a woman who applied for a job as a cave guide was turned down on the ground that it was 'a man's job'. In *Moyhing* v *Barts and London NHS Trust* (2006), the EAT deemed a policy requiring a male nurse to be chaperoned while undertaking intimate examinations of women, to be directly discriminatory to male nurses. No such requirement applied to the intimate examination of male patients by female nurses.

Direct discrimination includes associative and perceptive discrimination.

Qualities like physical strength and stamina must not be treated as sex specific. A woman cannot automatically be excluded from consideration for a job because it involves heavy lifting. Some women are stronger than some men, even if in general men are stronger than women.

Occupational qualification: Schedule 9, para 1

This defence may protect an employer who can prove that the essential nature of the job requires a specific gender.

A job may be reserved for a man or a woman specifically if this is essential for physiological reasons, such as lapdancers. Issues of privacy and decency may also be legitimate concerns, for example when staffing single-sex hospitals and prisons. It might be also legitimate to discriminate in appointments to residential jobs if appropriate separate sleeping or sanitary facilities cannot reasonably be provided.

Etam plc v Rowan (1996, EAT)

Held: being female was not essential for a shop assistant selling women's clothes. A male applicant could fulfil the bulk of the job. A female staff member could supervise changing rooms without any inconvenience to the employer or embarrassment to women customers.

Indirect discrimination: s 19

Indirect discrimination: covert discrimination. Selection criteria, policies, benefits, rules or conditions, that are applicable to the whole workforce, but discriminatory to members of a relevant characteristic.

Indirect discrimination or covert discrimination occurs when an employer imposes on an employee an apparently neutral 'provision, criterion or practice' (PCP) which puts an employee at a disadvantage when compared to employees of the opposite sex and which the employer cannot show to be a 'proportionate response to a legitimate aim'.

Home Office v Holmes (1984)

Held: a requirement that employees worked full time, not part time, was indirectly discriminatory against women. Their opportunities to go out to work full time were more likely to be limited by childcare responsibilities than men's. The nature of the job did not justify the full-time requirement.

Harassment: ss 26 and 40

Specific protection is provided against sexual harassment (s 26(2)).

Porcelli v Strathclyde Regional Council (1986)

Ms Porcelli worked as a technician in a laboratory with two male colleagues who mounted a campaign of sexual insults and physical intimidation to try to make her leave.

Held: she was the victim of discrimination, since the behaviour of her colleagues was 'a particular kind of weapon which . . . would not have been used against an equally disliked man'.

Equal pay

This has always been a particularly contentious area of sex discrimination against women. Historically, women's work has been undervalued, with low rates of pay in those areas of employment most often filled by women, like cleaning, nursing, catering and shop work. Where men have been employed alongside women, they have often been paid at a higher rate than women doing similar, or even identical, work. Legislation aimed at correcting this discrepancy was first introduced by the Equal Pay Act 1970, which was amended in 1983 under the Equal Pay (Amendment) Regulations to comply with the Equal Pay Directive (75/117/EEC) to cover work of equal value. Sadly, despite the legislation, women were still on average earning nearly 16 per cent less than men in 2014 according to statistics compiled by the TUC. Women bosses came off even worse; according to figures published the same year by the Chartered Institute of Management they received 35 per cent less than their male equivalent. By 2016 the overall pay gap narrowed to 9.4 per cent for full-time female employees. Part-time female employees on average earned 18.1 per cent less. Deloitte, the consultant accountants, estimate that at this rate it will be 2069 before the pay gap closes for full-time female employees.

Equality clause: implied term in an employment contract to ensure parties are treated equally favourably.

The EA 2010 largely replicates the previous legislation but with some minor expansion of protection. The **equality clause** (s 66) (see above) has particular relevance to equal pay issues, as it requires an entitlement to equal pay to be implied in a contract of employment that does not make it specific. Occupational pension entitlement is also included for the first time under the EA 2010 (s 67).

The equal pay provisions cover not only wages and salaries but also all monetary benefits such as paid holiday leave, sick pay and overtime. Non-monetary benefits, like access to social and sporting facilities, are also covered.

Equal work: s 65

A woman is entitled to claim equal pay and other contract terms with a male comparator who is doing:

Like work: work rated as equivalent to that of a comparator under a job evaluation scheme.

Equivalent work: work of the same or similar nature.

Work of equal value: work that is different in its general characteristics from that of a comparator but has the same monetary worth.

- **'like work'**, which means that the job is the same or largely similar; or
- **'work rated as equivalent'**, which means that although different in its nature it has been rated as similar under a job evaluation scheme; or
- **'work of equal value'**, which means that although the job is a different one, it should be viewed as of similar value with regard to such elements as the level of skill, decision-making or management responsibility it requires.

The court is required under EU law to interpret these provisions purposively.

These criteria will now be explored in a little more detail to see how they are likely to work in practice.

'Like work'

The woman must show that her work is identical or broadly similar to a male comparator looking at the job as a whole and considering any particular skill or responsibility that goes with it. Provided she can do this, she will succeed in her claim unless the employer can prove a material difference; for example, the qualification or training involved to do the job, the anti-social hours when it is performed; or that the physical *effort* required to perform it could be of practical importance.

A cosmetic difference, such as giving the man's job a superior title, does not fool the court.

Capper Pass v Lawton (1977)

Held: a woman employed to cook meals for the directors' dining room was doing essentially similar work to the assistant chefs in the canteen. The only differences were that the canteen chefs cooked more meals for greater numbers, were supervised and worked for four hours more every week than she did.

Heavy work may justify higher pay.

Noble v David Gold & Sons (Holdings) Ltd (1980)

Male warehouse workers were paid more than women working alongside them.

Held: this was justified by the fact that the men loaded and unloaded goods while the women's work was lighter and involved sorting, labelling and packaging goods.

Notional responsibilities that are not actually performed will not be treated as a material difference.

Shields v Coomes (Holdings) Ltd (1978)

It was claimed by the employer that a male counter assistant at a betting shop was paid more than a female counter assistant because he was there for security purposes.

Held: she was entitled to equal pay since the employer was unable to prove that the male assistant had received any security training, or that he had ever had to deal with troublemakers; there was no material difference between his function and the woman's.

Equivalent work

A woman is entitled to claim breach of the equality clause if her employer has a valid job evaluation scheme in operation, under which the woman's job is graded at the same level as a man's but he is paid more, or if the woman's job would have been graded at a higher level under the scheme if the evaluation had not been made according to different values for men and women. The same criteria must be applied to both men and women and the scheme must be drawn up in such a way as to avoid sex discrimination.

This provides a means whereby jobs may be systematically assessed to find their relative value. It rates the jobs on a points scheme using criteria such as level of responsibility, skill, effort and decision-making focusing on the jobs in their entirety, so comparison of very different types of job is possible.

Job evaluation schemes are not compulsory and, due to the relatively small number in operation, claims in this area are uncommon.

'Equal value'

To determine the value of the work, the demands of the relevant jobs must be assessed and compared by the tribunal. It must take into account the skill, knowledge, trade or professional qualification, physical and mental effort, and levels of responsibility and decision-making.

Hayward v *Cammell Laird Shipbuilders* (1988, HL)

Held: the work of a cook in the works canteen was of equal value to that of other skilled workers such as joiners, painters and insulation engineers. Therefore she was entitled to the same basic pay as they were. It was irrelevant that her entitlement to sickness benefits, holiday leave and meals entitlement were superior to other skilled workers.

This provision means that a wide range of jobs is comparable. A skilled manual job may be of the same or greater value than one involving an administrative role.

Comparators

The comparator must be, or have been, employed at the claimant's workplace or at another workplace associated directly or indirectly with the woman's employer.

The claimant has the choice of the comparator. This was originally determined by the House of Lords in *Pickstone* v *Freemans plc* (1988) as being necessary to prevent an employer from putting a 'token male' into the same line of work as the woman and paying him at the same rate. She may choose more than one comparator. Sometimes this may be essential to success if it is necessary to compare a number of terms in her contract that may not relate to the terms of service of just one comparator. The comparator need not be employed contemporaneously with the claimant (s 64(2)). This reflects the Court of Appeal's decision in *Macarthys* v *Smith* (1981) and prevents an employer from replacing a male employee with a woman on a lower rate of pay.

Hypothetical comparators

This provides new protection where no comparator may be found. For example, if an employer tells a woman that he would pay her more if she were male, but there are no comparable jobs in her own or an associated workplace, she can claim sex discrimination and use a hypothetical comparator (s 71).

Occupational pensions

Neither the EPA 1970 nor the SDA 1975 applied to pensions, but EC law led to anti-discrimination legislation:

Barber v *Guardian Royal Insurance* (1990, ECJ)

Held: it was contrary to Article 141 of the Treaty of Rome for a man who had been made compulsorily redundant to be entitled only to a deferred pension, if a woman of the same age and in the same position would be entitled to claim her pension immediately.

The Pensions Act 1995, ss 62–66 required equal treatment regarding pensionable service for all persons retiring since 17 May 1990.

The sex equality rule (s 67(1) EA 2010) now aims to enable men and women to obtain equal treatment both in terms of access to and benefits from an occupational pension. Section 61 requires a non-discrimination rule to be implied into every occupational pension scheme and prohibits 'a responsible person' from discriminating against or victimising or harassing anyone who wants to join the scheme or is a member of it.

Material difference

Under (s 69), an employer who can prove that the reason for a pay differential between men and women is 'a material factor', will not be liable. A material factor will be one that is genuine, relevant and significant and does not constitute direct sex discrimination. If it gives rise to indirect sex discrimination it will only be a valid defence if it is a proportionate means of securing a justifiable aim. Effectively, the employer is saying that the difference in pay between men and women is coincidental and that it is provably linked to material differences between the two parties other than their sex. Such differences have been held to include levels of qualification, length of service, place of work and anti-social hours of work. Organisational and economic factors may also justify a pay differential, but it is a question of fact for the court to decide in each case.

Staff shortages were held to represent a genuine material difference in the next case:

Rainey v Greater Glasgow Health Board (1987, HL)

The Board set up a prosthesis service within the NHS. Some prosthetists were recruited from the NHS sector and were paid at its current rate, but this was insufficient to recruit the numbers required and so a further 20 (all male) were recruited from the private sector and paid at a higher rate to reflect their previous, more favourable, salary. Ms Rainey, an NHS recruit, claimed that this was discriminatory.

Held: this pay differential was justifiable on the grounds of market forces.

The market forces argument is only relevant while the particular circumstances prevail. Once they ease, equal pay must be paid (*Benveniste* v *University of Southampton* (1989)).

Economic conditions were held not to be relevant in the following case:

North Yorkshire County Council v Ratcliffe (1995, HL)

Held: paying dinner ladies less than men judged to be doing work of equal value could not be justified on the ground that it was done to enable the employers to make the winning bid in compulsory competitive tender negotiations. This was 'the very kind of discrimination which the Act sought to remove'.

In *Blackburn and Another* v *Chief Constable of West Midlands Police* (2008) the Court of Appeal held that working night shifts was a material factor. Therefore, paying male police officers an enhanced rate for these shifts did not illegally discriminate against female officers who had opted out of night work because of childcare commitments. It could be objectively justified since it fulfilled the legitimate aim of rewarding people for working anti-social hours.

Equal pay during pregnancy and maternity

A woman should not be subject to inferior pay and conditions during pregnancy or while on maternity leave and a maternity clause is implied in her contract to that effect. No comparator is needed to determine such issues (s 73).

During her leave her normal pay arrangements will be suspended but she will obtain maternity pay if entitled under her terms of service. However, she is still entitled to any bonus or pay rise awarded while she is on leave if she would be entitled to it at work (s 74).

If she is a member of an occupational pension scheme, an implied maternity clause protects her against loss of pension rights while she is away from work on *paid* maternity leave (s 75(1)–(6) and (9)).

Pay transparency

In the interest of promoting equality, the Act aims to ensure that employers make pay structures clear and understandable to all employees and trades unions.

Some employers have promoted secrecy by including a gagging clause in employment contracts to prevent employees discussing and comparing salaries, which may enable continuance of hidden inequalities of pay. Such a clause is unenforceable under s 77 if it stops a person from making a 'relevant pay disclosure' or seeking disclosure from a current or previous colleague.

A disclosure is 'relevant' under the Act (s 77(3)) if it is about pay and aims to find out whether discriminatory practice is involved on the basis of any protected characteristic. An employer seeking to penalise an employee for making or seeking disclosure may be guilty of victimisation.

Section 78 gave the government power to make larger employers publish information indicating whether there are differences in pay scales between the men and women they employ but these powers were never used. However, the passing of the Small Business, Enterprise and Employment Act 2015, s 178 required the Secretary of State to 'make regulations under section 78 of the Equality Act 2010 (gender pay gap information) for the purpose of requiring the publication of information showing whether there are differences in the pay of males and females'. This resulted in the Equality Act (Gender Pay Gap) Regulations 2017. Since April 2017 these apply to all employers with a workforce of 250 or more and will require them to publish pay details including bonuses of all their employees on the company's website. Failure to comply may be sanctioned by a £5,000 fine. This is likely to be less than a fleabite to most businesses but the attendant publicity may be more of a deterrent. The first round of gender pay gap reporting has just been completed and the second round will occur in 2019.

Enforcing an equal pay claim

A woman is entitled to information from her employer if she believes she is receiving unequal pay, and failure to provide a clear response within eight weeks entitles an employment tribunal to infer that inequality exists (s 138(4) and (5)).

However, before taking the matter to the tribunal, the woman should attempt informal resolution and if this fails present a formal written grievance in line with the ACAS code. ACAS can also provide a conciliator.

The employment tribunal has special procedures for dealing with equal pay cases. If a claim is successful, the tribunal may issue a declaration setting out the woman's pay entitlement and if appropriate order payment of damages to cover arrears of pay and other lost benefits (s 132). Damages are not awarded for hurt feelings in an equal pay claim.

In 2017 the World Economic Forum announced that, at the present rate of change, parity of pay would not be achieved until 2186. It can only be hoped that the UK manages it rather sooner.

Sexual orientation

Introduction

Until 2003, an employee enjoyed little legal protection against discrimination on the grounds of sexual orientation. Human rights legislation provided some redress. The European Convention on Human Rights (Articles 8, 13 and 14, which prohibit discrimination) does not refer expressly to sexual orientation but can be interpreted purposively. The implementation of the Convention in the English courts by the Human Rights Act 1998 enabled further developments of English law in this area.

The ECHR, in *Smith and Grady* v *UK* (1998), held that the ban on lesbians and gay men in the armed forces violated their rights under Article 8 (the right to privacy and family life) and Article 13 (the right to an effective domestic remedy). This eventually led to a radical change in policy by the Ministry of Defence, which lifted the ban in 2005.

EC law eventually prompted change under the Equal Treatment Directive 2000, which was implemented by the Employment Equality (Sexual Orientation) Regulations 2003.

These regulations made it unlawful to discriminate against any employee by treating them less favourably on account of their sexual orientation. It thus became illegal to discriminate against a heterosexual, lesbian, gay man or bisexual because of their sexuality.

The EA largely replicates the rights under the regulations but has enhanced rights against harassment and victimisation.

The protected characteristic: s 12

Sexual orientation means a person's sexual orientation towards:

(a) persons of the same sex,

(b) persons of the opposite sex, or

(c) persons of either sex.

It therefore includes lesbians, gay men, heterosexuals and bisexuals.

Prohibited behaviour

Treating a person unfavourably because of sexual orientation is illegal under the Act.

Comparators

This should be someone in similar circumstances but who does not share the same characteristic. However, comparing a person who is a civil partner with one who is married is not a sufficient material difference (s 23(3)).

Direct and indirect discrimination: ss 13 and 19

As mentioned above, direct discrimination includes perceptive and associative discrimination and discrimination by association. Negative stereotyping of lesbians and gay men readily gives rise to unfavourable treatment.

Occupational qualification

Under Schedule 9, para 3, this is a defence to direct discrimination on the grounds of sexual orientation if it fulfils a legitimate aim and is carried out in proportionate manner. A support group for young lesbian and gay people might be justified in advertising for an advice worker as a position open to gay and lesbian candidates only on the grounds that its clients would be more prepared to approach someone of their own sexual orientation and shared experience.

Harassment: ss 26 and 40

People with this protected characteristic may claim harassment both by an employer (s 26) and third parties (s 40).

A heterosexual person may be harassed with homophobic 'banter' even though his colleagues do not actually believe him to be gay. In the case of *English* v *Thomas Sanderson* (2008), Collins LJ held on a preliminary issue:

> If one were to ask the question whether the repeated and offensive use of the word 'faggot' in the circumstances of this case was conduct 'on grounds of sexual orientation' the answer should be in the affirmative irrespective of the actual sexual orientation of the claimant or the perception of his sexual orientation by his tormentors. If the conduct is 'on grounds of sexual orientation' it is plainly irrelevant whether the claimant is actually of a particular sexual orientation.

Note, however, that Mr English's case ultimately failed when it came to trial because, although he had been made the subject of homosexual banter, harassment had not occurred, as he was found not to have been offended by the behaviour. As Mr English joined in the banter and remained good friends with his tormentors, no harassment occurred. The EAT upheld this decision (*Thomas Sanderson Blinds Ltd* v *English* (2011)).

Vicarious liability

An employer with knowledge of illegal behaviour by employees will continue to be vicariously liable if it takes insufficient steps to prevent the illegal behaviour continuing (s 109(4)).

Martin v Parkham Foods (2006)

In May 2005, abusive and homophobic graffiti naming Mr Martin appeared on the toilet wall at his workplace. He complained to the human resources department and a very limited cleaning operation took place which merely obliterated his name. Notices were put up telling staff not to deface the building, but homophobia was not mentioned.

In October 2005, his name reappeared on the graffiti. He complained again but was told that there was little that could be done to discover the culprit. He then wrote a formal complaint letter and Parkham suspended him to allow an investigation to take place.

In December 2005, while suspended, Mr Martin resigned and claimed harassment, direct discrimination and constructive dismissal.

Held: Parkham was vicariously liable for the harassment and had directly discriminated against Mr Martin.

It had not taken all reasonable steps to prevent the recurrence of the homophobic behaviour, which should have been addressed by appropriate training, team briefings or notes in pay-slips to make it crystal clear to all employees that homophobic behaviour would not be tolerated.

The grievance had not been diligently investigated and the failure to apologise to him was also culpable.

His suspension, given the connotations it carried, was inappropriate. All of these factors led to a breach of Mr Martin's trust and confidence and meant that he had been constructively dismissed.

Discrimination on the grounds of sexual orientation and religion or belief

There may be a tension between an employer or employees with particular religious beliefs and other personnel with a particular sexual orientation. This is well illustrated in the following cases which clearly demonstrate this clash:

Lee v Ashers Baking Company Ltd and Others (2015) UKSC

The owners of a bakery refused to supply a cake with the slogan 'Support Gay Marriage', as this was contrary to the owners' Christian values.

Held: this was not direct sexual orientation discrimination, as they would have refused to supply this cake to anyone who had requested it. It was the slogan that was objectionable rather than the claimants.

In contrast, in a case involving sexual orientation and services, the claimants were successful.

Bull and Another v Hall and Another (2013) UKSC

A Christian couple refused to allow a homosexual couple to stay at their hotel as their online terms and conditions stated that double bedrooms were available only to 'hetrosexual married couples'.

Held: this was direct discrimination on grounds of sexual orientation.

Enforcing anti-discrimination legislation

A complainant may apply to take the matter before an employment tribunal. An application must usually be made within three months of the alleged behaviour. Initially, grievance and possibly conciliation procedures are implemented, but if these fail the case will be heard by the tribunal.

The promotion of equality

The Act seeks to do more than right individual complaints of discrimination. It seeks to promote equality in general.

The public sector equality duty: s 149

This duty was implemented in April 2011.

Public Bodies listed in Schedule 19 to the Act have a three-part duty to:

(a) eliminate discrimination, harassment, victimisation and any other conduct that is prohibited by or under this Act;

(b) advance equality of opportunity between persons who share a relevant protected characteristic and persons who do not share it;

(c) foster good relations between persons who share a relevant protected characteristic and persons who do not share it.

Duty (a) applies to all protected characteristics but (b) and (c) are not relevant to marriage and civil partnership.

Schedule 19 indicates that s 149 covers ministers of the Crown, most government departments and local authorities. Other bodies which are not public bodies but exercise some public duties are subject to the requirement of s 149 with regard to their public duties.

The Equality and Human Rights Commission has the power to issue compliance notices and take whatever steps are necessary within its powers to ensure performance of the duty.

Specific equality duties

Under s 153, a minister has the power to issue by regulation specific equality duties 'for the purpose of enabling the better performance by the authority of the duty imposed by section 149(1)'. The government is consulting on this issue and so far no regulations have been created.

The socio-economic duty: s 1

The Act places public sector employers such as local authorities, health and primary care trusts and police forces under a legal duty to consider the impact their strategic decisions will have on individuals who are from disadvantaged backgrounds. However, the government has scrapped this provision.

Positive action: s 159

An employer may appoint or promote a candidate with a protected characteristic where people with that particular protected characteristic are underrepresented in the workforce. This can only be done where the relevant candidates are equally qualified: each case must be considered on its merit.

This section does not permit an employer to have a policy of appointing people with a specific protected characteristic in preference to others without it.

The Equality and Human Rights Commission

Equality and Human Rights Commission: body responsible for monitoring the operation of anti-discrimination law in the UK.

The **Equality and Human Rights Commission** (EHRC) was created under the Equality Act 2006, s 1. From October 2007, it replaced the Equal Opportunities Commission, the Commission for Racial Equality and the Disability Rights Commission, which had been responsible for overseeing the working of the legislation relevant to sexual, racial and disability legislation respectively. The EHRC took over their functions, but with additional powers enabling it to exercise a unifying role in monitoring anti-discrimination legislation as a whole. It is also responsible for the promotion of a culture of equality and human rights.

The core functions of the Commission

The Commission's core functions are currently:

1 Promoting and encouraging awareness and good practice in equality and diversity.

2 Promoting understanding of rights under the legislation through provision of easily accessible advice and information.

3 Enforcing rights under the legislation through individual case work support.

4 Working towards eliminating unlawful discrimination and harassment through promotion of awareness and provision of advice and through strategic enforcement, including the use of investigations and enquiries.

5 Promoting awareness, understanding and protection of human rights by initiating good practice in public authorities, in order to improve compliance with the Human Rights Act 1998.

6 Promoting good relations between the different groups covered by the equality laws and between them and society at large.

Reform of the Commission

In 2013 the Commission's budget was slashed by over two-thirds and its staff reduced by over a half. The government believes that it should not be a campaigning body and instead concentrate on making recommendations on the basis of facts. The Enterprise and Regulatory Reform Act 2013 (E&RRA) has left the Commission's main functions intact. However, some peripheral powers such as the duty to monitor continuing progress towards equality and the power to impose conciliation procedures have been axed.

Chapter summary

The scope of the Equality Act 2010

The Act protects individuals against less favourable treatment with reference to eight protected characteristics: age, disability, gender re-assignment, marriage and civil partnership, pregnancy and maternity, race, religion and belief, sex and sexual orientation.

Structure

The Act states the forms of relevant prohibited behaviour:

(a) direct/indirect discrimination (occupational qualifications may provide a defence; the legitimate aims defence is relevant only to indirect discrimination);

(b) harassment;

(c) victimisation.

An employer may also be vicariously liable for discriminatory behaviour of employees.

The Act imposes particular duties regarding people with certain specific protected characteristics. For example, it requires reasonable adjustments to be made for people with disabilities.

Positive discrimination is permitted to a limited extent.

Defences to liability are included. The defence of 'occupational requirement' applies in positive discrimination claims. It is a defence to indirect discrimination to show that it is a proportional means of attaining a legitimate aim.

Promotion of equality

Public service bodies are under a general duty to enhance and promote equality (s 149).

Section 159 permits limited positive action by employers making appointments to posts.

The Equality and Human Rights Commission

The Commission is responsible for the promotion of equality, by monitoring the operation of the EA 2010, assisting individuals in making claims, carrying out investigations and making recommendations for improvement.

Review questions 17

1 Freda, who is employed as a cleaner by Cheetah plc, is paid less than the male packers. Advise Freda.

2 Mr Jones was refused a job at the Warren Family Planning Clinic because he is male. Advise Mr Jones.

3 Explain the meaning of harassment.

4 When may it be legal to advertise a job as being open only to members of a particular ethnic group?

5 While Ms Rosey was on maternity leave she didn't get a bonus paid to all other employees on her grade. Her friend Ms Cole approached their boss, Mr Fox, and pointed out that Ms Rosey was entitled to the money under the Equality Act 2010. Two weeks later, Mr Fox dismissed Ms Cole. Advise Ms Rosey and Ms Cole.

6 Define and distinguish between direct and indirect discrimination.

Answers to all review questions can be found in Appendix 2.

Advanced questions 17

(A) To what extent do you consider that s 26 of the Equality Act 2010 affords comprehensive protection against harassment in the workplace?

(B) Critically evaluate the effect of the Equality Act 2010 in the area of disability discrimination.

Answers to the advanced questions can be found at **go.pearson.com/uk/he/resources.**

Take a closer look

The following cases provide important examples of how the law in this chapter has developed. They are primary sources illustrating the law in action and give more detail about their facts, as well as helping to understand the law and to appreciate how the judges reached their decisions.

Try looking them up in the law reports or accessing them via a database, e.g. BAILII (www.bailii.org/databases.html). LexisNexis or Westlaw may be available in the university or college library, or extracts may be found in a case book. (See Appendix 1: Additional resources.)

Achbita and Bougnaoui v *G4S Secure Solutions* [2017] CJEU C-157/15

Azmi v *Kirklees Metropolitan Borough Council* (2007) ICR 1154, EAT

Eweida and Others v *UK* [2013] ECHR 37

O'Neil v *Symm & Co.* [1998] IRLR 232, EAT

Rainey v *Greater Glasgow Health Board* [1987] AC 224, HL

Further reading

Patten, K. (2018) Workplace Bullying and Moral Urgency. *Industrial Law Journal.* 47(2), 169–191.

Web activity

On the website of ACAS click on 'Advice A–Z' then under E find 'Equality' to explore the wide range of resources on offer:
www.acas.org.uk/

Assignment 16

Trumpet Ltd provides public relations and publicity services. Madeline has been working for the company as a receptionist for seven years. Recently she was severely injured in a road accident unconnected with her job and is now confined to a wheelchair. Trumpet has given her notice saying that it cannot guarantee her safe evacuation from the building in the event of fire and that the toilet arrangements are not safely accessible to wheelchair users.

Raj, recently recruited to the company, receives an anonymous message through the internal mail saying 'Why don't you get a job nearer home?' and others follow containing website addresses for airlines providing bargain flights to Pakistan. He reports the matter to his manager, Gladys, who says he should ignore it and, anyway, there is nothing she can do about it.

Jane has worked in public relations for several years. She recently applied to Trumpet for a job and in her application was able to demonstrate conformity with all the essential and desirable requirements in the job description. At her interview, when asked to give examples of successful projects, she describes a publicity campaign that she ran for 'Outcome', a lesbian and gay organisation. She does not get the job and afterwards finds out that it has been given to another, less well-qualified applicant. She queries this with Trumpet's human resources manager, who tells her: 'We were not convinced that your professional experience fits the needs of our client group.'

Advise Madeline, Raj and Jane.

Rights at work:
Protection against termination of employment by wrongful and unfair dismissal including redundancy

Learning objectives

On completion of this chapter, students should be able to:

★ see the difference between wrongful and unfair dismissal;

★ explain the circumstances when a claim for unfair dismissal exists;

★ understand a claim for redundancy;

★ describe in outline the employee's remedies for unfair dismissal and redundancy;

★ appreciate the concept of transfer of undertakings.

Introduction

Generally, it is the employee who discharges their employment contract by giving in their notice and moving on to a new job. However, sometimes it is the employer who takes the initiative. This chapter will examine how this may occur and the remedies that an employee may obtain if the employer has broken the law protecting the employee's rights.

There are three ways in which the employer may unlawfully bring an employment contract to an end:

- *Wrongful dismissal*. At common law an employee dismissed without appropriate notice or where the employer has failed to follow contractual grievance and disciplinary procedures may sue in the civil courts for breach of contract at common law.

- *Unfair dismissal*. Provided that the required notice is given, dismissal is lawful at common law, but nonetheless may be deemed to be unfair dismissal as otherwise an employee is potentially vulnerable to dismissal at the whim of the employer. So since 1971, statutory rights have existed which protect employees found to have suffered an unfair dismissal. An employee may be entitled to bring a claim before an employment tribunal, whether dismissed with notice or not. Unless the employer can prove that it was fair to dismiss the employee which relates to the reason (because of incompetence, for example) and the procedure, he or she may have to pay compensation to the employee who might, in exceptional cases, be reinstated.

- *Redundancy.* One of the potentially fair reasons for dismissal is that an employer may need to reduce the size of the workforce, but an employee consequently made redundant has a right to be treated fairly in the process and may have a statutory entitlement to compensation.

These concepts are explained in detail below.

Wrongful dismissal

Wrongful dismissal: breach of contract by the employer.

Wrongful dismissal will occur if the contract of employment is terminated by the employer without the appropriate notice, or without following contractual procedures, or in the case of a fixed-term contract, if termination is enforced before the contract's completion date.

Summary dismissal: employee is dismissed without any notice.

Summary dismissal (without notice) may be justified only if the employer can prove that the employee was guilty of gross misconduct. This is serious misconduct which could include theft, fraud, violence or drunkenness, reckless behaviour or wilful refusal to obey a reasonable order.

Minimum notice periods

If an employer wishes to terminate an employee's employment, the notice period stated in the contract of employment must be given. If there is nothing specified in the contract, the minimum periods of notice required by s 86 of the Employment Rights Act (ERA 1996) must be given. Under the ERA 1996 the following notice periods apply unless a longer period is specified in the contract (s 86):

- up to one month in employment: no notice;
- one month to two years' employment: one week's notice;
- two to 12 years' employment: one week's notice for every completed year;
- over 12 years' employment: 12 weeks' notice.

Remedies for wrongful dismissal

An employee is entitled to sue for breach of contract in the courts to recover any lost earnings payable during the notice period, as well as any commission and gratuities that the employee would normally have acquired. An apprentice is entitled to be compensated for loss of prospects. An employee may also obtain compensation for benefits lost where the wrongful dismissal prevented the employee from completing the necessary period of continuous employment to entitle the employee to pursue a claim for unfair dismissal.

Alternatively, action may be brought in the employment tribunal, though here the damages are limited by the ERA 1996. Claims before the tribunal are usually time barred after three months from termination of the contract, while a limitation period of six years applies to court claims. (See also remedies for breach of contract in Chapter 9.)

Unfair dismissal

This area of the law, which has been subject to constant change since its inception, is currently largely governed by the ERA 1996 (as amended). Some important changes have been introduced through the Enterprise and Regulatory Reform Act 2013. All statutory references in this chapter refer to the ERA unless otherwise specified.

Any employee entitled to sue for wrongful dismissal may also be entitled to bring a claim for unfair dismissal at the employment tribunal. However, an employee who

Unfair dismissal: dismissal which cannot be justified as fair by the employer.

has not been dismissed wrongfully may still qualify to claim for **unfair dismissal**. Employers, therefore, are no longer necessarily free to dispense with an employee's services unless they can satisfy the tribunal that they acted fairly and with reasonable cause within the legislative criteria.

Certain types of employee are not eligible to claim unfair dismissal: for example, shareholder employees.

Eligibility to claim

Claims must be brought within *three months* of the termination of the contract. The following criteria must be satisfied:

1 continuous employment for at least two years;
2 the employee must prove the fact of the dismissal;
3 the employer must prove the dismissal was fair.

The employee must have been continuously employed for at least two years

This applies to both full- and part-time employees. The number of hours worked per week is irrelevant.

Employment remains continuous despite certain interruptions:

- sickness;
- pregnancy and maternity leave;
- temporary lay-offs;
- holidays;
- change of job with the employer or its associate;
- takeover by a new employer.

Continuous employment: minimum of two years working for the same employer which qualifies an employee to claim unfair dismissal at the employment tribunal.

The Unfair Dismissal and Statement of Reasons for Dismissal (Variation of Qualifying Period) Order 2012 raised the **continuous employment** requirement from one to two years. This was part of the implementation of Government policy aimed at cutting red tape for employers by simplifying the dismissal process and reducing the number of potential cases brought to the employment tribunal. A change can be introduced by order of the Secretary of State under the ERA, s 209.

There are certain situations where the two-year qualifying period does not apply (e.g. discrimination based dismissal) – these are called automatically unfair dismissals.

Employees must prove that they have been dismissed

Dismissal may be actual, constructive or deemed.

Actual dismissal: employer tells employee that he or she is dismissed.

Constructive dismissal: employee feels forced into resignation by employer's behaviour.

- **Actual dismissal**. The employer clearly indicates an intention to dispense with the employee's services.
- **Constructive dismissal**. The employer breaches a condition of the contract (a repudiatory breach) which entitles the innocent party to terminate the contract and or claim damages (see Chapter 11). The employee resigns claiming that the employer's behaviour made it impossible for the employee to stay. Breach of the employer's duty not to undermine the trust and confidence of the employee is

often the ground for such a claim. A number of such cases have arisen from an employer's failure to prevent sexual harassment and bullying. *Martin* v *Parkham Foods* (2006, EAT) is a good example of this (see above, Chapter 18).

Fletcher v *Countrywide Estate Agents* (2017, ET)

Fletcher had worked for Ashby Lowery estate agents in Northampton since 2003. She acted as deputy to the owner Darren Wilson and was left in charge when he was away. Fletcher dealt with the landlords and tenants, and was in charge of more than 20 staff, including the administration, lettings and management teams. The office ran smoothly, and staff morale was high until the business was taken over by Countrywide Estate Agents. Following the takeover, Fletcher encountered a number of difficulties including the payment of salaries, pension scheme enrolment, a lack of training and induction, the introduction of new systems and the failure to pay suppliers on time, which resulted in them withholding their services. This made it difficult for Fletcher to manage the office efficiently, and the late payment of invoices meant she was sometimes unable to get credit references for tenants.

The former owner, Mr Wilson, had become an employee of Countrywide but did not get involved in trying to overcome the day to day management problems. This put more pressure on Fletcher, who said she had to deal with 700 email complaints within four months. She also became the focus for complaints from unhappy staff.

Countrywide officials looked into the problem and accepted that staff were vociferous and negative, yet uncomfortable about approaching Mr Wilson with their complaints as he had told them off for doing so.

Fletcher resigned and brought a claim of constructive dismissal, saying there had been a lack of support and that Mr Wilson's conduct had been rude and hostile.

Held: The Employment Tribunal found there had been a constructive dismissal. The judge observed that Fletcher had been placed under severe stress following the takeover. He added: 'Mr Wilson may not have directed his anger at [her] personally, but . . . his hostility made her frightened and fearful for her own position.'

Deemed dismissal: an employer who refuses to permit an employee to resume her job after maternity leave is deemed to have dismissed her.

- **Deemed dismissal**. An employee who has been on maternity leave but has given appropriate notice that she wishes to return to work is deemed to be dismissed if the employer refuses to let her resume her job.

In the following circumstances dismissal does *not* occur:

1 *The employee fails to return to work after leave of absence has expired.* This may deprive an employee of the right to return but it is not a dismissal.

2 *Completion of purpose of employment.* Employees will not be able to claim that they were dismissed if they were appointed to complete a specific project. Once this is done, their employment ceases. This is common in seafaring and fishing contracts.

3 *Resignation.* Provided that the employee neither resigned voluntarily, nor was forced into doing so (see constructive dismissal, above).

The burden of proving the reason for dismissal was fair

The employer must prove:

(a) grounds for the dismissal;

(b) that in the circumstances it is fair.

Grounds for dismissal

Section 98 of the ERA 1996 lays down five grounds, any of which may justify dismissal:

1 lack of appropriate qualifications/capability to do the job;

2 the employee's conduct;

3 the employee was redundant: the job had ceased to exist;

4 continuance of employment would result in illegality;

5 any other substantial reason.

There are numerous cases to illustrate the application of these criteria, including the following examples. Each case is judged on its particular facts.

Lack of qualification or capability

The missing qualification must be essential to the proper performance of the current job.

Litster v *Thom & Sons Ltd* (1975)

Litster was given a job on condition that he obtained an HGV licence. However, he failed the test and was transferred to a fitter's post. Later he was given notice.

Held: he had been unfairly dismissed. The lack of a licence had not prevented him from serving his employer. (Presumably, if he had been sacked immediately on failing the driving test that might have been justifiable.)

Negligence

Negligence may justify dismissal. One isolated act of negligence is unlikely to be sufficient grounds for dismissal unless it is gross negligence and/or endangers the life and limb of third parties.

Taylor v *Alidair* (1978)

An airline pilot who once landed a plane in such a careless manner as seriously to disturb his passengers and crew was subsequently dismissed.

Held: this was not unfair because very high standards of safety needed to be maintained given the high risks attaching even to a momentary lapse in skill by a pilot.

Employer's fault

Dismissal is not deemed fair if the employee's lack of capability can be attributed to the fault of the employer. In *Davison* v *Kent Meters* (1975) a production line worker was held to have been unfairly dismissed for wrongly assembling several hundred components since she had been neither properly trained nor supervised.

Capability includes incapability caused by sickness

Long-term sickness may make dismissal fair if it places an unreasonable burden on the employer. The employer must prove that they made proper enquiries, including (where appropriate) with the employee's medical adviser. The employer must show that he/she used all practicable means to avoid dismissal, such as offering reduced hours or different duties to accommodate the employee's needs, or the employee may have the right to claim discrimination on grounds of disability.

Misconduct

Misconduct covers a multitude of obvious situations, including lying, fighting, theft, and dangerous and careless behaviour, but a wider range of behaviour may constitute grounds for fair dismissal. Employees who are guilty of rudeness to superiors, drinking on duty, or who refuse to cooperate with management instructions may also be fairly dismissed. The crucial factor is that the misconduct must be incidental to the job that the employee was employed to do.

In *Community Integrated Care Ltd* v *De Smith* (2008), the EAT held that Ms De Smith's dismissal for swearing at a resident of the care home where she worked was fair. Such behaviour was defined as gross misconduct under the employee rules at the home, which gave fair warning of the consequences of breach.

Conduct which occurs in the employee's spare time may be incidental to employment if it reflects adversely on the employee's suitability for the job or reasonably reduces the employer's confidence in the employee.

Moore v *C & A Modes* (1981)

Ms Moore worked as shop assistant for C & A. She was caught shoplifting in another shop.

Held: this was fair dismissal. Her conduct clearly reflected adversely on her integrity and made it reasonable for the employer to suspect that she might steal from her employer.

British Home Stores v *Burchell* (1980, EAT)

BHS dismissed Ms Burchell on the grounds of dishonesty in the BHS store where she worked.

Held: EAT determined it was a fair dismissal and made the following important points relevant to all misconduct dismissals.

Where misconduct is alleged:

(a) the employer must genuinely believe the employee is guilty of the misconduct;

(b) the employer must have reasonable grounds for that belief; and

(c) this belief must have been reached after a reasonable investigation.

Proof does not have to be proved to a criminal standard (beyond a reasonable doubt) and the employer does not have to adopt a procedure that would amount to a criminal investigation.

Dismissal for misconduct was held to be fair in all the following cases: *Atkin* v *Enfield Hospital Management Committee* (1975): failure to wear appropriate clothing; *Boychuk* v *Symons Holdings* (1977): wearing provocative badges in breach of instructions and several warnings; *Newman* v *Alarm Co. Ltd* (1976): conducting a sexual relationship in the company's time; *Parsons* v *McLoughlin* (1981): fighting; *Minter* v *Wellingborough Foundries* (1981): refusing to attend a training course.

Modern technology and social media provide new opportunities for misbehaviour. Posts which are likely to be damaging to the employer's business by bringing it into disrepute may well justify dismissal. Facebook was the first to feature in litigation after an employee published insulting comments about a fellow worker.

Teggart v *Teletech UK Ltd* (2012)

Mr T stated on his Facebook page that a fellow female colleague had a sexual relationship with most of the other Teletech staff. When she objected and tried to get the comment removed, he posted a comment suggesting that she indulged in bestiality. Teletech sacked him for gross misconduct in that he had brought the company into disrepute and harassed a fellow employee.

Held: he had been fairly dismissed for harassing a colleague. However, there was no evidence to suggest that the postings had brought the company into disrepute.

The Employment Appeals Tribunal held that abusive tweets were potentially grounds for dismissal in *Games Retail Limited* v *Laws* (2014).

Breaching the workplace smoking policy may also be sufficient to justify dismissal. This includes the use of E-cigarettes but only if they are specifically included in the policy: *Insley v Accent Catering* (2014). ACAS provides some useful guidance to employers on the best way to draft policies in relation to both smoking and the use of social media.

Worth thinking about?

What behaviour in relation to the use of social media do you think would be likely to justify dismissal?

Suggested solutions can be found in Appendix 2.

Facebook and YouTube are admissible as evidence of misconduct.

Gill v SAS Ground Services UK Ltd (2009, ET)

Mrs Gill was on sick leave after minor surgery and took the opportunity to attend London Fashion Week. She posted on Facebook that she had been 'auditioning 300 models' and had choreographed a fashion show, while footage on YouTube showed her on the catwalk, presenting a bouquet to the event organiser.

Held: she had been fairly dismissed as her presence at the event had been much more than purely social.

Redundancy

This topic is dealt with in depth later in this chapter.

Statutory restriction

This is where the employer claims that the employee can no longer be legally employed, or can no longer legally perform the job. Disqualification from driving is an obvious example, provided that driving is central to the job description. Dismissal is not automatically fair in such circumstances. The nature of the job, the length of disqualification, the type of criminal offence from which it arose and the possibility of redeployment must all be considered.

Mathieson v Noble (1972)

A travelling salesman who lost his driving licence arranged to pay for a driver out of his own pocket, but his employer dismissed him.

Held: he should not have been dismissed unless or until it was evident that this arrangement was unworkable.

Retirement

There is no longer a specific retirement age. An employer may be able to show that imposing one is justifiable in particular circumstances under equality legislation (see Chapter 18).

Some other substantial reason

A variety of circumstances which do not fit into any of the above categories may make dismissal reasonable. This might include having a sexual relationship with the employer's wife:

Whitlow v Alkanet Construction (1987)

Whitlow was asked by a senior executive to do some work at his house, where he departed from management instructions by starting a relationship with the executive's wife.

Held: he was fairly dismissed since he was in breach of his duty of good faith.

In *Gorfin* v *Distressed Gentlefolks' Aid Association* (1973) it was held that dismissal of an employee to resolve a personality clash may be reasonable to restore harmony to the workplace, when all other reasonable steps to resolve the situation have failed.

Farr v Hoveringham Gravels Ltd (1972)

A term in Farr's contract required him to live within reasonable travelling distance of his workplace, as he was sometimes needed to cope with emergencies outside working hours.

Held: it was fair for his employer to dismiss him after he had moved house to an address 44 miles away.

- *Long-term sickness* may amount to a 'substantial' reason to justify dismissal, though the employer must show that it has made all reasonable efforts to accommodate the employee. (See also disability discrimination, Chapter 18.)

- *Economic reasons* may also be treated as 'substantial', provided that the employer can show that these are based on good business practice. Employment tribunals seem readily convinced by such arguments. Employees who leave in protest at attempts to impose detrimental changes to their contracts may well fail in a claim that they have been constructively and unfairly dismissed. If, for instance, the employer can show that the new terms will result in cost saving, necessary to the continuance of the business and maintenance of most of the existing workforce, these are likely to be treated as substantial reasons.

St John of God (Care Services) Ltd v Brooks (1992, EAT)

A hospital, after large cuts in Government funding, offered its staff new contracts which reduced pay and overtime and removed paid holiday entitlement.

Held: the employer had provided substantial reasons for its decision, which must be examined with reference to all the relevant circumstances and not just to its impact on the employees.

Fairness of dismissal

It is not enough for the employer to prove that there were adequate grounds for dismissal. The appropriate procedures must also be followed.

Polkey v A.E. Dayton Services Ltd (1987, HL)

An employee claimed unfair dismissal on the grounds of redundancy because the employer had failed to carry out the required consultation procedure. The employer argued that this was irrelevant, as redundancy was inevitable regardless of consultation.

Held: the dismissal was unfair purely because the proper procedure had not been carried out, though where the procedure would have made no difference the amount of damages may be reduced.

Section 98(4) states that fairness is judged by deciding whether in all the circumstances of the case the employer acted reasonably. This 'shall be determined according to equity and the merits of the case'. It is not enough for the employer to prove that the employee received contractual notice and that one of the relevant criteria is satisfied. Good industrial practice demands that dismissal (except for gross misconduct, justifying summary dismissal) must not come out of the blue.

To justify the dismissal, the employer must prove that he or she dealt with the problem in a reasonable way in the particular circumstances. If the employee was dismissed after disciplinary proceedings, the employment tribunal should take into account whether the employer has complied with the ACAS Code of Practice on Disciplinary Practice and Procedures in Employment or the employer's own contractual grievance and disciplinary procedures, provided they are of an equivalent standard. This requires appropriate grievance procedures which may help to prevent situations escalating to the point where disciplinary proceeding may result.

Requirements of the grievance procedure

The grievance procedure requires that the employer must:

- notify the employee of the nature of the grievance;
- hold a meeting with the employee within a reasonable time;
- allow the employee to be accompanied to the meeting by a representative (e.g. union representative or lawyer);
- decide what action is appropriate;
- allow the employee to appeal against any decision taken by the employer.

Unreasonable failure by the employer to comply with the Code gives the tribunal the discretion to increase damages in a successful case by up to 25 per cent.

Disciplinary proceedings

The Code requires these to be timely and fairly constituted to prevent bias. The employee must be permitted to bring a colleague or trade union representative.

Dismissal should be the last resort and the employee must be given every opportunity to change. Verbal or written warnings should be given. Where appropriate the employer should provide training, support and supervision. In some cases, the employer should explore the possibility of redeployment.

Appeals

The Code requires appropriate appeal procedures. After any dismissal the employee is automatically entitled to an appeal hearing in person. Appeals in writing are not sufficient. Failure to follow these procedures entitles the employee to claim unfair dismissal and, if this claim is successful, his or her damages may be increased by up to 25 per cent.

Dismissal is automatically unfair in certain specified circumstances

The following employees, who are dismissed, are entitled to take their cases to the tribunal without having to satisfy the two-year continuous employment requirement; the reason for their dismissal must relate to:

- ERA 1996, s 99 (as amended by the Employment Relations Act 1999): women dismissed in connection with the exercise of maternity rights. This right covers *any person* exercising rights to parental leave to take time off for domestic incidents;
- ERA 1996, s 100: health and safety representatives;
- ERA 1996, ss 102 and 105: trustees of occupational pension schemes;
- ERA 1996, s 103: employees representing the workforce in redundancy consultations;
- ERA 1996, ss 103A and 105A (as amended by the Public Interest Disclosure Act 1998 and the ERRA 2013) protects employees dismissed for 'whistle blowing' provided the disclosure was made in the public interest to the appropriate person;

- ERA 1996, s 104: employees who have taken legal action against their employer to enforce statutory rights;
- ERA 1996, s 105: employees who have been made redundant;
- ERA 1996, s 108(4) as amended by E&RRA: political opinion or affiliation;
- Trade Union and Labour Relations (Consolidation) Act 1992 (TULR(C)A 1992), s 152: trade union membership or activity. This protection is extended by s 14 of and Schedule 5 to the Employment Relations Act 1999 (adding s 238A to TULR(C)A 1992) to include protection for employees participating in official industrial action;
- Employment Relations Act 1999, s 12: employees accompanying workers to a disciplinary hearing.

Real life

Sacha, trade union representative for his section at Smallville Borough Council, receives an email from Helga, a housing officer who is currently on leave. Helga explains that she is about to resign as she has been unhappy at work ever since Lucas became her line manager. She says Lucas has been endlessly and unjustifiably critical of her work, made her alter her leave plans to attend a tenants' conference, has been unsupportive when Helga sought his help in dealing with difficult and abusive tenants and reprimanded her for incompetence in front of a queue of people at the enquiry desk.

This all suggests that Helga may have a good case for constructive dismissal if she does leave. She would be able to cite these incidents as evidence that Smallville is in breach of its duty of trust and confidence to her. Sacha should suggest that she attempts to resolve the matter through Smallville's grievance procedure. However, if she does choose to resign she must make sure that she repeats all the information that she gave Sacha in her letter of resignation to indicate her grievance. Otherwise, she would be in danger of having her case struck out.

Redundancy

Redundancy: an employee's job ceases to exist because the employer restructures/changes business practices/ceases to carry on business/or closes location where employee works.

A redundant employee may have the right to make one or both of the following claims:

1 **Redundancy** *payment*. While it is legitimate to reduce the size of a workforce, thus rendering some employees, surplus to requirements, those employees may have statutory entitlement to compensation for losing their jobs (a redundancy payment).

2 *Unfair dismissal.* Employees who can prove that the method by which they were selected for redundancy did not meet the standards of good industrial practice, may additionally have a claim for unfair dismissal which might result in a compensatory award or an order for their reinstatement.

Redundancy payment

Eligibility

In order to be able to claim compensation the claimant must be able to prove the following:

1 *Two year's continuous service.* With the relevant employer.

2 *Relevant employee status.* Certain categories of employees excluded from claiming unfair dismissal are also excluded from statutory redundancy protection.

3 *Dismissal.* To be able to claim, employees must be able to prove that they have been actively or constructively dismissed within the meaning of ERA 1996, s 136. Dismissal includes the expiration of a short-term contract where renewal is not offered. An employee is also dismissed if the employer dies, or if the employer is a partnership or company which is dissolved or wound up. An employee who leaves voluntarily, having been warned of the threat of redundancy, is not dismissed.

4 *Redundancy has caused the dismissal.* Under ERA 1996, s 139 redundancy may occur where:

(a) the employer ceases to carry on business or ceases to carry on business at the location where the employee worked; or

(b) the employer restructures the business or changes production methods so that fewer employees are needed.

(An employee may also be redundant if dismissed by the employer who intends to take any of the above actions.)

Change of workplace location

Where the employee's contract contains a term that the employee may be required to work at any place of business the employer directs, the employee is not made redundant by being moved. If no term exists, it is a question of fact whether or not redundancy has occurred. Distance is often a material fact in deciding this. Where compliance with the employer's order would force the employee to move house or undertake a much longer journey to work than before, the employee will be able to claim to have been constructively dismissed in circumstances which make the employee redundant. Compare the following two cases.

O'Brien v Associated Fire Alarms (1969)

Reduction in the amount of business available in Liverpool resulted in the employer offering O'Brien a transfer to its Barrow-in-Furness branch. When he turned the offer down he was dismissed.

Held: he had been made redundant. Taking it up would have increased his journey to work very considerably.

Managers (Holborn) Ltd v Hohne (1977)

Held: an employee dismissed when he refused a transfer from an office in Holborn to one in Regent Street (a short tube ride) had not been made redundant.

Offers of suitable alternative employment

Employees offered suitable redeployment cannot, if dismissed, claim that they have been made redundant (ERA 1996, s 138(1)). What is 'suitable' is a question of fact to be determined by the tribunal in each case. Factors like travelling distances, domestic problems and lack of appropriate educational facilities for the employee's children may have to be taken into account. In *Devon Primary Care Trust* v *Readman* (2013, CA) it was held that when deciding if a refusal is reasonable the court must apply a two-pronged test. First, the court must determine whether judged objectively the employer's offer was reasonable. Secondly, a subjective test is used to decide whether the employee's refusal is unreasonable given their particular circumstances.

While an employer must show reasonable sensitivity and regard for the individual employee, there are limits. In *Fuller* v *Stephanie Bowman Ltd* (1977) a secretary working at her employer's Mayfair branch was held to have acted unreasonably when she refused to transfer to a Soho office because it was situated over a sex shop.

Under ERA 1996, s 138(2) an employee who takes up an alternative post has at least four weeks to decide if it is workable. If the employee gives up within the time limit, any rights to redundancy pay are not prejudiced.

Time limitation on redundancy claims

Employees must start their claims within six months of the date when a short-term contract expired or when their notice period expired. Late claims may be admitted by the tribunal if this is judged to be just and equitable.

Financial entitlement

This is calculated with reference to the age of the employee and the length of service up to a maximum of 20 years:

- 18–21: half a week's pay per year of service;
- 22–40: one week's pay per year of service;
- 41 or older: one-and-a-half weeks' pay per year of service.

A week's pay in 2019 is subject to an upper limit of £525. The maximum amount of statutory redundancy pay is £15,750, but there is, of course, nothing to stop an employer from voluntarily exceeding this. The Secretary of State is empowered to vary this sum (ERA 1996, s 227) and under the Employment Relations Act 1999 does so with reference to the Retail Price Index.

Unfair dismissal arising from redundancy

An employee who has been made redundant may have an additional claim for unfair dismissal (s 98). To avoid liability, the employer must show that he or she acted reasonably in selecting the employee for redundancy. Criteria determining selection should include safeguards against bias. The employee must have been given proper warning, adequate consultation must have taken place, and proper consideration must have been given to the provision of alternative employment. (The relevant awards of compensation are described below.)

Thomas v *BNP Paribas* (2016)

Mr Thomas had worked for BNP Paribas for over 40 years and become director of the property division. After a strategic review he was selected for redundancy from a pool of one. He was then sent immediately on garden leave and told not to contact colleagues or clients. A letter confirming this and sent the next day from the management addressed him as Paul, although his real name was Peter, which as a long-term employee he found upsetting. A list of possible alternative posts was also sent to him but all turned out to be unsuitable. A number of procedural errors followed. He was shocked and upset by the process. He appealed against the redundancy, claiming that the process had been a sham, but lost. His case failed at the employment tribunal which gave no reasons for its decision.

The EAT held: while defects in consultation did not necessarily make dismissal unfair, a tribunal must give reasons for its decision. It had described the process as 'perfunctory and insensitive' in its dealing with Mr Thomas but still found against him. The case must be remitted to a different tribunal for retrial with a reasoned decision on its conclusion.

What is reasonable is judged with reference to the size and resources of the employer's business. A successful claimant is entitled to the same levels of compensation as any other unfairly dismissed employee.

Transfer of undertakings

Transfer of undertaking: a new employer takes over an existing business.

In the event of a new employer taking over an existing business entity (a **transfer of undertaking**) current employees have enjoyed protection of their job security and existing conditions of service since 1981 when, prompted by the Acquired Rights Directive 1977 (ARD), the Transfer of Undertakings (Protection of Employment) Regulations 1981 (TUPE 1981) were introduced. These were replaced by the Transfer of Undertakings (Protection of Employment) Regulations 2006 (TUPE 2006). The rights and obligations of the previous regulations remain in place, but the 2006 regulations clarify and update them to reflect case law developments and increase the rights of employees and the duties of employers. The Collective Redundancies and Transfer of Undertakings (Protection of Employment) (Amendment) Regulations 2014 in turn amend and update the 2006 Regulations but do not replace them.

The regulations apply to a 'relevant transfer'.

In *Holis Metal Industries* v *GMB* (2007) part of a British-owned curtain-making business was transferred to an Israeli firm which refused to take on any of the current workforce. The EAT refused to strike out the GMB's claim and held that potentially TUPE may apply to transfers to business outside the UK. HHJ Ansell said:

> I am persuaded that the wording of both the ARD and Regulation 3 is precise in setting the application of the regulation to transfers of undertakings situated immediate before the transfer in the UK. Set against the purpose of protecting the rights of workers in the event of change of employer it seems to me that a purposeful approach requires that those employees should be protected even if the transfer is to be across borders outside the EU.

The meaning of 'relevant transfer'

Relevant transfer includes:

- transfer of a business, undertaking or part of one to another employer as a going concern (e.g. a company takeover or merger); or
- a 'service provision change', e.g. contracting out of services or re-tendering or bringing the work in-house.

The 2014 regulations require the activities carried out by the transferee employer to be 'substantially the same' as before the transfer. This provides clarity and brings the definition in line with case law which has developed in the intervening years.

A business transfer only takes place when the identity of the employer of a discrete group of employees changes. Certain types of transfer are, however, specifically excluded, such as transfer by share takeover, where the employer (the company) remains unchanged despite a change of shareholders.

The meaning of 'undertaking'

This has been interpreted widely by the courts and covers non-commercial operations as well as ordinary businesses, for instance, contracting out of public services by competitive tendering, or charities. No one factor is crucial to this definition and the ECJ has warned against the application of technical rules in this context. It may represent a small part of the transferor's enterprise as long as it remains 'an economic entity which retains its identity'. The bottom line is whether there is evidence that the unit transferred retains a minimum level of independence, enabling it to enjoy a separate existence either on its own, or as a discrete part of a larger undertaking.

Who is protected?

Any employee in the business or the part of the business being transferred who was employed immediately before the transfer took place is protected. Employees who can prove they were dismissed earlier for reasons connected with the transfer can also sue. Employees include not just those with a contract of service but also apprentices and workers supplied by an agency.

The rights of the employees

Both collective and individual rights are created by the regulations.

Information and consultation with employees

Both old and new employers must inform the relevant trade union or elected employee representatives of the transfer, when it will take place and why it is happening. Information as to the legal, economic and social implications of the transfer is also required, including any measures which either employer may need to take in relation to them. Consultation with union or elected representatives is generally required regarding such measures as, for example, a reduction in manpower. However, since 2014 direct consultation is possible in a business with fewer than 10 employees if they have no union representatives.

TUPE 2006 introduced liability for failure to supply the relevant information to employees and enabled the employment tribunal to order compensation to be paid jointly or severally by the old and new employers.

Provision of employee liability information

TUPE 2014 requires the transferor to provide information to the transferee prior to the transfer about the identity and age of the employees who will be transferred as well as details of collective agreements, grievances, and disciplinary proceedings concerning them within no later than 28 days before the transfer date. This has been extended from the 14 days required by the 2006 Regulations to help ensure better exchange of information and promote effective consultation. Failure to provide information enables an employee to claim for compensation of £500 at the employment tribunal if this is considered just and equitable.

Job security

The 2014 Regulations amend the 2006 Regulations to remove the words 'connected with' [the transfer]. Dismissal is now automatically unfair if it arises directly or indirectly from the transfer unless it is 'caused by an economic, technical or organisational reason' (**ETO**). Circumstances comprising an ETO have been extended by the 2014 Regulations to include an employee being required to work in a different location. However, an employee might still successfully claim that dismissal was unfair under the ERA 1996. Redundancy may be justified as an ETO.

ETO:
an economic, technical or organisational reason to justify changes to workforce/ conditions of service after the transfer of an undertaking.

Continuation of existing terms and conditions of employment

The transfer does not terminate the employee's contract of employment: all the existing rights, duties and liabilities of the old employer are generally transferred to the new one. The 2014 Regulations ensure that any variation by a transferee employer of a transferee will now be void if the sole or principal reason is the transfer, as opposed to merely *connected with* it as previously applied. The aim is to clarify the regulations and prevent unnecessary litigation.

Changes can only be justified if relevant to an ETO. Failure to comply with this may entitle the employee to claim constructive and unfair dismissal.

Insolvent businesses

TUPE 2006 makes it easier for transfer of a business which has become insolvent. The regulations prevent some of the transferor's pre-existing debts from passing to the transferee and in appropriate circumstances enable a transferee to take on a reduced workforce.

Claiming at the employment tribunal

ACAS conciliation

The E&RRA 2013 requires any employee who intends to take a case to the employment tribunal to inform ACAS of this first. No proceedings can be started until ACAS has issued an early Conciliation Certificate which proves that the parties have been informed about the process. Either party can refuse to proceed with conciliation after this point. If they decide to go through the conciliation process they may allow ACAS to help them achieve a settlement; but even then they are free to reject the proposal and proceed to the tribunal.

Claims are time limited

A claim must generally be started within three months less one day from the date of dismissal. In discrimination cases time runs from the date of the last discriminatory act. This time limit is extended where early conciliation takes place.

Cost

The E&RRA 2013 gave the Ministry of Justice the power to introduce fees at the employment tribunal which was exercised at the end of July 2013. In any case concerning disputes over pay and unpaid wages the claimant was required to pay £160 to issue a claim with a further £250 to pay if the case went to a hearing. In a claim for unfair dismissal or discrimination (apart from equal pay) the claimant had to pay £250 to start the claim with a further fee of £950 payable if a hearing took place. A successful claimant could recover the cost of fees from the defendant at the discretion of the court. Very limited financial assistance, based on a means test relating to income and savings, was available but it was helpful only to the very poorest claimants.

Adverse effects of fees on employees

From the outset there was concern from many about the ill effects of making fees payable in employment cases. The impact was immediate and considerable. Figures released by the Ministry of Justice in 2014 showed that overall the number of single claims to the employment tribunal between October to December 2013 dropped by 67 per cent for single claims and by 79 per cent overall. A Government review in January 2017 affirmed these figures and suggested that in some cases the cost of the fees may be greater than the sum to be claimed.

Judicial review proceedings instigated by the Unison trade union in 2014 claimed that the fees were unlawful because they interfered with access to justice and were also indirectly discriminatory to women, who were more likely to need to bring discrimination claims. Unison's case was unsuccessful until it reached the Supreme Court (*R (on the application of Unison)* v *The Lord Chancellor* (2017) UKSC. Here it was held that the imposition of fees at the employment tribunal was unlawful; the sharp drop in the number of claims evidenced by recent statistics indicated that fees substantially interfered with employees' rights to access the courts. Employment law rights existed to prevent an imbalance of power between employers and employees; they were only effective if an appropriate means to enforce them could be exercised. It was also held that the fees in discrimination cases were indirectly discriminatory to women and could not be justified as a proportionate means of obtaining a legitimate object. As a result of this case a refund of all fees on past and pending decisions has been ordered by the Government.

Unpaid award penalties

Penalties were increased in April 2016 by amendment to the Employment Tribunals Act 1996. If an award is unpaid the Government will issue a penalty notice to the defaulting employer. Failure to comply will result in a penalty of 50 per cent of the unpaid sum subject to a minimum of £100 up to a maximum of £5,000 payable to the Government.

Remedies

1 Reinstatement: ERA 1996, s 113

This may be ordered at the request of the employee if it is a practicable option. If granted, the employee resumes the job under the same pay and conditions as before.

2 Re-engagement

The employer may be ordered to find a reasonably comparable job for the employee. The new job may be with an associated employer (ERA 1996, s 114).

3 Compensation

An employer may be liable to compensate an employee who is unfairly dismissed. Compensation rates are assessed and adjusted in April every year by the Government.

Basic award: damages intended to cover an unfairly dismissed employee's loss of income while they seek new employment.

The **basic award** (ERA 1996, s 119) is intended to protect the employee against the losses caused by a break in continuous employment and is, therefore, calculated in the same way as the statutory redundancy award with reference to the employee's age, current gross weekly pay and years of service:

- an employee aged 18–21 is entitled to half a week's pay per year of service;
- an employee aged 22–40 is entitled to one week's pay per year of service;
- an employee aged 41 or older is entitled to one-and-a-half weeks' pay per year of service.

Compensatory award: damages intended to compensate an unfairly dismissed employee for losses arising from the dismissal which are the fault of the employer.

Under ERA 1996, s 120A the basic award may be increased to four weeks' pay if the employer failed to observe the statutory dismissal procedures and the employee would otherwise receive less than four weeks' pay. The maximum for a week's pay in the year beginning in April 2019 was £525 and the maximum basic award is limited to 30 weeks' pay. The minimum basic award in cases where a dismissal is unfair by virtue of health and safety, employee representative, trade union, or occupational pension trustee reasons is £6,408.

The **compensatory award** is intended to redress losses arising from the dismissal so far as these may be seen as the fault of the employer (ERA 1996, s 123).

The Secretary of State may vary the minimum of the basic award and the upper limit of the compensatory award with reference to the Retail Price Index (Employment Relations Act 1999, s 29). The conduct of the employee is relevant to the size of the compensatory award. It may be reduced if the behaviour of the employee contributed to the dismissal, or failed to take reasonable steps to mitigate his or her loss. It is unlimited in discrimination cases.

The E&RRA 2013 gave the power to impose a one year cap on the compensatory award. This power was exercised by the Secretary of State under the Unfair Dismissal (Variation of the Limit of Compensatory Award) Order 2013. The current cap is £86,444 or 52 weeks' pay if this is lower.

The **additional award** may be payable (ERA 1996, s 117, as amended by the Employment Relations Act 1999) where an employer fails to comply with an order to re-engage or reinstate an employee. It consists of 26–52 weeks' pay at the current rate.

Additional award: damages awarded against an employer who fails to comply with an order to re-engage or reinstate an employee.

Recommendations

The employer may be ordered to take practical steps to correct the situation *vis-à-vis* the claimant although there are no enforcement powers. In discrimination cases this originally extended to making recommendations for the benefit of the wider workforce, but the Deregulation Act 2015 abolished this power.

Penalties for non-payment of damages

Under the Small Business, Enterprise and Employment Act 2015, s 150 an employer may be fined for failing to comply with a tribunal judgment. If they fail to pay within 28 days of receiving an enforcement notice they may be fined up to 50 per cent of the total sum of damages.

Chapter summary

Wrongful dismissal: court/employment tribunal action.

Unfair dismissal: ERA 1996 employment tribunal action.

Employee must prove:

(a) dismissal (actual/constructive/deemed);

(b) 24 months' continuous employment;

(c) use of grievance procedure.

Employer must prove: dismissal fair (grounds and procedures).

Redundancy ERA 1996

Payment: employee entitled if:

(a) 24 months' continuous employment;

(b) relevant status;

(c) dismissed because of actual/imminent redundancy.

Unfair dismissal on account of redundancy

If employer cannot prove fair procedures (selection/consultation/suitable alternative work offer).

Transfer of Undertakings (TUPE 2006)

Current employment contract terms of the relevant body of workers continue to apply after takeover/merger/sale of business/part of business subject to ETO.
Any redundancy connected with the transfer is unfair subject to ETO.
Consultation with/information for employees is required prior to transfer.
Some adjustment of liability for employer taking on an insolvent business.

Remedies

(a) reinstatement;

(b) damages: basic/compensatory/additional award;

(c) recommendations.

Review questions 18

1 Define and distinguish between wrongful and unfair dismissal.

2 Explain the meaning of constructive dismissal.

3 On what grounds may Title Enterprises claim that they fairly dismissed the following employees?

   (a) Zora, who was given a job as a trainee lorry driver three years ago and has just failed the HGV test for the sixth time.
   (b) Carmel, who sexually harassed Ms Woodbine at the works' Christmas party.
   (c) Pable, a van driver who has crashed his vehicle three times.
   (d) Richard, who was recently convicted of being drunk and disorderly one Saturday night.

4 Have the following employees been made redundant by Linux plc?

(a) Adam, who heard rumours of redundancy and resigned.

(b) Poppy, a senior computer programmer, whose current workplace is being closed down. She is told that she is being transferred to another branch 80 miles away.

5 What procedures should be observed by an employer before making employees redundant?

6 What rights of employees are created by the Transfer of Undertaking Regulations 2006?

Answers to all review questions can be found in Appendix 2.

Advanced questions 18

(A) Critically evaluate the law of unfair dismissal.

(B) What difference is there between the requirements to consult a) unions, and b) employees where an employer is considering dismissing for redundancy?

Answers to the advanced questions can be found at **go.pearson.com/uk/he/resources.**

Take a closer look

The following cases provide important examples of how the law in this chapter has developed. They are primary sources illustrating the law in action and give more detail about their facts, as well as helping to understand the law and to appreciate how the judges reached their decisions.

Try looking them up in the law reports or accessing them via a database, e.g. BAILII (www.bailii.org/databases.html). LexisNexis or Westlaw may be available in the university or college library, or extracts may be found in a case book. (See Appendix 1: Additional resources.)

Farr v *Hoveringham Gravels Ltd* [1972] IRLR 104

Gorfin v *Distressed Gentlefolks' Aid Association* [1973] IRLR 290

Shergold v *Fieldway Medical Centre* [2006] ICR 304, EAT

St John of God (Care Services) Ltd v *Brooks* [1992] ICR 715, EAT

Web activity

See the ACAS website for more information about handling workplace disputes and discipline:

www.acas.org.uk/index.aspx?articleid=1364

ACAS also provide advice on the use of social media in the workplace:

www.acas.org.uk/index.aspx?articleid=3375

Read 'Why the *BHS* v *Burchell* decision is still relevant 40 years on' by James Medhurst on the Personnel Today website:

www.personneltoday.com/hr/british-home-stores-v-burchell-40-years-on/

Assignment 17

Critically evaluate the rights of employers in relation to social media postings by their employees.

PART

5

Introduction to company law

Business organisations

Learning objectives

On completion of this chapter, students should be able to:

★ define the different forms of business organisation described in this chapter;

★ understand the concept of legal personality;

★ distinguish between public and private companies;

★ explain what is meant by limited liability and how it is created.

Introduction

Anybody setting up a business has choices about its initial structure. The majority of businesses start as a sole trader operation, with the owner taking all the profits but entirely responsible for everything from raising capital to business liability. The partnership is a good option when two or more people want to set up a business together. Partners share the profits, but like the sole trader, remain personally liable for all the debts of the business. Both sole traders and partners have restricted opportunities for obtaining capital and often the only way to get a loan is to use personal assets, as security, so the financial risk may be substantial. Business owners may be able to reduce that risk by limiting their liability. The best way to do this is to set up a registered limited liability company. This makes the business corporate, an independent being from its members who stand to lose no more than their initial investment, if the company fails. This makes it a much more tempting investment prospect than a partnership or sole trader business. This chapter will more closely examine how these different types of business may be created. First, though, it is necessary to gain understanding of three concepts which are recurring themes in the law relating to business organisation – legal personality, incorporation and limited liability.

Legal personality, incorporation and limited liability

Legal personality

Legal personality: the bundle of rights and duties attaching to a human or legal/artificial person/corporation.

Under English law all human beings are endowed with a **legal personality** from birth until death. A person's legal personality is made up of that person's legal rights and duties. These are subject to change throughout the lifetime of the subject. A child has only very limited rights and few duties. The average adult has a complex bundle of rights and duties determined by the adult's current status: for example, as a married or single person, employer, employee, taxpayer, receiver of welfare benefit, debtor or creditor.

Incorporation

It is not just human beings who have legal rights and duties: the law permits the creation of artificial or legal persons (corporations) that have a legal personality, separate from the members.

Corporation: an office or organisation with its own legal personality distinct from holder/members.

A **corporation** is brought into being (incorporated) by operation of law. Some form of legal process must be completed before it comes into existence. This chapter is primarily concerned with corporations created exclusively for commercial purposes by registration in compliance with the Companies Acts. However, corporations may be created by other means and for different reasons. The Crown may create corporations by royal charter for a variety of different purposes, like education (the universities) or management of a profession (the Chartered Institute of Surveyors) or public service broadcasting (the BBC). Parliament may grant corporate status to an organisation by passing a special Act; the nationalised industries were all created in this way.

All types of corporation have certain characteristics in common:

1 *Creation by operation of law.* The necessary legal process (charter, Act or registration) must take place to bring the corporation into existence. Once created, the corporation will continue to exist unless or until the appropriate legal procedure takes place to bring it to an end. A registered company may be wound up, a chartered corporation may have its charter withdrawn and repeal of the relevant statute ends the life of a statutory corporation.

Corporation sole:
one-member
corporation.

2 *One or many members.* Incorporation may create an office held by one person (a **corporation sole**), like a bishop or the Public Guardian, but most corporate bodies have at least two members (a corporation aggregate).

3 *Its own legal personality.* The corporation's rights and duties are conferred by the charter or law under which it was created. The company's legal personality is distinct from that of the company's members. A change in membership does not affect the existence of the company. Even if all the members of a corporation were to die simultaneously, the company would continue to exist.

4 While company officers and employees may cause breaches of its contracts, or commit torts or crimes in the execution of its policies, it is the company which is legally liable for the wrongdoing. For example, a registered company which pollutes a river may be prosecuted and fined. Payment of the fine will come from the company's bank account, not the personal finances of the managing director whose order caused the pollution.

Limited liability

Limited liability:
limitation of financial
responsibility for
registered company's
liabilities enjoyed by
company members.

Most registered companies limit their liability by shares but it is also possible to limit it by guarantee. The members of such a company have **limited liability** which means that, while they do not enjoy complete immunity, their liability is generally limited to the sum which they have agreed to invest, even if the company runs out of money and cannot pay its creditors. A minority of companies have unlimited liability and their members will be responsible for any debts which the company cannot cover.

The sole trader

Sole trader:
one-man/woman
business.

Any person may set up in business and trade under his or her own name or a business name. Such a **sole trader** has independent control of the business and all the profits are his or hers. He or she also has total responsibility for the legal liabilities and financial risks of the business. The sole trader provides all the start-up capital; often this will involve a bank loan secured by a mortgage on the sole trader's home. Since he or she is personally liable for all business debts, the sole trader may be made bankrupt by the creditors of the business.

The partnership

Unincorporated association:
organisation with no
legal personality of
its own.

This is an **unincorporated association**, which simply means that it is an organisation without any legal personality distinct from its members. There are many different kinds of unincorporated associations which exist for social, educational, political and business purposes. Examples include sports clubs, pressure groups, local chambers of commerce, trade unions and political parties, not to speak of the Scouts, Guides and Brownies. What distinguishes a partnership from these organisations, is the motivation of the partners: they have joined together intending to carry on a business with a view to making and sharing profits.

Partnership:
two or more people working together with a view to sharing profit.

The **partnership** is traditionally the favoured method of business organisation for many professionals like doctors, solicitors and accountants. They can share facilities which a sole practitioner would be unable to afford. Also under the rules governing these professions they are not allowed to form limited companies. It is also very common for small businesses to operate from this base, as it enables start-up capital and expertise to be drawn from a number of people. Partners, like sole traders, often raise their contributions through a bank loan and are also personally liable for business debts.

There are three types of partnership:

1 The traditional partnership.
2 Limited partnership.
3 Limited liability partnerships.

1 The traditional partnership

The Partnership Act 1890 governs the creation and regulation of partnerships.

Forming the partnership

It is usual to formalise the existence of the partnership by written agreement; this might be written articles of partnership or a more formalised document, the deed of partnership. Writing is not essential, though. The partnership relationship may be implied from the conduct of two or more persons carrying on a business in common (as joint proprietors) with the intention of making and sharing the profits arising from their enterprise. The partnership relationship, with all its ensuing rights and duties, exists from the time when the business is up and running. Planning to run a business does not in itself create the partnership.

For clarity and for evidential purposes it is wise to have a written partnership agreement, which indicates the nature and purpose of the business, its name and address, the amount of capital invested by each partner, and how profits are to be shared and paid. If there are *sleeping partners*, whose only involvement is providing capital and taking a share of the profits, the agreement should specify which partners are actually responsible for the day to day management.

The partnership agreement, whether written or unwritten, is a contract governed by the rules considered in earlier contract chapters. Consequently, in *Valencia v Lupar* (2012), the Court of Appeal held that no partnership existed between the parties as the solicitor's letters made it clear that the parties' relationship was not intended to be a partnership until a formal partnership deed was executed. There was no evidence to suggest that the parties had moved from a subject to contract position to a legally binding partnership.

Naming the partnership

The partnership may trade under the names of the partners (Flacon Estates (Estate Agents), Bloggs Bros, Smith & Daughters), or under a business name (Speedy Cleaners). Choice of name must conform to the requirements of the Companies Act 2006 (see Chapter 21).

Numbers of partners

There must be at least two partners. Until 2001, the Companies Act 1985 imposed a maximum of 20 on commercial partnerships. It was believed that a business of such size should more appropriately be run as a registered company. However, the Partnership (Unrestricted Size) No. 17 Regulations 2001 removed this restriction completely. No such limits have ever applied to professional partnerships such as accountants and surveyors, since the rules of their professional organisations do not permit incorporation.

The partnership relationship is a fiduciary one

This means that the partners are placed in a position of trust with each other and have the following duties:

• to make full disclosure to each other of all issues relevant to the business;

• to declare any personal financial benefit received by a partner in carrying out the firm's business;

• not to compete with the firm without the consent of the other partners.

Each partner acts as the agent of the others

When transacting business on behalf of the firm, a partner is treated as its agent. Partners can act only within their legal authority and must carry out their duties with reasonable care and skill. The Partnership Act 1890 states that partners have apparent authority to carry out any transaction relating to the business, therefore, any resulting contract is binding on the other partners whether or not they actually authorised it. Failure to perform the contract could result in an action for breach against any or all of the partners. For example, if a partner ordered headed writing paper for the firm, the other partners will be jointly liable for its cost, even though it had previously been decided by majority at a partners' meeting that new supplies were not needed. Similarly, if a partner committed a tort while carrying out the firm's business, the other partners would be vicariously liable for it. A negligently performed job could give rise to this sort of liability.

The partners are jointly and severally liable for all partnership obligations

As the partnership has no legal existence distinct from its members, all the partners are personally liable for its debts and other legal obligations. If the firm does not have sufficient funds, the partners have to make good the shortfall out of their own funds.

Legal action can be taken against a partnership in its own name, but the partners remain jointly or severally liable for what is owed. This means that if a judgment debt is not paid, it can be enforced against all or any of the partners. This may result in one partner having to pay the entire debt, though that partner may seek a contribution from the others.

Like a sole trader, a partner may be made personally bankrupt if the assets of the business are not sufficient to cover its debts.

Dissolving the partnership

A partnership may come to an end for a number of different reasons.

1 *Lapse of time.* Most partnerships are formed in the belief that they will be continued indefinitely, but a specified period may be stated in the partnership agreement. For example, two people might decide to run catering facilities for the duration of an exhibition or a trade fair.

2 *The sole purpose of the partnership is achieved.* The example in 1 above is also relevant here.

3 *Death or bankruptcy of a partner.* Usually the partnership makes provision for such occurrences, but failure to do so could result in dissolution.

4 *Illegality.* If the purposes of the partnership subsequently become illegal, the partnership contract is frustrated (see Chapter 10). A partnership created for the import of certain goods would be dissolved if the import of those goods was subsequently banned by government regulations.

5 *Notice from a partner.* Unless the agreement provides otherwise, the partnership will terminate if one party decides to leave. Usually provision is made for this.

6 *Court order.* A partner may ask the court to order dissolution on the grounds of mental or physical incapacity of a partner, or because of misconduct by a partner prejudicial to the business or which amounts to wilful and persistent breach of the partnership agreement. The court may also dissolve the partnership if it is just and equitable to do so. Dissolution will be ordered if the business cannot be carried on without making a loss.

2 The limited partnership

Limited partnership: a partnership with limited liability.

The Limited Partnerships Act 1907 enabled the creation of a **limited partnership**. This comprises a number of sleeping partners who must take no active part in running the business and whose liability is restricted to the amount of capital each invested. The partners running the business have unlimited liability for partnership debts. In practice, such partnerships are relatively rare, as anyone seeking limited liability is more likely to seek registration of their business as a company (or a Limited Liability Partnership), though it is recognised as a useful tool for private equity and other investment funds. The Department for Business, Energy and Industrial Strategy (BEIS, formerly BIS) wished to encourage its use and brought in some minor reforms to improve regulation.

The Legislative Reform (Limited Partnerships) Order 2009 resulted in two main amendments to the 1907 Act:

- All limited partnerships must put 'Limited Partnership' or 'LP' after their names.
- The Registrar of Companies must issue a registration of partnership certificate as evidence of the date on which the limited partnership legally came into being.

Corporate status does not result from this process.

3 The limited liability partnership (LLP)

Limited liability partnership: registered partnership with corporate status whose members' liability is limited to the amount of their investment. They are governed by company and partnership law.

Limited liability partnerships are governed by the Limited Liability Partnerships Act 2000 and are partnership/company hybrids. They are corporate bodies and are thus much closer to registered companies than to partnerships. Note that they are quite different from limited partnerships.

A limited liability partnership (LLP) must be registered with the approval of the Companies Registrar. An incorporation document is required. Once registered, the LLP takes on a legal identity of its own, with each partner's liability limited to the amount of his or her investment in the firm. It enjoys all the advantages of incorporation and relatively few of the disadvantages. An LLP can hold property and sue and be sued in its own name. The *ultra vires* rule, which may bind companies to their stated objects (see Chapter 21) does not affect the LLP, so that it is free to pursue any business venture with the agreement of a majority of the partners. It is not subject to the same rules as companies concerning its internal governance and may regulate its relationships with its members and make its own management rules.

Despite incorporation, the LLP is still treated as a partnership for the purposes of tax. This is a key advantage and puts partners in a better financial position than if they were company shareholders. However, certain legal responsibilities follow incorporation. The LLP must present its annual audited accounts to the Companies Registrar and the accounts are then available for public scrutiny. Insolvency procedures governing companies also apply to an LLP.

Remember, limited liability partnerships are quite distinct from limited partnerships and are thus untouched by BIS's amendment of limited partnership law.

Public scrutiny of partnerships

Unless the partnership is an LLP, its affairs, unlike those of a registered company, are not generally subject to any more public scrutiny than those of an individual trader. However, a limited partnership does require registration. Relevant tax returns must be made and the planning requirements of the local authority concerning business use of the premises must be met. Members of the public have no right to inspect the accounts of the partnership and there is no legal duty to audit them.

If a business name is used, the names of the proprietors must be displayed at the place of business and on any letterheads of business stationery (Companies Act 2006, s 1202, which repealed and replaced s 4 of the Business Names Act 1985). This enables customers and traders to ascertain the identity of the people running the business. A partner (including one in a limited liability partnership) has the same duties and rights as any other employer and employee under the Equality Act 2010 (ss 44–45).

The registered company

This is a corporation created in compliance with the registration procedures in the Companies Act 2006 (CA 2006) and monitored by the Companies Registry.

The purposes of the registration process

This serves:

- to check that, before it starts trading, a business is financially viable, has a reasonable chance of success, and is likely to be reputably managed for legal purposes;
- to provide a public record of all such businesses, which may be inspected by interested parties before trading with or investing in them;
- to guard against fraud;
- to enable continuing supervision of the company by the Companies Registrar.

A registered company is generally required to provide a regular update of the information required on registration.

Types of registered company

The public company

Public company: registered company (plc) able to sell its shares to members of the public.

Under the CA 2006, a **public company** is a company which:

1 is limited by shares;

2 has 'plc' (or its Welsh equivalent) after the company name;

3 has limited liability;

4 is registered at Companies House; and

5 in its certificate of incorporation states that it is a public company.

A public company will only be registered as such if it has at least £50,000 of allotted/issued share capital. It is called a public company because its shares may be transferred freely to members of the public. If the company is *listed* the shares may be traded on the Stock Exchange. This enables capital to be raised easily. An applicant for listing must satisfy the requirements of the Financial Services and Markets Act 2000 and the Listing Rules issued by the United Kingdom Listing Authority. In practice, only large public companies will be eligible. Most of the members of a public company will aim to share in its profits without taking any part in its management.

The private company

Private company: registered company (Ltd) not able to sell shares to the public.

The CA 2006 states that any registered company, which is not a public company, is a **private company**. It must have 'limited'/'Ltd' (or the Welsh equivalent) after its name. This is the type of company usually formed by a sole trader or a partnership seeking the advantages (like limited liability) which incorporation may bring. Since the implementation of the Companies (Single Member Private Limited Companies) Regulations 1992, both private and public companies may be formed with only one member and the CA 2006 (s 270(3)) has dispensed with the requirement for a company secretary.

Shareholding in a private company is usually limited to participants in the business (and sometimes their families). Most, if not all, of the shareholders may be engaged in managing the business. Such companies are sometimes described as 'quasi-partnerships'. The transfer of the shares will be controlled by the company rules. If a member leaves, he or she may have to sell back his or her shares to existing members of the company, or obtain the company's permission before selling them to a third party.

A private company may later re-register as a public company if it grows to the point where this is appropriate.

The Companies Act 1989 began the process of deregulation of private companies to remove unnecessary bureaucracy and to lessen the administrative burdens of small businesses. The process of registration did not change, but a private company was able to choose by a unanimous vote of its members to opt out of certain obligations, like holding an annual general meeting or appointing auditors. This is clearly a sensible choice for a company incorporating a previous partnership of three or four people. The CA 2006 continues this process of simplification (reference will be made to these changes as relevant in the next three chapters).

Real life

Horace was recently left £20,000 in his great uncle Maurice's will. He is unde-
cided about how to invest it. His friend Cyril, who has just applied to patent a
mouse trap which he has invented, would like Horace to join in partnership with
him. He paints an optimistic picture of all the resulting profits in which Horace
would share in the future.

Horace should be cautious. While Cyril may ultimately be very successful,
Horace's money will be tied up and he will not see any return on his investment
unless and until sufficient profits come in. Unless it is a limited liability partnership, he has no security if the business fails. He might not only lose his entire
investment but, in a worst instance scenario, also find he has to pay out more,
since he has joint liability for business debts.

If he wants a safer business investment, he would be much better off buying
shares in three or four limited liability public companies. Then, at worst, he can
lose only what he has invested. If he chooses well, the shares will gain in value
and he may even get dividends (bonus payments) in a good year. He will also be
free to sell shares at any time he needs some liquidity, or reinvest elsewhere if a
particular investment is not doing well.

Holding and subsidiary companies

During the latter half of the twentieth century, it became increasingly common for
public companies to operate in groups. One (the holding company) controls the
others (subsidiary companies). Such a relationship exists where the holding company has the capability to control the voting majority within the subsidiaries. Under
the Companies Act 2006 there is a duty to disclose this relationship to ensure that
members of the public are not misled in their dealings with any of the members.
The holding company is also obliged to present group accounts as well as its own
(s 487).

The consequences of incorporation

Once registered the business is said to be incorporated. This has an effect on
the financial and general legal liabilities of the company, its directors, its
shareholders and any outsiders who have dealings with the company or are
affected by its actions.

The company is a separate entity distinct from its members

Once registration has been successfully completed a new legal person is created: its legal liabilities are entirely separate from those of its members. What the courts have described as a **veil of incorporation** prevents the members from being held responsible for the company's liabilities, however close their connections with it. This is clearly illustrated in the following case.

Veil of incorporation: protects the company from the liabilities of its members.

Salomon v *Salomon & Co. Ltd* (1897, HL)

Mr Salomon had a boot factory. He set up a company and sold the business to it for £39,000. He was paid £9,000 in cash and £20,000 in shares, the remaining six shares being held by members of his family acting as his nominees. Mr Salomon lent the company the remaining £10,000 of the purchase price, and this debt was secured by a charge on the company's property. In due course, the company got into financial difficulties and had to be wound up, leaving unpaid debts. As a secured creditor, Mr Salomon recovered what he was owed in full, but there were insufficient assets left to satisfy the other creditors. They argued that the company was a sham used by Mr Salomon as a front for his own business activities, and that he should have to pay off the creditors personally.

Held: the company had been created properly in accordance with the Companies Act and was a separate entity on whose behalf Mr Salomon acted as agent. It was irrelevant that after incorporation ownership and management stayed in the same hands as they had before. The company had borrowed the money and was legally liable to pay it back to its secured creditor who took preference over the other creditors.

Generally, the *Salomon* v *Salomon & Co Ltd* approach has been strictly adhered to, though to a very limited extent the courts have created exceptions to prevent fraud. In *Stone and Rolls* v *Moore Stephens* (2009), the House of Lords held that where a one-person company commits fraud, knowledge of that fraud is automatically imputed to the company. However there was no evidence of fraud in *Salomon* v *Salomon & Co Ltd*. Although Mr Salomon may seem to outward appearances to have been sailing rather close to the wind, he did not deceive anybody because his fellow shareholders knew what was going on. The charge on the company's assets was appropriately registered; the creditors could have found out about it before dealing with the company had they chosen to do so. In law they had notice of it.

The court may, however, be prepared to question whether a company owner is personally liable for its debts if it appears that the alleged company is a mere façade for the fraudulent activities of the owner. This is known as 'lifting the veil of incorporation'.

Jones v Lipman (1962)

Mr Lipman contracted to sell some land to Mr Jones and then changed his mind. He set up a company and conveyed the land to it to defeat Mr Jones's attempt to get a decree of specific performance.

Held: since Mr Lipman had absolute control and ownership of the company and had set it up specifically to defraud Mr Jones, he was personally liable and must perform the contract. The veil of incorporation did not protect him.

If the company is used as a façade to conceal criminal activities the court will hold that piercing the veil is justifiable.

Re K and Others (2005)

Under s 41(1) of the Proceeds of Crime Act 2002, Customs & Excise sought to restrain the assets of two companies as part of an investigation into a smuggling conspiracy involving the defendants. The companies argued that this could not be done, since the defendants did not control them and so it was not justifiable to pierce the corporate veil. Control of the companies was in the hands of the family of the defendants.

Held: although the defendants had no formal connection with the companies, they were clearly being used to assist the defendants' fraudulent activities in evading customs duty. Therefore, it was justifiable to pierce the corporate veil.

Where a director uses their company intentionally to cause loss to a third party the court may be prepared to make them personally liable.

Omnibill (Pty) Ltd v Egpsxxx Ltd and Another (2014)

The defendant was the sole director and shareholder of a company which owned a website that advertised escort services. Photographs which breached the claimant's copyright were displayed on the site.

Held: the defendant was personally liable as well as the company because he had used his position as a company officer and shareholder intentionally to commit a tort on the claimant.

A director may be personally liable for negligent advice given on behalf of the company provided that a 'special relationship' exists under the principle in *Hedley Byrne* v *Heller* (1963). (See Chapter 14 for a full explanation of the *Hedley Byrne* principle.)

Williams and Another v Natural Life Health Foods Ltd and Mistlin (1998, HL)

Natural Life was a very small company consisting of Mr Mistlin, the director, who owned all the shares except his wife's nominal holding. Apart from Mr Mistlin, there were only two company employees. Mr Williams and his partner bought a franchise to run a health food shop from Natural Life. They were given a brochure which described the company and Mr Mistlin's knowledge and expertise in glowing terms. They also received some financial projections of the potential of their franchise. All this information was compiled by Mr Mistlin, but he had no personal dealings at all with Mr Williams, who negotiated the sale with one of Mr Mistlin's employees. The turnover of Mr Williams's shop always fell substantially short of the projected levels and he went out of business within 18 months of opening. Mr Williams claimed that he had been negligently advised by Mr Mistlin.

Held: Mr Mistlin was not personally liable. The veil of incorporation could only be lifted in very exceptional circumstances, particularly where one-person companies were concerned, otherwise their owners would unreasonably be deprived of the protection of incorporation. Negligent advice by a director to an outsider dealing with the company could only give rise to personal liability of the director if the necessary special relationship under *Hedley Byrne* principles existed. This required a voluntary assumption of responsibility by the director and reasonable reliance by the recipient upon it.

Lord Steyn stated: 'In the present case there were no personal dealings between Mr Mistlin and the respondents. There were no exchanges or conduct crossing the line which could have conveyed to the respondents that Mr Mistlin was willing to assume personal responsibility to them. Contrary to the submissions of counsel for the respondents, I am also satisfied that there was not even evidence that the respondents believed that Mr Mistlin was undertaking personal responsibility to them. Certainly, there was nothing in the circumstances to show that the respondents could reasonably have looked to Mr Mistlin for indemnification of any loss.'

A voluntary assumption of responsibility by Mr Mistlin could not be presumed merely because he compiled the relevant literature: in any one-person company the owner was likely to be the individual with most of the skill and knowledge relevant to the running of the company. Mr Mistlin had no personal dealings with Mr Williams and there was no evidence that he or anybody on his behalf conveyed 'directly or indirectly to the prospective franchisee that the director assumed personal responsibility towards the prospective franchisee' (*per* Lord Steyn).

Objective assessment of the evidence indicated no grounds for reasonable belief by Mr Williams that Mr Mistlin was assuming personal responsibility, given the lack of direct dealings or undertakings to this effect.

There are several statutory exceptions to the separate entity rule, mainly relating to tax and insolvency law. For example, under s 213 of the Insolvency Act 1986, if during the liquidation of a company it becomes evident that the directors were trading fraudulently, they may be required personally to contribute to the payment of the company's creditors. (Fraudulent trading in this context includes continuing to trade when the directors are or should be aware that the company is unable to meet its current debts.)

Company members may enjoy limited liability for the company's debts

The company has unlimited liability to its creditors, but the liability of its members may be limited.

Company law does not permit a company's members to be completely free of financial liability, as this would promote irresponsible trading. Members' liability for company debts may, on registration of the company, be limited to the value of the capital which they have agreed to invest. Limitation of liability is seen to be in the public interest since it encourages investment in business enterprise and, therefore, promotes the economy.

Liability may be limited by shares or by guarantee.

1 *By shares.* The majority of companies raise their capital this way. If the company is unable to meet its debts, the maximum amount that any shareholders can be asked to contribute is the amount, if any, which they have still to pay for their shares. Their loss is therefore limited to the value of their shares when they joined the company.

2 *By guarantee.* A minority of companies limit their liability in this way. These companies generally exist for educational or charitable purposes, like private schools or museums. Since they are not formed for the purpose of making a profit, it is not appropriate for them to have a share capital. The liability of such a company's

members is limited to the amount which they have agreed to contribute if the company is wound up. The guaranteed sum is usually minimal.

Exceptionally, a company may be registered with *unlimited liability*. Its members agree to subsidise the company to an unlimited extent in the event of liquidation. This liability is owed, therefore, by the members to the company rather than to the company creditors.

The company may be legally liable

Criminal offences

There are certain crimes, like rape and bigamy, which a company cannot by its physical nature commit. Apart from these obvious exceptions, a company may be prosecuted for any crime which is committed in the course of carrying out the company's business. For example, prosecutions are common for using misleading trade descriptions, and for breach of health and safety regulations and anti-pollution controls.

After the Zeebrugge ferry disaster in 1987, it was established that at common law a company could be charged with manslaughter. The Corporate Manslaughter and Corporate Homicide Act (CMCH) 2007 s 1 creates a new offence of corporate manslaughter and came into force in April 2008. The offences may be committed by an 'organisation' if the way in which its affairs are managed (a) causes a person's death, and (b) amounts to a gross breach of a relevant duty of care owed by the organisation to the deceased. An 'organisation' includes both a corporation and a partnership (s 1(2)). The 'relevant duty of care' covers an employer's duty to employees and contractors, occupiers' liability, and duties arising from sale and supply of goods, construction and maintenance operations, use or keeping of plant or vehicles and any commercial activity of the organisation (s 2). Proceedings are taken against the company but its managers and other employees may be called to give evidence. Prosecution is reserved for the very worst cases of corporate mismanagement leading to death for which senior managers are substantially responsible. The offence is punishable by an unlimited fine.

The first proceedings under the Act were started in 2009 when Cotswold Geochemical Holdings was committed for trial for the unlawful killing of an employee who died while collecting soil samples for the company in a trench on a building site. It took two days for rescue workers to find his body which was buried in the several tonnes of mud that had landed on him when the trench collapsed. At trial in February 2011, Cotswold Geochemical Holdings was found guilty of corporate manslaughter and fined £385,000.

Two successful convictions for corporate manslaughter took place in 2012. JMW Farms Ltd (Co. Armagh) was convicted for corporate manslaughter and fined £187,000 plus £13,000 costs in May 2012 after one of their employees died as a result of being hit by a large feed mixing bin placed insecurely on a forklift loader driven by one of the company directors. In July 2012 Lion Steel Ltd in Manchester was convicted and fined £480,000 for corporate manslaughter after Steven Berry tragically died after sustaining injuries resulting from his fall through a fragile roof panel at the firm's premises.

Four more successful prosecutions followed from 2013–14; two others resulted in a not guilty verdict, though the defendants were fined for breaches of the Health and Safety at Work Act 1974.

There now appears to be several successful prosecutions every year for manslaughter and related offences brought against companies and/or senior members of staff. In 2015 Pyranha Mouldings and one of its directors were convicted and fined for corporate manslaughter arising from the death of an employee trapped in an oven used in plastics manufacture.

The cases above all relate to deaths of employees but in 2016 a care home and one of its directors were successfully prosecuted for causing the death of one patient. The home was closed down.

Elderly care home resident dies of neglect

Ivy Atkin who was 86 suffered from dementia. After a stay in hospital she was admitted to the care home run by Sherwood Rise Ltd, where her condition immediately deteriorated. She eventually died of pneumonia directly caused by neglect. No treatment plans had been implemented for any patients. She had a large untreated bed sore and had effectively been starved, having lost half her body-weight since being admitted to the home.

Sherwood Rise Ltd was fined £30,000 for corporate manslaughter. The director responsible for daily running of the home was found guilty of causing manslaughter by neglect, imprisoned for three years and banned from being a company director for five years.

Sources: Crown prosecution website: http://www.cps.gov.uk/news/; BBC News: http://www.bbc.co.uk/news/uk-england-nottinghamshire-35499865

Tort

The company is vicariously liable for the torts of its employees and agents committed in the course of their employment. Where the law imposes a non-delegable duty (for employee safety, for example) on the company, it remains personally liable even though the damage was caused by a third party.

Breaches of contract

Generally, a company is liable on its contracts in the same way as any other person. (This is dealt with in detail in the next chapter.)

Ownership and management

The company is owned by its members and managed by its directors. In a very small company, membership and management may be synonymous, but generally company membership does not give rights to dictate how the company is run on a day-to-day basis; it may not even entitle a member to vote at company meetings, since the rights of holders of some classes of shares may be limited under the internal rules of the company.

Public accountability

Once the company has been registered, certain information about it is open to public scrutiny through the Companies Registry. This information must generally be updated yearly through the *annual return*, though unlimited companies are exempt from this. Other company records may be inspected by the public at the company's registered office. BEIS has wide statutory powers to investigate companies where malpractice is suspected. It is legally entitled to obtain a warrant to search premises. A department inspector may require company officials to produce and explain any company document. A report of the investigation is usually made public.

Continuous succession

Once registered a company continues to exist until the legal process of liquidation brings its life to an end. 'Liquidation' means the realisation of the company's capital and other assets. These are distributed to creditors and shareholders according to strict rules of priority. The shareholders often lose much, if not all, of their investment.

There are two kinds of liquidation: compulsory and voluntary.

1 *Compulsory liquidation* by court order under the Insolvency Act 1986. This most commonly occurs where the company is unable to pay its creditors who then petition the court. The Official Receiver is appointed as liquidator.

2 *Voluntary liquidation.* Here the process depends on whether the company is still solvent. If so, the members control the liquidation process. If the company has become insolvent the creditors appoint a liquidator to distribute the company's assets.

The advantages of incorporation as a registered company

Turning a business into a registered company may be a sound move for its proprietors.

Limited liability of investors

Investors in a limited liability company are able to restrict their financial responsibility to the company. They cannot be personally bankrupted to pay business debts.

Worth thinking about?

Why did limited liability develop?

Suggested solutions can be found in Appendix 2.

Transferability of shares

When a member ceases to belong to the company, this does not affect the existence of the business, although it might destroy a partnership. The member's interest in the business can be transferred by sale or other means to a new member. In a listed public company such rights of transfer are unfettered and a sale of shares may take place under the auspices of the Stock Exchange. A private company's rules may impose considerable restrictions in order to protect the close personal relationship of the small number of members all actively engaged in running the business.

Tax

Incorporation and the subsequent separation of the financial interests of the business from the personal financial interests of the members may prove advantageous for tax purposes.

Separate property rights

The assets of a business become its own property on incorporation. This is advantageous in a number of ways. For example, a member who leaves cannot disrupt the business by claiming any particular asset as his or her own; he or she is entitled to recover only his or her financial stake at its current value. Similarly, if the company goes into liquidation members cannot be personally bankrupted when the company's assets are exhausted before all its debts are satisfied. All they will lose is their financial stake in the business.

Raising capital

Unincorporated businesses are very restricted as regards obtaining new capital. The only options are to increase the number of members or obtain a bank loan. Recruitment of new members, while increasing capital, results in business profits being spread more widely and perhaps more thinly. Bank loans involve large interest payments and usually are unobtainable without the security of a mortgage on the members' own homes. A company may be able to borrow money secured by a charge on its own assets. A public company may advertise publicly to attract loans through an issue of debentures (see Chapter 22).

This advantage is likely to be enjoyed only by a company with large enough assets to secure the loan. The members of very small private companies (quasi-partnerships) are usually required personally to secure the debt by mortgages on their homes.

Continuity

Once registered the company's existence continues regardless of any changes in membership. Only winding-up proceedings can bring the company to an end.

Changing the company law map: the Companies Act 2006

This massive piece of legislation (1,300 sections) consolidated most existing company law legislation, in particular the Companies Act 1985. The new Act introduced a number of reforms but also restated, without change, much of the previous legislation by putting it into plainer English. The law has been simplified in some respects in order to benefit small businesses and to reflect the way they operate, for example by abolishing the obligation to hold AGMs. One of the most important changes is the codification of directors' duties and other measures to encourage greater transparency in company dealings. The Act also seeks to encourage more participation by shareholders in running the company. (These changes will be looked at more closely in Chapters 23–4.)

The Act received Royal Assent in November 2006 and has been implemented in stages. Implementation was completed in 2009. All relevant references in this text are to the Companies Act 2006 unless otherwise stated.

The impact of the Human Rights Act 1998 (HRA 1998) on business organisations

Businesses directly bound by duties under the European Convention on Human Rights are those designated under the HRA 1998 as 'public authorities'. However, any business may have rights which can be protected by action under the HRA 1998 against state or other public authority interference. Additionally, the court, as a public authority itself, has a duty not to infringe any Convention rights of any party. This informs how decisions are reached and remedies awarded.

Property rights

A business may be able to protect its property by reference to Protocol 1, Article 1. This states that every human and *legal* person has a right to the peaceful enjoyment of property. This right is not absolute and interference may be justified in the public interest or where necessary to the collection of debts owed to the state. The right is breached if the interference prevents a fair balance being maintained between the rights of the claimant and the public interest. For example, a compulsory purchase order of business premises without adequate compensation would probably be judged to be in breach of the right.

Privacy

As an employer, an organisation may be subject to Convention duties regarding employees, such as Article 8, which protects respect for privacy and family life. A business may need to adjust working practices to accommodate requests by employees for more flexible working hours. Article 8 may also restrict employer access to employees' emails and phone conversations. Article 8 also protects business privacy, since the court must take care that it is not breaching this Article when granting search orders to premises in civil proceedings. The court must consider carefully whether the terms of the order are fairly balanced between the competing interests of the parties and that it is a proportionate response.

Fair trial

A business and its members enjoy the right to a fair trial under Article 6. This includes right of access to the courts and an impartial hearing. However, this right may be waived in civil proceedings where an arbitrator is used and in most cases where the parties settle out of court (see Chapter 4). Article 6 also includes the right to avoid self-incrimination. In *Saunders* v *UK* (1997) the ECtHR held that by subjecting Saunders to coercive questioning (refusal to answer was itself a criminal offence) DTI fraud investigators had breached his rights under Article 6.

Freedom of speech

Advertising, publishing, film, journalism and other media businesses may be protected by Article 10 (freedom of expression). The court, when granting an injunction to prevent publication, must ensure that it is not itself in breach of its Convention duties. Any restriction should be no more than is necessary in a democratic society to protect national security, public safety, health and morals, reputation or rights of others, or against breach of confidence. In *Venables* v *News Group Newspapers* (2001) the High Court issued a gagging order to prevent the press publishing information about the murderers of James Bulger. This was held to be justifiable, to prevent them being identifiable and thus in danger once they left prison. It can be seen from the examples above that, directly and indirectly, business organisations are just as likely to be affected by human rights law as any individual.

Conclusion

This chapter explains the different legal consequences of operating a business in three forms: sole trader, partnership and registered company. The next chapter looks in more detail at the formation and operation of a registered company. The concepts of legal personality, incorporation and limited liability underpin much of the content of the next four chapters. There follows a comparison of partnerships and registered companies.

The differences between a partnership and a registered company

The partnership	The company
Creation	
A written partnership agreement is usual but not essential. The parties' conduct (jointly doing business with a view to profit) will create a partnership.	The company does not exist until the registration procedures of the Companies Act have been complied with.
Numbers	
Minimum: at least two.	A one-person private company is possible.
Maximum: Not prescribed.	No maximum is prescribed.
Legal personality	
The partnership has no separate legal personality of its own: partners are vicariously liable for any breaches of civil law caused by a fellow partner in the course of the business.	Once registered, a company has its own legal personality separate from that of its members. Members cannot be made liable for its illegal activities.
Any partner may be personally liable for crimes relating to the business.	
Limited liability	
Partners have unlimited liability for the debts of the business, unless registered as a limited liability partnership.	The company's liability is unlimited.
Supervision and publicity	Members may have limited liability for company debts.
The operation of a partnership is not supervised by any outside authority.	A limited liability company is monitored by the Companies Registrar through its annual return. Particulars and accounts are open to public inspection.
Partnership accounts and other documentation are confidential to the partners unless the partnership is an LLP.	The Department for Business, Energy and Industrial Strategy has wide investigative powers.
Termination	
Completion of object, lapse of time, partner leaves, bankruptcy, mental disability or death of partner.	Once created, a company has continual succession. It will not cease to exist unless or until the legal processes involved in winding up are complete.

Chapter summary

Sole trader

Personal liability for business.

Partnership

Fiduciary relationship.

Partners are each other's agents.

Joint and several liability: limited liability possible.

Dissolution: lapse of time, purpose achieved, death/bankruptcy, illegality, resignation, court order.

Registered company

Process of incorporation regulated by the Companies Acts.

Public/private.

Incorporation by registration gives it legal personality distinct from members.

Limited liability (shares/guarantee).

Human Rights Act 1998

Action by company is possible (property rights, privacy, fair trial).

Review questions 19

1 Explain the concept of incorporation.

2 In relation to incorporation, what is meant by:
   (a) limited liability?
   (b) continuous succession?
   (c) a corporation aggregate?

3 What is the main difference between a partnership and a sole trader?

4 Thomas, Davide and Wong are members of a partnership called Outdoor Adventures. What is the legal position if:
   (a) Thomas, without consulting the others, bought two new four-wheel drive vehicles from Humber; and
   (b) as a result of Thomas's purchase, the partnership now has insufficient sums to pay its creditors?

5 Define and distinguish between a public and a private company.

6 Explain the advantages of trading as an LLP.

Answers to all review questions can be found in Appendix 2.

Advanced questions 19

(A) Analyse the circumstances in which a company may be prosecuted for corporate manslaughter.

(B) Define and explain the veil of incorporation and give examples of situations where the courts will disregard this principle.

Answers to the advanced questions can be found at **go.pearson.com/uk/he/resources.**

Take a closer look

The following cases provide important examples of how the law in this chapter has developed. They are primary sources illustrating the law in action and give more detail about their facts, as well as helping to understand the law and to appreciate how the judges reached their decisions.

Try looking them up in the law reports or accessing them via a database, e.g., BAILII (www.bailii.org/databases.html). LexisNexis or Westlaw may be available in the university or college library, or extracts may be found in a case book. (See Appendix 1: Additional resources.)

Jones v *Lipman* [1962] 1 WLR 832

Re K and Others (2005) *The Times*, 15 March

Salomon v *Salomon & Co. Ltd* [1897] AC 22, HL

Williams and Another v *Natural Life Health Foods Ltd and Mistlin* [1998] 2 All ER 577

Web activity

There is a wealth of information on the Bytestart website for small businesses. Check out the guides to setting up as a sole trader, partnership and registered company: www.bytestart.co.uk/index.shtml

See also the CPS web pages on corporate manslaughter: www.cps.gov.uk/legal-guidance/corporate-manslaughter

Assignment 18

Jackie and Simon run the Good Hair Day hair-dressing salon, which is a very successful business. They would like to expand their premises and staff and hope ultimately to open other salons in different locations. They are debating whether to continue to trade as a partnership or set up a limited company.

Advise Jackie and Simon.

Forming a registered company

Learning objectives

On completion of this chapter, students should be able to:

★ describe the process by which a company is registered;

★ define the functions of the memorandum and the articles of association;

★ explain how a company's objects are determined;

★ understand the rules governing a company's capacity to contract;

★ define the legal processes by which a company may be dissolved.

Introduction

Chapter 20 explains that if a sole trader or partnership wishes to incorporate its business and seek the advantages of limited liability which this can bring, it will need to comply with a statutory registration process. This chapter examines this process, which is currently laid down by the Companies Act 2006 (CA 2006). This Act largely consolidates the Companies Act 1985 and other previous relevant legislation. All section numbers cited in this chapter are from the CA 2006 unless otherwise indicated.

Promoting the company

Promoters: people responsible for setting up and registering a company.

The **promoters** of the company are the people who actually set it up, who may employ a solicitor, accountant or other professional, providing services to assist the process.

21

The promoters' role varies, but it always involves the formalities of registration. It may also involve finding directors and obtaining premises, plant and equipment. However, these latter functions may not be required of promoters, since large numbers of companies do not start from scratch on being registered. They have their origins in an established small business for which incorporation is the next logical step. The promoters of such a company will usually move from being partners to being directors.

Promoters' liability for pre-incorporation contracts

Section 51 of the CA 2006 makes promoters personally liable for all contracts entered into before the company has completed the registration process, even if made in the name of the future company. This is entirely logical since the company does not exist as an independent being until its registration is complete. While it may be essential for the promoters to make contracts on behalf of the business before incorporation, they cannot be treated as the agents of the company since it has no independent existence at this point. Therefore, it cannot legally authorise the making of a contract. Even when it is incorporated it cannot ratify any contracts made before incorporation brought the company into being. Thus, it is fair to give the other party to the contract the right to sue the promoters if the contract is not performed. The promoters may sue or be sued on such contracts regardless of whether the other party knew that the company did not yet exist. In *Phonogram v Lane* (1982, CA), the claimant contracted to supply finance to the defendant for the purposes of a company to manage a pop group called 'Cheap, Mean and Nasty'. The claimant knew that the company was still at pre-registration stage, but this did not prevent him from suing the defendant for breach of contract.

Section 51 of the CA 2006 allows a promoter to avoid personal liability by express agreement with the other party to the contract. Such agreements fall into two kinds:

1 the contract may stipulate that the liability of the promoter will cease once the company has been registered and has entered into a contract on the same terms;

2 a gentleman's agreement: the promoter may enjoy complete immunity if the other party agrees to enter into a gentleman's agreement from which the intention to form a legally binding relationship is excluded. This means that in reality the pre-incorporation contract does not have the status of a contract at all.

Forming the company

Memorandum of association: statement of intent by promoters to set up a company.

Section 7 states that a company is formed by one or more persons signing a **memorandum of association** and complying with the registration process as prescribed by the Act. Note that it is possible for a company to consist of one member, which helps small businesses to register.

The memorandum of association: s 8

The purpose of the memorandum is to state the intention of the subscribers to form the company and to become members of it. If the company is limited by shares, it must specify that they each hold at least one share.

The CA 2006 makes the memorandum much simpler and shorter than before. It used to contain some information like the objects of the company which may now be found in the articles of association of companies set up since the CA 2006. The memorandum no longer forms part of the company's constitution and has been relegated to being merely a historic document indicating who set the company up. It cannot be amended after registration.

The registration process: ss 9–13

The following documents must be delivered to the Companies Registry with the appropriate fee:

1 the memorandum of association;

2 the application for registration, which includes:

Registered office: the company's official contact point.

Articles of association: document identifying the company and its officers indicating its purpose and rules for transacting company business.

(a) the company's name, although the choice may not be as simple as it sounds (see below for more detail);

(b) the company's domicile (England/Wales/Northern Ireland);

(c) the address of the company's **registered office**; this is the official contact point for the company (s 86). It is here that official notices may be sent, or claim forms served. Information which may be inspected by members of the public is kept here (s 87). This includes the registers of members, directors and debenture holders.

(d) the **articles of association**;

(e) whether the company is limited or unlimited;

(f)   if limited, whether this is by shares/guarantee;

(g) a share statement (if the company is limited by shares) indicating the amount of share capital, how it is to be divided and initial share holdings;

(h) the terms of any guarantee;

(i)   names and addresses of the proposed officers (director(s), company secretary);

(j)   a statement of compliance with the registration procedure.

The company's name

The registrar will refuse to register a name if its use would constitute an offence or if it is offensive (s 53). For example, 'Hookers Ltd' has been rejected (*R* v *Registrar of Companies, ex parte Attorney-General* (1991)). The chosen name must not be the same as or to similar to an existing company (s 66). It also should not mislead the public about the company's purpose. The Company, Limited Liability Partnership and Business (Names and Trading Disclosures) Regulations 2014 have somewhat simplified requirements regarding the issue of similar names and have removed restrictions relating to for example 'exports', 'holdings', 'international' and 'services' and their Welsh equivalents.

Some names and expressions can be used only with permission from the Department for Business, Energy and Industrial Strategy (BEIS). These include any which suggest a connection with a government department or local authority. In 2013, as part of its 'Red tape challenge' aimed at removing unnecessary regulation in the business world, BIS (later BEIS) suggested that the list of over 160 names and expressions should be reduced to remove for example 'Accredited', 'British', 'Benevolent' and 'University'. After consultation, the Company, Limited Liability Partnership and Business (Sensitive Words and Expressions) Regulations 2014 were passed and came into operation in 2015. They include a considerable list of words (and their Welsh and Gaelic equivalents) no longer regarded as inappropriate, but interestingly none of those listed above as examples feature. The list includes the 'authority', 'international', 'pregnancy termination', 'registry', 'United Kingdom', and 'watchdog'.

Section 82 enables the Secretary of State to make regulations concerning publicising the company's name and other information. Previous legislation required the company's name to be displayed outside the business premises, and on all business stationery and on the company's seal. This has been extended. Since January 2007 a company is additionally required to list its name, registration number, country of registration and registered office address on its website and emails. The Company, Limited Liability Partnership and Business (Names and Trading Disclosures) Regulations 2014 simplified the display requirements concerning multi-occupancy business premises. Where six or more companies use the same building it is now only necessary for the name of each company to be displayed in a register available for inspection by any visitor to the building. In buildings accommodating less than six companies all the company names must still be displayed at the entrance to the building.

Failure to comply may result in criminal proceedings against the company and a fine. The officer responsible for the company's failure to display may also be personally liable for any transaction not honoured by the company, because the company was not clearly identified as being a party to it (s 83).

Where a company has limited liability this must be made evident by placing 'plc' after the name of a public company (s 58) and 'Ltd' or the Welsh equivalent after the name of a private company (s 59).

To protect use of a company name on the internet, it is wise to register its website's 'domain' with its internet service provider. Registrations are accepted on a 'first come first served' basis. Failure to act quickly could prevent a company from using its company name for internet purposes. Worse still, another company could use the name, and the only possible protection would be an action under the Trade Marks Act 1994 (see Chapter 25) or a passing-off action (see Chapter 26).

The effect of registration: ss 14–16

The registrar will register the company and issue the certificate of incorporation provided that the legal formalities have been complied with and the company is intended to pursue a legal object. This makes the subscribers to the memorandum, members of it and the named officers are deemed to be appointed. The company is now legally capable of exercising its functions stated in its constitution.

Streamlining the registration process

The Small Business, Enterprise and Employment Act (SBEEA) 2015 commits the government to streamlining the process by which companies are formed. Section 15 requires the minister to put a system in place during 2017 and to give annual reports to Parliament to indicate the progress of this reform (s 16) until completion. This process, now in operation, enables one person to provide once and in digital form all the necessary registration information to the Registrar, including registration for tax. The standard fee for web incorporation is £12.

The company constitution: the articles of association: s 17

Before the CA 2006, both the memorandum of association and the articles of association contained different aspects of the company's constitution. The memorandum contained matters governing the relationship of the company to the outside world, while the articles were purely concerned with rules governing the internal management of the company.

Under the CA 2006, the constitution is comprised by the articles and any special resolutions and shareholder agreements amending them (s 17). The articles of new companies include the information previously found in the memorandum. This reflects the recommendations of the 2005 White Paper. This called for reforms to make company formation simpler for small businesses and to ensure greater transparency in all company management and affairs. Under s 32, the company has a duty to provide copies of constitutional documentation to any member on request.

Section 19 enables the Secretary of State to prescribe draft model articles by regulation. A company may adopt all or some of these. They automatically apply by default to any company on formation if the promoters do not choose to register especially composed articles. Private companies often adopt draft articles, but public companies usually draft their own.

Under s 28, such provisions of the memoranda of existing companies, formed before implementation of the CA 2006, which are not relevant to the new-style memorandum will be treated as part of the articles of those companies.

Contents of the articles

These cover information relevant to all dealing with the business including the objects of the company.

Rules governing internal conduct of the company's business

These will include, for example:

- the number of directors;
- the method of their appointment;
- powers of directors;
- the procedures for calling and conduct of meetings;
- voting rights of members;
- keeping of accounts;
- the payment of dividends.

The company may, therefore, empower itself within the confines of the law. The Companies Act prohibits some activities (e.g. shares cannot be issued at a discount (s 580)) and permits others subject to compliance with certain procedures such as altering the articles (see below).

The next section explains the contents of the articles in more detail.

The objects clause

Ultra vires: in excess of legal authority. Describes behaviour by a company which is not permitted by its objects clause.

Historically the law required a precise statement of the objects to be pursued by the company, including the powers relevant to the fulfilment of the objects and specifying related transactions which the company might enter into. A contract exceeding the company's objects was totally void because it was **ultra vires** (see contractual capacity of a registered company, below). In *Ashbury Railway Carriage* v *Riche* (1875 HL) it was held that a company registered to manufacture, sell and hire railway stock was not empowered to build railways.

Promoters consequently often resorted to long, vague and complex objects clauses to avoid restrictions on later business development. As time went on, the courts adopted a more flexible approach, provided that the new enterprise was capable of being linked to the main purposes of the company. In *Bell Houses* v *City Wall Properties Ltd* (1966, CA) the court validated a clause giving a company the power to 'carry on any trade or business whatsoever which can in the opinion of the directors be advantageously carried on in connection with or ancillary to any of the above businesses and the general business of the company'.

The *ultra vires* rule became much less important after entry to the EC. The European Communities Act 1972 largely rendered it ineffective in actions for breach of contract *against* a company. Much greater flexibility was introduced by the Companies Act 1989. This amended the Companies Act 1985, providing (s 3A) that an objects clause might state that 'the object of the company is to carry on business as a general commercial company'.

The CA 2006 relaxes this requirement still further and s 31(1) provides that 'unless a company's articles specifically restrict the objects of the company, its objects are unrestricted'. Under s 31(2) any change to the objects must be reported to the company registrar.

The articles of the company represent contractual terms

Under s 33 the company's constitution (which comprises the current articles of a company) acts as a binding contract between the company and its members. It is as if the company and each of its members had promised to observe its provisions. Any money payable by a member is a debt due from the member to the company.

Failure by one of the parties to carry out its obligations under the constitution is actionable as a breach of contract by the company. The parties are bound by these terms, though the company is in the stronger position since it makes the rules and has the power to initiate their alteration.

Hickman v *Romney Marsh Sheep Breeders Association* (1915)

The articles of the association stated that in the event of a dispute between a member and the association, the matter must be referred to arbitration. Mr Hickman was expelled from the association and sued it, claiming breach of contract.

Held: he could not take court action until the arbitration process had taken place as required by the terms of his membership contract with the association.

A personal action by one member against another is possible.

Rayfield v Hands (1958)

The articles required the directors who were also shareholders to buy a retiring member's shares at a fair price.

Held: refusal to do so entitled a retiring member to obtain a decree of specific performance against the directors.

Members' capacity to sue on the terms imposed by the constitution is limited to enforcing their rights as members. The fact that a breach of the articles results in damage to them in their personal capacity does not allow them to sue for that breach.

Eley v Positive Life Assurance Co. (1876)

The articles stated that Eley would be the company's solicitor for life. When the company dismissed him, he unsuccessfully attempted to sue for breach of the articles.

Held: the interest which he was attempting to protect was a personal employment right, not one related to his status as a company member.

The articles may, however, provide evidence of terms to be implied in a separate contract giving rise to personal rights. For example, this enables directors to sue for remuneration owed to them under the terms of the articles. They must sue on the contract which appoints them, but its terms may be clarified by reference to the articles if necessary. In *Soden v British Commonwealth Holdings plc* (1997) it was held that the rights and obligations imposed by the Companies Act may also be implied terms within the contract. The court may be prepared to imply a term into a contract to give it business efficacy.

Cream Holdings Ltd v Davenport (2011, CA)

Cream's articles of association stated that on a transfer of shares the transferor was entitled to fair value, as determined by a third party accountant. Cream dismissed Mr Davenport, a director. Mr Davenport retaliated, refusing to agree to the appointment of the accountant chosen by Cream Holdings from the list of three that he had nominated, unless C Ltd disclosed certain documents.

> **Held:** (affirming the decision of the High Court): the company's articles represented contractual terms between the company and its shareholders and must be construed in the same way as any other contract in their entire context and having regard to any relevant commercial considerations.
>
> On the grounds that it was better that the contract should function rather than fail, a term would be implied that a shareholder could not unreasonably withhold consent to the appointment of an accountant. D's actions in withholding consent and demanding disclosure were unreasonable as nothing in the articles gave him a right to do so.

Changing the articles of association

The articles may be amended by a special resolution (s 21). This must be put to the vote and requires a majority of at least 75 per cent of the company's members. A copy of the amended articles must be sent to the registrar.

Provisions in the articles may be entrenched. Such provisions are not capable of amendment unless any conditions or procedures specified in the articles are complied with. Provision for entrenchment can be made in the articles before registration or result from later amendment passed unanimously by the company's members or result from a court order.

Real life

> Horace's friend Cyril set up a private limited company to market the mouse trap Cyril had invented. He registered it under the name of Hamlin Ltd with an authorised capital of £30,000 divided into shares of £1 each. Horace has 10,000 of them. Cyril and his wife Desiree hold the rest. The company's articles state that the objects of the company are 'to manufacture and trade in pest control products'. The mouse trap is selling well and Horace believes he has made a sound investment. However, he has yet to see any actual return on it. Should he wish to sell the shares at any point, he can only do so within the provisions of the company's articles, which say that sale of shares by one company member requires the approval of the rest. This enables Cyril and Desiree to control who joins the company.

The contractual capacity of a registered company

A company makes many contracts as part of the running of its business and these are enforceable by and against it. Before the UK's entry into the EU, a company might avoid its liability for a contract by hiding behind its objects clause and claiming that the contract exceeded the objects of the company and was therefore *ultra vires* (beyond its powers) and void. The other party could not plead ignorance of the limitations on the company's objects since it was deemed to have **constructive notice** of the memorandum of association because it is a public document which the other party could have inspected.

Constructive notice: exists where a party is deemed to be aware of relevant issues even though he or she may not actually have that information.

Re Jon Beauforte (London) Ltd (1953)

The company's objects were stated as dressmaking, but it had abandoned this and taken up manufacturing veneered panels. The company became insolvent, and those who had been supplying it with goods were unable to claim money owed.

Held: the creditors could not claim their money as the contracts with the company were *ultra vires* and they had notice of this. Orders had been placed on writing paper describing Beauforte as veneer panel manufacturers which gave the suppliers *actual* notice that the company had departed from its authorised objects. They had *constructive* knowledge of the true objects since the memorandum of association was open to their inspection.

When the UK entered Europe, reform was necessary for the law to conform to the First Company Law Directive. The European Communities Act 1972, s 9(1) stated that in favour of a person dealing with the company in good faith, any contract decided upon by the directors should be deemed to be within the company's capacity. This meant that if the company was sued for breach of contract it could not use the *ultra vires* principle in its defence. Although this was a step in the right direction, it was heavily criticised. First, it was restricted to contracts initiated by directors which in practice covers very few made by public companies. Secondly, it did not provide equal protection to a company which sued a defendant for breach. That defendant could still plead that it was not bound to perform the contract because it was *ultra vires*.

Consequently, the Companies Act 1985 was amended by the Companies Act 1989, which stated (s 35) that the company should be treated as having the capacity to make any contract even if it exceeds its objects clause. The good faith of the other party was irrelevant. The CA 2006, s 39 effectively re-states this unchanged.

The provisions introduced by the CA 1985 concerning the powers of the directors to bind the company are also unchanged. CA 2006, s 40 states that the power of the directors to bind the company or enable other people to do so is not restricted by the articles of the company. A third party which has dealings with the company in good faith need not worry about whether the company is acting unconstitutionally. They have no duty to enquire whether any restriction exists. Their good faith is presumed. Even if the third party knows that the contract does exceed the objects clause, this alone is not evidence of bad faith.

The company can sue for breach if the third party fails to perform the contract, as well as being liable for breach itself if it fails to perform.

The *ultra vires* rule still operates *within* the company

Section 40 does not prevent the operation of the *ultra vires* rule in the relationship of the company to its members. Where the directors have planned to exceed their authority but have not yet done so, a company member who finds out in time may seek an injunction to stop them.

The shareholders may ratify (confirm) the *ultra vires* activity by resolution. This absolves any director who authorised the transaction from liability for breach of duty. This must be contrasted with the situation when shareholders merely affirm the transaction. That has the effect of making the transaction binding on the company but it does not absolve the director who may be liable to pay compensation for breach of duty.

Although directors have a duty to act in good faith in their company dealings, there is still a danger that they may, in their personal capacity, enter into potentially fraudulent transactions with the company. To guard against this, s 41(2) provides that if the purported transaction by the company is made with:

1 a director of the company or its holding company; or

2 any person connected with the director or any company with which the director is associated, the transaction is *voidable* by the company.

This gives the company a choice not to go through with the transaction. Whether or not the company avoids the transaction, the director can be required to account for any profits arising and must indemnify the company for any damage caused to it.

Re-registering a company

It is possible to change the status of a company by re-registering it in accordance with the requirements of Part 7 of the CA 2006, ss 89–111. This makes it possible to change a private company into a public one and an unlimited company into a limited one and vice versa.

If a private company has done well and business is expanding, 'going public' may be advantageous as it permits the company to sell shares to the public at large, thus making it easier to raise capital. This is the commonest registration change.

The CA 2006 states that a private company (limited or unlimited) may apply to be registered as a public company limited by shares if its members have passed a special resolution to that effect (s 90) and it fulfils the minimum share capital requirements (s 91). Application is made to the registrar (s 94) including relevant accounts information, an auditor's report, a copy of the special resolution and a statement of the new name if relevant. If the registrar is satisfied that all the necessary requirements have been complied with, a certificate of incorporation on re-registration is issued.

Buying a company 'off the shelf'

Instead of going through the registration process, the promoters of a company may buy a ready-made company from a business specialising in providing such a service. The seller registers companies and then renders them dormant, relieving them of a duty to appoint auditors or prepare annual accounts. When the company is sold, the shares are transferred to the buyers, who then register themselves as the new directors and secretary. The name and objects of the company may have to be changed to fit the needs of the buyers' business. Apart from saving the promoters time and effort, buying a company off the shelf is generally cheaper than completing the registration process.

Worth thinking about?

Can you see disadvantages to making company formation so easy?

Suggested solutions can be found in Appendix 2.

Dissolution of the company

Just as formal procedures are required to form a company, they are also required to dissolve it. Dissolution (liquidation) most frequently occurs when the company is threatened by insolvency. The Insolvency Act 1986 governs the dissolution process, which may take various forms, as follows.

Members voluntary liquidation

The shareholders decide that they want to close down the company. This may be for a number of reasons, such as retirement of the director of a small family business where nobody else in the family wants to take it on, or the business is failing to make a profit and its members decide to close it down before the situation gets worse.

Creditors voluntary liquidation

If the company becomes insolvent it may call a meeting of its shareholders and provided 75 per cent agree, pass a resolution to wind up the company. The directors must then put the company into administration by appointing an insolvency practitioner who must call a meeting of the creditors to inform them of the situation, administer the remaining assets of the company and determine how much the creditors recover. The directors have no further control over the business or its assets.

Compulsory liquidation

It is illegal for a company to continue trading if it cannot pay its creditors. If the company owes £750 or more and at least 75 per cent of the shareholders agree, a director may apply to the court to get the company wound up. The director completes a winding up petition and submits it with other documentation to the High Court if the paid up capital of the company is £120,000 or more; otherwise proceedings will be dealt with at County Court level. At the court hearing a winding up order may be issued and then the court appoints an official receiver (an officer of the Insolvency Service) to liquidate the company.

Chapter summary

Forming the company

Promotion

The practicalities of starting up the business and preparing to register.

Off-the-shelf purchase possible.

Registration

The companies' registrar must receive and approve key documentation from the promoters: e.g. memorandum of association which includes Articles of Association, details of officers, registered office, authorised share capital, limitation of liability.

Registrar issues certificate of incorporation legally creating the company.

Re-registration possible later to change company from public to private, unlimited to limited, etc.

The articles of association

The company's identity card and internal rule book.

May be changed by 75 per cent majority vote at a company meeting.

The objects clause

Since CA 2006, objects unlimited except so far as restricted by the articles.

Company contracts

Contracts made in the company's name are binding. *Ultra vires* does not apply outside the company, though shareholders have remedies against the directors to protect company interests/may ratify an *ultra vires* contract.

Dissolution of the company

There are three possible procedures by which a company may be dissolved after which it ceases to exist.

Members voluntary liquidation: at the will of the shareholders

Creditors voluntary liquidation: the threat of insolvency by creditors makes the shareholders dissolve the company.

Compulsory liquidation: the company which has become insolvent submits to dissolution by the Court.

Review questions 20

1 What documentation must be received by the Registrar of Companies before a company can be registered?

2 What difference has EU law made to the contractual capacity of a company?

3 Dogger and Portland are the directors of Maritime Pursuits Ltd. They want to change their company to one with public status. What will they have to do?

4 How has the Companies Act 2006 changed the nature of the memorandum of association?

5 How may changes be made to a company's articles?

6 Explain the meaning of the phrase 'buying a company off the shelf'.

Answers to all review questions can be found in Appendix 2.

Advanced questions 20

(A) Critically evaluate the significance of the s 33 contract in respect of the articles of association.

(B) Examine the legal restrictions on the choice of names for a company.

Answers to the advanced questions can be found at **go.pearson.com/uk/he/resources.**

Take a closer look

The following cases provide important examples of how the law in this chapter has developed. They are primary sources illustrating the law in action and give more detail about their facts, as well as helping to understand the law and to appreciate how the judges reached their decisions.

Try looking them up in the law reports or accessing them via a database, e.g. BAILII (www.bailii.org/databases.html). LexisNexis or Westlaw may be available in the university or college library, or extracts may be found in a case book. (See Appendix 1: Additional resources.)

Phonogram v *Lane* [1982] QB 939, CA

R v *Registrar of Companies, ex parte Attorney-General* [1991] 2 QB 197

Rayfield v *Hands* [1960] 1 Ch 333

Soden v *British Commonwealth Holdings plc* [1997] 4 All ER 383

Web activity

Explore the resources at Companies House at:
www.gov.uk/government/organisations/companies-house

Assignment 19

(a) What is the purpose of the objects clause in the company's articles of association and to what extent may the wording restrict the trading activities of a company?

(b) How far does the objects clause affect the ability of a third party to enforce a contract against the company?

Running the company:
Raising and maintaining capital

Learning objectives

On completion of this chapter, students should be able to:

★ distinguish between the different types of share capital;

★ define ordinary/preference/redeemable/deferred shares;

★ appreciate how shares may be bought and sold;

★ understand how a company may obtain loans.

Introduction

In general terms, the company's capital includes all its business assets, including premises, equipment, stock in trade and goodwill. This chapter is concerned with capital in more specialised terms: that which can be raised through getting additional investors or through obtaining loans.

Capital therefore may be raised in two ways:

1 By selling shares (share capital): the buyers become company members. Their investment may be seen as a bit of a gamble, since its value is dependent on how well or badly the company fares. Shareholders risk losing their entire investment if the company fails.

2 By obtaining loans (loan capital) through issuing debentures. Debenture holders do not become members of the company. They will obtain interest on their debenture and provided the loan is secured by charges on the company's property which require registration under the Companies Act 2006, will be sure of recovering their investment if the company fails.

22

This area of the law is largely unchanged in substance by the Companies Act 2006, which restates the existing principles.

Share capital

Until implementation of the CA 2006, a company limited by shares was required to have an authorised share capital. This specified the capital which could be raised by shares, although it might be increased by an ordinary resolution passed by a simple majority of members. The CA 2006 abolished this requirement from October 2008. This means that the directors can issue shares without limitation, subject to any permission from members required by the company's articles. Each share must have a specified nominal value (s 542).

There are different categories of share capital:

Issued capital:
the number of shares issued.

Called-up capital:
funds from payment for shares when requested after issue.

Paid-up capital:
identical to called-up capital unless a shareholder has failed to pay.

Uncalled capital:
the difference between the called-up capital and the face value of the shares.

1 **Issued capital**. This refers to the number of shares issued to members and represents some guarantee of progress for the company's creditors.

2 **Called-up capital**. The amount of capital raised by a call on shares. A shareholder, on being allotted shares, may not have to pay for them at once but may be called on to do so at a later date.

3 **Paid-up capital**. This should be the same as the called-up capital unless a shareholder has failed to pay what is due. The amount of paid-up capital is a good indicator of the company's financial health.

4 **Uncalled capital**. The difference between the called-up capital and the nominal value of the shares.

Classes of shares

The articles prescribe the rights derived from the shares issued. For example, they might specify that the company may issue shares with whatever rights or restrictions may be determined by the passing of an ordinary resolution. Different classes of shares may give rise to different rights. A shareholder's rights are also to some extent governed by the size of its shareholding: this will govern the amount of dividend payable and the strength of the shareholder's voting power.

There are different classes of shares which a company might choose to issue.

Ordinary shares

Equity/ordinary shares: commonest type of share.

A company may choose to issue only **ordinary (equity) shares**. They commonly carry most of the voting rights.

Preference shares

Preference shares: give holders the right to a fixed rate of dividend, specified on issue of the shares and have very limited voting rights.

If the company chooses to declare a dividend, the members with **preference shares** are entitled to payment at a fixed rate promised to them when the shares were allotted to them. It will represent a percentage of the value of their shares. How great an advantage they enjoy is dictated by the fortunes of the company. They may be the only shareholders to receive a dividend, or may be paid at a higher rate than the ordinary shareholders. If the company is doing well, the ordinary shareholders may do better than the preference shareholders, since the latter, having received their dividend at the prescribed rate, are not entitled to share with the ordinary shareholders in the distribution of any surplus profits. The articles may entitle them to other benefits: they may take priority over ordinary shareholders with regard to recovery of capital during a winding up. Preference shareholders can only vote on a resolution affecting their rights or where their dividend has not been paid in whole or in part.

Redeemable shares

Redeemable shares: short-term shares, to be bought back by the company.

Redeemable shares are issued on a short-term basis. The holder takes them for a specified period of time, after which the company buys them back (redeems them). This can be a useful means of raising capital for a new small business. These shares may have preference or non-preference status. Section 684 permits the issue of any class of shares on a short-term basis.

Deferred/founders' shares

Deferred/founders' shares: held by the promoters.

Founders' shares: see deferred shares.

Ordinary shares: see equity shares.

Treasury shares: the company's own shares purchased from an existing shareholder.

Deferred (founders') shares may be held by the promoters of the company. They carry increased voting rights but rank below **ordinary shares** for payment of dividends and the return of capital.

Treasury shares

Treasury shares are shares purchased by the company from an existing shareholder, so reducing the outstanding shares on the open market (see Chapter 23). No dividends can be issued and no voting rights attach to them.

The issue of shares by a PLC

The first issue of shares can only be made on registration of a public company and is made to subscribers. Subsequent issues may be made provided that there is compliance with any procedures in the company's articles. A public company may make also make a **rights issue**, which is a sort of special offer, restricted initially at a favourable price, to existing shareholders.

Any company which intends to issue shares may issue a **prospectus** to describe the venture. A public company may advertise its shares for sale to the public, but that does not mean that it has an automatic right to sell through the Stock Exchange. The right to sell on the Stock Exchange is governed by rules administered by the Financial Conduct Authority under the Financial Services and Markets Act 2000.

A large public company may have the financial stature required to qualify its securities for admission to the Financial Conduct Authority Official List. The information given by the company in its listing application then becomes public knowledge and the shares may be marketed through the Stock Exchange.

The Companies Act places a number of restrictions on share issue. These exist to prevent the company reducing its capital to the prejudice of its creditors, for whom the company's share capital assets represent some security. The principal restrictions relate to the price of shares and a company's acquisition of its own shares.

Price

Under s 582, the company can generally transfer shares only in return for *money or money's worth*. Shares can be given in return for services rendered to a private company. A public company is prohibited from doing this.

Under s 580, on first issue the shares cannot be sold at *less than their face value* as stated in the memorandum, unless the sale is to underwriters when a discount of up to 10 per cent as commission is permissible (s 553).

Shares can be issued at a *premium*, i.e. at more than their face value. Any money so raised, is counted as part of the company's capital, not profits, and it must be treated as such. Funds from the premium issue must be kept in a separate account and may be used for certain purposes only (s 610):

1 paying up unissued shares for issue as bonus shares to members;

2 writing off the expenses of the issue of the shares and any commission paid.

A company's acquisition of its own shares

In the interests of capital maintenance, the *general* rule is that a company cannot acquire its own shares, unless the Articles specifically forbid it, since a likely (and undesirable) result is that Peter is robbed to pay Paul: the shareholder would be paid from the company's assets but, since the shares would be cancelled after purchase, the company's share capital would be reduced.

Rights issue:
new sale of shares restricted to existing shareholders.

Prospectus:
issued by a company to encourage investment in shares/debentures.

Under the CA 1985 a company might buy its own shares if its articles authorised this. Section 690 of the CA 2006 has changed this, enabling purchase as long as the articles *do not* impose restrictions and the provisions laid down in Part 18, Chapter 4 of the Act (Purchase of Own Shares) are complied with. These require that the company can purchase its own shares only if they are fully paid up and payment is immediately made on purchase (s 691). There are restrictions on how the purchase may be financed (s 692). The purchase can only be made if authorised by the shareholders (s 693). Share buyback schemes can be beneficial to company and remaining shareholders alike as it can be used to reduce permanently the number of issued shares with a consequent rise in the value of their shares. However, success is not automatic. Next plc consistently employed a share buyback policy for 10 consecutive years, and reduced the shares in issue by 50 per cent. The value of its shares rose dramatically in consequence. In the company's Annual Report in 2013 Lord Wolfson, the chief executive, gave some guidance on how to employ a buyback strategy successfully. He pointed out that a business should always prioritise investment and only buy shares back if there is surplus cash available. The scheme must enhance earnings and produce an equivalent rate of return in the remaining shares. It is only successful if the business is experiencing long-term growth.

Unless the purchase is made in accordance with s 690, the general rule (s 658) applies. This states that the company may *not* acquire its own shares by sale, subscription or any other means unless:

1 no valuable consideration is paid for the shares; or

2 the purchase is to effect a formal reduction of capital which has been approved by the court; or

3 the court orders the purchase of shares to protect the interests of a minority of shareholders; or

4 shares are forfeited or surrendered as required by the articles, by a shareholder who has failed to pay.

Worth thinking about?

Why do you suppose the law relating to a company purchase of its own shares has been changed?

Suggested solutions can be found in Appendix 2.

Becoming a shareholder

Acquiring shares from the company

When the shares are first issued by the company, an interested party, which could be a company or an individual, may apply to buy some. This is an offer which the

Allotment:
assignment of shares.

company may accept by a letter of **allotment**. At this point a contract for sale of the shares comes into existence. However, the shareholder does not become a member of the company until his or her name is placed on the company's register of shareholders. The company must issue a certificate of registration which is evidence of the shareholder's title to the shares. Under s 769, the company has a duty to do this within two months of the issue of the letter of allotment.

Acquiring shares from an existing shareholder

A shareholder in a public company may freely transfer his or her shares; restrictions may be imposed by private companies. Section 776 requires the transfer to be formally notified to the company. The company must register the change of shareholder and issue a new certificate of registration within two months of receiving the instrument of transfer (s 776).

Once registered, the buyer of shares acquires all the rights attaching to that class of shares as dictated by the articles. In a limited company the buyer's liability for the company's debts is limited to the value of its shares. The shareholding makes the shareholder part-owner of the company. Unless the company is wound up, a shareholder cannot withdraw his or her capital investment from the company, but may transfer his or her shares to somebody else.

The rights of shareholders

To be paid any dividend declared by the company

Dividend:
bonus payment for
shareholders which the
company may choose
to pay, out of its profits.

A **dividend** is a bonus payment which can only be paid out of profits (s 263). Dividends are declared at the company's discretion, so the shareholders have no automatic right to a dividend unless the company chooses to issue one.

To vote at company meetings

Shareholders may vote at company meetings provided that their shares attract voting rights. This is determined by the articles. Voting rights may be used for the personal benefit of the shareholder and do not have to be exercised in the best interests of the company.

To recover the capital value of their shares if the company goes into liquidation

This right can be exercised only subject to the superior rights of the company's creditors. The shareholders do not necessarily have equal rights in relation to each other. Those with superior status have a right to be repaid before others. The articles determine the status of shareholders in this respect.

To transfer their shares

Shareholders may transfer their shares subject to any restrictions laid down in the articles. Restrictions are usual in the articles of a private company. Disputes regarding interpretation of such restrictions may be brought to court. The court will interpret any ambiguity in favour of the shareholder. To be legitimate the restriction must be used in the best interests of the company; evidence of bad faith by the directors would invalidate it.

Who is in control? Greater transparency of share ownership required

The size and often multinational nature of companies in the twenty-first century can make it very difficult for the authorities, or anybody else dealing with them, to know who owns the company financially, or is able to control its activities in other ways. Measures introduced under the Small Business, Enterprise and Employment Act 2015 (SBEEA 2015) s 80 and Schedule 3, in operation since April 2016, are intended to prevent companies and shareholders from disguising their actual ownership of shares or control of a business behind a trust or another company.

SBEEA 2015 requires companies to maintain publicly accessible registers all of persons with beneficial ownership of the company showing who are the 'persons with significant control' (PSCs). These include:

- Persons with at least 25 per cent of issued share capital owned directly/indirectly/solely/jointly. If the company does not have shares, a PSC will be a person owning the rights to 25 per cent or more of its capital or profit share.
- Persons with at least 25 per cent of the voting rights in the company exercised alone/jointly with another person or company.
- Persons with the power to remove or appoint members of the board exercised directly/indirectly/alone/jointly.
- Anyone else able to exercise significant control.

Loan capital

Debentures: written evidence of secured loans to the company.

A company has powers to borrow money to develop the business; these are usually made explicit in the company's articles, which indicate how far the company's assets may be used as loan security. When it obtains loans in this way the company creates a mortgage of its property. This is described as issuing **debentures**.

Debentures

A debenture is the written evidence of a secured loan to the company. There are three forms of debentures.

Single debenture: secured loan to the company from individual/ organisation like a bank.

The single debenture

A **single debenture** is a loan to the company from any person or organisation prepared to lend it the money. In practice such loans most often come from a bank.

Series debentures

The company may look to its own members for loans and issue a **series of debentures** to participants who have equal rights to repayment. They are generally protected by a trust in the same way as holders of debenture stock.

Debenture stock

Public companies are entitled to issue **debenture stock**, which may be offered to the public through the Stock Exchange in the same way as shares.

In order to protect the debenture holders, the company creates a trust with control over the company's assets, with the power to appoint a receiver. The trustee, which is often an insurance company, has the status of a company creditor, with the legal duty to act on behalf of the debenture holders. The terms of the trust deed may require the company to take certain precautions to protect the lenders' interests, including insurance of company assets and limiting its borrowing powers.

The debenture holder agrees to lend a specific sum of money repayable with interest after a certain length of time. Additional benefits may also be offered as an inducement to buy debenture stock. When the facilities for the Wimbledon tennis championship were being expanded, the company responsible raised the capital through an issue of debentures. This concept has proved very popular in the sporting industry.

Investment entitled the debenture holders to special facilities at the ground and priority booking rights. In 2005, Welsh Rugby Union Ltd issued debentures on the 125th Anniversary of Welsh Rugby. For £6,000 each debenture holder got the right to book a designated seat in the Millennium Stadium and the right to purchase tickets for the Six Nations matches, all Welsh Rugby Union matches and UEFA qualifying matches involving Wales. The debentures will be redeemed in 2030, when the privileges will cease.

A debenture is a transferable security and may therefore be disposed of in the same way as shares. The company is required to keep a list of debenture holders and issue registration certificates which are evidence of ownership for the registered holder.

Charges: the security behind the loan

If the company does not have the funds to repay debenture holders at the appointed time, the company's assets securing the loan will have to be realised to honour the debt.

The **chargeable assets** of the company include its premises, plant, machinery and goods (including stock in trade). As well as this tangible property, intellectual property like patents and copyright are also chargeable assets, as are book debts and business goodwill.

Registration of charges

All charges issued to secure debentures must be registered with the companies' registrar within 21 days of being created. Failure to register within this timescale renders the charge void. This does not relieve the company from liability to pay the debt, but it prevents the debenture holder from having any enforceable security for its loan.

Types of charges

Two kinds of charges are possible: fixed and floating.

1 *Fixed charges.* Specific assets to the value of the loan link with it as soon as the charge is created. Such a charge prevents any disposal of the assets over which the charge exists and, therefore, only a limited variety of assets are suitable to being charged in this way. Land and large items of plant and machinery are the assets which are most appropriate for a **fixed charge**.

2 *Floating charges.* Here the charge relates to the company's assets at large. At the point the loan is created the security enjoyed by the debenture holder does not attach to any specified assets, but the debenture holder will be entitled to repayment of its loan from any of the assets held by the company at the time of repayment. A **floating charge**, therefore, may relate to any of the company's more fluid assets which are subject to constant change, like stock in trade. This facility, which is available only to registered companies and limited liability partnerships, is helpful to businesses with few fixed assets.

Any of the following circumstances will cause the floating charge to *crystallise* and attach to particular assets:

- the company ceases trading;
- winding up is commenced;
- the company fails to repay the debenture holder at the due date;
- the occurrence of any other event specified in the charge deed as triggering crystallisation.

A debenture holder is better protected by a fixed charge than a floating charge. The value of a floating charge is likely to fluctuate. In the event of a winding up, the fixed-charge holders or statutorily protected creditors (employees, for example) take preference over the floating-charge holder.

Fixed charge: like floating charge but attached to particular assets.

Floating charge: attached to the company's assets in general, to provide security for debenture holders.

Real life

Majid is a keen football fan and decides to invest in Smallville Wanderers plc, his local club which is currently doing very well and has aspirations to joining the Premiership. He spends £3,000 on shares and is delighted, a year later, to receive a generous dividend. A couple of weeks later he receives a prospectus saying that Wanderers wants to develop its grounds and build a large new grandstand. It invites shareholders to buy debentures to help finance the improvements. It offers ticket and other concessions to debenture holders. Majid, now thoroughly committed to investing in the club, splashes out another £3,000. The debentures are due to be repaid in five years' time.

Three years later, Smallville Wanderers are in trouble: two disastrous seasons have resulted in relegation to Division Two, and two of their key players are in prison for causing serious injuries to a referee after a disputed penalty decision. The current value of the shares has dived to 25 per cent of their original value. Majid is not unreasonably despondent about his investment. His debentures should be safe, as they are secured against the company's assets out of which he can be paid if necessary. However, things do not look good with the shares. Should the club slide further into financial difficulties, it may be faced with liquidation. If that happens, he may well lose his entire share investment as the company's creditors take priority over its members.

Summary of the differences between shares and debentures

Shares	Debentures
The shareholder is a member of the company with voting rights.	The debenture holder is a company creditor; he or she does not have voting rights.
Dividends are not payable out of capital. Since dividends are issued from profits at the company's discretion, a shareholder does not know if he or she will get any dividend, or what it will amount to.	The debenture holder must be paid interest on the loan, and this is payable out of capital. Debenture holders know how much interest they will get.
Risk: the entire value of the shareholding may be lost.	Since the loan is secured by a fixed or floating charge, the debenture holder has security.
The company cannot usually buy its own shares.	The company can buy its own debentures.
Shares cannot be issued at a discount.	Debentures may be issued at a discount.

Chapter summary

A company may have share and loan capital.

Share capital

This may be: issued, called up, paid up, uncalled.
Classes of shares: ordinary/preference/redeemable/treasury.

Issue of shares

May be advertised by prospectus.
Private companies may not advertise for sale to the public.

Rights issue possible.

Shares can only be transferred for money/money's worth of at least their face value.

Issue at a premium possible.

Issue must be registered at Companies House.

The company can only buy its own shares subject to the provisions of the CA 2006.

Shareholders have the right to:

1 dividends (if declared);

2 vote at company meetings (subject to nature of their shares);

3 recover the current value of their shares on liquidation of the company;

4 transfer the shares (subject to articles).

Loan capital

Single/series debentures

In effect, these are mortgages since they are loans secured on the company's assets by a fixed or floating charge.

Debenture holders

Lend the company money for a fixed term in return for interest and other benefits.

Unlike shareholders, they are not company members and have no voting rights.

Review questions 21

1 What is the difference between issued and called-up capital?

2 Why might a company issue redeemable shares?

3 Define and distinguish between ordinary and preference shares.

4 Silver, Gold, Copper and Brass all own shares in Metals plc and seek your advice on the following problems:

(a) Silver complains that he has never received a dividend.

(b) Gold, a preference shareholder, has just discovered that he has no right to vote at a company meeting.

(c) Copper, a preference shareholder, has heard rumours that Metals may soon be wound up and is worried about his investment.

(d) Brass, a debenture holder, is also worrying about whether he will recover his investment.

5 Can a company ever acquire its own shares?

6 Define and distinguish between a fixed charge and a floating charge.

Answers to all review questions can be found in Appendix 2.

Advanced questions 21

(A) Analyse the different types of share capital.

(B) Critically evaluate the law relating to a company's acquisition of its own shares.

Answers to the advanced questions can be found at **go.pearson.com/uk/he/resources.**

Web activity

On the website of the London Stock Exchange, click on 'For companies & advisers' then click on 'AIM' for information relevant to smaller companies considering going public:
www.londonstockexchange.com/home/homepage.htm
Read 'Wimbledon debentures: an ace investment for tennis fans?' by Emma Lunn on the Moneywise website:
www.moneywise.co.uk/investing/alternative-investing/wimbledon-debentures-ace-investment-tennis-fans
Read 'New Financial Reporting Requirements For Large Private Companies' by Caroline Williams on the Freeths website:
www.freeths.co.uk/2018/06/14/new-financial-reporting-requirements-for-large-private-companies/

Assignment 20

Rashida has won £1,000 in a raffle and wants to invest it in a company. She seeks your advice on whether she should buy shares or debentures. Explain the differences between the two investment methods to her, indicating the advantages and disadvantages of each.

The management and governance of companies:
Functions of directors, secretary and auditors

Learning objectives

On completion of this chapter, students should be able to:

★ distinguish between the different types of director and their functions;

★ explain the duties of directors;

★ appreciate the impact of the CA 2006 on directors' duties;

★ understand the functions of the company secretary;

★ describe the work and legal liability of an auditor;

★ give examples of how insider dealing may occur.

Introduction

The company is an independent legal entity, but manages its business through its staff. The key management figures are the directors who through their decisions determine the policies, culture, and ethos of the company. Their powers and duties are largely governed by statute but an independent Code of Practice issued by the Financial Reporting Council encourages good governance. The company secretary has important administrative duties, while the auditors are responsible for monitoring financial accountability.

This chapter will examine the work of these officers.

The directors

A private company must have at least one director and a public company must have at least two (s 154). The articles of the company state the means by which a director may be appointed. Usually this is by vote at an AGM. Nobody under the age of 16 may act as a director (s 157). The company must keep a register of directors (s 162) containing their particulars (s 163).

The directors are the agents of the company; they are primarily responsible for the daily management of the company and development of company policy. Decisions on such issues are made by the directors at **board meetings**.

Board meeting: a meeting of the company's directors.

A large company may have a correspondingly large board of directors. A number of these may be **lay (non-executive) directors**, who provide their services on a voluntary basis and whose primary function is attendance at board meetings. They do not play any direct role in the day-to-day management of the company, which is in the hands of its executive director(s). The value of lay directors is controversial: it is argued that their presence is important to ensure independent decision-making and an objective view of company policy. A more cynical view is that their lack of relevant knowledge and experience may render their contribution largely useless. It is also said that they are likely to be too readily influenced by **executive directors**.

Lay/non-executive director: attends meetings but is not actively involved in running the company.

Executive director: responsible for the day-to-day management of the company.

These concerns led to publication of the Stock Exchange Combined Code: Principles of Good Governance and Code of Good Practice 2008 which is regularly updated. It required lay directors to have regular meetings with the chair of the board without any executive directors present. They must also carry out an annual appraisal of the managing director's performance. It is also their responsibility to ensure that the minutes of meetings record their concerns about company business which they believe were not satisfactorily resolved.

At the time of writing, the most recent version of the Code had been issued in July 2018 (see below).

Appointing the directors

The first directors are named in the application for registration when the company is set up. Subsequent directors are appointed by ordinary resolution passed by a simple majority at a company general meeting. The articles of association state the procedure for replacement of a director who leaves or dies before a general meeting is due to be called. Directors need not be shareholders of the company, but the articles may require them to hold qualifying shares. To promote independence and transparency in the company's dealings, the Small Business, Enterprise and Employment Act (SBEEA) 2015, s 87 abolished the appointment of corporate directors. From 2016, subject to certain limited exceptions, only human persons can hold office.

Executive (managing) directors

Since they are responsible for the hands-on management of the company, executive directors work for the company full-time and have expertise and experience relevant to the company's business. They may be engaged by the company under a contract of service. Provided the articles do not state otherwise, a person may be both an employee and a director of a company, subject to some restrictions:

1 a contract of employment for more than two years cannot be offered to any person who is already a director without the approval of the shareholders in a general meeting (s 188);

2 company articles generally prohibit directors from voting on their terms of employment at a directors' meeting;

3 directors' service agreements are open to public inspection at the company's registered office.

In a small private company (quasi-partnership) all the directors will be full-time managers but will decide their salaries informally.

To prevent a conflict of interest for executive directors and to discourage malpractice in listed companies, the Combined Code introduced a requirement that companies put in place open and transparent procedures for appointing executive directors and formulating their remuneration. A company's annual report should state the relevant policies for the information of shareholders. The Code also requires that a committee of non-executive directors should decide, within agreed terms of reference, a company's policy for paying its executive directors. This committee is also responsible for determining the specific remuneration rights for each executive director, including pension entitlement and compensation payment.

Alternate directors

Alternate director: somebody nominated by an existing director as their representative at a company meeting.

If the articles permit, a director may appoint an **alternate director** to represent him or her at a board meeting if unable to attend. In practice, this function is usually exercised by another director.

Shadow directors

A **shadow director** uses their voting power to manipulate the directors and is defined (s 251) as 'a person in accordance with whose directions or instructions the directors of a company are accustomed to act'. They are bound by the general duties for directors (s 170(5) as amended by SBEEA 2015, s 89) (see below).

A person who merely gives professional advice to the board on which it acts is not a shadow director. The next case illustrates that there is a difference between giving advice and encouraging and cooperating in dishonest practice since such behaviour may result in liability as a shadow director.

Vivendi SA & Centenary Holdings III Ltd v *Richards and Bloch* (2013)

The defendant consultant Richards entered into a contract which bound him to faithfully serve Centenary Holdings and use his best endeavours to promote its interests. He and Bloch, the sole director of Vivendi, while knowing that the company was in financial difficulty, made it procure payments of over £10 million over several years. The company subsequently went into liquidation and the liquidators took action against Richards and Bloch for breach of their fiduciary duty, in particular their duty of good faith as directors. Richards argued that he was not a director.

Held: Richards must be deemed to be a shadow director of the company since he had contractual obligations to Centenary Holdings and he knew that Bloch relied upon his judgement and acted on his instructions. He must be assumed to have a fiduciary duty because of this and because he carried out similar functions to any *de jure* director [director in law]. The interests of the company's creditors must be considered and the actions of Bloch and Richards were clearly in breach of their fiduciary duty as they had been dishonest and acted prejudicially to the creditors. Their motive was to extract as much money as possible from what they knew to be an insolvent company before it failed.

De facto directors

A person who, while not formally appointed as such, performs the functions of a director is bound by the same statutory duties as any other director and owes a duty of good faith is a de facto director. It may sometimes be difficult to detect whether someone should be treated as a de facto director.

Smithton v Naggar (2014, EWCA)

Naggar was a director of Dawnay Day International, a holding company with just over half the shares in Smithton Ltd, a joint venture company. Clients introduced to Smithton by Naggar defaulted. Smithton claimed that Naggar, as a director of the holding company had, when bringing in new business, acted as a de facto director of Smithton and should therefore indemnify it for the losses resulting from his actions.

The High Court held that he had not acted as de facto director. The joint venture agreement governing the relationship between Smithton and its holding company specifically stated that Naggar was not a director. When he had introduced clients he was 'wearing a different hat' and representing his own rather than Smithton's interests.

Smithton appealed.

The Court of Appeal held: The appeal must be dismissed. There was no absolute test to be used here to determine the de facto director question. The court needed to decide on objective and contextual evidence whether Naggar had 'formed part of the corporate governance structure of the company'. Close examination of all Naggar's actions did not suggest any greater involvement in Smithton's affairs than might be expected of someone who was acting both as a major client and chair of the majority shareholding company.

The powers of the directors

These are indicated by the articles but basically involve managing company business. Examples of directors' powers include issuing shares and borrowing money on the security of the company's assets.

Limitation on the exercise of powers

The directors' powers must be exercised subject to the company's objects clause; they are the agents of the company and their powers are limited to those of the company.

The Companies Acts impose restrictions on the way directors may use their authority, and this may also be limited by the articles. The powers must be exercised in the best interests of the company to fulfil the purposes for which they were given.

Protecting third parties against abuse of directors' powers

If the directors exceed their power the company may be bound by a resulting transaction. The third party may enforce the transaction as long as he or she acted in good faith under s 40 (see Chapter 21 for detail). The law of agency also provides some limited protection: if the company board knows that a maverick director is exceeding his or her authority but does not disown that behaviour, the company is bound by any resulting contract with a third party. In law the directors are estopped (prevented) from denying that the contract was authorised. The director acts with apparent authority. (This is a good point at which to refresh one's memory on these principles (see Chapter 12) and look at *Newcastle International Airport Ltd* v *Eversheds LLP* (2012), which provides a good example.)

Freeman & Lockyer v *Buckhurst Park Properties (Mangal) Ltd* (1964)

The articles of the defendant company permitted the appointment of a managing director. None was appointed, but one of the directors was known by the others to be conducting business with outsiders as if he had these powers.

Held: the director had abused his authority and the company was held liable on the resulting contracts; the board had been fully aware of the director's behaviour and could not deny his apparent authority after the event.

The duties of directors

The directors have a number of duties arising from the exercise of their powers. Such duties are owed primarily to the company and the shareholders but also include the company's employees and creditors. Before the CA 2006 these were both statutory (under the CA 1985 and related legislation) and common law duties.

Directors' common law and equitable duties before the CA 2006

These duties fell into two categories:

A duty of care

The common law of negligence requires a director to act with reasonable care and skill when carrying on the company's business. However, the fact that damage has been caused by their behaviour is not in itself evidence of lack of reasonable care and skill provided that the directors have not acted *ultra vires* or fraudulently.

Re City Equitable & Fire Insurance Co. Ltd (1925)

Due to fraud by a managing director, the company suffered major losses resulting in its liquidation. The other directors were held not to be negligent in failing to notice the managing director's misconduct. The court laid down criteria for judgement of what is a reasonable standard of care.

Held:

1 the director must act honestly for the benefit of the business;

2 what is reasonable care must be judged with reference to the experience, knowledge and skill of the relevant director. Directors cannot be expected to exercise greater care than these qualities equip them for. Less would be demanded of a lay director than of a managing director;

3 a director is not generally expected to give continuous attention to the company's affairs, since directors' duties are essentially intermittent in their nature (today it is unlikely that any court would excuse a managing director who failed to exercise continuous attention);

4 delegation of duty by a director to an appropriate company official is not evidence of a breach of duty provided it is in accordance with business practice and does not infringe the company's articles.

Where it appears that a director has breached the duty of care, an action in negligence may be started, after members at a general meeting have voted in favour of such action. A director who is found to have been negligent must personally indemnify the company for its losses.

It is possible for the directors to be informally excused (without passage of a resolution) as concerns their negligent conduct by unanimous agreement of members with voting rights. This may be done even if the negligent directors themselves control the voting.

Fiduciary duty

This is imposed by the law of equity and requires directors to act with the *utmost good faith* in dealings with the company.

This has three consequences:

1 Directors must avoid any conflict between their own financial interests and those of the company. If they breach this duty, they must account to the company for any resulting profit.

2 Directors must make full disclosure of any personal interest which they have in company business. Generally, the articles provide that as long as directors fully declare their interests they may retain them, but they must not vote at a board meeting on any issue relating to those interests.

3 Directors must exercise their powers in good faith and for their proper purposes.

IDC v Cooley (1972)

Cooley was an architect employed as managing director of IDC. He was put in charge of negotiations with a gas board, which had approached IDC concerning the design of a gas holder. During the negotiations it became clear that the gas board was unwilling to place the contract with IDC. At this point Cooley resigned, falsely pleading ill health. Then he obtained the design contract with the gas board.

Held (Roskill J): Cooley must pay the profits from the contract to IDC, since he had abused his position as agent of the company and used his inside knowledge to obtain the contract, creating a conflict of interest. 'Information which came to him while he was managing director and which was of concern to the [company] and relevant for the [company] to know, was information which it was his duty to pass on.'

It was irrelevant that his behaviour had not necessarily caused IDC to lose the contract.

Hogg v Cramphorn Ltd (1967)

Hogg put in a bid to take over Cramphorn Ltd. The directors, who honestly believed that a threatened takeover was not in the company's best interests, issued 5,000 additional shares to a trust made up of employees to enable the bid to be outvoted.

Held: this was a misuse of the directors' powers. Their action had diluted the value of the company's stock. A shares issue could only be undertaken to raise capital, not to defeat a takeover bid.

If a contract is made in breach of the directors' fiduciary duty, the contract is voidable, and, therefore, the company is able to choose whether to go through with it or not. Provided that the directors have not acted fraudulently or in breach of the law, under the law of agency the shareholders might vote to ratify their actions. For example, in *Hogg v Cramphorn* it was held that, provided that the employees were excluded from the vote, the remaining shareholders could vote to ratify the directors' action.

Directors' duties since the CA 2006

The CA 2006 is intended to clarify directors' duties by codifying the obligations described above. These are now described as 'general duties' and comprise in effect a detailed analysis of the common law and equitable obligations.

These duties are owed to the company alone (s 170(1)) and replace the common law and equitable principles which form their basis. The Act indicates that they should be interpreted in that light and 'regard must be paid to the corresponding common law rules and equitable principles' (s 170(4)). Previous case law in this area therefore remains relevant unless and until changed. The new wording may have an impact on the interpretation of the scope of the duties.

The general duties: ss 171–177

These duties are not mutually exclusive, so more than one may arise in any one case. A director has a duty to:

1 *Act within his or her powers (s 171).* A director must comply with the company's constitution and only use their powers for the purposes for which they are conferred. This enacts the *ultra vires* rule.

2 *Promote the success of the company (s 172).* A director must in good faith promote the success of the company to benefit 'its members as a whole' (s 172(1)).

   This restates the director's duty to act in the company's best interests which is implicit in the original fiduciary duty. The wording appears somewhat contradictory as, although the duty initially sounds as if it is owed to the company, the Act continues by requiring the director to carry it out for the benefit of the shareholders, which could give rise to a conflict. However, any contradiction is arguably resolved by the criteria for decision making in s 172(1) which require a well-rounded approach.

   A director should take the following into account when making decisions:

   (a) likely long-term consequences;
   (b) interests of the company's workforce (replaces the CA 2006 duty to have regard to the employees' interests);
   (c) the need to foster good business relationships with all who deal with the company;
   (d) the environmental and community impact of the company activities;
   (e) the desirability of the company's maintaining a good reputation for business conduct; and
   (f) the need to act fairly as between company members.

Hellard and Others v Carvalho [2013]

Carvalho (the main director of the company) made repayments to some creditors (mainly family members) without having regard to the best interests of the company. The question arose as to whether Carvalho had acted in good faith.

Held: Carvalho was in breach of s 172. He also breached s 171 for failing to exercise his powers as a director for the purposes for which they were given.

BTI v *Sequana* [2019] (Court of Appeal Decision)

The Court was asked to consider whether the payment of dividends when the business was in financial difficulty constituted a breach by the directors of the fiduciary duties. Duty to consider creditors' interests is engaged when the directors know or should know that the company is or is likely to become insolvent. *Likely* in this context meaning 'probable'.

3 *Exercise independent judgement (s 173).* The directors' fiduciary duty has always required the exercise of unfettered discretion. Section 173(1) indicates that this duty is subject to any provision in the company's articles that authorises a restriction of discretion. Parliamentary debate during passage of the legislation indicates that it does not preclude delegation to committee or seeking expert advice where appropriate.

4 *Exercise reasonable skill, care and diligence (s 174).* This re-states the common law duty of reasonable care and skill as applicable to company directors and does not represent any real change.

   Previously the standard of care had been defined by the Insolvency Act 1986, s 214 which added an initial objective assessment to the existing subjective test in *Re City Equitable & Fire Insurance Co. Ltd* (1925) (see above).

   Section 174(2) adopts a similar definition. It provides that the duty requires:

the care, skill and diligence that would be exercised by a reasonably diligent person with –

(a) the general knowledge, skill and expertise that may reasonably be expected of a person carrying out the functions . . . [of] the director in relation to the company, and

(b) the general knowledge, skill and experience that the director has.

   Part (a) measures performance objectively to but (b) requires a subjective approach examining the skill, knowledge and experience of the director in question. The objective test therefore relates to the minimum standard of care required of the average reasonably competent director. The subjective test assesses whether, given their particular knowledge and experience in the particular circumstances, a higher standard should reasonably be expected of them.

   Students who have studied the tort chapters will recognise this as a specialised *Bolam* test. (See Chapter 13.)

5 *Avoid conflict of interest (s 175).* This general duty, which applies to the exploitation of the company's property, information or opportunity, is identical to the existing equitable duty as applied in *IDC* v *Cooley* (above). A director may be held to be liable for a breach regardless of the fact that the company suffered no loss and the director had no improper motive. (See *Towers* v *Premier Waste Management Ltd* (2011).)

6 *Refuse third party benefits (s 176).* This is another aspect of conflict of interest made specific by the Act. Benefits include bribes and gifts from those seeking to obtain business opportunities or advantageous terms. (See the *Towers* case below.)

Section 176(1) prohibits a director from obtaining a benefit from a third party which was conferred because he or she is a director or doing/not doing something as a director. A third party is defined (s 176(2)) as a person other than the company, its subsidiaries or any person acting on behalf of the company or subsidiaries. Benefits for services provided to the third party by the director are excluded (s 176(3)).

No breach occurs if the benefit could not reasonably be expected to give rise to a conflict of interest or duties (s 176(4) and (5)).

7 *Declare an interest in any proposed transaction or arrangement with the company (s 177).* Directors had a statutory duty to declare any interest in any proposed or existing contract with the company under s 317 of the CA 1985.

The CA 2006 splits this duty but the substance of the law remains the same. Existing contracts are now covered by s 182 which is explained below and s 177 concerns proposed contracts only.

Section 177(1) requires a director to disclose the nature and extent of any direct or indirect interest to all the other directors. An interest may arise indirectly if, for example, the director's spouse is involved in the proposed transaction. Provided the director has not breached his duties under s 175 and s 177, the transaction is not voidable without the approval of company members unless the articles of the company require this (s 180(1)).

A director is not in breach of this duty unless he should reasonably have been aware of the conflict of interest.

8 *Declare an interest in an existing transaction or arrangement.* Section 182(1) requires a director to disclose to all the other directors the nature and extent of any direct or indirect interest which he or she has in any transaction or arrangement which the company has entered into.

If the director has made a relevant declaration under s 177 at the point when the transaction was proposed, there is no need to make a second one (s 182(1)). He or she is not under a duty to declare an interest of which he or she could not reasonably have known (s 182(5)).

Failure to make a disclosure under s 182 is a criminal offence punishable by fine or imprisonment (s 183). Note that this does not apply to a breach of any other of the directors' duties (s 178); those are sanctioned by civil law only. Any contract involving an undeclared conflict of interest may be voidable and the director may be required to account for any profits.

Guinness plc v *Saunders* (1990)

During a takeover bid a payment of over £5 million was made to a director who had disclosed a relevant interest to a committee of the board consisting of only two other members and himself.

Held: this was not sufficient to discharge the duty because disclosure must be made to the whole board.

Case law indicates that the courts interpret these duties stringently even in the case of relatively minor breaches.

Towers v *Premier Waste Management Ltd* (2011, CA)

Mr Towers was a director of Premier. One of the company's customers offered him free loan of plant and equipment for his use in renovating his house. He did not disclose this advantageous arrangement to his company. When it became known, the company took action against him for breach of his duties.

Held: Mr Towers had breached his fiduciary duty to the company by failing in his duty of loyalty and by failing to avoid a conflict of interest. He had been disloyal in preventing the company from considering whether it objected to the diversion of a possible benefit from it. It was irrelevant that the company suffered no resulting loss and that he did not make a valuable profit, act in bad faith or that he would not have hired the equipment commercially had the offer of loan not been made.

A director may remain bound by their duties even after leaving the company.

Killen v *Horseworld Ltd* (2012)

Ms Killen, a director of Horseworld, was involved in negotiating a contract on behalf of the company to supply media broadcasting services to the organisers of the Badminton Horse Trials in 2009. Ms Killen then left Horseworld and set up her own company (Horse & Country Ltd) and exploited the information she had secured at Horseworld to get a contract to supply internet broadcasting services for the 2009 Horse trials.

Robinson J held: she was in breach of her duty to avoid conflict of interest and must account for the profits to Horseworld Ltd. 'Section 175(1) requires a director to avoid a situation where there is even the possibility of a conflict of interest, and Section 175(2) makes particular reference to the exploitation of an opportunity.' It was irrelevant that she was no longer a Horseworld director, as on leaving that company she had immediately engaged in negotiations in direct competition with it. Also '. . . she knew that Horseworld Ltd wanted the actual broadcast rights that were included in the package obtained by Horse and Country.'

Directors' duty to creditors

Insolvency Act 1986 s 214: if the directors should be aware that the company cannot reasonably avoid going into liquidation they have a duty to take reasonable steps to minimise losses to creditors of the company.

LRH Services v *Trew, Brewer and O'Neill* [2018]

In 2009 as part of a reorganisation LRH Services Ltd (LRH) reduced its share capital to £1 and made a distribution to its shareholders of around £21.3 million. While LRH was a non-trading company, it was the tenant of a number of commercial properties, some of which were occupied by its trading subsidiaries. When an occupier failed to pay its rent, LRH was unable to keep up with its lease payments, and eventually a landlord commenced winding-up proceedings against it. The reorganisation left the company unable to pay its debts, despite the company being balance sheet solvent. The company entered liquidation and the liquidators brought claims.

Held: the directors were personally liable for the actions taken. The unlawful capital reduction and distribution had breached their duty to promote the success of the company. The reduction in share capital and payment of the £21.3 million dividend was a breach of the directors' duties under the Companies Act 2006 to act in good faith in promoting the success of the company and exercise reasonable care and skill.

Transactions by directors which require shareholder approval

Certain transactions by the board of directors on behalf of the company require approval by ordinary resolution of the shareholders. The relevant transactions involve the possibility of unfair advantage accruing to a director. They include the following.

Substantial and material property transactions: s 190

Unless the shareholders have given their approval they may avoid any transaction involving the sale or acquisition of a noncash asset by the company to or from a director of the company or a person connected with him or her where the value of the property exceeds £5,000 and is in excess of 10 per cent of the company's net assets. Unless shareholder approval for the transaction is given, the director, or any connected person, is liable to the company for profits arising from the contract; and any directors who gave their approval may also be liable.

Persons connected with the director are stated in s 252 to include family (e.g. spouse, civil partner, children, and stepchildren) as well as a company in which the director can control 20 per cent of the shareholder vote.

Worth thinking about?

Before the CA 2006, directors considering two competing takeover bids could perform their duty of acting in the company's best interests by accepting the lower bid, if that was ultimately going to be more beneficial for the business. Arguably, this might be less financially beneficial to the shareholders.

Does the wording of s 172(1), which seems to suggest that the shareholders' benefit is paramount, prevent directors from legitimately opting for the lower bid?

Suggested solutions can be found in Appendix 2.

Directors' long-term service contracts: s 189

Without shareholder approval any provision in an executive director's employment contract restricting the company's rights to terminate the director's employment is void.

Loans to directors: ss 197–214

Subject to certain exceptions no loan can be made to a director without the company's approval and any loan is voidable without it. Exceptions cover expenses directly related to carrying out company business.

Golden handshakes: s 217

Compensation for loss of office of director or payments on retirement cannot be paid without approval from the shareholders. The UK Corporate Governance Code recommends that these should not be excessive (see below).

Reporting to shareholders

Shareholders need to be kept properly informed about the work of the company to enable them to play an effective role. As part of its campaign to promote transparency and to ensure compliance with existing legislation, the Companies Act 2006 (Strategic Report and Directors' Report) Regulations 2013 came into operation on 31 October 2013. These are aimed at making directors provide better information to shareholders about how well the directors have performed their duty to promote the success of the company (CA, s 172) during the past year. They apply to companies quoted on the Stock Exchange and require greater clarity and detail in reporting than was imposed previously.

Directors must now make a much fuller disclosure of the principal risks and uncertainties confronting the company. Overall the report should involve a fair and balanced review of the company's performance over the year.

The reports must now contain:

(a) Analysis of business trends showing the main factors in the business world affecting the company's operation.

(b) Environmental reporting to show the impact of the company's business.

(c) Gender diversity with reference to the company's employees and directors.

(d) Social, community and human rights issues, showing how the company's policies affect such issues and take them into account.

(e) A description of the company's policy.

(f) A description of the company's business model.

The rights of directors

Fees and expenses

Executive directors' remuneration is determined by the terms of their service contracts. Lay directors' entitlement is specified in the articles, but they are entitled to expenses.

The removal and retirement of directors

Removal by ordinary resolution with special notice: s 168

A director may be removed from office before the expiry of their term. This is done by passing an ordinary resolution of the company, for which special notice is given (see Chapter 24). This might occur, for example, in the event of a serious breach of duty by a director. The director must be given a copy of the special notice prior to its distribution to the shareholders so that the director can attach a written statement to it. Under s 169 the director is entitled to address the meeting and make representations in his or her defence.

Directors are entitled to use weighted voting rights even if these have been created specifically to prevent removal. Thus, in *Bushell* v *Faith* (1970, HL) a company's articles stated that in the event of a resolution to remove the directors, their shares would carry three votes per share instead of one. Mr Faith, a director, who held 100 shares, was able to use this measure to defeat his two sisters who held 100 shares each.

Although executive directors may be removed in the same way as any other director, the company may have to pay damages if the removal is in breach of an executive director's contract of employment (s 167(5)).

Real life

Heena owns shares in Smallville Wanderers plc. She has been invited to an extraordinary general meeting of the company and given special notice of a resolution to remove Bruno, one of the directors, from office. There is evidence that Bruno was wined and dined by a sales representative of Fleetfoot Sports Shoes plc just before a meeting of the board voted by a majority of only one, to place a large order with Fleetfoot and make it their preferred supplier. Bruno is also a shareholder in Fleetfoot but did not tell his fellow directors about this prior to the vote. Fleetfoot has now gone into liquidation before fulfilling an order worth £5,000, which Wanderers are very unlikely to recover.

It is alleged that Bruno has breached two duties: first, by accepting third party benefits; and, secondly, by failing to declare an interest in a proposed company transaction.

While accepting Fleetfoot's hospitality alone would not seem to justify removing Bruno, the shareholders may reasonably feel that this, combined with his failure to declare his interest in the deal with Fleetfoot, reflects very poorly on Bruno's integrity, particularly if Bruno spoke in favour of trading with Fleetfoot at the board meeting. If, in addition, Bruno should have been aware of Fleetfoot's perilous financial situation the shareholders would seem to be even more justified in getting rid of him, as this would seem to be a breach of his duty to act independently and with reasonable care and skill. Bruno may speak in his defence at the meeting.

Retirement and resignation of directors

Retirement and resignation rules are found in the company's articles. These may provide for retirement in rotation, at the AGM, for a proportion of the board after the lapse of a specified period of service. However, this is not practicable for many small private companies and in large listed companies directors will be required to stand for election every year.

Any circumstances preventing a director from being able to carry out his or her duties (for example, ill health or failure to attend company meetings without permission of the board) may be grounds for seeking their removal.

The disqualification of directors

Company Directors Disqualification Act 1986

Any person (not just an existing director) may be disqualified by order of the court from being a director, liquidator, administrator, receiver or manager of a company's property or from being in any way directly or indirectly concerned in running a company. Such an order may be made in the following circumstances:

(a) *Conviction for an indictable offence in the Crown Court.* The offence must be connected with setting up or managing a company. The maximum disqualification period is 15 years.

(b) *Persistent failure to make the annual return.* Persistent means three times over a five-year period. The maximum disqualification period is five years.

(c) *Fraudulent trading.* The maximum disqualification period is 15 years.

(d) *Unfit conduct by a director of an insolvent company.* Unfit behaviour includes:

- breach of directors' duties;
- misapplication or wrongful retention of company property;
- failure to comply with Companies Act requirements concerning accounts and annual returns;
- failure to cooperate with the liquidator in accordance with the requirements of the Insolvency Act 1986;
- bankruptcy: an undischarged bankrupt is disqualified.

The maximum period for disqualification is 15 years.

The company secretary

Company secretary: the principal administrator of a company responsible for ensuring compliance with the Companies Acts.

All public companies must have a company secretary but since the CA 2006 this is no longer obligatory for private companies (s 270).

This is a key post, since the **company secretary** is the company's principal administrative officer. The company secretary has a wide range of duties with responsibility for ensuring that the company fulfils its obligations under the Companies Acts. The secretary is not involved in managing the company or in carrying on its business, but has responsibility for running the registered office. In a large company, the company secretary's job may involve hiring staff, buying office equipment and administering a pension scheme, as well as carrying out any functions designated by the articles or statute.

Qualifications for office

In *private companies*, no specific qualifications are needed. In public companies the directors must be satisfied that their appointee has appropriate skills and experience to do the job (s 273). In addition, the appointee must satisfy one of the following requirements:

1 for three of the last five years have been the secretary of a public company; or
2 be called or admitted as a barrister/solicitor/advocate in the UK; or
3 be a member of an approved organisation (e.g. ICA, ACCA, ICSA, ICMA, CIPFA); or
4 appear to be capable of acting as a company secretary because of experience gained as the holder of another office or membership of an appropriate body.

The directors are responsible for appointing the company secretary.

The functions of the company secretary

Ensuring compliance with the Companies Acts

The secretary must make sure that all the documentation open to public inspection is kept in order and up to date. This includes the registers of share and debenture holders. The secretary is also responsible for supervising the completion of the annual return.

The **annual return** updates the information about the company which was required for registration, so that most of the information which may be obtained by looking at the register can be found in the return. Sections 855 and 856 require the following information to be included:

1 the names and addresses of the current directors and secretary;
2 particulars of other directorships held by board members;
3 the address of the registered office;
4 particulars of the company's share capital.

Further requirements may be imposed by the Secretary of State by regulation (s 857).

The return should be delivered to the Companies Registry every year on the anniversary of the company's incorporation or delivery of its last annual return. It may also be filed online under s 858, and failure to deliver it is a criminal offence by the company and its directors and secretary. However, the SBEEA 2015, s 92 amends the CA 2006 to enable a company to opt out of filing a return annually. Instead, any change of relevant details must be notified to the Companies Registry once a year.

The secretary has authority to act as the company's agent

Company secretaries have authority to make a wide variety of contracts incidental to their functions. These include engaging office staff, buying or hiring office equipment, and purchasing such other goods and services as are necessary to running the

Annual return: current information which the company secretary must file every year at Companies House.

company office. As long as the other party acts in good faith in the reasonable belief that the company has authorised the contracts, they will be enforceable against the company whether or not the secretary had actual authority or not.

Panorama Developments v *Fidelis Furnishing Fabrics Ltd* (1971, CA)

The company secretary of Fidelis Furnishings hired cars, claiming that they were to be used to transport customers to the company premises. In fact he was putting them to his own use.

Held: the company was liable on these contracts, which came within the scope of the secretary's apparent authority. The status of the company secretary had become greatly enhanced in the twentieth century and carried much greater responsibility than the largely clerical role of the office in the nineteenth century.

Some activities, however, do not come within the secretary's authority. These include borrowing money and making a trading contract, as these actions are not incidental to the administration of the company.

The role of the company secretary

In larger public companies the role of the company secretary has, in the last half century, grown considerably from the basic administrative role described so far to something much more complex and multifaceted. When performed well this enables them to make a substantial contribution to the success of the company. When they have been in post a long time they can provide useful continuity to the board as directors come and go; their wealth of background knowledge of the company's trading history is also valuable. They can play a significant role in aiding the success of the company by ensuring that all board members are appropriately supplied with the current information necessary to good decision-making; this is particularly important to keep non-executive directors in the loop and ensure the effectiveness of their role. The secretary may also provide a necessary link between executive and non-executive directors to enable good communication between them.

Annual report: comprehensive information on the company's activities and performance issued to shareholders.

Since the implementation of the Cadbury Report in 1993, the secretary's duties have become even more challenging. An **annual report** is sent to shareholders to give them a comprehensive review of the company's performance over the year. The secretary of a listed company must ensure that it includes a review of how far the company has complied with the requirements of the UK Governance Code issued by the Financial Reporting Council. Failure to declare progress to the Financial Conduct Authority on conforming to the code may result in the company having its listed status removed by the Stock Exchange.

The auditors of the company

The CA 2006 re-states this area of the law largely without change.

The duty to appoint an auditor

Auditor:
accountant appointed by the company to check on the company's accounts and report on them to the shareholders.

Every company must generally appoint an **auditor** for each financial year, but the procedure is now different for private companies. A public company appoints its auditor during an accounts meeting at which the company's annual accounts and reports are laid (s 489(2)). If a public company fails to appoint an auditor, the Secretary of State has the power to appoint one (s 490).

Under the CA 2006, private companies are relieved of the obligation of holding meetings, therefore a private company must generally appoint its auditor by ordinary resolution within 28 days of the accounts being issued (s 485(2)). If it fails to do this the existing auditor is deemed to be reappointed (s 487(2)) though this can be blocked by members (s 488).

A small private company, the turnover of which does not exceed £5.6 million in the current year, is completely exempt from the requirement to have an annual audit (s 477) though its accounts must be audited by an independent, appropriately qualified accountant.

The auditor must be a member of a recognised accountancy body. This includes the Institute of Chartered Accountants and the Chartered Association of Certified Accountants.

Under the Companies (Audit Investigations and Community Enterprise) Act 2004, the Professional Oversight Board for Accountancy has responsibility for monitoring the audits of all listed companies.

The functions of the auditors

The functions of the company's auditors are to check that the company's accounts genuinely reflect its actual financial position and to issue a report on the accounts to the shareholders. To perform these functions efficiently, the auditors will have to do more than just check the in-house accountant's arithmetic; the company's stock in trade and money-handling procedures will have to be inspected and the company advised of any undesirable practices taking place in the management of the business.

The powers of the auditors

Auditors have considerable powers to help them acquire the necessary information to perform their functions. They have access to all the company's books and records and may question company officials (s 499). It is a criminal offence knowingly or recklessly to make a misleading or materially false statement to an auditor.

The liability of the auditors

Contract

The auditors' contract with the company must be performed with reasonable care and skill. Failure to do so can make the auditors liable for breach of contract. Only the company has the right to sue, as there is no privity of contract between the auditors and individual shareholders.

Tort

Negligence liability will arise if the auditors do not act with reasonable care and skill, but this duty is owed only to the company, not to existing or potential shareholders. (See Chapter 13 and the House of Lords' decision in *Caparo Industries plc* v *Dickman* (1990).)

Insider dealing

Insider dealing: secretly using inside information about a company's share value for personal profit.

Anybody with inside information about the present or future value of the company's securities, who uses that information for their own profit and without disclosing it to any other relevant parties, may be guilty of **insider dealing**; this is a criminal offence. Insiders include the company's directors, shareholders and employees, and any other people who have access to relevant information about the company because of their office or professional status. Therefore, an auditor who bought shares in the knowledge that a takeover was imminent which would increase their value would be guilty of insider dealing if that information was not public knowledge.

Such dealing has been an infringement of the Companies Acts since 1980. The current law is to be found in the Criminal Justice Act 1993, Part IV, which was prompted by the need for the UK to comply with EC Directive 89/92 on insider dealing. It is an offence to deal in securities while in possession, as an insider, of inside information and if the price of securities is affected by this information. Defendants may avoid liability if they can prove that when they entered into the transaction they did not do so with the intention of making a profit or avoiding a loss.

The CA 2006 does not create civil liability for insider dealing; therefore the company or individual shareholders do not have any right to recover damages for the losses which they have suffered. Where the insider is a director, the profits from the deal are technically recoverable by the company, as by dealing in this way the director will have acted in breach of their duties. There are no reported decisions where such action has been taken.

Corporate Governance: monitoring corporate dealings – the UK Corporate Governance Code

Good governance by all directors and company officers of companies listed on the Stock Exchange has been encouraged by successive Combined Codes. These were published initially by the Stock Exchange in 1998 and subsequently by the Financial Services Authority (now the Financial Conduct Authority), each aiming to further improve directors' performance. The UK Corporate Governance Code 2010, published by the Financial Reporting Council (FRC), replaced and enhanced these. It provided new guidance on corporate governance for all directors but comprises principles rather than actual rules. Directors are required to report annually to the FRC indicating how far the company has conformed to Code requirements and explaining any deficiencies.

The Code stressed the need for a rise in standards by boards of companies to ensure value for money for their shareholders and the general good of the company. For example:

1 On appointment directors should conform to a role description prepared by the company's nomination committee and appointments to the board should be made on merit, judged against objective criteria.

2 Appropriate regard must be given to diversity on the board, including gender.

3 New directors should receive full, formal and appropriate induction on joining the board.

4 All directors should be able to give sufficient time to the effective fulfilment of their duties.

5 No non-executive director should be proposed for re-election by the shareholders without a performance evaluation indicative of his or her commitment and effectiveness in the role, since they are expected to challenge and help develop the company's strategies constructively.

6 Remuneration of executive directors should be regulated to ensure the long-term success of the company; and remuneration committees should clearly explain to shareholders how this is being done.

7 Remuneration committees are also required to take a robust line when determining the size of golden handshakes for retiring managing directors to ensure that they are proportionate.

8 The Code emphasises the responsibility of the board of directors for determining what and how much risk is involved in the company's dealings: this provision clearly reflects the concerns which emerged from the collapse of various financial institutions during the credit crunch which preceded the publication of the Code.

However, despite the Codes, concerns about corporate governance have continued. Public feelings of mistrust of the system have grown, especially in the last few years. A government policy of austerity and low wages in the public sector has been in contrast to the huge annual and retirement remuneration packages handed out to some CEOs and senior executives. At the same time there have been some spectacular business failures like the British Home Stores closure in 2016, Carillion in 2018, and the café chain Patisserie Valerie in 2019.

Substantial numbers of shareholders at company annual meetings have often voted against the size of such pay awards and other aspects of company policy. An important area of public criticism is the lack of sanctions for breaching the Code. The FRC's 'comply or explain' policy is often perceived to be ineffective if vague or superficial explanation of failings is accepted as sufficient.

In an attempt to improve matters and promote greater trust in the business world, the government published a Green Paper in November 2016 and requested feedback on its suggestions for reform from any interested persons. In April 2017 the Department for Business, Energy and industrial Strategy (BEIS, formerly BIS) published a report based on the questions raised in the Green Paper with recommendations for change.

CBEIS Committee report: mandatory regime threatened

The Business, Energy and Industrial Strategy Committee report stated that in principle it supported the 'comply or explain' policy imposed by the Combined Codes and did not think that prescriptive measures were necessarily the way forward. However, in the light of the recent high-profile failures in corporate governance and business, improvements to the effectiveness of the reporting system must be made.

A new corporate code must be introduced by the FRC to supervise the largest companies in private ownership. Another body would be set up to ensure that the code was satisfactorily fulfilled and to report on this.

It recommended a number of essential improvements to the reporting process, including:

Directorial duties under s 172: reporting must be enhanced with detailed evidence indicating how the board had considered the interests of all stakeholders in the company. Any breach could be sanctioned through legal proceedings by the FRC.

Diversity: all aspects of diversity should be addressed including the appointment of workers to the board. The government should set a target of 50 per cent female recruitment to new senior executive posts in all listed companies by May 2020.

Remuneration: CEOs should be paid by salary only with additions for long-term incentives. Bonuses should be payable only if rigorous targets were reached. All pay and benefits proposals from the remuneration committee must be accepted by at least 75 per cent of the shareholders or the chair of the committee must be sacked. There should be employee representation on the committee to aid realistic assessment of pay.

Power for the FRC: to name and shame companies failing to fulfil adequate reporting and achievement standards.

Following the government's consultation on corporate governance reform the most recent version of the UK Corporate Governance Code was introduced in July 2018 and will apply to accountancy periods beginning on or after 1 January 2019. The new Code stresses the importance of transparency and integrity in the management and leadership of a company, including:

- the overarching importance of good governance in delivering long-term sustainable performance;
- the board's responsibility for establishing a healthy corporate culture;
- improved shareholder and wider stakeholder engagement;
- diversity in board succession planning and proportionate remuneration which supports long-term success, with clearer reporting requirements (UK Corporate Governance Code – July 2018).

The likelihood is that if the latest version of the Code does not facilitate acceptable levels of performance, the government will introduce a mandatory system. Some commentators might argue that a mandatory system is long overdue.

Chapter summary

Directors

All private companies must have at least one director. Public companies must have two.
Larger companies have a board consisting of one or more executive director(s) plus lay directors.
Work of the board takes place largely at company meetings but the executive directors are responsible for the daily running of the company.

Duties of directors

Act within powers.
Promote success.

Exercise independent judgement.
Exercise reasonable care, skill and diligence.
Avoid conflicts of interest.
Not accept benefits from third parties.
Declare interests in proposed/existing transactions.

Transactions between company and directors requiring shareholder approval

Long-term service contracts.
Substantial property transactions with directors/connected persons.
Loans to directors.
Golden handshakes.

Payment of directors

Executive directors: under the terms of the employment contract.
Lay directors: only so far as the articles permit.

Disqualification of directors

CDDA 1986: e.g. fraudulent trading, conviction of an indictable offence, bankruptcy.

Retirement

Articles indicate length of service.

Removal by resolution of the shareholders

Ill health.
Failure to attend board meetings.

Review questions 22

1 Zara was approached by Lucy, a director of Textiles plc, and asked to supply catering services for Textiles' hundredth anniversary party. She incurred costs in preparing for the event, but has now been told that Lucy had acted without the authority of the board of directors, who had vetoed her proposal. What are Zara's rights?

2 Textiles plc is having severe financial problems. What duties does it owe to:

    (a) its creditors?

    (b) its employees?

3 Textiles' board has proposed that the company will employ Threads Ltd to carry out an efficiency study. The principal shareholder and managing director of Threads is Taffeta; she is married to Cotton, a director of Textiles plc. Cotton fails to mention the connection. What is the legal situation?

4 What is the legal position of the following Textiles directors?

    (a) Penny, who has gone bankrupt.

    (b) Damien, who has not attended a board meeting all year.

    (c) Twiggy, who was so consumed with worry over Textiles' affairs that he has become clinically depressed, refuses to communicate in any way with any of his fellow directors and sits silently weeping during board meetings.

5 Explain the meaning of insider dealing.

6 How can a director of a company be removed from office?

Answers to all review questions can be found in Appendix 2.

Advanced questions 22

(A) Explain the circumstances in which a company director can face criminal liability for 'insider dealing', and the possible penalties.

(B) Critically evaluate what is meant by the duty on directors to promote the success of the company, and explain how this should be applied.

Answers to the advanced questions can be found at **go.pearson.com/uk/he/resources.**

Take a closer look

The following cases provide important examples of how the law in this chapter has developed. They are primary sources illustrating the law in action and give more detail about their facts, as well as helping to understand the law and to appreciate how the judges reached their decisions.

Try looking them up in the law reports or accessing them via a database, e.g. BAILII (www.bailii.org/databases.html). LexisNexis or Westlaw may be available in the university or college library, or extracts may be found in a case book. (See Appendix 1: Additional resources.)

Caparo Industries plc v *Dickman* [1990] 1 All ER 568

Guinness plc v *Saunders* [1990] 2 AC 663

IDC v *Cooley* [1972] 1 WLR 443

LRH Services v *Trew, Brewer and O'Neill* [2018] EWHC 600 (Ch)

Panorama Developments v *Fidelis Furnishing Fabrics Ltd* [1971] 3 WLR 440, C

Web activity

Find out what resources the Institute of Directors provides for its members at:
www.iod.com

Read 'New Financial Reporting Requirements For Large Private Companies' by Caroline Williams at:
www.freeths.co.uk/2018/06/14/new-financial-reporting-requirements-for-large-private-companies/

The UK Corporate Governance Code (July 2018) can be found at:
www.frc.org.uk/getattachment/88bd8c45-50ea-4841-95b0-d2f4f48069a2/2018-UK-Corporate-Governance-Code-FINAL.pdf

Read 'Corporate governance reform: the new UK Corporate Governance Code' by Alyson Whale at:
www.burges-salmon.com/news-and-insight/legal-updates/corporate-governance-reform-the-new-uk-corporate-governance-code/

Assignment 21

'The changes to directors' duties under the Companies Act 2006 in practice made little difference to corporate governance.'

Discuss.

Company meetings, shareholder participation and minority protection

Learning objectives

On completion of this chapter, students should be able to:

★ know when and how a general meeting of a company must be called;

★ describe the conduct of a general meeting;

★ distinguish between the different types of resolution which may be passed by company members;

★ assess how far the law protects the rights of minority shareholders.

Introduction

Corporate governance concerns the nature and extent of rights and responsibilities held by different participants in the organisation, in particular, the relationship between directors and shareholders. This chapter is primarily concerned with the interaction of the company with its shareholders. The day-to-day management of the company is in the hands of the directors and usually there is little that the shareholders can do to influence this. However, the directors are accountable to the shareholders. The CA 2006 requires every public company to hold an annual general meeting (AGM) to which shareholders must be invited to get an overview of the company's progress in the previous year. A general meeting may have to be called if business has arisen that is too urgent to wait until the AGM. Occasionally shareholders may call such a meeting. At meetings shareholders generally are entitled to speak and vote on resolutions presented to them by the board. In certain circumstances they may be able to present a resolution themselves to get a matter discussed when the directors may be reluctant to do so.

The CA 2006 contains some measures that may be taken by minority shareholders who are concerned that the directors are in breach of their duties and all other measures to control them have failed. These will be examined at the end of the chapter.

General meetings

The annual general meeting (AGM)

Annual general meeting:
yearly meeting of company to which all members are invited.

Resolution:
a proposal to be voted upon by members.

The purpose of the **annual general meeting** is to allow the shareholders to question the directors about the annual report, to vote on any **resolutions** put before the meeting and to elect new directors.

Every public company must hold its annual general meeting within six months of its accounting reference date, in other words the end of its financial year (s 336). This is to help the shareholders to make the directors account for any problem showing up in the annual accounts and auditor's report. Twenty-one days' notice must be given.

A private company no longer needs to hold an AGM. This takes into account the 'think small' philosophy of the reforms which preceded the CA 2006. Large numbers of private companies are small businesses maybe consisting of only one, or at the most a few, members working together on a daily basis. An AGM for such companies is clearly redundant. Where a private company chooses to hold an AGM it is obliged to give 14 days' notice (s 307).

Additional general meetings may be called

General meeting:
meeting to which all members are invited.

It may be necessary to call a **general meeting** if something occurs which is so urgent that it cannot wait until the next annual general meeting. The CA 1985 described this as an 'extraordinary general meeting' but this concept no longer exists under the CA 2006. The directors' powers to call a general meeting are stated in the articles, but a duty is imposed by law in certain situations. Unless otherwise stated, 14 days' notice is required.

The CA 2006 requires a general meeting to be called in the following circumstances.

Serious reduction of capital

A director of a public company must call a meeting within 28 days of discovering that the company has suffered a serious loss of capital (s 656). A serious loss occurs where the company's net assets amount to half or less of its share capital. The meeting must be held within 56 days of notice being given.

The members requisition a meeting

The directors must call a general meeting if required to do so by members who hold at least five per cent of the paid-up share capital (s 303). Notice of the requisition, explaining why the meeting is needed, must be delivered to the company's registered office. It must be signed by the relevant shareholders. Within 21 days of the delivery, the directors must issue notice of the meeting. This must take place no later than 28 days after the date of issue of the notice.

Meeting by order of the court

A director or shareholder may ask the court to order that a meeting be convened with a specified agenda and a quorum of one when it is impracticable to call a meeting in the usual way or to conduct the meeting as prescribed by the Act or the company's articles (s 306). This is intended to resolve deadlock in a two-person company.

Requisition by retiring auditors

An auditor who has retired because of concerns about the financial management of the company may requisition a meeting to allow the members to consider the reasons for the auditor's resignation (s 518).

Rules concerning meetings

Notice of meetings

The length of notice

This varies according to the type of meeting and the nature of the business to be transacted. It may be reduced by agreement of the shareholders. An AGM of a public company generally requires 21 days' notice, but 14 days is sufficient for that of a private company (s 307).

Any other general meeting requires only 14 days' notice.

These notice periods may be reduced subject to agreement from the majority of the shareholders holding 5 per cent of the shares. The majority required is 95 per cent of the shareholders in a public company and 90–95 per cent in a private company (or as prescribed in a private company's articles). If a company does not have shares, members holding at least 95 per cent of the voting rights must agree (s 307).

How notice may be given: s 308

Notice may be given in the following manner:

- hard copy;
- email;
- company website; or
- by a combination of any of those means.

Electronic and website communication are changes introduced by the CA 2006. Since every member must be given notice (s 310) electronic means or a website notice alone would only be appropriate if all members have the relevant facilities. In practice, hard copy is likely to remain the most reliable method of communication in a company of any size.

Contents of the notice: s 311

The notice must contain the following information:

- the date, time and place of the meeting;
- the general nature of the business of the meeting (agenda).

Conduct of the meeting

Chairing the meeting

The articles usually specify who is to take the chair. If they do not, or if that person is not present, any nominated member may be chair. Usually this will be a director. The duty of the person in the chair is to run the meeting, but the permission of members must be sought before adjourning the meeting unless it becomes disorderly.

Quorum

Quorum:
the minimum number of members required to be present before a meeting can take place/continue.

The **quorum** is the minimum number of people who must be present to enable the business of a meeting to be legitimately transacted. This is usually specified in the articles; if not, two people are sufficient or one if the company has sole membership (s 318).

The meeting cannot take place if it is not quorate within 30 minutes of its starting time. If during the course of the meeting numbers drop below the required minimum, the meeting must be adjourned.

Resolutions

These are the proposals on which members may vote. Information regarding them may be circulated by email as well as hard copy since the CA 2006.

There are three categories of resolution:

Ordinary resolution:
requires a simple
majority.

1 *Ordinary resolution*. An **ordinary resolution** requires only a simple majority of members who vote to support it. This type of resolution is required, for example, to increase share capital or to remove a director.

2 *Special resolution*. A 75 per cent majority of members present and voting is necessary for a **special resolution** to be successful. This is required to make any change to the articles or to re-register a private company as a public one. Twenty-one days' notice is required though the articles may specify 28 days.

Special resolution:
requires a 75 per cent
majority.

Resolutions requiring special notice

The following resolutions cannot be put before the meeting unless the company received **special notice** of them at least 28 days before the date of the meeting:

Special notice:
28 days' notice, which
is required when cer-
tain types of resolution
are to be voted on.

1 a resolution for the removal of an auditor or to appoint a new one (s 510, s 515);

2 a resolution to remove a director (s 168).

When the company receives the special notice it must take the necessary steps to inform the members. Usually this accompanies notice of the meeting. Where a director or an auditor is threatened with removal, he or she must be sent a copy of the special notice and is entitled to defend him- or herself by circulating a written statement to members and to address the meeting.

Avoid confusion! A special notice is notice which must be given to the company, not to the members. A special notice has nothing to do with a special resolution. 'Special' in that context refers to the size of majority required for the resolution's success (75 per cent). Only an ordinary majority is necessary to remove a director or to appoint/remove an auditor.

Passing written resolutions

The CA 2006 distinguishes between private and public companies with regard to the passing of resolutions. Private companies may now pass most resolutions in writing while a public company can *only* pass a resolution at a general meeting (s 281). This reform is aimed at simplifying business for small companies, by reflecting their practical needs which may not involve meetings as such. A written record of decisions is all that is generally required. However, a **written resolution** is not sufficient to remove a director or auditor before the end of their term of service (s 288(2)).

Written resolution:
a written proposal to
which members of a
private company agree
by signing it rather
than voting at a gen-
eral meeting.

Written resolutions proposed by the directors must be circulated in advance to all members (s 291). Members may propose and circulate a written resolution provided those representing at least 5 per cent of the total voting rights (or any smaller percentage specified in the articles) request this (s 292). It may be accompanied by a 1,000-word explanatory statement. The members are responsible for the circulation costs unless excused by the company.

A written resolution is passed if the appropriate majority of company members communicate their agreement to it in writing within the appropriate time limits.

Passing resolutions at a general meeting

This is the only way a public company may pass a resolution. A resolution at a meeting is passed provided notice of the meeting and resolution was given to members and the meeting and voting were appropriately conducted (s 301).

Resolutions are often proposed by directors but a group of shareholders may do so too.

Section 338 enables shareholders of a public company to propose a resolution for an annual general meeting. The company must circulate the proposed resolution to all members if sponsored by at least 5 per cent of the total members with relevant voting rights, *or* by at least 100 members holding shares on which they have paid up at least £100 on average per member. While such motions are not necessarily successful, they do allow discussion to be opened up publicly with the board and sometimes to get wider publicity for the issue.

Resolutions may be amended at the meeting provided that this does not take them out of the scope of the notified business.

Voting at meetings

This may be by show of hands or by poll. A show of hands does not take into account the possible variation in voting strength of members specified in the articles.

Shareholders may register disapproval of company policy by voting against resolutions put forward by the board. Even though they may not succeed in defeating a resolution, a substantial minority vote will indicate significant objection and send a clear warning message to the board as well as attracting adverse publicity for the company.

Shareholder revolt

Since the end of the twentieth century a trend has developed for the UK's shareholders to become more militant by voting in substantial numbers against company proposals at the AGM. The main bone of contention has been remuneration packages for directors and chief executives. Substantial numbers of shareholders have voted against these on the grounds that they are disproportionately high in the context of the performance of the company and the record of the CEO or other office holder.

The biggest revolt so far was at the Royal Bank of Scotland in 2009, when there was a 90 per cent vote against a very generous pension award to Sir Fred

Goodwin, seen by many as the author of the near collapse of the bank, which led to its rescue by the taxpayer.

In 2012, shareholders voted against awards in six companies. At the advertising agency WPP close to 60 per cent voted against a proposed pay award for the chief executive.

In 2013, shareholders scored a notable win against the oil exploration company Afren when 80 per cent voted against a £3.4 million pay rise for the CEO. This trend continued in 2014 when WPP was back in the firing line. In 2015 the climate continued stormy for some boards. In the face of a likely defeat at its AGM, Aviva decided to reduce its proposals to award shares to its CEO which could have taken his 2015 earnings to £6.7 million; 2016 saw shareholders in substantial numbers disputing remuneration policies in eight major companies. BP's remuneration plan was rejected outright. The trend continued into 2017. Twelve companies suffered successful challenges by the end of April, including Imperial Brands (a tobacco firm), Thomas Cook and Next.

While there have not been many outright wins by shareholders, the threat of a substantial if not majority vote against their policies has often led a company to back down and reduce remuneration size. In May 2017, BP decided to stave off further rebellion and told shareholders at its general meeting that it was reducing its CEO's earnings by 40 per cent. In 2018 BT was subject to a rebellion over its outgoing chief executive's salary. At its AGM 34.2 per cent of investors voted against the remuneration report. As a consequence of the AGM outcome BT will be placed on a public register of firms in which more than 20 per cent of shareholders have voted against an executive pay resolution.

In 2019 42 per cent of shareholders at Standard Life Aberdeen voted against a remuneration report and pay package of £525,000 salary.

Sources: widely reported in the business media, including www.bbc.co.uk 2/5/12; www.guardian.co.uk 2/4/13, 11/6/13, 18/4/13 and 10/6/14; *Daily Telegraph* 9/4/13; this is money.co.uk 31/5/15; www.telegraph.co.uk 4/9/16 and 19/4/17; www.theguardian.com 27/4/17 and 11/7/17; www.aol.co.uk 17/5/17; and www.ft.com 14/5/19.

Proxy:
a person voting on behalf of a member at a general meeting.

Proxies may be appointed by any shareholder to vote in their place on their instructions. The articles may exclude the use of a vote to select the chair or adjourn a meeting. Otherwise, voting must be conducted by poll on the request of:

1 a minimum of five persons (proxies included); or
2 a member or members holding at least one-tenth of the voting rights; or
3 a member or members holding shares to the value of at least one-tenth of the paid-up capital.

Protecting the rights of minority shareholders

Derivative action: claim by minority shareholders to protect the company's interests from being harmed by mismanagement by directors.

The decisions of the directors may successfully be challenged by a majority of shareholders who disagree with their proposals. Problems may arise if the directors are also the majority shareholders, since this permits them to make decisions with which the minority disagree.

Shareholders may be able to bring a **derivative action** to protect the company.

The common law approach: the rule in *Foss* v *Harbottle*

The courts were generally reluctant to assist a minority of shareholders even where damage to the company's interests was alleged. The rule in *Foss* v *Harbottle* stated that, since only the damaged party can sue, the individual shareholder has no right to sue on the company's behalf, and that the court should not interfere with the internal management of a company acting *intra vires*. Three exceptions were acknowledged permitting an individual shareholder with permission from the court to intervene if:

1 the directors made an illegal or *ultra vires* decision;

2 the directors acted fraudulently;

3 the directors disregarded the procedures laid down in the articles.

The Law Commission's report of 1998 (*Shareholder Remedies* (Law Com. No. 246)) criticised this rule as being 'complicated and unwieldy' and commented that there were situations that fell outside the scope of fraud where nonetheless protection should be offered to shareholders. Reform has now been implemented by the CA 2006.

Statutory protection of minority rights

The CA 2006, s 260(1) in effect abolishes the rule in *Foss* v *Harbottle*. It states that a derivative action may be brought by a member of a company using only the procedures specified by the Act.

There are two of these:

1 proceedings under Chapter 11 of the CA 2006, ss 260–264, which is new;

2 proceedings under s 994, which replaces s 459 of the CA 1985.

Chapter 11 proceedings

Section 260 states that a member may issue a claim against a director regarding an 'actual or proposed act or omission involving negligence, default, breach of duty or breach of trust by a director'. The inclusion of negligence expands the grounds on which action can be taken as compared with those which could have been taken at common law.

A two-stage procedure must be negotiated before a claim will actually be heard (s 261):

- *Stage 1.* The member must first apply to bring the claim (s 261). Unless there is prima facie evidence to support the claim, it will be dismissed immediately. At this stage only the member's evidence is heard. Otherwise, the case proceeds to the next stage.

- *Stage 2.* The hearing: evidence from both sides is heard and the court comes to its decision.

Under s 262, a shareholder may request that a derivative action started by the company but halted, be fully heard. If the court is satisfied by evidence from both sides, then the claim will continue.

When deciding whether permission should be given, the court must take into account (s 263) whether the member is acting in good faith and whether the claim is really for the benefit of the company, rather than for the shareholder personally. A claim cannot continue if problematic conduct was authorised or subsequently ratified by the shareholders in accordance with required procedure. For example, s 239 requires that conduct by a director amounting to negligence, default, breach of duty or trust can be ratified by an ordinary resolution of the members of the company.

The CA 2006 has clarified the law in this area and potentially facilitated claims by shareholders. Concern has been voiced by some directors that they are now more vulnerable to claims due to the introduction of the new procedure (see directors' duties in Chapter 23) plus the many factors which must now be taken into account in taking duty-related decisions.

Worth thinking about?

Do you think the CA 2006 has got the balance of interests between directors and minority shareholders right? How does the CA 2006, Chapter 11 protect directors?

Suggested solutions can be found in Appendix 2.

Shareholder rights to petition the court on the grounds of unfair prejudice: s 994

This section is transferred unchanged from the CA 1985.

Unfair prejudice is a broad principle; it may exist even where the directors did not act intentionally or in bad faith, but a decision unfairly affects the interests of a minority of shareholders.

In order to take action under s 994:

1 the petitioner must be a member of the company;

2 the petitioner must have evidence that the company's affairs have previously been carried on in a way that is unfairly prejudicial to the interests of members, or at least to himself; or

Unfair prejudice: running the company in any way which unfairly affects the interests of a minority of shareholders.

3 the petitioner must have evidence that a proposed act or omission of the company would be similarly unfairly prejudicial (as in 2 above).

Whether or not unfairly prejudicial behaviour has actually occurred, is a matter for the court to decide on the particular facts of each individual case. It may exist without the directors being negligent or acting in bad faith.

Petitioners may succeed even though not entirely without fault themselves; but the morality of their behaviour is relevant to judging whether they have been unfairly treated.

Petitions have most commonly been sought on the following grounds:

- exclusion of the petitioner from the management of a small private company where the members are also directors and it is easy to vote someone off the board;
- failure to lay accounts before members;
- reduction in voting power;
- insufficient information and advice about a proposed takeover bid.

Under s 996, when a petitioner is successful, the court may make any appropriate order to give relief. This might include:

1 regulation of, or restrictions on, those eligible to manage the company;

2 an order requiring the company to purchase shares from a minority shareholder;

3 amendment of the company's articles, which can then be changed only with permission from the court.

The following case provides a useful example of the use of s 994.

Kohli v Lit and Others (2009)

Ms Kohli was a minority shareholder in Sunrise Radio. She applied to the court for an order requiring the directors, who were majority shareholders, to buy her shareholding because their behaviour had allegedly been unfairly prejudicial to her under the Companies Act 2006, s 994.

The defendant directors had:

1 Issued shares for a nominal price to a company in which one director had an interest.

2 Failed to disclose their remuneration when compiling the company accounts.

3 Been late in filing the accounts and company return.

4 Failed to get the agreement of shareholders before selling company property to one of the directors.

Held: the discounted shares sale was a breach of fiduciary duty; the defendants had not obtained the true and higher price of the shares and thus failed to promote the interests of the company or its shareholders.

Although the failure to disclose remuneration was unintentional, it was 'improper accounting', which might well destroy Ms Kohli's faith in the integrity of the board, making it unlikely that she would ever trust it again. The accounts, albeit prepared by accountants, remained the responsibility of the board.

Occurrences 2, 3 and 4 taken together clearly evidenced unfair prejudice and made it reasonable for Ms Kohli to feel that it was intolerable to continue as a shareholder in Sunrise.

The company must purchase her shares without a discount.

Such orders have been used successfully by minority shareholders of small private companies, but the procedure is less likely to be helpful to shareholders in large public companies who, in practice, are likely to remain largely powerless.

Shareholders' powers to initiate intervention by the Department for Business, Energy and Industrial Strategy

Where serious abuse of corporate powers is suspected, the shareholders may be able to instigate an inquiry by the Department for Business, Energy and Industrial Strategy inspectors. The relevant statutory provisions (which were *not* repealed by the CA 2006) are as follows:

1 under the CA 1985, s 431, a minority of at least 200 shareholders, or those holding at least one-tenth of the issued shares, may apply to the Secretary of State for an investigation to be carried out;

2 under the CA 1985, s 432, the Secretary of State may initiate an investigation in any circumstances suggesting that the company's members have not been kept appropriately informed, where there is evidence of fraud, unlawful behaviour by the company or misfeasance or misconduct towards members.

The Companies (Audit, Investigations and Community Enterprise) Act 2004, ss 21–24 give the Secretary of State considerable investigatory powers regarding production of documents, disclosure in a formal inquiry and the power to enter/remain on premises.

The following consequences may result from an investigation:

1 Under the Insolvency Act 1986, s 124A the Secretary of State may, if justified by the results of an investigation, petition for the company to be wound up on the grounds that it is just and equitable for this to happen.

2 Under the CA 2006, s 995 the Secretary of State may, if satisfied by an inspector's report that there is evidence of unfair prejudice to shareholders, petition the court for an order under s 994, in addition to/instead of an order to wind up the company.

Minority shareholder protection from specific types of abuse

1 The CA 2006, s 561 requires that new shares be offered to existing shareholders in proportion to their existing holdings to prevent further dilution of control or the issuing of shares to those who control the company for less than they are worth.

2 The CA 2006, s 630 provides a degree of protection for shareholders from changes in the rights attached to their shares. The class rights of shares can only be amended with the consent of a separate meeting of the class of shareholders by the passing of a special resolution if 75 per cent of the class cast their vote in favour of amendment.

3 A shareholder can sue in their own name to enforce personal rights provided by the company's regulations.

4 Where the class rights of a group of shareholders are undermined by the majority, the shareholders affected can take a representative action to challenge the decision to amend the class rights.

Real life

Hannah is a shareholder in Smallville Wanderers plc and was recently summoned to a general meeting to vote on a resolution to remove Mario, a director, from office for malpractice. Unfortunately, Mario used his influence to gather support from sufficient shareholders to defeat the motion.

However, the shareholders who had been responsible for raising concerns about Mario's conduct are taking advice. Chapter 11 proceedings might provide the answer. Permission to bring and continue the claim would be very likely to be given since there was no shortage of prima facie evidence. The shareholders seem to be acting in the interests of the company. Behaviour like Mario's was likely to have brought his company into disrepute and undoubtedly attracted undesirable publicity. This was evident from reports published in the *Smallville Chronicle* and subsequently in the business and sports sections of some national papers. However, the claim will not be allowed to proceed if the directors have ratified Mario's conduct. Given that he survived the resolution to remove him, it looks as if a resolution to ratify his conduct would probably also succeed.

If sufficient shareholder support is forthcoming, they could ask the Department for Business, Energy and Industrial Strategy to carry out an investigation. This might result in the company being wound up.

Chapter summary

General meetings

Company members are invited to these to debate and vote upon resolutions which have been circulated in advance.

A public company must hold an AGM. Other general meetings may be called where there is urgent business that shareholders need to vote upon. All resolutions must be passed at a general meeting.

Private companies are largely free of any duty under CA 2006 to hold general meetings of any kind and may pass written resolutions instead.

Notice of meetings

AGM of public company: 21 days.

AGM of private company: 14 days.

Other general meetings: 14 days.

CA 2006 has added email and company website as means by which notice and other company communications may be circulated to members.

Quorum

A meeting must have a minimum of at least two members present (one if company has only one member) before official business can be effectively transacted.

Voting on resolutions at the meeting

A resolution can be passed only by majority.

Some resolutions require special notice (28 days).

Ordinary resolutions: require only a simple majority and are used to transact most business.

Special resolutions: require a majority of 75 per cent and are needed to transact some business.

Proxies: may be appointed by members to vote on their behalf and according to their instructions.

Written resolutions: are only effective if used by private companies. Certain business cannot be transacted this way, e.g. removing a director before his or her period of office expires.

Protecting interests of minority shareholders

Common law procedure:

Foss v *Harbottle* exceptions effectively abolished.

Three types of statutory procedure:

Under CA 2006

Chapter 11 proceedings: permission from the court required (a) to bring and (b) to continue a previously existing claim.

Section 994: unfair prejudice claims.

Under CA 1985

Department for Business, Innovation and Skills (now BEIS) reform investigations.

Minority Protection in specific circumstances

s 561

s 630

Personal action

Representative action

Review questions 23

1 What is a general company meeting?

2 In what circumstances does the Companies Act 2006 require the directors of a company to call a general meeting?

3 Xanthe is an auditor of Atlanta plc who has just been sacked by Sam the managing director. What procedures must be fulfilled before Sam's decision to dismiss becomes effective?

4 Consider the rights of the following shareholders in Violet Ltd:
   (a) Bunny, who is unhappy about the company's decision to become a public company.
   (b) Rabi, who believes that the directors of Violet are trading fraudulently.

5 What is meant by a 'derivative' action by a shareholder?

6 Define and distinguish between an ordinary resolution and a special resolution.

Answers to all review questions can be found in Appendix 2.

Advanced questions 23

(A) Compare the protection offered to shareholders under CA 2006, s 994 with the protection offered to shareholders under CA 2006, s 260.

(B) Evaluate the following statement: 'UK company law enables most decisions to be taken by directors. Shareholders may be said to be disempowered in relation to the running of the company.'

Answers to the advanced questions can be found at **go.pearson.com/uk/he/resources.**

Web activity

Read 'UK regulator moves to protect minority shareholders' by Smith, A. and Kavanagh, M. (2014) on the website of the *Financial Times*:
www.ft.com/content/0c61d07e-d14b-11e3-81e0-00144feabdc0
Read 'Corporate governance and director's duties in the UK (England and Wales): overview' by Gibbon, N., Peel, G., Garston, C, and Salaman, B. (2018) at:
https://uk.practicallaw.thomsonreuters.com/3-597-4626?transitionType=Default&contextData=(sc.Default)&firstPage=true&comp=pluk&bhcp=1

Assignment 22

'Despite changes to the law, the minority interests of shareholders are still largely unprotected.'

Analyse this statement.

PART 6

General principles of intellectual property law

Statutory intellectual property protection:
Copyright, designs, patents and trade marks

Learning objectives

On completion of this chapter, students should be able to:

★ appreciate the nature of the different types of intellectual property protected by statute;

★ describe the scope of copyright protection;

★ explain in outline the registration process for designs, patents and trade marks;

★ be aware of the legal sanctions imposed for breach of statutory intellectual property rights.

Introduction

The law gives rights not only in relation to tangible property, i.e. goods capable of physical control like a car, but also in relation to the ownership of the intangible aspects of the work arising from the use of mental as opposed to physical energy. This is called *intellectual property* and enjoys both statutory and common law protection.

Mental effort is obvious in the creation of a book, film, piece of music or the invention of a 100 per cent efficient mousetrap. It is just as important in developing a successful business through original marketing strategy, or a novel way of packaging or labelling goods. This chapter explains statutory intellectual property rights including copyright, patents and registered trade marks.

25

Statutory regulation of intellectual property

Copyright

Copyright is regulated by the Copyright, Designs and Patents Act 1988 (CDPA 1988). The scope of copyright is very wide and includes (s 1):

- original literary, dramatic, musical and artistic works;
- sound recordings, films, TV and radio broadcasts and cable programmes;
- typographical arrangements of published works.

These terms have been defined in the Act or by the courts.

1 *Original: s 2.* This means 'not copied' rather than 'unique'. The issue of originality concerns the way an idea is expressed rather than the idea itself. It is also measured by the amount of independent work and effort which it required. A famous person may be the subject of a number of biographies. Information conveyed in the first biography does not become the exclusive property of the author and may well appear in subsequent works by different authors. The original author has rights to the 'copy' (the form of words or other form of expression used), not to the information which was conveyed. Commonly available knowledge may be 'original' because of its form of presentation. For example, in *McMillan & Co.* v *Cooper* (1923) a street directory was held to be original for copyright purposes.

2 *Literary: s 3.* This includes anything written, spoken or sung (other than a dramatic or musical work) if recorded in some tangible form. It covers tables, compilations and computer programs and their preparatory designs. Writing of any sort, including letters, lists of customers, reports and business plans may, therefore, attract copyright. To a limited extent copyright therefore protects privacy.

Prince Charles successfully used copyright to restrain publication of private journals in which he had recorded personal views and impressions during overseas tours (*HRH Prince of Wales* v *Associated Newspapers Ltd* (2007)).

3 *Artistic: s 4.* Again, the scope is wide. As well as covering works of 'artistic crafts-manship', like sculpture and paintings, textile patterns and clothing designs, it includes more commonplace items.

  Charts, maps, plans, graphs and diagrams may also be protected. It also covers buildings and models for buildings.

  In *Lucasfilm v Ainsworth* (2011), the Supreme Court held that the defendant, who was the designer of the Imperial Stormtrooper helmet for one of the films, had not breached Lucasfilm's copyright by marketing helmets to the public. They were not items of sculpture as Lucasfilm claimed but merely utilitarian (practical) items incidental to the production of the film.

To attract copyright the item must be more than a scheme or idea existing in the mind of the creator; it must be in a *tangible form* like a book, film, audio tape or a piece of writing, or a musical notation. If someone is told about a scheme for a business plan or hears a song before it is written down, they may possibly be liable for breach of confidence (see Chapter 26) if they steal the idea, but not for infringement of copyright.

Performers enjoy similar rights to copyright owners in relation to their work, under Part II of the Act. An unlawful recording at a pop concert would involve breach of copyright in the songs and breach of the performance rights of the members of the band.

Acquisition of copyright: ss 154–158

No formal process exists. Copyright is automatically acquired provided that the qualification criteria laid down in the CDPA 1988 are fulfilled.

A work will attract copyright if there is sufficient connection between it and the UK. It is sufficient that the author has British citizenship, or is domiciled or resident in the UK, or if the work is first published in the UK. Copyright also applies to works created or published in other countries to which the Act applies. This covers foreign states with which Britain has reciprocal copyright links.

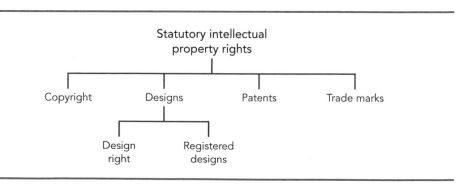

Figure 25.1

The duration of copyright: ss 12–15

How long the copyright period lasts depends on the type of work. Literary, dramatic, musical or artistic works enjoy copyright for 70 years from the end of the calendar year in which the author dies. Films are protected for 70 years from the end of the calendar year in which the last of the following die – director, writer, musical composer. Broadcasts and cable programmes enjoy copyright for 50 years from the first broadcast. Copyright in sound recordings lasts 70 years from the end of the calendar year in which they were released.

Crown copyright: s 163

The copyright in works created by civil servants and other Crown employees belongs to the Crown and lasts for up to 125 years.

The ownership of copyright: ss 9–11

The author (creator) of the relevant work is also generally the owner of the copyright. However, the copyright in any work created by an employee in the course of employment belongs to the employer. The course of employment is construed widely, and even relevant works created by employees in their spare time and without an express or implied order from the employer are likely to be treated as the employer's property, if relevant to the employee's job.

Copyright may be transferred in the same way as any other item of property. The owner may dispose of it by sale, gift or will. It may also be transferred by operation of law: if the owner becomes bankrupt, it will form part of the assets which may be sold towards satisfaction of the owner's creditors.

The rights of commissioners of photographs and films: s 85 – moral rights

This is relevant to anybody running a photography or video-making business. The photographer or film maker is the owner of the copyright in the photograph or film, but the party who commissioned it has the right to prevent its publication without that party's consent. This is called a moral right. This only protects commissions for domestic use. In *Williams* v *Settle* (1960) wedding photographs commissioned by the claimant included pictures of her father. He was subsequently murdered and the defendant photographer sold copies of the photographs to the press. It was held that this was a breach of the claimant's moral rights since she had not given permission for sale of the photographs which she had commissioned.

A person who is the subject of an unsolicited photograph (for example, by a street photographer) has no moral rights under the Act since the work was not commissioned.

Worth thinking about?

Do you have any rights in law if an unsolicited photograph is taken of you?

Suggested solutions can be found in Appendix 2.

The rights of the copyright owner

Copyright owners have exclusive rights to copy, adapt or present the work publicly.

Infringement of copyright

Any exercise of the owner's exclusive rights by a third party without lawful authority is a *direct infringement* (ss 17–21). It is irrelevant that it is being done for private use and that no profit is being made. Not surprisingly, a significant number of such infringements take place every day as many people copy music or 'pirate' their friends' computer software. It is highly unlikely that any action will be taken against them. However, where copyright materials are being used in public places, greater caution is required: for example, where a business uses background music.

Secondary infringement (ss 22–26) occurs if the copyright is exploited commercially and includes importation or sale of infringing items.

The CDPA 1988 provides some limited defences (ss 29–40). Where these apply, use of copyright material will not amount to an infringement: for example, making a copy for research or private study, limited use of quotations for the purpose of critical review or inclusion in a current affairs programme. Libraries and educational institutions also enjoy some limited protection. A new defence was introduced by the Copyright and Rights in Performances (Quotation and Parody) Regulations 2014/2356 to cover parodies (a work which mocks the original) and pastiches (imitation of the style) of existing copyright protected works.

Licensing

The copyright owner, or a collecting organisation such as the Performing Rights Society, may grant permission to do something which would otherwise be an infringement. The licensee may be required to pay royalties for this privilege. A business wishing to play background music should apply to the Performing Rights Society for a licence.

If the owners of copyright unreasonably refuse licences, they may be ordered compulsorily to grant them by the Secretary of State: for example, on the recommendation of the Competition Commission (s 144) where the public interest is prejudiced.

Sanctions

Breach of copyright entitles the owner to take civil action (s 96). Some forms of secondary infringement (including those mentioned above) also give rise to criminal liability (s 107) provided the defendant should reasonably have known that copyright existed.

Rights in performances and recordings

A composer of a piece of music is protected by copyright as explained above. Part II of the CDPA 1988 and the Copyright and Related Rights Regulations 1996 similarly protect the rights of performers and recording companies. Unlawful audio or video recordings of, for example, a rock concert will therefore breach the performers' rights as well as those of a company legitimately recording the event. Breaches also arise from the illicit copying of existing recordings.

Copyright and internet users

Everybody who accesses the internet should be aware of the copyright implications. If a person downloads or reproduces material found on a website, he or she may be infringing the copyright of the author, or the performance or recording rights of other people. The proprietor of a website will have copyright in the design of the website and materials on it, provided that these are their own original work, but they may be infringing the rights of others if they reproduce their materials from another's site without a licence. Internet service providers may also be infringing copyright if they are unable to show that they took reasonable steps to monitor the contents of the websites which they facilitate.

European Community Directive (2001/29/EC) was implemented in the UK through the Copyright and Related Rights Regulations 2003. Their purpose is to harmonise the basic rights of authors of materials transmitted through ecommerce and the information society. The details of these regulations are outside the ambit of this book.

Protection for design owners: the design right and registered designs

Design right:
protects ownership of an original design for a three-dimensional functional item excluding surface decoration.

The **design right** (governed by Part III of the CDPA 1988) attaches *automatically* to any sufficiently *original* design of three-dimensional objects and gives similar protection to copyright. An *inventive* design may also be registered under the Registered Designs Act 1949. The registered owner obtains a monopoly on the design similar to a patent.

The design right

The author of a design acquires copyright of that design, but that gives protection only against infringements of the copy (wrongful copying and publication). Ownership of the design right enables the owner to control the use of the design for manufacturing purposes. Nobody else may make items to that design without the owner's consent.

The design right protects a huge variety of items. Some qualify for registration under the Registered Designs Act 1949 (see below). Others might qualify for copyright protection as works of artistic craftsmanship. Where these other rights exist, the design owner may rely upon them rather than on the more limited design right.

The implicit intention of the CDPA 1988 is to ensure a limited protection for owners of sufficiently original designs for items capable of mass production. Such items are often functional, not necessarily visually attractive, and include a multitude of items in everyday use. The limits to design right protection are intended to prevent undesirable restraint on industrial development. Some areas of industrial design are very fast moving but would be put on hold if adaptations were an infringement of an existing design right. Also, it is unfair to restrict other designers, unreasonably, in the exercise of their creative skill.

Section 213(2) of the CDPA 1988 defines 'design' as: 'the design of any aspect of the shape or configuration (whether internal or external) of the whole or part of an article.' Only designs for *three-dimensional articles* are covered. Therefore, designs for surface decorations are not protected by the design right but may be protected by copyright. The design *must be original*. Original is described as 'not commonplace' in the relevant design field at the time of creation (s 213(4)). This is interpreted much more stringently than the originality test for copyright, but the design need not be unique.

The right does not exist unless and until it has been recorded in a design document or an article has been made to the design (s 213(6)). Like the law of copyright, it does not protect ideas. The design may be computer generated.

The person who creates the design is first owner provided that the design was not created in the course of employment or in carrying out a commission (s 215). If it was, the employer or the commissioner will be the first owner.

The right lasts for a maximum of 15 years from the end of the year when the design was created in a tangible form. If, however, goods made to the design are marketed within five years of the year of creation, the design right will last for only 10 years from the marketing date (s 216).

The design right is acquired in the same way as copyright (ss 217–220). It is part of the owner's personal property and may be sold, given away, or disposed of by will, or by operation of law (s 222). The owner has exclusive rights to exploit the design for commercial purposes, either by reproducing the design document or by making articles to the design (s 226).

The provisions of ss 226–227 concerning infringements mirror those explained above in relation to copyright. Infringement gives rise to civil liability only (s 229) and the remedies are the same as those available to a copyright owner.

Licences may be granted by the owner to third parties enabling them to exercise any of the exclusive rights to exploit the design (s 222). During the last five years of the right, anybody is entitled to a licence (s 237). Licences may be compulsorily ordered if it is in the public interest to prevent unreasonable restriction of competition (s 238). The Crown may, without a licence, use the design to supply articles for the use of the defence and health services. Compensation for loss of profit may be paid (ss 240, 243).

The Community design right

Since 2002 designers in the UK have a two-year right to protection throughout the EU and this covers two- and three-dimensional designs.

Registered designs

Some designs may qualify to be registered under the Registered Designs Act 1949 (RDA 1949) as amended by the Registered Designs Regulations 2001, Registered Designs (Amendment) Rules 2001 and the Registered Designs (Fees) Amendment Rules 2001. This amending legislation was necessary to implement the Designs Directive (98/71/EC) which aims to harmonize registration requirements across the EU, in order to eradicate differences which may adversely affect trade and to encourage free movement of goods. This legislation, implemented in December 2001, has extended the scope of the right and made the process more flexible.

Registered design: protects ownership of original design of three-dimensional items with individual character and capable of being produced industrially or as a handicraft.

The rights arising from a **registered design** relate to the appearance of the product, its shape and any patterns or design on it. Registered design is not concerned with its function, unlike a patent which is concerned with how a product works. In order to be registered the 'design' must relate to a 'product', which is 'new' and has 'individual character' as defined by the RDA 1949, s 1.

1 *Design.* This is the appearance of the whole or part of a product resulting from 'the lines, contours, colours, shape, texture or materials of the product or its ornamentation'. To be registered the design must therefore be visible to the user when the product is being used.

2 *Product.* This includes 'any industrial or handicraft item' except a computer program. It covers three-dimensional designs such as lamps, door furniture, water-filter jugs or one-dimensional designs such as patterns for wallpaper, floor covering, or clothing fabrics.

3 *New.* The design must differ materially from any existing 'publicly available' design. This is more generous to the designer than the old law, which required 'substantial' difference. 'Publicly available' means products being currently marketed as opposed to a museum exhibit.

4 *Individual character.* The overall impression of the design on the user of the product must be different from that of any similar publicly available design. Under the old law 'eye appeal' was required, which meant that the design had to be aesthetically pleasing. While this may be relevant to determining the existence of individual character, it is no longer essential. Designs for components of other products may be registered, as long as they fulfil the above criteria.

The Supreme Court's decision in *PMS International Group plc* v *Magmatic* (2016) is a good illustration of the application of these criteria.

PMS International Group plc v Magmatic (2016) UKSC

Magmatic had a UK registered design right and a Community Design Right (CRD) for its children's ride-on suitcase (the Trunki) which was shaped like a horned animal in two contrasting colours (grey with one black strip and black wheels). The PMS suitcase, the Kiddee Case, was also animal- or insect-shaped but with ears or antennae as a particular feature: it also involved more use of colour including stripes or spots. Magmatic claimed that PMS had breached their design rights.

Held: no breach had occurred: the overall impression of the design to the informed user was the key issue. The overall impression of the Trunki was of a horned animal in two contrasting colours only, not one with ears or antennae or different use of colours like the Kiddee Case. That was the design which had been registered. A registered design (or CRD) only protects designs of the nature actually registered, not the idea behind it, however clever.

Protection for spare parts remains very limited. The directive proved very contentious on this issue and member states were unable to agree on its operation. This part of the directive is suspended from operation currently, so the UK's existing law is retained. The design for a spare part must be for a product which is capable of standing alone. The product must not rely in its shape or configuration on another item. This is aimed at preventing unreasonable hindrance of development in the design field; it also prevents a designer of spare parts from acquiring a monopoly (*Ford Motor Co. Ltd and Iveco Fiat SpA's Design Application* (1993)). In *Ford Motor Co. Ltd*, designs for car doors, bonnets, boot lids and windscreens were held to be excluded.

The person who created the design is generally the owner, unless acting in the course of employment or carrying out a commission when ownership lies with the employer or the commissioner respectively (s 2). Only the owner can apply for registration. UK citizenship or resident status is not necessary. Applications are filed with the United Kingdom Intellectual Property Office (UKIPO). The procedure is complex so the owner of the design may need to use the services of a design agent to prepare the application.

The Registrar will register the design if searches indicate that the design is new, and the other statutory criteria are satisfied. Modifications may be required. Registration generally takes about six months. It must be completed within a maximum of 15 months from the time of application. A fee, currently £60 (£50 for online applications), is payable for registration.

A design will initially be registered for five years, which runs from the date of registration. This may be renewed for up to five further five-year periods (25 years maximum) on application to the registrar with payment of further fees (s 8). Most designs become outdated within about six to ten years as fashions and technology change, making it highly unlikely that renewal applications will be made more than once.

The owner of a registered design has the *exclusive rights* of commercial exploitation of the design (s 7): this entitles the owner to manufacture, import, sell or hire items made to the design. Items made to the design should be appropriately marked with the number under which it is registered. This is a clear indication of registration. Failure to do so may provide an infringing party with the defence that they acted innocently without knowledge that the design was registered. These rights are infringed by anybody who exercises them without a licence granted by the owner. Civil proceedings may be taken by the owner. The Intellectual Property Act 2014 introduced criminal penalties similar to those for infringement of copyright or trade marks for breaches of rights relating to a registered design. The Act also set up an opinions service to provide expert advice to owners and others on whether infringement has taken place.

The owner may issue *licences* to use the registered design. To protect unreasonable restrictions on the development and exploitation of designs, the Registrar has powers to grant *compulsory licences* (s 10) if, having registered the design, the owner fails to exploit it. The Registrar may also be ordered to issue licences on the recommendation of the Monopolies and Mergers Commission, where the owner is unduly restricting the issue of licences (s 11A).

The Crown is given rights to use the registered design under Sched. 1 to the Act. These are similar to those concerning the design right (see above).

It is a *criminal offence* to falsify the register (s 34) to register a design. Under s 35, it is also an offence to claim falsely that a design has been registered.

Registered Community designs

A registration process enables design owners in EU countries to obtain protection in all member countries.

Patents

Patent:
protects ownership of original invention of a product or process.

Patents are regulated by the Patents Act 1977 (PA 1977) as amended by the Patents Act 2004 (PA 2004). (All further references are to the PA 1977 unless the contrary is indicated.) The registration of a patent enables an inventor to obtain a monopoly over its exploitation. The invention may be a *device* (such as a mouse trap, an electric can-opener, or a solar-powered heating system) or a *process* (for example, making glass or waterproofing fabrics). The possibilities are endless.

The criteria for registration of a patent are stringently interpreted (ss 1–4):

1 *The invention must be new.* It must not currently form part of the state of the art in the UK or elsewhere (s 2). This means in effect that only the inventor and close associates must know of it and the information must clearly be confidential. Publication of information in, for example, a trade or academic journal anywhere in the world may put the invention into the public domain. Similarly, if the invention is already in use industrially its novelty is lost. Once an unpatented invention becomes part of the state of the art, it enables other people to develop it; the public interest would not be well served by the grant of a patent, as this would put a stranglehold on technological development already initiated by others.

2 *It must be an inventive step.* This is defined as something which would not be 'obvious to a person skilled in the art'. It must involve originality of thought and represent a new development in the relevant industry. It may be something deceptively simple, but which solves a problem which has existed for some time. It might cause even a lay person to say, 'Why didn't I think of that?' For example, in *Parks-Cramer Co. v Thornton Ltd* (1966, CA) the invention of an overhead vacuum cleaner with long vertical tubes reaching almost to the floor for cleaning narrow spaces between rows of fixed machinery was held to be original. It solved a problem which had caused a problem in the textile industry for many years.

3 *It must be capable of industrial application.* The invention or process must be capable of being produced or used under industrial conditions, which includes agriculture. Plant and animal varieties cannot be patented nor can biological processes which could be used to produce plants or animals. Micro-biological processes and the products of these processes may be patented. This includes genetic engineering processes.

Some inventions will not be registered: for example, those encouraging 'offensive, immoral or anti-social behaviour'. Current taste dictates what is appropriate here, but presumably ingenious instruments of torture are excluded. Public policy also plays a part. The Patents Act 2004 s 1 states that a patent is not to be granted for the invention of a surgical or therapy process. Registration of such processes would not be in the public interest given the cost implications for the NHS.

Certain things are not 'inventions' for the purposes of the 1977 Act. These include some things like computer programs and literary works which are protected by copyright. Scientific discoveries and theories also do not qualify; they are not directly capable of industrial application.

Real life

Simon is a member of a small private company called Hamelin Ltd which sells a mouse trap which was invented and successfully patented by Chloe.

The mouse trap is very ingenious. It consists of a small plastic box which gives off an infra-red beam. If a mouse comes within the field of the beam this triggers a tiny disc player inside the box to play at mouse-ear frequency a little tune, quite irresistible to mice. The creature is lured into the box, at which point a small but powerful hammer neatly disposes of it by a swift blow to the head. The mouse remains can later be removed hygienically in the replaceable lining of the trap.

With the help of a patents agent, Chloe was able to convince the Patents Registrar that this invention fulfilled the registration criteria. Fortunately, she acted swiftly and applied for the patent before publicly releasing any information about it or attempting to market it, so it is a *new* invention. It represents an *inventive step* as it is indeed an original concept in the vermin control trade. Finally, it is capable of mass production so is capable of *industrial application*.

The right to register a patent

The inventor is usually entitled to apply to patent the invention. This right is transferred to the employer, however, if the invention was created by an employee in the course of the employee's normal, or specially assigned, duties (s 39). Employers may try to protect themselves by putting a term in employment contracts, claiming ownership of employees' inventions. This will not be applicable if an employee's duties do not involve any potentially inventive activity. *Electrolux* v *Hudson* (1977) illustrates this well: Mr and Mrs Hudson invented an adaptor which allowed any brand of vacuum cleaner using disposable bags to be used with any brand of vacuum bags. Mr Hudson worked as a storekeeper for Electrolux, who tried to claim ownership. It was held that the invention belonged to Mr and Mrs Hudson and had been developed in their home. The nature of Mr Hudson's job did not cover such creative activity.

The inventor is entitled to be named in a patent application being made in some other person's name (usually an employer) (s 13).

If the patenting of the invention is of 'outstanding benefit' to the employer, the employee is entitled to be compensated by them (s 40). Section 10 of the PA 2004 extends the scope of compensation for employees. Before 2004, 'outstanding benefit' was only relevant to the patent itself, i.e. royalties from its being licensed, not the invention per se. A patent owner, however, may manufacture the invention itself and derive considerable profits. Under the PA 2004 these must be taken into account when computing the employee's compensation. The Comptroller of Patents or the court may order compensation if the employer does not voluntarily provide it.

Kelly and Another v *GE Healthcare* (2009)

Duncan Kelly and Ray Chiu, employees of GE Healthcare, were the co-inventors of a highly successful cardiac imaging agent that was patented by their employer. Marketed as Myoview, product sales are estimated at over £1.3 million, representing a hefty proportion of GE Healthcare's profits.

Held (Floyd J): the invention was an 'outstanding benefit' to GE Healthcare, particularly as it had protected the firm against generic competition and enabled it to make highly profitable deals. 'The benefits went far beyond anything which one could normally expect to arise from the sort of work the employees were doing.' Dr Kelly and Dr Chiu were entitled to £1 million and £500,000 respectively, based on the value of the patent estimated at £50 million.

The registration process: ss 14–19

This is a lengthy and highly complex business. A patent agent is usually employed. The different stages of the process have to be completed within certain time limits. Unless these are adhered to and the necessary fees paid, the application will be rejected. Here is an overview of the process, which concentrates on key features:

1 *The application.* An application for a patent must be made to the UKIPO in the required form and must include a full description of the invention. This must convey sufficient information to enable a reasonably skilled person in the relevant field to make the item or to carry out the process. It will involve lengthy written instructions and any necessary drawings. The inventor must indicate the specific purposes which the invention is intended to fulfil. The claim must not be too wide, or it will be rejected or at least require amendment. Some devices and processes have a very wide field of potential application, but the patent when granted may not necessarily cover them all. Some uses may not even exist yet as a twinkle in a technologist's eye, and it is not in the public interest to allow an inventor to monopolise their development.

2 *Search and publication.* Once the application has been received, initial checks and searches are carried out and the UKIPO publishes the application in its journal. This has two consequences:

  (a) the published invention is now part of the state of the art; subsequent applications for a similar patent may fail the novelty test. If the application fails it cannot be re-submitted;

  (b) on registration the applicant will be entitled to take action for any infringements occurring after the publication date.

3 *Substantial examination and registration.* Full examination of the specification and claim now takes place. Final checks are made against searches and any other information received since the publication date. Further amendments may be required. Provided the invention still meets the registration criteria, the patent will be granted. Notice of this appears in the *Patents Journal.*

Duration of patents

Patent rights exist for up to 20 years. Renewal fees are payable.

Ownership rights

A patent is the personal property of the owner and can be disposed of by operation of law or in any way the owner chooses: for example, by sale or by will. It can also be security for a mortgage (s 30).

Infringement

Protection under the PA 1977 is very wide: a large number of activities carried on without the consent of the patent owner are actionable. Infringements include the manufacture of patented products and the use of patented processes; they also arise from import into the UK of such products manufactured in breach of a patent (s 60). The owner of the patent may take civil action against infringement.

Defences to infringement include non-commercial use of products or processes and scientific investigations for the purpose of testing them.

The Intellectual Property Act 2014 implemented proposals to expand the Patents Advisory Service so that anyone can approach the Intellectual Property Office for advice about the validity or possible infringement of a patent. It is hoped that this will assist small businesses and encourage innovation, as well as preventing the necessity for expensive litigation.

Licensing

The owners of patents can grant licences to whomsoever they choose. The owner may request that the UKIPO indicates in the register that licences are available as of right (s 46), which could be a useful move if the owner has not been successful in marketing the licences privately.

After three years the UKIPO may grant licences either if the patent is not being worked, or if demands for relevant products are not being met (s 48). Wide Crown exploitation of certain patents by government departments is permitted (s 55), in connection with defence, health and nuclear energy policies.

Criminal liability

Under ss 109–113, offences include falsification of the register and false claims that a patent exists or has been applied for.

The Intellectual Property Act 2014 required a Patents Opinion Service to be set up to advise patent owners on potential patent validity.

The European Patent, available to applicants in all member states, enables inventors to obtain protection of their work throughout the EU.

Trade marks

The purpose of trade marks

Trade mark:
protects ownership of
distinguishing marks
used to advertise
goods and services.

Trade marks are used as a marketing strategy to enable providers of goods or services to ensure that their products are immediately and clearly recognizable by their potential customers. A competitor who markets a similar product in a similar way, may be breaking the law. If the distinguishing feature has been registered as a trade mark under the Trade Marks Act 1994, the competitor may be sued for infringement. Registration creates rights of ownership in the mark which can then be disposed of in the same manner as any other personal property.

Not all distinguishing characteristics can be registered, but the tort of passing off may provide a remedy for the misuse of unregistered marks and other distinguishing features. (See Chapter 26). The law relating to trade marks was updated and expanded by the Trade Marks Act 1994, which replaced the 1938 Act. The 1994 Act implements an EC directive aimed at harmonisation of trade mark law throughout the European Union.

The marks capable of registration

Section 1 of the Act defines a trade mark as any sign capable of being represented graphically which is capable of distinguishing the goods or services of one undertaking from another. 'Represented graphically' means capable of being represented in the form of pictures, words or numbers. This has greatly extended the scope of trade mark law. As well as designs, letters and numerals (which were all covered previously) it is now possible to register shapes of goods or their packaging (like the Coca-Cola^{TM} bottle). Moving images clearly come within this definition, as do advertising jingles, and potentially even perfumes since these can be graphically represented by their notation or chemical formulae, respectively.

A mark must be distinctive. It may be verbal or non-verbal in form. Verbal marks include the following:

1 *Names of people.* Names can be trademarked but will have to be represented in some way that makes them distinctive and immediately recognisable as that of one trader alone. This can be achieved by a signature (Walt Disney), or by a very distinctive style of lettering (McDonald's, Marks & Spencer). A business may prefer to trade under a made-up name (Kwikfit) to ensure a distinctive character.

2 *Names of products.* To prevent other businesses from being unreasonably restricted in the advertisement of their products, names will not be treated as distinctive if they relate to the character, quality, geographical origin, intended use or any other characteristics of the product. 'Wholemeal Flour' or 'Best Butter' could not be registered, but 'Floss Mill' and 'March Hare' would not offend. Invented words may well be distinctive for registration purposes: in themselves they convey no clear and ordinary meaning to the average person. 'Snickers' and 'Hovis', for example, without their associations with chocolate bars and bread, are completely meaningless. In this way monopolisation of the use of ordinary words is avoided.

Non-verbal marks include emblems, symbols and other pictorial representations, as well as combinations of letters or numbers. This enables lemonade to be marketed under the 7 Up trade mark. Advertising jingles come within the definition, which also embraces distinctively shaped goods or packaging: for example, Jif lemons.

A mark will not be registered if it is insufficiently distinctive, against the public interest or public morality, or identical or too similar to an earlier trade mark.

1 *Insufficiently distinctive.* As determined by the above rules. Thus, in *Phillips Electronics NV v Remington Consumer Products* (1998) it was held that a drawing of one of the heads of a three-headed electric razor was not sufficiently distinctive, because it did not sufficiently identify the manufacturer but merely referred to the function of the goods. Also in *Société des Produits Nestlé SA v Cadbury UK* (2016) Nestlé, which manufactures Kit-Kat chocolate bars, applied to register the shape of the confectionery (a four-fingered chocolate bar) as a trade mark. This application failed because the shape was not a distinctive feature of the product. Indeed, by

putting it in an opaque wrapper, the fact that it was divided into four segments was concealed. The buyer recognised the product by its distinctive coloured wrapping and the name which was printed on it. (Affirmed by the Court of Appeal in 2017.)

A trade mark, therefore, must be sufficiently distinctive to enable the public clearly to identify the origin of the product and not confuse it with others. In *Interlego AG's Trademark Application* (1998) the court refused to register a Lego brick shape on the grounds that it was insufficiently distinctive.

2 *Against the public interest or morally offensive (s 3).* These criteria are interpreted in the light of current taste and attitudes. 'Hookers' or 'Hustlers' condoms might prove problematic.

3 *Identical or too similar (s 5).* Marks which are identical or very similar to an earlier trade mark and applied to the same or similar goods or services. In *Berlei (UK) Ltd v Bali Brassiere Co.* (1969) both parties manufactured brassieres and corsets. Berlei successfully claimed that the use of the name Bali would lead to confusion with its product.

Some emblems enjoy special protection. These can be used as a trade mark only with permission from the registrar (s 4). They include Royal coat of arms, pictorial representations of members of the Royal family, and any of the flags of the UK. The use of any device or words suggesting that the product has been patronised or authorised by royalty is similarly protected.

The registration process

The applicant for registration must own the mark. There is no nationality or residence qualification. Application is made to the Trade Mark Registry. It must include a representation of the mark and state the product to which it may apply. A fee is payable (s 32) – £170 in 2019. The Registrar decides whether the mark is sufficiently distinctive and carries out any necessary searches (s 37). If the application is acceptable, the Registrar must publish notice of the application to enable interested parties to raise objections (s 38). Provided no objections are sustained, the Registrar will on payment of a fee register the trade mark (s 40), for use in relation to a particular class of goods or services.

Duration of protection

Registration lasts 10 years and renewal is possible every 10 years.

Infringements: s 10

Infringements may be committed only in the course of trade. They may arise from the wrongful application of an identical or similar mark in connection with identical or similar goods for which use of the mark is registered.

Phones 4u Ltd v Phone4u.co.uk Internet Ltd (2006, CA)

Phones 4U Ltd had a registered trade mark consisting of a red, white and blue logo including the words 'Phones 4U' in stylised form and had registered a domain name Phones4U.co.uk. It claimed that the defendant company had infringed its trade mark by registering and using the domain name Phone4u.co.uk to sell mobile phones.

Held: no infringement had occurred. The defendant was merely a similar name in a form not identical to or sufficiently similar to the claimant's registered trade mark, which involved the use of specific colours.

The defendant in the above case was, however, guilty of passing off (see Chapter 26).

'Application' of the mark includes not only putting it on the product or its packing, but also offering products for sale under the sign, or using it on business papers or in advertising.

Cosmetic Warriors Ltd and Lush Ltd v Amazon.co.uk Ltd (2014)

Amazon manipulated its search facility so that if anyone typed 'Lush' into Google it displayed a sponsored advertisement for Lush on the Amazon website. However, Amazon did not sell Lush products and nor did it openly state that it did not, on its website. Lush alleged that Amazon infringed its trade mark rights in three ways:

1 Customers who continued the search on the Amazon site found some pages carrying the Lush trade mark, showing products which closely resembled some of Lush's products like soap bombs.

2 Other pages illustrated goods similar to Lush products but did not carry its trade mark.

3 People who typed 'lush' into the site search facility found a drop down menu displaying various goods resembling or equivalent to those from Lush.

Held: Claim (1) did infringe Lush's trade mark, since the average shopper who saw the trademarked page would expect to find Lush products on sale by Amazon at a discounted price.

Claim (2) did not infringe the trade mark because the average customer using the Google search would not expect an un-trademarked page to be displaying Lush's products.

Claim (3): the onsite drop down menu did breach the trade mark because the average consumer would believe that he or she was being led to goods specifically produced by Lush and there was no indication that real Lush products were not available through the site.

Therefore an implication that a product is connected to a trademarked product may be sufficient to constitute infringement.

Using the mark merely to identify the relevant goods in accordance with honest commercial or industrial practice is not an infringement. Provided that the business is selling or servicing a particular product, it is perfectly legal to use the name on one's own advertising materials. Thus, Curry's can legally advertise that they stock Hotpoint and Hoover washing machines.

Ate My Heart Inc. v *Mind Candy Ltd* (2011)

Ate My Heart is Lady Gaga's company and owns the trade mark LADYGAGA. Mind Candy is an online computer game company which had created a number of characters which parodied real people. One of these was Lady Goo Goo, an animated cartoon baby who resembled Lady Gaga and sang one of her songs. The song was very successful on YouTube and Mind Candy wanted to promote it on iTunes.

Ate My Heart claimed breach of its trade mark and sought an interim injunction to prevent the song being promoted on YouTube and released through iTunes.

Held: Mind Candy had breached the trade mark and had diluted its effect. Evidence of comments made in blogs on the game and on YouTube showed that members of the public had been confused, as there was great similarity in appearance between Lady Gaga and Lady Goo Goo. Tags planted by Mind Candy relevant to Lady Gaga website tags prompted search engines to go to the YouTube listing of the Lady Goo Goo song. Searching for 'Lady Goo Goo' brought up the Lady Gaga trade mark, which gave the impression that Lady Gaga approved of this use of it. An injunction was granted to prevent the song and character of Lady Goo Goo being exploited via YouTube and iTunes, but its use in the computer game was allowed to continue.

Licensing the use of trade marks

Only the owner may grant licences for use of the mark by others (s 29). The licence may impose restrictions on the range of products to which the mark may be applied, or the manner of its use, or the locality within which the licence may be exercised.

Assigning the right to use a trade mark

Like all other intellectual property, a trade mark is part of the proprietor's personal property. It is transferable by assignment (in writing), by will or by operation of law.

The European Trade Mark (ETM)

Citizens of the EU may apply for registration which then protects them in all member states.

Remedies for infringement of statutory intellectual property rights

These are largely similar whichever type of intellectual property is involved.

Injunction

An injunction may be granted to prevent the commission or continuance of the infringement.

Damages

Damages may be awarded to compensate for consequential losses to the proprietor.

Account of profits

Any profit on the sale of relevant goods may be forfeit. This prevents the defendant from retaining any financial gain resulting from the illegal behaviour.

Seizure, delivery up or destruction orders

These remedies are relevant to infringement where goods have been manufactured or marked in breach of patent or trade mark rights.

The impact of EU law and international treaties on intellectual property rights

Intellectual property rights have considerable implications in relation to international trade. Consequently, their operation and development have been considerably influenced by EU law. A number of internationally binding treaties to which the UK is signatory are also important.

The EU context: conflict with English law – the position in 2019

EU law takes precedence over English law in the event of conflicting rights (see Chapter 3). This may or may not be the case if the UK leaves the European Union (Brexit). The Treaty of Rome imposes obligations to promote free trade within the European Union. Thus, free movement of goods must be encouraged, restrictive trade practices are prohibited and a dominant trading position must not be abused. Discrimination against nationals of other member states is also prohibited. It is easy to see that the exercise of some rights like licensing could be a breach of the treaty; the European Court of Justice (ECJ) has had to decide on issues like this in a number of cases. If and when the UK leaves the EU, it may be that future decisions of the ECJ will not form part of UK law.

In addition to the UK's treaty obligations, any relevant directives must be complied with. For example, the Trade Marks Act 1994 implements a directive aimed at harmonising this area of law throughout the EU; it has greatly widened the scope of trade mark protection in the UK. Future developments are awaited.

The EU's Protected Food Name scheme instituted in 1993 has been beneficial to some food producers. There are three marks under this scheme: the PDO (Protected Designation of Origin); the PGI (Protected Geographical Indication); and TSG (Traditional Speciality Guaranteed). Once registered with the EU, these protect the names and reputations and quality of a whole range of foods taking their names from the locality where they have originated or have been traditionally manufactured often with a particular recipe, and prevents those names being used for foods not manufactured in the relevant locality. Champagne and Parma Ham are famous examples internationally. In the UK there are currently 62 protected names, including Melton Mowbray Pork Pies, Stilton Cheese, Whitstable Oysters, Jersey Royal Potatoes and Anglesey Sea Salt.

A number of recent changes to copyright law have been the result of EU directives. The length of copyright was extended to its current limits in 1995 in compliance with EC law. Additional rights to protect copyright in databases were also added in response to EU requirements by the Copyright and Rights in Databases Regulations 1997.

Currently, under the European Patent Convention a proprietor may register their patent with effect in any member state specified in the application. An application may be filed directly with the European Patent Office or through the UKIPO in London. Infringements must be pursued in the courts of relevant state(s).

The Unitary Patent Court

Under the Unitary Patent Court Agreement signed by most EU countries in 2013, a Unified Patent Court will be established to enable enforcement of a patent across Europe in a single legal action. The Intellectual Property Act 2014 amends the Patent Act 1977 and gives the Secretary of State the power to implement the Agreement in the UK and to set up a branch of the Unitary Patent Court in London.

The Court is not yet in operation as the Agreement requires ratification by all EU states and it is not known how the UK will be affected after leaving the EU. The UK ratified in 2018 and Germany is the last country to ratify. Ratification will permit creation of a unitary patent which will be automatically enforceable in all the signatory EU states, unlike the European patent, which requires validation in each relevant state. The European patent will continue to exist. Owners of inventions will have a choice as to whether to opt for a European patent, which will protect them in any named state, or a unitary patent, which will protect them in all the signatory states.

Intellectual property law in the UK after leaving the EU

The Intellectual Property Office, which is responsible for registration of intellectual property and oversight of development of law in this area, is currently reassuring on this subject. In April 2017 it announced that the European Trade Mark (ETM) system will continue to benefit UK holders and new applicants. Design rights and patents in general will continue to be protected similarly. The IPO did admit that the future is more uncertain for copyright law as although EU regulations and directives which have added to its development will obviously continue to operate until the leaving process is over, the future will depend on the negotiation of the UK's exit deal.

It is certainly the case that there is mutual benefit for all businesses in the UK and in other member states to allow these practices to continue to operate in the UK.

The wider international context

The UK is signatory to a number of treaties with a large number of other countries, both in and outside the EU. These treaties give reciprocal rights to protection of intellectual property in signatory states. For example, through the Berne Convention and the Universal Copyright Convention, UK citizens and residents enjoy copyright protection of their work in any of the signatory states. Almost all countries are signatory to one or other of these. The Patent Cooperation Treaty enables patent holders from the UK to apply for registration in any signatory country.

International registration of trade marks has been possible since 1995 for members of states which are signatories to the Madrid Protocol.

Chapter summary

This chapter has examined how English statute law classifies and protects certain types of intellectual property. This is summarised in Figure 25.2, which provides a useful checklist of the principal legislation in this area, which has been gradually amended to bring it into line with a number of EC directives and treaty law.

Review questions 24

1 Advise Pippa whether she has copyright in the following works:
   (a) a piece of music which she has composed;
   (b) an idea for a short story which she and Bhatti discussed in the pub and which Bhatti has now written;
   (c) a flow chart which she produced at work and which is now being used by her employers in publicity leaflets;
   (d) a booklet of mathematical tables.

2 Heidi has designed a series of figurines representing different types of fish. She would like to know her legal rights over this design.

3 Pierre, who works for Fulmar Fish Foods, has designed a new fish-smoking process.

(a) What criteria will the process have to satisfy if it is to be patented?

(b) Who will own the patent?

4 Will the following parties be allowed to register their trade marks?

(a) Nitin Products advertise a peanut spread with a musical jingle.

(b) Bhijan plc markets fruit pies which it calls 'Yummies'. Chloe plc has registered its trade mark 'Yum-Yums' under which it markets lollipops.

(c) Merlin Ltd wants to market a game pie called 'Queen's Favourite'. The wrapper bears a picture of Windsor Castle.

5 What are the advantages of having a work protected by copyright?

6 Define and distinguish between a design right and a registered design right.

Answers to all review questions can be found in Appendix 2.

	Copyright	Design right	Registered design	Patents	Trade marks
Statute	Copyright, Designs and Patents Act 1988, Parts I and II	Copyright, Designs and Patents Act 1988, Part III	Registered Designs Act 1949 (as amended 2001)	Patents Act 1977 (as amended by Patents Act 2004)	Trade Marks Act 1994
Scope	Original, literary, dramatic and artistic works	Original design for 3D items excluding surface ornamentation	New design for any industrial or handicraft item, includes shape, pattern and ornamentation	New things/process, inventive step, industrial application	Distinctive identifying symbol for goods or services
Acquisition	By owner on creation, no formalities	By owner on creation, no formalities	Registration: UKIPO	Registration: UKIPO	Registration: UKIPO
Duration	Max: 70 years from author's death	Max: 15 years (No renewal)	Max: 25 years (5-year renewal)	Max: 20 years	Renewable indefinitely
Property rights	Personal property: transferable by assignment, will, intestacy, operation of law				
Licensing	Voluntary, compulsory, Crown	Voluntary, compulsory, Crown	Voluntary, compulsory, Crown	Voluntary, compulsory, Crown	Voluntary only

Figure 25.2

Advanced questions 24

(A) Consider the comparative advantages and disadvantages of registering a patent.

(B) Consider the types of intellectual property rights available to a manufacturer of a new perfume.

Answers to the advanced questions can be found at **go.pearson.com/uk/he/resources.**

Take a closer look

The following cases provide important examples of how the law in this chapter has developed. They are primary sources illustrating the law in action and give more detail about their facts, as well as helping to understand the law and to appreciate how the judges reached their decisions.

Try looking them up in the law reports or accessing them via a database, e.g. BAILII (www.bailii.org/databases.html). LexisNexis or Westlaw may be available in the university or college library, or extracts may be found in a case book. (See Appendix 1: Additional resources.)

Berlei (UK) Ltd v *Bali Brassiere Co.* [1969] 2 All ER 812

Electrolux v *Hudson* [1977] FSR 312

Levola Hengelo BV v *Smilde Foods BV* (2018) ECJ

Parks-Cramer Co. v *Thornton Ltd* [1966] RPC 407, CA

Williams v *Settle* [1960] 1 WLR 1072

Web activity

Explore the GOV.UK website to learn more about the Intellectual Property Office and check on current news:

www.gov.uk/government/organisations/intellectual-property-office

You might also find the archived website of the Intellectual Property Office interesting. Check out the famous cases section and take a look at the IP newsletters for the most up-to-date developments:

http://webarchive.nationalarchives.gov.uk/20140108134321/http://www.ipo.gov.uk/news.htm

See the 'Top 10 Copyright Myths' on the website of the UK Copyright Service:

www.copyrightservice.co.uk/copyright/copyright_myths

Read 'Copyright law does not protect the taste of cheese' by Estelle Derclaye on the website of the Copyright Licensing Agency:
https://cla.co.uk/blog/higher-education/copyright-cheese

Assignment 23

What types of work are protected by the Copyright, Designs and Patents Act 1988 and what rights does this give the owner?

Common law protection of intellectual property:
Passing off, malicious falsehood and breach of confidence

Learning objectives

On completion of this chapter, students should be able to:

★ define the torts of passing off, malicious falsehood and breach of confidence;

★ distinguish between passing off and malicious falsehood;

★ appreciate the scope of the tort of breach of confidence and its relationship to the HRA 1998;

★ explain the legal remedies for the above torts.

Introduction

The common law of tort protects certain aspects of intellectual property and the rights occur as a result of decided cases, unlike those arising from statute.

The tort of passing off protects a business from loss of sales or reputation if another business imitates the appearance of a product, its packaging or advertising by for example, using a very similar name. There is some overlap here with the law protecting trade marks.

The reputation of a business is easily damaged by bad publicity. Where statements made about a business are untrue and made intentionally with the intention of damaging the business, the owner may find a remedy through the tort of malicious falsehood (see *Kaye* v *Robertson* (1991, CA)).

The tort of breach of confidence was initially developed to protect a business owner from losses arising from the unfair trading of information, given in confidence to an employee who then breached the trust of the employer for personal gain.

However, its scope has gradually become much wider under the influence of the European Convention on Human Rights (ECHR) and the Human Rights Act 1998 (HRA 1998) so that it is now sometimes used to protect personal privacy.

Passing off

The tort of **passing off** protects the **goodwill** and reputation of a business. It is committed where the defendant falsely applies to its own product some distinctive feature (for example, packaging, logo, definitive or distinctively presented name) likely to persuade members of the public that it is associated with the claimant's business.

The tort may be committed in a number of different ways:

1 The defendant presents its goods or services in a distinctive manner similar to that used by the claimant for a similar product.

White Hudson & Co. Ltd v Asian Organisation Ltd (1964, PC)

The claimants had for five years marketed their cough sweets in distinctive red cellophane wrapping labelled 'Hacks', and people buying them often asked for 'red paper' cough sweets. The defendants started to market their brand of cough sweets in similar wrapping paper labelled 'Pecto'.

Held: the defendants were liable for passing off; the public associated that packaging's appearance with the claimant's product.

(See also *Numatic Ltd v Qualtex* (2010) below.)

2 The defendant uses a false description imputing a definitive characteristic of the claimant's product to its own.

Erven Warnink BV v *Townend & Sons (Hull) Ltd* (1979)

The defendants marketed a drink made of eggs and sherry under the name of 'Keelings Old English Advocaat'; this competed very favourably with the more expensive Warninks Advocaat which carried a heavier excise tax as it was made of brandy and eggs.

Held: the defendants were liable for passing off what should properly have been described as egg flip as Advocaat. Real Advocaat was recognised by the public as an entirely distinct drink because of its spirit base.

3 The defendant claims the claimant's work as its own.

  Thus, in *Bristol Conservatories Ltd* v *Conservatories Custom Built Ltd* (1989) the defendants were held to have acted illegally when they showed prospective customers photographs of conservatories constructed by the claimants, as evidence of the defendant's own work.

4 The defendant falsely suggests that the claimant endorses for the defendant's work.

  For example, in *Associated Newspaper Holdings* v *Insert Media Ltd* (1991) it was held that the insertion of an advertising leaflet between the pages of a newspaper without permission, would be likely to make readers believe that the newspaper approved of the products advertised.

The context of the defendant's behaviour may be crucial to proof of liability.

Fenty v *Topshop/Topman Ltd* (2015, CA)

In this case the claimant was Rihanna, the pop star, whom many people regard as a fashion icon.

Topshop sold a T-shirt with an image of Rihanna which had been used to publicise her most recent album. Previously Topshop had run a competition with a shopping trip and lunch with Rihanna as the prize; it had frequently referred to her in publicity including tweets about her visit to their main London branch.

Rihanna claimed Topshop's use of her image had implied that she had approved and authorised this, which would encourage people to believe that she was endorsing its products. Topshop argued that she was merely claiming rights to her image which English law does not support and appealed, when the High Court found in her favour.

The Court of Appeal held (upholding the High Court decision): Topshop was liable for passing off. Although selling a garment with an image of a pop star was not in itself sufficient to create liability, it became so in the context of Topshop's related publicity campaign. This was likely to confuse members of the public and make them think that, as a celebrity known for her interest in fashion, she approved of their product.

To succeed in an action the claimant must prove the following:

(a) *The defendant made a false statement.* The statement must be untrue, but the defendant need not have known this. The motive of the defendant is irrelevant.

The statement may be express or implied from conduct, e.g. by using a similar name to the claimant or packaging goods similarly. The next case provides a very clear example.

Numatic International Ltd v *Qualtex Ltd* (2010)

Numatic, the claimant, manufactures the well-known Henry vacuum cleaner. It is red and tub-shaped, decorated with a cheerful face surmounted by a black bowler hat-shaped lid.

The defendant, Qualtex, produced a prototype of a very similar shape in blue with the same black bowler hat lid, though without a face. Numatic claimed passing off and sought an injunction to prevent Qualtex marketing its model.

Held (Floyd J): the injunction should be granted. Numatic's protectable interest and goodwill in the shape and features of the Henry model were indisputable. A customer survey indicated that there was a real danger that members of the public might buy Qualtex's model mistaking it for Numatics's. It was not sufficient for Numatic's model merely to lack the facial characteristics of the real Henry. It 'does not mean that it necessarily follows that the absence of one or more of these features is sufficient to distinguish a replica product from the original'.

(b) *The statement was made in the course of trade.* 'Trade' has been defined widely by the courts and includes non-profit-making organisations.

(c) *The statement must be published to the claimant's customers.* The law of passing off exists to protect the goodwill of the claimant. Therefore, the claimant must currently be engaged in running an established business with the same geographical area as the defendant. Where a business organisation enjoys only very local goodwill, the use of a similar marketing technique 200 miles away will not be seen as unlawful. However, the court may take into account likely geographical expansion.

(d) *Damage to the claimant's business must be reasonably foreseeable.* The claimant does not have to prove that the defendant intended to cause damage. Where the public is not reasonably likely to connect the claimant's business with the defendant's activity, no liability exists.

Granada Group Ltd v Ford Motor Co. Ltd (1973)

Held: Ford Motors could not legally be restrained from marketing a car under the name 'Granada' merely because the claimant traded under the same name. The parties were not engaged in a similar field of business activity; therefore, it was unlikely that the public would be confused about the origin of the car and associate it with Granada TV.

Compare the outcome in:

NAD Electronics v NAD Computer Systems (1997)

Held: the public might well be confused by the use of the name NAD by these two companies. The claimant manufactured high-quality hi-fi equipment while the defendants were computer manufacturers. There were, therefore, similarities in their respective products since many computer systems include CD players and loudspeakers. Their products were also likely to be sold alongside each other in the same retail outlets.

(e) *Damage or sufficient probability of damage must result.* Any of the following may evidence actionable damage:

1 loss of sales to the claimant because customers believe the defendant's product was manufactured by the claimant;

2 loss of business reputation: the defendant's goods are inferior and people are likely to associate them with the claimant;

3 the unique character of the claimant's product is being undermined or its status diminished by the defendant's conduct.

Taittinger SA v Allbev Ltd (1993, CA)

Held: the limitation imposed by EC law on use of the name 'Champagne' to wines produced in the Champagne area of France gave the name a distinctive character. The defendant, by selling a soft drink described as 'Elderflower

Champagne', was marketing its product in a way which would inevitably lead to an erosion of the distinctiveness of the name Champagne.

(Note that 'Champagne' now enjoys protected status from the EU under its Protected Food Name scheme and can only be used to describe wine made in that area of France (see Chapter 25).)

Note the relationship of registered trade mark protection to passing-off actions.

If a product is marketed under a registered trade mark, the proprietor who alleges infringement merely has to prove that:

1 the mark is registered in relation to a relevant product; and

2 the conduct of the defendant amounts to an infringement within the definition of the Trade Marks Act 1994.

The mark is protected immediately on registration, even if, as yet, the product has not been marketed. So, it may be easier to assert one's rights under a registered trade mark than to commence a passing-off action. However, an action in passing off may be brought where the relevant product does not have the protection of a registered trade mark. Not all products are sufficiently distinctively marketed to qualify for registration. A passing-off action may also arise from conduct which does not amount to an infringement of a registered trade mark.

Real life

Jose has shares in Hamelin Ltd which produces an ingenious type of mousetrap. This is marketed in yellow and black packaging marked with the company's registered trade mark, which is a black and yellow drawing of a mouse dressed like the Pied Piper and playing a pipe drum. Jose recently came upon an advert for Pied Piper Bait, a new brand of mouse and rat poison sold in yellow and black containers. He reported this to Chloe, the company's managing director, who is considering taking proceedings against Wally Piper, the owner of Pied Piper Bait, for trade mark infringement and passing off.

The packaging and name of Wally's product does seem likely to encourage people to think that the two products are both Chloe's and permit Wally to take advantage of Chloe's existing reputation to boost sales of a product that has a similar purpose. However, Wally will argue that his packaging contains no mouse drawing and that he is using his own name. This might well defeat trade mark infringement proceedings as the dancing mouse image is a crucial part of the trade mark. Nonetheless, the superficial appearance of the two products does sound very similar and this may be good grounds for a passing-off action.

To succeed, Chloe will need to prove that there really is a danger that she will lose trade as a result of Wally's behaviour. Evidence that her customers are confused (e.g. if some have sought to order the rival bait) would be helpful. The geographical area in which the two products are marketed is also relevant. If Chloe's product enjoys nationwide goodwill, it will be no defence for Wally to argue that his sales are confined to one part of the country. Proof of damage is also crucial. Unless Chloe can prove that she has lost or, on the balance of probability, will lose sales as a result of Wally's marketing methods, her claim will fail.

Passing off on the internet

The owner of a website may obtain exclusive use of this *domain* by registering its address through the relevant internet service provider. However, if it bears a close resemblance to the name of another business, which has not sought registration and which the public might confuse with this one, then the owner may be liable in passing off. In *Marks & Spencer plc* v *One in a Million Ltd* (1998) the defendant registered the domain name, marks & spencer.co.uk, and then offered to sell it to the claimant. This was held to be a threat to pass off by the defendants. The claimant obtained an injunction that required the defendant to transfer the domain name to the claimant.

Malicious falsehood

Malicious falsehood: intentional or reckless statement causing damage to business interests.

Like passing off, an action for **malicious falsehood** protects a claimant against false statements damaging to the goodwill and reputation of its business. The claimant must prove the following:

1 *A false statement published by the defendant relating to the claimant's business.* The statement must be untrue and likely to cause damage to the claimant's business. It may consist of an express attack on the claimant's business reputation, but an untrue statement of an apparently innocent kind may give rise to liability.

Ratcliffe v *Evans* (1892)

The defendant untruthfully stated in a local newspaper that the claimant had ceased to trade from a particular address. He knew this was untrue, but wished to get the claimant to abandon his business premises.

Held: liability existed here since the statement was likely to deprive the claimant of customers.

Conduct may amount to a statement.

Wilts United Dairies Ltd v *Thomas Robinson & Sons Ltd* (1958)

Condensed milk manufactured by the claimant was bought and stockpiled by the government during the war. Years later when its quality had deteriorated, it was sold to the defendant on the condition that it was to be used only as animal feed. The defendant sold it for human consumption.

Held: the inferior quality of the milk sold suggested that this was the normal standard of the claimant's product and, therefore, the defendant was liable in malicious falsehood.

2 *Damage must be reasonably foreseeable*. It must be reasonably likely that potential customers will be influenced. Comparative advertising, where the defendant merely 'puffs' its goods by claiming that they are superior to those of the claimant, is unlikely to give rise to liability. In *White* v *Mellin* (1895) it was held that no liability existed where the defendant attached labels to the claimant's product, which the defendant sold in his shop, claiming that his own brand was superior.

The defendant will be liable if it has infringed normal business practice. In *De Beers Products Ltd* v *International General Electrics* (1975) apparently weighty statements about the accuracy of the claimant's instruments, backed up with reference to plausible, but actually specious scientific data, amounted to malicious falsehood.

Malice:
Intentional/reckless behaviour aimed at causing harm to someone.

3 *The statement must be made with* **malice**. The defendant must have made the statement either knowing it to be false or not caring whether it was true or false, or believing it to be true but publishing it because motivated by the intention to cause the claimant damage. An untrue statement made in good faith will not give rise to liability.

4 *The claimant must suffer damage as a result*. Proof of a general drop in custom will be sufficient.

Note the relationship between malicious falsehood and passing off:

1 *Dual liability may exist*. Where passing off involves the sale of inferior goods, this is also an implicit assertion that the claimant produces goods of poor quality and, therefore, may also be malicious falsehood.

2 *Both parties to a passing-off action must be in competition*. A passing-off action is limited to situations where both parties are engaged in competing businesses. Malicious falsehood can be pursued against any defendant who attacks another party's business reputation.

If the claimant has a choice, it is easier to succeed in a passing-off action. It is hard to prove the malice and falsity, crucial to success, in a malicious falsehood claim.

Breach of confidence and protection of privacy

This area of the law gives some protection to privacy in private and business life. If one party confides information to another, a legal duty may be created not to reveal that information to anyone else. Traditionally liability for **breach of confidence** existed only where the following criteria were satisfied:

Breach of confidence: revealing information to a third party, after it had been imparted by another party in circumstances indicating that it should be kept private.

1 the claimant expressly or implicitly reveals confidential information to another person;

2 a relationship of trust already exists between the parties or is created as a result. It will be apparent from the circumstances that this information is private and that the confidant is being relied upon to keep it confidential;

3 the confidant makes use of the information or passes it on to a third party;

4 as a result the claimant suffers damage.

However, since the end of the twentieth century, due in part to the implementation of the Human Rights Act (see below) the strict criteria of breach of confidence have been relaxed particularly in relation to proof of a relationship of trust. See *Campbell v Mirror Group Newspapers Ltd* (2004, HL) (see below). In *Max Mosley v News Group Newspapers Ltd* (2008), Eady J. held that the law protected privacy rights even where no existing relationship of confidence existed, provided that it was reasonable for a claimant to expect his or her privacy to be respected. This development of the scope of breach of confidence to give wider protection of privacy will be evident from the recent cases which are described below.

What information is confidential?

It is very difficult to define what type of information will be treated as confidential: it is a question of fact in every case and is judged objectively by the courts. Personal information will generally enjoy protection. In *Stephens v Avery* (1988) the claimant, Mrs S, confided in the defendant, Mrs A, details of her previous sexual relationship with Mrs T. This information was newsworthy because Mrs T had recently been murdered by her husband; Mrs A leaked the story to a newspaper and was held liable for breach of confidence. In 2007, an injunction was granted to protect Prince Charles's private journals containing his personal accounts of royal tours from publication in the *Mail on Sunday* (*HRH Prince of Wales v Associated Newspapers Ltd* (2007)).

In the context of business, confidential information includes trade secrets which do not enjoy statutory protection: for example, plans for an invention or industrial processes peculiar to the claimant's business. It may cover ideas and information not yet protected by copyright. It could also include information forming the subject of a competitive tender prior to its submission; leakage of such information could cause the claimant to lose the contract. For example, in *PSM International v Whitehouse &*

Willenhall Ltd (1992), drawings, price quotations and business plans were treated as confidential.

Equitable principles are very influential here; the moral justification for secrecy or revelation and the issue of public interest will be relevant to determining whether liability exists. However, even information that would have been treated as confidential ceases to be so once it enters the public domain.

Attorney-General v *Guardian Newspapers (No. 2)* (1990)

Memoirs of an ex-secret service officer were published in a book called *Spy Catcher* leading to a claim of breach of a confidence clause in his contract of employment. The information would have been regarded in law as confidential because of its national security implications.

Held: *The Guardian*, which published details from the book, was not liable for breach of confidence as the book had already been widely published and commented upon in the media abroad and, therefore, a duty of confidentiality no longer existed.

The issue of extent of public knowledge arose more recently in the case that follows.

PSJ v Newsgroup Newspapers Plc [2016] EWCA Civ 393

The claimant, who was married, had children and was well-known in showbusiness circles was alleged to have had extra-marital sex with a married couple. Newsgroup was approached by the couple who wanted to sell their story. The claimant obtained an interim injunction to prevent Newsgroup from publishing it. After 11 weeks a US magazine published details of the story and this began to spread. It was published in Canadian and Scottish newspapers and broadcast via the internet to the rest of the UK. Newsgroup then requested the court to lift the injunction and the claimant objected.

The Court of Appeal held: the injunction must now be lifted as it no longer served any legitimate purpose. While the claimant still had the right to sue for damages under The HRA, s 8 (breach of privacy) the formerly confidential material had been leaked into the public domain and anybody interested in such matters would be aware of the identity of the claimant and spouse.

It was necessary to balance the claimant's right to privacy against the defendant's right to free speech and the injunction no longer gave any meaningful protection to the claimant.

When does a duty of confidence arise?

This will be determined by reference to the nature of any relationship or legal obligation already existing between the parties. Such a relationship is capable of arising as a result of an informal request, or by operation of law or through a contract term.

Informally

An informal duty of confidence exists between friends, family members or business colleagues, employer and ex-employee. The confidant may be told of the need for discretion, or this will be obvious given the nature of the information and any other relevant circumstances. Recent cases involving the media indicate that no previous personal or business relationship between the parties is required, provided that the information published is clearly confidential. (See above, *Mosley* v *News Group Newspapers*.)

Operation of law

In the past a duty of confidence did not arise by operation of law unless the relationship of the parties was treated as fiduciary: for example, solicitor and client and doctor and patient. In such relationships there is an automatic duty of confidence. The fiduciary relationship exists regardless of whether or not the parties have a contract. A National Health Service doctor or a solicitor acting under the Legal Aid scheme is in a fiduciary relationship with the patient or client.

However, the courts indicated in the late twentieth century that a fiduciary relationship is not essential. This has widened the scope of the tort of breach of confidence, giving greater rights of privacy to claimants who in the past would not have been able to sue. In *A-G* v *Guardian Newspapers* (*No. 2*) (1990, HL), Lord Keith held that 'breach of confidence involves no more than an invasion of privacy . . . the right of privacy is one which the law should in this field seek to protect'. Potentially, this enables the bringing of claims by any person whose private life is exposed by a third party who passes on information about them without their consent.

Every case ultimately turns on its facts and not every breach of confidential information is actionable, however embarrassing the revelations may be for the claimant.

A v *B, sub nom Garry Flitcroft* v *Mirror Group Newspapers Ltd* (2002, CA)

A professional footballer who had had a one-night stand tried to obtain an injunction to prevent a report from the woman concerned being published in the press. His application was refused.

Held: breach of confidence had not occurred here. A transient sexual relationship may not be treated as confidential by the courts, if it involves an element of public interest and a party to such a relationship other than the claimant does not want it to remain confidential. A technical approach to the law was not required in such cases. A balancing of all the interests involved in the light of the particular facts was required.

While the court is unwilling to allow celebrities to use breach of confidence as a means of unfairly suppressing true information damaging to their reputation, some limited protection may be given to prevent publication of unnecessarily intrusive information, which is over and above what the public interest requires. Not everything that the public may find interesting is actually deemed to be in the public interest.

Campbell v *Mirror Group Newspapers Ltd* (2004, HL)

Held: a report by the *Daily Mirror* that Naomi Campbell had taken illegal drugs and was seeking treatment for addiction was not a breach of confidence, given her previous untrue assertion to the contrary. This was about exposing her hypocrisy. However, a photograph of her leaving a Narcotics Anonymous meeting and other details of her drug history was more information than the public interest required, so damages could be awarded for this disclosure. It was argued that this exposure might affect her continuing with her treatment. It is interesting how the courts treat photographs differently from the written word.

The issue of how far the privacy of celebrities should be protected is controversial and even the judges themselves may disagree. This is evident in a succession of cases involving Michael Douglas and Catherine Zeta Jones.

Douglas and Another v *Hello! Ltd* (*No. 3*) (2007) ended the saga of 12 cases triggered in 2000 by the 'spoiler' photographs of the wedding reception for Michael Douglas and Catherine Zeta Jones, published by *Hello* magazine in breach of the exclusive publication rights which *OK* magazine bought from the Douglases for £1 million.

In 2000, the Court of Appeal (*Douglas and Another* v *Hello! Ltd* (2001, CA)) held that an arguable case for damages in breach of confidence existed, but quashed an injunction previously ordered by the High Court, since by allowing publication of the photographs by *OK* they had surrendered their rights to the full privacy that such an event would normally enjoy.

No fewer than nine cases followed, before another Court of Appeal decision (*Douglas and Another* v *Hello! Ltd* (2005 CA)) approved a High Court award of £14,760 damages to the Douglases, on the ground that the photographs clearly related to their private life and therefore came within the protection of breach of confidence law.

However, it quashed an award to *OK* of £1 million, on the ground that it had *not* suffered breach of confidence just because the exclusivity contract had given it some proprietary interest in the photographs.

OK appealed to the House of Lords (*Douglas and Another v Hello! Ltd (No. 3)* (2007)) which, by a majority of only three to two, decided that *OK* had suffered a breach of confidence in relation to commercial information. The photographs were confidential since the opportunity to publicise them had been restricted to *OK* by the Douglases, in their sale of exclusive rights. This information was protected by the law because it was information of commercial value over which the Douglases had sufficient control to allow them to impose a duty of confidence. Lord Hoffmann commented that: 'being a celebrity or publishing a celebrity magazine are lawful trades and I see no reason why they should be outlawed from such protection as the law of confidence has to offer.'

Worth thinking about?

Lord Walker, one of the two dissenting Law Lords in *Douglas and Another v Hello! Magazine Ltd (No. 3)* (2007), said that breach of confidence law should not be employed to make a spectacle exclusive: 'The Douglases were content to have wedding photos published, for a handsome fee, so long as they had strict control over the selection of the pictures.'

What do you think about this controversial decision?

Suggested solutions can be found in Appendix 2.

Contract

In a business context it is very common for a confidence clause to be an express term of any consultancy contract, and in some other contracts for the provision of services, particularly employment contracts, where access to confidential information is involved. Such a term might also be implied in a contract of service as part of the duties of good faith and trust and confidence (see Chapter 17). This obliges both employer and employee not to reveal confidential information about each other to outsiders.

Lady Archer v Williams (2003)

Ms Williams was engaged as personal assistant to Lady Archer (Jeffrey Archer's wife) under a contract requiring her to work confidentially. After the contract was terminated, the defendant gave details of her employment with Lady Archer to a Sunday paper. Later it published an article saying that Lady Archer had had plastic surgery.

Held: an injunction would be granted to restrain Ms Williams from publishing any details which she had directly obtained through working for the claimant. The disclosure of such sensitive personal information as she had acquired was not in the public interest.

The nature of the employment is crucial to determining what will be treated as confidential. Ms Williams' contract was one of personal service. It is much harder to prove that information in a commercial contract is confidential, so a confidentiality clause does not give blanket protection to an employer, regarding all their business activity. Thus, in *Faccenda Chicken* v *Fowler* (1986) it was held that lists of the claimant's customers' names and details of van rounds compiled by the defendant (an ex-employee of the claimant) to assist him to set up a competing business were held not to be confidential information.

Tillery Valley Foods v *Channel Four Television* (2004)

Tillery manufactured and supplied foods for the public service market. A reporter working on a programme for Channel Four posed as a worker at Tillery's factory. The resulting programme contained allegations about lack of hygiene and also footage of production practices, secretly filmed at the factory.

Held: an employee filming in the workplace did not in itself amount to a breach of confidence unless confidential information was revealed. Tillery was unable to prove that any secret process which would attract confidentiality had been filmed. The blanket clause banning the employee from revealing information gained at work did not assist the employer, as no confidential information had been revealed. Public interest was paramount here.

Even a specific confidentiality clause will not be effective if it amounts to restraint of trade. (See also Chapter 10.) Breach of confidence may arise commercially without a breach of contract.

What sort of damage is actionable?

A claimant will have to prove that the breach of confidence operated to the claimant's detriment. Economic loss may have been suffered, but the courts also acknowledge the distress resulting from loss of privacy.

The public interest defence

As is evident from the *Flitcroft* and *Campbell* cases above, a defendant who can show that there was a duty to reveal the confidential information in the public interest may avoid liability. This defence does not just apply to celebrity cases. In *W* v *Edgell* (1990) a doctor, who informed the Mental Health Review Tribunal about his patient's psychopathic tendencies, was held not liable for breaching doctor–patient confidentiality, since this information was revealed in the interest of public safety.

The impact of the Human Rights Act 1998

Article 8 of the European Convention on Human Rights and Fundamental Free-doms (ECHR) gives the right to respect for privacy and family life, so an action under the HRA 1998 may be taken to enforce this right, providing an alternative to a breach of confidence action, if the defendant is a public authority. ECHR rights are not absolute. Article 8 states that interference by a public authority with the privacy of the individual may be justified so far as necessary 'in a demo-cratic society to ensure national security, public safety or the economic well-be-ing of the country, for the prevention of crime, the protection of health and morals or for the protection of the rights and freedom of others'. The courts as a 'public authority', therefore, must balance the rights of the claimant against the right to freedom of expression of the defendant and the public interest in receiv-ing the information.

The court as a public authority is bound by the ECHR. This means that in *every* case, not just those brought under the Human Rights Act, it has a duty to ensure a fair trial under Article 8 and have regard to the ECHR where relevant to the issues raised by the facts of the case. In *Douglas and Another* v *Hello! Ltd* (2001, CA) the Court of Appeal held that the ECHR required English law to respect a right of privacy and upheld their breach of confidence claim on that ground. The HRA 1998 is always likely to impact on cases involving breach of privacy, since the court must maintain a balance between the competing requirements of Article 8 (right to privacy) and Arti-cle 10 (freedom of information).

The following case provides a practical example of how the court balances the interests of each party.

Murray v Big Pictures UK Ltd (2008, CA)

David Murray (DM), son of Harry Potter author J. K. Rowling, appealed against a High Court decision which struck out his claim for breach of his rights of privacy against a photographic agency which had covertly obtained pictures of him in the street and sold them to Express Newspapers. The High Court held that since the pictures were taken in a public place and recorded a mundane activity, no right to privacy under ECHR Article 8 had been infringed.

Held: the action should not be struck out.

When deciding whether Article 8 had been breached two questions must be decided:

1 Was there a reasonable expectation of privacy? This must be decided objectively taking into account the facts of the case including the particular attributes of the claimant and the activity in which he was involved, and the means by which the defendant obtained the information.

2 If there was reasonable expectation, then a balance must be struck between the claimant's right to privacy and the defendant's right to publish.

It could be argued that DM, as the child of a famous parent, might reasonably expect not to be pursued by the press, since a child whose parents were not well known would not have been similarly targeted. Subject to the facts, children should be protected from unnecessary media attention. Consequently, David Murray was entitled to continue his case.

(See also *Douglas and Another* v *Hello! Ltd* (2001, CA); *A* v *B, sub nom Garry Flitcroft* v *Mirror Group Newspapers Ltd* (2002); and *Campbell* v *Mirror Group Newspapers Ltd* (2004) (above).)

In *Vidal-Hall* v *Google* (2015, CA) the Court recognised for the first time that there is a freestanding legal action for the tort of misuse of private information under English law.

Conclusion

There will therefore always be a potential conflict in privacy cases between the claimant's rights to privacy and the freedom of information. It may be argued that cases of the celebrity 'kiss and tell' kind may be more about reputation management than preserving privacy, with the claimant actually more concerned about loss of income than their privacy as such. However, it is often the tabloid press who protest the loudest in such cases and it is those papers that are most inclined to employ intrusive means to obtain such stories and portray them in the most lurid terms to boost sales. Motivation here is more about making money than keeping the public appropriately informed. The use of so-called 'super injunctions' which prevent the media reporting even that an injunction has been applied for, let alone the name of the applicant, have unsurprisingly proved controversial, even though applications often fail or are overturned on appeal and, if granted, are only in use in the short term. The Neuberger Report published in 2011 recommended that, in the interest of open justice, the Ministry of Justice should collate the numbers of such applications every year so that the number can be readily known. It also recommends that, before an application is heard, the relevant branch of the media should be informed so that it or any interested member of the public is able to contest the application. The Ministry of Justice has been monitoring the use of all injunctions since 2011.

Remedies for passing off, malicious falsehood and breach of confidence

The following remedies are available for each of the three torts:

Account for profits: judicial remedy requiring a defendant to hand over any financial advantage gained from their illegal activity.

1 *Injunction*: to prevent publication and/or require the defendant to hand over relevant goods or documentation.

2 *Damages*: to compensate the claimant for loss and damage.

3 *Account for profits*: the defendant may be required to **account for profits** by handing over the fruits of his or her wrongdoing.

Chapter summary

Passing off

***The defendant*:**

(a) presents its goods or services in a similar, distinctive get-up to those of the claimant's similar product; or

(b) falsely describes its product and suggests that it has the same definitive characteristics as the claimant's product; or

(c) presents the claimant's work as the defendant's own; or

(d) falsely suggests that the claimant vouches for the defendant's work.

***Claimant must prove*:**

(a) misrepresentation by the defendant;

(b) published in the course of trade;

(c) to the claimant's customers;

(d) which reasonably foreseeably would/did cause damage to the claimant.

Malicious falsehood

***Claimant must prove*:** malicious publication of a false statement concerning the claimant's business and resulting in reasonably foreseeable damage.

Breach of confidence

***Claimant must prove*:** information relating to the claimant was revealed by the defendant to a third party/parties in circumstances when privacy could reasonably be expected and resulted in damage to the claimant.

Public interest may be a defence.

Misuse of private information

Remedies

Account for profits.

Damages.

Injunction.

Review questions 25

1 What torts may have been committed in the following situations?

(a) Sadie told Dai, a fellow inventor, of her plans to develop a voice-activated tin opener. Dai has now patented the item.

(b) Wong, a professional photographer, discovers that Liora has been using samples of Wong's work to help her obtain photographic commissions.

(c) Farook, an opera singer, discovers that Pete, a professional rival, told Bhatti that Farook was temperamental, unreliable and given to cancelling engagements at the last minute.

2 What must a claimant prove in a claim for breach of confidence?

3 What remedies are available to a victim of malicious falsehood?

4 Why may a party seek to register a trade mark rather than rely on the common law protection of a passing-off claim?

5 What must a claimant prove to bring a claim for misuse of private information?

6 Define and distinguish between breach of confidence and misuse of private information.

Answers to all review questions can be found in Appendix 2.

Advanced questions 25

(A) Critically evaluate the use of super-injunctions by celebrities as a way of protecting their reputations.

(B) Analyse the law relating to the tort of passing off.

Answers to the advanced questions can be found at **go.pearson.com/uk/he/resources.**

Take a closer look

The following cases provide important examples of how the law in this chapter has developed. They are primary sources illustrating the law in action and give more detail about their facts, as well as helping to understand the law and to appreciate how the judges reached their decisions.

Try looking them up in the law reports or accessing them via a database, e.g. BAILII (www.bailii.org/databases.html). LexisNexis or Westlaw may be available in the university or college library, or extracts may be found in a case book. (See Appendix 1: Additional resources.)

A v B, sub nom Garry Flitcroft v Mirror Group Newspapers Ltd [2002] 2 All ER 545

Campbell v Mirror Group Newspapers [2005] UKHL 61

Douglas and Another v Hello! Ltd (No. 3) [2007] 2 WLR 920

Fenty v Topshop/Topman [2015] EWCA Civ 3

NAD Electronics v NAD Computer Systems [1997] FSR 380

Vidal-Hall v Google Inc [2015] EWCA Civ 311

Web activity

Protection of privacy is one of the aims of the charity Liberty. Try searching for information about its work in this area:
www.liberty-human-rights.org.uk

Assignment 24

Discuss how far it is true to say that application of the Human Rights Act 1998 has expanded the scope of breach of confidence actions.

Appendix 1:
Additional resources

Additional resources

Your studies will be more rewarding if you look beyond what is in this text. Coursework assignments may require some research from specialist textbooks. The internet is a very useful research tool. Here are some suggestions.

Background information

Apart from quality newspapers, TV and radio programmes are a useful source of information about current legal topics. 'You and Yours', 'Money Box' and 'Law in Action' on Radio 4 all deal interestingly with a variety of topical legal issues. *Which?* magazine is published monthly by the Consumers' Association and provides a lot of very accessible information on consumer rights.

Specialist texts

The English legal system

Allbon, E. and Kaur Dua, S. (2018) *Elliot and Quinn's English Legal System*. 19th ed. Pearson.

Contract Law

Chen-Wishart, M. (2018) *Contract Law*. 6th ed. Oxford University Press.
Finch, E and Fafinski, S. (2018) *Contract Law*. 6th ed. Pearson.
Taylor, R. and Taylor, D. (2019) *Contract Law*. 7th ed. Oxford University Press.
For reference: Furmston, M (2017): *Cheshire, Fifoot and Furmston's Law of Contract*. 17th ed. Oxford University Press.

Consumer law

Woodroffe, G., Twigg-Flesner, C. and Willett, C. (2016) *Woodroffe & Lowe's Consumer Law and Practice Consumer Law and Practice*. 10th ed. Sweet and Maxwell.

The law of tort

Cooke, J. (2019) *Law of Tort*. 13th ed. The Foundation Studies in Law Series, Pearson.
Horsey, K. and Rackley, E. (2019) *Tort Law*. 6th ed. Oxford University Press.
Horsey, K. and Rackley, E. (2019) *Kidner's Casebook on Torts*. 15th ed. Oxford University Press.

Employment law

Taylor, S. and Emir, A. (2019) *Employment Law*. 5th ed. Oxford University Press.
Smith, I., Baker, A. and Warnock, O. (2019) *Smith & Wood's Employment Law*. 14th ed. Oxford University Press.

Company law

Wild, C. and Weinstein, S. (2019) *Smith and Keenan's Company Law*. 18th ed. Pearson.
French, D. (2019) *Mayson, French and Ryan on Company Law*. 36th ed. Oxford University Press.
Hannigan, B. (2018) *Company Law*. 5th ed. Oxford University Press.

Intellectual property

Karapapa, S. and McDonagh, L. (2019) *Intellectual Property Law*. Oxford University Press.
Pila, J. and Torremans, P. (2019) *European Intellectual Property Law*. 2nd ed. Oxford University Press.

Useful websites

Subject to any specified copyright restraints, you may download and print off documents for your personal study use. Websites also often have useful links to other relevant sites.

Name	Nature of resources	Contact
ABTA (Association of British Travel Agents)	ADR process and other methods of resolving consumer disputes	**https://abta.com/help-and-complaints**
ACAS (Advisory, Conciliation and Arbitration Service)	Good employment law resource	**www.acas.org.uk**
Advice Guide	Consumer advice from the Citizens' Advice Bureau	**www.adviceguide.org.uk/**
BBC	Useful background information for many of the topics in this book	**www.bbc.co.uk/**
British and Irish Legal Information Institute (BAILII)	Large database of cases	**www.bailii.org/databases.html**
Business and Human Rights Resource Centre	Lots of useful information and news about business with a human rights perspective	**www.business-humanrights.org**
Bytestart	Advice on setting up and running a small business	**www.bytestart.co.uk/index.shtml**
The Carbolic Smokeball Company	Information about the famous case	**www.carbolicsmokeball.co.uk/**
Equality and Human Rights Commission	Non-departmental government body responsible for promoting equality, monitoring anti-discrimination law and ensuring its effectiveness	**www.equalityhumanrights.com**
Department for Business, Energy and Industrial Strategy	Consumer, company and employment law resource	**www.gov.uk/government/organisations/department-for-business-energy-and-industrial-strategy**
Europa	EU website: lots of news and information about the EU and how it works plus databases of legislation and cases	**europa.eu/index_en.htm**
Health and Safety Executive	Practical information about workplace safety and the law	**www.hse.gov.uk/index.htm**
Insolvency Helpline	Consumer debt advice	**www.insolvencyhelpline.co.uk/**
Institute of Directors	Information and resources for company directors	**www.iod.com**
The Liberty Guide to Human Rights	Lots of useful information about the ECHR, and the HRA 1998	**www.yourrights.org.uk/**
Parliament	Information about forthcoming legislation, Acts of Parliament from 1988, House of Lords cases	**www.parliament.uk/**
The Society of Motor Manufacturers and Traders	Useful example of ADR procedure	**www.smmt.co.uk/**
The Stock Exchange	Useful information about the operation of the stock market	**www.londonstockexchange.com/en-gb/**
Trading Standards Institute	Trading Law information and enforcement	**www.tradingstandards.uk/**
UK Intellectual Property Office	Lots of news and information about copyright, design right, patents and trade marks	**www.ipo.gov.uk/**

Appendix 2:
Worth thinking about? and Review questions – outline answers

Worth thinking about?

The idea behind these questions is to get students thinking and to prompt discussion, not just to test knowledge, so there may not necessarily be a definitive right or wrong answer.

Chapter 3

There are a number of possibilities here, the most obvious being that a case may have become so outdated that it no longer reflects current attitudes. In *British Railways Board* v *Herrington* (1972) where a child trespasser was badly injured by a live electric rail, the House of Lords departed from its previous decision in *Robert Addie & Sons Ltd* v *Dumbreck* (1929) in order to increase the duty of care owed by an occupier to trespassers, to reflect the more humane attitudes of the late twentieth century.

On occasion, the House of Lords has been prepared to acknowledge that a previous decision was misguided. In *R* v *Shivpuri* (1986) it departed from *Anderton* v *Ryan* (1985) which contained a statutory interpretation of attempt to commit a crime, which had been widely criticised. Lord Bridge described it as a serious error which should be corrected quickly.

Chapter 4

Out-of-court settlements work well if both parties are equally powerful. However, in many cases concerning personal injury or consumer problems the defendant is an insurance company or large business concern and the claimant, unless very well advised, may be squeezed into accepting an unprofitable deal for much less than would have been awarded by the court. Where small claims are concerned, the claimant will usually not be represented and have received a minimum of legal advice. The only real advantage to the claimant in cases like these is that at least they get some money; if the case had gone to court they might still have lost.

Chapter 5

The postal acceptance rule was developed to prevent uncertainty about when a contract, made at long distance, came into being. Acceptance is fixed at the earliest possible time in the communication process to ensure that a party cannot change its mind once a letter is posted. Once a letter is posted, any attempt on the part of the offeror to revoke would be a breach of contract.

Chapter 6

It is possible to see an element of potential duress in *Stilk* v *Myrick*. Also that case was decided at a time when mutiny at sea was greatly feared, so the court would have been inclined to take a strong line against the sailors. No threat was imposed by Mr Williams; in fact, the suggestion that the terms be varied seemed to come from Mr Roffey; who was concerned about avoiding a sanction imposed by a third party (the Housing Association). It is common business practice for the parties to vary the terms of a contract and happily go along with the change. This decision is in line with other current decisions on similar facts where lack of consideration has not been questioned and the outcome has been determined on the presence or absence of economic duress. (See Chapter 8.)

Chapter 7

Where the contract terms are incomplete or even unclear but one of the parties has embarked on performance by paying money or carrying out work prior to a dispute the court may use a purposive approach to imply a meaning to keep the contract alive and prevent one party unfairly gaining an advantage.

Chapter 8

Here we have two contracts in one. The 'buy one get one free notice' amounts to a unilateral offer which the customer accepts through making the contract to buy one of the products. This brings into being a collateral contract which the shopkeeper must perform by handing over the second product. Buying the first product forms the consideration for the second contract. The reality is that the customer in such situations is not getting a free item, they are just getting it more cheaply than usual. They are entering a contract and providing consideration for the goods. They are not getting anything free, just (maybe) a good bargain.

A shop which refuses to allow such a sale would, apart from any contractual liability, be breaking trading standards law and be liable for criminal prosecution.

Chapter 9

Here the contract has become impossible to perform. Provided this is not due to the fault of the seller, the contract is said to be discharged by frustration. (See Chapter 11.)

Chapter 10

The sale of a very basic mobile phone to a minor is arguably a contract for necessaries in our security-conscious age, so an excessive price could be challenged. However, the very fancy pieces of kit brandished by many children today would be likely to be treated as non-necessaries.

A monthly contract to supply phone services would be one of continuing obligation and therefore voidable by the minor at any time. You will find that phone companies are wise to this and refuse to enter into such contracts with anybody under 18 years of age.

Chapter 11

Mrs Beswick could sue John Beswick under the Contracts (Rights of Third Parties) Act 1999, as the contract between John and Peter was made for her benefit. (See Chapter 6.)

Chapter 12

Spearmint Rhino might try to argue that the contract with the lap dancers is illegal and void because it promotes sexual immorality, so it has no duty to pay. (See *Pearce* v *Brooks* (1866), Chapter 10.) In practice, however, it is unlikely to do so as presumably lap dancers encourage custom at the clubs and it makes some money directly for them as well. Many potentially illegal contracts go unchallenged while both parties are happy with the arrangement.

Chapter 13

Donoghue v *Stevenson* established a right of legal redress for claimants who suffered particular types of harm despite not having a contract. This has been extended to different types of products and the neighbour principle is relevant to determining whether a duty is owed in established duty situations. In new duty situations the *Caparo* test is used.

Chapter 14

Since *Hambrook* v *Stokes* it was the rule that a successful secondary victim must have witnessed the relevant accident through their own senses, not filtered through a third party, so in *Alcock* the House of Lords was affirming this principle. This was the first case of an accident directly injuring hundreds of victims which had been witnessed by countless people through TV. Their lordships held that the victims would not be sufficiently identifiable in the TV pictures. Maybe this was influenced by policy considerations concerning freedom of information in simultaneous broadcasts and the need to remove threat of litigation to broadcast media.

Chapter 15

Mr Piper has a potential action in negligence against the hospital which owes him a duty of care. He might try to claim that the hospital damaged the prosthesis when implanting it, thus breaching its duty of care.

Chapter 16

First, vicarious liability provides an identifiable defendant when this might be any one of many faceless employees. Secondly, the average employer is in a better financial position to meet the claim than the employee, since the employer should be fully insured against such losses.

Chapter 17

Perceptive students may ask why Ms Reid did not sue the landlord under the Occupiers' Liability Act 1957 as the occupier of the building. While she would have had a cause of action, she would have needed to ascertain who the occupier was, while the regulations led her straight to the employer. Further, under the OLA 1957 the occupier's duty is to take reasonable care to ensure reasonable safety. The regulations require the employer 'to ensure' safety, which imposes a higher level of duty. It was also more advantageous to sue the employer for breach of the regulations than at common law for breach of non-delegable duty, where only reasonable care is required and liability could be avoided if the employer could not reasonably have known of the state of the lift.

Chapter 18

Serco would appear to be a public authority and therefore under a duty (HRA 1998) to act compatibly with the ECHR. Mr Redfearn could argue that under Article 10 (freedom of expression) he is entitled to hold opinions. He was, after all, not even attempting to express them at work. *Redfearn* v *Serco Ltd* (2012) indicates that is a successful argument.

Like most of the Convention rights, this is not absolute and conditions and restrictions may be imposed upon it in the interests of public safety. Serco would no doubt have raised this argument, but, given where he actually worked and his good relationship with other staff, sacking him might be argued to be disproportionate. While most of us (author included) abhor the BNP, stopping its members from earning a living in the circumstances of this case seems a rather extreme response which should be corrected by the court.

However, since the amendment of ERA 1996, s 108, following the ECtHR decision in *Redfearn* v *Serco Ltd* (2012), which held that his rights to freedom of speech and association had been breached, he could take the much simpler route of suing for unfair dismissal, regardless of how long he has been employed there. His employer will have to show that he was fairly dismissed for other legally recognised reasons and that the procedures used to dismiss him were also fair.

Chapter 19

The employer's policies are the key here. These should be reasonable and clear so that the employee can understand in advance what behaviour will/will not be tolerated.

The amount of time spent during working hours, apart obviously from breaks may be an issue but appropriate warnings should be sufficient and it is highly unlikely to be a sacking issue. It's a sad fact of the modern workplace that employees often don't take the breaks they are entitled to and may be doing extra work from home, so sensitive treatment of this issue may be necessary. If there is no issue with the employee's output and efficiency a light touch is probably wise.

Any gross breaches involving harassment of colleagues or other people, defamatory comments or any other behaviour implicating the business and likely to bring it or the employer into disrepute may justify dismissal provided all appropriate disciplinary and appeal procedures have been used prior to the dismissal.

Chapter 20

Limited liability promotes investment. It is good for business, as it gives some guarantee of safety for investors in what is essentially a gamble: 'the value of your investment may go down as well as up.'

The history of limited liability is long, diverse and sometimes shameful. Dubious and often disastrous speculation protected by it, led to the Joint Stock Act 1844, which provided a registration system for companies which did not permit limited liability. However, public opinion aided by a disastrous slump in the economy led to a re-think and in 1855 the Limited Liability Act permitted it subject to certain controls.

Chapter 21

Company formation has become increasingly easier over the years, as successive governments have tried to help small businesses. However, this does promote opportunities for fraud, assisted by the ease and cheapness with which one can buy a company 'off the shelf'. Try Googling that phrase and you will find hundreds of firms ready to help, sometimes for as little as £30. All too often we hear of companies being set up as a cover for scams which enable the rogues behind the name to take the money and run. They may then cease trading or just disappear without trace or shelter behind limited liability in the event of proceedings being brought against them.

Chapter 22

This reform clearly reflects the policy behind the Act that seeks to simplify the transaction of company business and give greater flexibility to management. This is one less thing for company promoters to consider when drawing up the company articles, as it will not be necessary to include permission. The relaxation of the rule is arguably balanced by adequate protection for shareholder democracy.

Chapter 23

A decision to accept a lower bid may be justified once reference is made to the qualifying criteria in s 172(1). The directors must, for example, have regard to the long-term effects of their decision and how it will impact on the company employees. Maybe the lower bidder is offering a better long-term deal for them. The only real change made by the CA 2006 is to spell out decision-making criteria.

Chapter 24

The two-stage test will surely act as a powerful filter. If the directors are also major shareholders they will be able to support each other against a minority. Finally, given that a shareholder may be a company, there is the likelihood that a board of directors under threat may be able to rely on such institutional support, motivated by sympathy for a predicament which any board might face.

In practice, it seems likely, given its built-in protection for directors, that minority shareholders will be no better protected by the CA 2006 than they were by the rule in *Foss* v *Harbottle*. Directors' rather than the company's interests are arguably better protected by Chapter 11 proceedings.

Chapter 25

If the photograph is taken in a public place, the law generally regards you as fair game to any passing photographer. It may be irritating to individuals who feel that their privacy is being invaded, but restricting the activity would in most circumstances be incompatible with the ECHR (rights to free expression/ information). It is sad that the paparazzi so often abuse this. Photographs taken on private premises may in some circumstances amount to breach of confidence. (See Chapter 26.)

Chapter 26

We live in an age where celebrity has been described as a 'trade' by the courts (*per* Lord Hoffmann in this actual case) so in that context maybe it is reasonable to treat its 'products', such as a wedding, as a marketable entity. Any of us less famed human beings would probably prefer to control who takes photographs of us on such occasions. Maybe the Douglases thought that, as their wedding was going to attract a lot of media attention, the least disruption might be caused on the day by giving an exclusive to one magazine. These are reasonable wishes that deserve legal protection. When looking at a legal problem we have to try not to take the biased (though not necessarily unreasonable) view that Catherine Zeta Jones should 'get a life' and stop worrying about bootleg pictures of her engulfing a piece of cake, entering the public domain.

OK did pay £1 million for the exclusive photographic rights and it is arguable did not get their money's worth since some people wanting to see the pictures would doubtless have bought *Hello!* instead if that was their celebrity magazine of choice, so this would affect *OK*'s sales figures even though they got their pictures out first. Again, we need to have regard to the legal principle involved.

Review questions – outline answers

Review questions 1 – (Chapter 2: The nature of law)

1 Source: the state; scope: geographical limitations; sanctions: imposed by or with the authority of the state.

2 Antiquity; lengthy evolution unaffected by Roman law; creative power; authority of the judiciary; adversarial procedure.

3 Purpose and function to protect various rights and creation and enforcement of duties from infringement by individuals, organisations and government. This is done by civil, criminal and administrative law – see section 'Why do we need law'.

4 Retribution and protection for society through containment, deterrence, rehabilitation.

5 Compensation for damage caused by defendant; possibly an equitable remedy to make the defendant alter behaviour.

6 Sparticus may be prosecuted for drunken and careless driving. He may also be liable in negligence to Finch and breach of contract to Helen.

Review questions 2 (Chapter 3: How the law is made)

1 European law, parliamentary legislation, case law.

2 Regulations have immediate effect and aim at uniformity. Directives require state legislation and aim at harmonisation.

3 First and second reading; committee and report stages; third reading; transfer to the other House; procedures repeated; Royal Assent.

4 Two of the following: Orders in Council, statutory instruments, regulations, bye-laws.

5 Literal rule: face-value meaning of the statute's words. Mischief rule: purposive approach.

6 General words take their meaning from any preceding specific words.

Review questions 3 (Chapter 4: Resolving legal disputes)

1 (a) Crown Court. (b) Court of Appeal Criminal Division. (c) Crown Court/Divisional Court of QBD. (d) County Court. (e) High Court: QBD. (f) Employment tribunal. (g) County Court.

2 Letters of claim and pre-action protocols; issue of claim; defendants' response; allocation of case to relevant track; interlocutory stages; court trial; executing the judgment.

3 A freezing injunction prevents the defendant from transferring his or her assets abroad or otherwise concealing them.

4 Arbitration: arbitrator's decision binding. Conciliation: conciliator may suggest a solution. Mediation: parties reach their own decision.

5 Tribunals have specialist lay members, they are less formal, cheaper (but generally no legal aid), quicker and not necessarily bound by precedent. They have wide discretion.

6 Advantages: Less costly; relative informality; speed; flexibility. Disadvantages: No access to legal aid; increasingly legalistic proceedings; delays in dispute resolution particularly in employment tribunals.

Review questions 4 (Chapter 5: The law of contract – offer and acceptance)

1 Offer: promise to be bound on specific terms (*Carlill* v *Carbolic Smoke Ball Co* (1892)) Invitation to treat: expression of willingness to negotiate (*Fisher* v *Bell* (1963)).

2 A counter-offer is an attempt to vary the terms of the existing offer, to get more favourable terms, e.g. to get a price reduction (*Hyde* v *Wrench* (1840)).

3 Where post is the appropriate method of acceptance, the acceptance is made and the contract completed once the letter of acceptance is properly posted (*Adams* v *Lindsell* (1818)).

4 Termination of offer by: a) death; b) refusal or counter-offer; c) lapse of time; d) revocation; e) acceptance.

5 (a) No: invitation to treat. (b) No: invitation to treat. (c) Yes: unilateral. (d) No: lacks communication. (e) Counter-offer by Eli. (f) No: offer revoked, if Paul knew of sale.

6 (a) No: conditional. (b) No: failure to communicate. (c) Yes: if the postal rules apply. (d) No: failure to communicate.

Review question 5 (The law of contract – consideration, intention and privity)

1 Consideration is the concept of bargain – distinguishing a contract from any other sort of promise or bargain (*Curie* v *Misa* 1875; *Dunlop* v *Selfridge* (1915)).

2 Executory: exchange of mutual promises; Executed: promise in return for an act (*Carlill* (supra)).

3 The act is performed before any promise of payment is made (*Re: McArdle* (1951)).

4 Privity of contract: parties who have not given consideration for the contract cannot sue on the contract (*Tweddle* v *Atkinson* (1861)).

5 (a) Gratuitous: past consideration. (b) Binding: adequacy irrelevant. (c) Gratuitous: existing contractual duty. (d) Binding: exception to *Pinnel's* case. (e) Provides a defence under *High Trees* if Amira tried to repudiate.

6 The Contracts (Rights of Third Parties) Act 1999 may assist Gareth, since the contract is made for his benefit.

Review questions 6 (Chapter 7: The terms of the contract at common law)

1 Conditions: major terms, innocent party may repudiate and claim damages (*Poussard* v *Spiers* (1876)). Warranties: minor terms, damages only (*Bettini* v *Gye* (1876)).

2 Capable of being breached in a number of ways, some serious enough to justify repudiation (*Hong Kong Fir Shipping Co* (1962)).

3 The *Cehave* criteria indicate (a) Does contract indicate the consequence of the term? (b) Using the words condition/warranty does not give them specific status. (c) Is there a statutory right to repudiate? (d) Is there commonly accepted commercial practice? (e) If none of the above apply then assess status from the extent of the damage.

4 Limitation clause: limits financial liability. Exclusion clause: exempts the party in breach for legal and therefore financial liability for the breach.

5 (a) Yes, if it should be visible to customers before they enter the contract. (b) Yes, regardless of whether the signer read or understood it. (c) No: contract concluded at reception. (d) No: too late, contract already concluded.

6 This rule means that any unclear wording in the contract will be interpreted to give the meaning most favourable to the party who did not impose it.

Review questions 7 (Chapter 8: Statutory terms in contracts for goods and services)

1 Implied terms in B2B contracts are found in the Sale of Goods Act 1979. The seller is able to pass title (s 12), goods match description (s.13), are of satisfactory quality (s 14(2)), are suitable for their purpose (s 14(3)) and conform to sample (s 15).

2 Business buyer may reject goods within a reasonable time if the seller has breached any of the implied terms under SGA 1979, s 35.

3 In a B2B contract (between businesses) UCTA 1977, s 2 applies: negligence liability cannot be excluded for death or personal injury, damage to property may be excluded if reasonable. In a B2C contract (business to consumer) CRA 2015, ss 57 and 65 apply.

4 CRA 2015 and the Consumer Contracts (Information, Cancellation and Additional Charges) Regulations 2013.

5 Assuming that this is a consumer sale, Rosanna is entitled to reject the goods (s 22) or request repair or replacement under the CRA (s 23) within 30 days of delivery. If repair or replacement is not carried out within a reasonable time she then has a final right to reject.

6 This term may be voidable under the CRA 2015.

Review questions 8 (Chapter 9: Defects in the contract – misrepresentation, mistake, duress and undue influence)

1 (a) Voidable. (b) Void. (c) Void.

2 (a) Misrepresentation. (b) Mistake: subject matter. (c) Misrepresentation, mistake: identity. (d) Undue influence.

3 Statement of opinion genuinely held cannot amount to a misrepresentation (*Bisset* v *Wilkinson* (1927); compare *Smith* v *Land House Properties* (1884)).

4 Where there is a change of circumstances (*With* v *O'Flanagan* (1936)).

5 Duress is forcing a party to enter into a contract through physical threats to their person or by threatening their business interests (*Barton* v *Armstrong* (1975)); Undue influence is a contract entered into after abuse of a special relationship (*Williams* v *Bailey* (1866)).

6 Rectification: court's action or order to alter/amend wording or terms of a written contract to correct a mistake or to express true intentions of the parties.

Review questions 9 (Chapter 10: The consequences of illegality and incapacity – illegality and incapacity)

1 A contract for an illegal purpose (breaking the law) is completely void. Property is not generally recoverable. Severance is impossible. Under a contract perceived as merely undesirable to the public interest, property is recoverable and severance possible. Any void portion may be severed.

2 (a) To commit a crime. (b) Sexually immoral. (c) Dangerous to international relations.

3 (a) Necessary goods: reasonable price payable. (b) Non-necessaries: not enforceable. (c) Yes, if for his benefit. (d) No: contract of debt.

4 Restrictions on future employment of an employee must be reasonable in the interests of the parties and of the public. This is relevant to business interest, length of restriction and geographical area of restraint (*Nordenfelt* v *Maxim Nordenfelt* (1894)).

5 Contracts for necessaries (*Peters* v *Fleming* (1840)).

6 Knowledge of impairment of other contracting party; contracts for necessaries.

Review questions 10 (Chapter 11: Discharge of the contract and remedies for breach)

1 (a) (i) Yes: divisible contract. (ii) Yes: acceptance of part performance. (b) Yes: full performance prevented.

2 Barry committed an anticipatory breach. This would have entitled Laura to repudiate the contract but, as she did not exercise this right, it was lost when the contract was frustrated by destruction of the car. If the car was destroyed before the contract was made, the contract is void for mistake if neither party was aware that the goods no longer existed.

3 Remoteness: limits the amount of actionable damage. Quantum: concerns the amount of damages payable by the defendant to compensate for the actionable damage.

4 Specific performance will not be granted to enforce an employment contract, or one requiring continuing supervision. Discretionary: will not be granted to enforce any contract unless this is deemed fair to both parties.

5 An injunction can be used to prevent a negative stipulation (a promise not to break the contract) (*Warner Bros* v *Nelson* (1936)).

6 Mitigation is responsibility of the innocent party to minimise the effects of the losses suffered which could have been reasonably avoided (*Brace* v *Calder* (1895)).

Review questions 11 (Chapter 12: The law of agency)

1 (a) Actual express authority. (b) Actual implied authority.

2 Yes: Sanjay failed to notify Sparkles about Patricia's dismissal and is estopped from denying Patricia's apparent authority/ authority by estoppel (*Barrett* v *Deere* (1828)).

3 If the third party wished to contract with the agent personally (*Humble* v *Hunter* (1848)).

4 When the principal agrees/trade practice/routine tasks not requiring special skill.

5 When an irrevocable/enduring/lasting power of attorney exists.

6 In an emergency situation where one party takes action to protect another's property and communication with the other party is not possible.

Review questions 12 (Chapter 13: The tort of negligence)

1 Duty, breach, consequent damage.

2 Reasonable foreseeability, proximity, for established duty situations (*Donoghue* v *Stevenson*). For new duty situations: reasonable foreseeability, proximity and policy/public interest (*Hill* v *Chief Constable of West Yorkshire* (1988)).

3 The 'eggshell skull' rule is an exception to the *Wagon Mound* principle. If the claimant has some particular weakness that makes him or her susceptible to a type of harm which is not reasonably foreseeable, the defendant will nevertheless be liable (*Smith* v *Leech Brain & Co Ltd* (1962)).

4 Consent: express/implied consent by the claimant to the defendant's behaviour may be an effective defence (*Ratcliff* v *Harper Adams College* (1999)). Contributory negligence: damages may be reduced proportionally in relation to the claimant's failure to take care for their own safety (*Badger* v *Ministry of Defence* (2006)).

5 Contributory negligence.

6 Latin for 'the thing speaks for itself'. Allows a presumption of negligence to be drawn and the burden of proof to be put on the defendant where the cause of the accident/event is unknown, the thing causing the injury was under the control of the defendant and could not have occurred without negligence (*Scott* v *St Katherine Dock* (1865))

Review questions 13 (Chapter 14: Negligence and special duty situations)

1 (a) Yes: negligent misstatement (*Hedley Byrne* v *Heller* (1963)). (b) Yes: nervous shock (*Alcock* v *Chief Constable of South Yorkshire* (1992)). (c) No: damage caused by the third party (*Smith* v *Littlewoods Organisation* (1987)).

2 Standard of care of a reasonable professional adviser with their particular knowledge and experience (*Hedley Byrne* v *Heller* (1963)).

3 Nervous shock causing physical/psychiatric harm which must be medically recognised.

4 Primary victim: those directly involved in the accident or event, who, as a result, have been physically hurt or reasonably put in fear of their own safety (*Page* v *Smith* (1995)).

5 Secondary victim: a mere witness to the accident or event, not in danger or reasonable fear of it (*McLoughlin* v *O'Brian* (1982)).

6 There is no general liability for failure to act. Usually a defendant must act negligently, rather than fail to act. However, there are four situations where a failure to act does give rise to a duty to act: a) where there is a contractual duty to act; b) where there is a duty based on a special relationship such as doctor and patient; c) where the defendant has a duty to control another person's acts for whom he or she is responsible; and d) where the defendant has a duty to control events causing danger on his or her land.

Review questions 14 (Chapter 15: Product liability)

1 Limitation period (time that the law allows for claims to be brought), third party interference (*Evans* v *Triplex Glass* (1936), contributory negligence by claimant).

2 Basil, as the purchaser, has rights in contract against Tarragon. Basil and Rosemary also have rights in common law negligence and under the Consumer Protection Act 1987 against Marjoram.

3 Negligence liability is fault-based and duty, breach and damage must be proved (*Donoghue* v *Stevenson* (1932)); negligence action lies against the manufacturer and/or in some circumstances intermediaries who have some responsibility for the product.

4 Liability under CPA 1987 is strict. Defendant: producer/own brander/importer/supplier. Property damage: limited to claims over £275 under CPA 1987.

5 Under CPA 1987, s 4: (i) Goods comply with EC or UK safety standards and the defect is attributable to compliance with those standards; (ii) The goods became defective after they were supplied; (iii) The 'state of the art/developments risk' defence; and (iv) The defendant did not at any time supply the product to another in the course of business.

6 Remedies available depend upon the area of law in which a claim is brought: contract, negligence or CPA 1987. Contract: Any loss or damage to buyer as long as not too remote including purchase price. Tort: Any loss or damage to injured party as long as not too remote; excluding purchase price and other pure economic loss. CPA 1987: Death/personal injury. Damage to land and goods (over £275) excluding purchase price.

Review questions 15 (Chapter 16: Occupiers' liability, nuisance and vicarious liability)

1 (a) Public nuisance affecting the highway: non-delegable duty. (b) Under the Occupiers' Liability Act 1957, no liability if notice sufficient to discharge duty. (c) Lennie is a trespasser (Occupiers' Liability Act 1984). Reed likely to be liable, as he could easily have prevented a child from obtaining access to his storeroom and should have foreseen Lennie's likely presence if children regularly visit his shop. (d) Private nuisance.

2 Under OLA 1957, premises includes vehicles (a car), and failure to ensure the seat belt was functioning properly would be a breach of Chester's duty under OLA 1957, s 2(2).

3 Employers are vicariously liable for torts committed by an employee if incidental to the job. Generally there is no liability for independent contractors unless the employer's personal duty is non-delegable. However see *Barclays Bank* v *Various Claimants* (2018) where the courts have extended vicarious liability to include negligent actions of independent contractors in exceptional circumstances.

4 Vicarious liability enables the claimant to obtain compensation directly from the employer, who has financial means rather than the employee.

5 The occupier only owes a duty of care to trespassers under the OLA 1984 if the following criteria is satisfied: (a) the occupier must have reasonable knowledge

of the danger; (b) the occupier must know or reasonably suspect that potential entrants are in the vicinity of the premises or are reasonably likely to come into the vicinity; and (c) the risk is one against which, in all the circumstances, it is reasonable for the occupier to offer some protection.

6 An occupier is any person in control of the premises at the time of the accident (*Wheat* v *Lacon* (1966)).

Review questions 16 (Chapter 17: Rights at work – the contract of employment and health and safety at work)

1 Employer is responsible for paying employees' NI contributions and sick pay and deduction of income tax. Employer vicariously liable for wrongful acts of employee. No such responsibilities for contractors, who also have no rights to claim for unfair dismissal or redundancy. Lesser duty to contractors under the HSAWA 1974 than that owed to employees. Very limited vicarious liability for independent contractors.

2 ERA 1996, s 1 statement of particulars: parties' names and addresses, date employment commenced; date of continuous employment; notes of disciplinary and grievance procedures; pension rights/ holiday entitlement, etc.

3 Main sources of contractual terms for contracts of employment: custom and practice; works and staff rules; collective agreements; statute; common law rights and duties of employers and employees; business efficacy.

4 (a) Good faith: conflict with Juniper's interests (*Dalton* v *Burtons Gold Medal Biscuit Co. Ltd* (1974)); (b) Lack of reasonable care and skill; (c) Good faith: failure to account for profits.

5 Common law duties: competent staff, safe work systems. Criminal liability under the HSAWA 1974.

6 Prosecution, improvement/prohibition notices.

Review questions 17 (Chapter 18: Rights at work – protection from discrimination in employment)

1 Freda may claim that her work is of equal value under EA 2010 and that she is being treated unfavourably on the grounds of her protected characteristic of sex (*Hayward* v *Cammell Laird* (1988)).

2 Mr. Jones may be able to claim sex discrimination under the EA 2010, s 11 for direct discrimination (s 13) unless the occupational qualification (Schedule 9, para 1) is applicable (*Moyhing* v *Barts and London NHS Trust* (2006)).

3 Under EA 2010, s 26 there are three types of harassment: a) unwanted conduct relating to claimant's gender which has intention/effect of creating intimidating, hostile, degrading, humiliating environment; b) unwanted conduct of sexual nature as in a) above; c) less favourable treatment or harassment on grounds of sexual or gender reassignment.

4 If race (or sex) is deemed an occupational qualification because the employer can show that it is essential to the job and a reasonable and proportionate response (Schedule 9, para 1) (*Etam plc* v *Rowan* (1996)).

5 Ms Rosey has been subjected to unfavourable treatment because of being on maternity leave (s 18(2)). She is entitled to equal pay and therefore can claim the bonus under the EA, s 74. Ms Cole can claim victimisation (s 27) because she encouraged Ms Rosey to exercise her rights and may have been unfairly made redundant as a result.

6 Direct: overt restriction of employment opportunity resulting in unfavourable treatment of people with a protected characteristic under EA 2010. Indirect: provision, criteria or practice which negatively affects a protected group disproportionately and which cannot be justified as legitimate and proportionate (*Home Office* v *Holmes* (1984)).

Review questions 18 (Chapter 19: Rights at work – Protection against termination of employment by wrongful and unfair dismissal including redundancy)

1 Wrongful dismissal: breach of contract; no qualifying period of employment; common law action in the courts as well as the tribunal (damages in employment tribunal limited to £25,000); remedy – damages if claim brought in County Court or High Court determined by the court. Unfair dismissal: statutory right not to be dismissed except for a fair reason and following a fair procedure (employer has not necessarily breached the contract); requires employee to have one year's continuous employment; claim to be brought within three months of effective date of termination; hearing: employment tribunal only, compensation regulated by statute, reinstatement/re-engagement possible.

2 Constructive dismissal -employee resigns as a result of employer's serious breach of contract – repudiatory breach. *Martin v Parkham Foods (2006)*

3 (a) Lack of qualification. (b) Misconduct. (c) Negligence/incapability. (d) Conduct, but only if it reflects on Richard's suitability for the job.

4 (a) No: he was not dismissed. (b) If a contract term contains a reasonable mobility clause then she is not redundant; unless distance is too far to be considered reasonable.

5 Fair selection procedures, warnings, consultation procedures, redeployment offers.

6 Employees' rights under TUPE 2006: information and consultation; provision of employee liability information; redundancy connected with transfer is unfair subject to ETO; continuation of existing terms and conditions.

Review questions 19 (Chapter 20: Business organisations)

1 Incorporation is the process used to form a corporate entity or company with a separate legal personality from its owners. This legal process can be done by Royal Charter, Act of Parliament, or registration under the Companies Act 2006.

2 (a) Financial liability of corporation members may be limited to their investment. (b) Once incorporated, corporation continues to exist until extinguished by relevant legal process. (c) At least two members.

3 A partnership is defined as two or more persons coming together with a view to making a profit (PA 1890). A sole trader has total responsibility for the legal liabilities and financial risks of the business.

4 (a) Partners jointly bound if Thomas had apparent authority (*Freeman & Lockyer* v *Buckhurst Park Properties* (1964), Chapter 23); (b) All partners personally liable for partnership debts.

5 A company is public if: specified in the memorandum, limited liability, plc suffix, and it has at least £50,000 authorised capital, 25 per cent of which is paid up. Any other company is private.

6 Advantages of trading as a LLP: no minimum capital requirement; reduced taxation; limited personal liability of each partner; flexibility; corporate ownership; separate legal personality.

Review questions 20 (Chapter 21: Forming a registered company)

1 Memorandum and articles, details of directors and secretary, domicile of registered office, authorised share capital, whether/how liability is limited, statutory declaration.

2 Company may be bound by a contract which exceeds its objects clause.

3 This resolution must go to a meeting of the company: special resolution requires 75 per cent majority. Re-registration required.

4 Memorandum is merely evidence of the intention of the promoters to set the company up. It is no longer part of the company's constitution.

5 By a vote at a company meeting passed by a 75 per cent majority.

6 Rather than going through the company registration process, the promoters can buy a ready-made company from a specialist service provider.

Review questions 21 (Chapter 22: Running the company – raising and maintaining capital)

1 Issued capital: potential profit raised so far by the shares issued. Called-up capital: money actually raised by calls on issued shares.

2 As a short-term measure to raise capital.

3 Ordinary shares: commonest type of share, carry most voting rights and right to dividend if declared. Preference shares: fixed dividend – priority over ordinary shares in winding up.

4 (a) Company has no obligation to issue dividends. (b) Company's articles define voting rights: not all shareholders necessarily entitled. Preference shareholders enjoy no privileges in this respect: their preferential rights may compensate for lack

of voting rights. (c) Any shareholder may lose all/some of investment on winding up: shareholders rank below the company's creditors. Preference shareholders may be paid before the equity shareholders if the articles so require. (d) Brass has made a loan to the company which is secured against its assets and should recover his investment (*Salomon* v *Salomon & Co. Ltd* (1897), Chapter 20).

5 In the interests of capital maintenance, the general rule is that a company cannot acquire its own shares. However, s 690 of the CA 2006 changed the position, enabling purchase of their own shares as long as the articles do not impose restrictions and the provisions laid down in Part 18, Chapter 4 of the Act (Purchase of Own Shares) are complied with. These require that the company can purchase its own shares only if they are fully paid up and payment is immediately made on purchase (s 691).

6 A fixed charge is a claim against a specific asset of the company, e.g. property. A floating charge does not attach to any specific property of the company until it crystallises through the company committing some act or default, e.g. stock.

Review questions 22 (Chapter 23: The management and governance of companies – functions of directors, secretary and auditors)

1 Zara has rights in agency law: CA 2006, s 39.

2 (a) Insolvency Act 1986, s 214: continuing to trade when in financial difficulty could amount to wrongful trading in the event that the company is wound up. (b) CA 2006, s 172(1): directors have a general duty of good faith to promote the success of the company and to consider the interests of all stakeholders and this includes employees.

3 Cotton is in breach of his duty under CA 2006, s 177 to declare an interest in a proposed transaction: contract voidable.

4 (a) Penny is disqualified; (b) Damien is disqualified unless he has permission to be absent, per s 174, breach of duty to exercise reasonable skill, care and diligence using s 168 procedure; (c) Twiggy's ill health entitles the company to remove him from office.

5 Anybody with inside information about the present or future value of the company's securities, who uses that information for their own profit and without disclosing it to any other relevant parties, may be guilty of insider dealing; this is a criminal offence (Criminal Justice Act 1993).

6 Removal by ordinary resolution with special notice, s 168.

Review questions 23 (Chapter 24: Company meetings, shareholder participation and minority protection)

1 General meeting: all members whose shares entitle them to vote can vote in person or by proxy.

2 (a) Plc must hold AGM within six months of accounting reference date; private company does not need to hold an AGM; (b) or where there is a serious reduction

of capital; (c) or as a result of shareholder requisition; (d) or as a result of Court order; (e) or where retiring auditor requisitions a meeting.

3 Directors must pass a resolution to remove the auditor which requires special notice to the company 28 days prior to meeting. At this meeting Xanthe may address the meeting/ circulate any written defence to members. Resolution must be passed (ordinary majority required).

4 (a) Section 98: petition to court if at least 50 shareholders/ those who hold 5 per cent of shares agree. (b) Chapter 11 proceedings, s 994: if he can prove unfair prejudice, Department for Business, Innovation and Skills intervention.

5 Derivative: shareholder acts in the company's interests. Right to sue is derived from the company's rights.

6 Ordinary resolutions require only a simple majority and are used to transact most business. Special resolutions require a majority of 75 per cent and are needed to transact some business.

Review questions 24 (Chapter 25: Statutory intellectual property protection – copyright, designs, patents and trade marks)

1 (a) Yes: if written. (b) No: not a tangible form. (c) Employer owns the copyright. (d) If format sufficiently original. If created incidentally to her work, employer owns it.

2 Copyright: design drawings and figures (if works of art). Design right under CDPA 1988. Possibly design may be registered (Registered Designs Act 1949).

3 (a) New, inventive step, capable of industrial application. (b) Owned by Fulmar as the employer. Pierre may get compensation.

4 (a) If sufficiently distinctive it is registrable: capable of graphical representation. (b) Not if too similar. (c) Not if it unjustifiably suggests royal family endorsement.

5 Copyright owners have the exclusive rights to copy, adapt or present the work publicly. Maximum duration, 70 years from author's death.

6 The design right (governed by Part III of the CDPA 1988) attaches automatically to any sufficiently original design of three dimensional objects, and gives similar protection to copyright. The author of the design acquires copyright of that design, but that gives protection only against infringements of the copy (wrongful copying and publication). Ownership of the design right enables the owner to control the use of the design for manufacturing purposes. Nobody else may make items to that design without the owner's consent. Maximum duration of protection is 15 years (No renewal).

   Some designs may qualify to be registered under the Registered Designs Act 1949 (RDA 1949) as amended by the Registered Designs Regulations 2001, Registered Designs (Amendment) Rules 2001 and the Registered Designs (Fees) Amendment Rules 2001. The rights arising from the registered design relate to the appearance of the product, its shape and any patterns or design on it. Maximum duration of protection is 25 years (five-year renewal).

Review questions 25 (Chapter 26: Common law protection of intellectual property – passing off, malicious falsehood and breach of confidence)

1 (a) Breach of confidence. (b) Passing off. (c) Malicious falsehood.

2 (i) Confidential information disclosed. (ii) Relationship of trust between the parties. (iii) Information used by confidant/third party. (iv) Resulting damage.

3 Damages, injunction, surrender of profits.

4 Greater protection: goodwill need not yet exist. Simpler to prove.

5 Traditionally breach of confidence required a special relationship and information which was obviously confidential which was then disclosed causing damage to the confidante. More recently and particularly since the Human Rights Act 1998, these criteria have been relaxed (*Max Mosley* v *News Group Newspapers Ltd* (2008); *Campbell* v *MGN Ltd* (2004)).

6 'Private information' is personal information which is private because of its nature; for example, because it concerns an individual's health or sex life. It is information in which a claimant is said to have a 'realistic expectation of privacy'. The tort 'misuse of private information' is now a distinct feature of English law in its own right (*Vidal-Hall* v *Google* (2015)).

   'Confidential information' is effectively 'secret' information. It may be confidential by virtue of an agreement (e.g. an employment contract), an established relationship (e.g. doctor–patient) or simply because it is information which has the necessary nature and quality of confidence.

Index

ACAS conciliation 474–5, 482–3
acceptance 89–96
  battle of the forms 89
  communication 89, 91–6
    authorised persons 91
    conduct 92
    electronic communications 93–4
    Internet sales 94
    methods 92–4, 96
    offer 80
    particular method, requirement for a 96
    postal rule 94–6
    verbal communication 93
    waiver 96
  conduct, acceptance by 92
  counter-offers 85–6, 89
  electronic communications 93–4
  emails 93–4
  incomplete acceptance 88
  Internet sales 94
  mirror image of offer requirement 89
  offer 80, 85–6, 88–9
  postal rule 94–6
  reasonable expectations of honest men 90–1, 93
  rewards 96
  silence 96
  standard form contracts 89
  subject to contract 89–90
  unconditional, must be 89–90
  unilateral contracts 96
  waiver 93, 96
accord and satisfaction 228
account of profits 407, 604, 626
accountability 271, 506
acquisition of companies' own shares 533–4
Acts of Parliament 32–3

administration of justice, prejudicing 207
ADR see alternative dispute resolution (ADR)
adversarial procedure 18–19, 60
advertising 80–2, 610
age discrimination 426–9
  comparators 427
  definition 427
  direct discrimination 427–8
  European law 426
  harassment 429
  indirect discrimination 427–8
  occupational qualification 428
  prohibited behaviour 427–8
  proportionality 427
  retirement age 428–9
  social policy 428–9
  victimisation 429
agency 260–78
  accountability 271
  acts of parties, termination by 272, 273–4
  actual authority 262, 268, 275
  agent, definition of 261
  agreement between parties 262–3
  apparent authority 264, 272, 275
  auctioneers 275
  authority
    actual 262, 268, 275
    agreement between parties 262–3
    apparent authority 264, 272, 275
    express 262–3
    implied 262–3
    ostensible authority 266
    own interests, linked to agent's 273–4
    retrospective 262

bankruptcy 273
breach of contract 260, 270
brokers 275
capacity 267, 273
Commercial Agents Directive 272
commercial efficiency 262
commission 262, 269, 272, 274–5
company secretaries 559–60
confidential relationships 270
conflicts of interest 271
creation of agency 261–8
death 273
deed, creation by 262
delegation 270
directors 546–7
disclosure of principal 267, 268
estate agents 274–5
estoppel 264–6
express authority 262–3
factors 275
fiduciary relationships 270, 272
frustration 273
gratuitous agency 262, 269–70
implication, creation by 262–3
implied authority 262
indemnity 269
informal agreements 262
joint liability 268
lasting powers of attorney 274
mental incapacity 273
necessity 266–7
negligence 260
operation of law, termination by 272, 273–4
ostensible authority 266
payment 262, 269, 272, 274–5
performance 270, 273
powers of attorney 262, 273–4

agency (*continued*)
  principal
    capacity 267
    death 273
    definition 261
    disclosure 267, 268
    existence 267
    joint liability 268
    rights and duties 272
    undisclosed principal 268
    undue influence 197
  privity of contract 116
  ratification 267–8
  real life example 271
  reasonable skill 270
  repudiation 271
  retrospective authority 262
  revocation 273–4
  rights and duties of agents
      269–71
  specialist agents 274–5
  termination 272–4
    acts of parties 272, 273–4
    agreement, by 273–4
    notice 272
    operation of law, by 272,
        273–4
    revocation 273–4
  third parties 260, 261–2, 267,
      272
  tort 272
  undisclosed principal 268
  undue influence 197
  vicarious liability 272, 386
allocation to tracks 62–3
allurements 367
alternative dispute resolution
    (ADR) 66–9
  arbitration 66–7, 80
  conciliation 67–8, 482–3
  consumers 68–9
  encouragement by courts 68
  European law 68–9
  mediation 68
  ombudsmen services 67, 275
  Online Dispute Resolution
      Platform 69
  Property Ombudsman 275
  telephone mediation 68
  Woolf reforms 68
ambulance services 333–4
annual general meetings (AGMs)
    570, 571

annual reports 560
annual returns 506, 558, 559
anticipatory breach 238–42
appeals 57–60
  arbitration 67
  Chancery Division 58
  Court of Appeal 41, 42, 59–60
  Crown Court 56
  Employment Appeal Tribunal
      (EAT) 58, 70
  Family Division 58
  judges 57
  magistrates' courts 56, 57–8
  Queen's Bench 57–8
  statutory interpretation 59
appellants 23
arbitration 66–7
  advantages 67
  appeals 67
  arbitration clauses 66, 80
  arbitrator, role of 66–7
  code arbitration 67
  commercial arbitration 66–7
  consumers 67
  court, intervention by the 66
  Equality Act 2010 66
  procedure 66
articles of association 516,
    519–22
  changing articles 522
  contents 519–20
  contractual terms,
      representation of 520–2
  model articles 519
  object clauses 519–20, 522–3
  real life example 522
  ultra vires 519
assignment of debts 116
assignments, writing 5–11
  CLEO (claim, law, evaluation,
      outcome) formula 7, 8–10
  discursive assignments 10–11
  evidence 6
  general advice 5–6
  plagiarism, avoidance of 6
  problem questions 7–8
  style 5
  submission requirements 6–7
  techniques 7
association, discrimination by
    423–4, 431, 436, 446, 455
assumption of responsibility
    313–14, 316–17

attachment of earnings orders 65
auctions 86–7, 275
auditors 561–2
  appoint an auditor, duty to 561
  contract 562
  duty of care 283
  functions 561
  liability 562
  meetings, requisition of 572
  negligence 562
  powers 561

bail 56
bankruptcy 273, 492, 495
barter 154
best endeavours clauses 79–80
binding precedent *see*
      precedent, law of binding
blood products, contamination of
    350, 351
board meetings 543
Bolam test 289
brands 351
breach, discharge by 237–42 *see
    also* damages for breach
      of contract
  actual breach 242
  agency 260, 270
  anticipatory breach 238–42
  companies 505
  conditions 128, 130–2, 144,
      147–9, 151, 237–8
  exemption clauses 137–8
  frustration 241–2
  fundamental breach 137–8
  mitigation 240–1
  remedies 238, 242–56
  repudiation 130–3, 143, 238–
      41, 271
  sale of goods and services 144
  unfair contract terms and
      exemption clauses 156
  warranties 128–9, 237
breach of confidence 618–25
  account of profits 626
  actionable damage 623
  agency 270
  celebrities 620–2, 625
  damages 621–2, 626
  definition 618
  confidential information,
      definition of 618–19
  contract 622–3

employment contracts 407, 610
equity 619
European Convention on Human Rights 611
Human Rights Act 1998 611, 624–5
implied terms 622–3
informal duty 620
injunctions 619, 625–6
operation of law 620–2
private and family life, right to respect for 624–5
public interest defence 623–4
remedies 626
restraint of trade 623
super injunctions 625
trade secrets 618–19
unfair trading 610
when duty arises 620–1
breach of contract *see* breach, discharge by
breach of duty 284–92
  Bolam test 289
  breach of statutory duty 290, 368, 415
  burden of proof 291–2
  causation 291
  children 288
  clinical negligence 289
  Compensation Act 2006 289–91
  directors 571
  foreseeability 288
  good practice 288
  harm, extent of potential 285–6
  learner drivers 288
  likelihood of an accident happening 285
  precautions 286–7
  product liability 343, 348
  proof 348
  qualifications claimed by defendant 287–8
  reasonableness 284–6, 289–91
  res ipsa loquitur 291–2
  rescuers 290–1
  risk-benefit analysis 286–7
  risk management 290
  skilful claimants 287–8
  Social Action, Responsibility and Heroism Act 2015 290

unhappy outcomes 289
volunteers, protection of 290–1
breach of statutory duty 290, 368, 414–16
Brexit 31, 399, 605–6
brokers 275
business organisations 490–512
  fair trial, right to a 509
  freedom of expression 509
  Human Rights Act 1998 508–9
  incorporation 491–2
  legal personality 491–2
  limitation of liability 490, 492
  partnerships 490, 492–7, 510
  peaceful enjoyment of possessions 508–9
  private and family life, right to respect for 509
  registered companies 497–508, 510
  sole traders 490, 492
but for test 292–6
bye-laws 33

cancellation 118, 162
capacity *see* incapacity
capital *see* share capital, raising and maintaining
care and skill
  agency 270
  breach of duty 287–8
  directors 551
  employment contracts 405
  occupiers' liability 367
  partnerships 494
  reasonableness 154, 270
  supply of goods and services 154
case law and statute law 23–4
case management conferences 63
causation
  breach of duty 291
  but for test 292–6
  clinical negligence 292–3, 296, 298–9
  Compensation Act 2006 295
  consequential loss or damage, proof of 292–300
  eggshell skull rule 299–300
  fact, in 292–6
  foreseeability 292, 297–9

intervening acts 298–9
joint and several liability 295
law, in 292, 297–300
loss of a chance 296
mesothelioma 294–6
multiple causes 293–6
precautions 292
product liability 345, 352
public interest/policy 294
remoteness 292, 297–300
tort 292–300
caveat emptor 142
Chancery Division 57, 58
change of circumstances 176
changing the law
  common law 39
  Companies Act 2006 508
  economic and technological change 22
  Green Papers 32
  Law Commission 35, 253, 330, 356, 577
  political change 22
  public inquiry reports 35
  social change 22
  White Papers 32
Chapter 11 proceedings 577
characteristics of English law 18–19
  adversarial nature 18–19
  evolution over centuries 18
  judicial creativity 18
  precedent, law of binding 18
  Roman law influence 18
charges
  chargeable assets 537–8
  fixed charges 538
  floating charges 538
  loan capital 537–8
  registration 537–8
  security behind loans 537–8
charging orders 65
charterparties 129–30, 132–3
children *see also* minors, contractual capacity of
  breach of duty 288
  occupiers' liability 362
civil claims 62–5
  allocation to tracks 62–3
  bringing cases 60
  case management conferences 63
  Civil Procedure Rules 60–1, 68

civil claims (*continued*)
  claim forms 62
  costs 60–1, 63
  Court of Appeal 41, 42, 59
  criminal law, differences from
    20–1
  damages 64–5
  defendant's response 62
  execution of judgments 64–5
  fast track claims 63, 68
  funding 60
  industrial injuries 410–16
  injunctions 64
  interlocutory stages 63–4
  issue of claims 62
  legal aid 60
  letters of claim 62
  multi-track claims 63, 68
  pre-action protocols 62
  real life examples 20–1, 65
  reasons for not enforcing
    claims 60
  rights of audience 64
  small claims track 62–3
  starting civil actions 62–4
  tracing 60
  trials 64
  Woolf reforms 60
civil partnerships *see* marriage
  and civil partnership
claimants and defendants 23
CLEO (claim, law, evaluation,
  outcome) formula 7,
  8–10
clinical negligence 289, 292–3,
  296, 298–9
codification 35
collateral contracts 116–17
collective agreements 404
comfort letters 114
commercial agreements
  consideration 100
  course of a business 144
  intention to create legal
    relations 111, 114
  sale of goods and services
    143–52
commission 262, 269, 272, 274–5,
  407
commissioners of photographs
  and films, rights of 589
common law 34–5

change, presumption
  against 39
codification 35
directors 547–8
duty of care 410–14
employment contracts 398,
  404, 405–8, 410
Equality Act 2010 426
equity 23–4
formation of contract 77
illegality 204
implied terms 123–4, 405
industrial injuries 410–14
intellectual property 610–28
minority shareholders 577
quantum of damages 247
statutory interpretation 39
statutory law 23–4, 35
terms 122–41
unfair dismissal 464
Common Foreign and Security
  Policy (CFSP) 27
companies *see* auditors;
    company secretaries;
    directors; formation of
    companies; registered
    companies; share capital,
    raising and maintaining;
    shareholders
company secretaries 558–60
  agent, authority to act as
    company's 559–60
  annual reports 560
  annual returns 559
  compliance with Companies
    Acts, ensuring 559
  functions 559–60
  qualifications for office 559
  role 560
compensation *see also* damages
  breach of duty 289–91
  Compensation Act 2006 289–
    91, 295, 368
  Consumer Rights Act 2015 166
  defective buildings 313
  digital content 166
  employment tribunals 484–6
  occupiers' liability 368
  redundancy 465, 476, 477–9
  wrongful dismissal 466
competent staff, provision of
  410–11, 412

Competition and Markets
  Authority (CMA) 162
competitions 114
composition with creditors
  108–10
compulsory purchase 231
conciliation 67–8, 482–3
conditions 122–3, 128–32
  breach 128, 130–2, 144, 151,
    237–8
  implied terms 144, 147–9, 153
  innominate terms 129–30
  rejection 151
  sale of goods and services 144,
    147–9, 151
  supply of goods and
    services 153
  warranties 237
conduct
  misrepresentation, by 174
  mistake 189–90
  offer 83
  unfair dismissal 470–2
confidentiality *see* breach of
  confidence
conflicts of interest 271, 407,
  544, 548–9, 552
consequential loss or damage
  economic loss 310–11, 315,
    347
  product liability 348–9
  proof 292–300
consideration 101–11
  adequate consideration 104
  commercial agreements 100
  composition with creditors
    108–10
  definition 101
  economic duress 105–7
  executed consideration 101–2
  executory consideration 101
  existing legal duties 105–7
  gratuitous or bare promises
    100, 102, 110
  intention 100–1
  move from promisee,
    consideration must 103
  mutuality 100
  part payment 107–10
  past consideration 102–3
  privity of contract 101, 115–16
  promissory estoppel 110–11

promotions 104
real life examples 102, 108
rewards 102
rules 102–7
sufficient consideration 103–10
constructive dismissal 409, 467–8, 477
Consumer Rights Act 2015 162–8
compensation 166
consumer, definition of 163
definitions of key terms 163
digital content 162, 165–8
exclusion of liability 156, 162, 165, 166–8, 317
goods 162–8
misrepresentation 173, 179
reasonableness 166
reductions or refunds 166
rejection, right of 164
remedies for defective performance 166–7
repairs or replacements 164–5
repeat performance 165, 166
sale of goods and services 160
services 162–8
supply of goods 163–4, 165, 166
unfair contract terms and exemption clauses 143, 156, 162, 167–8
consumers see also Consumer Rights Act 2015
ADR 68–9
arbitration 67
consumer credit 78
Consumer Rights Directive 162
definition 160, 345
inequality of bargaining power 67
sale of goods and services 143, 160–2
unfair contract terms and exemption clauses 156, 160–1, 167
contra proferentem rule 137
contract law see also breach, discharge by; defects in contract; discharge of contracts; employment contracts; exemption clauses (limitation or exclusion

clauses); formation of contracts; implied terms; terms of contract
arbitration 66
articles of association 520–2
auditors 562
breach of confidence 622–3
contractual capacity 204, 217–20, 522–3
directors, long-term service contracts of 555
illegality 204, 205–17
pre-incorporation contracts, company promoters' liability for 515–16
privity of contract 101, 115–18
rescission 253–4
standard form contracts
standard term contracts 77, 89, 156
supply of goods and services 152–9
contributory negligence 302–3, 370, 373
damages
quantum 245, 253
reduction in 302
industrial disease 303
product liability 346
smoking 303
copyright 587–91
acquisition 588
artistic works 588
Berne Convention 606
commissioners of photographs and films, rights of 589
defences 590
definition 587
design right 591–2
duration 589
employees, creation by 589
European law 591, 605
exclusive rights 590
films 589
infringement 590–1
Internet users 591
licensing 590
literary works 587
moral rights 589
originality 587
ownership 589, 590

performances and recordings, rights in 588, 591
Performing Rights Society (PRS) 590
photographs 589
regulation 587–91
sanctions 590
tangible form, items must be in 588
transfer 589
UK, connection with 588
Universal Copyright Convention 606
corporations see auditors; company secretaries; directors; formation of companies; registered companies; share capital, raising and maintaining; shareholders
corruption in public life, contracts promoting 207–8
costs 60–1, 63
county courts
Court of Appeal 59
financial limits 56–7
High Court, transfers from the 57
judges 56
precedent 41
small claims track 63
Court of Appeal
Civil Division 41, 42, 59
county courts 59
Criminal Division 41, 42, 59–60
Crown Court 59
employment tribunals 70
High Court 59
Lord and Lady Justices of Appeal 58–9
precedent 41, 42
Supreme Court 59
tribunals 58
court system 55–60
appellate functions 57–60
county courts 56–7
Crown Court 56
hierarchy of courts 55
High Court 57
law-making 26, 34–43
magistrates' courts 55–6

criminal offences *see also* fraud
  civil law, differences from 20–1
  companies 504–5, 518
  contracts to commit crime, tort
      or fraud 205
  corporate manslaughter 504–5
  Court of Appeal 41, 42, 59–60
  Crown Court 56, 59
  directors 552, 558
  either way offences (hybrid
      offences) 55
  fines 56
  imprisonment 56
  indictable offences 56, 558
  insider dealing 562–4
  nuisance 381
  patents 599
  Police and Judicial
      Cooperation in Criminal
      Matters (PJCCM) 27–8
  real life example 20–1
  regulatory offences 55
  safety in the workplace 399,
      416–18
  sentencing 56
  summary offences 55
Crown Court
  appeals 56, 59
  bail 56
  indictable offences 56
  judges 56
  legal aid 56
  magistrates' courts 59
  precedent 41
  sentencing 56
Crown, use of term 23
custom and practice
  employment contracts 404
  implied terms 127
  terms of contract 127, 130,
      132–3

damages *see also* compensation;
      damages for breach of
      contract; quantum of
      damages
  adequacy of damages 253–4
  breach of confidence 621–2
  breach of statutory duty 414
  contributory negligence 302
  employment tribunals 485
  equal pay 453

equitable remedies 253
execution of judgments 64–5
inhuman or degrading
    treatment 45–6
insider dealing 562
intellectual property 604
malicious falsehood 617, 626
nuisance 385
passing off 626
payments into court 61
penalties for non-payment of
    damages 485
Rylands v Fletcher, rule in 385
specific performance 254
unfair dismissal 467
damages for breach of contract
    242–53
  anticipatory breach 238
  breach of confidence 626
  foreseeability 244
  Hadley v Baxendale 243–5
  misrepresentation 180, 181–4
  purpose 242–3
  remoteness 242–5
  repudiation 238
  special damage 243
  usual damage 243
debentures 536–7, 538–9
  distinguished from shares 539
  loan capital 507–8, 536–7
  real life example 538–9
  series debentures 537
  single debentures 536
  stock 537
deceit 179–80
deeds 78
defective buildings 312–13
defective products *see* product
    liability
defects in contract 172–200 *see
    also* misrepresentation;
    mistake
  duress 194–6
  undue influence 196–200
  void contracts 173
  voidable contracts 172
defence and prosecution 23
defendants and claimants 23
delegated legislation 32, 33–4
  advantages and
      disadvantages 34
  bulk of legislation 34

bye-laws 33
flexibility 34
frequency of changes 34
Orders in Council 33
parliamentary control,
    loss of 34
regulations to implement
    European law 33
saving of Parliamentary time 34
scrutiny 34
sitting, passing legislation
    when Parliament not 34
specialist knowledge 34
statutory instruments 33
delegation 270, 391–2, 401, 410
delivery up 604
derivative actions 577, 578
description, sale by 144,
    145–7, 153
  examination of goods 146–7
  form of description 145
  quality 146
  reliance 146
  samples 145, 151
design rights 591–5
  Community design right
      593, 595
  copyright 591–2
  definition 591
  design, definition of 592
  exclusive rights 595
  individual character 593
  industrial designs 592
  inventive design 591
  licensing 592, 595
  novelty 593
  ownership 594
  product, definition of 593
  registered Community
      designs 595
  registered designs 591,
      593–5
  spare parts 594
destruction orders 604
development risks defence
    350, 356
digital content 162, 165–8 *see
    also* Internet
directives 30
directors 543–58
  agency 546–7
  alternate directors 544

annual general meetings
    (AGMs) 570
annual returns, failure to
    make 558
appointment 543–4
articles of association 523
board meetings 543
breach of duty 571
care, skill and diligence,
    exercise of reasonable 551
codification of duties 508
Combined Code 543–4
common law duties 547–8
Companies Act 2006 550–6
conflicts of interest 544,
    548–9, 552
creditors, duties to 554
criminal offences 552, 558
de facto directors 545–6
disclosure 548, 552, 556
disqualification 558
duties 547–56
    codification of duties 508
    creditors, to 554
    general 550–4, 564
duty of care 547–8
equitable duties 548–9
executive (managing) directors
    543, 544
fees and expenses 556
fiduciary duties 548–9
Financial Reporting Council
    (FRC) Code of Practice 564
fraudulent trading 558
golden handshakes, approval
    of 555
good faith 546, 548, 550
independent judgment,
    exercise of 551
indictable offences, conviction
    for 558
insolvent companies, unfit
    conduct by 558
interests in proposed
    transactions or
    arrangements with
    company, declaration
    of 552–3
lay (non-executive)
    directors 543
liquidation 554
loans, approval of 555

long-term service contracts,
    approval of 555
minority shareholders 571,
    577–81
negligent statements 502
powers 546–7
    abuse 546–7
    limitations 546
promotion of success of
    company 550–1
removal 556–7
remuneration 544, 556, 563
reporting 556
resignation 557–8
retirement 556–7
rights of directors 556
service agreements 544
shadow directors 545
shareholders
    annual general meetings
        (AGMs) 570
    approval, transactions
        requiring 554–5
    minority 571, 577–81
    relationship with 570
    reporting 556
substantial and material
    property transactions,
    approval of 555
third parties 546–7, 552
ultra vires 547, 550
disability discrimination 429–33
    addictions 430
    association, discrimination
        by 431
    comparators 432
    consequential unfavourable
        treatment 431
    depression 430
    direct discrimination 431
    disability, definition of 429
    enquiries about disability and
        health 433
    European law 431
    frustration 230
    impairment, definition of 430
    indirect discrimination 431–2
    long-term, how long is 430
    normal day-to-day
        activities 429
    obesity 430
    occupational requirement 431

perception, discrimination by
    431
prohibited conduct 431
provisions, criteria or practices
    (PCPs) 432
reasonable adjustments 432–3
recruitment 433
substantial and long-term
    adverse effect 428
discharge of contracts 225–42 see
    also breach, discharge by
accord and satisfaction 228
agreement, discharge by 228
bilateral discharge 228
frustration 228–37, 241–2
performance, discharge by
    225–8
unilateral discharge 228
disciplinary procedures 464–5,
    474–5
disclaimers 315, 317, 319
disclosure
    directors 548, 552, 556
    equal pay 453
    insurance 177
    misrepresentation 175–7
    principal and agent 267, 268
    search orders 64
    volunteer information, failure
        to 175–6
discretion 253, 333–8
discrimination see also Equality
    Act 2010
    employment tribunals 483, 485
    recommendations 585
dishonesty 253
dismissal see unfair dismissal;
    wrongful dismissal
dispute resolution 54–73 see
    also alternative dispute
    resolution (ADR)
    civil courts, bringing a case in
        the 60, 62–4
    civil litigation procedures 62–5
    court system 55–60
    execution of judgments 64–5
    payments into court and offers
        to settle 61
    settlements out of court 61–2
    trials 64
    tribunal system 69–70
    Woolf reforms 60–1, 68

disqualification of directors 558
distance contracts 162
distraint orders 65
dividends 535
Divisional Courts 41
domain names 518
domestic or social situations
        111–14
    car pool agreements 112
    detrimental reliance 112
    financial detriment 112
    maintenance agreements 112
    prizes 113–14
    reliance 317
dress 49, 440–1, 444
duress 194–6
    costs, rise in 185
    economic duress 105–7, 194–6
    factors to be considered 194
    threats 194
    voidable contracts 194–5
duty of care 282–4 see also
        breach of duty
    auditors 283
    common law 410–14
    development of duty 282–3
    directors 547–8
    fair, just and reasonable test
        283
    foreseeability 282, 283
    incremental approach 338
    industrial injuries 410–14
    neighbour principle 282, 308,
        343–5
    nervous shock 322, 324, 326,
        329–30
    new situations 282
    occupiers' liability 370–2
    omissions 331
    product liability 343, 346–8
    proximity 283, 284
    public interest/policy 283, 284
    reasonableness 283
    special duty situations 308 9,
        318, 338
    standard of care 289–90, 365,
        367–8

economic duress 105–7, 194–6
economic loss 308–9, 310–15
    alternative remedies, existence
        of 312–13, 318

consequential loss
    distinguished 310–11, 315,
    347
criteria determining existence
    of a special relationship
    315–21
defective buildings 312–13
insurance 311–12
negligent statements 314–21
nuisance 382
product liability 346–8
proximity 313–21
    degree of proximity 313–14
    reliance 313–155
    voluntary assumption of
        responsibility 313–14
pure economic loss 308–9,
    310–15, 346–8, 357, 382
quasi-fiduciary relationships
    315
reliance 313–14, 319
special duty situations 308–9,
    310–21
education 337
effective remedy, right to an 454
eggshell skull rule 299–300
either way offences (hybrid
        offences) 55
ejusdem generis rule 36
electronic communications 82,
    93–4
employment see employment
    contracts; employment
    tribunal claims; safety in the
    workplace; unfair dismissal
employment contracts 399–410
    account of profits 407
    breach of confidence 610
    Brexit 399
    business efficacy 404
    care and skill, duty to work
        with reasonable 405
    collective agreements 404
    common law 398, 404, 405–8,
        410
    confidential information 407
    conflict with employers'
        interests 407
    constructive dismissal 409
    continuation of existing terms
        and conditions after
        transfer 482

continuity of employment, date
    for 402–3, 408
contracting out 400
contracts for services 387, 399
contracts of services 387, 392,
    399, 403–4
control test 401
copyright 589
custom and practice 404
delegation or personal
    performance 401
divisible contracts 226
employees
    definition 399, 400–1
    delegation or personal
        performance 401
    factors which help determine
        status 400–3
    independent contractors,
        distinguished from 387–8,
        399–401
    labels 500
employee shareholders 400
express terms 404
factors which help determine
    status 400–3
financial risk and capital outlay
    400
form of contract of services
    402–3, 404
gig economy 401–3, 408
good faith 406–7, 409
implied terms 404, 405
independent contractors
    399–403
    definition 399–401
    delegation or personal
        performance 401
    employees, distinguished
        from 387–8, 399–401
    factors which help determine
        status 400–3
    labels 400
    vicarious liability 400
industrial action 406
injunctions 255–6
labels 400
minimum wage/living wage
    407–8
minors, contractual capacity of
    218–19
mutuality of obligation 408

negligence 405
oral contracts 402
orders, duty to obey
    reasonable 405–6
performance, discharge by 226
provide work, obligation
    to 408
red tape challenge 398
restraint of trade 210–15
safe working conditions
    407, 410
sex equality clauses 446
shams 400
sources of terms 404, 405
statute as source of terms
    404, 405
summary dismissal 465
transfer of undertakings 482
trust and confidence 407, 409
unfair dismissal 400, 402,
    408–9
vicarious liability 400
wages, duty to pay 407–8
work and staff rules 404
worker, definition of 399–400
working time 405, 408
written statement of terms
    contents of 402–3
    penalties for failure to
        provide 403
wrongful dismissal 465–6
zero hours contracts 408
employment tribunal claims
    482–5
ACAS conciliation 482–3
appeals 69–70
compensation 484–5
Employment Appeal Tribunal
    (EAT) 58, 70
equal pay 453
Equality Act 2010 457
fees 483
judges 70
jurisdiction 69
penalties for non-payment of
    damages 485
recommendations 485
reinstatement and
    re-engagement 484
remedies 484–5
sex discrimination and fees 483
time limits 483

unfair dismissal 60, 465, 466–7
unpaid award penalties 484
wrongful dismissal 466
enemy aliens, contracts with 207
enforcement
    Equality Act 2010 357
    judgments, execution of 64–5
    specific performance 253,
        254–5
    state, enforcement of law by
        the 17
    unfair contract terms and
        exemption clauses 162,
        168–9
Equality and Human Rights
    Commission (EHRC) 458–9
equal pay 448–54
    benefits 448
    bonuses 453
    comparators 450–1, 452
    damages 453
    disclosure 453
    employment tribunals 453
    enforcement 453–4
    equality clauses 448, 449–50
    equal value 448, 450
    equal work 448–50
    equivalent work 448, 449–50
    European law 448, 451
    gagging clauses 453
    gender pay gap reporting 453
    hypothetical comparators 451
    information, entitlement to 453
    job evaluation 449–50
    like work 448–9
    market forces 452
    material differences 449, 451–2
    part-time workers 448
    pensions 448, 451, 453
    pregnancy and maternity
        452–3
    transparency 453–4
    victimisation 453
Equality Act 2010 422–62 see
    also equal pay
    age discrimination 426–9
    arbitration 66
    association, discrimination by
        423–4
    combined discrimination 424
    common law 426
    comparators 424

core provisions 423–62
defences 424
direct discrimination 423–4,
    425
disability discrimination 429–33
employment tribunals 457
enforcement 457
Equality and Human Rights
    Commission (EHRC) 458–9
    core functions 458–9
    reform 459
gender re-assignment
    433–4
harassment 425, 457
indirect discrimination 424
irrelevance of discriminator's
    characteristics 424
justification 425
knowledge 426
marriage and civil partnership
    434–5
occupational requirements
    424, 425
offer 82
operation of Act 426
perception, discrimination
    by 423
positive action 458
potential claimants and
    defendants 426
pregnancy and maternity
    435–6
prohibited conduct 423–6
promotion of equality
    457–8
protected characteristics
    423–62
provisions, criteria or practices
    (PCPs) 424
public sector equality duty
    457–8
race discrimination 436–41
religion or belief 441–5
sex discrimination 445–54
sexual orientation 454–7
socio-economic duty 458
specific equality duties 458
vicarious liability 426
victimisation 425, 457
volunteers 426
equality of bargaining power 67,
    156–9, 167, 213, 408

equitable remedies 253–6 *see also* injunctions
   damages, adequacy of 253
   discretion 253
   dishonesty 253
   mistake 189–90, 192–3
   oppression 253
   rectification 192–3
   rescission 179–80, 183–5, 200, 253–4
   specific performance 253, 254–5
equity *see also* equitable remedies
   breach of confidence 619
   case law 23–4
   directors 548–9
   estoppel 110–11, 264–6
   fiduciary relationships 176, 197–9, 270, 272, 315, 494
   statutory law 23–4
estate agents 274–5
estoppel 110–11, 264–6
EU law *see* European law
European Convention on Human Rights (ECHR) 43–50
   breach of confidence 611
   EU, confusion with 44
   European Court of Human Rights 44–50
   law-making 26–7
   sexual orientation discrimination 454
   statutory authority, defence of 303
European law 26, 27–31
   Acquired Rights Directive 480
   ADR 68–9
   age discrimination 426
   Brexit 31, 399, 605–6
   Commercial Agents Directive 272
   Common Foreign and Security Policy (CFSP) 27
   Community design right 593, 595
   Consumer Rights Directive 162
   copyright 591, 605
   Council of the EU 28, 29
   decisions 30
   directives 30
   disability discrimination 431

Economic Community 27
equal pay 448, 451
Equal Treatment Directive 441
EU, creation of 27
EURATOM 27
European Coal and Steel Community (ECSC) 27–8
European Commission 28, 29
European Convention on Human Rights 44
European Council 28
European Court of Justice (ECJ) 29
   advocates-general 29
   breach of EU legal obligations 29
   Court of First Instance (CFI) 29
   functions 29
   judges, number of 29
   penalties 29
   preliminary references 29
   priority of European law 29
   workload 29
European Parliament 29
European Trade Mark (ETM) 599, 603, 605
First Company Law Directive 523
impact on English law 30–1
implement European law, regulations to 33
insider dealing 562
institutions 28–9
intellectual property 604–6
Internet sales 94
law-making 26, 27–31
patents 599, 605
Police and Judicial Cooperation in Criminal Matters (PJCCM) 27–8
pregnancy and maternity 435
priority of European law 28
product liability 349–50, 354, 358
Protected Food Name scheme 605
registered Community designs 595
regulations 30
religion or belief 441
safety in the workplace 414, 416, 418

sexual orientation discrimination 454
sources of European law 30
statutory interpretation 38
three pillars 27–8
trade marks 599, 603, 605–6
treaties 30, 31
ultra vires 520
unfair contract terms and exemption clauses 143, 161–2, 167
Unitary Patent Court 605
examination of goods 146–7, 149, 150, 343, 345
examination techniques 14–15
execution of judgments 64–5
exemption clauses (limitation or exclusion clauses) 133–9 *see also* unfair contract terms and
exemption clauses
   ambiguity 134, 137–8
   clarity 134
   Consumer Rights Act 2015 165, 166, 317
   contra proferentem rule 137
   definition 123
   digital content 166
   disclaimers 315, 317, 319
   exclusion clauses, definition of 133
   fundamental breach 137–8
   incorporation 134
   insurance 137
   limitation clauses, definition of 133
   misrepresentation 179
   notice 123, 134–9
      real life example 138–9
      signatures 136–7
      sufficiency 134, 136
      timing 134–5
   occupiers' liability 369
   real life example 138–9
   signatures 136–7
   unfair contract terms 138–9
express terms 122–3, 404

factors 275
fair, just and reasonable test 283, 318–21, 322, 334, 347–8
fair trial, right to a 335, 509

Family Division 57, 58
Family Proceedings Court (FPC)
    56
fast track claims 63, 68
fiduciary relationships 176, 197–9,
    270, 272, 315, 494
films 589
Financial Reporting Council (FRC)
    Code of Practice 542,
    564–5
fines 56, 407, 418
fire brigade 333–4
fixed charges 538
floating charges 538
food 342, 605
force majeure clauses 233
foreign relations, contracts
    damaging to 206
foreseeability
    breach of duty 288
    causation 292, 297–9
    damages 244
    duty of care 282, 283
    frustration 232, 233
    industrial injuries 410, 413
    malicious falsehood 617
    negligence 309, 318, 338
    negligent statements 314, 317,
        320
    nervous shock 321–7, 330
    nuisance 373, 377–9, 382, 383
    occupiers' liability 362–3, 366
    passing off 614
    product liability 343, 349
    remoteness 244
    Rylands v Fletcher, rule in 384
    stress 413
formation of contracts *see also*
    acceptance; consideration;
    offer
    essentials of binding contracts
        77–8
    common law 77
    deeds 78
    formalities 76
    intention to create legal
        relations 111–15
    simple or parol contracts 76
    writing 77–8
formation of companies 514–28
    articles of association 516,
        519–22

changing articles 522
contents 519–20
contractual terms,
    representation of 520–2
object clauses 519–20,
    522–3
real life example 522
ultra vires 519
charter companies 491
constitution 516, 518–19
constructive notice 523–4
contractual capacity 522–3
corporations sole 492
dissolution of companies
    525–6
effect of registration 518
liquidation 525–6
    compulsory 526
    voluntary 525
memoranda of association 516,
    518–19, 523
names 517–18
object clauses 519–20, 522–3
off the shelf, buying companies
    525
operation of law, creation by
    491
pre-incorporation contracts,
    promoters' liability for
    515–16
process of registration 516–17
promotion of the company
    514–16
registered officers 516
re-registration of companies
    498, 524
statute, creation by 491
streamlining registration
    process 518
ultra vires 519–20, 524
Foss v Harbottle, rule in 577
franchises 214
free gifts 154
freedom of expression 45, 47,
    49, 509
fraud
    contracts to commit crime, tort
        or fraud 205
    fraudulent trading 503, 558
    misrepresentation 174–5, 179–
        80, 188–9
    Statute of Frauds 78

freedom of assembly 47
freedom of expression 45, 47, 49
freezing injunctions 64
frustration 228–37
    advance payments, recovery of
        235–7
    agency 273
    breach 241–2
    burdensome, where contract
        has become more 232
    compulsory purchase 231
    consequences 234–5
    Coronation cases 231
    death or illness of one of
        parties 229–30
    delay in performance 229, 232,
        233
    destruction or unavailability of
        subject matter 229, 234
    disability discrimination 230
    expense, increase in 232
    expenses, recovery of 234–6
    failure of event on which
        contract is based to occur
        229, 231
    force majeure clauses 233
    foreseeability 232, 233
    government intervention 229,
        231
    impossibility 228
    imprisonment 231
    inconvenience 232
    Law Reform (Frustrated
        Contracts) Act 1943 235–6
    limitations of rule 232–3
    mistake 234
    radical change in obligation 228
    real life example 234
    risk 233
    self-induced frustration 233–4
    supervening illegality 228, 229,
        230–1, 232
    valuable benefit, right to cost
        of a 236–7
    wartime 231, 242
fundamental breach 137–8
funding 56, 60, 68, 70

gagging clauses 453
gender *see* equal pay; gender
    re-assignment; sex
    discrimination

gender re-assignment 433–4
  certificates 434
  Gender Recognition Act 2004
      434
  harassment 433, 434
  indirect discrimination 433
  medical treatment 433
  occupational requirement 434
  prohibited behaviour 433
  victimisation 433
general meetings 571–6
  additional meetings 571–2
  annual general meetings
      (AGMs) 571
  auditors, requisition by retiring
      572
  chairing the meeting 573
  conduct of meetings 573–4
  court orders 472
  notice 572–5
    contents 573
    length 572
    method of giving notice 573
    passing resolutions 574–5
    resolutions 574
    written resolutions, passing
      574–5
  proxies 576
  quorum 573
  requisition by members 572
  resolutions 571, 573–4
    ordinary 574
    special notice, resolutions
      requiring 574
    special resolutions 574
  revolts by shareholders 575–6
  rules 572–3
  serious reduction of capital 572
  voting 575–6
gig economy 401–3, 408
golden handshakes 555
good faith 161, 167, 406–7, 409,
      546, 548, 550
goods see sale of goods and
      services, statutory terms
      for; supply of goods and
      services
goodwill 611
governance of companies see
      also auditors; company
      secretaries; directors
  CEOs, remuneration of 563–5

diversity 564
Financial Reporting Council
      (FRC) Code of Practice
      542, 564–5
  UK Corporate Governance
      Code 562–4
Green Papers 32
grievance and disciplinary
      procedures 464–5, 474–5
guarantee, companies limited by
      503–4
guarantees 78, 220

Hadley v Baxendale 243–5
Hansard 36, 39
harassment
  age discrimination 429
  Equality Act 2010 425, 433,
      434–6, 447, 457
  gender re-assignment
      433, 434
  marriage and civil partnerships
      435
  pregnancy and maternity 436
  sex discrimination 447
  sexual orientation
      discrimination 454, 455–6
health and safety at work see
      safety in the workplace
hierarchy of courts 40–1, 55
High Court
  Chancery Division 57
  county courts, transfers from
      57
  Court of Appeal 59
  divisions 57
  Family Division 57
  judges 57
  precedent 41
  Queen's Bench Division 57
  Supreme Court 59, 60
Hillsborough disaster 324–30
hire contracts 155
hire purchase 144, 155
holidays 117, 247–9
homosexuality see sexual
      orientation discrimination
human rights see European
      Convention on Human
      Rights (ECHR); Human
      Rights Act 1998
Human Rights Act 1998 43–50

Bill of Rights, proposals for
      replacement with 50
breach of confidence 611,
      624–5
business organisations 508–9
controversial decisions 50
damages 45–6
direct effect 46–7
effective remedy, right to an 454
European Convention on
      Human Rights 43–50
European Court of Human
      Rights 44–50
fair trial, right to a 335, 509
freedom of assembly 47
freedom of expression 45, 47,
      49, 509
impact of Act 46–9
indirect effect 46–7, 49
injunctions 45, 49
judges
  function of 44–6
  law-making 43–50
law-making 43–50
legal background 44
liberty and security, right to
      47–8
life, right to 47
list of rights 44
nuisance 385–6
operation of HRA 44–6
peaceful enjoyment of
      possessions 385, 508–9
persuasive precedents 44
political background 44
prisoners' right to vote 45
private and family life, right to
      respect for 47, 49, 385–6,
      509, 624–5
proportionality 47–9
public authorities 44, 46, 335,
      337, 508
reform 50
remedies 45–6
repeal, calls for 50
sex offenders' register 47
sexual orientation
      discrimination 454
statutory interpretation 44–5, 49
thought, conscience and
      religion, freedom of 49,
      441, 444

identity, mistakes as to 187–92
illegality 205–17
    administration of justice,
        prejudicing 207
    common law 204
    competition 205
    consequences 208–10
    contract law 204, 205–17
    corruption in public life,
        contracts promoting 207–8
    crime, tort or fraud, contracts
        to commit 205
    definition 204
    enemy aliens 207
    foreign relations, contracts
        damaging to 206
    marriage, contracts prejudicial
        to 208
    partnerships 495
    price-fixing 205
    public interest 204, 205,
        209–10
    public policy 205, 209–10
    public safety, contracts
        endangering 207
    purposes which are against the
        law 204
    restraint of trade 210–17
    Revenue, contracts to defraud
        the 207
    sexually immoral purposes,
        contracts for 206
    statute, by 205
    unjust enrichment 206, 208,
        210
    void contracts 204, 205, 208
    vulnerable parties 209
    waiver 209
    withdrawal from contracts
        208–9
immigration rights 69
implied terms 123–8
    breach of confidence 622–3
    business efficacy 124–6
    business sense 126–7
    business to business
        agreements 128
    common law 123–4, 405
    conditions 144, 147–9, 153
    definition 122
    employment contracts 404,
        405

hire purchase 144, 155
    offer 80
    purposive interpretation 124
    sale of goods 127–8, 144–52,
        160
    satisfactory quality 144, 147–9
    sources 123–8
    statute, implied by 127–8
    supply of goods and services
        154, 155
    trade custom and practice 127
    unfair contract terms and
        exemption clauses 156,
        161
impossibility 228
imprisonment 56
improvement notices 418
incapacity 217–21
    agency 267, 273
    contractual capacity 204, 217–20,
        522–3
    mentally impaired persons 204,
        220, 273
    minors, contractual capacity of
        204, 217–20
incorporation of companies 491–2,
        499–508
independent contractors 399–403
    definition 399–401
    delegation or personal
        performance 401
    employees, distinguished from
        387–8, 399–401
    factors which help determine
        status 400–3
    labels 400
    non-delegable duties 391–2
    occupiers' liability 368
    safety in the workplace 417
    vicarious liability 387–8, 391–2,
        400
inducement 156–7, 173, 177–9
industrial diseases 303
industrial injuries, employers' civil
    liability for 410–16
    breach of statutory duty
        414–16
    common law duty of care
        410–14
    competent staff, provision of
        410–11, 412
    foreseeability 410, 413

    negligence 410
    non-delegable duty 410
    precautions 413
    real life example 412
    safe premises, plant and
        equipment, provision of
        410, 411, 412, 415–16
    safe system of work, provision
        of 410, 411–12
    stress-related illnesses 412–14
    tort 410–16
inequality of bargaining power
    67, 156–9, 167, 213, 408
information, requests for 64
inhuman or degrading treatment
    337
injunctions
    breach of confidence 619,
        625–6
    compelling performance 256
    employment contracts
        255–6
    freezing injunctions 64
    Human Rights Act 1998 45, 49
    intellectual property 604
    interlocutory injunctions 64
    malicious falsehood 626
    nuisance 381, 385
    passing off 626
    restraint of trade 255–6
    Rylands v Fletcher, rule in
        385
    super injunctions 625
innominate terms 123,
    129–33, 154
    breach 129–33
    charterparties 129–30
    conditions 129–33
    definition 123, 129
    warranties 129–30
inquisitorial procedure 19, 63
insider dealing
    definition 562
    monitoring corporate dealings
        562–4
    UK Corporate Governance
        Code 562–4
insolvency 65, 482, 558 *see also*
    liquidation
instructions 148, 149, 348, 352
insurance 116, 137, 168, 177,
    311–12, 334

intellectual property *see also* copyright; patents; trade marks
  account of profits 604
  common law protection 610–28
  damages 604
  delivery up 604
  design rights 591–5
  destruction orders 604
  European law 604–6
  injunctions 604
  mental effort 586
  passing off 611–16
  remedies 604
  seizure 604
  treaties and conventions 606
intention 130–1, 175, 297 *see also* intention to create legal relations
intention to create legal relations 111–15
  business agreements 111, 114
  comfort letters 114
  domestic or social agreements 111–14
  negotiations 8203
  offer 78, 80–4
Internet
  acceptance 94
  Consumer Rights Act 2015 162, 165–6
  copyright 591
  domain names 518
  electronic communications 82, 93–4
  European law 94
  passing off 616
  social media 471–2
  unfair dismissal 471–2
interpretation *see* statutory interpretation
intervening acts 298–9
invitations to treat 80–2, 84–5
  advertisements 80–2
  electronic commerce 82
  mere puffs 80
  self-service shops 81
  shop displays 81–2
  tenders 84–5

joint and several liability 295, 495
judges
  appeals 57, 58–9
  common law 34–5
  county courts 56
  creativity 18, 34–5
  Crown Court 56
  district judges 55
  European Court of Justice (ECJ) 29
  High Court 57
  Human Rights Act 1998 43–50
  law-making 26, 34–43
  Lord and Lady Justices of Appeal 58–9
  Lords of Appeal in Ordinary 59
  magistrates' courts 55
  statutory interpretation 35–6, 39–40
  Supreme Court 59
jurisdiction 17, 69
justices of the peace (JPs) 55

kettling 48

land *see* occupiers' liability; sale or transfer of land
law, definition of 16–17
  enforcement by the state 17
  jurisdiction 17
  rules 17
  state, created by the 17
law-making 26–52
  courts 26, 34–43
  European law 26, 27–31
  European Convention on Human Rights 26–7
  Human Rights Act 1998 43–50
  Parliament 26, 32–4
law reporting system, importance of 42
leap-frog procedure 60
learner drivers 288
legal funding 56, 60, 68, 70
legal personality 491–2
legislation *see* delegated legislation; statutory law
letters of claim 62
liberty and security, right to 47–8
life, right to 47
limited liability partnerships (LLPs) 496

limited partnerships 495–6, 497
limitation of liability *see also* exemption clauses (limitation or exclusion clauses)
  companies 503–4, 506–7
  business organisations 490, 492, 500–4, 506–7
  limitation clauses, definition of 133
  names 518
  product liability 345–6
  sale of goods and services 148–9
liquidation 525–6
  compulsory liquidation 526
  continuous succession 506
  creditors' voluntary liquidation 525
  directors 554
  fraudulent trading 503
  members voluntary liquidation 525
  separate property rights 507
  share capital, raising and maintaining 535
  voluntary 506, 525
living wage *see* minimum wage/living wage
loan capital 507–8, 530, 536–9
loss of a chance 296
loss of profits 243–4, 245

magistrates' courts 55–9
  appeals 56, 57–8
  Crown Court 56, 59
  district judges 55
  either way offences (hybrid offences) 55
  Family Proceedings Court 56
  fines 56
  imprisonment 56
  justices of the peace (JPs) 55
  precedent 41
  Queen's Bench Division 57–8
  regulatory offences 55
  sentencing 56
  summary offences 55
  Youth Court 55
maintenance agreements 112
malicious falsehood 616–17
  account of profits 626

business, relating to 616
damage requirement 617
damages 626
definition 610
dual liability 617
foreseeability 617, 626
goodwill 616
injunctions 626
malice, definition of 617
passing off 617
manufacturers 160, 343–7, 350–1,
    355–6, 358
marriage and civil partnerships
    425, 434–5
  brokerage contracts 208
  contracts prejudicial to
      marriage 208
  harassment 435
  indirect discrimination 435
  occupational qualification
      defence 435
  pre-nuptial agreements 208
  prohibited behaviour 435
  protected characteristic 434
  LGBT couples 434
  undue influence 198–9
  victimisation 435
maternity see pregnancy and
    maternity
media 3, 471–2
mediation 68
medical negligence 289
medication
  Pearson Commission 349, 356
  Thalidomide 349
meetings see also general
    meetings
  annual general meetings
      (AGMs) 570, 571
  board meetings 543
  resolutions 570
  shareholders 570
memoranda of association 516,
    518–19, 523
mental distress, hurt feelings and
    disappointment, damages
    for 245, 247–9
mentally impaired persons
  agency 273
  contractual capacity 204, 220,
      273
  incapacity 204, 220

knowledge of impairment 220
  necessaries 220
  powers of attorney 273
mere puffs 80
mesothelioma 294–6
minimum wage/living wage 407–8
  bands 407
  fines 407
  name and shame system 407
  tips 407
minority shareholders 577–81
  abuse, protection from specific
      types of 581
  Chapter 11 proceedings 577
  common law 577
  Department for Business,
      Energy and Industrial
      Strategy, initiation of
      intervention by 580
  derivative actions 577, 578
  directors, breach of duties by
      571
  Foss v Harbottle, rule in 577
  Law Commission 577
  real life example 581
  statutory protection 577–80
  unfair prejudice petitions
      578–80
minors, contractual capacity of
    204, 217–20
  contracts capable of binding a
      minor 217–18
  employment, beneficial
      contracts of 218–19
  guarantee of minors' debts 220
  minor, definition of 217
  necessaries 217–18
  ratification of debts 220
  restitution 220
  services 218
  unenforceable contracts 219–20
  voidable contracts 219
misrepresentation 173–84
  actionable misrepresentation
      173
  carelessness 181–2
  change of circumstances 176
  conduct 174
  Consumer Rights Act 2015
      173, 179
  damages 180, 181–4
  deceit 179–80

disclosure 175–7
exemption clauses 179
fiduciary relationships 176
fraud 174–5, 179–80, 188–9
future performance, estimates
    as 175
half-truths 176
incorporation as term 173
inducement 173, 177–9
innocent misrepresentation
    181–3
intention 175
material inducements 177–9
negligence 180–1
opinions 174
reasonableness 177, 179–80
reliance 178
remedies 173, 179–80, 184
rescission 179–80, 183–4
statements of fact 174–7
statements of law 175
unfair contract terms and
    exemption clauses 179
voidable contracts 173, 176–9,
    184, 188–9
volunteer information, failure
    to 175–6
mistake 184–94
  common mistake 185–92
  conduct 189–90
  equitable remedies 185, 192–3
  fraudulent misrepresentation
      188–9
  frustration 234
  identity
    contracting party 187–92
    subject matter 187
  non est factum 193–4
  operative mistakes 194–5
  mutual mistake on identity of
      subject matter 187
  quality 185
  real life example 194
  reasonableness 189
  rectification, equitable remedy
      of 192–3
  rescission 184–5
  sale of land 185
  signatures 193–4
  subject matter 185–92
  terms of contract, unilateral
      mistake as to 192

mistake (*continued*)
  unilateral mistake 187–8,
    192–3
  void contracts 184–6, 192
  voidable title 188–9
mitigation 240–1, 245, 252–3
multi-track claims 63, 68
Muslim dress and school uniform
  49

names
  companies 517–18
  partnerships 494, 497
  trade marks 600
National Health Service (NHS),
  ADR in 68
nationality discrimination 437,
  438, 439
nature of law 16–25
  changing the law 22
  characteristics of English law
    18–19
  criminal and civil law,
    differences between 20–1
  essential legal terms 22–4
  law, definition of 16–17
  need for law, whether there is
    a 19
necessaries 217–18, 220
necessity 266–7
negligence 280–306 *see
  also* breach of duty;
    contributory negligence;
    duty of care;
negligence and special duty
    situations; negligent
    statements
  agency 260
  auditors 562
  employment contracts 405
  industrial injuries 410
  occupiers' liability 363, 365,
    373
  product liability 342–3, 346–9,
    355, 358
  public authorities and statutory
    discretion 333–8
  reasonable care 280
  unfair contract terms and
    exemption clauses 155,
    160, 168, 317
  unfair dismissal 469–70

negligence and special duty
    situations 308–41
  criteria determining existence
    of a special relationship
    315–21
  duty of care 308–9, 318, 338
  economic loss 308–9, 310–21
  fair, just and reasonable test
    318–21
  foreseeability 309, 318, 338
  negligent statements 314–18,
    325–30, 502
  neighbour principle 308
  nervous shock 321–30
  omissions 330–1
  proximity 309, 313–21, 338
  public authorities and statutory
    discretion 333–8
  public interest 318
  restrictions on liability 308–9
  third parties 331–3
negligent statements
  directors 502
  disclaimers 315, 317, 319
  economic loss 314–21
  fair, just and reasonable test
    318
  foreseeability 314, 317, 320
  Hedley Byrne principle 180–1,
    315, 317, 325, 502
  misrepresentation 180–1
  nervous shock 325
  proximity 315–21
  real life example 320–1
  reasonableness 314, 316–17
  reliance 314, 316–17, 321
    circumstances in which
      advice given 317
    disclaimers or conditions 317
    foreseeability 317
    reasonable 314, 316–17
    reliable advice, ability to
      give 317
    social situations 317
  restrictions on *Hedley Byrne*
    principle 317
  special duty situations 314–18,
    325–30
  third parties 315–16
  voluntary assumption of
    responsibility 316–17
negotiations 82–3

neighbour principle 282, 308,
  343–5
nervous shock (psychiatric harm)
  321–30
  aftermath 322, 326–8
  bad news, delivery of 325
  close bonds of love and
    affection 327–8, 330
  definition 321
  duty of care 322, 324, 326,
    329–30
  fair, just and reasonable test
    322
  foreseeability 321–7, 330
  Hillsborough disaster 324–30
  involuntary participants 323
  Law Commission 330
  medically recognisable
    illnesses or conditions 321
  negligent statements 325
  physical injury distinguished
    322
  pleural plaques 322–3
  primary victims 321, 322–3,
    325
  proximity 326–30
  public interest 324
  rescuers 324–5
  secondary victims 321–2, 326–30
  special duty situations 321–30
  sudden and immediate shock
    327, 330
  television, witnessing events
    on 327
  witnesses 321–2, 326–30
noise 248–9, 373, 376–8, 381
non est factum 193–4
note-taking 4, 12–13
novus actus interveniens 298–9
nuisance 363, 373–81 *see also*
    private nuisance
  foreseeability 373
  Human Rights Act 1998
    385–6
  inconvenience 373
  peaceful enjoyment of
    possessions 385
  private and family life, right to
    respect for 385–6
  public nuisance 373, 381–3
  Rylands v Fletcher, rule in
    384–5

obiter dictum 42
objects clauses 519–20
obstruction 382, 391, 417
occupiers' liability 362–73
    actionable damage 369, 373
    allurements 367
    breach of statutory duty 368
    children 367, 371
    Compensation Act 2006 368
    compliance 366
    consent to presence 365
    contractors, liability for 368
    contributory negligence 370,
        373
    control of premises 364
    dangerous premises, definition
        of 364
    defences 370, 373
    discharging the duty 368–9
    duty of care 370–2
    exclusion of liability 369
    extent of duty 365, 372
    foreseeability 362–3, 366
    knowledge 371, 373
    negligence 363, 365, 373
    neighbours 362–3
    notices 370, 373
    nuisance 373, 379–80
    occupier, definition of 364
    Occupiers' Liability Act 1957
        363, 364–70, 386
    Occupiers' Liability Act 1984
        368, 370–2, 386
    performance of the duty 372
    precautions 365, 368–70
    premises, definition of 364
    reasonable care 365, 368,
        372–3
    resources 371
    risk assessment 366
    roam, right to 370–1
    special skills, visitors with 367
    standard of care 365, 367–8
    trespassers 370–3
    unfair contract terms and
        exclusion of liability 369
    visitors 364, 365, 367, 370–1
    volenti non fit injuria 370
    voluntary assumption of
        responsibility 373
    warnings 368–9, 373
    when duty is owed 371–3

offer 78–88
    acceptance 85–6, 89
    best endeavours clauses
        79–80
    bilateral offers 78
    clearly stated terms 78–80
    communication of intention 78,
        83–4
    conduct, by 83
    counter-offers 85–6, 89
    death, effect of 85
    Equality Act 2010 82
    intention to create legal
        relations 78, 80–4
    invitations to treat 80–2, 84–5
    lapse of time 86
    mirror image of offer
        requirement 89
    negotiations 82–3
    offeree, definition of 78
    offeror, definition of 78
    open, promises to keep offers
        87–8
    prices, misleading 82
    rejection 85–6
    revocation, notice of 86–8
    rewards 78, 84
    tenders 84–5
    termination of offers 85–8
    unilateral offers 78, 83–4, 88
ombudsmen 67, 275
omissions 330–3
    duty of care 331
    false omissions 331
    foreseeability 332
    legal duties to act 331
    misfeasance 330
    moral justifications for
        intervention 330–1
    nonfeasance 330
    pre-existing relationships
        332–3
    special duty situations 330–1
    third parties, acts of 331–3
Online Dispute Resolution
    Platform (ODRP) 69
opinions 174
oral contracts 402
orders, duty to obey reasonable
    405–6
Orders in Council 33
overdraft charges 168

pain and suffering, damages for
    246
Parliament 32–4
    Acts of Parliament 32–3
    delegated legislation 32, 33–4
    direct legislation 32
    Hansard 36, 39
    law-making 26, 32–4
    Pepper v Hart 36, 39
    reports 36
    sovereignty 43, 35, 37
    statutory interpretation 25–7
part payment 107–10
partnerships 490, 492–7, 510
    agents of the others, partners
        as 494
    agreements 493
    care and skill 494
    court orders, dissolution
        through 495
    death or bankruptcy 495
    definition 493
    dissolution 495
    fiduciary relationships 494
    formation of partnerships 493
    illegality 495
    joint and several liability 495
    lapse of time, dissolution
        through 495
    limited liability partnerships
        (LLPs) 496
    limited partnerships 495–6,
        497
    names 494, 497
    notice of dissolution 495
    number of partners 494
    professions 493, 494
    public scrutiny 497
    purpose of partnership,
        achievement of 495
    registered companies,
        distinguished from 510
    registration 496
    tax 496
    traditional partnerships
        493–5
    unincorporated associations
        492–3
    vicarious liability 494
passing off 611–16
    account of profits 626
    actionable damage 614

passing off (*continued*)
advertising 610
damages 626
definition 610
foreseeability 614
goodwill 611, 613
injunctions 626
Internet 616
malicious falsehood 617
packaging 610
real life example 615–16
registration 615
trade marks 599, 602, 610,
610
patents 595–9
applications 598
criminal liability 599
definition 595
duration 598
European patent 599, 605
industrial application 596
infringement 598–9
inventive step 596
licensing 599
novelty 595
ownership 598
patent agents 597–8
real life example 596
registration
process 597–8
right to register 597
substantial examination and
registration 598
search and publication 598
substantial examination and
registration 598
Unitary Patent Court 605
pay *see* equal pay; minimum
wage/living wage; wages
payments into court 61
peaceful enjoyment of
possessions 385, 508–9
pensions 448, 451, 453
per incuriam 40–1
perception, discrimination by
423, 431, 446, 455
performance
acceptance of performance
227
agency 270, 273
delay 229, 232, 233
delegation 401

digital content, remedies for
defective performance of
165, 166
discharge by performance
225–8
divisible contracts 226
employment contracts 226
entire contracts 226
exceptions 225, 226–8
frustration 229, 232, 233
future performance, estimates
as to 175
injunctions compelling
performance 256
occupiers' liability 372
part performance 225–8
prevention of completion by
one party 226–7
remedies for defective
performance 165, 166–7
repeat performances 165, 166
specific performance 253,
254–5
substantial performance 227–8
photographs 589
planning permission 375–6, 378
pleural plaques 322–3
police
discretion 334–7
duty of care 335–6
Human Rights Act 1998 337
life, right to 335–6
Police and Judicial
Cooperation in Criminal
Matters (PJCCM) 27–8
private and family life, right to
respect for 337
positive action 458
postal rule 94–6
powers of attorney 262, 273–4
enduring 274
irrevocable 274
lasting 274
mental incapacity 273
pre-action protocols 62
precautions
breach of duty 286–7
causation 292
contributory negligence 346
nuisance 377
occupiers' liability 365, 368–70
product liability 346

safety in the workplace 413,
417
stress 413
precedent, law of binding 18,
40–3, 55
advantages and disadvantages
43
certainty 43
county courts 41
Court of Appeal Civil Division
and Criminal Division 41, 42
Crown Court 41
distinguishing 42
Divisional Courts 41
flexibility 43
haphazard development 43
hierarchy of courts 40–1, 55
High Court 41
Human Rights Act 1998 44
law reporting system,
importance of 42
magistrates' courts 41
obiter dictum 42
overruling decisions 42
parliamentary sovereignty 43
per incuriam 40–1
persuasive precedents 40,
42–3, 44
practical nature 43
Privy Council, Judicial
Committee of 42–3
ratio decidendi, scope of 41–2
relevance of previous decisions
40, 41–2
retrieval problems 43
reversing decisions 42
speed 43
Supreme Court 40–1, 42
undemocratic, system as
being 43
pregnancy and maternity 435–6
association, discrimination
by 436
direct and indirect
discrimination 436
equal pay 452–3
European law 435
prohibited behaviour 436
protected period 436
victimisation and
harassment 436
prescription 380–1

prices
  fixing prices 205
  misleading prices 82
  reasonableness 154
  shares 533
prisoners' right to vote 45
Privy Council, Judicial Committee
    of 42–3
prizes 113–14
private and family life, right to
    respect for 337, 385–6,
    454, 509, 624–5
Private Members' Bills 32
private nuisance 373–81
  amenity damage 373–5
  burden of proof 378–9
  damages 385
  foreseeability 377–9
  inconvenience 373
  injunctions 385
  landlords 380
  licences 380
  locality 375–6
  motive 377
  naturally occurring events 379
  noise 373, 376–8, 381
  occupiers 373, 379–80
  owners 379
  planning permission 375–6,
      378
  precautions 377
  prescription 380–1
  prevention, practicability of 377
  proof of liability 373
  public benefit 378
  reasonableness 375–9
  sensitivity 377–8
  smells 373
  smoke 373
  standing to sue 379–80
  tenants 379–80
  timing, level, duration and
      frequency of nuisance 377
  unreasonable interference
      373–5
  vibration 373
  who may be sued 380
privity of contract 115–18
  agency 116
  assignment of contractual
      debts 116
  cancellation 118

collateral contracts 116–17
consideration 101, 115–16
Contracts (Rights of Third
    Parties) Act 1999 101,
    117–18
double liability 118
exceptions 116–17, 118
group, contracts for the benefit
    of a 116
holidays 117
insurance 116
reform 117–18
trusts 116
variation 118
withdrawal 118
problem questions 7–8
product liability 342–61
  actionable damage 356–7
  agricultural products 352
  blood products, contamination
      of 350, 351
  brands 351
  breach of duty 343, 348
  carelessness 352
  causation 345, 352
  consequential damage 348–9
  consumer, definition of 345
  Consumer Protection Act 1987
      349–58
  contributory negligence 346
  control, goods no longer under
      defendant's 345
  dangerousness 352–4
  defences 354–7
  defendants, identity of 351
  duty of care 343, 346–8
  economic loss 346–8
  European law 349–50, 354, 358
  examination 343, 345
  fair, just and reasonable test
      347–8
  fault 349–50
  food 342
  foreseeability 343, 349
  importers 351
  instructions 348, 352
  lapse of time 346
  Law Commission 356
  limitation of liability 345–6
  manufacturers 343–7, 350–1,
      355–6, 358
  medication 349

negligence 342–3, 346–9, 355,
    358
neighbour principle 343–5
normal uses of product 352
own brands 351
packaging 352
precautions 346
privity of contract 342
product, definition of 344,
    351–2
producers 351
proximity 348
quality 347
real life example 347, 358
remoteness 343, 349
risk/benefit analysis 354
safety standards 353–4
standing to sue 350
state of the art defence/
    development risks defence
    350, 356
strict liability 349–50, 355, 358
substances won or abstracted
    351
suppliers 351
supply, methods of 351
tampering 345
time limits 357
time when product was issued
    352
trade marks 351
ultimate consumers 343, 345
warnings 348, 352, 354
prohibition notices 418
promises
  gratuitous or bare promises 88,
      100, 102, 110
  open, promises to keep offers
      88
  promissory estoppel 110–11
  unilateral promises 102
Property Ombudsman 275
property rights 385, 508–9
proportionality
  age discrimination 427
  Human Rights Act 1998 47–8
  race discrimination 440–1
  religion or belief, discrimination
      on grounds of 442–3
  sexual orientation
      discrimination 455
prosecution and defence 23

prospectuses 533
proxies 576
proximity 309, 313–21
  degree of proximity 313–14
  duty of care 283, 284
  economic loss 313–21
  negligent statements 315–21
  nervous shock 326–30
  product liability 348
  public authorities 334, 336–7
  reliance 313–155
  special duty situations 309,
    313–21, 338
  trust 315
  voluntary assumption of
    responsibility 313–14
psychiatric harm *see* nervous
  shock (psychiatric harm)
public authorities 333–8
  alternative remedies 336
  ambulance services 333–4
  discretion 333–8
  education 337
  fair, just and reasonable test
    334
  fair trial, right to a 335
  fire brigade 333–4
  Human Rights Act 1998 44, 46,
    335, 337, 508
  insurance 334
  negligence 333–8
  police 334–7
  private and family life, right to
    respect for 337
  proximity 334, 336–7
  public policy 333
  public sector equality duty
    457–8
  social services 336–7
  statutory authority, defence of
    303
  statutory discretion 333–8
public companies 497–8, 507,
  533–4
public interest/public policy
  breach of confidence 623–4
  causation 294
  duty of care 283, 284
  illegality 204, 205, 209–10
  nervous shock 324
  public authorities 333
  rescuers 324–5

special duty situations 318
  trade marks 601
public nuisance 373, 381–3
  criminal behaviour 381
  damage requirement 382
  damages 385
  economic loss 382
  foreseeability 382, 383
  injunctions 381, 385
  obstruction 382, 391
  occupational rights 381
  pollution 381
  potential defendants 381
  proof of liability 382
  public, definition of 382
  reasonableness 382–3
  scope of liability 381
  special damage 381
  standing to sue 381
  statutory offences 381
  vicarious liability 391
public policy *see* public interest/
  public policy
public safety, contracts
  endangering 207

quality
  description 146
  implied terms 144, 147–9
  mistake 185
  product liability 347
  sale of goods and services 144,
    146, 147–9
  satisfactory quality 144, 147–9,
    153, 160
  supply of goods and services
    153
quantum of damages 242–3,
  245–53
  agreed damages 245, 249–51
  common law 247
  contributory negligence 245,
    253
  dismissal from employment,
    manner of 246
  liquidated damages 249–52
  loss of profits 243–4, 245
  mental distress, hurt feelings
    and disappointment 245,
    247–9
  mitigation 245, 252–3
  noise 248–9

pain and suffering 246
  peace of mind obligations
    247–9
  penalties 245, 249–52
  physical inconvenience 248–9
  quantifiable loss 245–6
  reliance losses 245–6
  reputation 245, 247
  stigma damages 245
  unfair dismissal 246–7
Queen's Bench Division 57–8
questions and answers 632–50

race discrimination 436–41
  colour 437, 439
  defences 439
  direct discrimination 439
  dress codes 440–1
  ethnic or national origins
    437–8, 439
  indirect discrimination 439–41
  nationality 437, 438, 439
  occupational qualification 439
  prohibited conduct 439–40
  proportionality 440–1
  protected characteristics 437–8,
    439–40
  racial group, definition of 438
  real life example 440–1
  unfair dismissal 439
  vicarious liability 440
ratification 220, 267–8, 549
ratio decidendi, scope of 41–2
real property *see* occupiers'
  liability; sale or transfer of
  land
rectification 192–3
reductions or refunds 166
redundancy 476–80
  cause of dismissal 477
  change of workplace location
    477
  compensation 465, 476, 477–9
  constructive dismissal 477
  consultation 474
  continuous service 402, 477
  definition 476
  dismissal, existence of 477
  eligibility 477
  financial entitlement 479
  payments 465, 476, 477–9
  status of employees 477

suitable alternative
employment, offers of 478
time limits 478
unfair dismissal 472, 474, 477
reform see changing the law
registered companies 497–508,
510 see also auditors;
company secretaries;
directors; formation of
companies; share capital,
raising and maintaining;
shareholders
accountability 506
advantages of incorporation
506–8
breach of contract 505
capital, raising 507–8
Companies Act 2006 508
Companies Register 506
consequences of incorporation
499–506
continuity 508
continuous succession 506
corporate manslaughter 504–5
criminal offences 504–5, 518
deregulation 498
guarantee, companies limited
by 503–4
holding and subsidiary
companies 499
incorporation 491–2, 499–508
insolvency 65, 482, 558
legal personality 491–2
limited liability 492, 500–4,
506–7
liquidation 506–8, 525–6
ownership and management
506
partnerships 510
private companies 498
public accountability 506
purpose of registration process
497
public companies 497–8, 507,
533–4
real life examples 499, 505
re-registration as public
company 498, 524
separate entity distinct from
members, company as
500–3
separate property rights 507

shares, companies limited by
497, 503
shares, transferability of 507
tax 507
tort 505
types 497–9
unlimited liability 504
veil of incorporation 500–3
regulatory offences 55
reinstatement and
re-engagement 484
rejection, right of 143, 151–4,
160, 164
relationship breakdowns,
mediation and 68
reliance
circumstances in which advice
given 317
damages 245–6
description 146
disclaimers or conditions 317
domestic or social agreements
112
economic loss 313–14, 319
explicit reliance 150
foreseeability 317
implicit reliance 149–50
misrepresentation 178
negligent statements 314,
316–17, 321
proximity 313–15
reasonableness 314, 316–17
reliable advice, ability to give
317
sale of goods and services 146,
149–50
social situations 317
religion or belief 441–5
belief, definition of 441–2
direct discrimination 442
dress 49, 440–1, 444
education, right to 49
employers with a religious
ethos 445
Equal Treatment Directive 441
indirect discrimination 442–3
manifest religion or belief, right
to 443
occupational requirement
444–5
organised religions 445
prohibited behaviour 442–4

proportionality 442–3
religion, definition of 441
school uniform and Muslim
dress 49
sexual orientation 443–4, 445,
456–7
thought, conscience and
religion, freedom of 49,
441, 444
remedies see also damages
for breach of contract;
equitable remedies;
injunctions
account of profits 407, 604, 626
breach of confidence 626
breach of contract 242–56
Consumer Rights Act 2015
165–6
defective performance 165,
166–7
delivery up 604
destruction orders 604
digital content 166
effective remedy, right to an
454
employment tribunals 484–5
Human Rights Act 1998 45–6,
454
intellectual property 604
misrepresentation 173, 179–80,
184
public authorities and statutory
discretion 336
wrongful dismissal 466
remoteness
causation 292, 297–300
foreseeability 244
intention 297
product liability 343, 349
trespass 297
remuneration see equal pay;
minimum wage/living
wage; wages
repairs or replacements 151–2,
160, 165, 166
repudiation 238–41
agency 271
damages 238
notice 239–40
sale of goods and services 143
terms of contract 130–3
reputation 245, 247

res ipsa loquitur 291–2
rescission 179–80, 183–5, 200, 253–4
rescuers 290–1, 300–1, 324–5
resignation 469
resolutions 571, 573–4
    ordinary resolution 574
    shareholders' meetings 570
    special notice, resolutions requiring 574
    special resolutions 574
resources 629–31
    background information 629–30
    specialist texts 629–30
    websites 630–1
respondents 23
restitution 220
restraint of trade 210–17
    breach of confidence 623
    competition 212
    employment contracts 210–15
    franchises 214
    inequality of bargaining power 213
    injunctions 255–6
    purposive interpretation 214, 217
    real life example 212–13
    reasonableness 212–17
    sale of a business 210, 215
    severance 216–17
    solus agreements 210, 216
    void restraint, consequences of 216
retrospectivity 39, 262
retirement
    age 428–9, 473
    directors 556–7
    unfair dismissal 473
Revenue, contracts to defraud the 207
revision techniques 11–13
    battle plans, working out 13
    morale, maintaining 13
    note-taking while reading 12–13
    testing knowledge 13
    thorough reading 12
    time planning 11–12
revocation
    agency 273–4
    offer 86–8

rewards 78, 84, 96, 102
rights issues 533
rights of audience 64
roam, right to 370–1
Roman law 18
Rylands v Fletcher, rule in 383–5
    accumulation 383
    damages 385
    defences 384
    escapes from land 383–4
    foreseeability 384
    injunctions 385
    non-natural user 383–4
    nuisance 384–5
    statutory authority, defence of 303
    strict liability 384
    things within the rule 383

safety in the workplace 416–18
    breach of statutory duty 414
    contracts of employment 407, 410
    corporate manslaughter 504–5
    criminal law 399, 416–18
    employees, duties of 417
    employers, duties of 417
    European law 414, 416, 418
    fines 418
    Health and Safety Executive (HSE) 416, 417–18
    improvement notices 418
    independent contractors 417
    industrial injuries, employers' liability for 410–16
    ministerial regulations 418
    obstruction 417
    policies 417
    precautions 413, 417
    premises, plant and equipment, provision of 410, 411, 412, 415–16
    prohibition notices 418
    prosecutions 417
    resources 417
    safe system of work, provision of 410, 411–12
    statutory duties 416–17
    strict liability 414, 416–17
    third parties, duty to 417
    time limits 418
    tort 399

trade unions 417
    visitors 417
    working conditions 407, 410
sale of goods and services, statutory terms for 142–52
    see also unfair contract terms
    breach 144, 151
    caveat emptor 142
    commercial sales 143–52
    conditions 144, 147–9, 151
    consumers 143, 160–2
    course of business 144
    description 144, 145–7, 151
    European law 128
    examination of goods 146–7, 149, 150
    implied terms 127–8, 144–52, 160
    instructions 148, 149
    limit of liability 148–9
    mistreatment of goods by buyers 149
    notice of defects 148–9
    packaging 148
    quality 128, 144, 146, 147–9
    real life example 150
    rejection, right of 143, 151–2, 160
    reliance 146, 149–50
    repairs 151–2, 160
    replacement 160
    repudiation 143
    sale of goods contract, definition of 144
    samples 144, 145, 150–1
    satisfactory quality 144, 147–9, 160
    secondhand goods 144, 148
    strict liability 144
    suitable for purpose 144, 149–50
    title 145
    transfer ownership, lawful authority to 144
    unfair contract terms and exclusion clauses 143
    warranties 151
sale or transfer of land
    deeds 78
    estate agents 274–5
    gazumping 89–90

mistake 185
Property Ombudsman 275
rescission 185
specific performance 254
subject to contract 89–90
trespass 297, 370–3
writing 77
samples 144, 145, 150–1, 153
satisfactory quality 144, 147–9,
    153, 160
school uniform and Muslim
    dress 49
search orders 64
secondhand goods 144, 148
self-employed see independent
    contractors
sentencing 56
services see sale of goods and
    services, statutory terms
    for; supply of goods and
    services
settlements
    costs penalties 61
    fast track claims 68
    offers to settle 61
    payments into court 61
severance 216–17
sex discrimination 445–54 see
    also equal pay
    association, discrimination
        by 446
    comparators 446
    direct discrimination 446
    employment tribunal fees 483
    harassment 447
    indirect discrimination
        447–53
    men 446
    occupational qualification 447
    perception, discrimination
        by 446
    prohibited behaviour 446–7
    protected characteristics of
        sex 446
    provisions, criteria or practices
        (PCPs) 447
    sex equality clause 446
sex offenders' register 47
sexually immoral purposes,
    contracts for 206
sexual orientation discrimination
    454–7

armed forces 454
association, discrimination
    by 455
comparators 455
direct discrimination 455, 457
effective remedy, right
    to an 454
European Convention on
    Human Rights 454
European law 454
harassment 454, 455–6
Human Rights Act 1998 454
indirect discrimination 455
occupational qualification 455
perception, discrimination
    by 455
private and family life, right to
    respect for 454
prohibited behaviour 454–6
proportionality 455
religion or belief 443–4, 445,
    456–7
stereotyping 455
vicarious liability 455–6
victimisation 454
share capital, raising and
    maintaining 507–8, 530–41
acquisition of own shares
    533–4
called-up capital 531
charges
    chargeable assets 537–8
    fixed charges 538
    floating charges 538
    registration 537–8
    security behind loans 537–8
classes of shares 531–2
debentures 507–8, 536–7,
    538–9
    distinguished from
        shares 539
    real life example 538–9
    series debentures 537
    single debentures 536
    stock 537
deferred/founders' shares 532
dividends 535
issued capital 531
liquidation 535
loan capital 507–8, 530, 536–9
ordinary/equity shares 532
paid-up capital 531

preference shares 532
price of shares 533
prospectuses 533
public limited companies
    (PLCs), issue of shares by
    498, 533–4
redeemable shares 532
reduction 572
rights issues 533
sale of shares 530
serious reduction of capital 572
shareholders
    acquiring shares from the
        company 534–5
    existing shareholders,
        acquiring shares from 535
    rights 535–6
    transfer of shares 535–6
    transparency 536
    treasury shares 532
    uncalled capital 531
    voting at company meetings
        535
shareholders
    acquiring shares from the
        company 534–5
    allotment of shares 535
    approval, transactions requiring
        554–5
    articles of association 521
    directors 554–6, 570
    dividends 535
    employee shareholders 400,
        466
    existing shareholders,
        acquiring shares from 535
    meetings 535, 570
    memoranda of association 516
    minority shareholders
        577–81
    ownership and management
        506
    reporting 556
    resolutions 570
    rights 531–2, 535–6
    transfer of shares 535–6
    transparency of share
        ownership 536
    ultra vires 524
    voting 535
shares, companies limited by
    497, 503

signatures 136–7, 193–4
skill *see* care and skill
small claims track 62–3
smells 373
smoke 373
smoking 303
Social Action, Responsibility and Heroism Act 2015 290
social media 471–2
social policy 428–9
social services 336–7
social situations *see* domestic or social situations
sole traders 490, 492
solus agreements 219, 216
special duty situations *see* negligence and special duty situations
specific performance 254–5
  damages, adequacy of 254
  debt, enforcement of 254
  hardship 255
  sale of land 254
  supervision 254
spouses *see* marriage and civil partnerships
standard of care 289–90, 365, 367–8
standard term contracts
  acceptance 89
  battle of the forms 89
  unfair contract terms and exemption clauses 156
  writing 77
state of the art defence/development risks defence 350, 356
Statute of Frauds 78
statutory instruments 33
statutory interpretation 35–40
  appeals 59
  common law, presumption against changing the 39
  contextual approach 36
  ejusdem generis rule 36
  European law 38
  external aids 35–6, 38
  golden rule 37–8
  Hansard 36, 39
  Human Rights Act 1998 44–5, 49

Interpretation Act 1978 35
intrinsic aids 35
judicial presumptions 39–40
judicial principles 35–6
Law Commission or public inquiry reports 35
literal rule 36–7, 38
mischief rule 38
parliamentary reports 36
parliamentary sovereignty 35, 37
Pepper v Hart 36, 39
purposive approach 38–9, 124, 214, 217
real life example 39
retrospectivity, presumption against 39
strict liability, presumption against 39–40
statutory authority, defence of 303
statutory law *see also* statutory interpretation
  Acts of Parliament 32–3
  common law 23–4, 35
  employment contracts 404, 405
  equity 23–4
  Green Paper 32
  illegality 205
  implied terms 127–8
  pre-legislative stage 32
  Private Members' Bills 32
  procedure 32–3
  sale of goods and services 142–52
  White Paper 32
stereotyping 455
stigma damages 245
stress-related illnesses 412–14
strict liability
  presumption against strict liability 39–40
  product liability 349–50, 355, 358
  Rylands v Fletcher, rule in 384
  safety in the workplace 414, 416–17
  sale of goods and services 144
  statutory interpretation 39–40
study skills 2–15
  assignments, writing 5–11

  examination techniques 14–15
  good habits 4–5
  knowledge, application of 4
  learning checks 5
  media 3
  misconceptions 2
  note-taking 4
  practice 4
  reading 4, 5
  relevant, law as 2–3
  revision techniques 11–13
  starting to study 2–4
  structure for learning, creation of 4
  time management 4
subject to contract 89–90
summary dismissal 465
summary offences 655
supply of goods and services 152–9
  barter 154
  conditions 153
  Consumer Rights Act 2015 163–4, 165, 166
  description 153
  free gifts 154
  goods and services contracts, definition of 152–3
  hire contracts 154
  hire-purchase 155
  implied terms 154, 155
  innominate terms 154
  minors, contractual capacity of 218
  price, reasonable 154
  reasonable care and skill 154
  reasonable time 154
  rejection 153–4
  samples 153
  satisfactory quality 153
  suitability for purpose 153
  supply of services, definition of 154
  title 153
Supreme Court 59–60
  Court of Appeal 59
  High Court 59, 60
  House of Lords, replacement of 40, 59
  Judicial Appointments Committee 59

Law Lords 59
leap-frog procedure 60
Lords of Appeal in Ordinary 59
per incuriam 40–1
precedent 40–1, 42
statutory interpretation 59
sureties 198–9

tax 207, 496, 507
telephone mediation 68
tenders 84–5
termination of contracts see
        discharge of contracts
terminology
    appellant and respondent 23
    case law and statute law 23–4
    Civil Procedure Rules 61
    claimant and defendant 23
    equity, case law as statute law
        as opposed to 23–4
    essential legal terms 22–4
    prosecution and defence 23
terms of contract 122–41 see
        also conditions; exemption
        clauses (limitation or
        exclusion clauses); implied
        terms; sale of goods and
        services, statutory terms
        for
    charterparties 129–30, 132–3
    clearly stated terms 78–80
    common law 122–41
    employment contracts 402–4,
        405
    express terms 122–3
    importance of terms 123,
        128–33
    innominate terms 123, 129–33,
        154
    intention 130–1
    mistake 192
    repudiation 130–3
    statutory terms 404, 405, 123
    time of the essence 131–2
    trade custom and practice 130,
        132–3
    warranties 122–3, 128–30, 151,
        237
    written statement of terms of
        employment 402–3
textbooks 629–30
Thalidomide 349

third parties
    agency 260, 261–2, 267, 272
    directors 546–7, 552
    negligent statements 315–17
    omissions 331–3
    privity of contract 101, 115–18
    safety in the workplace 417
    special duty situations 331–3
    third party debt orders 65
    undue influence 200
thought, conscience and religion,
        freedom of 59, 441, 444
time management 4
time of the essence 131–2
title
    fraudulent misrepresentation
        188–9
    mistake 188–9
    sale of goods and services 145
    supply of goods and services
        153
tort see also duty of care;
        negligence
    agency 272
    auditors 562
    causation 292–300
    companies 505
    consequential loss or damage,
        proof of 292–300
    contracts to commit crime, tort
        or fraud 205
    defences 300–3
    industrial injuries
    statutory authority, defence
        of 303
tracing 60
trade custom and usage see
        custom and practice
trade marks 599–603
    assignment 603
    definition 599
    distinctiveness 600–1
    duration of protection 601
    emblems 601
    European Trade Mark (ETM)
        599, 603, 605–6
    identical or similar marks 601–2
    infringements 599, 601–3
    licensing 603
    Madrid Protocol 6–6
    morally offensive, marks which
        are 601

names 600, 603
non-verbal marks 600
passing off 599, 602, 610, 615
people, names of 600
product liability 351
products, names of 600
public interest 601
purpose 599
registration
    marks capable of registration
        600–1
    process 601
trade secrets 618–19
trade unions 404, 417, 493
transfer of land see sale or
        transfer of land
transfer of undertakings 480–2
    Acquired Rights Directive 480
    continuation of existing terms
        and conditions 482
    economic, technical or
        organisational reasons
        (ETOs), transfers for 482
    European law 480–1
    information and consultation
        with employees 481
    information, provision of
        employee liability 481–2
    insolvent businesses 482
    job security 482
    relevant transfer, definition
        of 480
    rights of employees 481–2
    service provision change 480
    undertaking, definition of 481
    who is protected 481
transparency 453–4
trans-persons see gender
        re-assignment
trespass 297, 370–3
tribunal system 69–70 see also
        employment tribunal
        claims
    advantages and
        disadvantages 70
    cheapness 70
    flexibility 70
    immigration rights 69
    informality 70
    legal aid, no access to 70
    legalistic, proceedings as
        having become 70

tribunal system (*continued*)
  reform 69
  speed 70
  urgent cases 70
trust and confidence, mutual duty
    of 407, 409
trusts 116

UK Corporate Governance Code
    562–4
ultra vires 519–20, 524, 547, 550
undue influence 196–200
  affirmation 200
  burden of proof 197
  constructive notice 198–9
  delay 200
  doctor and patient relationship
    197
  fiduciary relationships 197–9
  independent legal advice 197,
    199
  presumed undue influence 197
  principal and agent
    relationship 197
  rescission 200
  solicitor and client relationship
    197
  spouses/partners 198–9
  sureties 198–9
  third parties 200
  voidable contracts 196, 200
unfair contract terms and
    exemption clauses 155–9
  ambiguity 161
  breach of contract 156
  business liability 155, 156
  cancellation rights 162
  Competition and Markets
    Authority (CMA) 162
  consequences of unfair
    terms 168
  Consumer Rights Act 2015
    138–9, 143, 156, 162,
    167–8
  Consumer Rights Directive 162
  consumers 156, 160–1, 167
  core terms 167–8
  digital content, purchase
    of 162
  distance contracts 162
  effect of an unfair term 161

  enforcement 162, 168–9
  European law 143, 161–2
  examples of unfair terms 167–8
  exclusions 155
  good faith 161, 167
  implied terms 156, 161
  inducements and choices
    156–7
  inequality of bargaining power
    156–9, 167
  information, provision of 162
  insurance 168
  misrepresentation 179
  negligence 155, 160, 168, 317
  notice 155, 168, 319
  occupiers' liability 369
  overdraft charges 168
  plain and intelligible language
    167
  prior knowledge 157
  real life example 138–9
  reasonableness 155–9, 317,
    369
  regulators 168
  sale of goods and services 143
  special requirements 157
  standard form contracts 156
  Unfair Contracts Term Act 1977
    155–61, 167, 317, 319
  unfair, definition of 167
  Unfair Terms Directive 161–2
  Unfair Terms in Consumer
    Contracts Regulations
    1999 161–2, 167
  unfairness of term 161
unfair dismissal 466–76
  actual dismissal 467
  automatic unfair dismissal 467,
    475–6
  burden of proof 469–75
  common law 464
  completion of purpose of
    employment 469
  constructive dismissal 409,
    467–8, 477
  continuous employment 402,
    408, 467, 475
  damages 246–7, 467
  deemed dismissal 468–9
  definition 464–5
  economic reasons 473–4

  eligibility 467–75
  employee shareholders 400
  employer's fault 470
  employment tribunals 69, 465,
    466–7
  failure to return to work after
    absence 468
  fair, proof that dismissal was
    467, 474
  grievance and disciplinary
    procedures 464–5, 474–5
  grounds for dismissal 469–70
  manner of dismissal, damages
    for 246
  misconduct 470–2
  negligence 469–70
  personality clashes 473
  proof of dismissal 467–8
  qualification or capability, lack
    of 469–70
  race discrimination 439
  real life example 476
  redundancy 472, 474, 477
  resignation 469
  retirement 473
  shareholder employees 466
  sickness 470, 473
  social media and technology
    471–2
  some other substantial reason
    473
  statutory restrictions 472
  statutory rights 465
  wrongful dismissal 466
  zero hours contracts 408
unfair prejudice petitions
    578–80
unincorporated associations
    492–3, 507
unjust enrichment 206, 208, 210

veil of incorporation 500–3
vibration 373
vicarious liability 363, 386–92
  agency 272, 386
  authorised acts 388
  close connection test 388–91
  contracts for services 387
  contracts of service 387, 392
  course of employment test
    388, 505

control 388
Equality Act 2010 426
extent 388–91
hospitals 392
independent contractors
    employees, difference from
        387–8
    non-delegable duties 391–2
    unlawful acts 400
non-delegable duties 391–2
obstruction of the highway
    391
partnerships 494
public nuisance affecting the
    highway 391
race discrimination 440
servants, injuries to 392
sexual orientation
    discrimination 455–6
supervision 388
unauthorised acts 388–9, 400
victimisation 425, 429, 433, 435,
    453–4, 457
visitors 364, 365, 367, 370–1,
    417, 436
volenti non fit injuria 300–2
    carelessness 301–2
    occupiers' liability 370
    rescue cases 300–1

volunteers *see also volenti non
    fit injuria*
    assumption of responsibility
        313–14, 316–17
    breach of duty 290–1
    Equality Act 2006 426
    information, failure to
        volunteer 175–6
voting
    company meetings 535,
        575–6
    dividends 535
    prisoners' right to vote 45

wages *see also* equal pay;
        minimum wage/living
        wage
    chief executive officers (CEOs),
        remuneration of 563–5
    deductions 408
    directors 544, 556
    duty to pay wages 407–8
    provision of work 408
warnings 348, 352, 354, 368–9,
    373
warranties 128–30
    breach 128–9, 237
    conditions 237
    definition 122–3

innominate terms 129–30
    sale of goods and services 151
websites 630–1
White Papers 32
winding up *see* liquidation
Woolf reforms 60–1
    ADR 68
    adversarial system, abuse
        of 60
    Civil Procedure Rules 60–1, 68
    costs 60
working time 405, 408
writing, contracts which require
    77–8
wrongful dismissal 465–6
    compensation 466
    definition 464, 465
    employment tribunals 466
    grievance and disciplinary
        procedures 464
    minimum notice periods
        465–6
    remedies 466
    summary dismissal, definition
        of 465

Youth Court 55

zero hours contracts 408